Beginning Visual Web Programming in VB .NET

From Novice to Professional

DANIEL CAZZULINO
VICTOR GARCIA APREA
JAMES GREENWOOD
CHRIS HART

Apress®

Beginning Visual Web Programming in VB .NET: From Novice to Professional

ISBN (pbk): 1-59059-359-6

9 8 7 6 5 4 3 2 1

Distributed to the book trade in the United States by Springer-Verlag New York, Inc., 233 Spring Street, 6th Floor, New York, NY 10013, and outside the United States by Springer-Verlag GmbH & Co. KG, Tiergartenstr. 17, 69112 Heidelberg, Germany.

In the United States: phone 1-800-SPRINGER, fax 201-348-4505, e-mail `orders@springer-ny.com`, or visit `http://www.springer-ny.com`. Outside the United States: fax +49 6221 345229, e-mail `orders@springer.de`, or visit `http://www.springer.de`.

For information on translations, please contact Apress directly at 2560 Ninth Street, Suite 219, Berkeley, CA 94710. Phone 510-549-5930, fax 510-549-5939, e-mail `info@apress.com`, or visit `http://www.apress.com`.

The source code for this book is available to readers at `http://www.apress.com` in the Downloads section. You will need to answer questions pertaining to this book in order to successfully download the code.

To Any, for believing in me, changing for me, and risking with me on this seemingly never-ending journey though new challenges. I hope I can get to be as supportive with you as you have been with me. You have been the most amazing companion I could have ever dreamed of.

*To Agustina, my little baby, for giving me yet another reason to love working at home. Watching you grow every day up close is a great gift from God (I hear Any say I shouldn't be *just* watching :o)).*

To my father, for being such a life warrior. I'll never give up, just as you never do. Thanks for staying with us and giving me the opportunity of making you feel proud of me. I can clearly see now that it wasn't your time, and God really wanted you to see everything that came after.

To all my girls, mum and sisters, for showing me what great women look like. I must listen to you more. I'm working on that.

To my dear friends (you know who you are), for always being there and bringing me back to earth. Talking to you makes me understand there's a beautiful life outside (along with?) .NET.

To Olga, for being like a second mother, and to Pedro, for doing all the things I should do at home so I can spend more time programming, without getting Any mad at me. I never thank you enough. With regards to Pedro, it's already too late. I hope I never make that mistake again. We miss you a lot.

Daniel Cazzulino

Contents at a Glance

Contents

About the Authors

DANIEL CAZZULINO, one of the original authors of this book, is the main editor of this edition. He reviewed and modified the original text to make it an even more consistent book and to adapt it to the latest changes in the ASP.NET product.

Daniel (also known as "kzu") is cofounder of Clarius Consulting (`http://clariusconsulting.net`), providing training, consulting, and development in Microsoft .NET technologies. He coauthored several books for Wrox Press and Apress on web development and server controls with ASP.NET, has written and reviewed many articles for *ASP Today* and *C# Today*, and currently enjoys sharing his .NET, XML, and ASP.NET experiences through his weblog (`http://clariusconsulting.net/kzu`). He also works closely with Microsoft in key projects from the Patterns and Practices group, shaping the use of OO techniques, design patterns, and frameworks for .NET. Microsoft recognized him as a Most Valuable Professional (MVP) on XML Technologies for his contributions to the community, mainly through the XML-savvy open source project NMatrix (`http://sourceforge.net/projects/dotnetopensrc`) he cofounded and his weblog. He also started the promising Mvp.Xml project with fellow XML MVP experts worldwide (`http://mvp-xml.sf.net`). Surprisingly enough, Daniel is a lawyer who found a more exciting career as a developer and .NET/XML geek.

JAMES GREENWOOD is a technical architect and author based in West Yorkshire, England. He spends his days (and most of his nights) designing and implementing .NET solutions—from government knowledge-management systems to mobile integration platforms—all the while waxing lyrical on the latest Microsoft technologies. His professional interests include research into distributed interfaces, the automation of application development, and human-machine convergence. When he can be pried away from the keyboard, James can be found out and about, indulging in his other great loves: British sports cards and Egyptology. You can reach James at `jsg@altervisitor.com`.

CHRIS HART is a full-time developer, part-time author based in Birmingham (UK). Chris took the long route into development, having originally studied Mechanical Engineering. She is currently working at Trinity Expert Systems (`www.tesl.com`), and her most recent project has involved developing a heavily customized Microsoft CMS Server application. In her spare time, she enjoys writing about ASP.NET, and she has contributed chapters to many books, published by both Apress and Wrox Press. In the remaining hours of the day, she enjoys cooking, going to the gym, and relaxing with her extremely supportive husband, James.

VICTOR GARCIA APREA, one of the authors of the original version of this book, also served as the technical reviewer of this edition. You can read about him on the "About the Technical Reviewer" page.

About the Technical Reviewer

VICTOR GARCIA APREA is cofounder of Clarius Consulting, providing training, consulting, and development in Microsoft .NET technologies. Victor has been involved with ASP.NET since early in its development and was recognized as a Microsoft MVP for ASP.NET since 2002. He has written books and articles, and also has done a lot of reviewing for Wrox Press, Apress, and Microsoft Press. Victor is a regular speaker at Microsoft Argentina (MSDN DevDays, Ask the Experts panel, and other events) and .NET local user groups.

You can read Victor's weblog at `http://clariusconsulting.net/vga`.

Acknowledgments

Special thanks to Chris Hart for sharing her writing skills with me and turning a chaotic, spasmodic writer into a bearable author. To Ian Nutt for letting me learn the intricacies of the editing work, which ultimately made my role in this book possible. The editorial industry misses you!

Thanks to Dominique, for remembering my name after the lunch, our meeting, and the years, and for believing in the strong and concise material we created for this book. Hey, I slipped Mono release only by a year :o)!

And thanks to Ewan, Marilyn, Beckie, and Kelly for their help in getting this book out the door.

And thanks to Victor for being the most amazing technical reviewer (besides being an excellent author and partner, too). It's great to see that just as we began, we continue (not that you being the reviewer and me the editor means I'm sort of your boss...).

—Daniel

Introduction

The introduction of .NET has blurred the lines between previously distinct programming disciplines, and it has done so to great effect for developers. With so much functionality encapsulated by the .NET Framework class library, some diverse tasks have gained a common programming interface.

One area in which this change is particularly striking is that of web development. Before .NET, web application programming "the Microsoft way" was all about ASP. At the time, ASP was new, accessible, and exciting. But it was also script-based and inefficient. It led to serious maintainability problems, and the IDEs were disjointed. Microsoft has channeled the lessons it learned from ASP into its .NET Framework. Now, with ASP.NET (the .NET web development technology), you can create efficient, interactive Internet applications using the same languages that you use for Windows desktop applications.

In Visual Studio .NET (VS .NET), Microsoft has taken this idea even further; not only does the *code* look similar, but the *GUI* looks similar, too. Visual Basic .NET's (VB. NET's) familiar form-based interface is used for development of web applications, as well as for desktop programs. If you want to, you can create a web application without ever seeing a line of HTML code, and you can take advantage of all the facilities for testing and debugging that VS .NET provides to programmers of all disciplines.

The structure of class libraries in the .NET Framework is such that the methodology you use is the same, regardless of whether you're developing desktop applications or web applications. ASP.NET is really just a series of classes in the .NET Framework, just like the Windows Forms classes. From this perspective, the move from desktop application development to web development shouldn't be too much of a leap.

Yet there *are* some major differences that you need to consider when you move to web development. We are no longer talking about applications installed and running on individual machines; instead, we're talking about hosting an application on a central server, ready to be accessed by hundreds or thousands of remote clients every hour. This means that you need to be more concerned with performance, scalability, and security issues to ensure that the end user's experience is as smooth and secure as possible.

In this book, we'll explain the issues involved in the web development paradigm and how they're different from those you're used to in desktop application development. To demonstrate how to apply these principles, beginning in Chapter 3, this book guides you through building a feature-rich, interactive web application called Friends Reunion, using VB .NET, ASP.NET, and VS .NET.

The emphasis is on learning by practice. Every example in the book is described step by step, and we'll outline and explain each stage in the development, debugging, and deployment of the Friends Reunion application.

Who Is This Book For?

This book is predominantly targeted at developers who have some experience in the VB .NET language (perhaps through practical application of the language or simply from a VB .NET tutorial book). These developers may fall into one of two groups:

- Readers who have little or no web development experience, have gained their VB .NET experience mostly in the context of desktop applications, and are seeking to apply this VB .NET expertise in web development in .NET

- Readers who have gained some web development experience using ASP, PHP, or other technologies, and are seeking to move into web development using .NET and VB .NET.

This book does not assume that you have programmed for the web environment before, but it does assume that you have some familiarity with VB .NET. Previous experience with the VS .NET integrated development environment (IDE) is not essential, but it is helpful. Similarly, we assume no previous experience with HTML, XML, databases, or any of the other technologies mentioned in this book—though a little background knowledge does no harm.

What Does This Book Cover?

The first two chapters of this book are introductory. They provide the basic foundation you need to begin working on the Friends Reunion web application in Chapter 3.

The remaining chapters examine different aspects of web application development using VB .NET and ASP.NET. In each chapter, we study an aspect both in general terms and within the context of the Friends Reunion application. Over the course of these 11 chapters, we build, test, debug, and deploy a rich interactive web application—and you'll see every single step. You can obtain all of the code presented in this book from the Downloads section of the Apress web site (`http://www.apress.com`). Appendix A contains an overview of the code and explains how to install and run it for each chapter.

Here's a summary of the contents of this book:

- Chapter 1 is an introduction to the web environment. It discusses the similarities and differences between web applications and desktop applications, and explains what happens behind the scenes when a user employs a browser to request a web page. The intention is to clarify the issues that influence the way we design applications for the Web and to set the scene for the remainder of the book. We also set up the web server here and create a couple of simple examples to get things started.

- In Chapter 2, we move on to create some basic ASP.NET web forms using VS .NET. We look at how web forms are processed and the lifecycle of a page, and we demonstrate it all by walking through our first ASP.NET application.

- Chapter 3 is all about the server control. The server control is the core part of any web form; it's at the heart of the development of dynamic, interactive web sites in .NET. VS .NET allows you to drag-and-drop server controls onto your web forms in exactly the same way that you insert Windows Forms controls into a Windows desktop application. And you can add code to your forms to interact with these controls in much the same way, too.

- In Chapters 4 and 5, we turn our attention to data. Most interactive web applications rely on the existence and manipulation of data of some form, and on storage of that data (either in a full-scale database or some other format). In Chapter 4, we use ADO.NET to access and manipulate data. In Chapter 5, we demonstrate how data binding techniques make it easy to display data on your pages in a user-friendly manner. You will also see how to apply templates to your web forms to alter the look and feel of your data-bound controls.
- Chapter 6 is about applications, sessions, and state. By nature, the Web is a stateless medium—when you request a web page, the web server delivers it, and then forgets about you. If you want your web applications to recognize users when they make multiple page requests (for example, as they browse an e-commerce application adding items to a shopping basket), you need to know about the different techniques you can use to retain state across pages, for a session, or across an application.
- Chapters 7 and 8 focus on XML, a topic that has become very important as widespread Internet connectivity becomes the norm. In Chapter 7, we look at the concept of markup and how it is widely relevant to data-driven applications, and we create our own XML language by way of an XML Schema. In Chapter 8, we explore how to use that XML Schema to facilitate a data-transfer feature—exploiting XML's nature as the perfect vehicle for data transfer across the Internet.
- In Chapter 9, we turn briefly away from web sites to explore a different type of web application: the web service. Web services enable you to expose your application's functionality to other "client" applications. These applications make requests using standards and protocols over the Internet. This also means that you can use other people's web services in your code as if they were components on your own system, even though they are only accessible across the Internet. We'll examine both how to create web services and how to consume existing services.
- Chapter 10 is about ASP.NET authentication, authorization, and security. The role of security in an application is motivated by the need to restrict a user's (or application's) access to certain resources and ability to perform certain actions. For example, you may want to include administrative tools in your web application and to prevent access to these administrator pages for all but authorized users. This chapter looks at the ASP.NET tools for authenticating and authorizing users of your applications.
- Chapter 11 tackles two distinct but related subjects: debugging and exception handling. Debugging is much easier when you understand the different types of bugs that can occur, and easier still with the array of debugging tools and techniques made available by VS .NET and the .NET Framework. We'll study all that in the first half of the chapter. In the second half, we use the .NET exception mechanism to handle some potential input errors that could occur at runtime and prevent the application from crashing in a heap.
- In Chapter 12, we focus on two more different but related subjects: performance and caching. We set out to clarify what we mean by "good performance," and suggest a number of techniques you can use to analyze your application in realistic conditions. We'll apply some of those techniques to our Friends Reunion application, putting the application under stress to see what happens, and identifying and fixing a number of

different bottlenecks. We'll explain the issues related to caching and employ some caching techniques to save our application some processing effort, thereby optimizing the use of the server's resources.

- In Chapter 13, we describe how to prepare your application for deployment. VS .NET provides some easy-to-use tools that enable you to build your own deployment wizards. We demonstrate how to prepare the application for deployment—web site, database, and all—by wrapping it all up into an easy-to-use installation wizard.

- Appendix A contains a brief overview of the structure and functionality of the Friends Reunion web application, the design of the database, and the structure and use of the downloadable code.

- Appendix B contains more information about the setup and configuration of the Internet Information Server (IIS) web server and the Microsoft SQL Server Desktop Engine (MSDE).

What You Need to Use This Book

The following is the list of recommended system requirements for running the code in this book:

- A suitable operating system—server versions, such as Windows 2000 Server or Windows Server 2003 Web Edition, or professional versions, such as Windows 2000 or Windows XP Professional Edition

- Internet Information Server (IIS), which is shipped with the suitable operating systems (the version will depend on the operating system, but all of them are suitable for ASP.NET development)

- Visual Studio .NET (or Visual Basic .NET) Standard Edition or higher

- The Microsoft SQL Server Desktop Engine (MSDE) or Microsoft SQL Server

---

Note Windows XP Home Edition does *not* come with IIS and cannot run IIS. For ASP.NET web development on Windows XP Home Edition, you may consider the ASP.NET Web Matrix tool, available for free download from `http://www.asp.net`. This tool offers limited ASP.NET web server functionality, and you won't be able to run web projects in VS .NET with this version.

Read Appendix B for details on how to download and install MSDE if you don't have a full SQL Server. VS .NET provides a useful user interface for any SQL Server or MSDE database.

CHAPTER 1

Environment and Architecture

Windows desktop applications and web applications have many differences, but one difference is fundamental. This difference lies in the relative locations of the *application* itself and its *user interface*:

- When you run a Windows desktop application, the user interface appears on the screen of the machine on which the application is running. Messages between the application and its user interface are passed through the operating system of the machine. There's just one machine involved here and no network.
- When you run a web application, the user interface can appear in the browser of *any* machine. Messages between the application and its user interface must also pass across a network, because, typically, the web application and its user interface are on two *separate* machines.

This single difference in architecture manifests itself in many ways. If you're used to writing desktop applications and you're coming to web applications for the first time, it brings many new issues for you to consider. Let's begin with an overview of these considerations.

Web Application Considerations

Arguably, the most significant advantage of web applications is that the end users don't need to be on the same machine on which the application is running. In fact, they don't even need to be in the same country! But there are many other technical, practical, and design considerations, such as these:

Messaging: Since a running web application must communicate with its user interface across a network, there needs to be a way of passing messages between the two that is "network-proof."

Manipulating the user interface: How can a web application tell its browser-based user interface which buttons, text, labels, and so on to show, and how to arrange and style them?

Security: If a web application is available across a public network, you need to prevent unwanted users from accessing the application or from tapping in on authorized users.

Multiple users: A web application can be executed via a remote machine, so it can effectively be executed by two or more users at the same time (potentially millions of them if it's a successful one!).

Identification and state: How does a web application identify a user for the first time and recognize that user when she returns? This is especially important because of the stateless nature of the Web (see the "An Introduction to State Management" section later in this chapter).

If you're migrating from desktop application development to the Web, these are just a few issues that derive from the simple fact that an executing web application is (usually) physically separate from its user interface. We'll address all of the issues over the course of the book.

This chapter focuses on the web environment and on the architecture of web applications, to give you an idea of the implications of having an application and its user interface on different machines. In this chapter, we'll look at these aspects:

- How the web works, from the time the user requests a page to the time the user receives the response
- What a web application is and how it is composed
- The purpose of HTTP (the protocol underlying the Web) and its role in the request/response interaction between a browser and the web application server
- The role of the web server in hosting a web application
- The use of virtual directories in organizing web applications
- The difference between static content and dynamic content
- How client-side code and server-side code bring different effects to the world of dynamic content

We'll start by taking a look at how the web works and how requests for web pages are processed.

The Web Model

You can take advantage of the Web to set up an application that runs in one central location and can be accessed by users located anywhere in the world, through just a browser and an Internet connection.

The earliest web applications weren't really "applications" in the functional sense, but they took advantage of this basic concept to host documents in a single, central location and enable users to access those documents from distant places. With the global explosion of interest in the Internet, developers all over the world are now creating web applications that are much more functionally rich in their design.

Web applications no longer exist just as a central resource for shared documents. Now, they're still a central resource, but we use them interactively to buy groceries, to calculate our taxes, and to send and receive e-mail. Our children use the Web as an exciting, interactive learning experience. We're now using web applications to perform all those interactive tasks that were previously only in the domain of the desktop application. We don't need to install the software anymore; we just need to point the browser across the Internet to the application.

Desktop Applications vs. Web Applications

If you've built a Windows desktop application in a language like Visual Basic .NET (VB .NET), then it's not too difficult to sit down and write a VB .NET *web* application that looks and feels quite similar to that desktop application, as illustrated in Figure 1-1. You can design the forms in the user interface (UI) to be similar, have the forms react to mouse clicks and button presses in a similar way, and make the back-end processing of the two applications quite similar.

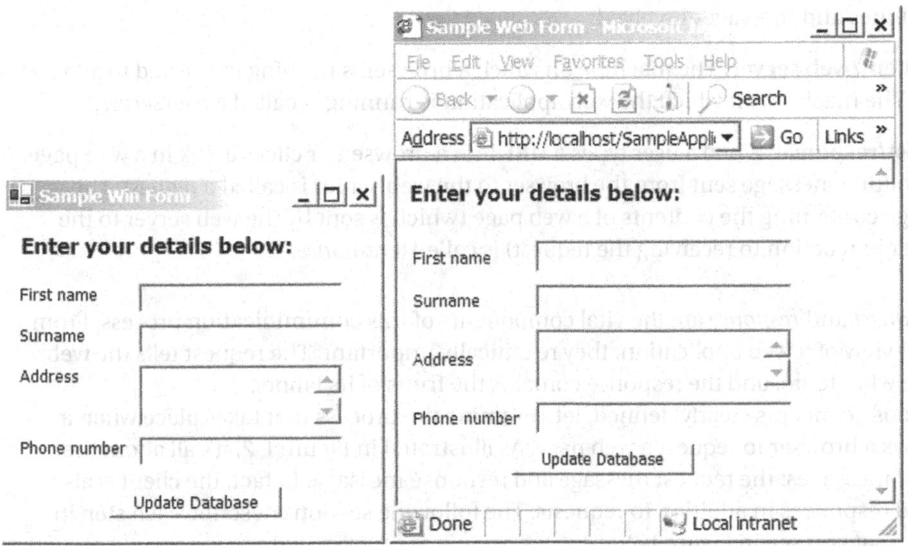

Figure 1-1. *A desktop application (left) and a web application (right) can look and feel quite similar.*

To use the desktop version of an application, you need to install it on a machine, and then sit at that machine while you use it. When you ask the operating system to run the application, it will create a new *process* for it, where the application will execute. Afterwards, your mouse clicks and keypresses will be detected by the operating system and passed to the process in which the desktop application is running. The application interprets these messages, does whatever processing is necessary, and tells the operating system what changes should be made to the UI as a result. All the communication between the application process and the UI is done via the operating system of that machine.

To use the web version of an application, you need to use a web browser. You type a URL into the web browser, which tells it where to find the machine on which the application is running. The browser arranges for a message to be sent across a network to this other machine. When the message is received by that machine, it's passed to the application, which interprets the message and decides what the UI (a web page) should look like. Then it sends a description of that web page back across the network to the browser.

Far more players are involved in the use of the web application than are involved with the desktop application, but the advantages of this remote-access concept are nothing short of phenomenal. To build an effective web application, you need to understand these interactions between the browser and web application in finer detail, because they shape the way you write web applications.

Web Servers and Web Clients

You know that by entering a URL into the Address box of a browser window, you can surf and navigate to a web site. But what actually happens, behind the scenes, when you press Enter or click the browser's Go button to submit that URL?

Before looking into the process, you need to understand the distinctions between the different machines and messages involved:

> **Web client/web server:** The machine on which a browser is running is referred to as a *web client*. The machine on which the web application is running is called a *web server*.
>
> **Request/response:** When a user types a URL into a browser, or clicks a link in a web page, the resulting message sent from the browser to the web server is called a *request*. The message containing the contents of a web page (which is sent by the web server to the browser in reaction to receiving the request) is called a *response*.

The *request* and *response* are the vital components of this communication process. From the point of view of a web application, they're critically important. The request tells the web application what to do, and the response contains the fruits of its labors.

With those concepts clearly defined, let's examine the process that takes place when a user employs a browser to request a web page. As illustrated in Figure 1-2, it's all about the exchange of messages: the request message and response message. In fact, the client is also able to send responses in addition to requests. The following sections describe each step in the process that you see in Figure 1-2.

Step 1: Initiating the Client Request

In the first stage, the user clicks a link, types a URL into a browser, or performs some similar action that initiates a request. The *request* is a message that must be sent to the web server.

In order to send any request (or response) message, the browser needs to do three things:

- *Describe* the message in a standard way so that it can be understood by the web server that receives it. For this, it uses the Hypertext Transfer Protocol (HTTP), the protocol used by the Web to describe both requests and responses. The described request message is called the *HTTP request,* and it has a very particular format that contains information about the request plus the information required to deliver it to the web server.
- *Package* the message so that it can be safely transported across the network. For this, it uses the Transmission Control Protocol (TCP).
- *Address* the message, to specify the place to which the message should be delivered. For this, it uses the Internet Protocol (IP).

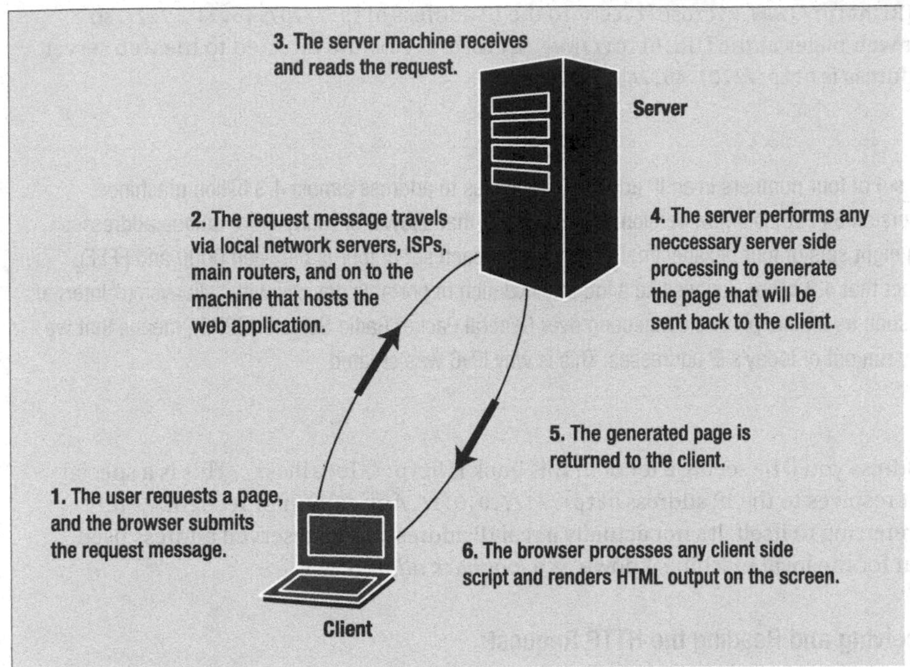
3. The server machine receives and reads the request.
Server
2. The request message travels via local network servers, ISPs, main routers, and on to the machine that hosts the web application.
4. The server performs any neccessary server side processing to generate the page that will be sent back to the client.
5. The generated page is returned to the client.
1. The user requests a page, and the browser submits the request message.
6. The browser processes any client side script and renders HTML output on the screen.
Client

Figure 1-2. *What happens when a user requests a web page from a browser*

Note TCP and IP are often grouped together and referred to as TCP/IP. When you hear people talking about TCP/IP, they're discussing packaging and addressing Internet messages.

After the browser has described the message, packaged it, and addressed it, the request is ready to be dispatched across the network to its intended target: the web server.

Step 2: Routing the Request

Thanks to the HTTP, TCP, and IP protocols, the request message is formatted in such a way that it can be understood by each of the machines involved in *routing* the request—that is, passing the request from one machine to another as it finds its way from the web client to the web server.

The web server machine will be connected to the Internet (either directly or via a firewall) and will be uniquely identified on the Internet by its *IP address*. An IP address is a set of four numbers, each of which ranges between 0 and 255.

However, the original request probably didn't contain an IP address. More likely, it was made using a URL that began with a named web site address (this is usually something more memorable, like `http://www.apress.com/`). The link between an IP address and its named equivalent is mapped using the Domain Name Service (DNS). For example, DNS currently maps the URL `http://www.microsoft.com/` to the IP address `http://207.46.245.222/`, so requests for web pages at the URL `http://www.microsoft.com/` are directed to the web server whose IP address is `http://207.46.245.222/`.

Note The set of four numbers in an IP address enables us to address almost 4.3 billion machines uniquely. IP version 6 (IPv6) is a new version of the protocol that allows for many more unique addresses by employing eight sets of four hexadecimal digits (so that each set of four is between 0000 and FFFF). Despite the fact that 4.3 billion sounds like a lot, the invention of portable devices with "always on" Internet connections, such as mobile phones connecting over General Packet Radio Service (GPRS), means that we will eventually run out of today's IP addresses. This is why IPv6 was created.

One address you'll be seeing a lot of in this book is `http://localhost/`. This is a special address that resolves to the IP address `http://127.0.0.1/`. Any computer recognizes this address as referring to itself. It's not actually a real IP address, but a reserved address used as a shortcut for the local machine, known as a *loopback address*.

Step 3: Receiving and Reading the HTTP Request

The standardized format for web requests is defined by HTTP, so when the HTTP request arrives at its destination, the web server knows exactly how to read it.

In HTTP, a web client can make two principal types of requests of a server:

`GET` request: The client can ask the server to send it a resource such as a web page, a picture, or an MP3 file. This is called a `GET` request, because it gets information from the server. This is a commonly used method, for example, when developing a search facility on a web site, where the same request will be made on more than one occasion. It's also how you request simple web pages and images.

`POST` request: The client can ask the server to perform some processing in order to generate a response. This is called a `POST` request, because the client posts the information that the server must process, and then awaits a response. This method is more likely to be used, for example, when submitting personal data to an online shopping site or in any other situation where you are sending information to the server.

Step 4: Performing Server-Side Processing

The web server is the place where the application is running. It is responsible for ensuring that any necessary server-side processing takes place in order to complete its task and generate a response.

If the HTML request contains a request for a simple HTML page, the web server will locate the HTML page, wrap it into an HTTP response, and dispatch it back to the client. In contrast, if the request is for an `.aspx` page, for example, the web server will pass the request to the ASP.NET engine, which takes care of processing the page and generating the output (usually HTML), before the web server wraps that newly generated output into an HTTP response, ready to be sent back to the client.

The HTTP response consists of two parts: the header and the body. The *header* contains information that tells the browser whether the request was successful or there was an error processing it. For example, if the web server received the request but was unable to locate the requested page, the header will contain an HTTP 404 (File Not Found) error code. The response *body* is where a successfully requested resource (such as a block of HTML) is placed.

Step 5: Routing the Response

The HTML page, generated at the web server, has been described in terms of an HTTP response message, and is packaged and addressed using TCP/IP. The return address is an IP address, which was included in the HTTP request message sent in step 1.

The HTTP response message is routed back across the network to its target destination: the web client that made the original request.

Step 6: Performing Client-Side Processing and Rendering

When the HTTP response reaches the web client, the browser reads the response and processes any client-side code. This processed code is now displayed in the browser window.

Now that you know what goes on when a user requests a page, it's time to start using some code.

System Configuration for Web Development

The best way to understand the web application process is to create some web pages and look at them from the perspective of both the end user and web server. You'll begin to do this shortly (and you'll create plenty of web pages during the course of the book), but before you can start, you need to install and configure a web server, which you'll use to host your web applications.

If you are running Windows 2000, Windows XP, or even Windows Server 2003, you'll be able to use Microsoft's own web server—Internet Information Services (IIS)—to host your applications. Other web servers are available for Windows (such as Cassini, a web server written in .NET) and for other development platforms (notably Apache, which can be installed on Windows machines, Linux machines, and now even comes preinstalled on Mac OS X machines). For this book, we'll use IIS to host the sample web applications, because it's the platform provided by Microsoft in order to run ASP.NET applications (although not the only one).

Different versions of IIS are supplied as part of different versions of the Windows operating system:

- Windows 2000 Professional or higher has IIS 5.0
- Windows XP Professional has IIS 5.1
- Windows Server 2003 has IIS 6.0

IIS 5.0 and IIS 5.1 are very similar (in fact, IIS 5.1 is just a minor update of IIS 5.0). IIS 6.0 is a more substantial revamping of the IIS architecture, providing improvements in security and speed, as well as a deeper level of integration with ASP.NET applications.

Having said that, the front-end interface for all of these versions is very similar; therefore, the configuration process described in this chapter works equally well for all of these IIS versions. For the remainder of the book, we'll limit the discussions mainly to the features available to IIS 5.*x* developers, because it's the main platform for workstations. We've included an overview and setup instructions for IIS 6.0 in Appendix B, as there are some differences that should be taken into account when setting up web development or deploying the application on a server with Windows Server 2003.

Installing and Configuring IIS for .NET Web Applications

The IIS installation process itself is a fairly painless operation. If you haven't installed any of the necessary software yet, then it's recommended that you install IIS *before* either the .NET Framework or Visual Studio .NET (VS. NET), because the installation of the latter configures the former so that it is able to deal with the ASP.NET files that are central to web applications in .NET.

If You Haven't Installed the .NET Framework or VS .NET Yet

If you have not yet installed the .NET Framework or VS. NET, open the Control Panel and head to Add/Remove Programs. In the dialog box that appears, select Add/Remove Windows Components. In the list of components that appears, select Internet Information Services (IIS), as shown in Figure 1-3. Accept all the default settings, and the installation process will commence. Now, you can go ahead and install the .NET Framework and VS. NET, too.

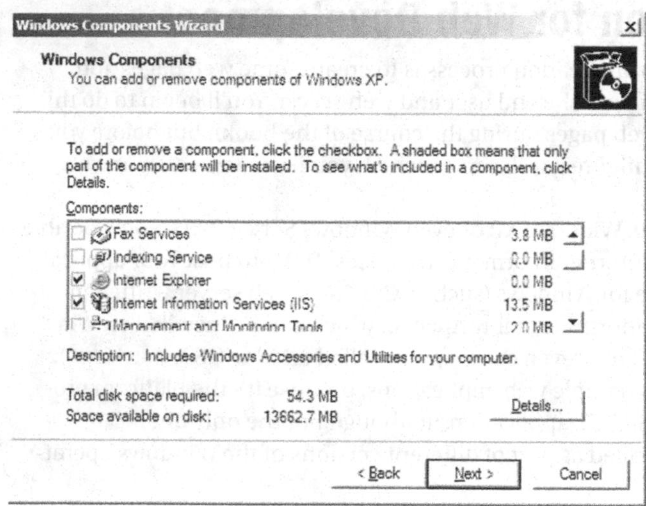

Figure 1-3. *Choosing to install IIS*

If You've Already Installed the .NET Framework or VS .NET

If you have already installed the .NET Framework and/or VS .NET, you could proceed by uninstalling VS .NET, and then uninstalling the .NET Framework (via the Add/Remove Programs group in your Control Panel). Then you could install IIS, and finally, reinstall VS .NET. But this is an aggressive (and time-consuming) process. Instead, we recommend that you try to use one of the following tools to "repair" the .NET Framework, and use the uninstall/reinstall method only as a last resort.

First, try to run the ASP.NET IIS registration utility. Select Start ➤ Run. In the dialog box that appears, type the following command:

```
%systemroot%\Microsoft.NET\Framework\[Version]\aspnet_regiis.exe
```

`[Version]` is the .NET version you have: `v1.0.3705` for .NET 1.0 or `v1.1.4322` for .NET 1.1.

If that doesn't work, you should be able to do the job using the VS. NET DVD or CDs.

If you own the VS .NET DVD, insert the DVD, and then select Start ➤ Run. In the dialog box that appears, type the following command (on one line):

```
<Drive>:\wcu\dotNetFramework\dotnetfx.exe
                    /t:c:\temp
                    /c:"msiexec.exe
                    /fvecms c:\temp\netfx.msi"
```

If you have the VS .NET CDs, insert the VS .NET Windows Component Update CD, and then select Start ➤ Run. In the dialog box, type the following command (on one line):

```
<Drive>:\dotNetFramework\dotnetfx.exe
                         /t:c:\temp
                         /c:"msiexec.exe
                         /fvecms c:\temp\netfx.msi"
```

Administering IIS

Once the IIS installation has completed, you can check that it was successful by viewing the IIS console. The IIS console is the key administration tool that you will use to configure your IIS web server software.

To run the console, select Start ➤ Run, type **inetmgr** in the dialog box, and click OK. Alternatively, you can use the Internet Services Manager shortcut in the Administrative Tools group in your Control Panel (if you are running Windows XP, this link is named Internet Information Services). The IIS console appears, and it should look something like the window shown in Figure 1-4.

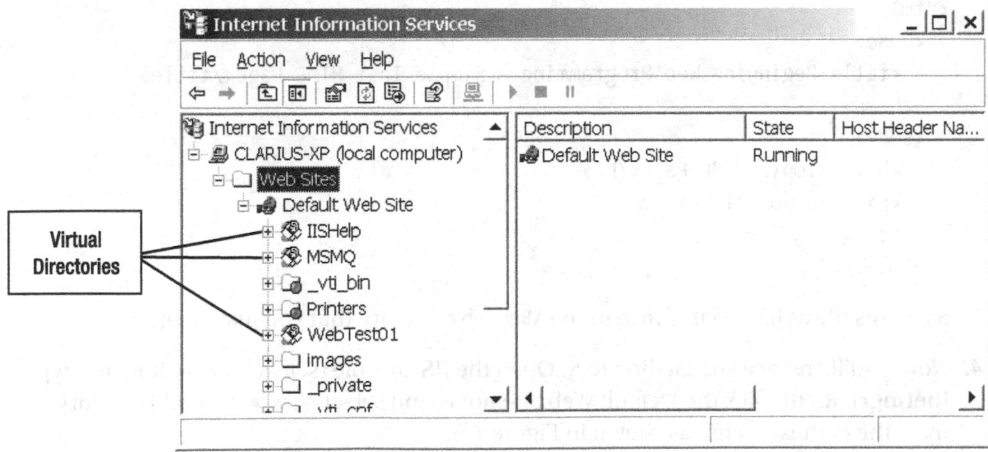

Figure 1-4. *IIS console is an administration tool for configuring IIS web server software.*

Creating Virtual Directories

In the folder list, you will notice that several of the folders are marked with a package-like (gear-like in IIS 6.0) icon (shown in Figure 1-4). This icon indicates that the folder is a *virtual directory*, which is also configured to be a root location for a web application.

IIS maps each virtual directory to a physical directory on the web server machine. This mapping works as follows:

- The virtual directory structure is the structure that the end users see when they browse the pages of the web site though a browser.
- The physical directory structure is the *actual* folder structure that is used on the web server's hard disk for organizing and storing the pages and resources of the web application.

Thus, web developers can use this mapping of virtual directories to physical ones to place the web application's source files in the most convenient place on their server and to hide their server's physical organization from end users (each virtual directory is just the alias of a physical directory). Let's see how this works and examine the process in more detail in an example.

Try It Out: Create a Virtual Directory In this example, you'll use the IIS console to create a virtual directory that points to a physical folder on your system. You'll write a simple HTML page and place it inside the physical directory, so that it will be possible to use a browser to navigate to that page via HTTP, using the virtual directory structure you created.

1. Use Windows Explorer to create a directory called `Apress` anywhere on your drive, and then create a subdirectory called `BegWeb` within it, so that you have a physical directory structure like `C:\Apress\BegWeb`.
2. Fire up a text or code editor such as Notepad. (You'll be using VS .NET in every other example in the book, but for this example, it's really not necessary.) Enter the following simple HTML code into a new file:

```
<html>
  <head>
    <title>Beginning Web Programming - Simple Test HTML Page</title>
  </head>
  <body>
    <h2>A Simple HTML Page</h2>
    <p>Hello. world!</p>
  </body>
</html>
```

3. Save this file as `HelloWorld.htm` in the `\BegWeb` directory that you just created.
4. Now, you'll create a virtual directory. Open the IIS console (select Start ➤ Run and type **inetmgr**). Right-click the Default Web Site node, and select New ➤ Virtual Directory from the context menu, as shown in Figure 1-5.

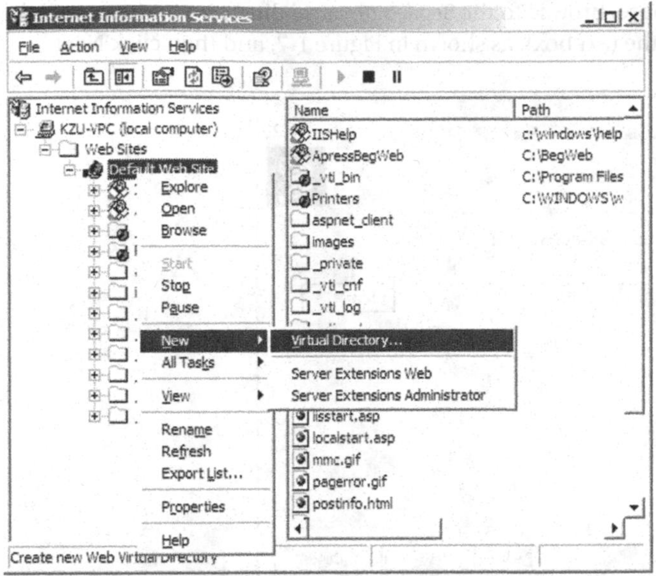

Figure 1-5. *Choosing to create a new virtual directory*

5. At this point, an introductory dialog box will appear. Just click Next to continue.
6. In the first page of the wizard, you'll be prompted for the name that you want to give to your virtual directory. This is the name that end users will see in the Address box of a browser when they request the page. Name your directory `ApressBegWeb`, as shown in Figure 1-6. Then click Next.

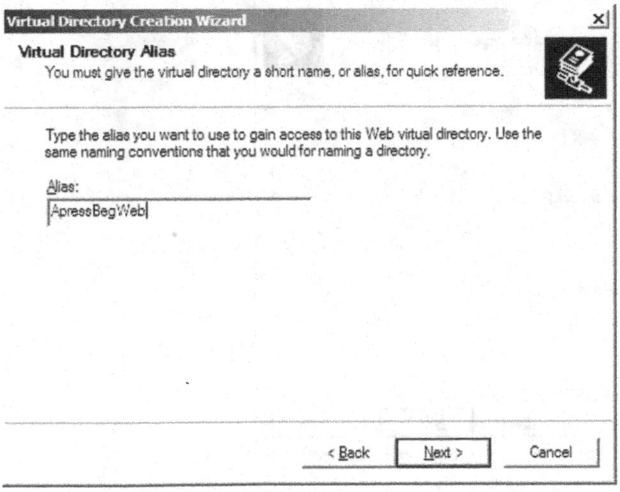

Figure 1-6. *Naming your virtual directory*

7. In the next wizard page, browse to the BegWeb physical directory (or just enter the directory path into the text box), as shown in Figure 1-7, and then click Next.

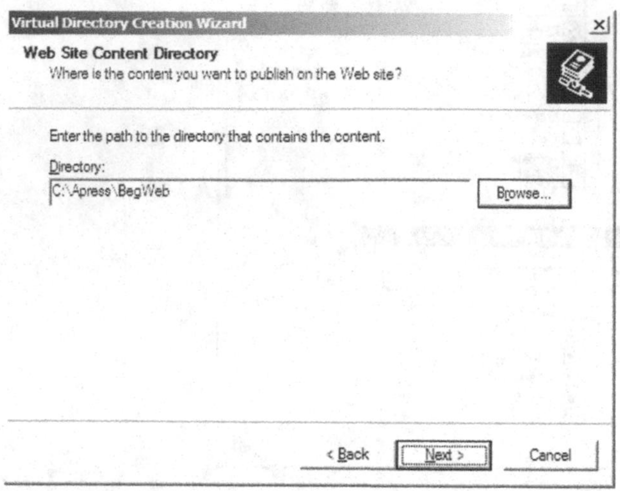

Figure 1-7. *Specifying the physical directory that contains the web page contents*

8. The next page, Access Permissions, presents a number of options relating to the permissions enabled on resources contained within this virtual directory, as shown in Figure 1-8. By default, users will be able to read files and run script-based programs. For now, leave the default settings and click Next to continue.

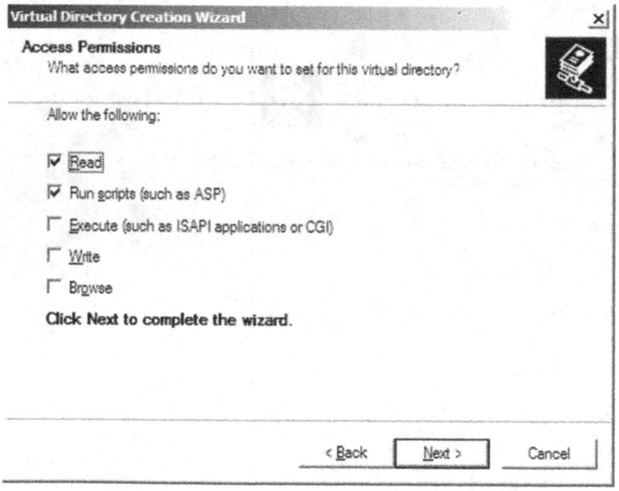

Virtual Directory Creation Wizard

Access Permissions

What access permissions do you want to set for this virtual directory?

Allow the following:

- [x] Read
- [x] Run scripts (such as ASP)
- [ ] Execute (such as ISAPI applications or CGI)
- [ ] Write
- [ ] Browse

Click Next to complete the wizard.

< Back | Next > | Cancel

Figure 1-8. *Setting access permissions*

9. The last page of the wizard confirms that the virtual directory has been created successfully. Click Finish to close the wizard. Your new virtual directory should now appear in the directory list in the IIS console, as shown in Figure 1-9.

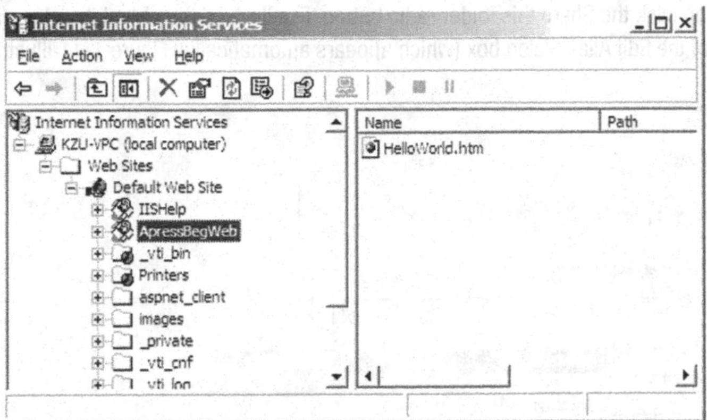

Figure 1-9. *Your new virtual directory appears in the IIS console.*

10. You can now run the example by opening your web browser and entering `http://localhost/ApressBegWeb/HelloWorld.htm` in the Address box. You should see the page shown in Figure 1-10.

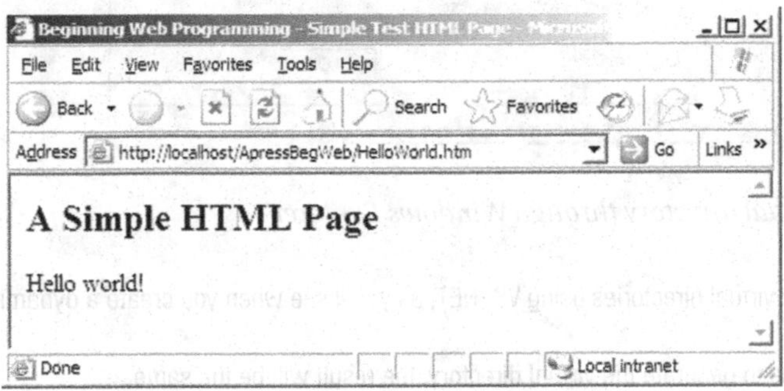

Figure 1-10. *Running the example in a web browser*

OTHER METHODS FOR CREATING VIRTUAL DIRECTORIES

It's also possible to create a virtual directory using Windows Explorer. To do that, right-click the physical directory in question (such as `C:\Apress\BegWeb`) and select Properties from the context menu. Then select the Web Sharing tab and click the Share this folder radio button. Finally, type the virtual directory (alias) name into the Alias text box of the Edit Alias dialog box (which appears automatically). Figure 1-11 illustrates the process.

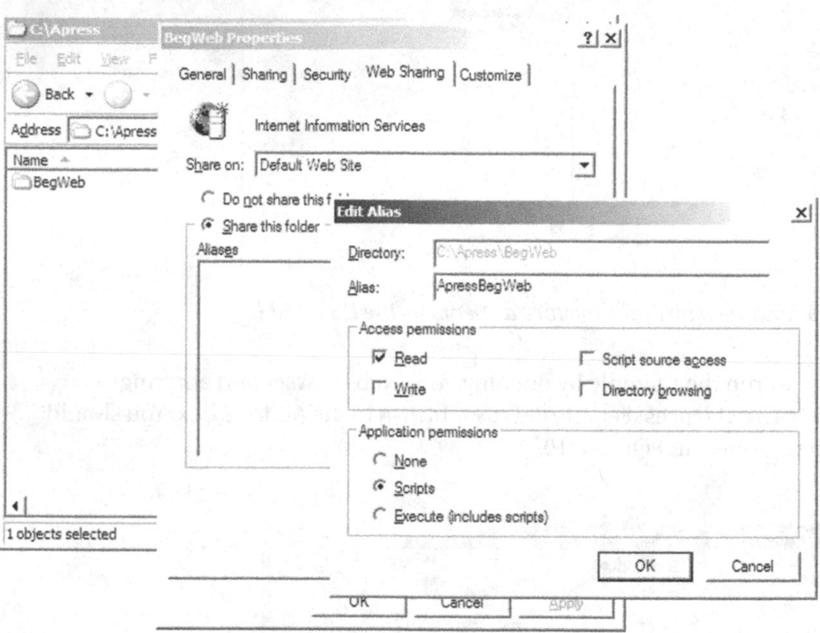

Figure 1-11. *Creating a virtual directory through Windows Explorer*

It's also possible to create virtual directories using VS .NET, as you'll see when you create a dynamic web page later in this chapter.

Whichever method you use to generate the virtual directory, the result will be the same.

How It Works

At the end of the example, you played the part of the end user by typing a URL into the Address box of the browser and sending the request. The destination of the request is determined by examination of the first part of the URL: `http://localhost/`. The machine name `localhost` very quickly resolves to the loopback IP address, `http://127.0.0.1/`, so the request is sent to the web server software (the IIS installation) that is running on the local machine.

When the web server receives the request, it reads and processes it. To establish exactly which resource was requested, it reads the remaining part of the URL: `/ApressBegWeb/HelloWorld.htm`. This tells the web server that the required resource is the HTML page,

HelloWorld.htm, and that it should be located in the directory whose alias is /ApressBegWeb. The web server knows that this virtual directory alias corresponds to the physical directory, C:\Apress\BegWeb, so it is able to fetch the .htm file from that location. All this processing is invisible to the end user who requested the page.

When it's ready, the web server sends the required output back to the requester. In this example, the request was for a simple HTML page, and the HTML is sent back to your browser.

The browser understands HTML and knows what to do with it. The HTML in this example is designed to display a simple page in the browser window. HTML is a *markup language*, constructed using plain text, and you don't need any fancy tools to create it. The browser interprets the HTML that it received and renders the page on-screen (by putting the contents of the <title> element into the title bar, rendering the contents of the <h2> element as a level 2 heading, and so on). We'll discuss the subject of markup languages in more detail in Chapter 7.

Finally, you've probably noticed that if you double-click an .htm file in Windows Explorer, it appears in a web browser (by default). It looks the same as requesting it in HTTP, but it's not. The file is opened in a browser because, by default, the operating system is configured to open .htm files in a browser. As you can see in the Address box in Figure 1-12, this page is not the result of an HTTP request, so it was served locally by the operating system, not by the web server.

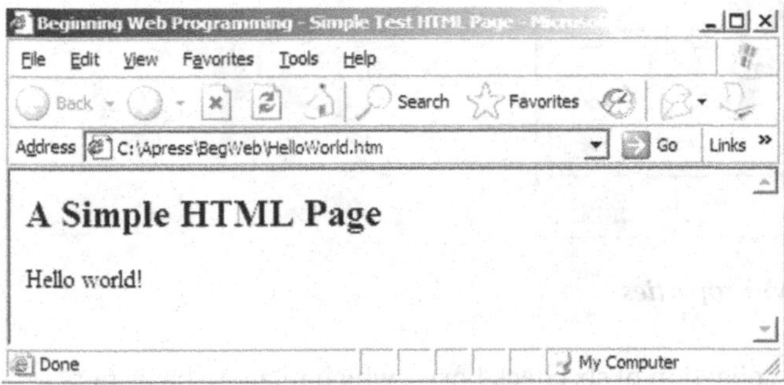

Figure 1-12. *Running the example from Windows Explorer*

Note It's the web server, not the operating system, that is responsible for arranging that any necessary server-side code is executed. And it's HTTP that allows the requests to be carried between web client and web server machines in a network. For a web application to work, requests must be made using http:// URLs and virtual directories, not through physical directories.

If you want, you can add more HTML pages and other web resources to the physical directory C:\Apress\BegWeb, and those pages and resources will be accessible via a browser in the same way: by browsing to the virtual directory http:\\localhost\ApressBegWeb\....

Configuring Virtual Directories

When you were setting up the virtual directory in the previous example, you chose to accept the default access settings. Of course, it's possible to influence the amount of access users have to your applications by adjusting these settings after the virtual directory has been created. You can alter the settings for your virtual directory by right-clicking the virtual directory in the IIS console and selecting Properties. You'll see the Properties dialog box for the virtual directory, as shown in Figure 1-13.

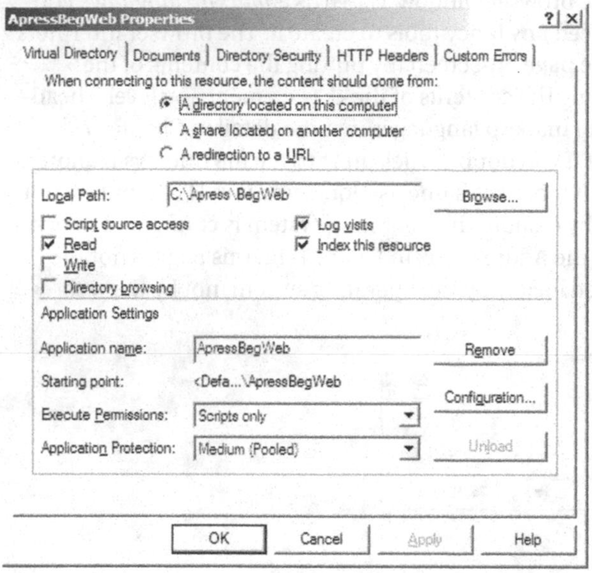

Figure 1-13. *Setting a virtual directory's properties*

In the dialog box, you can see a collection of six check boxes, which relate to basic permissions. You can alter these as required, but note that you always need to have the Read check box enabled if anyone is to view any of the pages in your directory! Out of the other available options, you will find the following two to be the most useful:

Write: This needs to be set if the user is to be allowed to update files within the virtual directory.

Directory browsing: This is a useful permission to enable when you're developing a web application by hand, because it allows you to examine the contents of the virtual directory through a web browser by browsing to that virtual directory. It's highly recommended that you disable this permission for production web applications, however, because it exposes potentially sensitive information about your file listing to anyone who cares to try it out.

Tip You can try out the Directory browsing permission. Select the check box, click OK, and then browse to `http:\\localhost\ApressBegWeb` on our web server. You'll see a Windows Explorer-like display of the contents of the corresponding physical directory.

You can apply more security settings to your virtual directories to further control access to pages, as discussed in a bit more detail in Appendix B. We'll also discuss security controls set at the ASP.NET level in Chapter 10.

If you choose to do so, you can create multiple virtual directories on your web server, with each one pointing to a different physical location. You can even create multiple aliases for the same physical directory, each with different permissions and settings.

Also in the Properties dialog box is a section for Application Settings. We mentioned earlier that the icon in the IIS console represents a virtual directory that is configured to be the root location for a web application. In this section, you can configure aspects of that application, its permissions, and its relationship with the web server itself. These settings are automatically configured by VS .NET when it creates the web application. There are additional details that are important about this section for IIS 6.0, as explained in Appendix B.

Dynamic Web Applications

One of the things about the `HelloWorld.htm` HTML page is that, no matter how many times you look at it, it's always the same. The entire contents of the page are contained in that one file. In fact, the contents of that page don't need to be generated at all. The web server feeds the HTML from the `.htm` file straight into the HTTP response and back to the browser, and the browser renders the HTML straight onto the screen. Content like this is called *static content.*

Static content doesn't need to be generated at the time it is requested, because it has already been generated before the request was made. (That's why it's the same each time.) It's fine to store your content as a bunch of static `.htm` files; indeed, if your content is static, it's unlikely to be a great burden to your web server when someone requests it. But static content alone doesn't make for an interactive web experience.

If you want your web users to be able to read or update data stored in a database, or if you want you web application to react to the user's actions or make calculations at the time the request is made, your web pages need to be backed up with the processing code that can perform those actions. Additionally, you need that processing code to be executed on request. The result is a more interactive web application involving a certain amount of *dynamic content.*

So, the main difference between static content and dynamic content is simple: static content is generated only once, at the time the file was created, *before* the request is made; dynamic content is generated *after* the request is made. You gain two clear advantages by generating the content after the request is made:

- The web application can tailor the content it generates according to values submitted as part of the request. For example, if you're using an e-commerce web site, and you submit your username and password, the next page you would expect to see is a dynamically generated page containing information about your personal account.

- The web application can tailor the content it generates according to the most recent information available. For example, plenty of sites include a display of the number of users currently using the site. That display is generated using up-to-the-minute information taken at exactly the moment the request is received by the web server.

The main disadvantage of dynamic content is that it takes processor power to generate it. If you have a web server that serves web pages to many consecutive users, and your dynamic pages depend on server-side processing, your web server must be able to support all those users. If you have content that rarely changes, it's better to store it statically and save your server's resources. We'll talk about performance issues in much more detail in Chapter 12, but suffice it to say that static content *does* have its place in web application development, and dynamic, server-side processed pages are *not* for free.

Client-Side Processing and Server-Side Processing

You can create a dynamic, interactive feel to our web applications in two ways: through server-side processing and through client-side processing. This book is largely about the former, and the two certainly play very different roles within the request/response process.

Client-Side Code

You can design your web pages to include *client-side code* that is passed to the browser, along with HTML, as part of the HTTP response. This code executes on the browser, *after* the response is finished (step 6 of the diagram in Figure 1-2, shown earlier in the chapter) and is an effective way to give pages a more lively and interactive feel.

Client-side code can take the form of JavaScript, Java applets, ActiveX controls, and even Flash applications. As we've said, it's the browser that processes this code. Client-side code is often code that is intended to give an instant reaction to button clicks and keyboard presses within the browser. Most modern, rich browsers support JavaScript scripting. To view something like a Flash movie, the browser is likely to need the appropriate plug-in. Some browsers come with Flash preinstalled, but this doesn't mean that *all* browsers do.

Placing large amounts of client-side code in a page comes at a cost. It increases the size of the page, and that makes it slower to load. Moreover, not all browsers can handle client-side code (some users disable client-side scripting to eliminate annoying features like pop-up ads; others use stripped-down browsers to speed up browsing times), and even different types of browsers may handle client-side code differently.

Server-Side Code

The *server-side code* is the place where your application can react to user input and respond with customized results. For example, if you search the Amazon web site for the latest CD by your favorite artist, Amazon's web server executes server-side code to search its datastores for the relevant item. It sorts any items that match the search according to whatever sort criterion you may have specified (perhaps by album name, artist name, or release date) and uses this information to generate HTML that is returned to your browser for display.

The server-side processing takes place much earlier than the client-side processing in the request/response process (step 4 of the diagram shown earlier in Figure 1-2). It's here that the web application can react to data passed as part of the HTTP request, query databases, perform other processing as necessary, and generate the page content (HTML plus client-side code) to be sent back to the browser.

As well as generating HTML, server-side code can also serve to generate client-side code to be sent back to the browser for execution there. This is the sort of feature that ASP.NET has built into some of its server controls (a subject that we'll cover in depth in Chapter 3).

Although server-side code is powerful, it isn't the perfect solution to every requirement. Plenty of features are better coded using client-side code. Often, you can reduce the overall load on the web server with a little judicious application of some client-side code. For example, you can use client-side techniques to prevalidate a registration form before it's submitted to a server, as you'll do in Chapter 3. And you certainly should never use server-side code to handle mouse rollover events (just imagine your clients waiting for a server response every time they moved the mouse!).

Ultimately, a good, interactive, efficient web application is the right blend of dynamic server-side code, client-side code, and static content. Keep in mind that server-side code incurs the cost of network latency, meaning that even if you have a smooth experience at development time (if everything is running locally, which is the most common scenario), an end user accessing the Internet through a modem may not feel the same way.

It's time for an example. The simple HTML example that you tried earlier didn't use any dynamic elements, so let's look at an example that contains some server-side and client-side functionality in an ASP.NET web page.

Try It Out: Create a Dynamic Page You'll use VS .NET to create your first dynamic example, using both server-side code and client-side code. In the next chapter, we'll look at the VS .NET environment and creating ASP.NET applications in more detail. Here, we'll concentrate on a simple example, constructed with a minimum of fuss.

1. Open VS .NET and create a new Visual Basic project: an ASP.NET Web Application project using the address `http://localhost/ClockExample`, as shown in Figure 1-14.

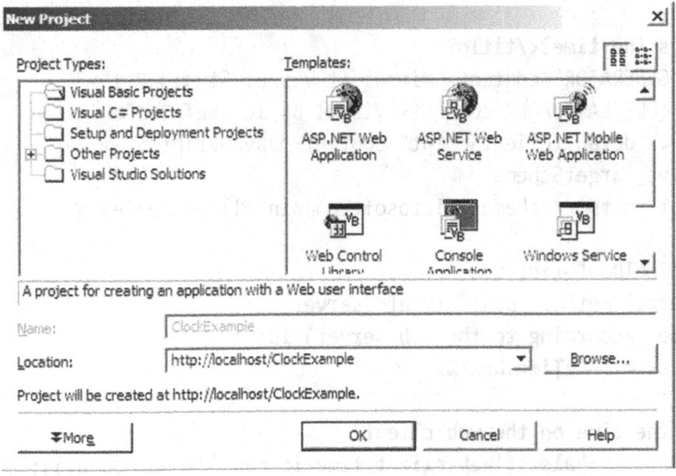

Figure 1-14. *Creating an ASP.NET Web Application project*

2. Once the blank application has been created (this may take a while), you will be presented with a design-time view of a web form. Click the HTML button at the bottom of the form to switch to the HTML view of your page, as shown in Figure 1-15.

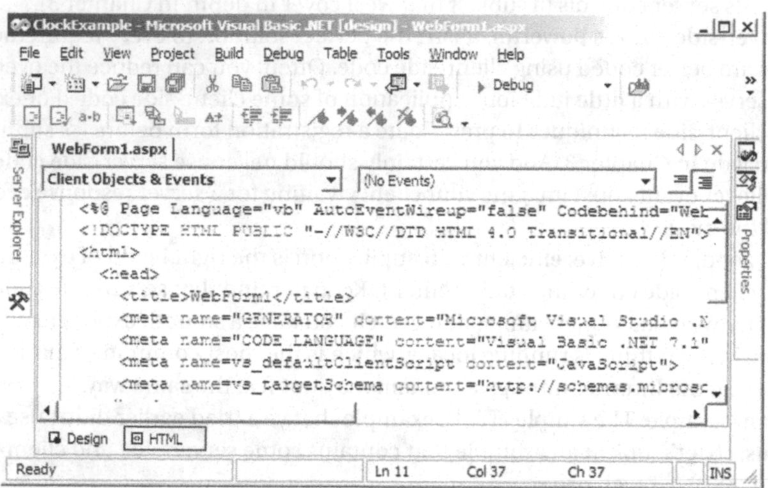

Figure 1-15. *Viewing the HTML display*

3. In the main window with your HTML source code, adjust the code as shown in the following highlighted lines:

```
<%@ Page language="vb" Codebehind="WebForm1.aspx.vb"
         AutoEventWireup="false" Inherits="ClockExample.WebForm1" %>
<!DOCTYPE HTML PUBLIC "-//W3C//DTD HTML 4.0 Transitional//EN" >
<html>
  <head>
    <title>What's the time?</title>
    <meta name="GENERATOR" content="Microsoft Visual Studio 7.1">
    <meta name="CODE_LANGUAGE" content="Visual Basic .NET 7.1">
    <meta name="vs_defaultClientScript" content="JavaScript">
    <meta name="vs_targetSchema"
          content="http://schemas.microsoft.com/intellisense/ie5">
  </head>
  <body MS_POSITIONING="GridLayout">
    <form id="Form1" method="post" runat="server">
      <p>The time (according to the web server) is:
          <%= System.DateTime.Now %>
      </p>
      <p>What's the time on the web client?
        <input onclick="alert('Web client time is now ' + new Date());"
               type="button" value="Client Time"/>
      </p>
```

```
    </form>
  </body>
</html>
```

4. Run the application by pressing F5 or by clicking the Start button on the toolbar.

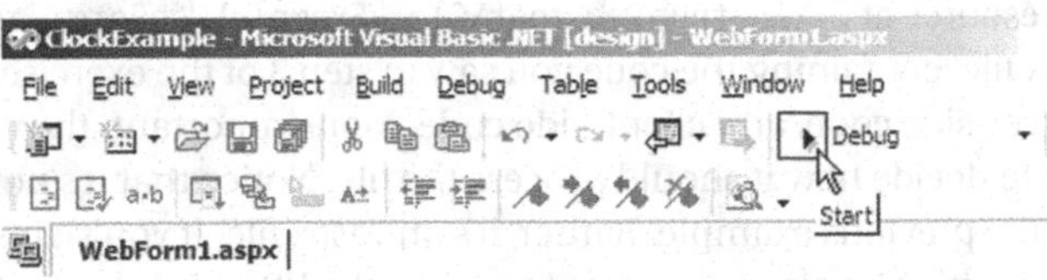

5. When the application runs, you should see the time at which the page was loaded on your web server. Wait a few seconds, and then click the button, and a window should pop up, as shown in Figure 1-16.

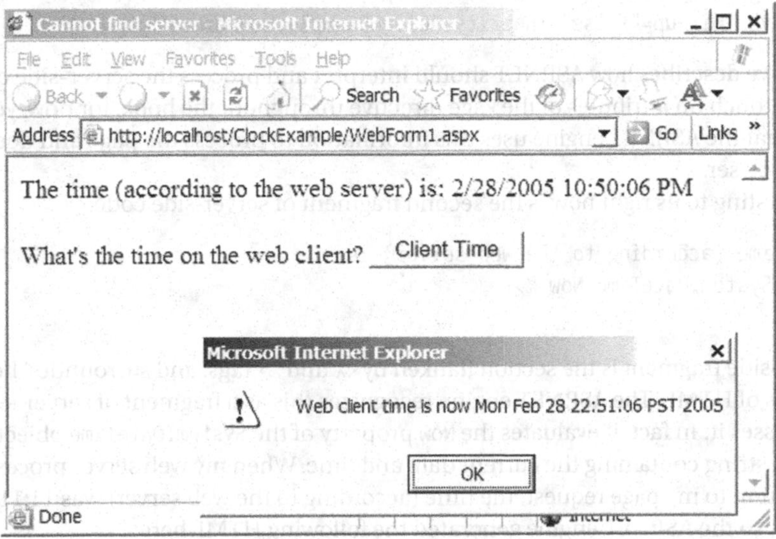

Figure 1-16. *Running you dynamic application*

How It Works

The server-side processing and client-side processing occur at different stages in the overall request/response process, as described in the six-stage diagram shown in Figure 1-2 earlier in the chapter. Figure 1-16 shows what happened when I ran this example.

When I made the request, the browser packaged it into an HTTP request and sent it off to the web server. When the web server received the request, it examined the URL to find out what resource was requested. In this case, it's the web page called `WebForm1.aspx`, located in the physical directory whose alias is `ClockExample`.

This time, you didn't create the `ClockExample` virtual directory yourself. Instead, VS .NET did it for you when you first created the `ClockExample` web application. By default, VS .NET creates a virtual directory for each new ASP.NET web application, and it creates a corresponding physical directory as a subfolder of `C:\Inetpub\wwwroot\` (assuming that C: is the local hard drive on the web server).

So, the web server reads the virtual resource location, `/ClockExample/WebForm1.aspx`, and searches its hard drive for the resource at `C:\Inetpub\wwwroot\ClockExample\WebForm1.aspx`. The resource it finds is an `.aspx` file, containing the code you saw in step 3 of the exercise. This code is a mixture of HTML, server-side code, and client-side code. More important, the web server uses the suffix of the file to decide how it should process the file. Notice that it's not an `.htm` file, like the static page in the previous example. Rather, it's an `.aspx` file. If you've installed IIS and the .NET Framework correctly on your web server machine, the IIS web server software knows that it needs to send `.aspx` files to the ASP.NET engine for server-side processing.

The ASP.NET engine examines the contents of the `.aspx` file, looking for server-side code to process. In fact, it finds only two fragments of server-side code here. The first is a `Page` directive:

```
<%@ Page language="vb" Codebehind="WebForm1.aspx.vb"
        AutoEventWireup="false" Inherits="ClockExample.WebForm1" %>
```

This directive describes how ASP.NET should interpret and process the server-side code in the file. We'll touch on attributes of the `Page` directive throughout the book; for now, you just need to know that the ASP.NET engine uses this information to process the page and does not send it to the browser.

More interesting to us right now is the second fragment of server-side code:

```
<p>The time (according to the web server) is:
    <%= System.DateTime.Now %>
</p>
```

The server-side fragment is the section flanked by `<%` and `%>` tags, and surrounded here by a couple of lines of HTML. The ASP.NET engine recognizes this as a fragment of server-side code and processes it. In fact, it evaluates the `Now` property of the `System.DateTime` object, which returns a string containing the current date and time. When my web server processed this line in reaction to my page request, the time (according to the web server) was 11:11 PM and 39 seconds, so the ASP.NET engine generated the following HTML here:

```
<p>The time (according to the web server) is:
    3/4/2004 11:11:39 PM
</p>
```

There isn't any more server-side code in this `.aspx` file; so with this action, the ASP.NET engine has done its job. The resulting HTML and client-side code are sent to the browser and rendered on the screen. To see what the web server sends to the browser, you can just use View ➤ Source (or a similar option) on the browser, as shown in Figure 1-17.

```
WebForm1[1] - Notepad
File  Edit  Format  View  Help
<!DOCTYPE HTML PUBLIC "-//W3C//DTD HTML 4.0 Transitional//EN">
<html>
  <head>
    <title>What's the time?</title>
    <meta name="GENERATOR" content="Microsoft Visual Studio .NET 7.1">
    <meta name="CODE_LANGUAGE" content="Visual Basic .NET 7.1">
    <meta name=vs_defaultClientScript content="JavaScript">
    <meta name=vs_targetSchema content="http://schemas.microsoft.com/intellisense/ie5">
  </head>
  <body MS_POSITIONING="GridLayout">
    <form name="Form1" method="post" action="WebForm1.aspx" id="Form1">
<input type="hidden" name="__VIEWSTATE" value="dDwxNDEzNDIyOTIxOzs+MyiAiGz/BRQ+S4JR8Nm1j

      <p>The time (according to the web server) is:
          2/28/2005 10:12:58 PM
        </p>
        <p>What's the time on the web client?
          <input onclick="alert('Web client time is now ' + new Date());"
                type="button" value="Client Time"/>
        </p>
      </form>
  </body>
</html>
```

Figure 1-17. *Viewing the source code in a browser*

Most of this is HTML, and there's one bit of client-side script. In the HTML, you have a `<head>` element that contains the title of the page and a few elements of metadata (information about how the page was created, and so on). You also have a `<body>` element that contains what you see on the page. It consists of a `<form>` containing the following:

- A hidden `<input>` element, named `__VIEWSTATE`, which contains encoded information that is generated by ASP.NET and used when working with forms (this is related to the concept of maintaining *state* in applications, introduced in the next section)
- A `<p>` paragraph element containing the time information created by the server
- Another `<p>` paragraph element, which itself contains more text and an `<input>` element of type `button`

It's the button that arouses our interest now. Let's look at that `<input>` tag more closely:

```
<input onclick="alert('Web client time is now ' + new Date());"
       type="button" value="Client Time"/>
```

When the user clicks this button, the `onclick` event is fired and the `alert()` method runs on the browser, producing a message box. This is client-side processing, and the time and date reported are the time and date as calculated by the browser on the client machine, not the web server.

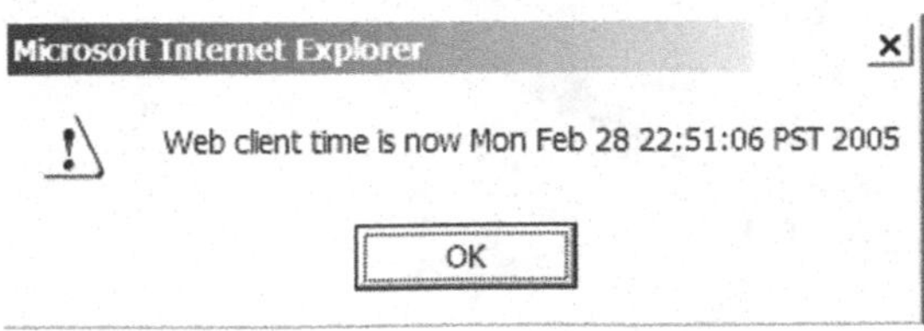

An Introduction to State Management

When you request a resource from a server, using `GET` or `POST`, the server responds to your request and returns the appropriate data. After the HTTP response has been sent back to the client, the server then forgets all about the client. HTTP is known as a *stateless* protocol. This means that state (that is, information relating to the connection and who is at the other end of it) is not retained from one request to the next.

If you were to accept this limitation as unavoidable, it would certainly restrict the usefulness of your web applications. Being able to remember a user is necessary in all kinds of situations. For example, imagine using a site that requires you to log in and being forced to log in for every single page! It would be much easier if you could log in once and have the web server recognize you when you make subsequent requests. Also, consider how important this for an e-commerce site with shopping baskets, in which the web application must remember what shoppers have ordered as they make their way through the pages of the site.

To counter this problem, two important techniques are available. One way is to instruct your application to store state on the server in an object of some type. You could store selected information about the client in a temporary location that exists for as long as the user is browsing the site. The server can then remove this temporary data when the user navigates out of scope of the application or closes the browser.

Alternatively, you can store selected information about the client on the client's machine. The following are two of the most common methods for doing this:

- Place the data in a small file called a *cookie*. You can use cookies to store small amounts of data up to a limit, such as general preferences or login details. Each time a user navigates to your site, those nuggets of data can be passed up as part of the request and used by the web application to achieve an "automatic login" or to personalize the interface.
- Place data in a hidden `<input>` field within the HTML for the page—a technique also used by an ASP.NET feature known as *viewstate*, which you saw in the preceding example. You'll learn more about viewstate and how you can use it in Chapters 2 and 6, and you'll learn about how it affects performance in Chapter 12.

State management is a fundamental aspect of dynamic web applications. We'll have more to say on the subject of statelessness, and strategies for dealing with it, in Chapter 6.

Web Application Architecture

A web application is more than just a collection of web pages. For example, a web application can contain configuration files, stylesheet files (used to control the visual appearance of the site), and files that link to a database server to retrieve information. Figure 1-18 illustrates how a basic web application fits together.

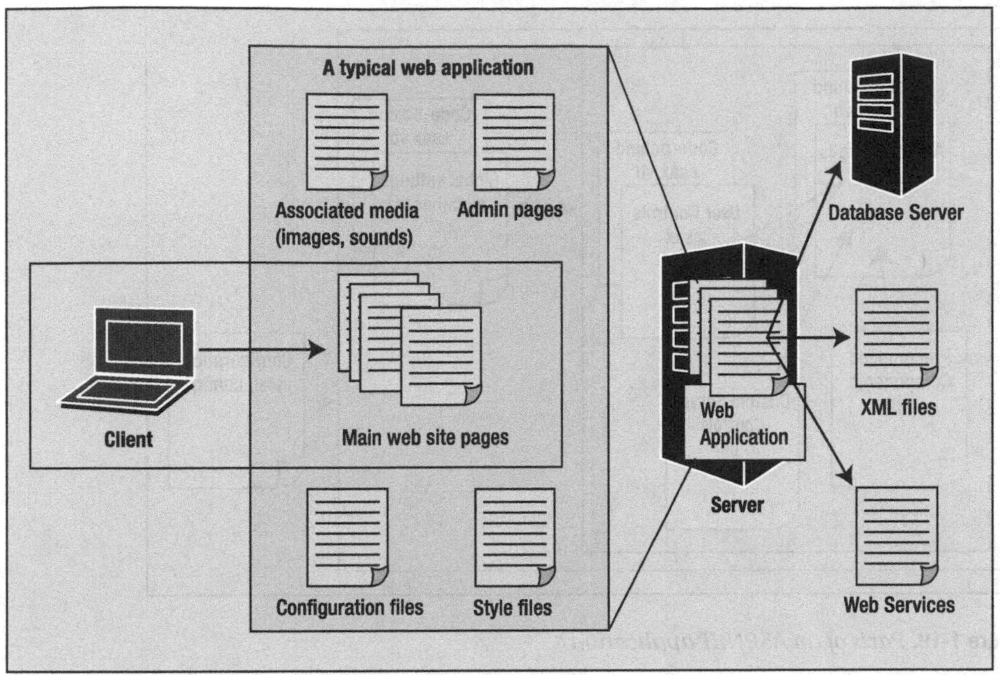

Figure 1-18. *Web application architecture*

The web client (that is, the machine employed by the end user browsing to the web application) can see only the main web site pages. This main site can itself link to images, music files, or pictures that are displayed on the main pages. The site can use separate style files to customize the appearance of the site. The site's configuration can be controlled by individual configuration files, and you can administer your site by using custom administration pages, if you want. The application can draw on information stored in databases, XML files, and even web services.

As you will see in later chapters, ASP.NET web applications follow this model very well. Compared to older technologies like ASP 3.0, ASP.NET web applications can separate each part of the application into a separate file. The architecture of ASP.NET lends itself to *encapsulation* and *reuse*, which means that it's much easier to modularize your applications and avoid reams of repeated code.

When you create an ASP.NET application, you split your application into pieces, as shown in Figure 1-19.

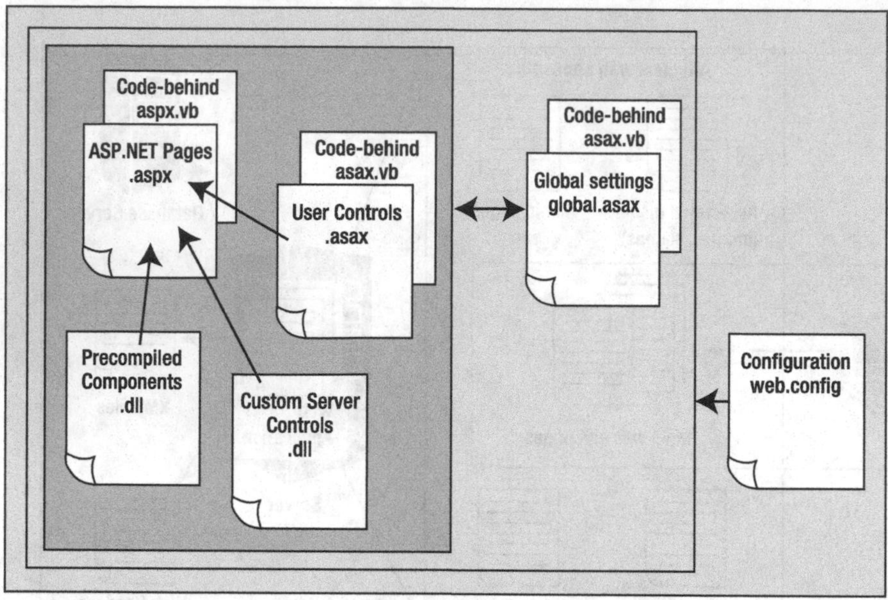

Figure 1-19. *Parts of an ASP.NET application*

At the core of an application is the ASP.NET page, which may have an associated *code-behind* page. This page can use functionality and presentation elements from user controls, precompiled components, and custom server controls, as follows:

User controls: These contain presentation code that is intended to be reused across many pages and can even be cached to improve loading times. An example is a header control that contained links to other parts of your site. You'll see an example of a user control in Chapter 3.

Components: These contain application code that can be reused as required by compiling it into classes that can be used in your ASP.NET pages.

Custom server controls: These are a sort of mixture of precompiled components and the visual characteristics of user controls, in the sense that they are designed for providing reusable visual elements that can be placed on your ASP.NET pages and packaged as independent assemblies (that is, dynamic link libraries). There is a rapidly growing market for professional compiled custom server controls for UI elements such as toolbars, menus, and so on, which can be downloaded, installed, and then deployed in your own applications, much as you could do with ActiveX on the past, but specifically tailored for the web architecture and standards.

The ASP.NET application also has a *global settings file*, `Global.asax`, which can provide application-level support, such as session management, application-level events, storage of information that you can use throughout the application or for the duration of a session, and so on.

Finally, the web application's files are governed by a *configuration file*, `Web.config`, which controls exactly how your application operates; for example, the security settings in place on your application and other settings such as how long each session should last. We'll discuss available settings in the context of each feature in ASP.NET throughout this book.

In Chapter 2, you'll start to learn more about the core ASP.NET components and how an ASP.NET application is constructed. You can gain a lot of insight into the construction of ASP.NET web applications just by using the VS .NET environment, which can create basic template files ready for you to extend and customize as appropriate.

Summary

Windows desktop applications and web applications can be made to behave in similar ways, but under the covers, they are fundamentally different. A desktop application must be installed and executed on the user's machine. In contrast, a web application runs on a machine that could be anywhere in the world, and the user interacts with it remotely through a web browser.

The physical separation of a web client machine and a web application machine means that you need a network-proof set of protocols to allow them to communicate. Each interaction takes the form of a request message and a response message. The web uses HTTP to describe a message, TCP to package it, and IP to address it. At the client end, the user interacts with the web application through a browser or similar piece of software. At the server end, the web application is hosted by web server software, such as IIS.

There are two types of web content. One type is static content, which is generated only once, at the time the corresponding file is created, *before* the user requested it. The other type is dynamic content, which is not generated until *after* the request arrives at the server. Web content can be made to be more interactive by means of dynamic techniques, specifically server-side processing and client-side processing. Most web applications consist of some combination of static content, server-side code, and client-side code.

Typically, a web application is made up of many client/server relationships. For example, a user triggers a browser to request a page from the web server. For the web server to respond, it may, in turn, need to make requests of server-side components, databases, file systems, and other services.

.NET's answer to the problems of web application programming is *ASP.NET*. You've seen a little of how ASP.NET makes it easy for you to design applications in a modular way, to get good organization of your application, and to encourage encapsulation and reuse. In Chapter 2, we'll examine the task of creating ASP.NET web applications in more detail, and we'll explore the VS .NET web development environment and the ASP.NET architecture. Then, in Chapter 3, you'll be ready to start work on the Friends Reunion web application, which is the sample full-scale application you'll develop in this book.

CHAPTER 2

Web Development in .NET

In this chapter, we'll look at how ASP.NET web applications work and how you can create them. We'll examine the structure and elements of an ASP.NET page, and put together some very simple pages that demonstrate basic techniques. All this will help to get you ready to start building the Friends Reunion application in Chapter 3.

Along the way, you'll make good use of the VS .NET integrated development environment (IDE), and you'll start to discover some of the VS .NET tools you'll take advantage of in the web application development tasks covered in this book.

In this chapter, you'll learn more about the following:

- The features available when developing web applications in .NET
- Building web applications using VS .NET
- What goes on behind the scenes of an ASP.NET application and how .NET applies the object-oriented design paradigm to web applications
- What happens when a user requests an ASP.NET page and how server-side code results in client-side content

ASP.NET is at the center of web application development in .NET, so let's start with an introduction to this technology.

An Introduction to ASP.NET

As you saw in Chapter 1, a large-scale web application can be a complicated thing, which takes advantage of many different technologies. If you write your application using the .NET Framework, the technology at the center of it all, pulling everything together, is *ASP.NET*.

So what is ASP.NET? Here's a definition that summarizes the key characteristics:

ASP.NET is an event-driven, control-based, object-oriented architecture that generates content and dynamic client-side code from server-side code using functionality described mostly in the System.Web classes of the .NET Framework.

Let's unravel this statement, so that you can get a better understanding of all the implications of this definition and how ASP.NET is important to web application developers:

ASP.NET generates content and client-side code, either static or dynamic. In Chapter 1, you saw that when a web server receives a web page request, it performs any necessary processing to generate the page response before sending that response back to the browser. ASP.NET is the technology at the center of that processing.

ASP.NET generates responses from server-side code. ASP.NET works on the web server. It takes the page request and executes the necessary server-side code to generate the web page that is sent back to the browser in the response.

ASP.NET is event-driven. ASP.NET pages fire events, and you can write code to react to those events. These events include user-input actions (such as when a user clicks a button or selects an item from a drop-down list on the page) and events that occur as part of the lifecycle of the page (like the `page Load` event, which fires when a page is loaded).

ASP.NET is control-based. ASP.NET relies heavily on reuse of elements of visual functionality known as *server controls*. In this chapter, we'll look at server controls in generic terms. In Chapter 3, we'll cover the different types of server controls, how they work, and how they're used.

ASP.NET uses functionality described in the `System.Web` classes of the .NET Framework. ASP.NET achieves all this using a comprehensive set of .NET Framework classes contained within the `System.Web` namespace and all other namespaces that begin `System.Web.*` (these are sometimes called the ASP.NET classes). It includes functionality for simple ASP.NET pages, web forms, web services, controls, and so on. You'll meet all of these over the course of this book.

ASP.NET is object-oriented. ASP.NET brings the full power of object-oriented techniques to web development. Everything in ASP.NET is extensible and reusable through inheritance and polymorphism, and all features take advantage of abstraction and encapsulation through classes that you can leverage to perform all sorts of actions during the life of the web application. Even so, you don't need to master object-oriented programming in order to start developing attractive and interactive web applications quickly, as you'll discover as you work with ASP.NET.

Two terms that you need to know are *ASP.NET page* and *web form*. An ASP.NET page is a web page that contains server-side elements written using a .NET language, such as VB .NET. An ASP.NET page has a file extension of `.aspx`. A web form is a type of ASP.NET page that contains an interactive form.

Since many ASP.NET pages contain forms, the terms *web form* and *ASP.NET page* are often used interchangeably.

Web Form Construction in VS .NET

If you're familiar with the process of building Windows forms in VS .NET or in Visual Basic 6.0 (VB6), you're probably already comfortable with the way in which these IDEs allow you to work with the interface:

- Use a drag-and-drop technique to add different controls (such as text boxes, labels, drop-down lists, buttons, and so on) to your forms.
- Double-click a control in order to add an event handler to the control's default event, allowing your application to respond to events.

In VS .NET, Microsoft has worked hard to create a web development environment that is similar in look and feel to the Windows development environment you're already used to. So, VS .NET makes the same drag-and-drop techniques available for creating web forms and provides a similar experience whenever you need to code an event handler for your web form.

VS .NET also gives you control over the positioning of your form elements, a Properties browser that allows you to assign features and properties to your controls, and other tools. VS .NET is not the *only* tool available for coding .NET web applications. For example, you can use the ASP.NET Web Matrix, which is a free tool available from `http://www.asp.net`, and it's even possible to code everything using Notepad. But the VS .NET IDE is familiar in look and feel, and it offers a lot of help (IntelliSense, shortcuts, wizards, code generation, and more) when developing applications for the Web.

Note You are not required to use VS .NET when developing ASP.NET web applications in VB. Whatever development tools you choose to use for developing web projects, you'll encounter the same problems (in areas like security, usability, maintainability, debugging, and error handling) that all other web developers encounter. Different IDEs will help you to tackle these problems in different ways. Microsoft has learned a lot of lessons from the limitations of its pre-.NET IDEs and has applied them effectively to VS .NET. The result is a highly usable and integrated IDE, which is why we chose to use it in this book.

Understanding Web Form Structure: Presentation and Processing

In Chapter 1, you saw a very basic example of a web form. It consisted of some HTML code and some in-line VB code. When a user requests this web form, the server runs the simple VB code to work out the current time on the web server, and then sends a page to the browser that has the web server's time (at that instant) displayed on the browser.

Looking back at that code, you'll see that all the presentation code and server-processing code is mixed together in the page:

```
<body MS_POSITIONING="GridLayout">
  <form id="Form1" method="post" runat="server">
    <p>The time (according to the web server) is:
        <%= System.DateTime.Now %>
    </p>
    <p>What's the time on the web client?
      <input onclick="alert('Web client time is now ' + new Date());"
             type="button" value="Client Time"/>
    </p>
  </form>
</body>
```

For a simple page such as this one, mixing the presentation and server-processing code is not too much of a problem. But it's good practice to separate these two different types of code. The standard method for doing this in ASP.NET is to use two different files:

- A file with an `.aspx` extension, which contains all of the *presentation code,* including the HTML and server controls.

- A file with an identical name, but with an added `.vb` file extension, which contains all the *functional code* and is known as a *code-behind* file. It contains only the language-specific (in our case, VB-specific) code in which your classes, methods, and event handlers are coded. Everything in this file is executed on the server.

When you create a web form, VS .NET automatically creates both the `.aspx` file and the `.aspx.vb` file for you.

Keeping the presentation and code-behind information separate is a great way to organize code. It makes the code much more maintainable, and even allows a web page designer and a VB developer to work side-by-side on different elements of the same page.

In addition to these two files, and the automatically generated code contained within them, VS .NET also creates many other files that relate to configuration and setup of your web application. You'll look at these in more detail as you build the main example in this chapter. Let's begin that example now.

Try It Out: Control the Presentation Elements on a Web Form The best way to see all this in action is in an example. Here, you'll create a new VB ASP.NET web application, with a single web form. You'll concentrate on the basic presentational elements of the web form for now, and work on the style (and other) properties and functionality of this web form later in the chapter.

1. Open VS .NET. Create a new Visual Basic ASP.NET Web Application project. Call it `Chapter2Examples` by typing `http://localhost/Chapter2Examples` into the Location box, as shown in Figure 2-1. Then click OK.

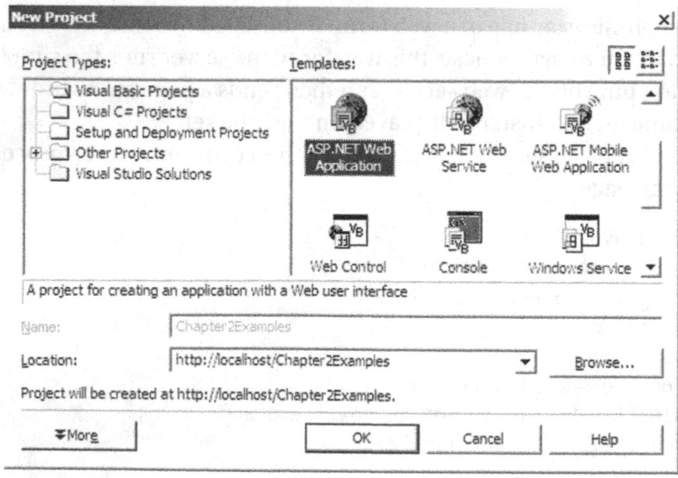

Figure 2-1. *Creating a new ASP.NET Web Application project for the examples in this chapter*

2. Wait a few seconds while VS .NET creates a new web application. During this time, VS .NET is performing all the necessary file creation and configuration of the new web application on your local machine (since you specified `localhost` as the machine name). You should now see the screen shown in Figure 2-2.

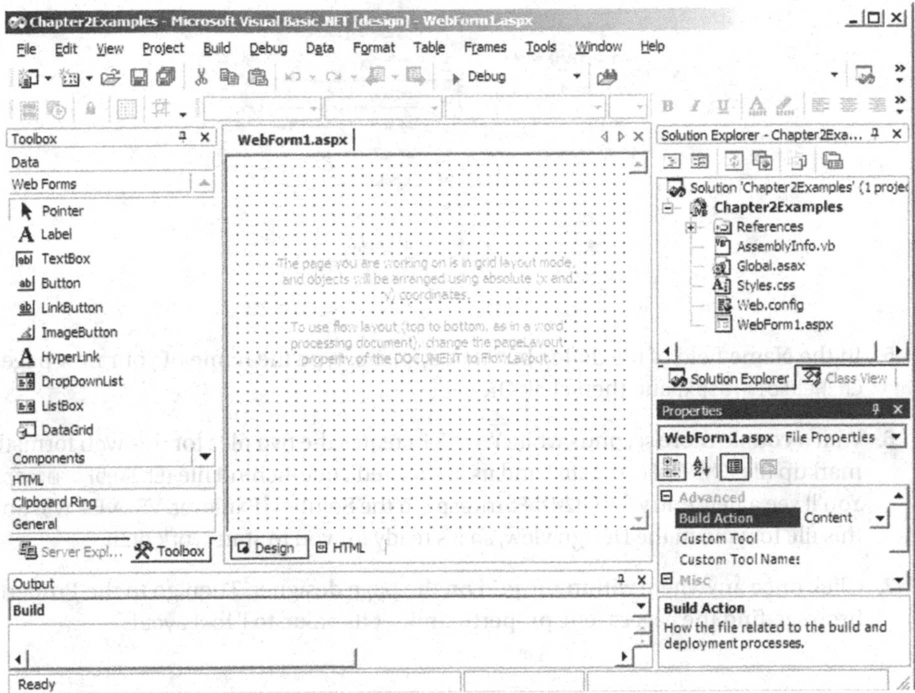

Figure 2-2. *Starting to build a web form*

3. Now you can start to build your web form. As it happens, VS .NET has created a web form, `WebForm1.aspx`, already. You'll remove this web form and create one that has a name of your own choosing. Go to the Solution Explorer (shown at the top right in Figure 2-2), select `WebForm1.aspx`, and delete it. (If you don't see the Solution Explorer, press Ctrl+Alt+L or select View ➤ Solution Explorer.) VS .NET will warn you that `WebForm1.aspx` will be deleted permanently; just click OK.

4. To create a new web form, right-click the `Chapter2Examples` project in the Solution Explorer and select Add ➤ Add Web Form from the context menu.

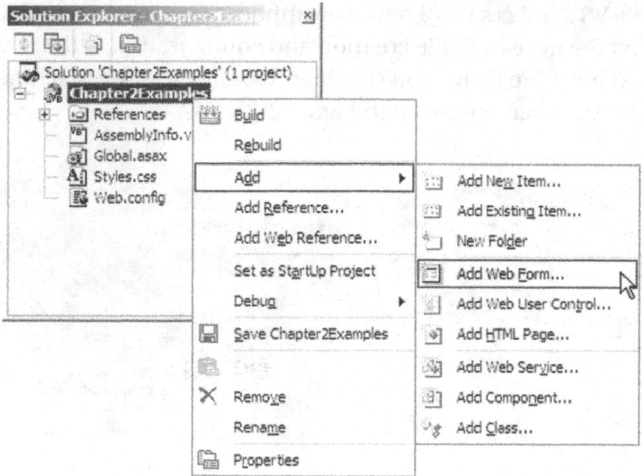

5. In the Name field of the dialog box that appears, type the name of your new page, `Ch2WebForm.aspx`, and then click OK.

6. Wait a couple more seconds while VS .NET creates the two files for this web form: the markup file (`Ch2WebForm.aspx`) and its associated code-behind file (`Ch2WebForm.aspx.vb`). You'll see a new entry for `Ch2WebForm.aspx` in the Solution Explorer. VS .NET will open this file for you, in the Design view, so it's ready for you to start work on it.

7. Click once anywhere within the grid on the page designer. Then go to the Properties browser, find the `pageLayout` property, and set its value to `FlowLayout`.

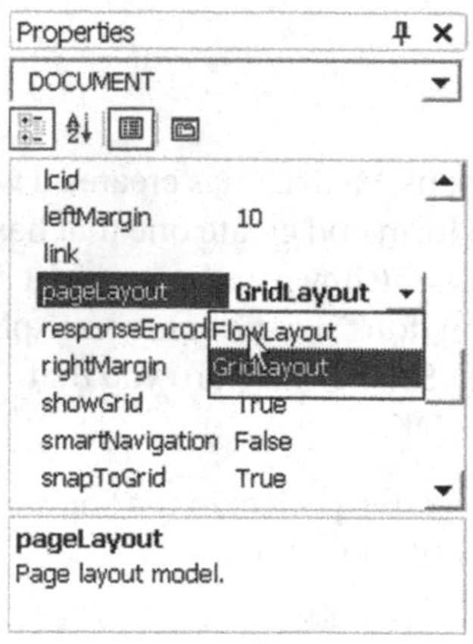

8. Return to the Design view of the page, and you'll see that the grid marks have disappeared.

9. Now you can start adding visual elements to the page. Place your cursor in the Design view of the page and start typing text so that it looks like this:

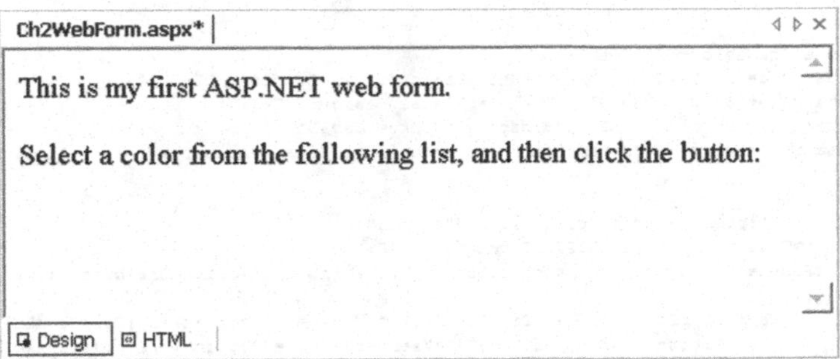

Make sure you press the Enter key at the end of each line of text, so that when you've finished, the cursor is below the second line of text.

10. Look at the Toolbox on the left of the IDE (press Ctrl+Alt+X or choose View ➤ Toolbox if it's not already visible). Select the Web Forms tab, and add a DropDownList control to the page (either double-click the DropDownList item in the Toolbox or drag-and-drop it from the Toolbox onto the page).

11. Add a Button control to the page in the same way, so that it is positioned just after the DropDownList control. Then position your cursor at the end of the line and press Enter to create a new line.

12. Add a Label control to the new line, in the same way you added the other two controls. The Design view for `Ch2WebForm.aspx` should now look like Figure 2-3.

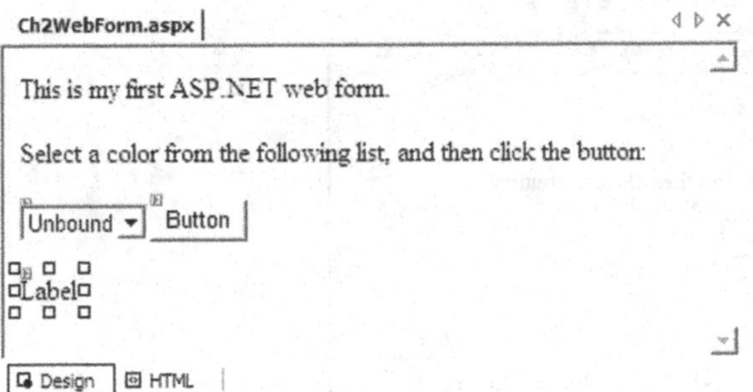

Figure 2-3. *The Ch2WebForm.aspx file in the Design view*

13. Take a look at the presentation code that you've generated by adding these items to the page. Click the HTML button at the bottom of the Design view, and you'll see the code, as shown in Figure 2-4. (We'll discuss this code in more detail in the next section.)

Ch2WebForm.aspx

Client Objects & Events | (No Events)

```
<%@ Page Language="vb" AutoEventWireup="false" Codebehind="Ch2WebForm.aspx.vb" Inherits="(
<!DOCTYPE HTML PUBLIC "-//W3C//DTD HTML 4.0 Transitional//EN">
<HTML>
    <HEAD>
        <title>Ch2WebForm</title>
        <meta name="GENERATOR" content="Microsoft Visual Studio .NET 7.1">
        <meta name="CODE_LANGUAGE" content="Visual Basic .NET 7.1">
        <meta name="vs_defaultClientScript" content="JavaScript">
        <meta name="vs_targetSchema" content="http://schemas.microsoft.com/intellisense/i(
    </HEAD>
    <body>
        <FORM id="Form1" method="post" runat="server">
            <P>This is my first ASP.NET web form.</P>
            <P>Select a color from the following list, and then click the button:</P>
            <P>
                <asp:DropDownList id="DropDownList1" runat="server"></asp:DropDownList>
                <asp:Button id="Button1" runat="server" Text="Button"></asp:Button></P>
            <P>
                <asp:Label id="Label1" runat="server">Label</asp:Label></P>
        </FORM>
    </body>
</HTML>
```

Design | HTML

Figure 2-4. *Viewing the presentation code for the added controls*

14. You can run the project at this stage. To do this, go to the Solution Explorer, right-click `Ch2WebForm.aspx`, and select Set As Start Page. Then press F5 to build the project and run it in Debug mode. This will start up a new browser window with the page displayed, as shown in Figure 2-5.

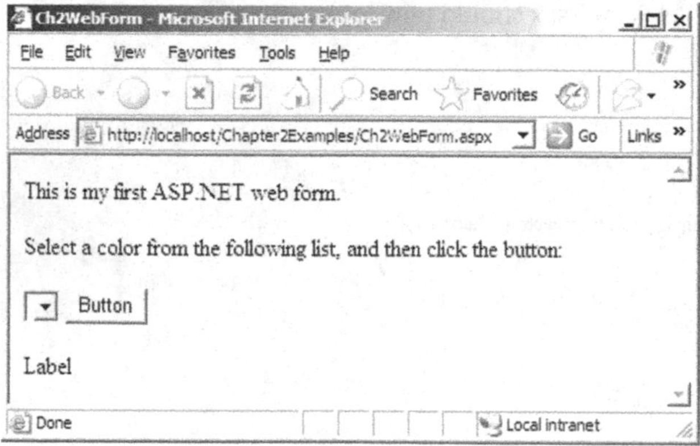

Figure 2-5. *Running the sample form*

How It Works

The first thing you'll notice is that the page displayed in the browser doesn't do very much. There are no entries in the drop-down list, and nothing happens when you click the button. You'll add this functionality later in the chapter (in the "Using Code-Behind" section). For now, let's look at what you've done so far.

The first interesting thing you did was change the page's pageLayout property from GridLayout to FlowLayout.

- *Grid layout mode* is useful for absolute positioning of elements, but it is based on a standard that not all browsers support. It's the only way you can develop Windows applications.

- *Flow layout mode* is a more natural approach to layout. It assumes a top-down, left-right approach and reduces the clutter in the Design view of your pages in the IDE. The layout is more widely used in web applications.

In the next few steps, you created the content that you see on the page. You have a couple of lines of text and three controls. By adding this text and these controls to the page, you've generated a number of new tags in the presentation code in Ch2WebForm.aspx. You may have noticed these new items in step 13, when you looked at the HTML view of the Ch2WebForm.aspx file. Let's examine some aspects of that code more closely.

The first line is a Page directive:

```
<%@ Page language="vb" Codebehind="Ch2WebForm.aspx.vb"
      AutoEventWireup="false"
      Inherits="Chapter2Examples.Ch2WebForm" %>
```

This contains information that ASP.NET uses when it executes the page to generate output for the browser. In particular, note that it indicates that the code-behind file for your Ch2WebForm.aspx page is the file Ch2WebForm.aspx.vb. By default, you don't see this file in the Solution Explorer. In order to see it, you need to select Project ➤ Show All Files or click the appropriate button in the Solution Explorer:

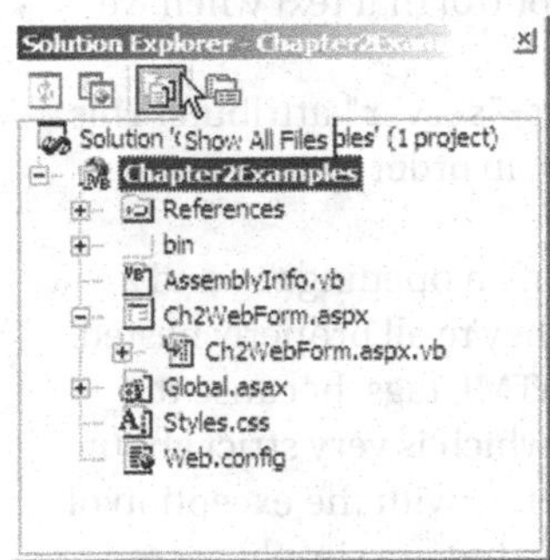

You will be able to see all of the files created by VS .NET this way. We'll take a closer look at these files later in this chapter, in the "ASP.NET Application Files" section.

In the remainder of the code in Ch2WebForm.aspx, most of the interesting stuff is happening inside the <body> element:

```
<html>
  ...
  <body>
    <form id="Form1" method="post" runat="server">
      <p>This is my first ASP.NET web form.</p>
```

```
      <p>Select a color from the following list, and then click the button:</p>
      <p>
        <asp:dropdownlist id="DropDownList1" runat="server">
        </asp:dropdownlist>
        <asp:button id="Button1" runat="server" text="Button">
        </asp:button>
      </p>
      <p>
        <asp:label id="Label1" runat="server">Hello World!</asp:label>
      </p>
    </form>
  </body>
</html>
```

The code here consists of two types of content:

- Simple HTML tags (the `<html>` and `<body>` tags, and the `<p>` tags, which delimit paragraphs on the page)
- The three server controls (represented by the `<asp:dropdownlist>`, `<asp:button>`, and `<asp:label>` elements) that you added to the page via the Toolbox

Each of the three server controls also has the `runat="server"` attribute, which means that when the page is requested, each element is processed at the server, in order to generate HTML to be sent to the client. Each server control also has an automatically generated `id`, which you'll use later (in the "Using Code-Behind" section) to attach functionality to these controls. The `<asp:label>` control has some default text (the string `Hello World!`), which you saw when you viewed the page. Again, you'll add functionality to control that text when we explore using the code-behind file.

The HTML `<form>` tag is special here because it also has a `runat="server"` attribute. This tag is also processed on the server at the time the page is requested, in order to generate HTML for the browser.

It's interesting to note that each of the elements here consists of an opening tag and a closing tag (for example, `<asp:label>` and `</asp:label>`) and that they're all properly nested. In fact, this is more important for the server controls than for the HTML tags, because the server controls are processed on the server by the ASP.NET parser, which is very strict about how each ASP.NET element is arranged. The standard HTML elements (with the exception of the `<form runat="server">` element) are not processed at the server, but are simply passed to the browser. Most browsers tend to be much more forgiving about missing end tags and poor nesting, and they can often compensate for such errors.

VS .NET helps out by ensuring that all of the tags are *well-formed*. Well-formedness is a set of rules about syntax of tags, which includes the rules about nesting and matching start and end tags, which we'll discuss in Chapter 7. For now, VS .NET will take care of the syntax for you, but it's worth being aware of it.

Tip You've probably noticed that all the HTML tags have been created using lowercase characters. You can control this using a setting in VS .NET. Select Tools ➤ Options from the main VS .NET menu. In the Options dialog box, select the Text Editor, then HTML/XML, then the Format node on the left. In the dialog box, look for the two drop-down lists that specify how to format HTML tags and attributes. To make them all lowercase, select Lowercase and click OK. Again, most browsers are forgiving about the use of case in HTML elements; you can use uppercase, lowercase, or a mixture. We think that lowercase is the most visually pleasant, which is why we've used that setting in this book.

You've seen the code that is processed on the server. What about the code that actually gets sent to the browser? You can see this code by looking at the source code in the browser (the exact menu option depends on the browser; in Internet Explorer, right-click the page and select View Source).

You'll see that the HTML code that you saw in the `.aspx` file is still there when the page reaches the browser. However, the ASP.NET `Page` directive is gone. Also, the `<asp:...>` tags are gone, and they have been replaced by more HTML tags. In addition, the `<form runat="server">` element has been processed at the server, to generate more new HTML:

```
<html>
  ...
  <body>
    <form name="Form1" method="post" action="Ch2WebForm.aspx" id="Form1">
      <input type="hidden" name="__VIEWSTATE"
             value="dDwtMTU2OTI3MDUzMzs7Pg8RF9otUlFlTXjrUdHbFIc3CwRT" />
      <p>This is my first ASP.NET web form.</p>
      <p>Select a color from the following list, and then click the button:</p>
      <p>
        <select name="DropDownList1" id="DropDownList1">
        </select>
        <input type="submit" name="Button1" value="Button" id="Button1" />
    </p>
      <p>
        <span id="Label1">Hello World!</span>
      </p>
    </form>
  </body>
</html>
```

The newly generated HTML is shown in bold font here. Essentially, the ASP.NET engine has converted your server-side controls into elements that the browser can understand. For example, the `<asp:dropdownlist>` server control has been converted into an HTML `<select>` element. The ASP.NET engine has also added some information about something called *viewstate,* which we'll mention again when we talk about the code-behind file later in this chapter and study in Chapter 6.

Now let's continue to work on the web form to make it do some interesting things.

Using the Properties Browser

The Properties browser in VS .NET is an extremely useful tool. The Properties browser shows the values of the properties of whatever element, control, or other item is currently in focus and allows you to change those property values. You used it earlier to change the `pageLayout` property of the `Ch2WebForm.aspx` page from `GridLayout` to `FlowLayout`.

The Properties browser is incredibly versatile. In the next simple example, you'll use it to change the `id`s of your controls and to add some basic styling to the text. You'll be using it throughout the book for changing all sorts of properties.

Try It Out: Set Properties on Your Page Let's use the Properties browser to make some adjustments to the property values of elements on the page, ready for the next stage of the example.

1. Return to the Design view of `Ch2WebForm.aspx` (click the Design tab at the bottom of the main window). Check that the Properties browser is visible (if not, press F4 to display it).
2. Place the cursor within the first line of text. The Properties browser will display a `<P>` tag in the drop-down list at the top, which means that the properties you are about to assign apply to the paragraph element at just that point in the page.
3. Set the `align` property to `center`, as shown here.

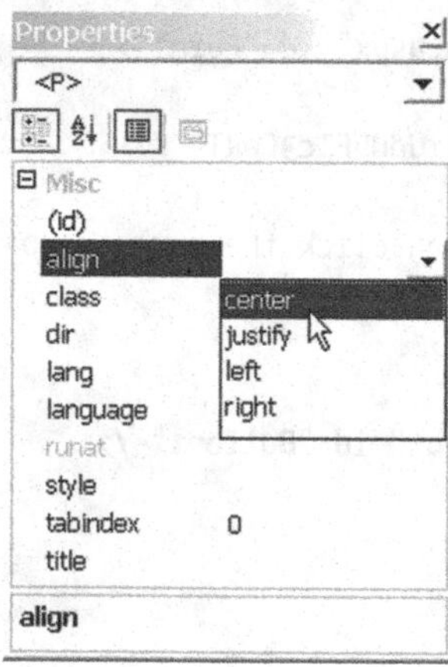

4. Select the `style` property. You can add a lot to the `style` property, so VS .NET provides an editor, the Style Builder, to help. To start the Style Builder, click the ... (ellipsis) button next to the `style` entry in the Properties browser.

5. In the Style Builder, select the Font tab on the left. Click the ... button next to the Family text box to bring up the Font Picker dialog box. Use it to add the two installed fonts Verdana and Arial, and the generic Sans-Serif, in that order. (These fonts will be used in that order of priority; the final one will result in the default sans-serif font being used, if neither of the others is available.) Click OK in the Font Picker dialog box when you're finished.

6. Still in the Style Builder, set the Color to Maroon; set the Specific size to be 12 pt; set the Effects to None; and set the Bold property to Bold. The dialog box should look like Figure 2-6.

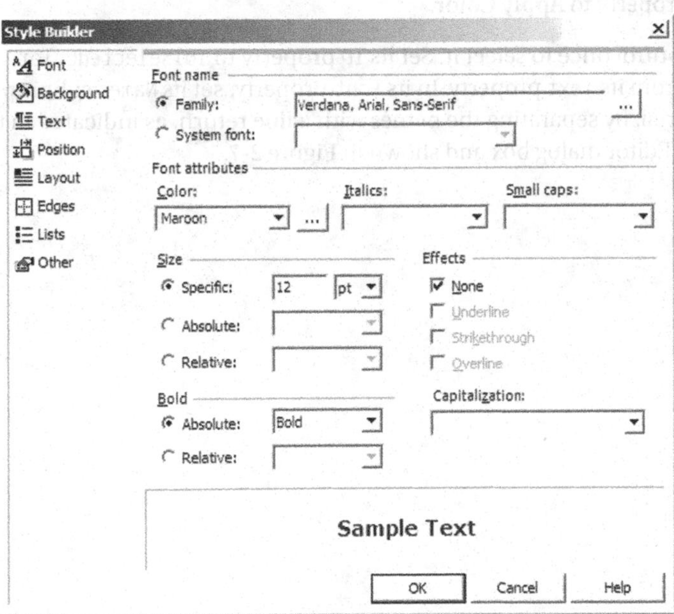

Figure 2-6. *Using the Style Builder to set the style*

7. Click OK to close the Style Builder and apply the styling. You'll see the changes reflected immediately in the Design view.

8. Place the cursor on the second line of text. Leave this line as left-aligned (which is the default), but set the font for this paragraph as in step 5 (Verdana, Arial, generic Sans-Serif).

9. Click the DropDownList control once to select it, and then look in the Properties browser. Change the `ID` of this control to `ddlColorList`.

10. Click the Button control once to select it. Set its `ID` property to be `btnSelectColor`, and change its `Text` property to **Apply Color**.

11. Click the Label control once to select it. Set its `ID` property to `lblSelectedColor`, and remove any text from its `Text` property. In its `Font` property, set its `Names` subproperty to Verdana and Arial, by separating the names with a line return, as indicated in the String Collection Editor dialog box and shown in Figure 2-7.

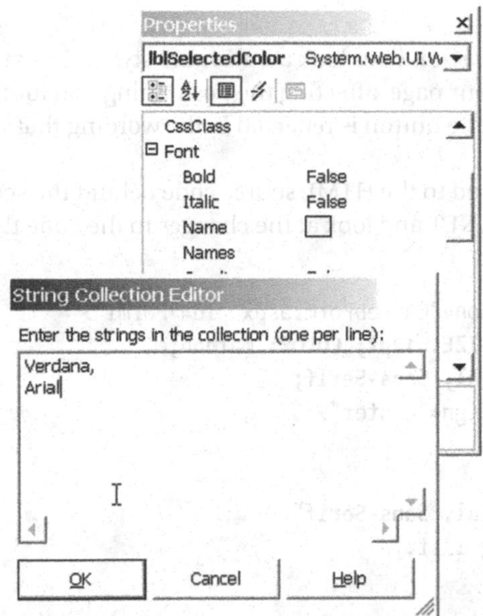

Figure 2-7. *Assigning multiple names to a Label control*

12. Run the project again by pressing Ctrl+F5. You should see the page shown in Figure 2-8 in your browser.

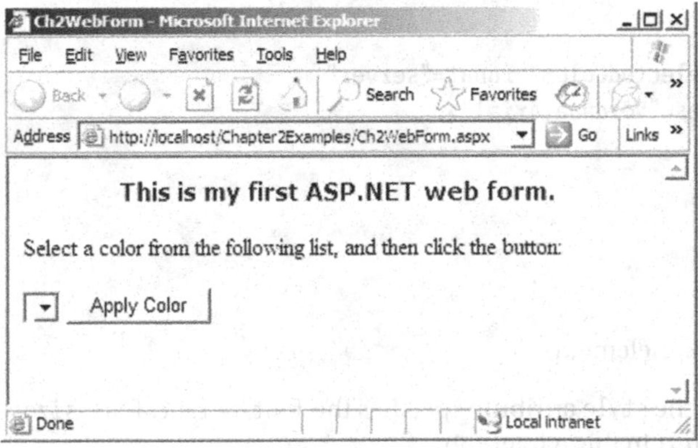

Figure 2-8. *Running the sample form after adding some properties*

How It Works

The page still does not have any functionality, but it does look a little more styled. The style properties control the visual appearance of your page, affecting the positioning and font of the text. Also notice that the Text property of the button is reflected in the wording that you see on the button now.

Let's look at the changes that have occurred to the HTML source code behind the scenes. Go back to the HTML view for the page in VS .NET and look at the changes to the code there:

```
<body>
    <form name="Form1" method="post" action="Ch2WebForm.aspx" id="Form1">
      <p style="FONT-WEIGHT: bold; FONT-SIZE: 12pt; COLOR: maroon;
                FONT-FAMILY: Verdana, Arial, Sans-Serif;
                TEXT-DECORATION: none" align="center">
        This is my first ASP.NET web form!
      </p>
      <p style="FONT-FAMILY: Verdana, Arial, Sans-Serif">
        Select a color from the following list,
        and then click the button:
      </p>
      <p> 
        <asp:dropdownlist id="ddlColorList" runat="server">
        </asp:dropdownlist>
        <asp:button id="btnSelectColor" runat="server"
                    text="Apply Color">
        </asp:button>
      </p>
      <p>
        <asp:label id="lblSelectedColor" runat="server"
                   font-names="Verdana,Arial">
        </asp:label>
      </p>
    </form>
  </body>
</html>
```

Notice the changes in the <p> elements:

- In the first <p> element, the style attribute specifies the font-weight, font-size, color, and font-family of the text in this paragraph.
- In the second <p> element, the style attribute just specifies the font-family.
- The third <p> element doesn't have a style attribute, because you didn't set one there. However, you did set the font-names attribute of the <asp:label> control, and that change is reflected in the code here.

Tip Setting style properties like this gets a bit tiresome when there are a lot of elements on the page and when you're trying to get many elements across many pages to look the same. The solution is to place style definitions into classes in a Cascading Style Sheets (CSS) file, link that file from all your pages, and then use the classes to style the elements. You'll learn more about CSS in Chapter 3, when you begin working on the Friends Reunion application.

Finally, you can see that the changes you made to the `ID` properties of the three server controls are reflected in the page HTML view. These new `ids` are chosen to reflect the purpose of the controls, as you'll see in the next section.

You may have noticed that setting styles for HTML elements and styling server controls are done in different ways. We will look at this and other differences between the types of controls in the next chapter.

Using Code-Behind

So far, you've just been working on the `Ch2WebForm.aspx` file, which contains the presentation elements of your page. You also have the code-behind file, `Ch2WebForm.aspx.vb`, into which you can place code that adds functionality to the elements of the page, making for a more interactive experience. In the code-behind file, you can place the event handlers that handle events raised during the life of the page.

Earlier in the chapter, we pointed out the `<%@ Page %>` directive that appears in the first line of the `Ch2WebForm.aspx` file. As we noted, this line of code contains a reference to the code-behind file, and its purpose is to act as the link between the two files:

```
<%@ Page language="vb"
        Codebehind="Ch2WebForm.aspx.vb"
        AutoEventWireup="false"
        Inherits="Chapter2Examples.Ch2WebForm" %>
```

The `Codebehind` attribute points to the file name of the code-behind file. The `Inherits` attribute points to the namespace and class name defined in the code-behind file, as you'll see in the next example. The `language` attribute specifies that you're going to use VB whenever you write server-side code; hence, your code-behind file must be written in VB.

Finally, the `AutoEventWireup` attribute tells ASP.NET how to associate an event with an event-handler method. If it is set to `true`, the specially named event handlers `Page_Load()` and `Page_Init()` are called automatically by ASP.NET when the page runs. If it is set to `false`, you must explicitly specify which method handles each event. At the end of this example, we'll return to this and take a look at what has been generated.

Try It Out: Add Functionality Using Code-Behind Let's create some interactivity in our example by adding some functional code to the code-behind file. You'll create an array of three colors and list them in the drop-down list. You'll invite the user to select a color and click the button, and you'll arrange that the button click causes some text to appear in the Label control, reflecting the user's choice of color.

1. In the Solution Explorer, right-click `Ch2WebForm.aspx` and select View Code. This will cause the code-behind file, `Ch2WebForm.aspx.vb`, to open in the IDE. Alternatively, you can double-click the web form design surface. VS .NET interprets this as a sign that you want to write code for the page-loading event, and you'll be taken directly to the `Page_Load()` method.

2. In `Ch2WebForm.aspx.vb`, look for the event-handler method called `Page_Load()`, and add the code shown here in bold:

```
Public Class Ch2WebForm
  Inherits System.Web.UI.Page
  ...
  Private Sub Page_Load(ByVal sender As System.Object,
    ByVal e As System.EventArgs) Handles MyBase.Load
    If Not Page.IsPostBack Then
      ddlColorList.Items.Add("Red")
      ddlColorList.Items.Add("Green")
      ddlColorList.Items.Add("Blue")
    End If
  End Sub
End Class
```

3. Return to `Ch2WebForm.aspx` and select the Design view. Double-click the Button control. VS .NET interprets this double-click as a signal that you want to write an event handler for the `Click` event on this Button control, which is designated (by the control developer—in this case, someone on the ASP.NET team) as the default event on the control. It creates an empty method called `btnSelectColor_Click()` in `Ch2WebForm.aspx.vb` that handles the `Click` event. Then it changes the display to show the code-behind file, `Ch2WebForm.aspx.vb`, with the cursor placed inside the `btnSelectColor_Click()` method, ready for you to begin typing.

4. Type the code shown in bold into the `btnSelectColor_Click()` event-handler method:

```
Public Class Ch2WebForm
  Inherits System.Web.UI.Page
  ...
  Private Sub btnSelectColor_Click(ByVal sender As System.Object, _
    ByVal e As System.EventArgs) Handles btnSelectColor.Click
    lblSelectedColor.Text = _
      "You selected " + ddlColorList.SelectedItem.Text()
    lblSelectedColor.ForeColor =
      Color.FromName(ddlColorList.SelectedItem.Text)
  End Sub
End Class
```

5. That's it! Now run the project by pressing Ctrl+F5. When the page loads, select a color from the drop-down list and click the Apply Color button. Your page should look something like the one shown in Figure 2-9.

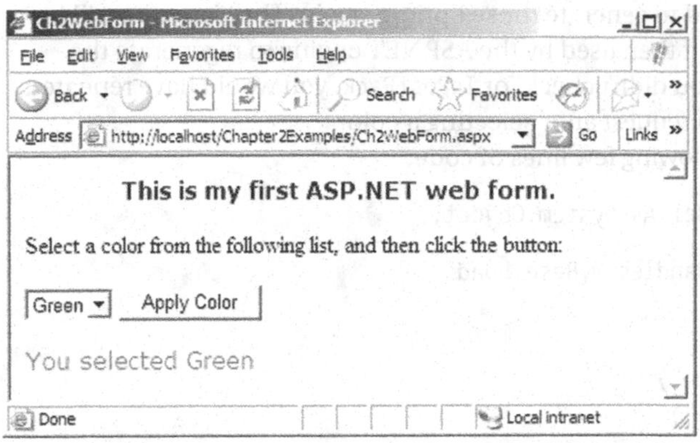

Figure 2-9. *Running the sample form after adding some functionality*

How It Works

All you've done here is add a few lines of functional code to the code-behind page. It didn't take much effort to add an interactive feature to the page (albeit a very simple one).

The first thing you needed to do was to add the colors to the list of options in the drop-down list. You need this to be done at the time the page loads, so that it's already set up and ready for the first time the user clicks the Apply Color button. For this reason, you add the code for this to the `Page_Load()` event-handler method. This method is a private method of the `Ch2WebForm` class, which is the class holding server-side code for this page, and it runs when the page is requested by the user. (We'll talk more about page-related events in the "The Lifecycle of a Page" section later in this chapter.)

The `Page_Load()` event handler runs *every* time the page is loaded. So, as expected, it runs when the page is first called. However, the Apply Color button is a server control, so when the user clicks this button, the browser sends a request to the server for processing, and the page is reloaded. Therefore, the `Page_Load()` event handler *also* runs each time the user clicks the Apply Color button.

So, to handle this, each time the page is loaded, the `Page_Load()` code uses the `Page.IsPostBack` property to find out whether the request is a first-time request or a *postback*; that is, the page is being re-requested by the user so that the web server can process an event and regenerate the page. If `Page.IsPostBack` is `false`, it's a first-time request. In this case, you need to add the three options to the drop-down list. If `Page.IsPostBack` is `true`, it's a postback. In this case, the data for the options has already been generated once and used to create the options in the drop-down list. Then those options are stored within the HTML that's sent to the browser, in Base64-encoded format, in a hidden HTML `<input>` tag called *viewstate*:

```
<form ...>
  <input type="hidden" name="__VIEWSTATE"
         value="dDwONDY2MjMzMjtoPDtsPGk8MT47 ... ... QFJWeORw=" />
  ...
</form>
```

Using this method, you don't need to generate those options again. The viewstate will be sent to the server with the request, and then used by the ASP.NET engine to regenerate the three items in the drop-down list. If you didn't check for `IsPostBack`, you would have repeated items added each time the user sent a request after selecting a color.

You achieve all that in just the following few lines of code:

```
Private Sub Page_Load(ByVal sender As System.Object,

  ByVal e As System.EventArgs) Handles MyBase.Load
  If Not Page.IsPostBack Then
    ddlColorList.Items.Add("Red")
    ddlColorList.Items.Add("Green")
    ddlColorList.Items.Add("Blue")
  End If
End Sub
```

Each of the three `Add()` method calls adds an item to the `Items` collection of the control, which lists the available options.

Tip Adding and displaying dynamic data on controls is so common in web development that it has been greatly simplified and enhanced with a powerful concept called *data binding*, which frees the developer from linking data to controls manually. We'll study this subject in more detail in Chapter 5.

The button's `Click` event handler is much easier. When you double-click the Button control, the IDE creates an event-handler method in the code-behind file. Note that the IDE chose to name this event-handler method `btnSelectColor_Click()`, after the `ID` property of the Button control (which you set to `btnSelectColor` earlier in the chapter) and the event it's intended to handle. As is usual in VB, the method is wired to the appropriate button event through the `Handles` keyword:

```
Private Sub btnSelectColor_Click(ByVal sender As System.Object,
  ByVal e As System.EventArgs) Handles btnSelectColor.Click
```

In the event-handler method, there are just two lines of code. The first assigns some text to the `Text` property of the Label control, and the second changes its foreground color. Both use the expression `ddlColorList.SelectedItem.Text`, which returns the value of the option that the user selected in the drop-down list before clicking the Apply Color button:

```
Private Sub btnSelectColor_Click(ByVal sender As System.Object, _
  ByVal e As System.EventArgs) Handles btnSelectColor.Click
  lblSelectedColor.Text = _
    "You selected " + ddlColorList.SelectedItem.Text()
  lblSelectedColor.ForeColor =_
    Color.FromName(ddlColorList.SelectedItem.Text)
End Sub
```

There is one extra bit of work to do in the second line. Notice that the selected color value is a string, but the `ForeColor` attribute expects an object of type `System.Drawing.Color`. Therefore, you use the static `FromName()` method of that class to create a `Color` object based on the string name of the color. The `System.Drawing` namespace is imported for all web projects by default.

We'll revisit many of these concepts in later chapters. In particular, in the next chapter, we'll concentrate on the different types of controls and how they're used.

A Brief Tour of An ASP.NET Application

ASP.NET is an order of magnitude more structured than any other web development environment Microsoft has ever produced. You've already seen that it is object-oriented, event-driven, and control-based. Its design also heavily promotes the benefits of code reuse and compiled versus interpreted code execution. In the remaining pages in this chapter, you'll take a brief tour of some of these aspects of ASP.NET.

ASP.NET Application Files

You've already seen some of the files in an ASP.NET application; specifically, each web form consists of an `.aspx` file and its associated `.aspx.vb` code-behind file. A quick look at the Solution Explorer (or, indeed, through Windows Explorer, a look at the folder that contains the application) indicates that a number of other files are created by default when VS .NET creates a new VB ASP.NET web application.

Let's look at some of these files. Return to the Solution Explorer, click the Show All Files button, and expand the resulting nodes. You'll see a number of files that were previously hidden from view.

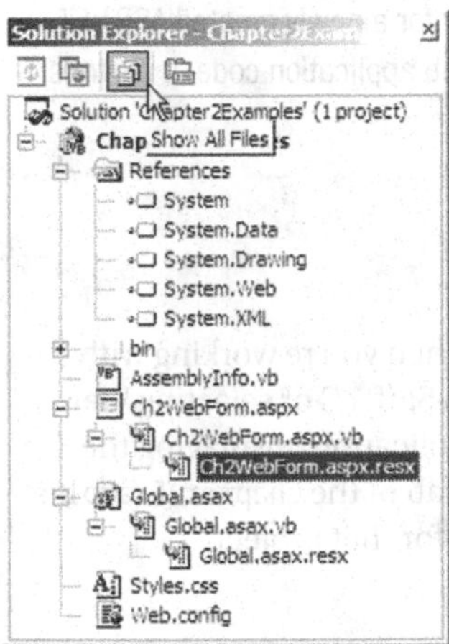

Notice that besides the `Ch2WebForm.aspx.vb` code-behind file that was created automatically when you created your web form, there's another file associated with the web form: an `.resx` file. This is known as a *resource file,* which contains any other information external to the form itself. VS .NET uses it for its drag-and-drop visual designer.

What other files do you see here? Here's a brief résumé of the more important files, from the point of view of this book:

References files: Under the References node are a number of child nodes. Each one looks as if it relates to a namespace. In fact, these are the names of the assemblies that are linked to the application. Each assembly contains compiled code. These five hold the compiled classes contained in five namespaces. (For convenience, many of .NET's namespace classes are compiled into assemblies of the same name as the namespace; for example, the `System.Data` namespace classes are compiled into `System.Data.dll`.) The five shown in the example are the five assemblies linked to an ASP.NET application by default when it's created in VS .NET, so the classes in these namespaces are available to you immediately.

`Global.asax` and `Global.asax.vb`: Further down the list, the next important files are `Global.asax` and `Global.asax.vb`. This pair is where you put the methods that handle application-level and session-level events (for example, the `Application_Start()` method, which runs when the application starts up, and the `Session_Start()` method, which runs whenever a new user session starts). It's also the usual place to keep global variables. You'll find some uses for `Global.asax` during the development of the Friends Reunion application, in subsequent chapters.

`Web.config`: At the bottom of the list, the `Web.config` file is used to customize the configuration of your web application. It can contain all sorts of information about application settings, security settings, session-state timeout settings, compilation settings, error-handling options, and so on. You'll see this file mentioned in quite a number of the following chapters, whenever you need to apply application-specific settings.

Note You'll also notice the `AssemblyInfo.vb` file in the Solution Explorer for a newly created ASP.NET application. This file contains assembly attributes relating to the compiled web application code. It controls versioning, signing of the assembly, culture information, and so on.

The Class View

The Class View window is another tool that often comes in handy when you're working with ASP.NET applications. You can display this window by pressing Ctrl+Shift+C or selecting View ➤ Class View. This window offers a slightly different view of your application, displaying the *class hierarchy* of the web application. If you look at the Class View tab of the `Chapter2Examples` project and expand a couple of nodes, you'll see the class hierarchy for that project.

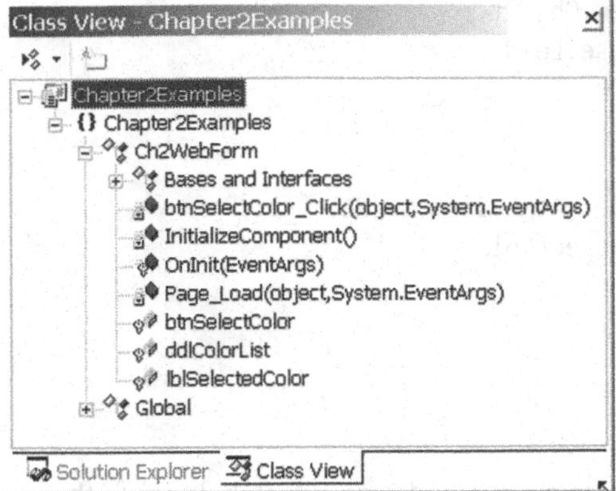

In this example, you can see a few methods:

- The `btnSelectColor_Click()` method, which runs in response to the `Click` event of the `btnSelectColor` Button control
- The `InitializeComponent()` method, which is involved in initialization by the page designer
- The `Page_Load()` method, which runs when the page loads
- The `Page_Init()` method, which handles the page's `Init` event and calls `InitializeComponent()`

Under these methods, you can see variables representing the button, drop-down list, and label that you created.

If you double-click any of these nodes, VS .NET takes you immediately to the point in the code at which that item is defined. As your applications grow more complex, you may find this to be a useful tool for finding your way around in the code.

Object Orientation in ASP.NET

The .NET programming environment is fully object-oriented, and that holds true in .NET *web* application programming, too. Take a look at the simple `Chapter2Examples` project. It contains a class called `Ch2WebForm`, which is the page class for your `Ch2WebForm.aspx` web form (you can see this in the code in `Ch2WebForm.aspx.vb`):

```
Public Class Ch2WebForm
  Inherits System.Web.UI.Page
  ...
  Protected WithEvents ddlColorList As System.Web.UI.WebControls.DropDownList
  Protected WithEvents btnSelectColor As System.Web.UI.WebControls.Button
  Protected WithEvents lblSelectedColor As System.Web.UI.WebControls.Label
  ...
```

```
    Private Sub Page_Load(ByVal sender As System.Object,
      ByVal e As System.EventArgs) Handles MyBase.Load
      ...
    End Sub

    Private Sub btnSelectColor_Click(ByVal sender As System.Object, _
      ByVal e As System.EventArgs) Handles btnSelectColor.Click
      ...
    End Sub
End Class
```

From this code fragment, you can see that:

- The `Ch2WebForm` page class inherits from a base class called `Page`, which belongs to the `System.Web.UI` namespace.
- The `Ch2WebForm` page class contains member declarations and can contain public and private properties, and so on.
- Each of the controls in the page (the drop-down list, the button, and the label) is declared as a protected member of the `Ch2WebForm` page class, whose events can be handled by methods on the class (`WithEvents` keyword). Each member is an instance of a class that resides in the `System.Web.UI.WebControls` namespace.

All this comes from the fact that ASP.NET provides a truly object-oriented approach to web application development.

Reusability and Encapsulation

The object-oriented nature of ASP.NET also manifests itself in the level of *code reusability* that is possible. The `Ch2WebForm` page provides a simple example of this: each of the three controls in the `Ch2WebForm.aspx` page is a reuse of an existing class. Each class is developed and tested by Microsoft; it's compiled, ready to use, and easy to deploy. When you're developing web forms, you don't need to think about the internal complexities of these controls' classes—you can just drag-and-drop to create instances of the classes in your code.

The three controls you used in this chapter's example are just a small sample of the vast library of classes made available in the .NET Framework. There are some 17 namespaces, which contain the classes that make up ASP.NET's core functionality. These namespaces organize the classes into logical groups; each of them is prefixed with the name `System.Web`.

Much of the structure of ASP.NET applications is built up from these classes, so you spend some of your time creating instances of ASP.NET classes or writing your own classes that inherit from them (as you saw in the `Ch2WebForm` example). There isn't space to list all of the namespaces here, but it's worth noting a few of the most commonly used ones:

`System.Web`: This namespace contains classes for processing ASP.NET pages at their lowest level and defining how ASP.NET relates to the web server. It contains classes for handling information passed via HTTP, as discussed in Chapter 1, such as `HttpRequest` and `HttpResponse`.

System.Web.UI: This namespace contains a lot of functionality that you use when constructing your pages. It's one level of abstraction higher than the classes contained in the System.Web namespace. When you construct an ASP.NET page, the classes in this namespace are used to ensure the page has the correct structure. (The page class is one of the classes in this namespace.) These classes define the functionality available to all ASP.NET pages. You'll understand this better when we discuss how pages are loaded and processed a little later in this chapter, in the "Lifecycle of a Page" section.

System.Web.UI.WebControls and System.Web.UI.HtmlControls: These namespaces contain the control elements that you add to the page. (For example, the DropDownList, Button, and Label controls you added to the Ch2WebForm page are all instances of classes contained in the System.Web.UI.WebControls namespace.) Each of these controls inherits some basic functionality from the System.Web.UI.Control class, but they also add their own functionality on top of this to provide a rich UI element. You'll learn a lot more about the classes in these namespaces in Chapter 3.

System.Web.Services and its child namespaces: These namespaces are somewhat different from all the rest. They are specifically designed for the development of web service applications. We'll defer discussion of them until Chapter 9, which covers web services.

Finally, note that ASP.NET applications are not restricted to using the classes of the System.Web.* namespaces. Elsewhere in the .NET Framework, there are many other (non-ASP.NET-specific) namespaces, whose classes can be used in ASP.NET applications to connect to data sources, build complex graphical interfaces, manage file systems and configuration, and perform many other tasks. In fact, you'll be making good use of some of them during the course of the book.

Compilation

You're probably already aware that a program created in VB must be compiled before it can be run. The same is true of VB ASP.NET applications, where there is a three-stage compilation process:

- In the first stage, all the classes are compiled into Microsoft Intermediate Language (MSIL), in the form of a .NET Assembly. This is done at design-time, when you *build* the web application project.
- In the second stage, the first time an .aspx page is requested, it's compiled into a temporary assembly, too.
- In the final stage, the Just-In-Time (JIT) compiler compiles the MSIL to be used (both from the code-behind and from the compiled page) into machine code, and it is finally executed.

Thus, the first call to a web page demands significant more work (page compilation and the JIT compilation from MSIL to machine code). Second and subsequent calls to the page will receive a much faster response, because the page class is already fully compiled to native machine code by then.

When you prepare a VS .NET web application for execution, all of the code files within the application (including the code-behind files) are compiled into an MSIL *assembly*; the web application depends on this assembly to run.

When you run an application (as you did earlier in the chapter by pressing the Ctrl+F5 shortcut), VS .NET first creates the assembly, and then it uses the assembly file to run the application. The assembly file for the example in this chapter is called `Chapter2Examples.dll`.

The Lifecycle of a Page

In the first chapter, we described the sequence of processing steps that occurs, beginning when a user requests a static page. It's helpful to expand the steps fulfilled by ASP.NET when the incoming request is processed by the server, and ending with the content being routed back to the user's browser. Given the event-based nature of ASP.NET, we'll focus on the events fired at each stage during processing.

The sequence depends on whether the request is the *first* request for a page or a *subsequent* request for the same page that is initiated via a postback. You saw this in the `Ch2WebForm` example, in which the task of getting the options in the drop-down list was achieved by loading it programmatically when the user first loaded the page or automatically by using the encoded data in the viewstate (when the user clicked the Apply Color button and generated a postback).

Figure 2-10 shows what happens each time the client requests a page, via either an original request or a postback.

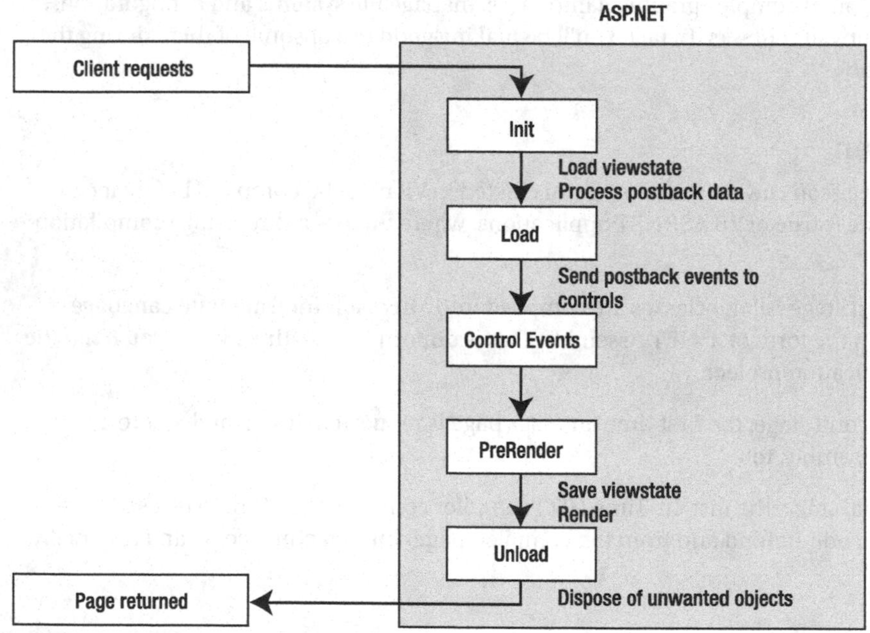

Figure 2-10. *What happens each time the client requests a page*

The System.Web.UI.Page class, from which every page ultimately inherits, exposes these stages for you to consume and customize. There's a common pattern for customizing these phases: you can attach a handler for an event, such as Init or Load, or you can override a corresponding method on the page class, such as OnInit or OnLoad.

In Figure 2-10, there are five main stages—Init, Load, Control Events, PreRender, and Unload—and you are able to add code that is processed at each of them. Other actions also occur between these main phases, completing the picture of how a page is processed. As we said, the main events can be handled in two ways: by attaching to the event itself or by overriding the corresponding method. For example, there's an Init event and an OnInit virtual method you can override. When you override, you must always remember to call the base class method, as in the following example:

```
Protected Overrides Sub OnPreRender(ByVal e As System.EventArgs)
  MyBase.OnPreRender(e)
  ' Do our stuff
End Sub
```

This ensures that all built-in processing implemented in the base class is properly executed. Most notably, calling the base method implementation ensures the appropriate event is fired.

Let's analyze each of the five stages of a page's lifecycle.

The Init Stage

When the page request is first received by the ASP.NET engine, the Init stage ensures proper setup of the framework of the page and preparation of the controls on the page for rendering. Most controls perform their initialization at this moment. By default, the VS .NET-generated code-behind class handles the Init event of the base class to hook the InitializeComponent() method, where further component initialization may happen:

```
Private Sub Page_Init(ByVal sender As System.Object, _
  ByVal e As System.EventArgs) Handles MyBase.Init
  'CODEGEN: This method call is required by the Web Form Designer
  'Do not modify it using the code editor.
  InitializeComponent()
End Sub
```

Following this phase are a couple of smaller processes. First, if there is any viewstate, it is loaded. In other words, the ASP.NET engine looks for data that was contained in the page in a hidden <input name="__VIEWSTATE"> tag and has been included in the page request. If it finds any such data, it reads and decodes it, ready for use in the (re)generation of the page. In the Ch2WebForm example, this equates to collecting encoded data contained in the <input name="__VIEWSTATE"> tag that relates to the options in the drop-down list.

Second, the *postback* data is processed. In the Ch2WebForm example, when the user clicks the Apply Color button, the web form fires a postback containing information for the server to process (specifically, the color selected by the user in the drop-down list).

The Load Stage

When a page is fully initialized and any state has been properly restored (either from viewstate or postback), the main event raised is the `Load` event. The corresponding method you can override is `OnLoad()`. By default, VS .NET always adds the `Page_Load()` method and sets it to handle this event:

```
Private Sub Page_Load(ByVal sender As System.Object,
  ByVal e As System.EventArgs) Handles MyBase.Load
End Sub
```

This is a useful facility for the developer, as this is usually the best place to add code that controls global page behavior. (In the `Ch2WebForm` example, you used the `Page_Load()` method to check whether the request was a postback, and if not, to populate the options in the drop-down list.)

The Control Events Stage

In the Control Events stage, the ASP.NET engine deals with a series of events that are raised and handled. If the page is being posted back, this includes events raised by the user. For example, the `Click` event of the `btnApplyColor` Button control would be handled here.

The PreRender Stage

The corresponding method for handling the `PreRender` event is called `OnPreRender()`. At this stage, you can perform last-minute changes to the way the page is rendered and have these changes preserved across postbacks. ASP.NET will save the state of your page just after this phase, into the viewstate that will be returned to the client.

The single most important process in the page lifecycle that is not an event is the call to the `Render()` method. By default, this method renders each server control by generating the HTML that the browser will need to display. You can override it to make more last-minute changes that affect how your page is rendered. These changes, however, are not preserved across postbacks, because the viewstate has already been saved.

The Unload Stage

In the final stage, you have code that cleans up unused objects, such as data connections that you don't need anymore. Here again, you can either use the `Unload` event or override the `OnUnload` method. Immediately after this event, the page is disposed of.

Summary

We started this chapter with a definition of ASP.NET. We said that it is an event-driven, control-based, object-oriented architecture that generates content and dynamic client-side code from server-side code using functionality described in the `System.Web` classes of the .NET Framework. The intention of this chapter was to explore this definition, expanding and clarifying the assertions it makes, and demonstrating the concepts and techniques that derive from it. You've seen that:

- A web form is a special kind of ASP.NET page, which contains an HTML `<form>` element processed on the server (`runat="server"` attribute).
- A web form developed in VS .NET with VB consists of an `.aspx` file and an associated `.aspx.vb` code-behind file. These two files represent the separation of presentation markup and functional code.
- The VS .NET IDE makes it easy to rapidly create web forms using drag-and-drop techniques in the visual designer.
- Events and event handling are core to ASP.NET, since events occur at many stages in the life of an ASP.NET page. The lifecycle of a page runs through initialization, loading, event handling, prerendering and rendering, and finally, unloading and disposal.
- Adding a control to a web form page is simple, and setting properties for a control is equally simple using the VS .NET tools. It's also easy to write event handlers, which contain the code to run on the server so that it reacts to events raised by your controls, originating from client actions.
- The functionality available to ASP.NET comes from a series of classes built into the .NET Framework. The `System.Web.*` namespaces contain a huge number of classes that provide much of the functionality you need to write web forms. This functionality includes class definitions for your controls, for handling the rendering process, and much more. The non-ASP.NET Framework namespaces are also available for you to work with.
- ASP.NET is a part of the object-oriented world of .NET, and its object-oriented nature brings flexibility and extensibility.

In the next chapter, you'll begin the task of building a web application called Friends Reunion. By the end of that chapter, you'll have a simple working application with a few pages. In each subsequent chapter, you'll continue to add functionality and features to the application.

Along the way, we'll build on the foundation of Chapters 1 and 2, and we'll explore a number of concepts and technologies that help to enhance web applications. We'll look at controls, data access and data binding, state, XML and schemas, web services, and security. We'll also consider some important development-related issues: debugging, exception handling, performance, and deployment.

We'll start at the beginning, with an exploration of user interfaces and server controls in ASP.NET.

CHAPTER 3

■ ■ ■

User Interfaces and Server Controls

In Chapter 2, we examined the architecture and purpose of web forms, and discussed how they improve the concept of a web page. You began to see how, in combination with the IDE provided by VS .NET, ASP.NET's *server (or server-side) controls* can transform web page design into the drag-and-drop ballet that our colleagues in the Windows desktop programming department have enjoyed for so long. The way that server controls work is ingenious. While you're designing your web application, server controls behave like any other controls, allowing you to position them and set their properties through the familiar Properties browser. At runtime, they generate the HTML code necessary to render themselves identically in web browsers, using nothing but standard HTML elements and possibly client-side scripts if needed.

Mastering ASP.NET server controls will make you a highly productive web developer, with an intuitive feel for which controls should be used when. This chapter aims to teach this proficiency by describing:

- How ASP.NET's HTML controls compare with HTML elements
- How to react to events fired by controls, on both the server side and the client side
- Different ways to change the appearance of controls, using attributes and stylesheets
- The advantages of web server controls, especially their design-time benefits and unified object model (common set of properties, methods, and events)
- How to make web-based data capture more reliable by using the validation controls
- How to create user controls and custom controls that expand on built-in functionality
- How to use dynamic content to generate user-aware web applications

In this chapter, you'll have your first look at a sample application that you'll be returning to in each remaining chapter of this book. The Friends Reunion application is a simplified take on a class of web sites that is currently quite popular. The idea is to allow registered users to enter details of schools and colleges they've attended or places they've worked. Then people who were at the same place at the same time are given the opportunity to contact one another. As you progress, this application will become ever more complex, but you'll start here with some basics: a login form, registration form, and a page for general news items. You will also work on some header and footer components, which are common in web applications.

Server Controls

In the examples in Chapter 2, you had some experience with server controls: the Button and DropDownList controls. In this chapter, you'll soon discover that most of the other server controls at your disposal in VS .NET are just as easy to place and use. While a page is being designed, server controls appear as controls that you can configure through the Properties browser, changing their appearance, default values, and so on. At runtime, ASP.NET transforms them into plain old HTML code that it sends to the browser.

Server controls offer real productivity gains over other methods of web page design, not only because of their ease of use, but also because they conform to the .NET programming model. They make the process of building a page as easy as designing a Windows Forms application. You drag controls onto your pages, tinker with their properties, and there's your user interface. You don't need to grapple with HTML—unless, of course, you really want to. Once you get used to the new model, you may never want to mess with HTML source code again!

Note If you've done some ActiveX controls programming before, perhaps with ASP, it's worth pointing out that server controls are a very different thing. They don't need any client-side installation, and they're not Windows-specific.

When you open a web form for editing in VS .NET, two areas of the Toolbox contain UI elements that you can place on your web pages. As shown in Figure 3-1, the HTML area contains the HTML controls, and the Web Forms area contains the web controls.

The namespace hierarchy looks like this:

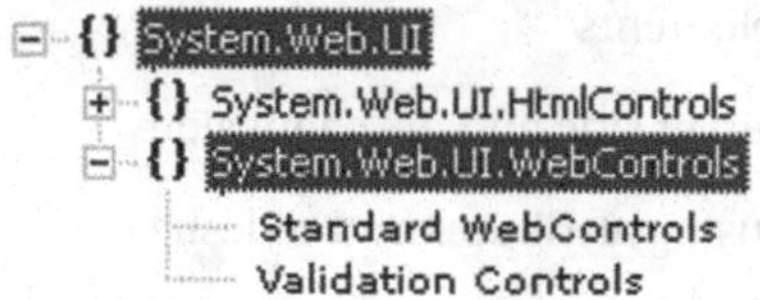

All of these controls can be dropped and configured in the VS .NET IDE, their settings modified using the Properties browser, and so on. The first division of these control types is between HTML controls and web server controls. HTML controls map exactly to the HTML tags. An HTML *server* control is a special type of HTML control, which runs on the server side. A web server control always runs on the server side.

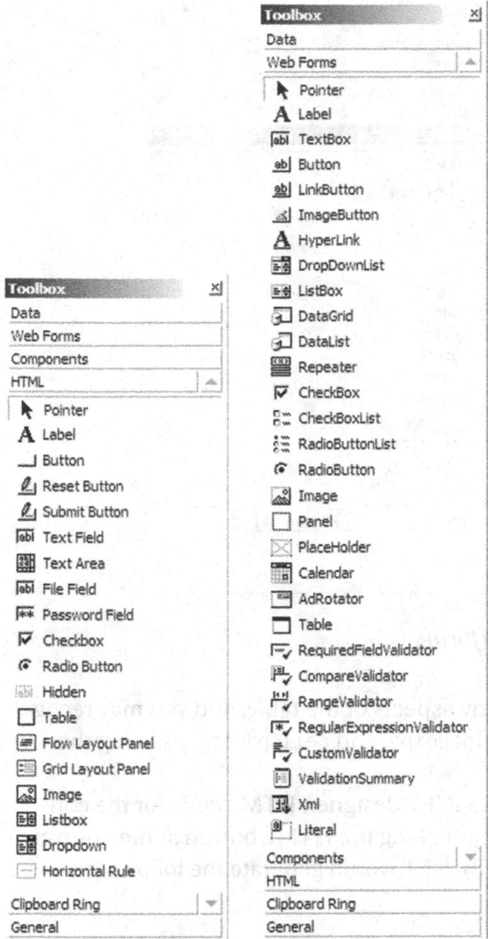

Figure 3-1. *The HTML area (left) contains the HTML controls, and* the *Web Forms area (right) contains the web controls.*

HTML Controls

The HTML controls correspond exactly with standard HTML elements; they have all the same properties, and they render precisely, as you would expect. For example, the ASP.NET HTML Table control is equivalent to the HTML <table> element. If you were to drag one from the Toolbox onto an empty web form, it would appear in the designer as shown in Figure 3-2.

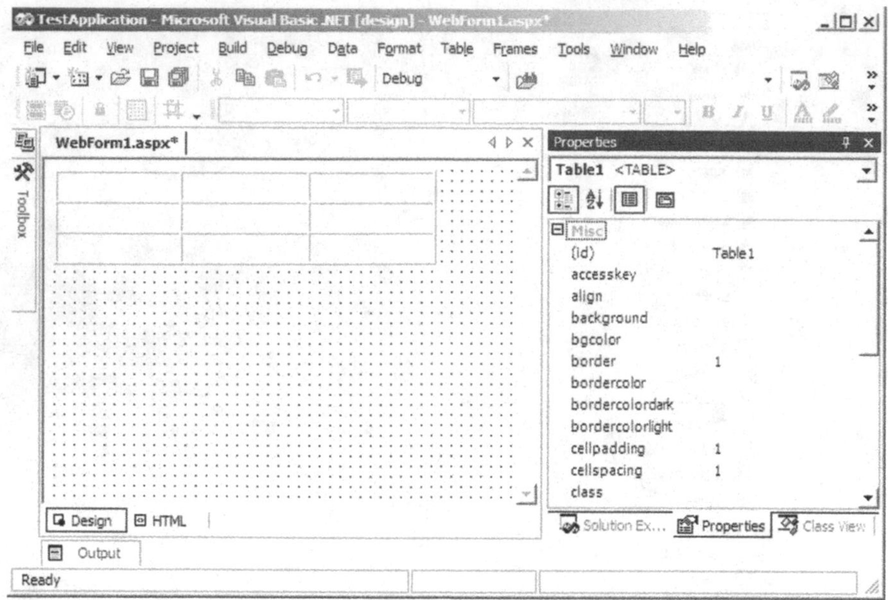

Figure 3-2. *An HTML Table control on an empty web form*

In the Properties browser, you can change many aspects of the table, and you may recognize the names in the window (such as `border`, `cellpadding`, and `cellspacing`) as being the attributes of a traditional HTML table.

When you add a control to a web form in the VS .NET designer, HTML code for the control is generated, and you can see (and modify) it by clicking the HTML button at the bottom of the designer. For the table shown in Figure 3-2, VS .NET would generate the following HTML:

```
...
<body>
  <form id="Form1" method="post" runat="server">
    <table id="Table1" cellSpacing="1" cellPadding="1"
           width="300" border="1">
      <tr>
        <td></td>
        <td></td>
        <td></td>
      </tr>
      <tr>
        <td></td>
        <td></td>
        <td></td>
      </tr>
      <tr>
        <td></td>
```

```
      <td></td>
      <td></td>
    </tr>
   </table>
  </form>
 </body>
</html>
```

There's nothing strange or magical here—just plain old HTML elements.

Because the HTML controls are represented by regular HTML code, there's almost no processing required, and ASP.NET simply passes the markup to the client browser pretty much as-is. Also, you can use all of the traditional techniques for manipulating HTML controls, such as setting attributes or executing client-side script.

Let's start the ball rolling with a demonstration of some HTML controls.

Try It Out: Build a Login Form For this first example, you're going to create a simple login form that provides minimal authentication for users of the Friends Reunion site. As you'll see, it's amazing what you can do with little more than a table and a couple of text controls!

1. Create a new ASP.NET Web Application project in VS .NET. Give it the name `FriendsReunion`, as shown in Figure 3-3.

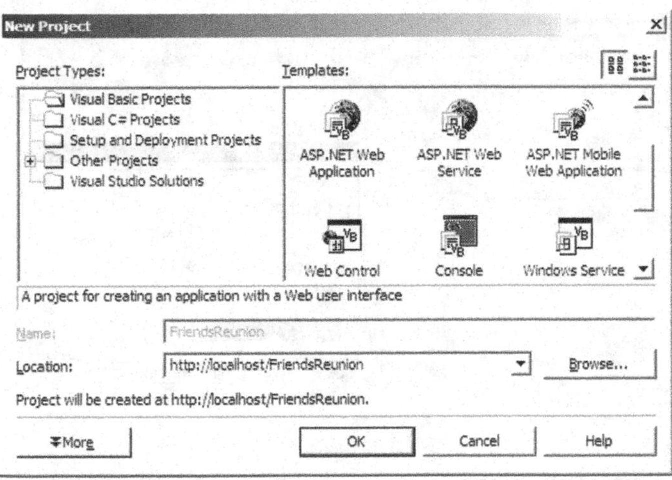

Figure 3-3. *Creating the Friends Reunion project*

2. When the project is created, go to the Solution Explorer (press Ctrl+Alt+L to bring it up, if it is not already visible), right-click the `FriendsReunion` project, and select Properties. Then select Designer Defaults, set the `Page Layout` property to `Flow`, and select OK.

3. Back in the Solution Explorer, delete the `WebForm1.aspx` web form that was created by default.

4. Later in the book, you will endow the Friends Reunion application with secure login functionality. As a signal of that intent, you're going to place the Login page in a subfolder of its own, called `Secure`. So, in the Solution Explorer, right-click the `FriendsReunion` project and choose Add ➤ New Folder to add a new folder. Name it `Secure`.

5. Right-click the newly created folder and select Add ➤ Add Web Form to add a new web form. Name it `Login.aspx`.

6. Double-click the Table control in the HTML tab of the Toolbox to add this control to the form.

7. Place the cursor on one of the empty cells in the third column, right-click the same cell, and select Delete ➤ Columns, so that your table now has just two columns.

8. Click the top-left cell and type **User Name:**. In the cell below it, type **Password:**.

9. Drag-and-drop a Text Field control and a Password Field control, respectively, into the next cells in the table.

10. The last control to add is a Button. Place it in the first cell in the last row of the table. Using the Properties browser, set its `value` property to `Login`, so that the page now looks like Figure 3-4.

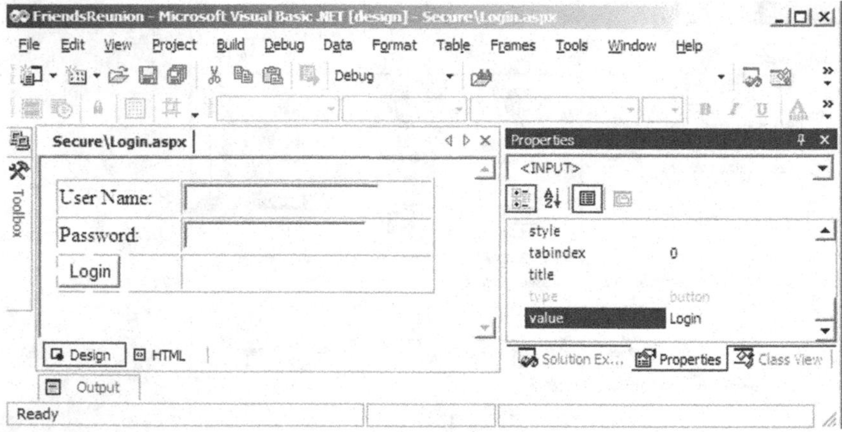

Figure 3-4. *The Login page with some controls*

11. To remove the unused cell to the right of the button, right-click it and choose Delete ➤ Cells.

12. Select the cell containing the button, and in the Properties browser, set its `colspan` property to **2**. If you now switch to the HTML view using the HTML button at the bottom of the web form, you should see something like this:

```
<%@ Page Language="vb" AutoEventWireup="false"
                    Codebehind="Login.aspx.vb"
                    Inherits="FriendsReunion.Login"%>
<!DOCTYPE HTML PUBLIC "-//W3C//DTD HTML 4.0 Transitional//EN" >
<html>
  <head>
    <title>Login</title>
    <meta name="GENERATOR" content="Microsoft Visual Studio .NET 7.1">
    <meta name="CODE_LANGUAGE" content="Visual Basic .NET 7.1">
    <meta name="vs_defaultClientScript" content="JavaScript">
    <meta name="vs_targetSchema"
          content="http://schemas.microsoft.com/intellisense/ie5">
  </head>
  <body>
    <form id="Form1" method="post" runat="server">
      <table id="Table1" cellSpacing="1" cellPadding="1" width="300"
             border="1">
        <tr>
          <td>User Name:</td>
          <td><input type="text"></td>
        </tr>
        <tr>
          <td>Password:</td>
          <td><input type="password"></td>
        </tr>For this
        <tr>
          <td colspan="2"><input type="button" value="Login"></td>
        </tr>
      </table>
    </form>
  </body>
</html>
```

13. Let's add a client-side handler for the Login button being clicked. Position the cursor next to the last <input> tag and press the spacebar to view the IntelliSense options available, as shown in Figure 3-5.

14. Scroll down to the onclick event (or just type its first few letters), and insert it (by double-clicking, pressing the Tab key, or pressing the equal sign key).

15. Add the following small amount of code, which will bring up a simple message box:

```
<td colSpan="2">
  <input onclick="alert('About to log in!');"
         type="button" value="Login"></td>
```

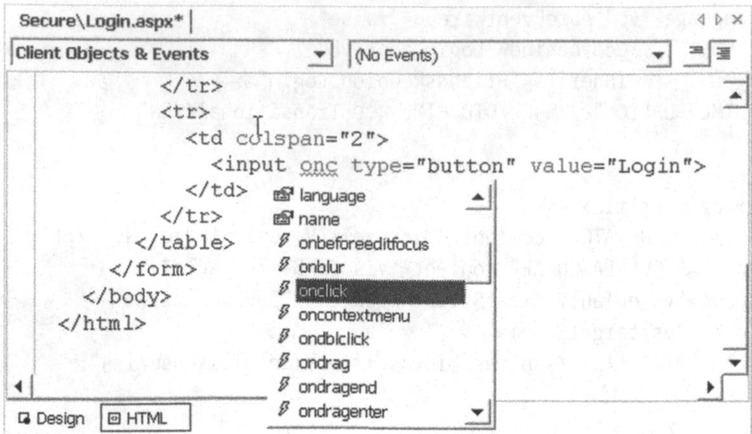

Figure 3-5. *Viewing the IntelliSense options for the Login button*

16. Right-click the `Login.aspx` page in the Solution Explorer and select Set As Start Page. Compile and run the solution by pressing Ctrl+F5 (shortcut for Debug ➤ Start Without Debugging), which also saves all files.

How It Works

The first thing you do is change the project's `Page Layout` property from `Grid` to `Flow`. This is because you will build all the pages in this application using `FlowLayout`, as you did in the examples in Chapter 2.

Tip Setting the property at the *project* level like this saves you the trouble of setting the `pageLayout` property each time you create a new page. This kind of layout is the most common and browser-compatible for web application development. It causes elements to be positioned according to their location in the page HTML source, rather than using absolute positioning. Absolute positioning, which involves specifying the coordinates at which elements should appear, is more frequently used in Windows applications than in web applications.

As you drop and set the controls' properties, the IDE automatically generates the corresponding HTML source code, as you saw when you switched to the HTML view. In this view, you also get the benefit of IntelliSense, which (among other things) lists all of the valid attributes for any HTML element.

When you view the page in a browser, the HTML code that you see in VS .NET is sent straight to the browser, which interprets it to render the controls that you placed in the designer. (In Internet Explorer, you can check this by right-clicking the page and choosing View Source.) When you click the Login button, you should see the message shown in Figure 3-6.

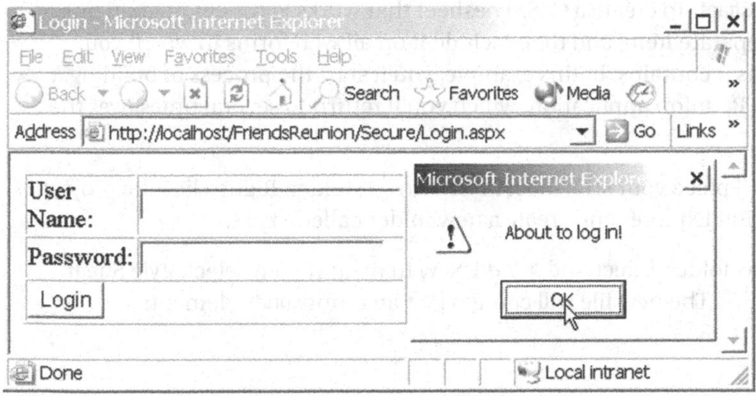

Figure 3-6. *Clicking the Login button brings up a message box.*

This demonstrates that you can perform client-side event handling as usual, by attaching a script to the element's corresponding onXXX attribute, as you did here with `onclick`. If you want more sophisticated functionality, this script can call further client-side methods. Right now, however, let's address a more pressing concern: the Login page looks quite ugly, doesn't it? You need to add some *style* to your page.

Tip Client-side script code can perform some complex tasks, and it's a subject to which whole books are dedicated. For more information about script code, see *Practical JavaScript for the Usable Web*, by Paul Wilton, Stephen Williams, and Sing Li (Apress, 2003; ISBN: 1-59059-189-5).

Finally, it's important to say that all those `<meta>` tags in the `<head>` section can be completely removed. We won't show them in upcoming examples.

Using Visual Styles

You can use *Cascading Style Sheets* (CSS) to define visual characteristics, which you can then apply uniformly to a range of items on one page or a range of pages. As you saw in Chapter 2, VS .NET comes with the Style Builder editor, which makes creating CSS styles easy. You open the Style Builder by clicking the ellipsis (...) button next to the `style` property of an HTML control in the Properties browser. The Style Builder allows you to change every aspect of a particular control's appearance.

Unfortunately, adding the style for each control on the page can be tedious, and it is certainly error-prone. Furthermore, if you decided at a later date to change the font of all the `<input>` text boxes in your application, for example, you would have some serious work to do, and it would be all too easy to miss one or two, spoiling the consistent feel. There's a better approach: using the Style Builder, you can create a single stylesheet file defining *all* the styles that you use, throughout your site. Let's see how that might work.

Try It Out: Create a CSS Stylesheet To create a CSS stylesheet that works across more than one web form, create it as a separate item, and then include it on all web forms in which you want to use the definitions it contains. In this example, you'll start the process of building a stylesheet for the Friends Reunion application, which you'll return to several times over the course of this chapter.

1. For neatness, you'll place your stylesheet in its own subfolder. Right-click the project name in the Solution Explorer and create a new folder called `Style`.

2. Right-click the new folder, select Add ➤ Add New Item, and then select Style Sheet. Name it `iestyle.css`. The new file will contain just an empty `body` element:

```
body
{
}
```

3. Right-click the `body` element and select Build Style from the context menu. This brings up the Style Builder editor, which you will now use to specify appearance characteristics that will apply to all pages that use this stylesheet.

4. Select the Background category from the list on the left side of the Style Builder, and choose a color from the Color drop-down, such as sensible Silver (but feel free to be as garish as you like!). Select OK when you're finished.

5. You're going to ensure that all the tables in the application have the same basic appearance. Right-click anywhere on the stylesheet and select Add Style Rule. From the Element drop-down list in the dialog box that appears, select TABLE, and then click OK.

6. Right-click the new `TABLE` element and select Build Style again. Choose the Tahoma font as the Family value, and set 8 pt for the Specific field in the Size section, as shown in Figure 3-7.

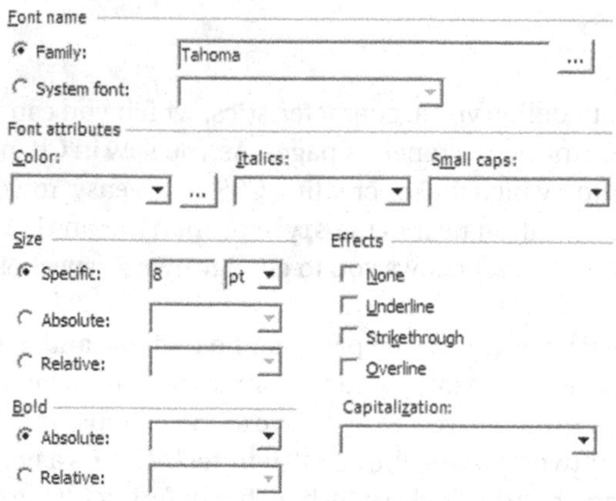

Figure 3-7. *Setting the style for tables in the application*

7. Click OK and save the stylesheet.

8. You can now associate the new stylesheet with the Login page you built earlier by adding the following line at the top of the file's HTML code:

```
<html>
   <head>
      <title>Login</title>
      <link href="../Style/iestyle.css" rel="stylesheet" type="text/css">
       ...
```

Tip You can drag-and-drop the stylesheet file directly on the form, and the link will be added automatically.

---

9. Save, compile, and run the application, again by pressing Ctrl+F5.

How It Works

The CSS stylesheet groups together the layout attributes that should be applied to all instances of a particular HTML element. By linking the stylesheet with a page through the <link> element, the styles it contains are applied to items on the page. The path to the stylesheet is relative, based on the location of the current web form; hence, the need for the .. syntax to step back to the application's root directory.

Once you've saved the stylesheet and linked it to your page, you can see the effect of your handiwork when you reopen the page, as shown in Figure 3-8.

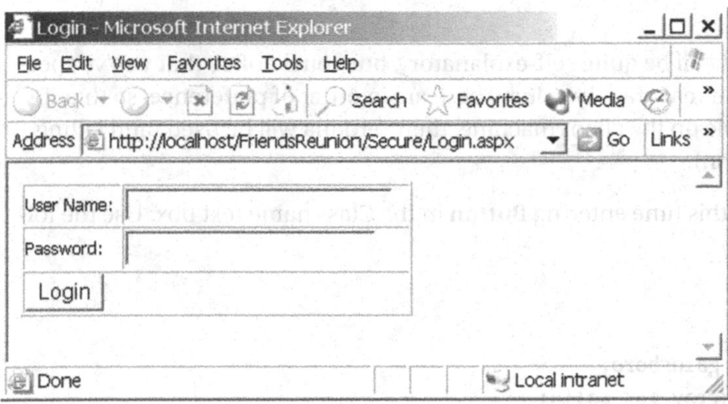

Figure 3-8. *The Login page after applying a CSS stylesheet*

Without any further work on your part, the color you set for the <body> element is shown, and the text inside the table has taken on its new font. If you were to make changes to any of the values in the stylesheet, they would be automatically reflected on this page and any other page that links to it.

Creating a More Flexible Stylesheet

Associating one style with all instances of a particular element isn't very flexible. What if you want to display some text boxes with one style and other text boxes with a different style? (Consider the HTML `<input>` element, which represents text boxes, buttons, password fields, check boxes, and more!) There's another way to group styles together and associate them with elements: you can use a CSS *class*.

Try It Out: Group Styles by Class Name In this example, you'll use CSS classes to provide different styles to the text boxes and buttons in the application. Both of these are facets of the `<input>` element, so it would be impossible to do this by associating style rules with the element name.

1. If necessary, reopen the `iestyle.css` stylesheet in VS .NET. Then right-click anywhere in it and select Add Style Rule.

2. This time, instead of selecting an item in the Element drop-down list, select the Class name radio button, and type **TextBox** (this will also appear in the preview box in the lower-right corner, preceded by a period). Click OK.

3. Add the following code inside the new rule's braces:

```
.TextBox
{
  border: #c7ccdc 1px solid;
  border-top: #c7ccdc 1px solid;
  border-left: #c7ccdc 1px solid;
  border-bottom: #c7ccdc 1px solid;
  font-size: 8pt;
  font-family: Tahoma, Verdana, 'Times New Roman';
}
```

   These additions should all be quite self-explanatory, but you'll notice that you've specified three fonts for the `font-family` value. These are in order of preference, so that if Tahoma is not available on the client machine, then Verdana will be used (and failing that, Times New Roman).

4. Repeat steps 2 and 3, this time entering **Button** in the Class name text box. Use the following code:

```
.Button
{
  background-color: gainsboro;
  border-right: darkgray 1px solid;
  border-top: darkgray 1px solid;
  border-left: darkgray 1px solid;
  border-bottom: darkgray 1px solid;
  font-size: 8pt;
  font-family: Tahoma, Verdana, 'Times New Roman';
}
```

5. Open the Login page in the Design view, select each of the two input boxes in turn, and set the `class` property of both to `TextBox`. Also, set the Button's `class` property to `Button`. When you compile and run the page again, you'll see the controls change, reflecting the styles defined by each class.

6. Finally, select the table and set its `border` property to **0**, and then save and run the page.

How It Works

In this example, you added new style rules to your stylesheet manually, but if you now open the Build Style dialog box for any of them, it will be populated with the values you typed. Furthermore, IntelliSense is there to help you whenever you add a new line inside a rule, showing the styles currently available.

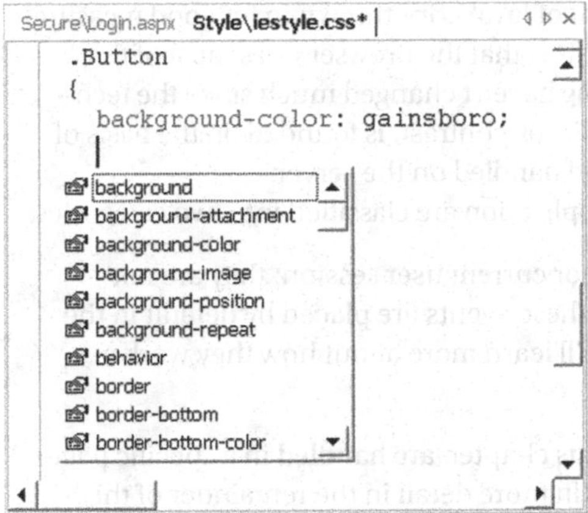

When you instruct a control to use a CSS class that you've defined in a stylesheet, VS .NET makes the association by using the HTML `class` attribute on the tag in the code that is sent to the browser. The `class` attribute is a standard attribute available to all HTML elements, and it's equally possible to associate controls with the styles in a stylesheet by adding it manually. When you open the Login page in the browser, you'll see the page shown in Figure 3-9.

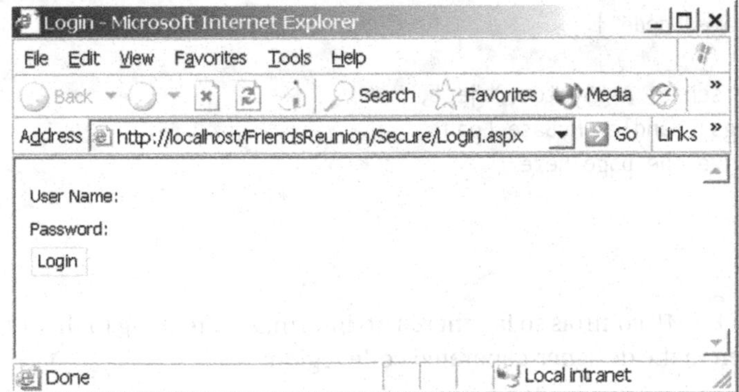

Figure 3-9. *The Login page after using CSS classes*

Well, that's an improvement! Better yet, you can now reliably and quickly apply the same style to any text box you create, just by setting its class property to TextBox. If you then made any further changes to the style rule, the associated controls would reflect them automatically.

Tip For comprehensive information about CSS, we recommend *Cascading Style Sheets*, by Owen Briggs, et al (Apress, 2004; ISBN: 1-59059-231-X). *Usable Web Interface Components*, by Jon Stephens (Apress, 2004; ISBN: 1-59059-354-5) is also useful.

HTML Server Controls

So far, you've seen some useful features of the VS .NET IDE, but what you've ultimately produced has been old-fashioned HTML, with a little bit of JavaScript thrown in for good measure. One of the characteristics of web applications like this is that the browser does most of the work, and the principles of client-side event handling haven't changed much since the technique first began to appear several years ago. ASP.NET, by contrast, is founded on the basis of server-side programming: events can be trapped and handled on the server.

In ASP.NET, the events associated with a web application are classified into two categories:

- *Global events* apply to the whole application or current user session; they are not specific to any particular page. Handlers for these events are placed by default in the code-behind of the Global.asax file, and you'll learn more about how they work in Chapter 6.

- *Page-specific events*, as you saw in the previous chapter, are handled in a specific page's code-behind file. We'll examine these events in more detail in the remainder of this chapter.

Start by taking a look at the code-behind page for Login.aspx, by right-clicking the page (in the Solution Explorer or the designer) and choosing View Code:

```
Public Class Login
  Inherits System.Web.UI.Page

    [ Web Form Designer generated code ]

  Private Sub Page_Load(ByVal sender As System.Object,
    ByVal e As System.EventArgs) Handles MyBase.Load
    'Put user code to initialize the page here
  End Sub

End Class
```

Since you've used only plain HTML controls so far, there's no information relating to them in the code-behind page, not even in the designer-generated code region:

```
#Region " Web Form Designer Generated Code "

  'This call is required by the Web Form Designer.
  <System.Diagnostics.DebuggerStepThrough()> Private Sub InitializeComponent()

  End Sub

  'NOTE: The following placeholder declaration is required by the Web Form Designer.
  'Do not delete or move it.
  Private designerPlaceholderDeclaration As System.Object

  Private Sub Page_Init(ByVal sender As System.Object,_
    ByVal e As System.EventArgs) Handles MyBase.Init
    'CODEGEN: This method call is required by the Web Form Designer
    'Do not modify it using the code editor.
    InitializeComponent()
  End Sub

#End Region
```

Placing HTML *server* controls on the page, on the other hand, *does* result in code being placed in the code-behind file, as you'll see in the following example.

Try It Out: Convert to HTML Server Controls Converting an HTML control to an HTML server control is simply a matter of right-clicking the control in the designer and choosing Run As Server Control from the context menu. In this example, you'll do precisely that for the three `<input>` elements already on the Login page, and you'll add a new element that provides the users with some feedback that their actions have had an effect.

1. Right-click the two text boxes and the button in turn, and select Run As Server Control. As you do this, a small, green arrow will appear in the top-left corner of each control, to indicate that it is indeed now a server control.

2. To make the ensuing VB code a little clearer, use the Properties browser to change the IDs of the controls to `txtLogin`, `txtPwd`, and `btnLogin`. Save the file.

3. Underneath the login table, add a new HTML Label control, and convert it to a server control as you did for the other controls in step 1. Then set its `ID` to `lblMessage`, delete its text content, and clear its `style` property.

4. Double-click the `btnLogin` control and add the following line of code to the event handler:

   ```
   Private Sub btnLogin_ServerClick(ByVal sender As System.Object, _
     ByVal e As System.EventArgs) Handles btnLogin.ServerClick
     lblMessage.InnerText = "Welcome " + txtLogin.Value
   End Sub
   ```

5. Save and test the page by pressing Ctrl+F5.

How It Works

When you select Run As Server Control for an HTML element, a runat="server" attribute is added to that element's HTML declaration, and a protected class member field representing that element is added to the class in the code-behind page, inside the code region labeled Web Form Designer Generated Code. In the case of Login.aspx, the following member fields were added:

```
#Region " Web Form Designer Generated Code "

  'This call is required by the Web Form Designer.
  <System.Diagnostics.DebuggerStepThrough()> Private Sub InitializeComponent()

  End Sub
  Protected WithEvents txtLogin As System.Web.UI.HtmlControls.HtmlInputText
  Protected WithEvents txtPwd As System.Web.UI.HtmlControls.HtmlInputText
  Protected WithEvents btnLogin As System.Web.UI.HtmlControls.HtmlInputButton
  Protected WithEvents lblMessage As _
    System.Web.UI.HtmlControls.HtmlGenericControl
...
```

VS .NET takes care of a lot of the necessary-but-tiresome details of writing pages, such as the skeleton code for event handlers. When you double-clicked the btnLogin control, the empty event handler was generated and specified as the handler of the default event of the button control, ServerClick.

Additional handlers can also be attached in this way in other places in the code-behind page, such as in the Page_Load() handler. In the discussion of the page lifecycle in the previous chapter, you learned that control events are raised at a stage following the Init and Load stages. If you choose a later stage, however, your handlers will never be called, as it's already too late in the page processing.

Inside the click handler, the code simply tells the label to display a message. You can dynamically access and modify the properties of any of the HTML server controls in the code-behind page. (You cannot access the <table> itself, because you didn't convert it to a server control.) Note that the field pointing to the control is named *exactly* after the ID of the HTML control, and that is what ties things together. When you test the page now, you first get the alert message from the client-side script that you added before, and then, when the form is posted to the server, a message is returned, as shown in Figure 3-10.

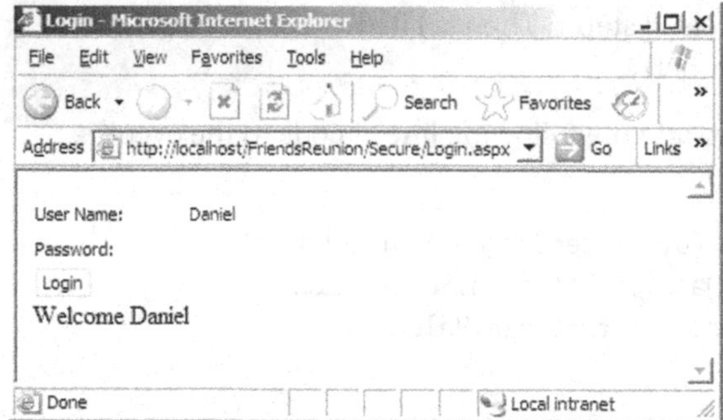

Figure 3-10. *The Login page after converting to HTML server controls and performing a postback*

A Side Note: Inside the Postback Mechanism

At this point, it would be reasonable to ask how the server-side code knows which control was clicked. In general, a form could contain any number of buttons, so how does ASP.NET determine which handler to call? To discover the answer to this, take a look at the HTML code that's generated at runtime by ASP.NET (choose View ➤ Source, View ➤ Page Source, or a similarly named menu option in your browser). When the application is first launched, this is the code sent to the browser:

```
<body>
  <form name="Form1" method="post" action="Login.aspx" id="Form1">
    <input type="hidden" name="__EVENTTARGET" value="" />
    <input type="hidden" name="__EVENTARGUMENT" value="" />
    <input type="hidden" name="__VIEWSTATE"
     value=" dDwtNzMONDUyNDg2Ozs+XKvwk77EGvG1aOoaaieqYyUCsv4=" />
    <script language="javascript">
    <!-
    function __doPostBack(eventTarget, eventArgument) {
      var theform;
      if (window.navigator.appName.toLowerCase().indexOf("netscape") > -1) {
        theform = document.forms["Form1"];
      }
      else {
        theform = document.Form1;
      }
      theform.__EVENTTARGET.value = eventTarget.split("$").join(":");
      theform.__EVENTARGUMENT.value = eventArgument;
      theform.submit();
     // ->
    </script>

    <table id="Table1" cellSpacing="1" cellPadding="1"
          width="300" border="0">
      <tr>
        <td>User Name:</td>
        <td>
          <input name="txtLogin" id="txtLogin" type="text"
                 class="TextBox" />
        </td>
      </tr>
      <tr>
        <td>Password:</td>
        <td>
          <input name="txtPwd" id="txtPwd" type="password"
                 class="TextBox" />
        </td>
      </tr>
      <tr>
```

```
            <td colSpan="2">
              <input language="javascript"
                onclick="alert('About to log in!'); __doPostBack('btnLogin','')"
                name="btnLogin" id="btnLogin" type="button" value="Login"
                class="Button" /></td>
          </tr>
        </table>
        <div id="lblMessage"
            ms_positioning="FlowLayout">Authenticated on the server!</div>
      </form>
    </body>
  </html>
```

Notice the three hidden input fields that have been added and the new script block containing a JavaScript function called `__doPostBack()`. This function receives two arguments, saves them in the first two hidden fields, and then submits the form to the server.

Further down the listing, you come to the `onclick` handler for `btnLogin`. In addition to the call to `alert()` that you added to this attribute earlier, there is now a call to the `__doPostBack()` function, which is passed the button's `id` attribute and a blank string.

The result is that when you click the button, the function saves the `id` of the control that caused the postback in a hidden field and submits the form to the server. ASP.NET receives the form and uses the hidden `__EVENTTARGET` value to determine the appropriate handler for the event, which, in this case, would be your `btnLogin_ServerClick()` method.

Web Server Controls

As well as all of the HTML controls (and their server-side variants), ASP.NET offers another set of controls for the use of web form programmers. These are the *web server controls* (or just *web controls*, since they're *always* server controls), and they're located in the Web Forms tab of the Toolbox. Many of these controls have direct HTML equivalents, but there are several new ones, too.

Of the many reasons for choosing web server controls over HTML controls, here are the most important ones:

- Web server controls offer a layer of abstraction on top of HTML controls. At runtime, some of them comprise a number of HTML elements, and therefore offer greater functionality with less design-time code. In a moment, we'll look at an example featuring the Calendar control, which demonstrates this idea quite nicely.
- Since web controls are independent of the markup that will render them at runtime, some of them will render different HTML depending on the browser they're being viewed with, to improve compatibility. An example is the Panel control, which renders as a `<div>` on Internet Explorer, but as a `<table>` on Netscape browsers.
- Web server controls have a more consistent and logical object model than HTML elements, with some properties common to all web controls (including style-related properties such as `BackColor`, `BorderColor`, `Font`, and so on).

- Web server controls have a richer event model, making it easier to write server-side code for them.
- Design-time support for web server controls is greatly enhanced and more flexible. Some of these controls, for example, have their own wizards, custom property pages, and the like.
- Web server controls provide typed values; in HTML controls, all values are strings.
- Since web server controls always run at the server, they are always available from within your server-side code (in the code-behind page).

Try It Out: Create the News Page In this example, you'll add a News page to the Friends Reunion application, which will eventually fulfill the role of notifying the user of potential new contacts. For the time being, though, you'll just use it to display a calendar that allows the user to select a date. You've got to start somewhere!

Note Along with the code used in this book, the image files used in examples are available from the Downloads section of the Apress web site (`http://www.apress.com`).

---

1. You'll be using some images on this page, so create a new folder in the project and call it `Images`. Select all the files from the `Images` directory in the code download, and drag-and-drop them onto the new folder in the Solution Explorer.
2. Add a new web form to the root directory of the project and call it `News.aspx`. Its `pageLayout` property should already be set to `FlowLayout` (because you changed this property at the project level earlier in the chapter).
3. From the Web Forms tab of the Toolbox, drop a Panel control onto the new page. Set the following properties for it:
   - BackColor: `#336699`
   - Font ➤ Bold: `True`
   - Font ➤ Name: `Tahoma`
   - Font ➤ Size: `8pt`
   - ForeColor: `White`
   - HorizontalAlign: `Right`
4. Set the panel's inner text to **Friends Reunion**. Then drop a new Image control inside the panel, to the right of the text.

5. Set the properties of this Image control as follows:

    - ImageUrl: `Images/friends.gif`
    - ImageAlign: `Middle`

    Your form should look something like the one shown here.

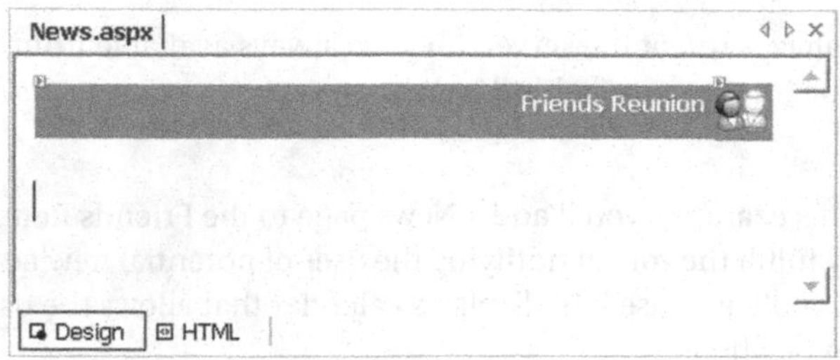

6. Below the panel, insert an HTML paragraph tag (<p>) by pressing the Enter key, and then enter this text: **Welcome to the news for today! Here is the current calendar:**.
7. Press Enter again after the text and double-click a Calendar control in the Web Forms tab of the Toolbox. When it appears in your web form, set its `ID` to `calDates`.
8. Below the calendar, drop a Label control and set its `Text` property to `Selected Date: `. The ` ` is an HTML character entity that inserts a space (`nbsp` stands for new blank space) after the colon.
9. For a little extra complexity, you'll add a drop-down list that allows the user to go straight to yesterday, today, or tomorrow. Next to the label, place a DropDownList control, and change its `ID` to `cbDay`. Click the ellipsis next to its `Items` property to bring up the ListItem Collection Editor. Click the Add button three times to add three items to the Members pane on the left, and set their properties as follows:

    - **ListItem 0:** Selected = True, Text = Today, Value = 0
    - **ListItem 1:** Selected = False, Text = Tomorrow, Value = 1
    - **ListItem 2:** Selected = False, Text = Yesterday, Value = –1

10. Click OK, and the page will now appear in the designer as shown in Figure 3-11.
11. Set this page as the start page, and then press Ctrl+F5 to run the project.

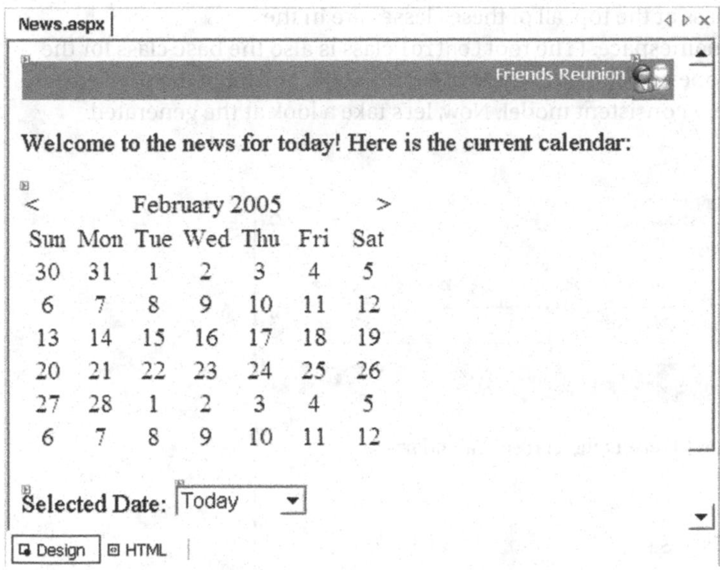

Figure 3-11. *Adding a Calendar control to the News page*

How It Works

The first thing to observe here is that, even if you used the font only on the Panel control, the Calendar, Label, and DropDownList controls all have a `Font` property, too, which behaves exactly the same in all of them. This consistency derives from the fact that the controls inherit from more general controls, which provide the common properties. For the controls you used on this page, the hierarchy is as shown here:

Except for the Control class at the top, all of these classes are in the System.Web.UI.WebControls namespace. (The root Control class is also the base class for the HTML controls.) The Font property belongs to the WebControl class, and all of the derived controls inherit it, providing a very consistent model. Now, let's take a look at the generated output, shown in Figure 3-12.

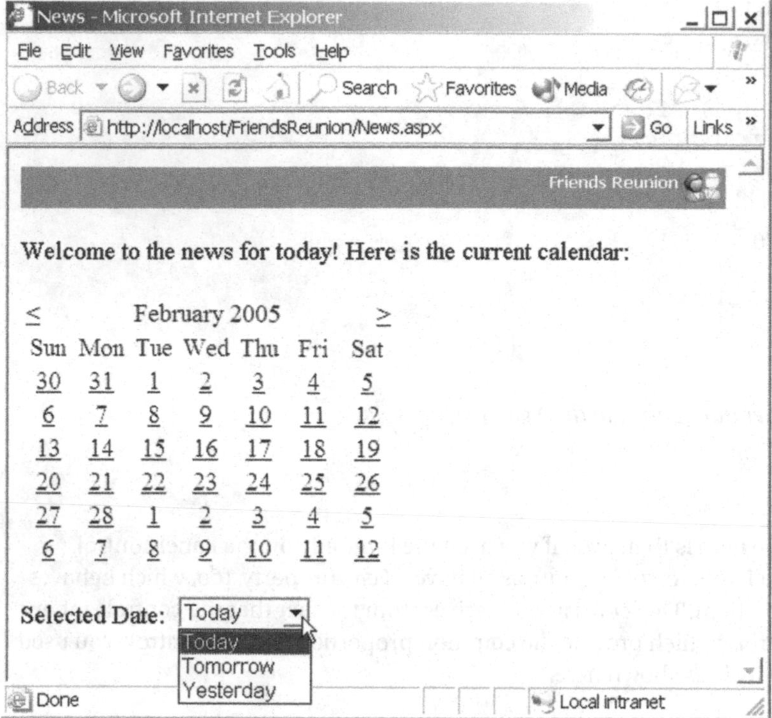

Figure 3-12. *The News page*

The Calendar control is one of the most sophisticated built-in web server controls. You didn't need to write a single line of code, and yet you have a full-featured calendar that automatically allows the user to select other months by using the links displayed at the top of the control (to the left and right of the month name), as well as the date.

That's not all. ASP.NET tailors the control to work optimally in different browsers. Furthermore, some controls can even automatically localize their UI for the culture of the user currently accessing the page (such as for Spanish users). Let's try this "intelligent" rendering with the Calendar control.

Try It Out: Customize the Calendar Control In this exercise, you'll customize the application so that it takes advantage of automatic localization and predefined Calendar control formatting options.

1. In order to achieve this localization, a single line of code is required to tell the running thread to use the language supported by the browser. This can be done in the Global.asax file, on the Application_BeginRequest event handler:

```
Sub Application_BeginRequest(ByVal sender As Object, ByVal e As EventArgs)
  Try
    System.Threading.Thread.CurrentThread.CurrentCulture = _
      New System.Globalization.CultureInfo( _
        Context.Request.UserLanguages(0))
  Catch
    'Will simply use the default language
  End Try
End Sub
```

2. To change the Calendar's appearance, right-click the calendar and select the Auto Format option from the context menu. You'll see the dialog box shown in Figure 3-13.

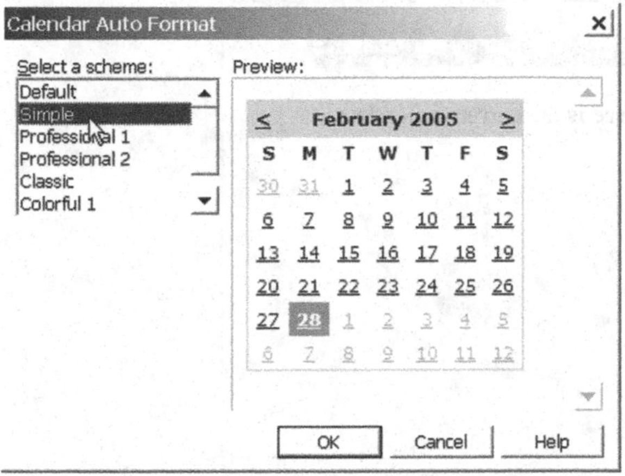

Figure 3-13. *The Calendar Auto Format dialog box lets you apply predefined designs to the control.*

3. In the Select a scheme list, choose the Simple format for the Calendar control. (Feel free to experiment with the different built-in formats.) Then click OK.

4. Through the Properties browser, set the Calendar `DayNameFormat` property to `Short`, so that the names of the days in the calendar appear as localized short names.

5. Set the page as the start page, and then run it (press Ctrl+F5) to test the results.

How It Works

The first step sets the culture to use during execution of the current request. This is done by creating a new `CultureInfo` object based on the preferred culture specified by the user through the browser. This information is exposed by the `Context.Request.UserLanguages` property.

Note that you're just *trying* to change the current language. Things may fail at this point, for example, because the user doesn't have a user language selected, or because the client browser sent wrong data for that value, or for some other reason. This example just ignores any error that could happen and lets ASP.NET continue processing as normal, using the default culture. We will discuss exception handling in Chapter 11.

At runtime, the calendar is rendered as an HTML table, with all the formatting in place. There is strong design-time support through the Calendar Auto Format dialog box, which you used to apply a predefined design. The calendar also renders at design-time with the style you chose. Figure 3-14 shows an example of the runtime rendering using a browser accepting the Spanish language.

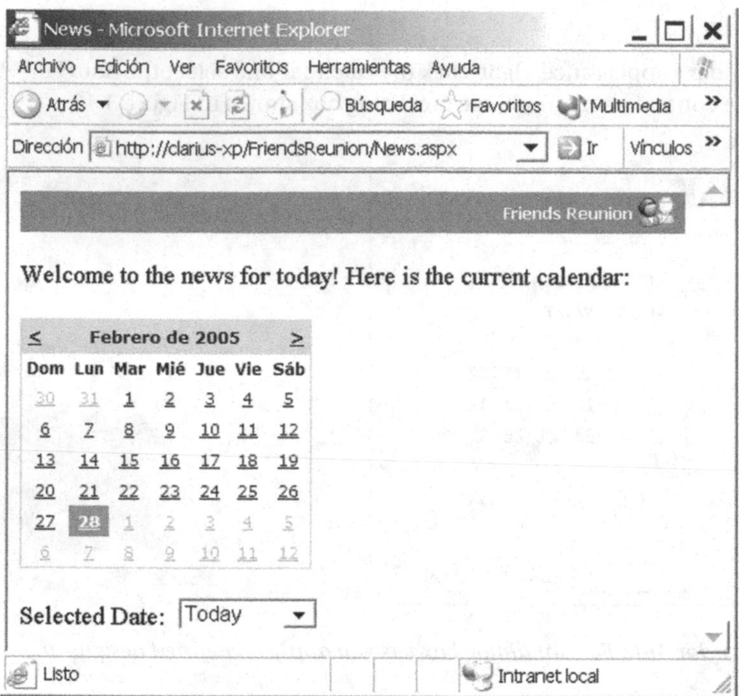

Figure 3-14. *A Calendar control with customized format and automatically localized for Spanish users*

Applying CSS Styles to Web Server Controls

All of the more complex web controls, such as the DataGrid that you'll see in Chapter 5, offer easy formatting in a similar way, and you can also set these properties manually, of course. Also, just as for HTML controls, you can define CSS styles that apply to the web server controls throughout your application. To assign a style rule to a web server control, specify its name in the control's `CssClass` property, and link the stylesheet to the page using the `<link>` element inside the `<head>` section, just as you did in the previous examples. However, rather than adding the link in the file's HTML code, you will surely find it easier to simply drag-and-drop the CSS file onto the web form and let VS .NET add the link automatically.

Try It Out: Use CSS Styles with Web Controls In this exercise, you'll do more to standardize the appearance of the controls in your application by creating some new style rules and applying them to your `News.aspx` web form.

1. Define a style that will apply fundamental formatting to any element that doesn't require something more specialized. Reopen the `iestyle.css` file and add the following `Normal` style rule:

```
.Normal
{
  font-size: 8pt;
  font-family: Tahoma, Verdana, 'Times New Roman';
}
```

2. Change the color scheme. Modify the `body` style rule to match the following:

```
body
{
  background-color: #f0f1f6;
  font-size: 8pt;
  font-family: Tahoma, Verdana, 'Times New Roman';
}
```

3. Add the CSS file by dropping it onto the form from the Solution Explorer.

4. Set the `CssClass` property of the label that reads "Selected Date:" to `Normal`. Set the `class` property of the "Welcome..." message paragraph to `Normal`, too.

5. Set the `CssClass` property of the DropDownList control to `TextBox`, and then run the project.

How It Works

Just as HTML controls have the `class` attribute, web server controls have a `CssClass` attribute, and it has exactly the same effect, because CSS styles work the same way for both control types. Once the styles have been applied, your News page should look like Figure 3-15.

Handling Events

Handling events for web server controls is exactly the same as for HTML controls. To associate a new handler with a control, switch to the code-behind file, select the control in the left drop-down list at the top of the code editor, and then select the event you're interested in. Let's try that now.

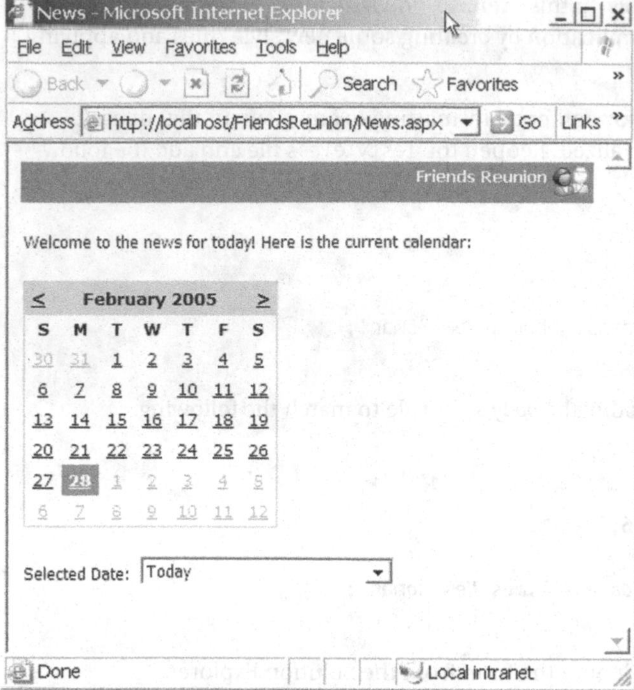

Figure 3-15. *The News page with CSS styles*

Try It Out: Handle Events for Web Server Controls To extend the example, you'll use some server-side event handling to make the link between the calendar and the drop-down list, and to report the currently selected date to the user. You'll arrange for selections in the drop-down list to change the selected date in the calendar, as well as for any selection change to result in the current date being displayed in a label.

1. Add a new Label control at the bottom of the `News.aspx` file. Set its `ID` to `lblMessage` and its `CssClass` to `Normal`. Clear its `Text` property.

2. Set the `cbDay` DropDownList control's `AutoPostBack` property to `True`. Then double-click the control and add the following code to the handler:

```
Private Sub cbDay_SelectedIndexChanged(ByVal sender As System.Object, _
  ByVal e As System.EventArgs) Handles cbDay.SelectedIndexChanged
  calDates.SelectedDate = DateTime.Now.AddDays( _
    Convert.ToDouble(cbDay.SelectedItem.Value))
  calDates.VisibleDate = calDates.SelectedDate
  lblMessage.Text = "Current Date: " + _
    calDates.SelectedDate.ToLongDateString()
End Sub
```

3. Open the code-behind page for the form. From the drop-down list in the top-left corner of the code editor, select the calDates item. From the drop-down list in the upper-right corner, select the SelectionChanged item.

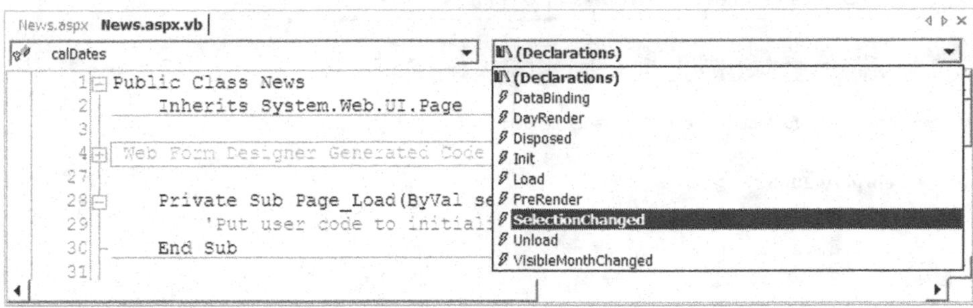

Then add the following code to the event handler that will be automatically created:

```
Private Sub calDates_SelectionChanged(ByVal sender As System.Object, _
  ByVal e As System.EventArgs) Handles calDates.SelectionChanged
  lblMessage.Text = "Current Date: " + _
    calDates.SelectedDate.ToLongDateString()
End Sub
```

4. The News.aspx page is now set up so that when you select an option from the drop-down list, the relevant day is highlighted in the Calendar control. Run the project in the usual way to see this in action.

How It Works

In the handler for the drop-down list, you use the SelectedItem property to retrieve the drop-down box value (either 0, 1, or -1, as defined when you set up the list items earlier). You convert the value it contains to a Double using the Convert.ToDouble() method, and then add this value to the current date before setting that as the SelectedDate property of the calendar. You also set the VisibleDate property to the new date to ensure it's visible in the calendar. Finally, you update the label to show this date.

In order to create a handler for the SelectionChanged event, instead of double-clicking the control, you explicitly selected the control and event you wanted to handle. You needed to do this because SelectionChanged is not the default event for this control. For all events except the default one for a control (like the Click event for a button or the SelectedIndexChanged for a drop-down list), you will use this procedure to create an event handler.

To ensure that the event fires as soon as a change occurs in the drop-down list, you need to set the AutoPostBack property to True. This is an important step, because unlike the button and the calendar, drop-down lists don't cause a postback by default. Figure 3-16 shows the typical output of the page as it now stands.

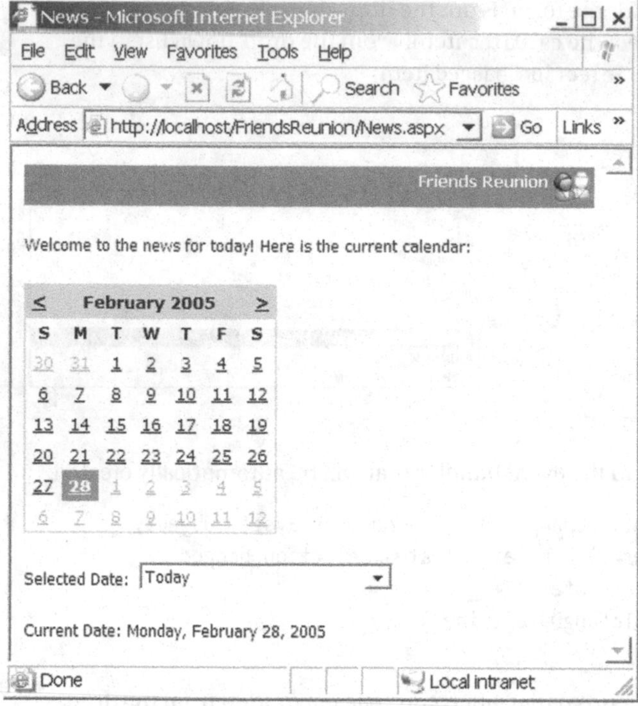

Figure 3-16. *The News page after adding event-handling code and selecting a date*

What stage have we reached? You now know that web server controls offer several features above and beyond those of the HTML controls, and those features can make your time more productive. Their consistent object model is also beneficial, since once you've learned the set of properties that are available for one control, chances are that you will see those properties again in other controls.

The events available for web controls are different from the HTML events that you can use in the attribute list of an HTML tag; there are no `onclick`, `onmouseover`, `onkeydown`, and the like. This is because web control events are exposed on the server, and so comprise only those events appropriate for server-side processing. Imagine what would happen if your page caused a postback for every single mouse move operation! Even the `Click` event, which roughly corresponds to HTML's `onclick` event, is available only for those controls (such as buttons) where it makes sense.

Tip For a complete description of all of the web server controls and the events that each can fire, check out the information in the VS .NET help files or MSDN online.

Validation Controls

When you're creating a web form, especially one in which you hope to collect some data from users, you'll often come across situations in which you need to place constraints on exactly what data they can submit. For example, you might want to mandate that a particular field must always be completed (say, a user name), or must adhere to a particular format (say, a Social Security number). In the past, this validation process had to be done manually, but ASP.NET comes with a set of *validation controls* that perform this task automatically.

Technically speaking, the validation controls are a subset of the web server controls, but there are enough new things to say about them that they deserve a section of their own here. Usually, they take the form of fields that are invisible most of the time, but become visible when a validation error occurs.

A number of validation controls are available, and their names are almost self-explanatory:

- RequiredFieldValidator
- CompareValidator
- RegularExpressionValidator
- RangeValidator
- CustomValidator

In the examples to come, you'll see the first three of these in use. RangeValidator doesn't apply to our example (but it's not complicated to understand). CustomValidator is used only to create your own validation controls.

The ASP.NET validation controls are capable of performing validation on the server and (for Internet Explorer 5 and later browsers) on the client as well, via JavaScript. To force validation to take place, you can call the `Page.Validate()` method, or you can call the `Validate()` method of every validation control on the page, which has the same effect. Validation controls are associated with the control to validate, and they have an `IsValid` property that indicates whether its data is currently valid. There is a similar property at the page level that indicates whether all the validation controls on the page are in a valid state.

Try It Out: Build a New User Form In this example, you'll build a form for capturing the details of a new user and employ the validation controls to ensure that you receive valid information in certain fields.

1. Create a new web form in the `Secure` folder and name it `NewUser.aspx`.
2. Link the `iestyle.css` stylesheet file by dropping it onto the form from the Solution Explorer.
3. Back in the Design view, place the cursor at the top left of the page and type **Fill in the fields below to register as a Friends Reunion member:**. Press Enter when you're finished.

4. Drop an HTML Table control onto the page, and give it ten rows with two columns each. (You can add a new row by placing the cursor on a cell and pressing Ctrl+Alt+down arrow.) Set the table's `ID` to `tbLogin`, its `cellspacing` and `cellpadding` properties to **2**, and the `colspan` property of the last row to **2**. Delete the rightmost cell in this row. Finally, set the `border` property for the table to **0**.

5. Enter text into the cells as shown in Figure 3-17. Also, add nine TextBox web server controls to the right-hand column, setting their `CssClass` property to `TextBox`. The simplest way to do this is to place the first TextBox control, set its `CssClass` property, and then copy-and-paste it into the other locations.

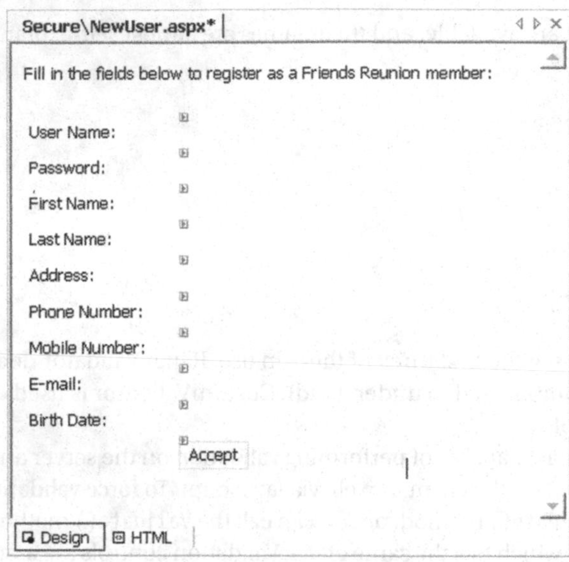

Figure 3-17. *The fields in the New User form*

6. Now let's modify the `TextBox` element in the `iestyle.css` stylesheet slightly. Add an extra line as follows to make the text boxes wider:

```
.TextBox
{
  border-right: #c7ccdc 1px solid;
  border-top: #c7ccdc 1px solid;
  border-left: #c7ccdc 1px solid;
  border-bottom: #c7ccdc 1px solid;
  font-size: 8pt;
  font-family: Tahoma, Verdana, 'Times New Roman';
  width: 200px;
}
```

7. Set the width of the table containing the controls to **400** in order to accommodate the longer text boxes and labels.

8. The last row contains a Button control with an `ID` of `btnAccept`, a `Text` property of `Accept`, and a `CssClass` of `Button`. To have it centered in the cell, set the cell's `align` property to `center`.

9. Give the TextBox controls the following `ID` properties, in the order they are displayed: `txtLogin`, `txtPwd`, `txtFName`, `txtLName`, `txtAddress`, `txtPhone`, `txtMobile`, `txtEmail`, and `txtBirth`. Set the `TextMode` property of `txtPwd` to `Password`.

10. To narrow the Birth Date field, which doesn't need to be as wide as in Figure 3-17, add the following style rule to the stylesheet, and then set `txtBirth`'s `CssClass` property to `SmallTextBox`:

```
.SmallTextBox
{
  border-right: #c7ccdc 1px solid;
  border-top: #c7ccdc 1px solid;
  font-size: 8pt;
  border-left: #c7ccdc 1px solid;
  border-bottom: #c7ccdc 1px solid;
  font-family: Tahoma, Verdana, 'Times New Roman';
  width: 70px;
}
```

11. Drop a RequiredFieldValidator control next to the `txtLogin` text box, and set its properties as follows:

   - ID: `reqLogin`
   - ControlToValidate: `txtLogin` (choose this from the drop-down list that contains the names of all the web server controls on the form)
   - Display: `None`
   - ErrorMessage: **A user name is required!**

12. Copy this RequiredFieldValidator control, and then paste it next to the `txtPwd` text box. Set its properties as follows:

   - ID: `reqPwd`
   - ControlToValidate: `txtPwd`
   - ErrorMessage: **A password is required!**

13. Continue to paste RquiredFieldValidator controls next to the `txtFName`, `txtLName`, `txtPhone`, and `txtEmail` text boxes. For each, change the `ID`, `ErrorMessage`, and `ControlToValidate` properties as appropriate, making particularly sure that the latter refers to the correct text box.

14. Drop a CompareValidator control next to the `txtBirth` text box, and then give it these properties:

    - ID: `compBirth`
    - ControlToValidate: `txtBirth`
    - Display: `Dynamic`
    - ErrorMessage: **Enter a valid birth date!**
    - Operator: `DataTypeCheck`
    - Type: `Date`

15. Drop a RegularExpressionValidator control next to the RequiredFieldValidator control for `txtPhone` (there is no problem with using these controls in tandem), and then set these properties:

    - ID: `regPhone`
    - ControlToValidate: `txtPhone`
    - Display: `None`
    - ErrorMessage: **Enter a valid US phone number!**
    - ValidationExpression: `U.S. Phone Number` (click the ellipsis next to this property's field and select this from the list)

16. Drop another RegularExpressionValidator control next to the RequiredFieldValidator control for `txtEmail`, and then set these properties:

    - ID: `regEmail`
    - ControlToValidate: `txtEmail`
    - Display: `None`
    - ErrorMessage: **Enter a valid e-mail address!**
    - ValidationExpression: `Internet E-mail Address` (click the ellipsis next to this property's field and select this from the list)

17. Drop a Label control below the table. Set its `ID` to `lblMessage` and clear its `Text` property. Set its `CssClass` property to `Normal`.

18. Drop a ValidationSummary control below this label. Set its `ID` to `valErrors` and its `CssClass` to `Normal`. The form should now look something like Figure 3-18.

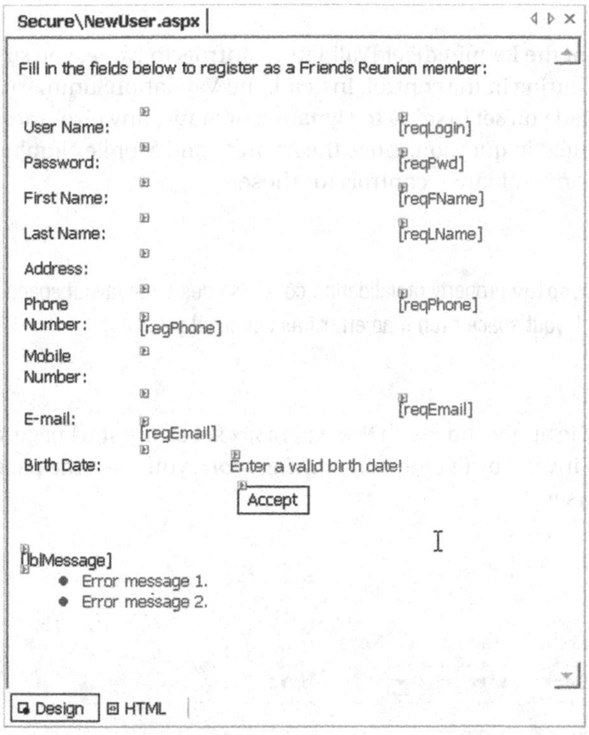

Figure 3-18. *The New User form with validation controls*

19. Finally, let's handle the `Accept` button's `Click` event and populate the message label with a string indicating the current status of the page. Double-click the button in the designer and add the following code:

```
Private Sub btnAccept_Click(ByVal sender As System.Object, _
  ByVal e As System.EventArgs) Handles btnAccept.Click
  If Page.IsValid Then
    lblMessage.Text = "Validation succeeded!"
  Else
    lblMessage.Text = "Fix the following errors and retry:"
  End If
End Sub
```

The validation controls on your `NewUser.aspx` form are now set up and ready to go.

How It Works

By setting the `Display` properties of the RequiredFieldValidator controls to None, you suppress any errors they produce from appearing in the control. Instead, the ValidationSummary control displays errors on the page. Had you set `Display` to Dynamic or Static, any error messages would have appeared next to the field in question. Since the Address and Mobile Number fields are optional, you didn't use any validation controls for those.

Note The Dynamic setting for the `Display` property of validation controls uses page layout space only if validation fails. The Static setting uses layout space even if no error has occurred yet.

If you now compile and run the application with `NewUser.aspx` set as the start page, and submit the page after entering an invalid birth date *and nothing more*, you'll see the page shown in Figure 3-19 in your browser.

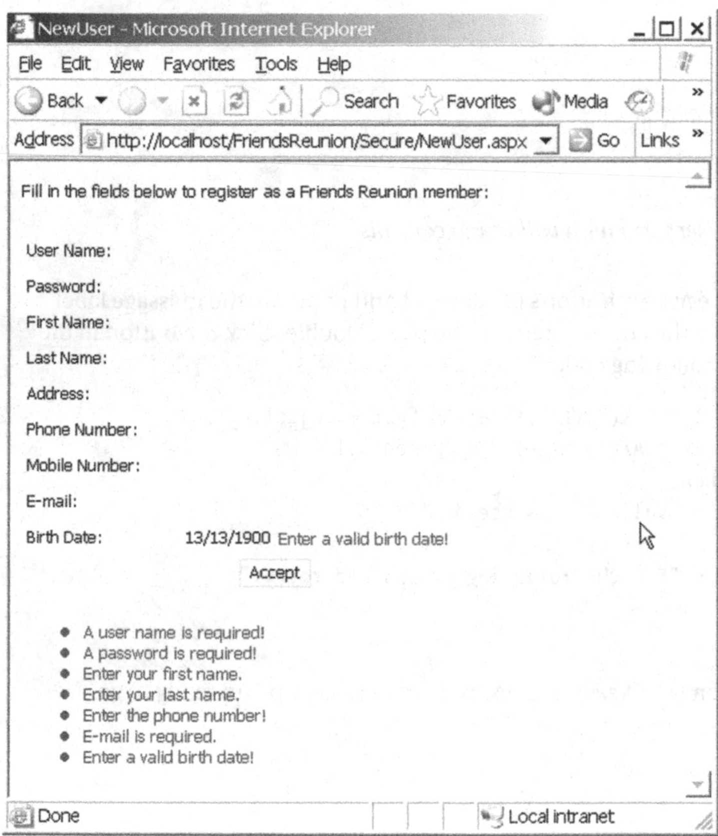

Figure 3-19. *Failing to provide valid information in the New User page*

Notice how the validation errors are automatically collated in the summary control (you can change the format used for this control through its `DisplayMode` property). Also notice that the individual validation controls don't display their error messages, just as you specified. For `compBirth`, whose `Display` property you set to Dynamic, the error message appears in the summary as well as in the validation control itself.

The `compBirth` validation control checks that the value entered matches a Date data type (as a result of setting `Operator` to `DataTypeCheck` and `Type` to `Date`). When a CompareValidator control is configured to perform this sort of check, the `ControlToCompare` and `ValueToCompare` properties are ignored. In other circumstances, you might use these properties to validate the field against another control's value or against a constant value.

The RegularExpressionValidator controls for `txtEmail` and `txtPhone` contain a somewhat complicated string in the `ValidationExpression` property, which you were able to set with the aid of the VS .NET IDE. As you would expect, it's quite possible to enter your own strings here, should you need to do so.

The final step, where you added the event handler for the Accept button, demonstrates a subtle difference between handling validation with client-side JavaScript code and causing a postback when the Accept button is clicked. Even if there are errors, the second message (set when `Page.IsValid` is `False`) will never appear in Internet Explorer 5 and later versions. This is because validation occurs on the client side, thus preventing the user from submitting invalid values. The postback will not occur until all fields contain valid data. Using Netscape/Mozilla, however, you will see the second message while invalid data remains. It's worth noting, from a security point of view, that in *either* case, validation will always be performed on the server side, to ensure valid data has been received.

REGULAR EXPRESSION RESOURCES

Using regular expressions is a fairly advanced topic in its own right. The classic reference to learn more about it is *Mastering Regular Expressions, Second Edition*, by Jeffrey E. F. Friedl (O'Reilly, 2002; ISBN: 0596002890). Also, if you're a subscriber to *ASP Today*, you can find a number of related articles there:

- Regular Expressions in Microsoft .NET (`http://www.asptoday.com/Content.aspx?id=711`)
- Validating user input with the .NET RegularExpressionValidator (`http://www.asptoday.com/Content.aspx?id=1378`)
- String Manipulation and Pattern Testing with Regular Expressions (`http://www.asptoday.com/Content.aspx?id=85`)

Another resource available is an amazing tool called The Regulator. This free tool, which you can download from `http://regulator.sf.net/`, is a great help in learning and testing regular expressions

Finally, you can find an ever-growing library of well-tested regular expressions ready for use at `http://www.regexlib.com`.

User Controls

In our Friends Reunion application, it would be good to have a common header and footer for every page, a common navigation bar, and so on. ASP.NET provides a straightforward reusability model for the page features that you create, in the form of the *user controls*. You create these controls in much the same way as you create web forms, but they're saved with the `.ascx` extension.

A user control doesn't contain the tags that usually start off a page, such as `<html>`, `<head>`, `<body>`, and so on. Also, instead of the ASP.NET `<%@ Page %>` directive, it uses the `<%@ Control %>` directive to customize certain features of the control. Without further ado, let's build an example, so that you can see what's going on.

Try It Out: Build a Header Control To begin, let's build a header control that you can put to use on every single page in the Friends Reunion site. It will look a little like the blue banner that currently sits at the top of the News page.

1. Create a new folder called `Controls`, right-click it, and choose Add ➤ Add Web User Control from the context menu. Name the new file `FriendsHeader.ascx`.

2. Drop a Panel web server control onto the page, and give it the following properties:

   - ID: `pnlHeaderGlobal`
   - CssClass: `HeaderFriends`

3. Set the text inside the panel to **Friends Reunion**.

4. Drop an image web server control inside the panel, to the right of the text, and set the following properties:

   - ID: `imgFriends`
   - CssClass: `HeaderImage`
   - ImageUrl: `../Images/friends.gif`

5. Drop another Panel web control below the previous one. Clear the text inside it, and set the following properties:

   - ID: `pnlHeaderLocal`
   - CssClass: `HeaderTitle`

6. Drop an Image web server control inside this panel, and set the following properties:

   - ID: `imgIcon`
   - CssClass: `HeaderImage`
   - ImageUrl: `../Images/homeconnected.gif`

7. Drop a Label web control inside the same panel, to the right of the image, and set these properties:

   - ID: lblWelcome
   - Text: **Welcome!**

8. Save the control, which should now look like this:

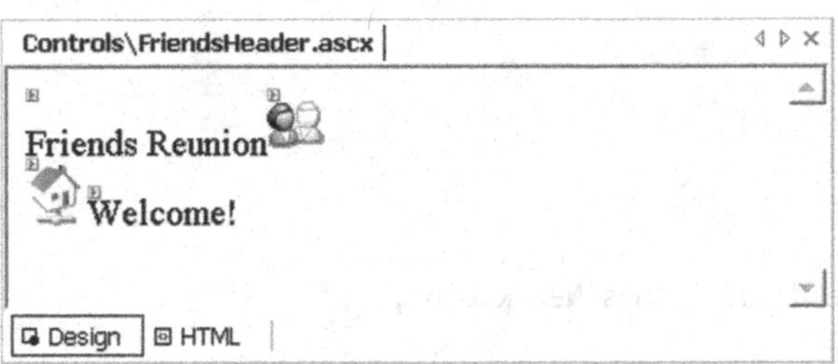

9. Just to see how the control has been created, switch to the HTML view. Notice the absence of any "normal" HTML elements around the ASP.NET elements:

```
<%@ Control language="vb" AutoEventWireup="false"
  Codebehind="FriendsHeader.ascx.vb"
  Inherits="FriendsReunion.Controls.FriendsHeader"
  TargetSchema="http://schemas.microsoft.com/intellisense/ie5"%>
<asp:panel id="pnlHeaderGlobal" runat="server" cssclass="HeaderFriends">
  Friends Reunion
  <asp:image id="imgFriends" runat="server" cssclass="HeaderImage"
    imageurl="../Images/friends.gif"></asp:image>
</asp:panel>
<asp:panel id="pnlHeaderLocal" runat="server" cssclass="HeaderTitle">
  <asp:image id="imgIcon" runat="server" cssclass="HeaderImage"
    imageurl="../Images/homeconnected.gif"></asp:image>
  <asp:label id="lblWelcome" runat="server">Welcome!</asp:label>
</asp:panel>
```

10. As you will have noticed, you've used some CSS styles that haven't yet been defined: `HeaderFriends`, `HeaderImage`, and `HeaderTitle`. Let's add those to the `iestyle.css` stylesheet now:

```
.HeaderFriends
{
  padding-right: 5px;
  padding-left: 5px;
  font-weight: bold;
  font-size: 8pt;
  font-family: Tahoma, Verdana, 'Times New Roman';
  width: 100%;
  color: white;
```

```
  background-color: #336699;
  text-align: right;
}
.HeaderImage
{
  vertical-align: middle;
}
.HeaderTitle
{
  padding-right: 5px;
  padding-left: 5px;
  padding-right: 10px;
  font-weight: bold;
  font-size: 8pt;
  font-family: Tahoma, Verdana, 'Times New Roman';
  width: 100%;
  color: white;
  background-color: #336699;
}
```

11. Open the NewUser.aspx form and drag the FriendsHeader.ascx file from the Solution Explorer onto it, placing it just before the first line of text on the page. Add a new paragraph after the newly added control by pressing Enter.

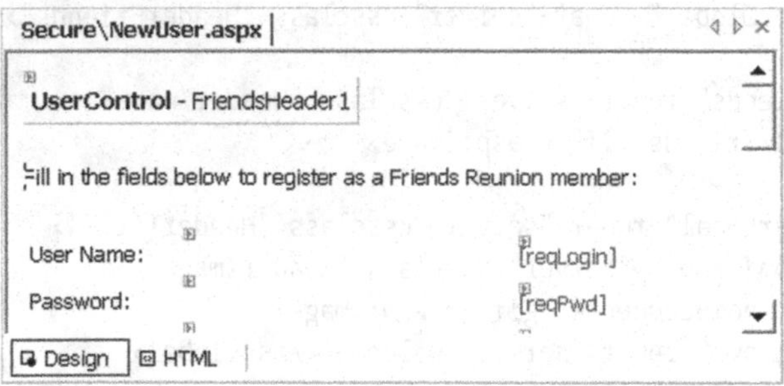

12. Save, compile, and run the application, and see what you get.

How It Works

The process of designing a new user control is just like creating a page: you drop controls and set their properties in the same way. Apart from the lack of page-level elements, the HTML looks just like the code for a regular web form. Once the user control is created, you can place it on the page just as if it were a control from the Toolbox. At that moment, the control is registered with the page with the Register directive, and the following lines are added to the page's HTML code:

```
<%@ Register TagPrefix="uc1" TagName="FriendsHeader"
          Src="../Controls/FriendsHeader.ascx" %>
  ...
 <body>
   <form id="NewUser" method="post" runat="server">
     <p><uc1:friendsheader id="FriendsHeader1" runat="server">
       </uc1:friendsheader></p>
     ...
```

The Register directive at the top of the page tells ASP.NET where to locate and load the appropriate user control, from the relative path specified in the Src attribute. It also associates the control with a prefix that's used when you define control instances, which you can change if you want to. When you open the NewUser.aspx page, you see something like Figure 3-20.

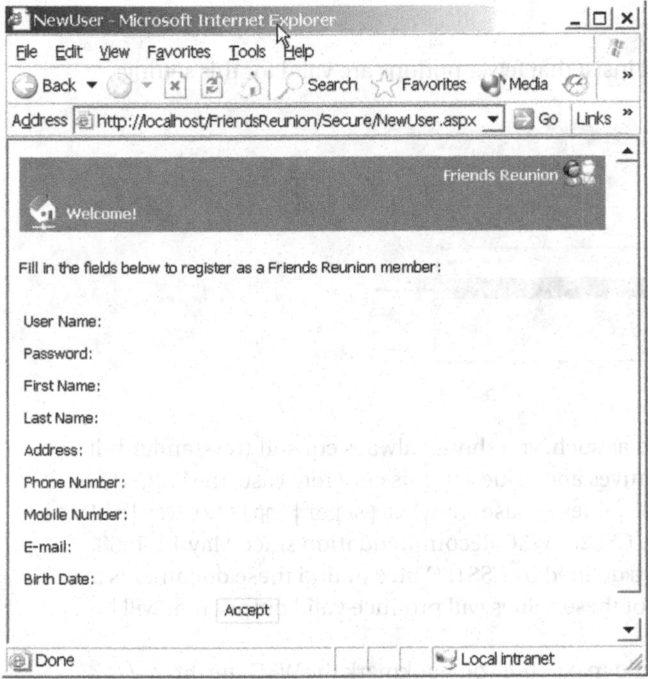

Figure 3-20. *The New User page with a header user control*

As long as you use server controls for the images in the header (in other words, you don't use an HTML Image element without the runat="server" attribute), the relative paths will be properly resolved, no matter where the page using the control is located.

Just dropping this control onto every page of the Friends Reunion site will help to provide it with a consistent look and feel, building on the work you've already done with stylesheets. However, always having the same icon and message on the left isn't ideal, so in a moment, you'll see how to customize it for the current page. First, though, we'll deal with a problem that you may have noticed a couple of pages ago.

A Side Note: Style Builder, IntelliSense, and CSS

Sometimes, there's a lack of synchronization between what IntelliSense and the Style Builder show. One example is the `vertical-align` property you used to style the images. IntelliSense will show you the following available values:

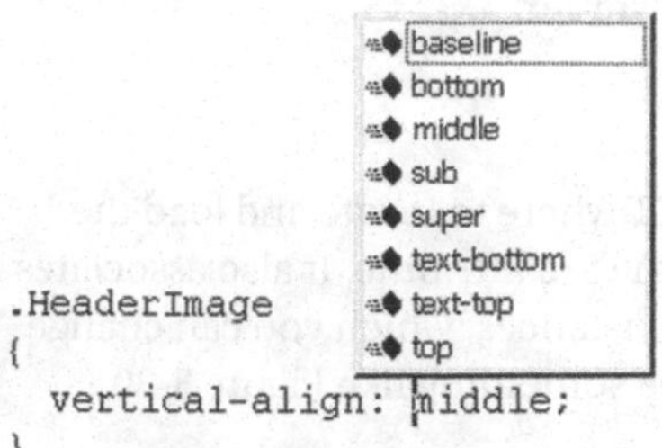

The Style Builder, however, will insist that fewer options are valid for this setting:

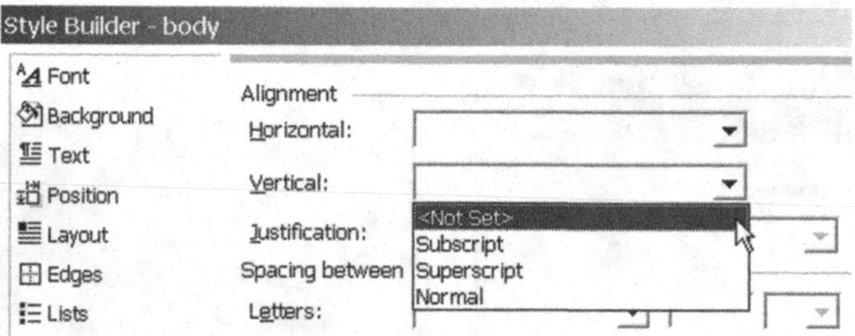

The CSS is a W3C standard, and as such, you should always consult the standards if you are in doubt about valid alternatives and values. In this concrete case, the W3C's CSS1 Recommendation specifies the legal values as `baseline` | `sub` | `super` | `top` | `text-top` | `middle` | `bottom` | `text-bottom` | <*percentage*>. CSS2, a W3C Recommendation since May 12, 1998, adds <*length*> | `inherit` to the values defined by CSS1. (You can find these documents at `http://www.w3.org/Style/CSS`.) All of these values will produce valid output that will be properly rendered by most browsers.

The bottom line is that you should make sure you bookmark the W3C site (`http://www.w3.org/`) and go there as often as you need to ensure that you're using standards-compliant options and that you're not missing something.

Try It Out: Add Properties to User Controls Returning to our Friends Reunion sample application, we were talking (before our little diversion) about customizing the user control for different pages. The technique for doing this is to define some properties for the control that you can set when the control is instantiated. In this example, you'll make it possible to set the image and the message on the left side of the user control banner.

1. Open the code-behind file for the user control (right-click it and select View Code), and add the following code to it:

```
Public Class FriendsHeader
  Inherits System.Web.UI.UserControl

  [ Web Form Designer Generated Code ]

  Private Sub Page_Load(ByVal sender As System.Object,_
    ByVal e As System.EventArgs) Handles MyBase.Load
    'Put user code to initialize the page here
  End Sub

  Private _message As String = ""
  Private _imageurl As String = ""

  Public Property Message() As String
    Get
      Return _message
    End Get
    Set(ByVal Value As String)
      _message = Value
    End Set
  End Property

  Public Property IconImageUrl() As String
    Get
      Return _imageurl
    End Get
    Set(ByVal Value As String)
      _imageurl = Value
    End Set
  End Property

  Protected Overrides Sub Render(ByVal writer As System.Web.UI.HtmlTextWriter)
    If Message <> "" Then lblWelcome.Text = Message
    If IconImageUrl <> "" Then imgIcon.ImageUrl = IconImageUrl
    MyBase.Render(writer)
  End Sub
End Class
```

2. Open the `News.aspx` page. Delete the panel and image you added previously as a header. Drop the new user control in its place, and then insert a new paragraph after it.

3. Switch to the HTML view and find the line containing the control's declaration:

```
<uc1:friendsheader id="FriendsHeader1" runat="server">
</uc1:friendsheader>
```

4. Add a Message attribute to it, like so:

```
<uc1:friendsheader id="FriendsHeader1" runat="server"
               message="Welcome to the news page!"></uc1:friendsheader>
```

5. Open the NewUser.aspx page in HTML mode. Change the control's declaration to include both a Message attribute and an IconImageUrl attribute:

```
<uc1:friendsheader id="FriendsHeader1" runat="server"
               message="Registration form"
               iconimageurl="../Images/securekeys.gif">
</uc1:friendsheader>
```

6. Save, compile, and run the page to see how your changes have affected the output displayed in your browser.

How It Works

You can add properties to a user control, just as you can add them to any other custom class. In this example, you've implemented two properties that control the message and the icon of the second panel through a couple of private member fields:

```
Private _message As String = ""
Private _imageurl As String = ""
```

You initialize the variables to empty strings in order to be able to determine whether values have been supplied. In the Render() override, you change only the default image and message if you have nonempty values for the properties. (This method is called just before the HTML code is sent to the client.) In order to create a method that overrides one on the base class, you use the same procedure you used to handle events, but you choose the item named (Overrides) in the top-left drop-down list within the code editor. The drop-down list on the right will show all of the methods that you can override.

When you now open the NewUser.aspx page, you see something like Figure 3-21.

Try It Out: Create the Footer Control Let's complement the header you just created with a corresponding footer control.

1. Right-click the Controls folder and choose Add ➤ Add Web User Control from the context menu. Name the new file FriendsFooter.ascx.

2. Open the code-behind file for the user control (right-click it and select View Code), and then add the following code to it:

```
<%@ Control Language="vb" AutoEventWireup="false"
    Codebehind="FriendsFooter.ascx.vb"
    Inherits="FriendsReunion.Controls.FriendsFooter"
    TargetSchema="http://schemas.microsoft.com/intellisense/ie5" %>
<asp:panel id="pnlFooterGlobal" CssClass="FooterFriends" runat="server">
  Friends Reunion Application - Courtesy of Apress<br>
  <b>Beginning Web Applications </b>
</asp:panel>
```

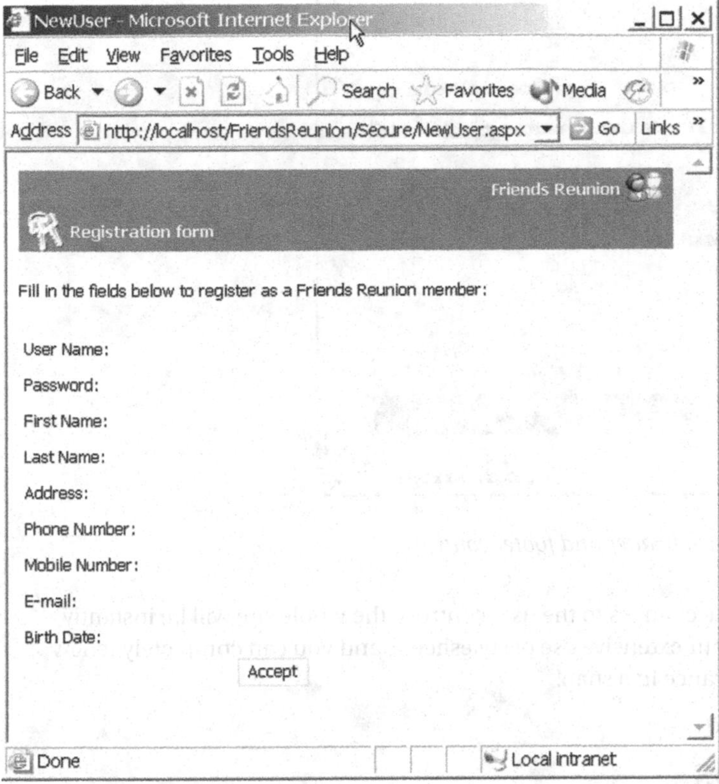

Figure 3-21. *The New User page with a customized header user control*

3. Add the `FooterFriends` CSS style class used by the control to the `iestyle.css` stylesheet:

```
.FooterFriends
{
  font-size: 8pt;
  font-family: Tahoma, Verdana, 'Times New Roman';
  width: 100%;
  color: white;
  background-color: #336699;
  text-align: center;
}
```

4. Now you can go back to each of the pages you have created so far in the Friends Reunion application and add the new header and footer controls to each one. Figure 3-22 shows what the `Login.aspx` page will look like after you have added your user controls for the header and footer.

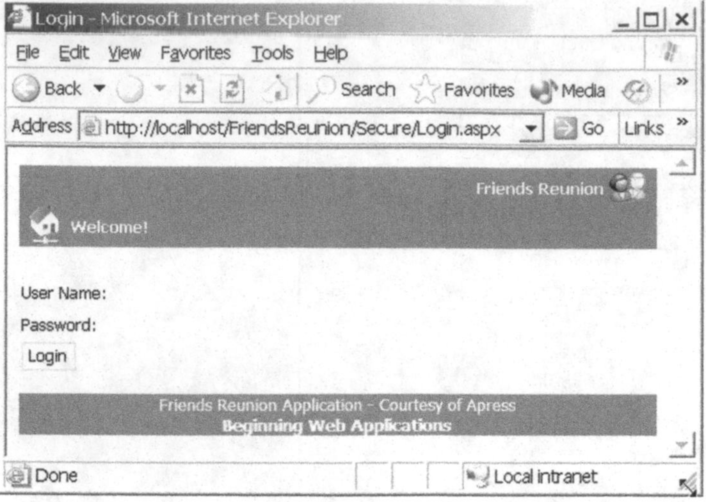

Figure 3-22. *The Login page with header and footer controls*

Now whenever you make changes to the user controls, the whole site will be instantly updated. Couple this with your extensive use of stylesheets, and you can completely renew the web application's appearance in a snap!

Custom Controls

Most of the built-in ASP.NET server controls offer great features, but the ASP.NET object model also allows you—and even encourages you—to extend the controls through *inheritance.* A control that extends base functionality like this is called a *custom control.*

When creating a custom control, the particular base class you choose to inherit from will depend on the situation. You could inherit from the TextBox control if you wish to incorporate some custom processing into its behavior, or you might inherit from the top-level `WebControl` base class to provide fully customized UI rendering.

In this section, we'll start by working with some simple custom controls, and then increase their complexity by incorporating more advanced features.

Tip Our aim here is just to raise your awareness of custom controls, which can be an invaluable addition to the ASP.NET web designer's toolset. For a comprehensive study of this important feature, take a look at *Building ASP.NET Server Controls*, by Dale Michalk and Rob Cameron (Apress, 2003; ISBN: 1-59059-140-2).

Try It Out: Build the SubHeader Custom Control In this example, you're going to create a simple custom control that displays a subheader beneath your page header control, containing today's date and a link to the registration form.

1. Right-click the project name and select Add ➤ Add Class. Give the new class the name `SubHeader.vb`.

2. Add the following code to the code-behind file:

```
Public Class SubHeader
  Inherits WebControl

  Private _register As String

  Public Sub New()
    'Initialize default values
    Me.Width = New Unit(100, UnitType.Percentage)
    Me.CssClass = "SubHeader"
  End Sub

  'Property to allow the user to define the URL for the
  'registration page
  Public Property RegisterUrl() As String
    Get
      Return _register
    End Get
    Set(ByVal Value As String)
      _register = Value
    End Set
  End Property

  Protected Overrides Sub CreateChildControls()
    Dim lbl As Label

    ' If the user is authenticated, we will render their name
    If (Context.User.Identity.IsAuthenticated) Then
      lbl = New Label
      lbl.Text = Context.User.Identity.Name

      ' Add the newly created label to our
      ' collection of child controls
      Controls.Add(lbl)
    Else
      ' Otherwise, we will render a link to the registration page
      Dim reg As New HyperLink
      reg.Text = "Register"
```

```
      ' If a URL isn't provided, use a default URL to the
      ' registration page
      If _register = "" Then
        reg.NavigateUrl = "~\Secure\NewUser.aspx"
      Else
        reg.NavigateUrl = _register
        ' Add the newly created link to our
        ' collection of child controls
        Controls.Add(reg)
      End If
    End If

    ' Add a couple of blank spaces and a separator character
    Controls.Add(New LiteralControl(" - "))

    ' Add a label with the current data
    lbl = New Label
    lbl.Text = DateTime.Now.ToLongDateString()
    Controls.Add(lbl)
  End Sub
End Class
```

3. Add the following style to the `iestyle.css` stylesheet:

```
.SubHeader
{
  border-top: 3px groove;
  font-size: 8pt;
  color: white;
  font-family: Tahoma, Verdana, 'Times New Roman';
  background-color: #4f82b5;
  text-align: right;
  width: 100%;
  display: block;
}
```

4. Open the `News.aspx` page in the HTML view and add the following directive at the top of the page, which will allow you to use your new custom control:

```
<%@ Register TagPrefix="ap"
             Namespace="FriendsReunion" Assembly="FriendsReunion" %>
```

5. Directly below the header user control you added earlier, add the following line:

```
        <ap:subheader id="SubHeader1" runat="server" />
```

6. Set `News.aspx` as the start page, run the project, and sit back and admire your handiwork!

How It Works

Your new custom control derives from the WebControl base class, just like most intrinsic ASP.NET web controls. The base class provides properties for setting the control's layout, such as its Width, its CssClass, and so on, which you set at construction time. You've added a property to hold a URL, similar to what you did for your user control:

```
Private _register As String

Public Sub New()
  'Initialize default values
  Me.Width = New Unit(100, UnitType.Percentage)
  Me.CssClass = "SubHeader"
End Sub

'Property to allow the user to define the URL for the
'registration page
Public Property RegisterUrl() As String
  Get
    Return _register
  End Get
  Set(ByVal Value As String)
    _register = Value
  End Set
End Property
```

The main difference between the user control and the custom control is the way that the control's interface is built. For the user control, you just dropped controls onto the design surface, as you would have done for a web form. For the custom control, a special method named CreateChildControls () is called whenever ASP.NET needs to rebuild your control so it is ready for display. For *composite* custom controls—those made of other child controls like your SubHeader control—this method is the appropriate one to override for creating the control hierarchy. You do so by specifying the controls that make up your custom control through the Controls collection property. (This property comes from the Control base class, so any server control can be a container for any other controls in this model.) You need to create and set up the new controls programmatically before they are appended to that collection:

```
' If the user is authenticated, we will render their name
If (Context.User.Identity.IsAuthenticated) Then
  lbl = New Label
  lbl.Text = Context.User.Identity.Name

  ' Add the newly created label to our
  ' collection of child controls
  Controls.Add(lbl)
Else
  ' Otherwise, we will render a link to the registration page
  Dim reg As New HyperLink
  reg.Text = "Register"
```

```
    ' If a URL isn't provided, use a default URL to the
    ' registration page
    If _register = "" Then
      reg.NavigateUrl = "~\Secure\NewUser.aspx"
    Else
      reg.NavigateUrl = _register
      ' Add the newly created link to our
      ' collection of child controls
      Controls.Add(reg)
    End If
  End If

  ' Add a couple of blank spaces and a separator character
  Controls.Add(New LiteralControl(" - "))

  ' Add a label with the current data
  lbl = New Label
  lbl.Text = DateTime.Now.ToLongDateString()
  Controls.Add(lbl)
```

Also of note here is that you used the `Context.User.Identity.IsAuthenticated` property to display the Register link selectively. As you'll see in Chapter 10, this property identifies an authenticated user, according to the authentication method selected. If the user is authenticated, the `Identity.Name` property will contain the correct user name.

Note If you expect more than one instance of your custom control to be used on a page, you need to implement the marker interface `INamingContainer` to avoid naming conflicts for child controls, such as the label or hyperlink you are using to build your control.

When you open the `News.aspx` page, you should see something like Figure 3-23.

Tip The tilde char (~) you used to specify the default location of the registration page (`~\Secure\NewUser.aspx`) can be used on any server control property expecting a URL to signify that a path is relative to the current application root.

Figure 3-23. *The News page with the SubHeader custom control*

You'll learn more about security settings in Chapter 10, but for now, you can simulate an unauthenticated user by enabling Anonymous access and disabling Integrated Windows authentication. To do this, open the IIS console (Start ➤ Settings ➤ Control Panel ➤ Administrative Tools ➤ Internet Information Services). In the Default Web Site node under your server name, right-click the `FriendsReunion` application and select Properties. Select the Directory Security tab, and click the Edit button in the Anonymous access and authentication control section. Check Anonymous access, and uncheck Integrated Windows authentication and Basic authentication, as shown in Figure 3-24.

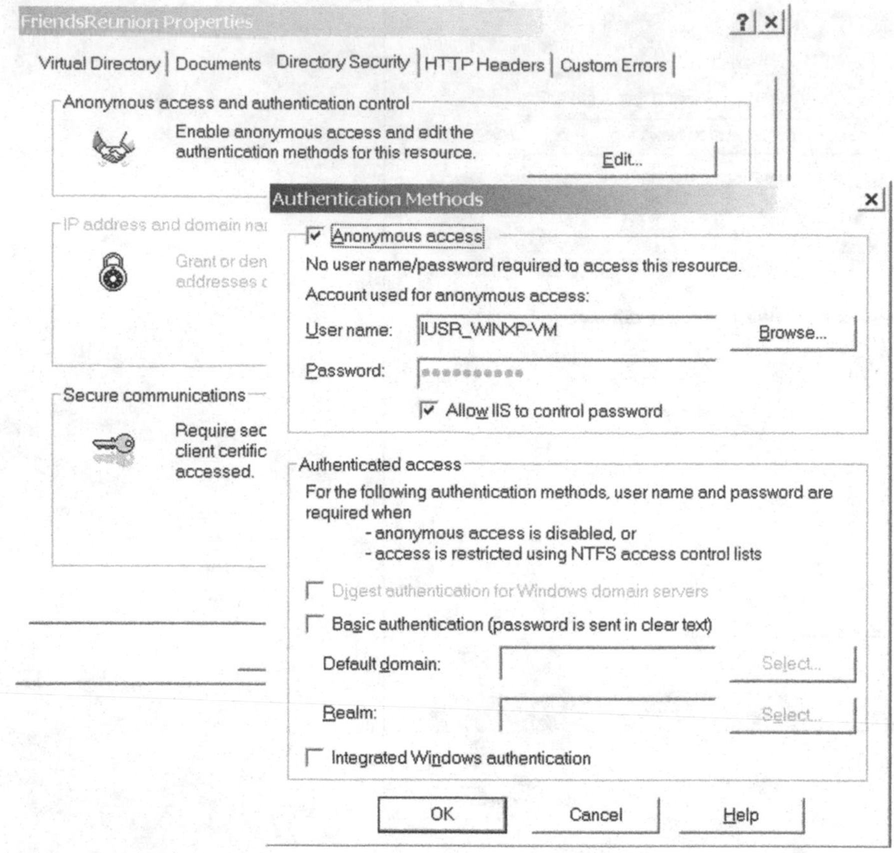

Figure 3-24. *Enabling Anonymous access and disabling Integrated Windows authentication*

You can switch from an authenticated user to an unauthenticated user just by alternating from Integrated Windows authentication only to Anonymous access. After enabling the latter, you will see the link to the registration form instead of the Windows user name.

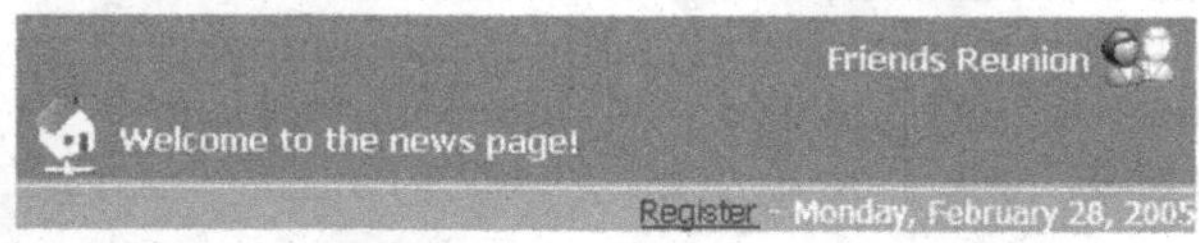

At runtime, there's not much difference between this control and the user control you created for the header, but the custom control stands out at design-time. With the `News.aspx` page in the Design view, you can immediately see the difference, as shown in Figure 3-25.

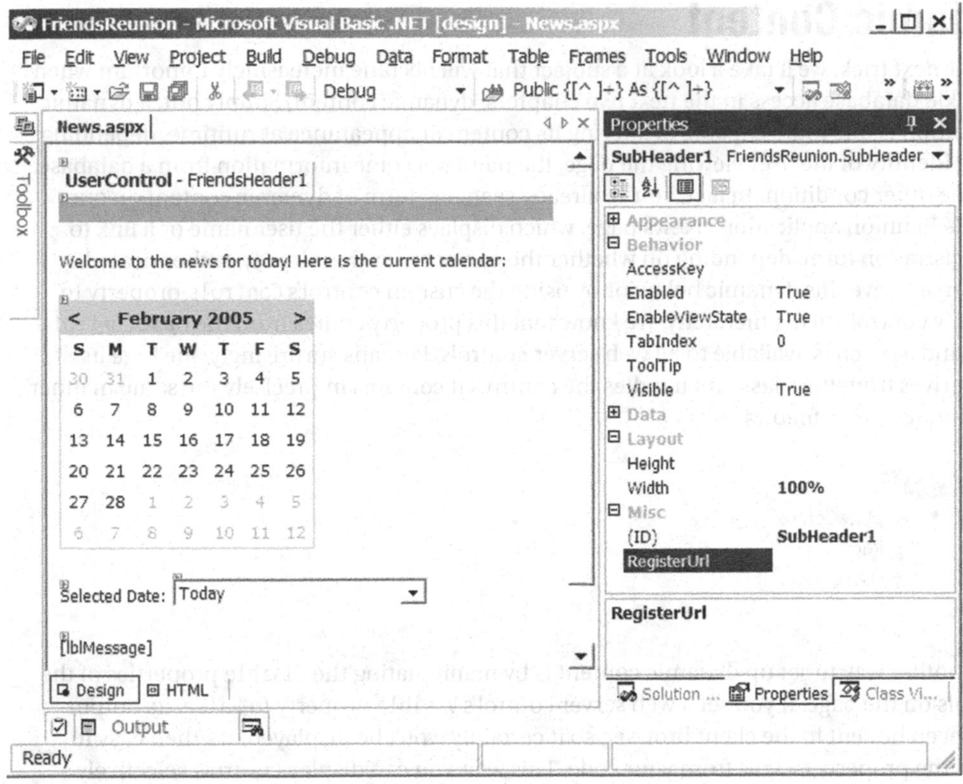

Figure 3-25. *The custom control in the Design view*

Unlike the user control, which isn't even rendered at design-time (other than that ugly gray box), your custom control renders itself on screen and provides the complete set of visual properties available for all web server controls through the Properties browser. Toward the bottom of the Properties browser, you can see the `RegisterUrl` property that you added. This is far more intuitive than the user control approach, at the cost of some extra effort on the part of the control developer.

Note ASP.NET version 2.0 will provide about the same design-time support for both user controls and custom controls.

Dynamic Content

For our next trick, we'll take a look at a subject that will become increasingly important when we tackle database access in the next two chapters: dynamic content. Simply put, a dynamic application is one that's capable of altering its content or appearance at runtime, depending on the identity of the user viewing the page, the nature of some information from a database, or some other condition. In fact, you've already seen one form of dynamic content on our Friends Reunion application's News page, which displays either the user name or a link to the registration form, depending on whether the current user was already authenticated.

You achieve this dynamic behavior by using the custom control's `Controls` property to add new controls to the hierarchy. We know that this property comes from the base `Control` class, and as such is available to all web server controls. Perhaps surprisingly, the `Page` itself *also* derives from this class and handles the controls it contains in precisely the same manner. The hierarchy is as follows.

Another way to set up dynamic content is by manipulating the `Visible` properties of the controls on the page. If you set a web server control's `Visible` property to `False`, its output won't even be sent to the client browser, so it certainly won't be displayed! It's then easy to switch the property to `True` from your code. This way, you can display controls selectively according to certain conditions.

Try It Out: Dynamically Build Navigation Controls As a further example of dynamic content, you will now create the `Default.aspx` entry page for the Friends Reunion site. This will be the page that all users visit after they've logged in, and the links it offers will vary according to who they are. In it, you'll use a PlaceHolder control to define the location of the controls you add to the page programmatically.

1. Add a new web form to the project's root directory and call it `Default.aspx`.

2. Drop the `FriendsHeader.ascx` and `FriendsFooter.ascx` controls onto it. Set their `ID`s to `ucHeader` and `ucFooter`.

3. Add the `SubHeader` custom control by switching to the HTML view, and adding a `Register` directive and a `<wx:subheader>` element, just as you did for the `News.aspx` page. This time, set its `ID` to `ccSubHeader`.

```
<%@ Register TagPrefix="ap"
           Namespace="FriendsReunion" Assembly="FriendsReunion" %>
     ...
       <ap:subheader id="ccSubHeader" runat="server" /></P>
```

4. While in the HTML view, add a `<link>` element for the `iestyles.css` stylesheet (or drag-and-drop the `.css` file on the design surface).

5. Below the headers, type a description for the page: **Welcome to the Friends Reunion web site – the meeting place for lost friends!** Set its `class` property to `Normal`, and start a new paragraph after it.

6. Drop a PlaceHolder web control, and then set its `ID` to `phNav`. This marks the location on the page where all of the controls you add will be placed.

7. Add the following code to the `Page_Load()` method:

```
Private Sub Page_Load(ByVal sender As System.Object, _
  ByVal e As System.EventArgs) Handles MyBase.Load

  Dim tb As New Table
  Dim row As TableRow
  Dim cell As TableCell
  Dim img As System.Web.UI.WebControls.Image
  Dim lnk As HyperLink

  If (Context.User.Identity.IsAuthenticated) Then
    ' Create a new blank table row
    row = New TableRow

    ' Set up the News image
    img = New System.Web.UI.WebControls.Image
    img.ImageUrl = "Images/winbook.gif"
    img.ImageAlign = ImageAlign.Middle
    img.Width = New Unit(24, UnitType.Pixel)
    img.Height = New Unit(24, UnitType.Pixel)

    ' Create a cell and add the image
    cell = New TableCell
    cell.Controls.Add(img)

    ' Add the new cell to the row
    row.Cells.Add(cell)

    ' Set up the News link
    lnk = New HyperLink
    lnk.Text = "News"
    lnk.NavigateUrl = "News.aspx"

    ' Create the cell and add the link
    cell = New TableCell
    cell.Controls.Add(lnk)
```

```
        ' Add the new cell to the row
        row.Cells.Add(cell)

        ' Add the row to the table
        tb.Rows.Add(row)
      Else
        ' Code for unauthenticated users here...
      End If

      ' Finally, add the table to the placeholder
      phNav.Controls.Add(tb)
    End Sub
```

8. Set `Default.aspx` as the start page, and save and run the application. Turn on and off Anonymous access in IIS (as described in the previous section) to see how the results differ. Figure 3-26 shows the Default page.

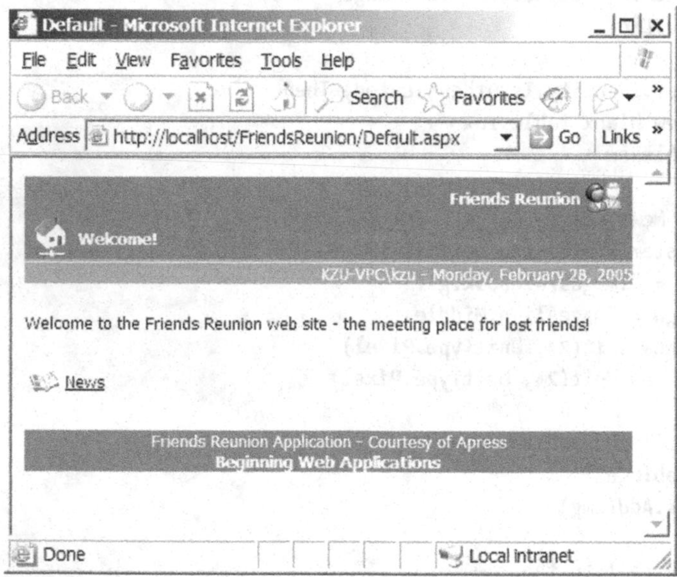

Figure 3-26. *The Default page with dynamic content*

How It Works

The special PlaceHolder control has been designed with dynamic control loading in mind. It forms an invisible container for controls that you insert later and positions them correctly in the hierarchy that's defined by the `Page.Controls` collection. The PlaceHolder control doesn't render HTML to the client itself; it's useful only for this sort of scenario.

The Page_Load() event handler instantiates a new Table web control that will hold the links you add. When you finish the process of adding links, you add the table to the Placeholder control. You can add as many controls to the placeholder as you need; it's not limited to just one.

Avoiding Code Duplication

At this point, you've developed a set of controls that will help to create a consistent look and feel for the application. At the moment though, you need to add the user controls and the custom control to every new page manually. You can avoid this tedious task with a custom base page that can load user and custom controls dynamically.

Try It Out: Build a Custom Base Page Our technique for this final example will be to create a new class that inherits from and builds on the System.Web.UI.Page class. Once you've set it up with the header and footer controls you want to use, you'll inherit from the new class in all of your web forms, providing them with that functionality by default.

1. Add a new class named FriendsBase.vb to the project.
2. Add the following code to the class:

```
Public Class FriendsBase
  Inherits Page

  Protected HeaderMessage As String = ""
  Protected HeaderIconImageUrl As String = ""

  Protected Overrides Sub Render(ByVal writer As System.Web.UI.HtmlTextWriter)
    ' Get a reference to the form control
    Dim form As Control = Page.Controls(1)

    ' Create and place the page header
    Dim header As FriendsHeader
    header = CType( _
      LoadControl("~/Controls/FriendsHeader.ascx"), _
      FriendsHeader)

    header.Message = HeaderMessage
    header.IconImageUrl = HeaderIconImageUrl
    form.Controls.AddAt(0, header)

    ' Add the SubHeader custom control
    form.Controls.AddAt(1, New SubHeader)

    ' Add space separating the main content
    form.Controls.AddAt(2, New LiteralControl("<p/>"))
    form.Controls.AddAt(form.Controls.Count, _
      New LiteralControl("<p/>"))
```

```
    ' Finally, add the page footer
    Dim footer As FriendsFooter
    footer = CType( _
      LoadControl("~/Controls/FriendsFooter.ascx"), _
      FriendsFooter)

    form.Controls.AddAt(Page.Controls(1).Controls.Count, footer)

    ' Render as usual
    MyBase.Render(writer)
  End Sub
End Class
```

3. Add a new web form to the project called `Info.aspx`. Its `pageLayout` property should already be set to `FlowLayout`.

4. Type some place-holding text in a paragraph (such as: **This is an information page.**) on the new form.

5. As usual, drop the `iestyles.css` stylesheet file from the Solution Explorer onto the form to link it.

6. Open the code-behind page and change the class declaration to this:

```
Public Class Info
  Inherits FriendsBase
```

7. Add the following lines to the `Page_Load()` method:

```
Private Sub Page_Load(ByVal sender As System.Object, _
  ByVal e As System.EventArgs) Handles MyBase.Load
  HeaderIconImageUrl = "~/Images/winbook.gif"
  HeaderMessage = "Informative Page"
End Sub
```

8. Save and run the project with `Info.aspx` as the start page. It should look like Figure 3-27.

How It Works

By default, web forms inherit directly from the base `Page` class, but this is not a requirement. It's possible to inherit from any `Page`-derived class, creating a great opportunity for adding common behavior across pages. Our web application takes advantage of this to insert header, subheader, and footer controls on every page automatically, relieving the page developer from the chore of dropping and placing these controls all the time. Now it's just a matter of inheriting from the new base page, as you did in step 6 of the previous example, by changing the `System.Web.UI.Page` default base class to point to the `FriendsBase` class.

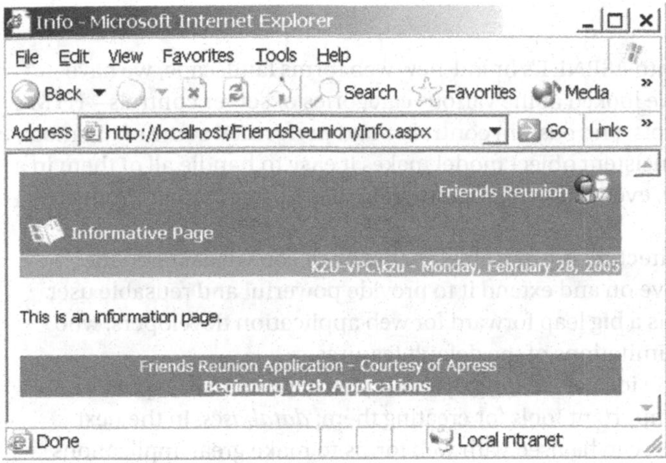

Figure 3-27. *Starting the project with a custom base page*

The base page class loads controls onto the page by two methods. For user controls, you need to use the special `LoadControl()` method, provided by the `TemplateControl` class from which both `UserControl` and `Page` derive.

Once the control is loaded and assigned to a variable of the correct type, you can access the properties and methods of the `UserControl`. After configuring the loaded control, you add it to the form's `Controls` collection, specifying *where* you want to add it by using the `AddAt()` method. The form itself is the control with index `1`, as you saw in the example. This is the case for your page because ASP.NET treats everything from the page startup to the opening `<body>` tag as a single literal control. Note that if you add any other controls between the `body` tag and the `form` tag, its index will no longer be 1.

In order for inheriting pages to set the message and the icon to use (these were previously set directly in every page), the base page defines two protected variables called `HeaderIconImageUrl` and `HeaderMessage`, and uses them to set the controls appropriately. The footer works in the same way as the header.

The SubHeader custom control, on the other hand, doesn't need any special handling, because it is treated just like any other server control. You add a new instance directly, without declaring a variable, as it doesn't need any further settings. At this point, you also add a couple empty paragraphs to separate the header and footer from the main content.

The special processing to set up the pages has been created by overriding the `Render()` method in the base page, and before exiting the function, you call `MyBase.Render()` to let the base `Page` class perform the usual rendering of the modified control hierarchy. Any derived class that wants to override this method *must* also call `MyBase.Render()`, passing in the `writer` object that's used to create the appropriate output.

The custom base page gives exactly the same result as you achieved with the `Default.aspx` and `News.aspx` pages, but with almost no code at all required in `Info.aspx`!

Summary

During this exploratory journey into ASP.NET's brand-new web forms landscape, we have uncovered a lot of new features. We looked at the various categories of server controls—HTML controls, web controls, user controls, and custom controls—and performed some of the most common tasks with them. The consistent object model makes it easy to handle all of them in a standard manner, and server-side, event-driven programming raises programmer productivity to a new level.

Almost every part of the architecture is extensible, so that once you've mastered the built-in functionality, you can move on and extend it to provide powerful and reusable user controls or custom controls. This is a big leap forward for web application developers, who are no longer constrained by the limitations of the default features.

Although we've touched on the idea of creating dynamic web sites in this chapter, we haven't yet considered the most important tools for creating them: *databases*. In the next chapter, you'll learn how databases can be used with web forms to make great applications with minimal code.

CHAPTER 4

ADO.NET

In Chapter 3, while we were talking about the various types of controls, we made a number of references to the myriad of additional functionality that becomes available when data access is brought into the mix. In our nascent Friends Reunion application, for example, we could keep a permanent store of all the people who have entered their details into the form and allow the creation of links between those records, so that users returning to the site are immediately presented with a list of the people who want to contact them. We could also let them see complete details about each other, so that they can get in touch.

To manipulate the data stored in databases, ASP.NET uses *ADO.NET*, Microsoft's data-access strategy in .NET. ADO.NET contains many classes that ease the process of building dynamic web applications. We will be discussing the most interesting of these classes over the course of the next two chapters. As we do so, we will be considering the following topics:

- The overall architecture of ADO.NET
- An overview of how to use ADO.NET to access different data sources, using *data providers*
- How to add and read data to and from a database, and display it on a web form
- How to modify data that is already stored in a database
- What datasets are and how to use them

Before we start coding, we'll take a brief tour of the ADO.NET architecture. If you're already familiar with the terms and concepts of ADO.NET, feel free to skip the first section of this chapter. On the other hand, if you're not familiar with ADO.NET, the description of the architecture will give you an idea of how it works, and then this will become clearer as you work through the examples in the later sections.

The Architecture of ADO.NET

Before we go any further, let's get something out of the way: the name *ADO.NET* doesn't actually stand for anything at all. Before you raise a hand to point out that ADO originally stood for *A*ctiveX *D*ata *O*bjects, just remember that Microsoft has decreed that ADO.NET is the name of a technology and *not* an acronym. More significantly, ADO.NET is an important technological leap forward from ADO and has a substantially different architecture, so it's well worth taking a look at its overall design.

Whenever developers want to access data in a database, the most common technique for doing so involves first connecting to the database, and then issuing a SQL statement. ADO.NET supports these two tasks, which together allow interaction between your code and a source of data. Figure 4-1 shows how ADO.NET works: a *command object*, which will usually contain a SQL statement, uses a *connection object* to reach the database. Besides direct SQL statements, a command object can also be used to execute a stored procedure that's already present in the database.

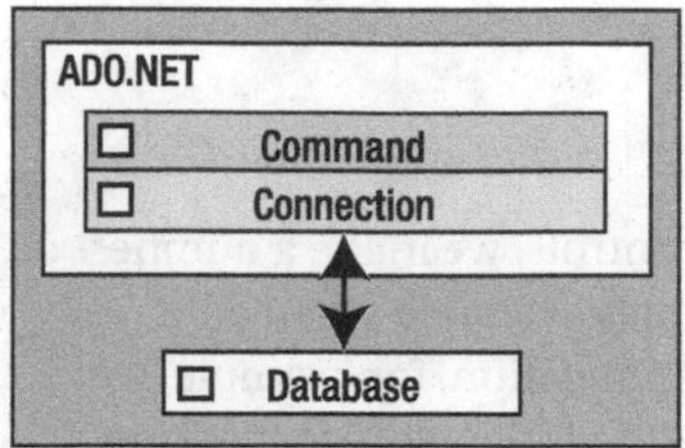

Figure 4-1. *ADO.NET command and connection objects for interacting with a database*

Depending on the query being executed, you may expect to retrieve a single value (from a `SELECT COUNT(1) ...` statement, for example), a result set (from a `SELECT * FROM ...` statement), or no result at all (from an `INSERT` or `UPDATE` statement). Even in the latter case, however, it can be useful to know the number of table rows that were affected. For each of these options, you can use different methods of the command object to execute the command:

- `ExecuteScalar()`returns an `Object` containing the value.
- `ExecuteReader()` returns a data reader object, for accessing a result set.
- `ExecuteNonQuery()` returns an integer with the number of rows affected by the command.

The first and last of these methods are really quite simple, and you'll see them in action shortly. The second, however, is more complex, and the data reader object it returns deserves a little more explanation here.

The Data Reader Object

A *data reader object* is a fast, read-only, forward-only, connected cursor to the data returned from the database. As such, it represents a very efficient way to display the results of a SQL statement.

Using a data reader object is very similar to using the other "reader" objects in the .NET Framework, such as `StreamReader`, `XmlReader`, and so on. You get a reference to it (by calling `ExecuteReader()` in this case) and call `Read()`, and if that returns `True` (meaning that more data is available to be read), you use its methods to access data in the current position. Typically, for result sets containing multiple rows of data, you'll have a code pattern like this:

```
reader = Command.ExecuteReader()
While (reader.Read())
  ' Process current row
End While
```

From this point, you can use the data reader object's methods or its default property to access the values contained in the columns inside the current row.

The data reader object has `GetXXX()` methods for retrieving typed values. Methods such as `GetBoolean()`, `GetString()`, and `GetInt32()` receive the index of the column as an argument and return a value of the appropriate type. Inside the preceding code block, you could write:

```
Response.Write(reader.GetString(0))
```

If you know the name of a column but not its index, you can use the data reader object's `GetOrdinal()` method, which receives the column name and returns its position:

```
Dim pos As Integer = reader.GetOrdinal("CategoryID")
```

The data reader object's `GetValues()` method fills an array with the values in the columns. This method receives an `object` array and fills it with the values in the current row:

```
 Dim values(3) As Object
reader.GetValues(values)
```

If you wish, you can use the data reader's `FieldCount` property to initialize the array. In the preceding code, the array will be filled with the values from the first three columns of the current record.

The data reader object also has a default property that provides direct access to the column values. You can pass either an integer representing the column's position or a string with the column's name. The value returned is of type `Object`, so you'll need to convert it to the target data type explicitly:

```
Dim id As Integer = CType(reader("UserId"), Integer)

' Or accessed by column order
Dim id As Integer = CType(reader(0), Integer)
```

Before you head off and try to find classes called `Connection`, `Command`, and `DataReader` in the .NET Framework, we should tell you that they don't actually exist as such. In ADO.NET, each different type of database must be accessed using its own version of these objects. A particular set of these objects for a particular database is called a *data provider*. The methods we've mentioned so far are the core ones common to all data providers, but a provider may expose additional features that are unique to its database.

Data Providers

Why do we need to use data providers? Wouldn't it be less complicated to have a single set of objects for accessing any kind of database? This is an approach that has been taken in the past, but there's a problem with it: in order to have a common set of objects across disparate databases, an abstraction layer must be implemented on top of database-specific features. A lowest-common-denominator approach must be taken in the design of the classes, which hinders the possibility of making database-specific features easily available. This also adds overhead and causes a performance impact.

In ADO.NET, each database can be accessed using classes that take best advantage of its specific features. At the time of writing, the following .NET data providers exist:

SQL Server: This provider is located in the `System.Data.SqlClient` namespace and provides classes for working with SQL Server 7.0 (or later) databases. It contains the `SqlConnection`, `SqlCommand`, `SqlDataReader`, and `SqlDataAdapter` classes. It is built into the `System.Data` assembly.

OLE DB: This provider is located in the `System.Data.OleDb` namespace and provides classes for working with any data source for which an OLE DB driver exists. It contains the `OleDbConnection`, `OleDbCommand`, `OleDbDataReader`, and `OleDbDataAdapter` classes. It is built into the ADO.NET `System.Data` assembly.

ODBC: This provider is located in the `System.Data.Odbc` namespace and provides classes to work with any data source with an installed ODBC driver. It contains the `OdbcConnection`, `OdbcCommand`, `OdbcDataReader`, and `OdbcDataAdapter` classes. It is built into the ADO.NET `System.Data` assembly.

Oracle: This provider is located in the `System.Data.OracleClient` namespace, and its assembly must be explicitly referenced in a project, as it's part of the `System.Data.OracleClient` assembly, not `System.Data`. It contains the `OracleConnection`, `OracleCommand`, `OracleDataReader`, and `OracleDataAdapter` classes.

Third party: Additional providers exist for IBM DB2, MySQL, PostgreSQL, SQL Lite, Sybase, and even embedded database engines. There's a growing industry of commercial as well as free data providers. A search for "ADO.NET data provider" using a search engine will reveal many of them. An interesting place to look for open-source providers is the Mono project (`http://go-mono.com/ado-net.html`).

Clearly, the data providers will have different implementations as a result of the variety of database technologies they need to deal with. However, they're very similar as far as developers are concerned, because they have common methods and properties for us to use. This means that, generally speaking, choosing a provider is a matter of performance, not of features. The product-specific providers (SQL Server and Oracle, for example) offer superior performance for the databases they target, compared with the generic OLE DB or ODBC providers. The SQL Server provider, for example, communicates with the database using its own proprietary format, Tabular Data Stream (TDS), resulting in significant performance gains.

For the examples in this chapter, we'll use the SQL Server data provider to connect to the Microsoft SQL Server Desktop Engine (MSDE). If you haven't explored MSDE before, there's relevant information about it in Appendix B. As far as the data provider is concerned, MSDE is indistinguishable from SQL Server, which means that the actual classes we'll be using to read data are the same as those for SQL Server, as shown in Figure 4-2.

However, this picture is still incomplete. Specifically, there are two kinds of objects left out of the diagram in Figure 4-2: *data adapters*, which are components of the data providers, and the generic `DataSet` object. We'll take a look at both of these objects later in the chapter (in the "The Rest of the Picture: The DataSet and Data Adapter Objects" section). For now, let's explore some concrete uses of what you've already learned.

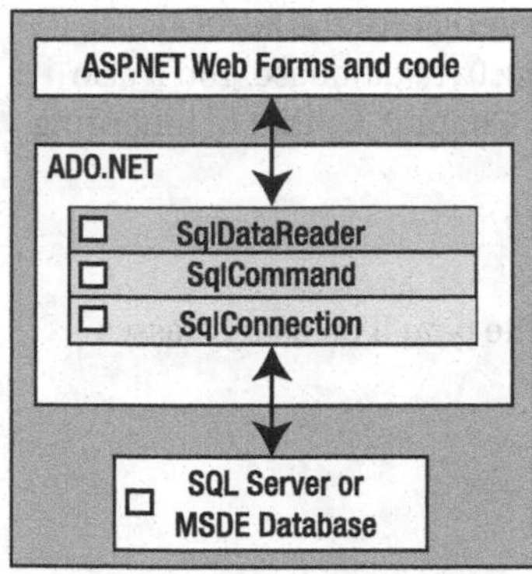

Figure 4-2. *ADO.NET classes for interacting with MSDE and SQL Server*

Programmatic Use of ADO.NET

Now that you've had an introduction to how data access works in ADO.NET, let's make a start on improving our Friends Reunion application to take advantage of it. First, you'll see how to use a database to store new user information.

The database that you're going to use for your data is called `FriendsData`. It is a ready-to-use, detached SQL Server database, provided with the code for this book (which you can download from the Downloads section of `http://www.apress.com`).

Note If you haven't used MSDE before, take a look at Appendix B. That appendix contains details about how to install and set up MSDE, how to use the Server Explorer window, and how to connect to databases using the built-in features of the VS .NET IDE. It also showcases the `FriendsData` design.

Adding Data to a Database

In Chapter 3, you built a form called `NewUser.aspx` that accepts data from the user. Clearly though, such a form is pretty useless unless you're able to save that data somewhere! That's precisely what you'll do now, and you'll use a `SqlCommand` object to achieve it.

After the user has finished entering details into the form, you'll insert a new row into the `User` table of the `FriendsData` database. This table has the following structure:

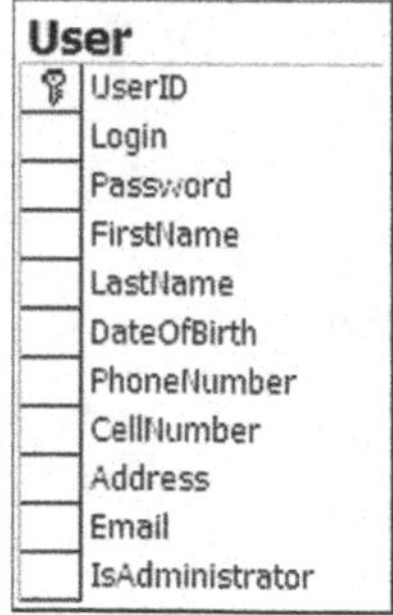

Try It Out: Add a New User For this first example, you'll rewrite the handler for the `NewUser.aspx` form's Accept button to store the details in that form in the `FriendsData` database. You'll also add the improvement that you began to implement at the end of Chapter 3—that of inheriting the `FriendsBase` base class for all forms.

1. Open the `NewUser.aspx` code-behind page.

2. Add the following imports at the top of the code-behind file (you'll be using classes from these namespaces):

```
Imports System.Data.SqlClient
Imports System.Text
```

Tip It's common practice to arrange imports alphabetically, so they can be easily located.

---

3. To take advantage of the common base page you created in Chapter 3, change the base class for your page:

```
  Public Class NewUser
    Inherits FriendsBase
```

4. Now remove the header and footer user controls from this page, because they will be added by the base page from which you're inheriting.

5. As you learned in Chapter 3, change the page icon and the message text in the `Page_Load()` event handler:

```
Private Sub Page_Load(ByVal sender As System.Object, _
  ByVal e As System.EventArgs) Handles MyBase.Load
  MyBase.HeaderIconImageUrl = "~/Images/securekeys.gif"
  MyBase.HeaderMessage = "Registration Form"
End Sub
```

6. Now modify the handler for the Accept button. When you initially added it to the form in the previous chapter, it tested only whether the page was valid. In its new form, it will be responsible for building and executing the SQL `INSERT` statement that will add a new user to the database. This method takes advantage of string formatting, which makes replacing placeholders in a string with values a breeze.

```
Private Sub btnAccept_Click(ByVal sender As System.Object, _
  ByVal e As System.EventArgs) Handles btnAccept.Click
  If Page.IsValid Then
    Dim values As New ArrayList(11)

    ' Optional values without quotes as they can be the Null value
    Dim sql As String
    sql = "INSERT INTO [User] " + _
     "(UserID, Login, Password, FirstName, LastName," + _
```

```
"PhoneNumber, Email, IsAdministrator, Address," + _
 "CellNumber, DateOfBirth)" + _
 "VALUES " + _
 "('{0}', '{1}', '{2}', '{3}', '{4}'," + _
 "'{5}', '{6}', '{7}', {8}, {9}, {10})"

' Add required values to replace
values.Add(Guid.NewGuid().ToString())
values.Add(txtLogin.Text)
values.Add(txtPwd.Text)
values.Add(txtFName.Text)
values.Add(txtLName.Text)
values.Add(txtPhone.Text)
values.Add(txtEmail.Text)
values.Add(0)

' Add the optional values or Null
If (txtAddress.Text.Length <> 0) Then
  values.Add("'" + txtAddress.Text + "'")
Else
  values.Add("Null")
End If

If (txtMobile.Text.Length <> 0) Then
  values.Add("'" + txtMobile.Text + "'")
Else
  values.Add("Null")
End If

If (txtBirth.Text.Length <> 0) Then
  values.Add("'" + txtBirth.Text + "'")
Else
  values.Add("Null")
End If

' Format the string with the array of values
sql = String.Format(sql, values.ToArray())

' Connect and execute the query
Dim con As New SqlConnection( _
 "data source=.;initial catalog=FriendsData;" + _
 "user id=apress;pwd=apress")
Dim cmd As New SqlCommand(sql, con)
con.Open()

Dim doredirect As Boolean = True
```

```
      Try
        cmd.ExecuteNonQuery()
      Catch ex As SqlException
        doredirect = False
        lblMessage.Visible = True
        lblMessage.Text = _
          "Insert couldn't be performed. User name may be already taken."
      Finally
        ' Ensure connection is closed always
        con.Close()
      End Try

      If (doredirect) Then Response.Redirect("Login.aspx")
    Else
      lblMessage.Text = "Fix the following errors and retry:"
    End If
  End Sub
```

7. To make the text of the `lblMessage` label stand out better in case of any errors, set its `ForeColor` property to `Red`.

8. Save and run the project with `NewUser.aspx` as the start page. If you now try to create a new entry for a user who already exists, you'll see something like the message shown in Figure 4-3.

For the sake of simplicity, if the row is successfully inserted (that is, a new record is created in the database), the user will be redirected to the Login page, where the new user will (eventually) be able to enter a user name and password for the account just created.

Note The password on the connection string must match the one you chose at database installation time, as explained in Appendix B. If you have problems authenticating with SQL accounts (for example, the `apress` account we're using), the appendix contains information about how to enable Mixed (Windows and SQL) mode authentication on MSDE.

How It Works

As you saw in Chapter 3, the `Page.IsValid` property represents an accumulation of the validation state of all the validation controls on the page. If all of them are in a valid state, the property will return `True`; otherwise, its return value will be `False`.

The process of building the SQL `INSERT` statement itself isn't too complicated. You just split the query over multiple lines to make the SQL statement more readable. For the values to replace in the statement, you use an `ArrayList`, taking into account that optional fields will be `Null` if no value is specified on the form. When you're finished, you simply format the SQL string with the values, assigning it again to save another variable declaration:

```
sql = String.Format(sql, values.ToArray())
```

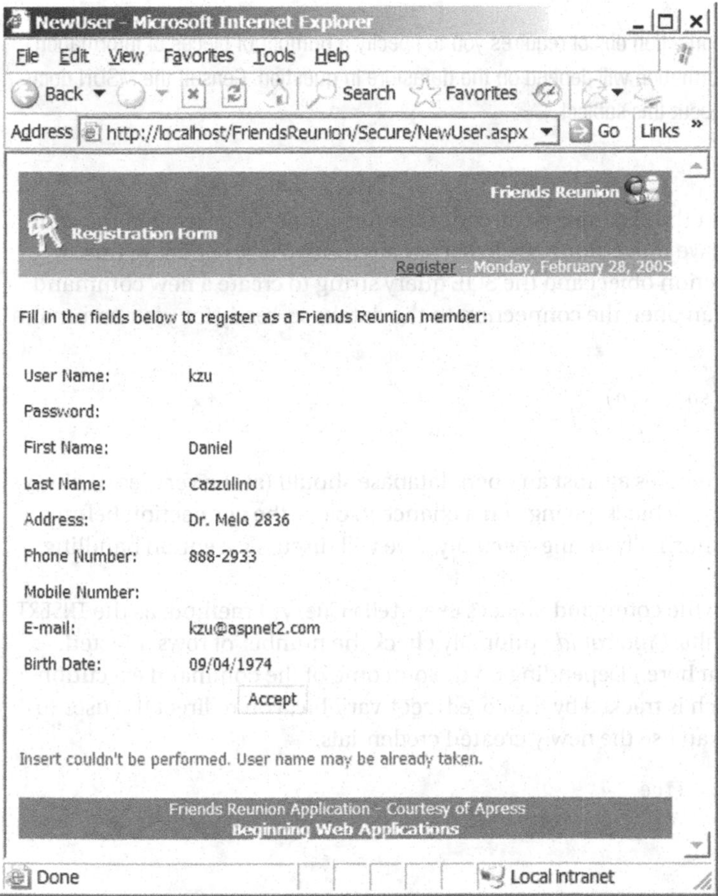

Figure 4-3. *An error message appears when you try to add a user whose name already exists in the database.*

As far as our focus in this chapter is concerned, the database connectivity code comes next. The first order of business is to create connection and command objects, and the very next line of code achieves the first of these two tasks:

```
Dim con As New SqlConnection( _
   "data source=.;initial catalog=FriendsData;" + _
   "user id=apress;pwd=apress")
```

Here, you're supplying the following arguments:

- `.` is the name of our MSDE instance. The dot is a shortcut for (local), which means the default MSDE instance in the local machine.
- `FriendsData` is the name of the database to connect to.
- `user id` is the name of the user with rights to access that database.
- `pwd` is the user password.

Note The constructor for a connection object requires you to specify a number of pieces of information, and the precise nature of this information will depend on the datastore in question. Consult the MSDN documentation for more information about this subject.

It's important to note that this example hard-codes the full connection string in the code, which is not a good thing. As we move along, we'll discuss alternative ways of doing this.

Next, you use the connection object and the SQL query string to create a new command object. With that done, you can open the connection to the database, ready for your command to be executed against it:

```
Dim cmd As New SqlCommand(sql, con)
con.Open()
```

Any block of code that executes against an open database should (at the very least) always be placed inside a `Try...Finally` block, giving you a chance to close the connection before execution terminates, either normally or unexpectedly. (We will discuss exception handling in detail in Chapter 11.)

Inside the block, you use the command object's `ExecuteNonQuery()` method, as the `INSERT` statement doesn't return results. (You *could* optionally check the number of rows affected, but we're simply ignoring that here.) Depending on the outcome of the command execution, either success or failure, which is tracked by the `doredirect` variable, you redirect the user to the Login page, so that user can use the newly created credentials:

```
Dim doredirect As Boolean = True

Try
  cmd.ExecuteNonQuery()
Catch ex As SqlException
  doredirect = False
  lblMessage.Visible = True
  lblMessage.Text = _
   "Insert couldn't be performed. User name may be already taken."
Finally
  ' Ensure connection is closed always
  con.Close()
End Try

If (doredirect) Then Response.Redirect("Login.aspx")
```

As you can see, using `ExecuteNonQuery()` is fairly simple, and it's all you need in order to execute `INSERT`, `UPDATE`, and `DELETE` statements.

Retrieving Data from a Database

Now that you have a means by which to add new users to a database, the obvious next step is to learn how to retrieve that information at a later date. In the Friends Reunion application, there is nowhere more in need of this ability than the Login page. When someone enters a user name and a password, you want to discover whether such a user exists and whether the password supplied is correct. Once you have the ability to log in users, you'll be able to offer them a way to view and edit their own information, but one thing at a time!

Before we look at the data-access code, however, you need to make a few changes to the application's security settings. This topic will be explained in more detail in Chapter 10, but we'll run through the specifics of this particular case here.

Try It Out: Set Up Security Simply put, you need to configure the Friends Reunion application so that the Login page is *always* the first one that users see, regardless of how they try to access our application. Furthermore, you need to arrange things so that unregistered users can navigate from the Login page to `NewUser.aspx`, but to no other pages. Here's how to do that:

1. Just as you did in Chapter 3, use the IIS console (Start ➤ Programs ➤ Administrative Tools ➤ Internet Information Services) to enable Anonymous access for the application, as shown in Figure 4-4. This setting means that IIS won't handle authentication, delegating that responsibility to ASP.NET and its settings. Integrated Windows authentication is also enabled, by default, and is needed to debug the application from VS .NET.

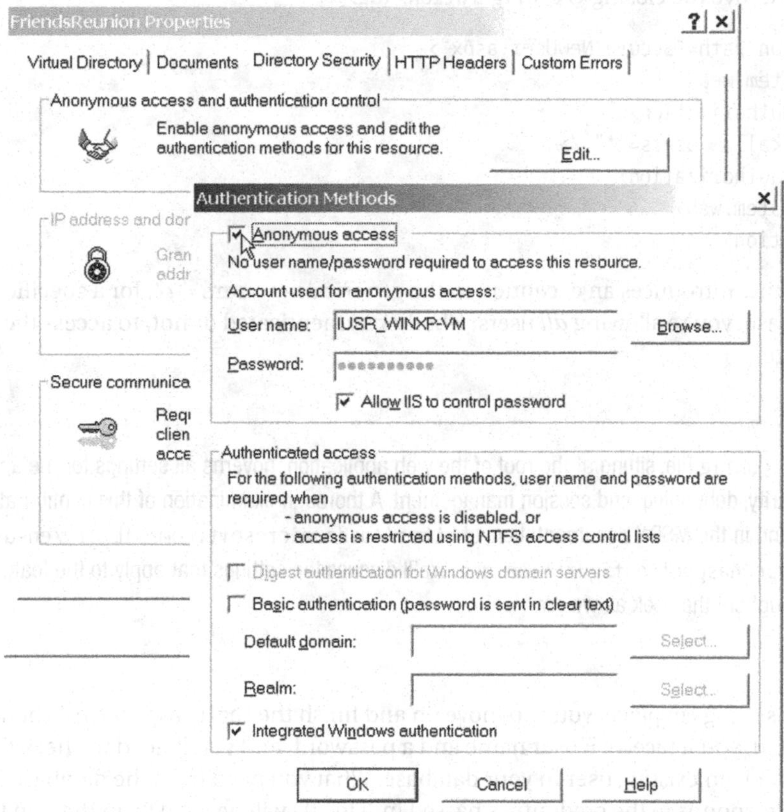

Figure 4-4. *Enabling Anonymous access*

2. Open the Web.config file for the application, locate the <authentication> element, and modify it so that it looks like the following, noting the inclusion of a child <deny> element inside the <authorization> element:

```
<authentication mode="Forms">
  <forms loginUrl="Secure/Login.aspx" />
</authentication>
<authorization>
  <deny users="?" />
</authorization>
```

   Briefly, this tells ASP.NET that you will use a form to authenticate users and also specifies its location. Then you specify that Anonymous (not authenticated) users cannot access any page in this application (deny users="?"). If you had specified "*", you would be denying access to *all* users, whether they are authenticated or not. With this setting in effect, clients will be automatically redirected to the Login.aspx page whenever they try to open *any* ASP.NET page in this application.

3. Anonymous users will need to access the NewUser.aspx form in order to register, so you need to enable Anonymous access to that. Add the following code to the Web.config file, just above the closing </configuration> tag:

```
<location path="Secure/NewUser.aspx">
   <system.web>
      <authorization>
         <allow users="*" />
      </authorization>
   </system.web>
 </location>
```

   This setting introduces an exception to the generic deny users="?", for a specific path. In this case, you're allowing *all* users, whether authenticated or not, to access the specific page.

Note The Web.config file, sitting at the root of the web application, governs all settings for the application, such as security, debugging, and session management. A thorough examination of this configuration file format can be found in the MSDN documentation, at http://msdn.microsoft.com/library/en-us/cpguide/html/cpconaspnetconfiguration.asp. We'll discuss the settings that apply to the features we introduce throughout the book as we go.

With these settings in place, you can move on and finish the Login.aspx form. When the form is submitted, you'll receive a user name and a password, and you'll need to check that those values match an existing user in your database. What you need from the database is the user ID that corresponds to the credentials passed in. This ID will be used from then on to retrieve various pieces of information for the current user.

Once you have a valid user ID, you need to tell ASP.NET that the user is authenticated, and let the user see the page originally requested. This is achieved by calling the `FormsAuthentication.RedirectFromLoginPage()` method found in the `System.Web.Security` namespace, passing in the user ID. After this method has been called successfully, the user will be able access any resource in the application. In addition, you'll be able to retrieve the ID at any time, from any page, by reading the `Context.User.Identity.Name` property. This makes it easy to customize the content of a page according to the current user. We'll analyze security and authentication in detail in Chapter 10.

Try It Out: Verify User Credentials in the Login Form In this example, you'll put the things we just talked about into code. In the handler for the Login button, you'll use the `ExecuteScalar()` method to retrieve the ID of a user with a given login name and password.

1. Open the `Login.aspx` form. Delete the header and footer controls that you added previously, leaving only the table with the text boxes and the Login button. Add a line of explanatory text, such as **Enter your user name and password to access the special features of this application**.

2. Switching to the HTML view, remove the `div` you used as a label before, and then add a panel containing an image and a label at the bottom of the page to hold any authentication error messages that may occur:

```
      <p>
        <asp:panel ID="pnlError" Runat="server" Visible="False">
          <img src="../Images/error.gif" align="absmiddle"> 
          <asp:label ID="lblError" Runat="server" ForeColor="Red">
          </asp:label>
        </asp:panel>
      </p>
    </form>
  </body>
</html>
```

3. Remove the `onclick` attribute on the Login button, as it would now be sort of annoying for a real user!

```
<input onclick="alert('About to log in!');" ...
```

4. Switch back to the Design view so that the code-behind file is synchronized with these new web controls.

5. In the code-behind page, change the code to match the following:

```
Imports System.Data.SqlClient
Imports System.Web.Security

Public Class Login
  Inherits FriendsBase
```

```
[ Web Form Designer Generated Code]

Private Sub Page_Load(ByVal sender As System.Object, _
  ByVal e As System.EventArgs) Handles MyBase.Load
  MyBase.HeaderIconImageUrl = "~/Images/securekeys.gif"
  MyBase.HeaderMessage = "Login Page"
End Sub

Private Sub btnLogin_ServerClick(ByVal sender As System.Object, _
  ByVal e As System.EventArgs) Handles btnLogin.ServerClick
  Dim con As New SqlConnection( _
    "data source=.;initial catalog=FriendsData;" + _
    "user id=apress;pwd=apress")
  Dim cmd As New SqlCommand( _
   "SELECT UserID FROM [User] " + _
   "WHERE Login=@Login and Password=@Pwd", con)

  ' Add parameters for the values provided
  cmd.Parameters.Add("@Login", txtLogin.Value)
  cmd.Parameters.Add("@Pwd", txtPwd.Value)
  con.Open()
  Dim id As String = Nothing

  Try
    ' Retrieve the UserID
    id = CType(cmd.ExecuteScalar(), String)
  Finally
    con.Close()
  End Try

  If Not id Is Nothing Then
    ' Set the user as authenticated and send him to the
    ' page originally requested
    FormsAuthentication.RedirectFromLoginPage(id, False)
  Else
    pnlError.Visible = True
    lblError.Text = "Invalid user name or password!"
  End If
 End Sub
End Class
```

6. Save all your changes, and then run the application with `Default.aspx` as the start page. You should find that you're taken to the Login page automatically, as shown in Figure 4-5.

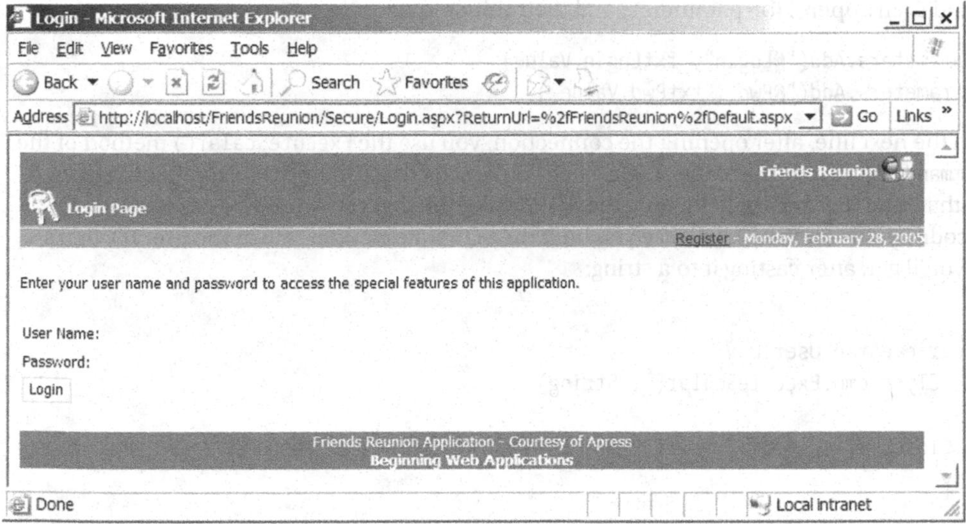

Figure 4-5. *The Login page appears automatically after your changes.*

How It Works

From now on, all of the web forms that you add to this project will inherit from the FriendsBase class that you created in Chapter 3. You'll also always use the two fields provided by the base class to set the text and the image for the current page. On this occasion, that was done in the Page_Load() handler:

```
Private Sub Page_Load(ByVal sender As System.Object, _
  ByVal e As System.EventArgs) Handles MyBase.Load
  MyBase.HeaderIconImageUrl = "~/Images/securekeys.gif"
  MyBase.HeaderMessage = "Login Page"
End Sub
```

The settings you've applied to the Web.config file will redirect the browser to the Login.aspx page when you start the project. After entering values for the user name and password and clicking the button, the code in btnLogin_ServerClick() is executed. The first step performed there is to create a new SqlConnection object, using the same connection string as last time. After the object is created, it remains closed until you explicitly call the Open() method later on:

```
Dim con As New SqlConnection( _
  "data source=.initial catalog=FriendsData" + _
  "user id=sapwd=apress")
```

Next, construct a SqlCommand object whose SQL statement contains parameter references:

```
Dim cmd As New SqlCommand( _
 "SELECT UserID FROM [User] " + _
 "WHERE Login=@Login and Password=@Pwd", con)
```

And then append the parameters and their values to it:

```
cmd.Parameters.Add("@Login", txtLogin.Value)
cmd.Parameters.Add("@Pwd", txtPwd.Value )
```

In the next line, after opening the connection, you use the `ExecuteScalar()` method of the `SqlCommand` object to retrieve the single value you're selecting. (If the SQL expression returned more than one row and/or field, only the first field of the first row would be passed back to your code by this method.) Because you built the SQL statement to return the user ID, that's what you'll get, after casting it to a string:

```
Try
  ' Retrieve the UserID
  id = CType(cmd.ExecuteScalar(), String)
Finally
  con.Close()
End Try
```

Next, check whether a valid user ID was returned. If it wasn't, either the user name or the password must have been incorrect, so you show an error message. If everything is fine, you use the `RedirectFromLoginPage()` method to send the user to the page the user requested in the first place. If you take a closer look at the URL in Figure 4-5, you'll notice that a `ReturnUrl` query string value has been appended to it. This is how `RedirectFromLoginPage()` knows where to redirect the user:

```
If Not id Is Nothing Then
  ' Set the user as authenticated and send him to the
  ' page originally requested
  FormsAuthentication.RedirectFromLoginPage(id, False)
Else
  pnlError.Visible = True
  lblError.Text = "Invalid user name or password!"
End If
```

Once a user has been authenticated here, you can access that user's ID from any code-behind page through the `Context.User.Identity.Name` property.

The new piece of functionality you used here was adding values with parameters to the `SqlCommand` instead of direct string formatting. Note that parameters must be prefixed with the `@` sign, but they don't need to match the corresponding field name. For example, this code uses `@Pwd`, although the field name is `Password`.

From now on, we'll use the word `apress` as both the user name and password in our examples. The database comes preloaded with some information for this user. After a successful login, the user is presented with a Welcome page, in which (if you remember your work in Chapter 3) the subheader that displays the date also includes the following code:

```
Protected Overrides Sub CreateChildControls()
  Dim lbl As Label

  ' If the user is authenticated, we will render their name
  If (Context.User.Identity.IsAuthenticated) Then
```

```
    lbl = New Label
    lbl.Text = Context.User.Identity.Name

    ' Add the newly created label to our
    ' collection of child controls
    Controls.Add(lbl)
  Else
    ...
```

As a result of the changes you've made, the label now displays the user's ID, rather than the name, but we'll be correcting that in Chapter 10.

Finally, for now, `Context.User.Identity.IsAuthenticated` is working just as it did before: it returns `True` if the user has entered valid credentials in the `Login.aspx` form. One difference, however, is that the code after the `Else` statement will never be executed, because in that case (an unauthenticated user accessing the page), the browser will automatically be redirected to the Login page.

Changing the Data in a Database

In general, details of the kind collected in the application's registration form do not remain the same forever, so it seems only reasonable that you should give your users the opportunity to change the data you have about them. Since the updated information is of exactly the same format as they used when they first registered, you can use the same form and just change some of its code. Specifically, you can discover if the user accessing `NewUser.aspx` is a new user seeking to register or a registered user trying to modify personal information, by testing `Context.User.Identity.IsAuthenticated`.

Try It Out: Edit a User's Profile In the case of a registered user, you will preload the form with the existing data by using the command object's `ExecuteReader()` method. When the time comes to save the data back to the database—that is, when the Accept button is clicked—you'll test the same property to determine whether an `UPDATE` or an `INSERT` is appropriate. The `INSERT` code is already in place, so you just need to add the `UPDATE`, again using the `ExecuteNonQuery()` method.

You'll also make a slight modification to the `SubHeader.cs` custom control that you built in Chapter 3, so that it shows a link to allow users to change their profile. Since the register link and the edit profile link both point to the same page, `NewUser.aspx`, you need to change only its text.

1. Open the `SubHeader.cs` file and modify the code in `CreateChildControls()` as follows:

```
Protected Overrides Sub CreateChildControls()
  Dim lbl As Label
  ' Always render a link to the registration/edit profile page
  Dim reg As New HyperLink

  ' If a URL isn't provided, use a default URL to the
  ' registration page
  If _register = "" Then
```

```
    reg.NavigateUrl = "~\Secure\NewUser.aspx"
  Else
    reg.NavigateUrl = _register
  End If

  If (Context.User.Identity.IsAuthenticated) Then
    reg.Text = "Edit my profile"
  Else
    reg.Text = "Register"
  End If

  ' Add the newly created link to our
  ' collection of child controls
  Controls.AddAt(0, reg)

  ' Add a couple of blank spaces and a separator character
  Controls.Add(New LiteralControl(" - "))

  ' Add a label with the current data
  lbl = New Label
  lbl.Text = DateTime.Now.ToLongDateString()
  Controls.Add(lbl)
End Sub
```

2. If you have not already done so, set the `Default.aspx` page to inherit the `FriendsBase` class and, from the page Design view, delete all the existing controls except the placeholder. Also, modify the introduction line for the page to something like **Welcome to the Friends Reunion application. Select the desired link to access the functionality on the site:**.

3. If you recompile the project after making just these changes, and then reopen the `Default.aspx` page (you may need to log in again), you'll see the page shown in Figure 4-6.

4. Now modify the `Page_Load()` handler in the `NewUser.aspx` page to preload the form with a registered user's data:

```
  ...
  Imports System.Data.SqlTypes
  ...

Private Sub Page_Load(ByVal sender As System.Object, _
  ByVal e As System.EventArgs) Handles MyBase.Load
  MyBase.HeaderIconImageUrl = "~/Images/securekeys.gif"
  MyBase.HeaderMessage = "Registration Form"
```

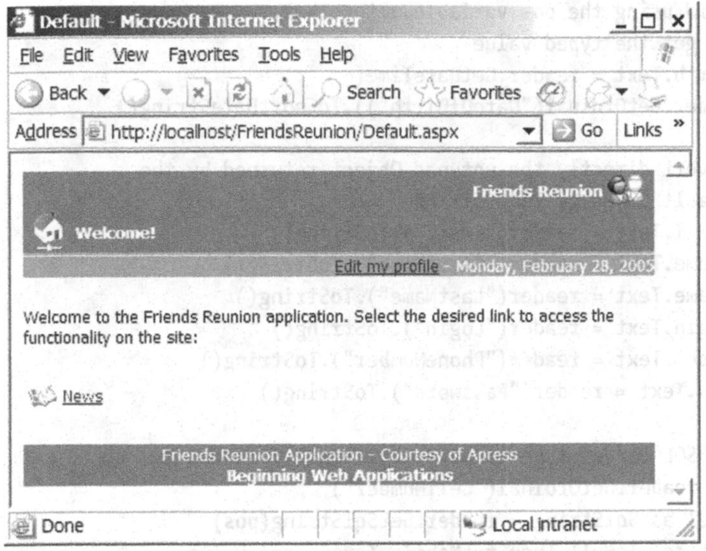

Figure 4-6. *The Default page after modifications*

```
' Postbacks will typically be caused by the validator
' controls in non-IE browsers
If Page.IsPostBack Then Return

' If this is an update, preload the values
If Context.User.Identity.IsAuthenticated Then
  ' Change the header message
  MyBase.HeaderMessage = "Update my profile"

  Dim con As New SqlConnection( _
   "data source=.;initial catalog=FriendsData;" + _
   "user id=apress;pwd=apress")
  Dim cmd As New SqlCommand( _
   "SELECT * FROM [User] WHERE UserID=@ID", con)
  cmd.Parameters.Add("@ID", Page.User.Identity.Name)

  con.Open()
  Try
    Dim reader As SqlDataReader = cmd.ExecuteReader()

    If reader.Read() Then
      ' Retrieve a typed value using the column's ordinal position
      Dim pos As Integer = reader.GetOrdinal("Address")
      txtAddress.Text = reader.GetString(pos).ToString()
```

```
            ' Avoid using the pos variable altogether,
            ' but get the typed value
            txtBirth.Text = reader.GetDateTime( _
              reader.GetOrdinal("DateOfBirth")).ToShortDateString()

            ' Convert directly the untyped Object returned by the
            ' default property to a string
            txtEmail.Text = reader("Email").ToString()
            txtFName.Text = reader("FirstName").ToString()
            txtLName.Text = reader("LastName").ToString()
            txtLogin.Text = reader("Login").ToString()
            txtPhone.Text = reader("PhoneNumber").ToString()
            txtPwd.Text = reader("Password").ToString()

            ' Use SQL Server type to have additional features
            pos = reader.GetOrdinal("CellNumber")
            dim cel as SqlString = reader.GetSqlString(pos)
            If Not cel.IsNull Then txtMobile.Text = cel.Value
          End If
        Finally
          ' Ensure connection is ALWAYS closed
          con.Close()
        End Try
      End If
    End Sub
```

5. Test this code by compiling the project and refreshing the previous page. If you click the Edit my profile link, you'll see that the values are preloaded on the form, as shown in Figure 4-7.

6. Next, to organize the code, create a private method called `InsertUser()`, and move the code inside the `If` statement from the `btnAccept_Click()` handler to it:

```
Private Sub InsertUser()
  ...
End Sub
```

7. The code in the button `Click` event handler should now be as follows (you'll complete the `If` statement later):

```
Private Sub btnAccept_Click(ByVal sender As System.Object, _
  ByVal e As System.EventArgs) Handles btnAccept.Click
  If Page.IsValid Then

  Else
    lblMessage.Text = "Fix the following errors and retry:"
  End If
End Sub
```

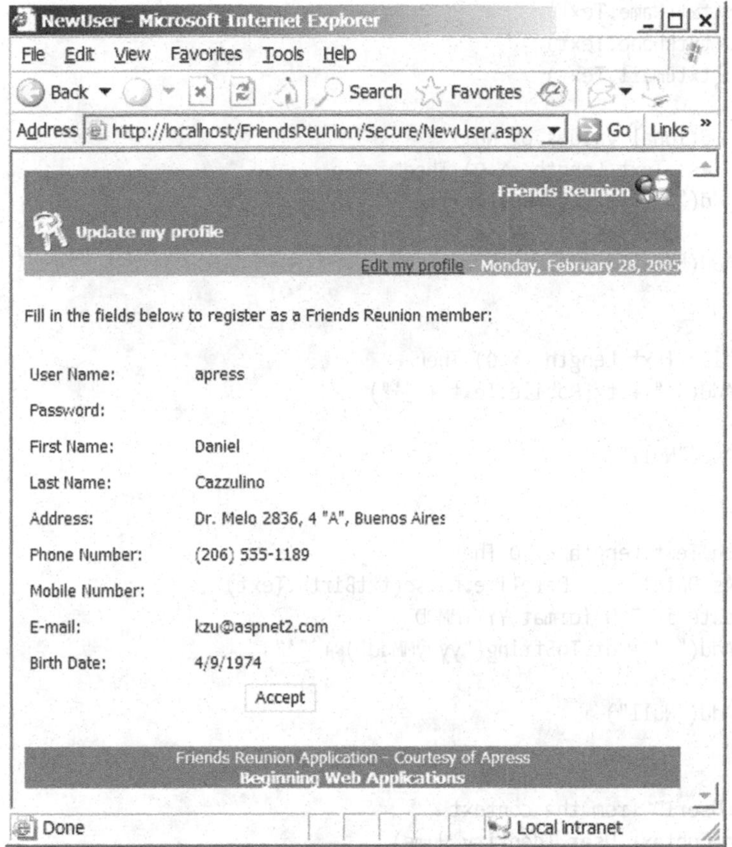

Figure 4-7. *Values are preloaded for editing a user profile.*

8. With that in place, now create another new method, called `UpdateUser()`, to handle the update scenario. Inevitably, it's similar to the code for inserting new entries.

```
Private Sub UpdateUser()
  Dim values As New ArrayList(10)

  ' Optional values without quotes as they can be the Null value
  Dim sql As String
  sql = "UPDATE (User) SET " + _
   "Login='{0}', Password='{1}', FirstName='{2}', " + _
   "LastName='{3}', PhoneNumber='{4}', Email='{5}',  " + _
   "Address={6}, CellNumber={7}, DateOfBirth={8} " + _
   "WHERE UserID='{9}'"

  ' Add required values to replace
  values.Add(txtLogin.Text)
  values.Add(txtPwd.Text)
  values.Add(txtFName.Text)
```

```
values.Add(txtLName.Text)
values.Add(txtPhone.Text)
values.Add(txtEmail.Text)

' Add the optional values or Null
If (txtAddress.Text.Length <> 0) Then
  values.Add("'" + txtAddress.Text + "'")
Else
  values.Add("Null")
End If

If (txtMobile.Text.Length <> 0) Then
  values.Add("'" + txtMobile.Text + "'")
Else
  values.Add("Null")
End If

If txtBirth.Text.Length <> 0 Then
  Dim dt As DateTime = DateTime.Parse(txtBirth.Text)
  ' Pass date in ISO format YYYYMMDD
  values.Add("'" + dt.ToString("yyyyMMdd") + "'")
Else
  values.Add("Null")
End If

' Get the UserID from the context
values.Add(Context.User.Identity.Name)

' Format the query with the values
sql = String.Format(sql, values.ToArray())

' Connect and execute the query
Dim con As New SqlConnection( _
  "data source=.;initial catalog=FriendsData;" + _
  "user id=apress;pwd=apress")
Dim cmd As New SqlCommand(sql, con)
con.Open()

Dim doredirect As Boolean = True

Try
  cmd.ExecuteNonQuery()
Catch ex As SqlException
  doredirect = False
  lblMessage.Visible = True
  lblMessage.Text = "Couldn't update your profile!"
Finally
```

```
      con.Close()
    End Try

    If doredirect Then Response.Redirect("../Default.aspx")
  End Sub
```

9. Finally, add the following code to the now empty If statement in the btnAccept_Click() handler:

```
  Private Sub btnAccept_Click(ByVal sender As System.Object, _
    ByVal e As System.EventArgs) Handles btnAccept.Click
    If Page.IsValid Then
      If Context.User.Identity.IsAuthenticated Then
        UpdateUser()
      Else
        InsertUser()
      End If
    Else
      lblMessage.Text = "Fix the following errors and retry:"
    End If
  End Sub
```

10. Save and compile the project. If you run the project again and log in to the application, you can click the new link in the subheader and not only see the form preloaded with values, but also change any of its values. It's even possible for the users to change their user name, because that's not being used as the primary key for the table!

How It Works

The change in the SubHeader control is very straightforward: just change the text of the link according to the IsAuthenticated property for the current request. The interesting thing is happening in the Page_Load() method, where you create the database connection and command objects as usual, but assign the result of executing the command to a variable of type SqlDataReader:

```
Dim reader as SqlDataReader = cmd.ExecuteReader()
```

To read the values that form the result of our query, you start by checking that a row has actually been returned, by calling the Read() method:

```
If reader.Read() Then
```

After that, and in order to show all the available ways to retrieve the values, you use several options that are available with the reader. First, you use the GetOrdinal() method to retrieve the position of a column in the reader, so that you can get a typed string using the GetString() method, which needs this value:

```
 ' Retrieve a typed value using the column's ordinal position
Dim pos As Integer = reader.GetOrdinal("Address")
txtAddress.Text = reader.GetString(pos).ToString()
```

The next line takes the same approach, but avoids the need for an extra variable by calling the GetOrdinal() method from inside the GetDateTime() method call:

```
' Avoid using the pos variable altogether,

' but get the typed value
txtBirth.Text = reader.GetDateTime( _
  reader.GetOrdinal("DateOfBirth")).ToShortDateString()
```

This reduces the amount of code you need to write, at the expense of a little added complexity. Because the value returned is a typed DateTime object, you can use its methods to format the date. The following lines show the most common approach, where you simply use the data reader object's default property, which receives the column name and returns an Object. You can convert this object to a string very easily indeed:

```
' Convert directly the untyped Object returned by the
' default property to a string
txtEmail.Text = reader("Email").ToString()
txtFName.Text = reader("FirstName").ToString()
txtLName.Text = reader("LastName").ToString()
txtLogin.Text = reader("Login").ToString()
txtPhone.Text = reader("PhoneNumber").ToString()
txtPwd.Text = reader("Password").ToString()
```

The last bit of code is a peek at the extra features you can get from a SqlDataReader object. Accessing the native data types of a SQL Server database can improve application performance, since by doing so, you avoid the conversion between SQL Server data types and .NET data types. However, this does make it harder to change the data provider if you decide to use a different database in the future. In this block, you use the SqlString type, which has (among other things) an IsNull property that can tell you whether a value is present:

```
 ' Use SQL Server type to have additional features
pos = reader.GetOrdinal("CellNumber")
Dim cel As SqlString = reader.GetSqlString(pos)
If Not cel.IsNull Then txtMobile.Text = cel.Value
```

When the user clicks the Accept button, you check the IsAuthenticated property and call the update or the insert method accordingly:

```
If Context.User.Identity.IsAuthenticated Then
  UpdateUser()
Else
  InsertUser()
End If
```

If you compare the code for the UpdateUser() method with that for the insert method that you created earlier, you will find that the two are almost identical. The only difference lies in the SQL statement building process, so we don't need to go any deeper there.

The Rest of the Picture: The DataSet and Data Adapter Objects

Until now, we've been looking at a *connected* model for accessing a database; that is, your code retains a connection to the database for the duration of your interactions with it. Data reader objects are very useful if you just need to move forward through the results of a query and display some values quickly, but an open connection is a valuable resource. Also, if you need to pass the retrieved data between methods, perform some processing before displaying it, or move back and forth through the results, a data reader simply doesn't cut the mustard.

What you need is some way to extract data from the database on a semipermanent basis, so that you can close the database connection for a while and manipulate the data as you see fit. In other words, you need a way to deal with data that's *disconnected* from the data source.

Dealing with Disconnected Data

An ADO.NET object that we mentioned earlier but haven't examined so far is the `DataSet`. Unlike the data reader, command, and connection objects that we've been using, `DataSet` objects are not data provider-dependent. `DataSet` is a class in the `System.Data` namespace, and instances of it can be used with any data source. A `DataSet` object can be thought of as an in-memory relational database, as it contains a collection of `DataTable` objects, which, in turn, contain collections of `DataColumn` and `DataRow` objects, as illustrated in Figure 4-8.

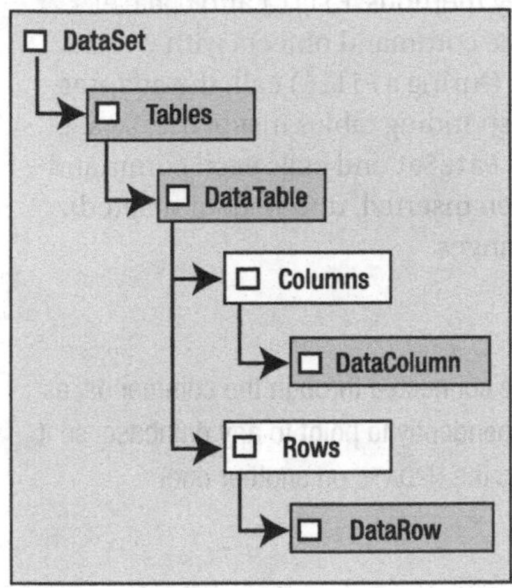

Figure 4-8. *The DataSet object model*

The data in a `DataSet` object can be inserted, updated, and deleted, and the object retains the details of any such modifications. However, being a generic, disconnected store for data, the `DataSet` object is completely unaware of the data source, which means that a dataset can be created from a database, a file, or programmatically, and it will always remain independent from the original source.

The connection between the data provider-agnostic DataSet and a specific database store is the responsibility of another object in the ADO.NET architecture: the data adapter. The data adapter *is* data provider-specific. Each data provider contains its own data adapter version: SqlDataAdapter, OleDbDataAdapter, OracleDataAdapter, and so on.

The data adapter's job is to handle the process of filling the DataSet with data from a database and post changes back to that database. The data adapter uses command objects to retrieve data from a database and later to post changes (insertions, updates, or deletions) back to it. Figure 4-9 diagrams the interaction between these objects.

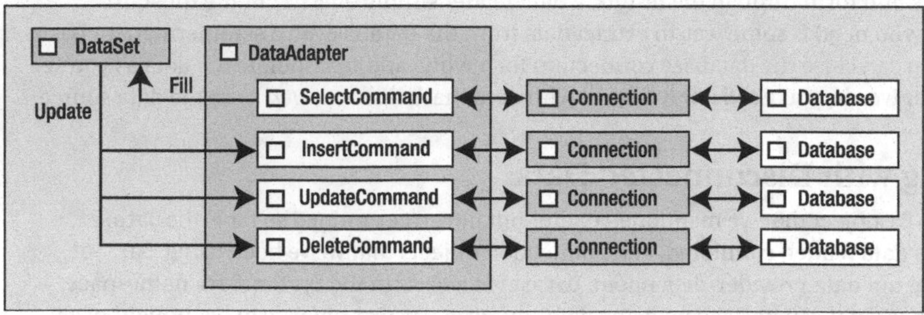

Figure 4-9. *The interactions between the DataSet and data adapter objects*

As shown in the figure, a data adapter object has two key methods: Fill() and Update(). Both of these take a DataSet as an argument, and they use the command objects with which the data adapter is configured to interact with the database. During a Fill() call, the adapter executes its SelectCommand and loads the data into the corresponding tables inside the DataSet. During an Update() call, the adapter inspects the data in the DataSet and calls each command depending on what's happened to each row (it may have been inserted, updated, or deleted). As stated earlier, the DataSet itself keeps track of all such changes.

Tip The data adapter isn't actually connected to the database; it's connected through the commands, as shown in Figure 4-9. Each of the commands can be configured independently to point to any database, so it is actually possible to perform the SELECT from one database and do the UPDATE on another one.

So, let's recap. Connection and command objects are used *every* time there is a need to access a database. From there, you can do either of the following:

- Choose to use a connected mode, and use a data reader that's retrieved as a result of executing a command.
- Take advantage of the disconnected DataSet object, and use a data adapter to provide the link between it and the database.

The complete picture for ADO.NET is shown in Figure 4-10. (With the exception of `DataSet`, the names of the other elements shown in the figure are abstractions, since the actual class names are specific to each data provider.)

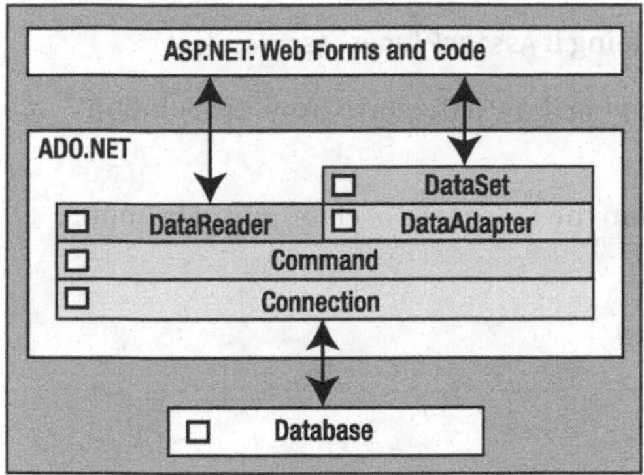

Figure 4-10. *The complete ADO.NET model*

Using a DataSet Object

In our Friends Reunion application, users can enter information about the places they have studied or worked in the past, so that fellow users can contact them. This information is kept in the following tables in the database:

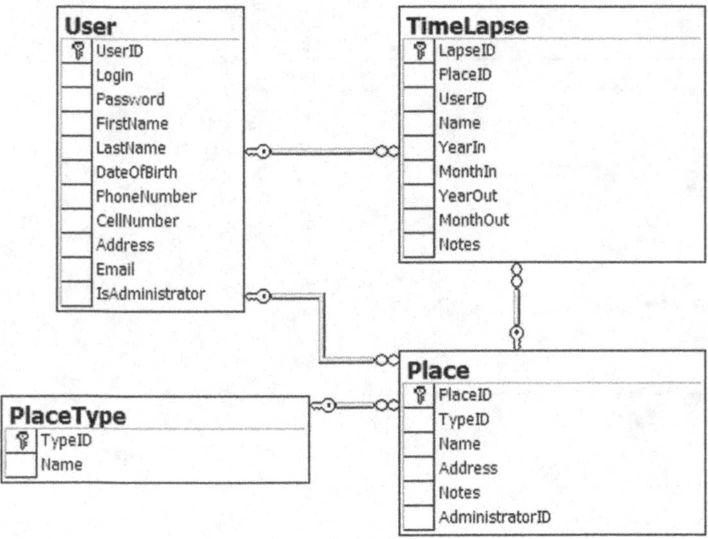

The `TimeLapse` table has a `Name` field, where users can describe what they were doing in that place. For example, if the place were Columbia University, the name of the time lapse could be Systems Engineer, meaning that the user was studying that career at that place for the period of time in question.

Try It Out: Assign Places For the next addition to the application, you'll build a form to allow users to enter all of this information. You'll need to load any existing places they've registered, and allow the editing of this list as well as the creation of new records in the `TimeLapse` table. As you've probably guessed, you'll be filling a `DataSet` object with all of the relevant information.

1. Add a new web form to the application, naming it `AssignPlaces.aspx`.
2. Link the `iestyle.css` stylesheet file by dropping it onto the form from the Solution Explorer.
3. Change the code-behind page to inherit from the `FriendsBase` class, and also import the namespace you'll be using:

```
Imports System.Data.SqlClient

Public Class AssignPlaces
  Inherits FriendsBase
```

4. To set up this form, add a Panel control called `pnlExisting`, containing a `PlaceHolder` control with an `ID` of `phPlaces`, which will be filled dynamically with a control for each `TimeLapse` record found, in much the same way that you saw in Chapter 3. Also add an HTML table with eight rows and two columns, and the `border` property set to **0**, with text boxes and a combo box for the creation of a new record. Finally, add a button for performing the insert operation. Figure 4-11 shows what the page should look like. Use the `ID` properties shown inside the control in Figure 4-11 for each control. The `Add` button's `ID` should be `btnAdd`.

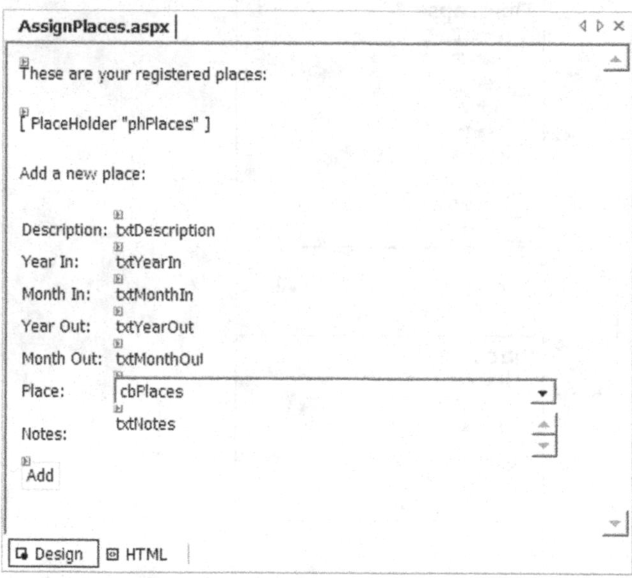

Figure 4-11. *The design of the Assign Places form*

5. Create a new style class called BigTextBox in iestyle.css. This will be for descriptions and notes, which are usually longer than can be contained in regular text boxes. This style is just a copy of the TextBox style with a bigger value for width:

```
.BigTextBox
{
  border-right: #c7ccdc 1px solid;
  border-top: #c7ccdc 1px solid;
  border-left: #c7ccdc 1px solid;
  border-bottom: #c7ccdc 1px solid;
  font-size: 8pt;
  font-family: Tahoma, Verdana, 'Times New Roman';
  width: 350px;
}
```

6. Set CssClass to BigTextBox for txtDescription, cbPlaces, and txtNotes. All of the other text boxes have the SmallTextBox value, and the button has Button. Set the txtNotes text box Multiline property to True.

Note You could use RequiredFieldValidator controls on each of the required fields here, and you could use a CompareValidator control to ensure that the period is sensible (so that YearIn is forced to be equal to or less than YearOut, for example. In this example, however, we'll focus on only the data-access aspects.

---

7. Add the following code to the Page_Load() method (it just sets the agenda for the work to come):

```
Private Sub Page_Load(ByVal sender As System.Object, _
 ByVal e As System.EventArgs) Handles MyBase.Load
  MyBase.HeaderMessage = "Assign Places"

  LoadDataSet()
  InitPlaces()
  InitForm()
End Sub
```

8. The first method, LoadDataSet(), will load a DataSet with all of the information needed by this page, and it will necessarily be available as a class-level variable. Once you finish loading the data, the other two methods will initialize the user interface. Add the following code block below the Page_Load() method:

```
Dim ds As DataSet

Private Sub LoadDataSet()
  Dim con As New SqlConnection( _
   "data source=.;initial catalog=FriendsData;" + _
   "user id=apress;pwd=apress")
```

```
' Select the place's timelapse records, descriptions, and type
Dim sql As String
sql = "SELECT " + _
 "TimeLapse.*, Place.Name AS Place, " + _
 "PlaceType.Name AS Type " + _
 "FROM " + _
 "TimeLapse, Place, PlaceType " + _
 "WHERE " + _
 "TimeLapse.PlaceID = Place.PlaceID AND " + _
 "Place.TypeID = PlaceType.TypeID AND " + _
 "TimeLapse.UserID = '" + _
 Context.User.Identity.Name + "'"

' Initialize the adapters
Dim adExisting As New SqlDataAdapter(sql, con)
Dim adPlaces As New SqlDataAdapter( _
 "SELECT * FROM Place ORDER BY TypeID", con)
Dim adPlaceTypes As New SqlDataAdapter( _
 "SELECT * FROM PlaceType", con)

con.Open()
ds = New DataSet

Try
  ' Proceed to fill the dataset
  adExisting.Fill(ds, "Existing")
  adPlaces.Fill(ds, "Places")
  adPlaceTypes.Fill(ds, "Types")
Finally
  con.Close()
End Try
End Sub
```

9. The InitPlaces() method uses the DataSet you just filled to add items to the panel at the top of the page: a summary of each existing place and a link to allow the user to delete it. You saw how to create dynamic content in Chapter 3, but now you use data from the DataSet to drive the process. Add this method below to the previous one:

```
Private Sub InitPlaces()
  phPlaces.Controls.Clear()
  Dim msg As String = _
   "Type: {0}, Place: {1}. From {2}/{3} to {4}/{5}. Description: {6}."

  Dim row As DataRow
  For Each row In ds.Tables("Existing").Rows
    Dim lbl As New LiteralControl
```

```
      ' Format the msg variable with values in the row
      lbl.Text = String.Format(msg, _
         row("Type"), row("Place"), _
         row("MonthIn"), row("YearIn"), _
         row("MonthOut"), row("YearOut"), row("Name"))

      Dim btn As New LinkButton
      btn.Text = "Delete"

      ' Pass the LapseID when the link is clicked
      btn.CommandArgument = row("LapseID").ToString()

      ' Attach the handler to the event
      AddHandler btn.Command, AddressOf OnDeletePlace

      ' Add the controls to the placeholder
      phPlaces.Controls.Add(lbl)
      phPlaces.Controls.Add(btn)
      phPlaces.Controls.Add(New LiteralControl("<br>"))
    Next
    ' Hide the panel if there are no rows
    If ds.Tables("Existing").Rows.Count > 0 Then
      pnlExisting.Visible = True
    Else
      pnlExisting.Visible = False
    End If
  End Sub
```

10. In the previous method, you attached the same handler to all of the link buttons, but because each of them has a different CommandArgument, you can use that value to determine which row to delete. The code to perform the deletion is very similar to what you have seen so far. Add this method, which will handle the user action:

```
  Private Sub OnDeletePlace(ByVal sender As Object, _
    ByVal e As CommandEventArgs)
    ' e.CommandArgument receives the LapseID to delete
    Dim con As New SqlConnection( _
     "data source=.;initial catalog=FriendsData;" + _
     "user id=apress;pwd=apress")
    Dim cmd As New SqlCommand( _
     "DELETE FROM TimeLapse WHERE LapseID='" + _
     e.CommandArgument.ToString() + "'", con)

    con.Open()

    Try
      cmd.ExecuteNonQuery()
```

```
  Finally
    con.Close()
  End Try

  LoadDataSet()
  InitPlaces()
End Sub
```

11. The InitForm() method initializes the combo box with the available places the first time the page is accessed. Add it as follows:

```
Private Sub InitForm()
  ' Initialize combo box
  If Not Page.IsPostBack Then
    ' Access the table by index
    Dim row As DataRow
    For Each row In ds.Tables(1).Rows
      ' Find the related row in Types data table (by name now)
      Dim types() As DataRow = ds.Tables("Types").Select( _
        "TypeID='" + row("TypeID") + "'")

      ' Access row columns by name, using default property
      Dim text As String = types(0)("Name") + ": " + row("Name")
      ' We can access the row's column by index too
      Dim value As String = row(0).ToString()

      cbPlaces.Items.Add(New ListItem(text, value))
    Next
  End If
End Sub
```

12. Double-click btnAdd in the Design view, and add the following code to the event handler:

```
Private Sub btnAdd_Click(ByVal sender As System.Object, _
 ByVal e As System.EventArgs) Handles btnAdd.Click
  If Page.IsValid Then
    Dim values As New ArrayList(9)

    Dim sql As String = "INSERT INTO TimeLapse " + _
   "(LapseID, PlaceID, UserID, Name, " + _
   "YearIn, YearOut, MonthIn, MonthOut, Notes) " + _
   "VALUES " + _
   "('{0}', '{1}', '{2}', '{3}', " + _
   "{4}, {5}, {6}, {7}, '{8}')"

    values.Add(Guid.NewGuid().ToString())
    values.Add(cbPlaces.SelectedItem.Value)
```

```
      values.Add(Context.User.Identity.Name)
      values.Add(txtDescription.Text)
      values.Add(txtYearIn.Text)
      values.Add(txtYearOut.Text)

      If txtMonthIn.Text.Length <> 0 Then
        values.Add(txtMonthIn.Text)
      Else
        values.Add("Null")
      End If

      If txtMonthOut.Text.Length <> 0 Then
        values.Add(txtMonthOut.Text)
      Else
        values.Add("Null")
      End If

      If txtNotes.Text.Length <> 0 Then
        values.Add(txtNotes.Text)
      Else
        values.Add("Null")
      End If

      sql = String.Format(sql, values.ToArray())

      ' Connect and execute the query
      Dim con As New SqlConnection( _
       "data source=.;initial catalog=FriendsData;" + _
       "user id=apress;pwd=apress")
      Dim cmd As New SqlCommand(sql, con)
      con.Open()
      Try
        cmd.ExecuteNonQuery()
      Finally
        con.Close()
      End Try

      LoadDataSet()
      InitPlaces()
    Else
      Throw New InvalidOperationException("Invalid page data.")
    End If
End Sub
```

As you can see, it's just a simple INSERT statement that creates a new row for the TimeLapse table.

13. Compile and run the project with `AssignPlaces.aspx` as the start page. After logging in as the `apress` user, you should see something like the page shown in Figure 4-12.

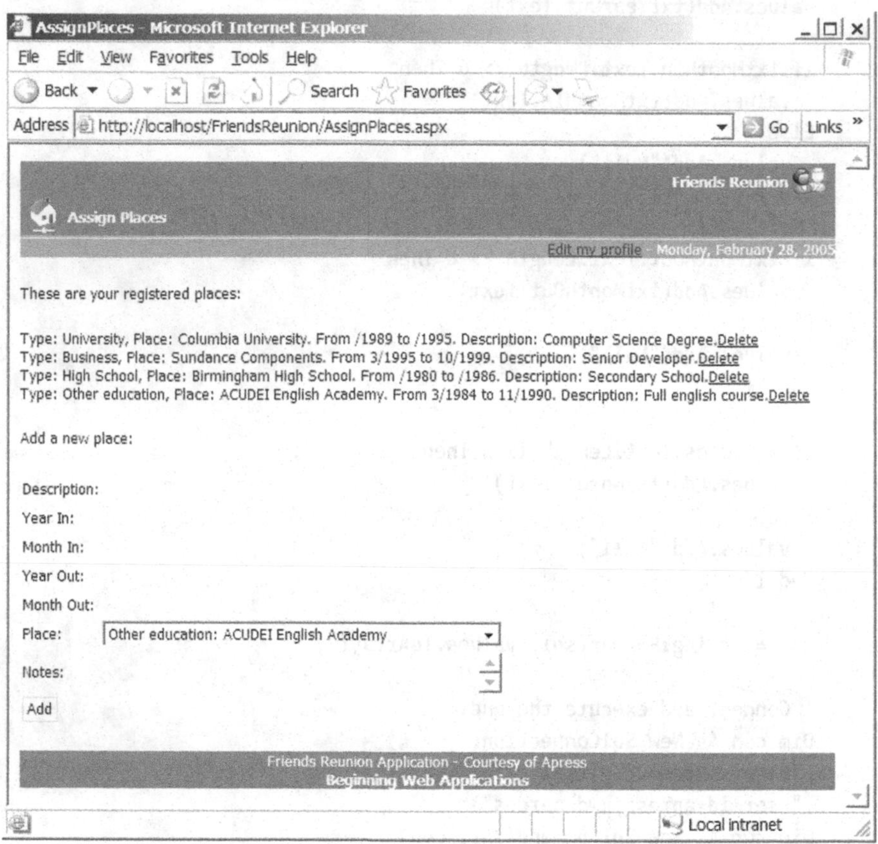

Figure 4-12. *The Assign Places page*

How It Works

Of the three methods that deal with what the user sees on the screen, the only one that interacts directly with the database is `LoadDataSet()`. Once the `DataSet` object has been filled with data by this procedure, you don't need to refer to the database in `InitPlaces()` or `InitForm()`. This is a direct result of the disconnected nature of `DataSet` objects.

The data adapter class has a constructor that receives a SQL statement that's used to initialize its `SelectCommand` property. This has the same effect as setting this property to an existing command later on. To the same constructor, you also pass the `SqlConnection` that the command should use. In the code, you can see three adapters being created: one to retrieve full details, one that's just for places, and one that's just for place type names.

```
' Initialize the adapters
Dim adExisting As New SqlDataAdapter(sql, con)
Dim adPlaces As New SqlDataAdapter( _
 "SELECT * FROM Place ORDER BY TypeID", con)
Dim adPlaceTypes As New SqlDataAdapter( _
 "SELECT * FROM PlaceType", con)
```

Because you're only retrieving data here (as opposed to editing or updating it), you don't need to configure anything else, so you can just proceed to connect to the database and create a new `DataSet` object:

```
con.Open()
ds = new DataSet
```

Inside the `try` block, you just call each adapter's `Fill()` method, passing the `DataSet` object and name that you want to give to the `DataTable` that's created as a result. If you didn't specify a name here, you would get tables called `Table1`, `Table2`, and so on.

```
Try
  ' Proceed to fill the dataset
  adExisting.Fill(ds, "Existing")
  adPlaces.Fill(ds, "Places")
  adPlaceTypes.Fill(ds, "Types")
Finally
```

Once you've filled the `DataSet`, you can access its data using various approaches. In `InitPlaces()`, which fills the placeholder at the top of the user's screen, you use a couple of different methods. First, you access the table from the `DataSet`'s `Tables` property, using the table name you specified when you filled it:

```
Dim row As DataRow
For Each row In ds.Tables("Existing").Rows
```

Now, you can use the `For Each` construct to iterate through the rows of the table in the same way that you would iterate through any standard collection or array. The `DataRow` class contains a default property that takes the column name (or its index), and retrieves the value in that column:

```
lbl.Text = String.Format(msg, _
   row("Type"), row("Place"), _
   row("MonthIn"), row("YearIn"), _
   row("MonthOut"), row("YearOut"), row("Name"))
```

The `InitPlaces()` method is just creating a literal control and a link button that's initialized with the values of each row. The link button will pass the row's `LapseID` column value, which is the primary key of the `TimeLapse` table, to the corresponding event handler:

```
Dim btn As New LinkButton
btn.Text = "Delete"

' Pass the LapseID when the link is clicked
btn.CommandArgument = row("LapseID").ToString()

' Attach the handler to the event
AddHandler btn.Command, AddressOf OnDeletePlace
```

This way, the handler you attached to all the buttons will know which record to delete, as this value is used to build the DELETE SQL statement:

```
Private Sub OnDeletePlace(ByVal sender As Object, _
 ByVal e As CommandEventArgs)
  ' e.CommandArgument receives the LapseID to delete
  Dim con As New SqlConnection( _
   "data source=.;initial catalog=FriendsData;" + _
   "user id=apress;pwd=apress")
  Dim cmd As New SqlCommand( _
   "DELETE FROM TimeLapse WHERE LapseID='" + _
   e.CommandArgument.ToString() + "'", con)
```

Finally, in InitForm(), which sets up the values in the combo box, you use some of the other choices offered by a DataSet. The most interesting one is that while you iterate through the records in the Places table, you perform a Select in the Types table to find the row corresponding to the current TypeID:

```
Dim types() As DataRow = ds.Tables("Types").Select( _
  "TypeID='" + row("TypeID") + "'")
```

The Select() method of the DataTable object receives an expression that's equivalent to an SQL WHERE expression and retrieves an array of DataRow objects matching the criteria. In this case, you know there will be only one row returned. This way, you're recovering the relationship between these two tables without any dependence on the database store! Next, you use the row's default property to retrieve a field value by name:

```
Dim text As String = types(0)("Name") + ": " + row("Name")
```

The value can also be retrieved using the default property overload that receives the field index:

```
Dim value As String = row(0).ToString()
```

Then you add a new item to the combo box, using the values you recovered:

```
cbPlaces.Items.Add(new ListItem(text, value))
```

Now that you've added the Add Places page, to round off our application for this chapter, you need to update Default.aspx to reflect the latest addition in functionality to the Friends Reunion application.

Try It Out: Update Default.aspx Previously, when you were transferred to the `Default.aspx` page after logging in to the application, there was only one link present, namely to the `News.aspx` page. Now that you have another page that the user can access, you should include this also.

1. Open the `Default.aspx` code-behind page.
2. Add the following code in the `Page_Load()` method:

```
' Create a new blank table row, this time for Assign Places link
row = New TableRow

' Assign Places link
img = New System.Web.UI.WebControls.Image
img.ImageUrl = "Images/flatscreenkeyb.gif"
img.ImageAlign = ImageAlign.Middle
img.Width = New Unit(24, UnitType.Pixel)
img.Height = New Unit(24, UnitType.Pixel)

' Create the cell and add the image
cell = New TableCell
cell.Controls.Add(img)

' Add the cell to the row
row.Cells.Add(cell)

' Set up the Assign Places link
lnk = New HyperLink
lnk.Text = "Assign Places"
lnk.NavigateUrl = "AssignPlaces.aspx"

' Create the cell and add the link
cell = New TableCell
cell.Controls.Add(lnk)

' Add the new cell to the row
row.Cells.Add(cell)

' Add the new row to the table
tb.Rows.Add(row)
```

It will come as no surprise to you that it looks very similar to the code required to render the News link. With this modification to the code, the `Default.aspx` page looks like Figure 4-13.

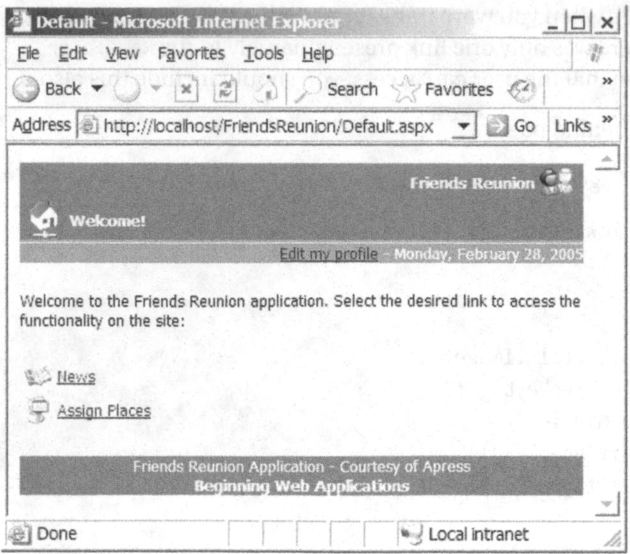

Figure 4-13. *The modified Default page*

Summary

Data access is essential for all but the most trivial web applications. You have learned the basics of ADO.NET, Microsoft's new strategy for data access, and you have seen how the various pieces fit in the whole picture of web application development.

Tip For a more complete discussion of ADO.NET, refer to *A Programmer's Guide to ADO.NET in C#*, by Mahesh Chand (Apress, 2002; ISBN: 1-893115-39-9), or *Applied ADO.NET: Building Data-Driven Solutions*, by Mahesh Chand and David Talbot (Apress, 2003; ISBN: 1-59059-073-2).

In this chapter, you started to add some data-aware pages to your application, which allowed you to leverage the power of data-driven pages. We discussed how to programmatically access a database and handle its data. You were able to display that data in web forms, taking advantage of the techniques you learned about in previous chapters.

Up to now, however, you have been typing a lot of code manually. VS .NET goes much further in programmer productivity, introducing the key concept of *components*. In the next chapter, we'll discuss this concept, and you'll discover what components are and how they work in conjunction with the IDE to perform some automatic coding tasks. We'll also dig into some exciting new features introduced by VS .NET to simplify web forms and data interaction through *data binding*. You'll learn how to use the more advanced wizards provided by components, and how to leverage web server controls to display and edit data in highly customizable ways through the use of another technique: *templates*.

CHAPTER 5

Data Binding

In Chapter 4, you learned how to interact with a database using the ADO.NET classes, and in this chapter, we'll build on that. We'll first take a look at VS .NET's new component architecture. This opens the door to the automatic generation of data-access code, and you'll see how that works in the latter part of this chapter.

We'll also take a tour of the new data-binding capabilities provided by ASP.NET, a feature that allows developers to write less code and let the platform do the heavy work of transferring data from ADO.NET objects to web forms. You'll then learn how to take advantage of another feature that can be used in combination with data binding: *templates*. Templates allow you to customize the look and feel of the controls in which your data is displayed—from the IDE and with full drag-and-drop support.

In this chapter, we will cover the following topics:

- An introduction to components, to get you up and running
- Simple data binding to show data on a form
- More complex data binding that involves sets of data and presents it in tabular fashion, automatically
- The interaction between .NET components and the IDE that lets VS .NET generate code on your behalf
- Typed datasets, which improve the experience of data binding at design-time, and offer some other improvements to your code
- Templates, which you can apply to customize the display of complex sets of data
- How to enable the editing of data through your web pages

Introduction to Components

Having come this far in the book, you may be starting to wonder what happened to the *Visual* part of VS .NET and VB .NET. We've been writing code as if we had nothing better than Notepad! Fortunately, VS .NET does come with some great productivity enhancements, including wizards and designers that can make most data-related work a breeze. Now that you know the basics of ADO.NET, you'll have a better understanding of what's going on behind the scenes when you use these VS .NET features.

The fundamental concept that supports these features of the VS .NET IDE is the *component*. Putting out of your mind for a moment the various other meanings that have been ascribed to this word over the years, a *component* in VS .NET is a class that (directly or indirectly) implements the `System.ComponentModel.IComponent` interface. Most of the time, such a class will inherit from `System.ComponentModel.Component`.

Placing a Component on a Form

A VS .NET component closely interacts with the IDE. You can drop a component onto a designer (like the Web Forms Designer) page, and it will appear as an item in a separate section on the page, below the UI elements. All of the ADO.NET classes you've seen are components, and as such, they also cooperate with and use services provided by the designer. For example, Figure 5-1 shows a `SqlConnection` component that's been dropped from the Toolbox's Data tab onto an empty page.

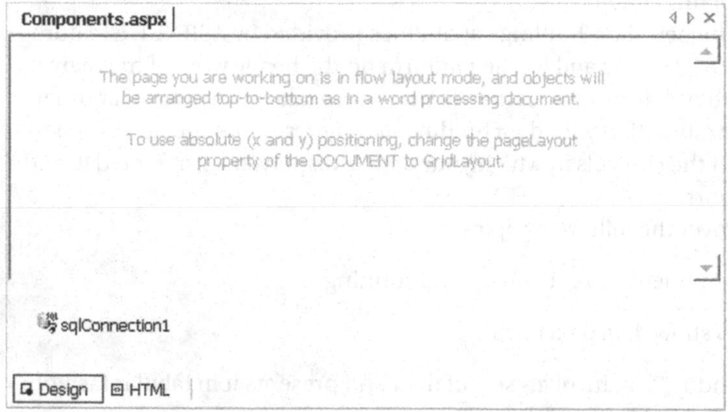

Figure 5-1. *A SqlConnection component added to an empty page*

When a component is placed on a designer page, it starts interacting with it, providing properties and wizards that the developer can use to configure the component. Behind the scenes, the designer works together with the component to generate source code representing the actions the developer performs. As always, the best way to understand what's going on is to build an example.

Try It Out: Configure a Connection Component In this very short demonstration, you'll see what happens when you place a database component onto a form in a VS .NET designer.

1. To your `FriendsReunion` project, add a new web form called `Components.aspx`. We'll use this form to experiment with components.

2. In the Toolbox, from the Data tab, drag-and-drop a `SqlConnection` component onto the form. Use the Properties browser to change its `Name` property to `cnFriends`. Also, from the drop-down list next to the `ConnectionString` property, you can select <New Connection...> and use the Data Link dialog box to configure a new connection,

or you can use the FriendsData connection created as explained in Appendix B. (This is another advantage of creating database connections with the Server Explorer, as described in Appendix B.)

3. Switch to the Code view and take a look at the code that has been generated for you.

How It Works

Components don't have a UI, so they appear in a separate section at the bottom of the page. In this example, you used the component to build the value for the ConnectionString property. After the steps you performed, the code-behind page contains the following:

```
Public Class Components
  Inherits System.Web.UI.Page

#Region " Web Form Designer Generated Code "

  'This call is required by the Web Form Designer.
  <System.Diagnostics.DebuggerStepThrough()> _
  Private Sub InitializeComponent()
    Me.cnFriends = New System.Data.SqlClient.SqlConnection
    '
    'cnFriends
    '
    Me.cnFriends.ConnectionString = [YOUR_CONNECTION_STRING]

  End Sub
  Protected WithEvents cnFriends As System.Data.SqlClient.SqlConnection

  'NOTE: The following placeholder declaration is required by the Web Form...
  'Do not delete or move it.
  Private designerPlaceholderDeclaration As System.Object

  Private Sub Page_Init(ByVal sender As System.Object, _
    ByVal e As System.EventArgs) Handles MyBase.Init
    'CODEGEN: This method call is required by the Web Form Designer
    'Do not modify it using the code editor.
    InitializeComponent()
  End Sub

#End Region

  Private Sub Page_Load(ByVal sender As System.Object, _
    ByVal e As System.EventArgs) Handles MyBase.Load
    'Put user code to initialize the page here
  End Sub

End Class
```

The Web Forms Designer generated the code in the #Region section automatically. It also defined a protected variable, cnFriends, for the connection you added. The InitializeComponent() method creates the connection and sets the ConnectionString that you assigned through the Properties browser. This method is called when the page is initialized, in the Page_Init() event handler. There is no magic here; there are just plain old variables and initialization code that you could have written by hand.

In truth, the component that you've added here offers only limited advantages over manual coding. But later on in the chapter, you'll see how other components, such as the SqlDataAdapter component, can perform some quite complex tasks on your behalf.

Configuring Dynamic Properties

Another advantage of components is the availability of *dynamic properties*, which can be configured to load their values from the application configuration file, Web.config. In VS .NET, dynamic properties live in a special section under the Configurations heading in the Properties browser. Once again, the designer works together with the component to generate the appropriate code, this time for retrieving data from Web.config. Let's see how that happens.

Try It Out: Configure a Dynamic Connection String In this example, you will modify the SqlConnection component you just added to use a dynamic property for the connection string. This is a significant improvement over the approach you've been using so far, which involved hard-coding the value everywhere you needed access to the database.

1. Open the Components.aspx web form in the Design view and select the cnFriends component.

2. In the Properties browser, expand the (DynamicProperties) element. Click the ellipsis button next to ConnectionString, and then check the option to map the property to a key in the configuration file, as shown in Figure 5-2. Then click OK.

In the Properties browser, you'll see that a small icon has appeared next to the ConnectionString property under the Data category, indicating that this is now a dynamic property.

How It Works

The (DynamicProperties) section in the Properties browser works in conjunction with components, showing only the properties that can be dynamically configured. If you now take a look at the Web.config file, you'll see that something similar to the following element has been added:

```
<appSettings>
  <!--   User application and configured property settings go here.-->
  <!--   Example: <add key="settingName" value="settingValue"/> -->
  <add key="cnFriends.ConnectionString" value="[YOUR CONNECTION STRING]" />
</appSettings>
```

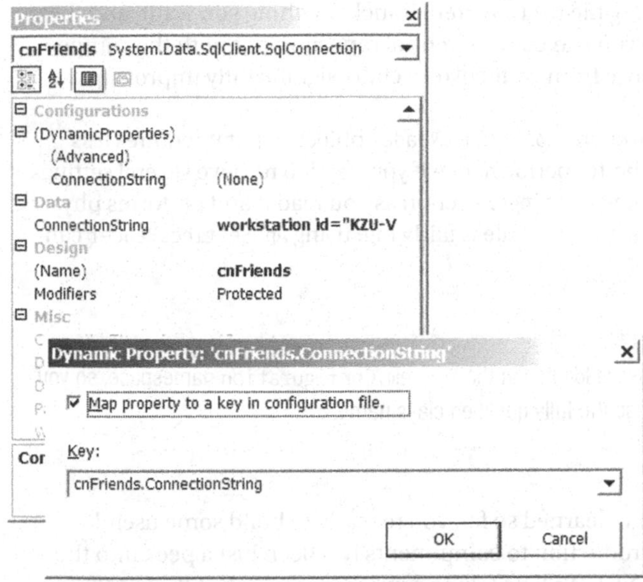

Figure 5-2. *Setting a dynamic property for a component*

If you look again at the code-behind page, you'll see that there have been some changes there, too:

```
<System.Diagnostics.DebuggerStepThrough()> _
Private Sub InitializeComponent()
  Dim configurationAppSettings As System.Configuration.AppSettingsReader = _
    New System.Configuration.AppSettingsReader
  Me.cnFriends = New System.Data.SqlClient.SqlConnection
  '
  'cnFriends
  '
  Me.cnFriends.ConnectionString = CType(configurationAppSettings.GetValue( _
    "cnFriends.ConnectionString", GetType(System.String)), String)

End Sub
```

The new `configurationAppSettings` variable is an instance of the `AppSettingsReader` class, which allows access to the values in the `Web.config` file. The property's value is retrieved with this object, using the key that was built by the dynamic property, and cast explicitly to a string. Whenever you change the setting in the configuration file, this page will automatically use the new value.

There's actually another method of getting the values that you store in `Web.config` file. You can modify the code that you've been using to create connection objects so far to use the following syntax:

```
Dim con As New SqlConnection( _
  ConfigurationSettings.AppSettings("cnFriends.ConnectionString"))
```

In fact, you can use the `Web.config` file to store pretty much anything you want, and then retrieve it with this syntax. This way, you can use this central repository for both the components added through the IDE and those from your custom code, significantly improving maintenance.

The advantage of this shortcut over an `AppSettingsReader` object is that it requires less code, but the reader object can offer better performance if you need to retrieve several settings at once. This is because it caches the `<appSettings>` section as you read it and performs physical access to the file only once. If the `Web.config` file is fairly big, using `AppSettingsReader` can be more suitable.

Tip The `ConfigurationSettings` class is located in the `System.Configuration` namespace, so you can either add an `Imports` statement or use the fully qualified class name.

With the database concepts you've learned so far, you're ready to build some useful data-aware applications, but this introduction to components has been just a peek into the possibilities that are available in VS .NET. We'll be taking a much closer look at these components later in this chapter. You'll see how they reduce the amount of code you need to type and provide advanced functionality for your applications, with hardly any effort. For now though, we'll move on to the main topic of this chapter: data binding.

Data Binding

Recall your work with the `NewUser.aspx` page in Chapter 4. When you added the capability to preload the form with information from the database (for the current users, to allow them to edit their profiles), you used code in the code-behind page to set the values to be displayed in the various controls. The code looked like this:

```
txtEmail.Text = reader("Email").ToString()
txtFName.Text = reader("FirstName").ToString()
txtLName.Text = reader("LastName").ToString()
txtLogin.Text = reader("Login").ToString()
txtPhone.Text = reader("PhoneNumber").ToString()
txtPwd.Text = reader("Password").ToString()
```

The need to display data from a data source— a data reader object, in this case—is a situation that crops up time and time again. For this reason, ASP.NET supports the concept of *data binding*, which frees you from writing code like this. The idea behind data binding is that the link between the data source and the controls that will display it is known at design-time, and this link will rarely (if ever) change at runtime.

To use data binding, you provide each control property that will display data at runtime with a *binding expression* that represents that data at design-time. At runtime, ASP.NET resolves the binding expression to its actual value and assigns that to the control property instead.

Using Binding Expressions

A binding expression can be specified in HTML source code, in place of any web server control's property value, such as:

```
<asp:Label id="lblPending" runat="server" Text='<%# EXPRESSION %>' />
```

Here, you see a data binding expression, `<%# EXPRESSION %>`, replacing the `Text` property value of a Label web server control. This is probably the most common use, but there's nothing to stop you from using data binding for the label's `BackColor` property, if that's what you want to do. This use of data binding is called *simple binding*, because resolution of the expression results in a single value.

To get the expression evaluated and have the results placed in the control's property, you need to call the control's `DataBind()` method. This method is inherited from the `Control` base class, and as such, it is available to all controls, even the page itself. Its effects propagate to all child controls, too, so a call at the page level will cause all of the data binding expressions on a page to be evaluated, and the results will be placed in the corresponding properties.

A binding expression is evaluated in the context defined by the actual Page class instance built from the code-behind source; that is, all of the page-level variables, methods, and properties that are available in the code-behind page can be used as binding expressions. For example, you could have a method called `GetPending()` that performs a database query and returns a string to be bound, and use that as follows:

```
<asp:label id="lblPending" runat="server" Text="<%# GetPending() %>" />
```

Similarly, if you had a page-level variable called `userID`, you could bind that to any control you wanted with the following code (for a label in this case):

```
<asp:label id="lblPending" runat="server" Text="<%# userID %>" />
```

Just as easily, you could refer to a dataset variable defined in the code-behind page to show the count of the rows in a table:

```
<asp:label id="lblPending" runat="server"
         Text="<%# dsUser.Tables(0).Rows.Count %>" />
```

As you can see, the mechanism is very flexible. You just need to perform the appropriate variable initialization or method coding.

If you intend to use data binding, though, you need to do a little advance planning. Typically, you'll define a page-level variable to hold the data (say, a dataset), fill it using a data adapter as you saw in Chapter 4, and finally call `DataBind()` in the page itself. This will cause all the controls that have binding expressions to be populated with the values from the just-filled dataset.

Note The code-behind members to be used in binding expressions must be either `Public` or `Protected` in order to be accessible at the moment binding occurs.

Formatting with the DataBinder Class

If you need to format a value prior to displaying it, you can use a helper class that's provided in the System.Web.UI namespace, called DataBinder. This class contains a static method called Eval(), which receives an object, an expression, and (optionally) a format string. The object is used as the context in which to evaluate the expression, and the result of the evaluation is formatted using the last parameter, if specified.

If you wanted to apply special formatting to a user's birth date, for example, you could use this:

```
<asp:label id="lblBirth" runat="server"
        Text='<%# DataBinder.Eval(dsUser.Tables(0).Rows(0), _
        "(DateOfBirth)", "{0:MMMM dd, yyyy}") %>'>
</asp:label>
```

Here, the first parameter to Eval() is the row to display the value from, and it is used as the context in which the second parameter is evaluated—the result of retrieving the DateOfBirth field through the Row default property; that is, the default property for the row at index 0. If you were retrieving a direct property, you wouldn't need the parentheses. Note that you must obey VB rules when splitting lines. Finally, the format string is applied. Notice that this part of the expression includes double quotes. That's why single quotes surround the code that assigns the Text property value (Text='...'). You cannot replace quotes the other way around, because single quotes cannot be used to enclose strings in the VB language.

You may have noticed that the default property of the DataRow object (the object accessed by dsUser.Tables(0).Rows(0)) receives a string. However, the code uses the opening parenthesis, followed directly by the column name and then the closing parenthesis, without quotes. This facility of the DataBinder class saves you a lot of duplicate quotes. The "true" value that would be used is as follows:

```
DataBinder.Eval(dsUser.Tables(0).Rows(0), "(""DateOfBirth"")", "{0:MMMM dd, yyyy}")
```

This relaxed syntax is valid only for the DataBinder.Eval() method, and it certainly makes the code more readable!

Caution DataBinder makes pretty heavy use of reflection for its dynamic evaluation capabilities, which hinders performance. You may want to consider alternative ways of getting at the data, such as explicit simple data binding through methods or properties at the page level.

Now let's see how this functionality can be useful in the Friends Reunion application.

Using Data Binding

The Friends Reunion application is intended to allow users to get in touch with "old friends." To handle this, when users make requests for fellow users to contact them, a record will be placed in the Contact table. This table has the following structure:

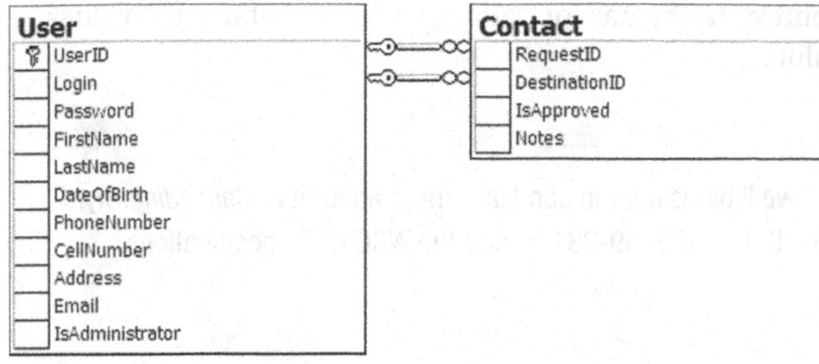

In order to respect the user's privacy, the site will never disclose a contact's details without approval. Therefore, when a new request for contact is placed in the `Contact` table, it will have its `IsApproved` flag set to `0`, indicating that this is a request waiting to be approved. After the user has approved the contact, the `IsApproved` flag is updated, and the other user will be able to access the contact information.

For example, say that you spot your old friend Victor listed at the Friends Reunion site, and he has said it's okay for you to contact him. You would then be given access to his personal information to arrange a meeting or whatever. In the following discussion, we'll focus on the view of the target user—the one specified in the `DestinationID`, your friend Victor.

Before the target user approves a contact that has placed a request, he will surely want to see that user's details; that is, Victor will want to make sure that you're really an old friend. To allow this verification, the application will use a form that receives a `RequestID` as a query string parameter and displays information about the user who is requesting contact (you, in this example) in a table, taking advantage of data binding. The form's code-behind page will include a method that counts the number of pending requests the user has, and use data binding to display this value, too. Finally, a button will allow Victor to update the `IsApproved` flag, and thus approve the contact. Once the flag has been updated, Victor will be redirected to the page he came from, which will be `News.aspx`.

Try It Out: Display Information About Fellow Users Using Data Binding Eventually, the page you're about to create will arrive as a result of navigation from `News.aspx`, in the course of which the `RequestID` will be passed as a query string. For now, while testing this example, you'll assemble the string, but don't let that put you off—we'll deal with `News.aspx` later.

1. Add a new web form called `ViewUser.aspx` to the project, adding the link to the `iestyle.css` stylesheet (you can drag-and-drop the file to the design surface as usual), and changing the code-behind page to inherit from the `FriendsBase` class.

2. Add a style rule called `TableLines` to the stylesheet. This will help to make the HTML tables look consistent across the site:

```
.TableLines
{
  border-bottom: #c7ccdc 1px solid;
  border-left: #c7ccdc 1px solid;
  border-right: #c7ccdc 1px solid;
  border-top: #c7ccdc 1px solid;
  padding: 5px 5px 5px 5px;
}
```

Notice that we're using the abbreviated syntax for padding, which contains the values for all four sides in a single value.

Tip There's a lot more to CSS than what we'll be using. You can learn more about it in *Cascading Style Sheets*, by Owen Briggs, et al (Apress, 2004; ISBN: 1-59059-231-X) and the W3C CSS specifications (`http://www.w3.org/Style/CSS/`).

---

3. Add an HTML table with six rows and two columns. Set the following properties for it:
   - (id): `tbLogin`
   - class: `TableLines`
   - border: 0
   - cellpadding: 2
   - cellspacing: 2
   - width: blank (remove the default value)
4. Add Label web server controls to the cells on the right, except for the last row, which will contain a Hyperlink control, with an `ID` of `lnkEmail`. Below the table, add some text and a label to reflect the form layout, as shown here.

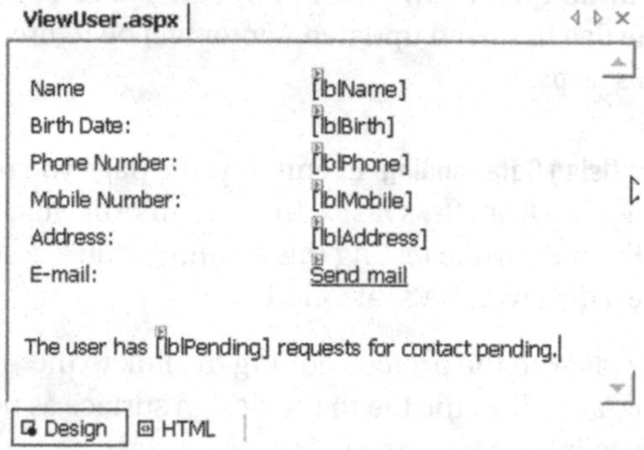

5. Below the text, add a web server Button control. Set its `ID` to `btnAuthorize`, its `CssClass` to `Button`, and its `Text` property to **Authorize Contact**.
6. Switch to the HTML view, and make the following changes to add data binding expressions to the controls:

```
...
<body ms_positioning="FlowLayout">
  <form id="Form1" method="post" runat="server">
    <p>
```

```
<table class="TableLines" id="tbLogin"
       cellspacing="2" cellpadding="2"
       width="300" border="0">
  <tr>
    <td>Name</td>
    <td>
      <asp:label id="lblName" runat="server"
      text='<%# dsUser.Tables(0).Rows(0)("FirstName") + " " + _
                  dsUser.Tables(0).Rows(0)("LastName") %>'>
      </asp:label></td>
  </tr>
  <tr>
    <td>Birth Date:</td>
    <td>
      <asp:label id="lblBirth" runat="server"
        text='<%# DataBinder.Eval( _
                  dsUser.Tables(0).Rows(0), _
                  "(DateOfBirth)", "{0:MMMM dd, yyyy}") %>'>
      </asp:label></td>
  </tr>
  <tr>
    <td>Phone Number:</td>
    <td>
      <asp:label id="lblPhone" runat="server"
        text='<%# DataBinder.Eval( _
                  dsUser.Tables("User").Rows(0), _
                  "(PhoneNumber)") %>'>
      </asp:label></td>
  </tr>
  <tr>
    <td>Mobile Number:</td>
    <td>
      <asp:label id="lblMobile" runat="server"
    text='<%# dsUser.Tables("User").Rows(0)("CellNumber") %>'>
      </asp:label></td>
  </tr>
  <tr>
    <td>Address:</td>
    <td>
      <asp:label id="lblAddress" runat="server"
        text='<%# DataBinder.Eval( _
                  dsUser.Tables("User").Rows(0), _
                  "(Address)") %>'>
      </asp:label></td>
  </tr>
  <tr>
    <td>E-mail:</td>
```

```
        <td>
          <asp:hyperlink id="lnkEmail" runat="server"
            navigateurl='<%# DataBinder.Eval( _
                                  dsUser.Tables("User").Rows(0), _
                                  "(Email)",  "mailto:{0}") %>'>
            Send mail
          </asp:hyperlink></td>
      </tr>
    </table>
    </p>
    <p>You have
      <asp:label id="lblPending" runat="server"
        text="<%# GetPending() %>">
      </asp:label> pending requests for contact.</p>
    <p>
      <asp:button id="btnAuthorize" runat="server"
                text="Authorize Contact" cssclass="Button">
      </asp:button>
    </p>
  </form>
</body>
```

7. Open the code-behind page and add the following `Imports` statements to the top of the page:

```
Imports System.Configuration
Imports System.Data.SqlClient
```

8. Also add the `DataSet` as a protected variable, and perform the database access in the `Page_Load()` event handler:

```
...
protected dsUser as DataSet

Private Sub Page_Load(ByVal sender As System.Object, _
  ByVal e As System.EventArgs) Handles MyBase.Load
  Dim userID As String = Request.QueryString("RequestID")

  ' Ensure we received an ID
  If userID Is Nothing Then
    Throw New ArgumentException( _
     "This page expects a RequestID parameter.")
  End If

  ' Create the connection and data adapter
  Dim cnFriends As New SqlConnection( _
   ConfigurationSettings.AppSettings("cnFriends.ConnectionString"))
  Dim adUser As New SqlDataAdapter( _
   "SELECT * FROM [User] WHERE UserID=@ID", cnFriends)
```

```
    adUser.SelectCommand.Parameters.Add("@ID", userID)

    ' Initialize the dataset and fill it with data
    dsUser = New DataSet
    adUser.Fill(dsUser, "User")

    ' Finally, bind all the controls on the page
    Me.DataBind()
  End Sub
```

9. The next method, `GetPending()`, will return the value that's used in the `lblPending` label to show the number of pending requests for the current user:

```
  Protected Function GetPending() As String
    ' Create the connection and command to execute
    Dim cnFriends As SqlConnection = New SqlConnection ( _
      ConfigurationSettings.AppSettings("cnFriends.ConnectionString"))
    Dim cmd As SqlCommand = New SqlCommand ( _
      "SELECT COUNT(*) FROM Contact " _
      "WHERE IsApproved=0 AND DestinationID=@ID", cnFriends)
    cmd.Parameters.Add("@ID", Page.User.Identity.Name)
    cnFriends.Open()
    Try
      Return cmd.ExecuteScalar().ToString()
    Finally
      cnFriends.Close()
    End Try
  End Function
```

10. The last piece of code that you need to add here is the handler for the Authorize button. This will just perform an update of the `IsApproved` flag. Double-click the button and add the following code to the event handler:

```
  Private Sub btnAuthorize_Click(ByVal sender As System.Object, _
    ByVal e As System.EventArgs) Handles btnAuthorize.Click

    ' Create the connection and command to execute
    Dim cnFriends As New SqlConnection( _
      ConfigurationSettings.AppSettings("cnFriends.ConnectionString"))
    Dim cmd As New SqlCommand( _
      "UPDATE Contact SET IsApproved=1 " + _
      " WHERE RequestID=@RequestID AND DestinationID=@DestinationID", _
      cnFriends)
    cmd.Parameters.Add("@RequestID", Request.QueryString("RequestID"))
    cmd.Parameters.Add("@DestinationID", Page.User.Identity.Name)
    cnFriends.Open()

    Try
      cmd.ExecuteNonQuery()
```

```
        Finally
            cnFriends.Close()
        End Try

        Response.Redirect("News.aspx")
    End Sub
```

11. Finally, save and compile the project. Open a browser window, and point it to the newly created page with the following parameter appended to the URL: `?RequestID=1A1CF6BD-9EEE-4b7d-9AB1-BEE3C3365DC9`. After you log in to the application (again, with apress as the user name and password), you should see the page shown in Figure 5-3.

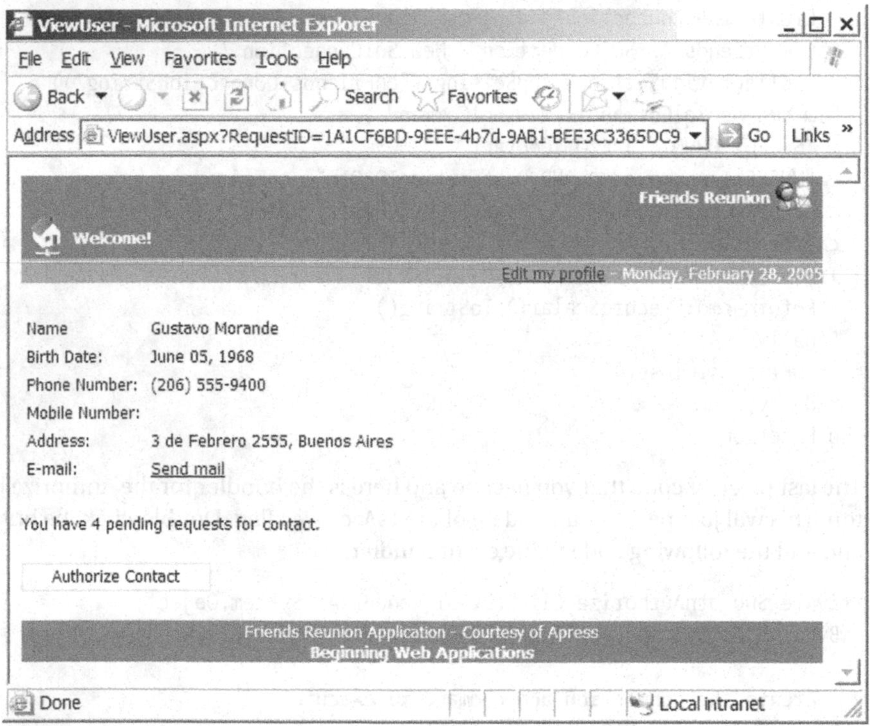

Figure 5-3. *The View User page*

How It Works

The code in `Page_Load()` starts by checking for the existence of the `RequestID` parameter, and then creates a connection and a data adapter to perform the query. As you learned earlier in this chapter, you are no longer hard-coding the connection string. Instead, you are using the value stored in the configuration file:

```
Dim cnFriends As New SqlConnection( _
  ConfigurationSettings.AppSettings("cnFriends.ConnectionString"))
```

You are using the adapter SelectCommand property to assign the value to the parameter, as explained in the previous chapter:

```
Dim adUser As New SqlDataAdapter( _
  "SELECT * FROM [User] WHERE UserID=@ID", cnFriends)
adUser.SelectCommand.Parameters.Add("@ID", userID)
```

After you have the objects configured, you create and fill the dataset that you defined at the class level as a protected variable:

```
dsUser = new DataSet()
adUser.Fill(dsUser, "User")
```

Now, instead of manually assigning each property to the corresponding value in the dataset, you let the data-binding mechanism do its work and evaluate the expressions used in the page's HTML source. You do this by explicitly calling DataBind() at the page level, so that every control on the page is evaluated:

```
Me.DataBind()
```

To see exactly what's going on, though, we need to take a look at the different binding expressions in the example, starting with the first one:

```
<asp:label id=lblName runat="server"
  text='<%# dsUser.Tables(0).Rows(0)("FirstName") + " " + _
           dsUser.Tables(0).Rows(0)("LastName") %>'>
</asp:label>
```

Here, you directly specify the values from the dataset variable that you defined in the code-behind page. You're accessing the table by its index, as well as the row, and finally retrieving the field you're interested in by using the default property overload that receives the column name. Notice that you can also perform simple string concatenation inside the expression.

The next binding expression uses DataBinder.Eval() to give the date a special format:

```
<asp:label id=lblBirth runat="server"
  text='<%# DataBinder.Eval( _
             dsUser.Tables(0).Rows(0), _
             "(DateOfBirth)", "{0:MMMM dd, yyyy}") %>'>
</asp:label>
```

You split the expression just after the row to evaluate is selected (dsUser.Tables(0).Rows(0)), and let the method resolve the default property access with "(DateOfBirth)". Notice how you can take advantage of the relaxed syntax we talked about: you don't need additional quotes around the column name. The expression below it is just the same, but without formatting, for the PhoneNumber column.

```
<asp:label id=lblPhone runat="server"
  text='<%# dsUser.Tables("User").Rows(0)("CellNumber") %>'>
</asp:label>
```

This is just to show that if you don't use DataBinder.Eval(), you need to code the expression as valid VB code. In this case, that means passing the proper quoted string to access the column value. The next expression after that follows the pattern with DataBinder.Eval().

You're also taking advantage of named access to the tables:

```
<asp:hyperlink id=lnkEmail runat="server"
  navigateurl='<%# DataBinder.Eval( _
                    dsUser.Tables("User").Rows(0),
                    "(Email)", "mailto:{0}") %>'>
Send mail
</asp:hyperlink>
```

The third argument to the Eval() method here applies formatting, just as if the following were called directly in the code:

```
String.Format("mailto:{0}", dsUser.Tables("User").Rows(0)("Email"))
```

Actually, in this case, you could even use this String.Format statement instead of the original one, which would result in a slightly better performance.

At the bottom of the page is a simpler data binding expression, where you bind the lblPending label to the GetPending() method created in the code-behind page:

```
<asp:label id=lblPending runat="server"
  text="<%# GetPending() %>">
</asp:label>
```

The GetPending() method itself simply returns the count of pending requests for the current user in the Contact table:

```
Dim cmd As SqlCommand = New SqlCommand ( _
  "SELECT COUNT(*) FROM Contact " _
  "WHERE IsApproved=0 AND DestinationID=@ID", cnFriends)
```

The btnAuthorize handler just performs an update and redirects the user to the News.aspx page. To use the command, you call ExecuteNonQuery(), as you don't expect a result to be returned.

Binding to Sets of Data

Up to now, you have been binding to *single* items of data; each of the binding expressions has selected just one value from the database. In order to generate the table on the ViewUser.aspx page, you needed to write a different expression for each cell. But there's an easier way: to display *sets* of data, you can use some of the controls provided with ASP.NET that support binding to multiple items.

ASP.NET comes with three controls for displaying sets of data: DataGrid, DataList, and Repeater. These controls provide a DataSource property that can be set to point to the data you want to display. When this type of binding is used, the control itself is in charge of iterating through the data source and formatting the data for display, in a fashion that's configured using the control's properties.

The concept of a *data source* is fairly wide here, and is by no means a synonym for *dataset*. These controls can be bound to *any* set of data, provided that the object containing the data implements the IEnumerable interface. This definition certainly includes the DataSet object, but also encompasses the ArrayList, a collection, and even an array or arbitrary objects.

In our application, we want to display the current user's list of pending requests for contact. This information can be easily displayed in tabular format, so we will use a DataGrid control.

Try It Out: Display Pending Contacts in a DataGrid The process you'll follow here involves filling a DataSet object with the data, setting it to be the data source for the grid, and calling the grid's DataBind() method. In addition, the control will be placed inside a panel, so you can later hide it if there are no pending requests. As the starting point, you'll use the News page that you created in Chapter 3.

1. Open the News.aspx page. Remove its existing controls (calendar, a combo box, the user controls, and so on), because they aren't of much use any more. Also, you'll recall that the header and footer controls were moved to the FriendsBase base class, so you should make this page inherit from that one. Once you've tidied up a little, the page source should look like the following:

```
<%@ Page language="vb" Codebehind="News.aspx.vb"
         AutoEventWireup="false"
         Inherits="FriendsReunion.News" %>
<!DOCTYPE HTML PUBLIC "-//W3C//DTD HTML 4.0 Transitional//EN" >
<html>
  <head>
    <title>News</title>
    <link href="Style/iestyle.css" rel="stylesheet" type="text/css">
</head>
  <body ms_positioning="FlowLayout">
    <form id="Form1" method="post" runat="server">
    </form>
  </body>
</html>
```

2. In the Design view for the News.aspx file, drop a Panel web control onto the form and set its ID to pnlPending.

3. Change the text inside the panel to something meaningful, such as **These users have requested to contact you:**, and add a carriage return.

4. Drop a DataGrid web control inside the panel and set its ID to grdPending.

5. Add the following namespace Imports statements:

```
Imports System.Configuration
Imports System.Data.SqlClient
```

6. Switch to the code behind page, delete the `cbDay_SelectedIndexChanged()` and `calDates_SelectionChanged()` methods, and change the `Page_Load()` handler as follows:

```
Private Sub Page_Load(ByVal sender As System.Object, _
  ByVal e As System.EventArgs) Handles MyBase.Load
   ' Configure the icon and message
   MyBase.HeaderIconImageUrl = "~/Images/winbook.gif"
   MyBase.HeaderMessage = "News Page"
   Dim sql As String = _
     "SELECT " + _
     "[User].FirstName, [User].LastName, " + _
     "Contact.Notes, [User].UserID " + _
     "FROM [User], Contact  WHERE " + _
     "DestinationID=@ID AND IsApproved=0 AND " +_
     "[User].UserID=Contact.RequestID"

  ' Create the connection and data adapter
  Dim cnFriends As New SqlConnection( _
    ConfigurationSettings.AppSettings("cnFriends.ConnectionString"))
  Dim adUser As New SqlDataAdapter(sql, cnFriends)
  adUser.SelectCommand.Parameters.Add("@ID", Page.User.Identity.Name)
  Dim dsPending As DataSet = New DataSet

  ' Fill dataset and bind to the datagrid
  adUser.Fill(dsPending, "Pending")
  grdPending.DataSource = dsPending
  grdPending.DataBind()
End Sub
```

7. Set `News.aspx` as the start page, and then save and run it. After the usual apress login, you'll see a list of users who have asked to contact you, as well as their user IDs on the far right of the table, as shown in Figure 5-4.

8. Once you're satisfied that everything works as described, go back to `News.aspx`, right-click the DataGrid, and select Auto Format. Play with the different styles, which will surely remind you of Excel's auto-format feature. Look at how the page source changes when you modify the look and feel of the grid, and how these settings are also available for modification in the Style section of the Properties browser for the DataGrid. For now, set the format of the DataGrid to `Simple1`.

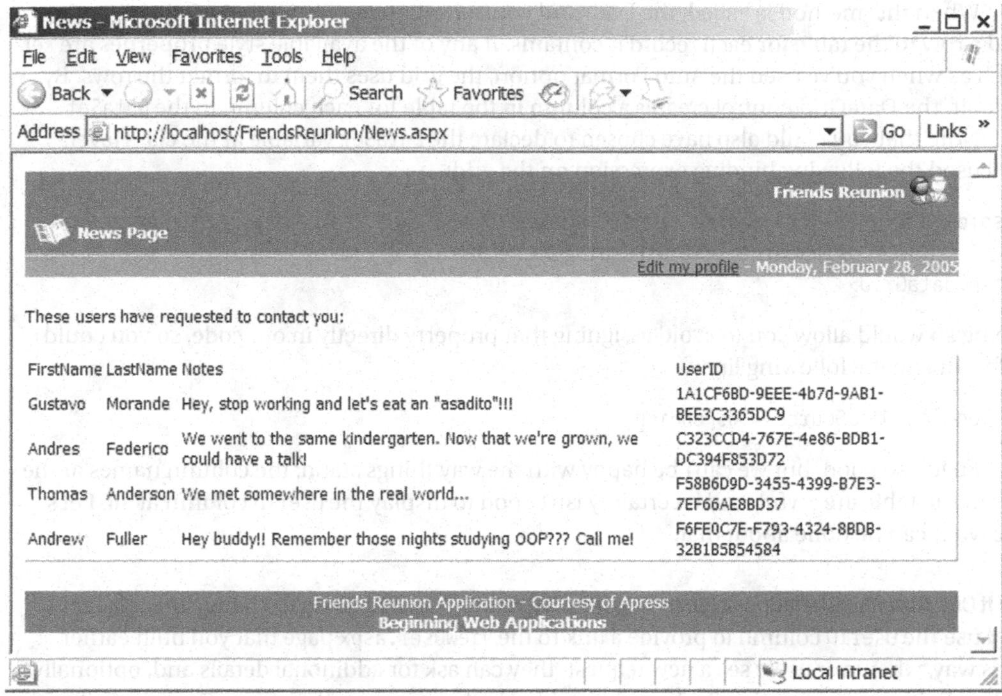

Figure 5-4. *The News page with a DataGrid control*

How It Works

Once again, you perform the data binding programmatically, at page-loading time. To do so, you first query the database for records in the `Contact` table that have the `IsApproved` flag set to 0 and for which the `DestinationID` matches the current user:

```
Dim sql As String = _
  "SELECT " + _
  "[User].FirstName, [User].LastName, " + _
   "Contact.Notes, [User].UserID " + _
   "FROM [User], Contact  WHERE " + _
   "DestinationID=@ID AND IsApproved=0 AND " + _
   "[User].UserID=Contact.RequestID"
```

You then create the connection and the data adapter as usual, set the `@ID` parameter, and fill a new `DataSet`. Finally, you set this `DataSet` to be the data source for the grid, and call the grid's `DataBind()` method:

```
grdPending.DataSource = dsPending
grdPending.DataBind()
```

When this method is called, the DataGrid control will iterate through the DataSet and add a row to the table for each record it contains. If any of the available style properties are set, such as when you've used the Auto Format option, the grid uses them to format the rows. By default, the DataGrid control creates a column in the table for each column in the DataSet.

Note that you could also have chosen to declare the DataSet variable at the class level, and used the following binding expression on the grid:

```
<asp:dataGrid id="grdPending" runat="server"
              DataSource="<%# dsPending %>">
</asp:dataGrid>
```

Doing so would allow you to avoid assigning that property directly in our code, so you could safely delete the following line:

```
grdPending.DataSource = dsPending
```

So far, so good, but we can't be happy with the way things stand: the column names at the top of the table are awful, and it certainly isn't good to display the UserID column at all. Let's see what can be done about that.

Try It Out: Customize DataGrid Columns To improve matters, you're going to change the headers and use the UserID column to provide a link to the ViewUser.aspx page that you built earlier. This way, whenever users see a new request, they can ask for additional details and, optionally, authorize that request using the button provided in the corresponding form. Operationally speaking, you need to override the automatic column generation feature and provide your own column definitions instead.

1. Return to the Design view of News.aspx, right-click the DataGrid, and select Property Builder. Notice how this user interface looks similar to that of the Style Builder you saw in Chapter 3.
2. Select the Columns category, and uncheck the Create columns automatically at run time check box at the top of the form.
3. From the Available columns list box, select Bound Column and click the > button three times, to add the first three columns. Select each of the new columns from the list and set the following property values for them:
   - Header text: **First Name**, Data Field: **FirstName**
   - Header text: **Last Name**, Data Field: **LastName**
   - Header text: **Notes**, Data Field: **Notes**

4. From the Available columns list box, select HyperLink Column and click the > button again. Set its properties as follows:

    - Header text: **Details**
    - Text: **View**
    - URL field: `UserID`
    - URL format string: `ViewUser.aspx?RequestID={0}`

5. If you wish, you can play with the various formatting options that are available under the Format and Borders sections of the Property Builder. When you're finished, the Property Builder should look something like Figure 5-5.

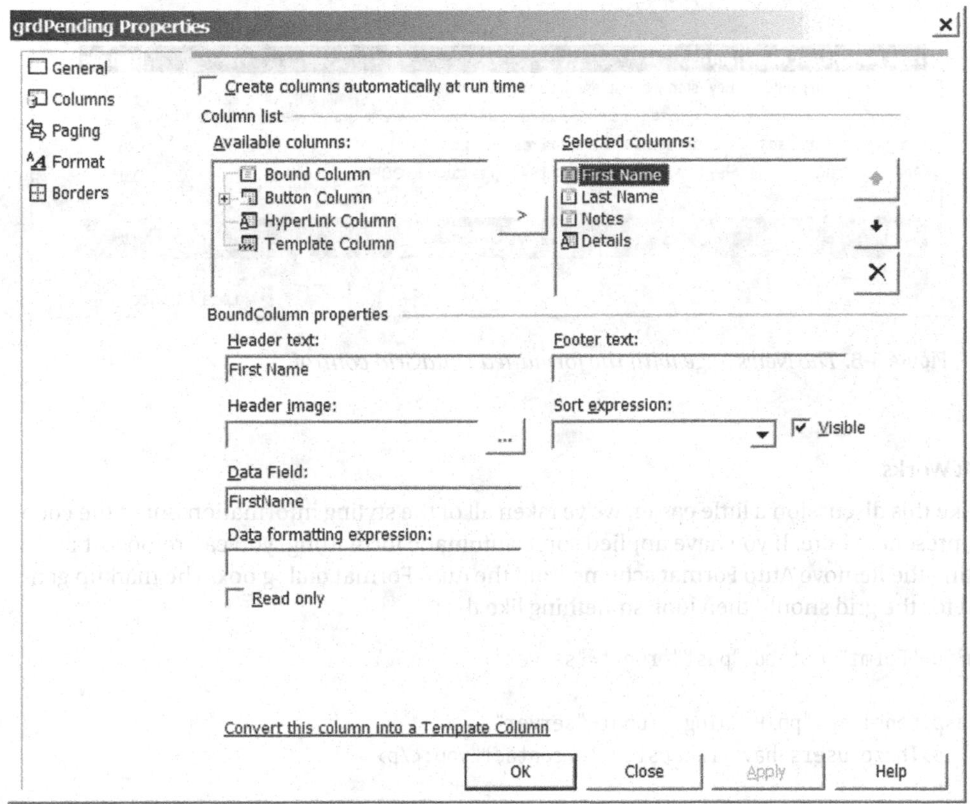

Figure 5-5. *Using the Properties Builder to control the appearance of the DataGrid*

6. Save the changes and run the application again. You should find that the appearance of the application has improved significantly, as shown in Figure 5-6.

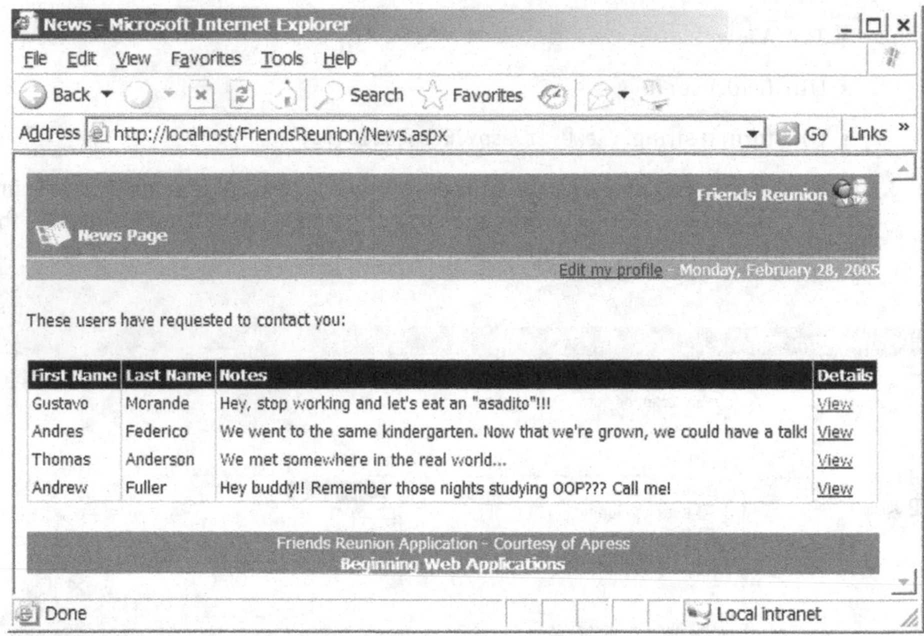

Figure 5-6. *The News page with the formatted DataGrid control*

How It Works

To make this discussion a little easier, we've taken all of the styling information out of the code being presented here. If you have applied some automatic formatting, you can remove it by selecting the Remove Auto Format scheme from the Auto Format dialog box. The markup generated for the grid should then look something like this:

```
<form id="Form1" method="post" runat="server">
  <p>
    <asp:panel id="pnlPending" runat="server">
      <p>These users have requested to contact you:</p>
      <p>
        <asp:datagrid id="grdPending" runat="server"
                      autogeneratecolumns="False">
          <columns>
            <asp:boundcolumn datafield="FirstName"
                             headertext="First Name">
            </asp:boundcolumn>
            <asp:boundcolumn datafield="LastName"
                             headertext="Last Name">
            </asp:boundcolumn>
```

```
            <asp:boundcolumn datafield="Notes"
                             headertext="Notes">
            </asp:boundcolumn>
            <asp:hyperlinkcolumn text="View"
              datanavigateurlfield="UserID"
              datanavigateurlformatstring="ViewUser.aspx?RequestID={0}"
              headertext="Details">
            </asp:hyperlinkcolumn>
          </columns>
        </asp:datagrid>
      </p>
    </asp:panel>
  </p>
</form>
```

The DataGrid control now has a child element called `<Columns>`, which contains four new elements that correspond to the four columns you set up in the exercise. The first three of these are `BoundColumn` elements, and you can see how their `DataField` and `HeaderText` attributes correspond with the columns in your `DataSet` and the labels in the DataGrid control, respectively. The fourth column in the table is implemented with a `HyperLinkColumn` element, in which the `DataNavigateUrlFormatString` attribute provides a skeleton within which to perform string formatting, using the `DataNavigateUrlField` as the first argument.

Note If you chose to output all attributes as lowercase (Tools ➤ Options ➤ Text Editor ➤ HTML/XML ➤ Format), you will see the output shown here. Each attribute usually maps to a corresponding property of a .NET class, such as `DataGrid.AutoGenerateColumns`.

This apparent complexity simply renders the appropriate link to the `ViewUser.aspx` file, with the expected `RequestID` parameter being added according to each row in turn. The DataGrid control is performing most of the binding work itself, using the properties that you set, so you don't need to provide the binding expressions directly.

Working Visually with Data

Aside from the help provided by the DataGrid control, so far, the VS .NET IDE hasn't provided much assistance with our data-related tasks. We've done all of the data binding manually, and we've been accessing the database directly from our code, just as we did in the previous chapter. But the IDE actually does provide a number of facilities to make your coding easier.

The VS .NET IDE can generate code automatically (both HTML source, and the code-behind page), based on settings you specify through the Properties browser or in dedicated wizards. This capability is provided through the data components we introduced at the beginning of this chapter. Now you'll see how to take advantage of these features.

Working with Data Components

Earlier in this chapter, you dropped a SqlConnection component onto a web form, resulting in the automatic generation of some code. However, we noted at the time that the benefits of using that particular component weren't exactly compelling. A better example of potential benefits is provided by the SqlDataAdapter component, which we've used frequently in our programs so far. In VS .NET, you can visually configure this component, including all its internal Command objects for SELECT, INSERT, UPDATE, and DELETE statements. In fact, provided that the SELECT is reasonably straightforward, VS .NET can even create the INSERT, UPDATE, and DELETE statements on your behalf!

When you drop a SqlDataAdapter component onto a web form, you're presented with a wizard. (If you close the wizard, you can reopen it by right-clicking the component and choosing Configure Data Adapter.) The wizard is very complete, allowing not only the creation of SQL statements, but also the creation of new stored procedures (or the reuse of existing ones) and even testing their execution. Figure 5-7 shows the Query Builder that the wizard makes available for this purpose.

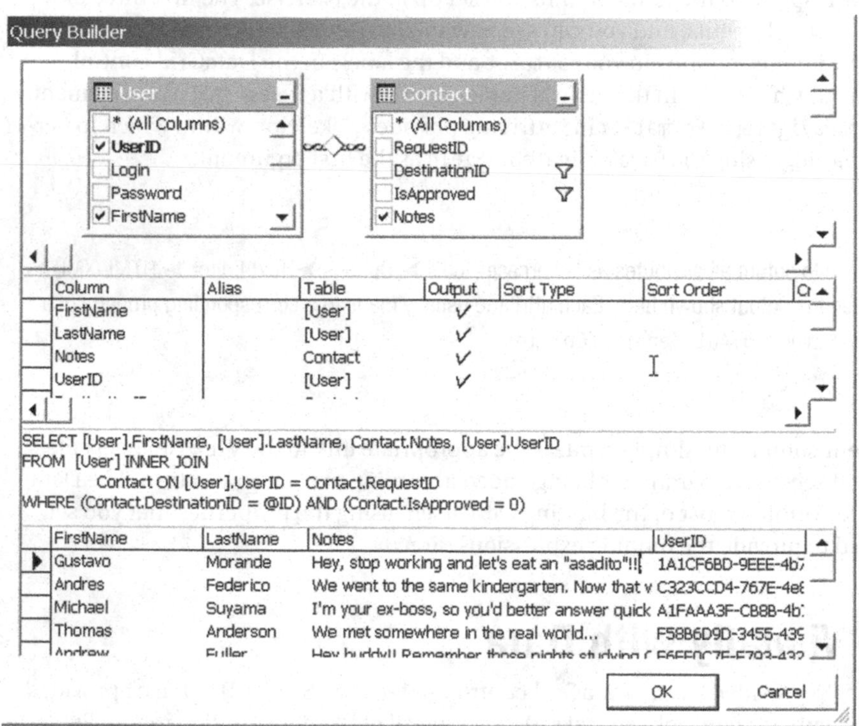

Figure 5-7. *The Query Builder lets you create SQL statements.*

What you see in Figure 5-7 is the result of building the same query you used previously to fill the grid of pending requests for contact. Right-clicking anywhere inside the Query Builder shows the menu of available actions, including running the current query. When you use a parameter, you're even presented with a proper UI to fill in for that parameter!

To see how the data adapter is being "magically" configured, you only need to look at the `InitializeComponent()` method in the code-behind page, which will contain the code that corresponds to the settings you've made through the wizard. The `TableMappings` property that appears in the Properties browser and the initialization code tell the adapter which tables and fields in the `SelectCommand` to map to which tables and columns in the `DataSet`. This means that the names of the columns, or even the tables, in the `DataSet` don't need to match those in the source database.

It's also possible to use the Properties browser to set the property of one data component to point to another one that is present on the same page. For example, you can set a `SqlDataAdapter` component's `SelectCommand` property to point to an existing `SqlCommand` component on the page, and set the latter's `Connection` property to point to an existing `SqlConnection` component in turn. This makes it easy to share a common connection object, for example, among multiple data adapters or commands.

Using Typed Datasets

Another VS .NET data-retrieval feature is a special type of dataset: a *typed dataset*, which offers some additional benefits, both for the visual design of applications and for code. When we discussed how to access the tables, rows, and column values in a `DataSet` object, you saw that you could do so using the string name of the element:

```
dsUser.Tables("User").Rows(0)("FirstName")
```

Or you could access those values using the element's index:

```
dsUser.Tables(0).Rows(0)(0)
```

The code is simple in both cases, but it shows a drawback of the `DataSet` object: a mistake in the name of a table or a field won't be trapped at compile-time. Instead, it will produce a runtime exception. The alternative, which is to access the values with indexes, introduces a dependency on the SQL statement that's used to acquire the data. If you happen to change the fields returned (or even just their order), the code will not work as expected.

ADO.NET introduces the concept of a typed dataset, which is an automatically generated class that inherits from the generic `DataSet` class, but adds properties and classes to reflect the tables and rows in a type-safe manner. Once instantiated, you can use it to write code like this:

```
Dim ds As New UserDataSet()
' Fill the dataset

' Render the user ID
Dim row As UserDataSet.UserRow = CType(ds.User.Rows(0), UserDataSet.UserRow)
Response.Write(row.UserID)
```

Notice how you can access the tables as direct properties of the dataset (as in `ds.User`), and after a straightforward cast to the specific row type, you can access the fields as properties of the row itself (as in `row.UserID`). This feature improves your productivity, because you don't need to worry about getting the names and indexes of tables and fields right. If you get them wrong, IntelliSense (and the compiler itself) will tell you about it! Furthermore, the values in the columns of a typed dataset also have properly defined types, making it impossible to (say) assign a string to a column that's expecting an integer.

A typed dataset can be generated from a data adapter component that's been placed on a web form. Provided that it has a valid `SelectCommand` assigned, you can right-click it and choose the Generate Dataset option, and a typed dataset will be created based on the structure of the information that's retrieved by the command. You can give the new dataset a name and choose to add an instance of it to the current form, in order to use it immediately.

Going through this process creates a *schema* for the dataset that contains a definition of its structure (such as tables, columns, and their types) in a file that has an `.xsd` extension. This file is an XML document with a special format (also known as an XML language), which we will examine more closely in Chapter 7. It can be opened inside the IDE, where the designer will show the various pieces that make up the dataset's structure.

As is so often the case, a lot of these ideas will become clearer with an example. In the next exercise, you'll improve the `News.aspx` page further, to display a list of approved contacts as well as the pending ones. The query will be similar to the one you used earlier, except that you'll be looking for the `IsApproved` flag to be set to 1. The new list will appear above the existing one, and since the contacts on the list have already been approved, you'll show the user more complete data about those contacts and provide a link to send them e-mail. You'll also provide a link to another page showing the contact's complete information. This linked page will be the `ViewUser.aspx` form, with a slight change to hide the Authorize Contact button, as that won't be necessary.

Try It Out: Retrieve Contacts from the Database In this example, as well as implementing the features just described, you'll see how using a typed dataset results in improvements to the support that's available through the IDE for configuring the way data is bound to the grid.

1. Open the `News.aspx` page and add a carriage return before the panel where the pending requests appear. Add a new Panel web server control, set its `ID` to `pnlApproved`, and change the text inside it to **These are your approved contacts:**.

2. Drop a DataGrid control inside the panel, next to the text, and set its `ID` to `grdApproved`. Add a carriage return to separate it from the text.

3. Now let's configure the data components. First, drop a `SqlConnection` component onto the form, set its `(Name)` property to `cnFriends`, and use the `ConnectionString` property under the DynamicProperties category to map this value to the value in your `Web.config` file: `cnFriends.ConnectionString`. As the value will be already present in the `Web.config` file (you put it there earlier in this chapter), the value will be loaded and shown in the `ConnectionString` property under the Data category, with an icon to indicate that it's a dynamic value.

4. Drop a `SqlDataAdapter` component from the Toolbox's Data tab onto the Web Forms Designer page, and a wizard will appear. Click Next, and select the `FriendsData` data connection from the drop-down list. (The list is populated from the connections in the Server Explorer that point to a SQL Server database.)

5. In the next step, the wizard offers the option to use SQL statements or stored procedures to access the database. Select the first option and click Next.

6. The next step allows you to set various advanced options, use the Query Builder, or directly type the SQL statement to use. Whichever method you choose, the final SQL statement should be as follows:

```
SELECT [User].FirstName, [User].LastName,
       [User].PhoneNumber, [User].Address,
       [User].Email, [User].UserID
FROM [User]
INNER JOIN Contact ON [User].UserID = Contact.RequestID
WHERE (Contact.DestinationID = @ID) AND (Contact.IsApproved = 1)
```

You can also uncheck the Generate Insert, Update and Delete statements check box in the dialog box that opens when you click the Advanced Options button. You won't be making changes to the dataset's data, and those additional commands won't be needed.

7. Click Next, and then click Finish to close this wizard.

8. Change the data adapter's `(Name)` to `adApproved`. Optionally, expand the `SelectCommand` property and set its `(Name)` to `cmApproved`. Notice how the wizard automatically detected that an existing `SqlConnection` on the page was already pointing to the same SQL Server connection and used it for the command's `Connection` property.

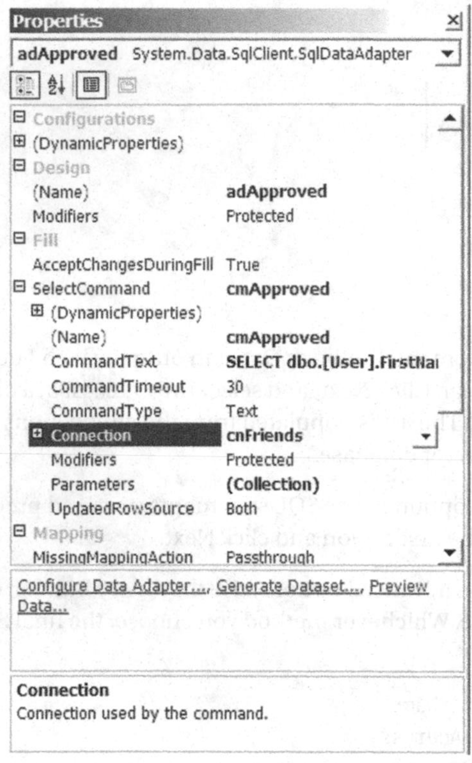

9. If you like, you can take a look at the `SelectCommand`'s `Parameters` collection. You'll see that the `@ID` parameter you used is already configured with the appropriate type. You'll fill this parameter with the current user's `ID` before filling the dataset, so that you get only the contacts for the current user.

10. Let's now generate a typed dataset to be filled by this data adapter. Click the Generate Dataset link that appears in the Properties browser, or right-click the data adapter and select the similarly named menu option. In the dialog box that appears, type `ContactsData` as the new dataset name; this will be the name of the generated `DataSet`-derived class. The check box near the bottom of this dialog box specifies that you want to add an instance of this dataset to the current Web Forms Designer page. Click OK.

11. Change the newly added dataset component's `(Name)` to `dsApproved`.

12. Set the DataGrid's `DataSource` property to point to `dsApproved`. Now you should see the real column names displayed in the grid, instead of the dummy columns you saw before.

13. Open the Property Builder for the DataGrid. In the Columns pane, the list of fields is now shown in the Available columns list box. This makes it much easier to choose which columns to display. Add all of them except for `Email` and `UserID`, and remember to uncheck the box at the top of the pane (Create automatic columns).

14. Add a hyperlink column (as described earlier in the "Try It Out: Customize DataGrid Columns" section) to allow the sending of e-mail, using the following values:

    - Header text: **Contact**
    - Text: **Send mail**
    - URL field: `Email`
    - URL format string: `mailto:{0}`

15. Add another hyperlink column to allow the viewing of user details, using the following values:

    - Header text: **Details**
    - Text: **View**
    - URL field: `UserID`
    - URL format string: `ViewUser.aspx?UserID={0}`

    Notice that URL field is now a combo box that shows the list of columns in the typed dataset. You're passing a different query string parameter to `ViewUser.aspx`, so that it knows you're not asking for the details of a pending request for contact (it receives a `RequestID` in that case).

16. Now for the "hard" part. In the code-behind page, below the existing code in `Page_Load()`, add the following to complete the command, fill the dataset, and bind to the DataGrid:

```
' Fill approved contacts
adApproved.SelectCommand.Parameters("@ID").Value = _
  Page.User.Identity.Name;
adApproved.Fill(dsApproved)
grdApproved.DataBind()
```

17. That is really all you need to code! To finish things off, though, let's add two lines at the end to hide the panels if there is no data to show:

```
 If dsPending.Tables(0).Rows.Count = 0 Then
  pnlPending.Visible = False
End If
If dsApproved.User.Rows.Count = 0 Then
  pnlApproved.Visible = False
End If
```

18. Let's apply a little auto-formatting. Right-click the DataGrid, choose Colorful 4 in the Auto Format dialog box, and click OK.

19. Now let's modify the `ViewUser.aspx` page, to take into account the fact that it can now receive a user ID query string parameter. If that happens, it needs to hide the Authorize Contact button. Change the `if` statement that checks for the ID in its `Page_Load()` event handler to match this:

```
' Ensure we received an ID
If userID Is Nothing Then
  userID = Request.QueryString("UserID")
  If userID Is Nothing Then
    Throw New ArgumentException("This page expects either a RequestID " +
      "or a UserID parameter.")
  Else
    btnAuthorize.Visible = False
  End If
End If
```

20. Save the page, set `News.aspx` as the start page, and run the project. After the usual login process, you will see something like the page shown in Figure 5-8, after a couple contacts have been approved.

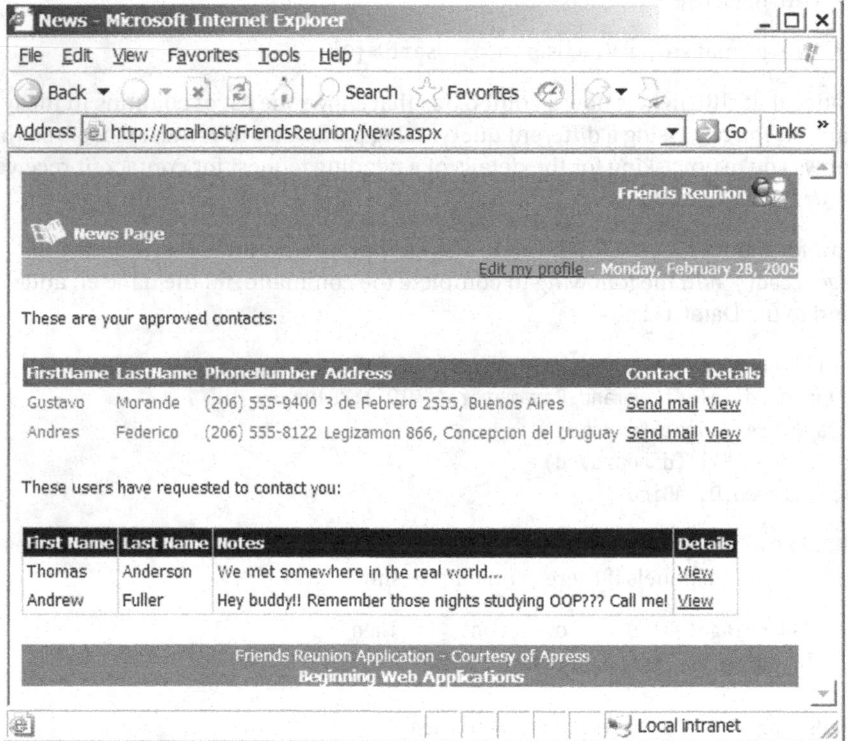

Figure 5-8. *The News page with approved contacts added*

How It Works

The data components you dropped on the page, the wizards, and the settings you specified are all reflected in the code-behind page by variable declarations at the class level:

```
Public Class News
  Inherits FriendsBase

  ' Web server controls here...
  Protected WithEvents cnFriends As System.Data.SqlClient.SqlConnection
  Protected WithEvents adApproved As System.Data.SqlClient.SqlDataAdapter
  Protected WithEvents cmApproved As System.Data.SqlClient.SqlCommand
  Protected WithEvents dsApproved As FriendsReunion.ContactsData
```

Each component has its own variable, and the last one—the dataset—is the most interesting. It's not defined as a generic `DataSet`, but rather as the custom `FriendsReunion.ContactsData` class. This is the class that was generated by the adapter when you asked it to do so. The components instances, just like their server controls counterparts, are initialized inside the `InitializeComponent()` method, which is placed inside the `Web Form Designer generated code` region. You can take a look inside that method, and you'll realize there's no magic there—just raw VB code you could have written yourself.

The key point to bear in mind about this demonstration is that the code you wrote to load the list of pending requests in the previous section performs exactly the same task as the code here, and that code took 12 lines to achieve the same results as 3 lines here! That's four times less code—certainly *not* a minor detail. The code has been greatly simplified because all of the variable initialization code is generated automatically. You just need to pass the adapter the value for the current user ID, fill the dataset, and call `DataBind()` on the grid:

```
' Fill approved contacts
adApproved.SelectCommand.Parameters("@ID").Value = Page.User.Identity.Name
adApproved.Fill(dsApproved)
grdApproved.DataBind()
```

Note Just in case you're concerned with the database connection, it is opened by the data adapter, and it's closed as soon as the data adapter doesn't need it anymore.

Finally, note that when you checked for the existence of rows in the two datasets, you could use the new property in your typed dataset that points to the correct table:

```
If dsApproved.User.Rows.Count = 0 Then
  pnlApproved.Visible = False
End If
```

This is instead of the following syntax, which you had to use for the generic dataset:

```
If dsPending.Tables(0).Rows.Count = 0 Then
  pnlPending.Visible = False
End If
```

When the user clicks the View link, the browser navigates to the `ViewUser.aspx` page passing the `UserID` of the current row. When that page is loaded, it will hide the Authorize button, because it received a `UserID` parameter instead of a `RequestID`. Otherwise, it will throw an exception, as either one or the other is required in order to display the information.

Advanced Data Binding

Sometimes, you need more flexibility in the rendering of data than is provided by a table with simple row and cell values. ASP.NET supports better customization of output through the use of *templates*. A template is a piece of ASP.NET/HTML code that can contain binding expressions, and it is used inside a DataGrid column (for example) as a skeleton for each row/cell's representation. The Web Forms Designer offers great integration with this concept, and makes designing with templates a breeze.

Tip Controls that support templates include DataGrid, DataList, and Repeater. Third-party controls may also support templates.

Try It Out: Use a Templated Column in a DataGrid In this example, you'll use a template to display four items in a cell: two small images, and the user's phone number and address. This display will replace the columns that you previously used for this purpose. You'll need to first create a template for that cell, and then take advantage of what you learned earlier about simple data binding to link values to the labels inside it.

1. Open the `News.aspx` page, right-click the `grdApproved` DataGrid, and select Property Builder.

2. In the Columns pane, remove the PhoneNumber and Address columns. Next, select the Template Column element from the Available columns list box, and add it to the list of Selected columns. Using the arrows at the right of the list box, move the column up and position it above the Contact column.

3. Set the Header text form field to Info, and then click OK.

4. To add controls inside the template column, you need to start editing it. Right-click the DataGrid again, and a new menu option will be available: Edit Template. It contains a submenu that displays all template columns available in the control. Select the only item available: Columns[2] - Info. You will see that the grid layout changes to show the template, with four sections named HeaderTemplate, ItemTemplate, EditItemTemplate, and FooterTemplate.

5. Drop two Image and two Label web server controls inside the ItemTemplate section. Separate them by a line break (`<br>`) by pressing Shift+Enter. Set the `ImageUrl` property of the images to `Images/phone.gif` and `Images/home.gif`, respectively. The section should then look like this:

These are your approved contacts:
grdApproved - Columns[2] - Info
HeaderTemplate
ItemTemplate
Label
Label
EditItemTemplate
FooterTemplate

6. Select the first label, and then open the DataBindings dialog box for it by clicking the ellipsis in the Properties browser.

7. In the Simple binding list box, locate the Container ➤ DataItem ➤ PhoneNumber node. Note that once again, the complete list of fields available is shown, because you're using a typed dataset.

8. Do the same for the other label, this time binding it to Container ➤ DataItem ➤ Address.

9. Right-click the template and choose the End Template Editing menu option.

10. Save everything you've done so far, make this the start page, and then run the project. You will now see something like the page shown in Figure 5-9.

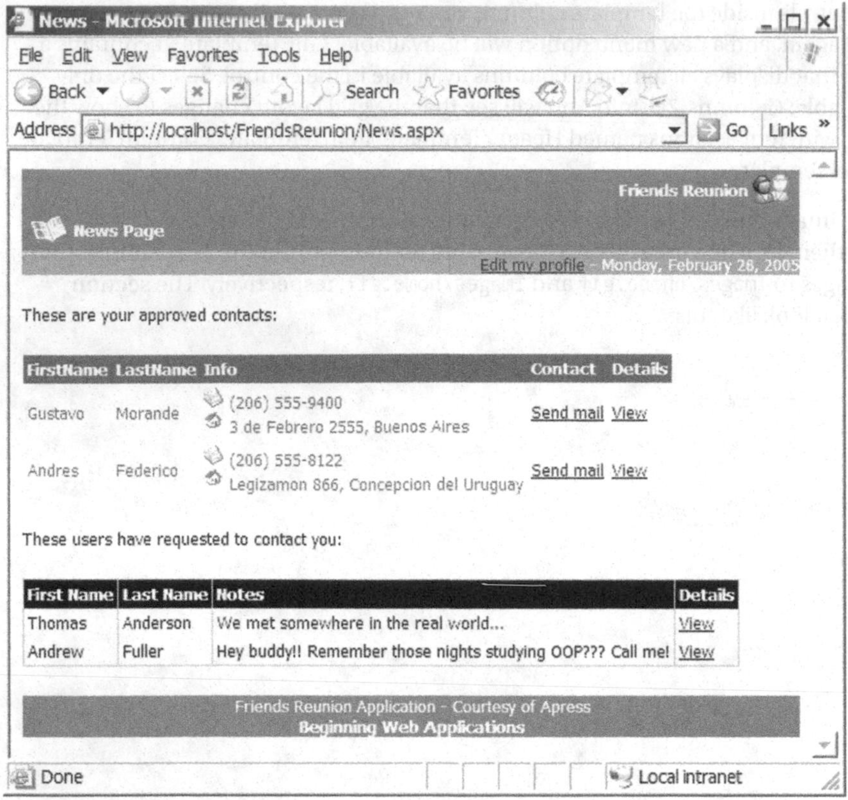

Figure 5-9. *The News page after applying a template to a column*

How It Works

When you add templated columns to a DataGrid, the Edit Template context menu option is enabled. After selecting the template column to edit from its submenu, the template design process is exactly the same as for the page itself: you drop controls on the sections you want, set the controls' binding, and so on. You also used the DataBindings dialog box for the first time. You could directly bind to the column you wanted, thanks to the typed dataset. In that dialog box, you saw that the binding can be applied to any control property.

As a result of the template editing, the Web Forms Designer generates the following HTML code (again, we've removed the auto-formatting information to make the code more readable):

```
<asp:datagrid id="grdApproved" runat="server" DataSource="<%# dsApproved %>"
                      AutoGenerateColumns="False">
 <columns>
   <asp:boundcolumn datafield="FirstName" headertext="FirstName">
   </asp:boundcolumn>
   <asp:boundcolumn datafield="LastName" headertext="LastName">
   </asp:boundcolumn>
```

```
    <asp:templatecolumn headertext="Info">
      <itemtemplate>
        <asp:image id="Image1" runat="server"
                   imageurl="Images/phone.gif">
        </asp:image>
        <asp:Label id="Label1" runat="server"
          Text='<%# DataBinder.Eval(Container, _
                    "DataItem.PhoneNumber") %>'>
        </asp:label><br>
        <asp:image id="Image2" runat="server" imageurl="Images/home.gif">
        </asp:image>
        <asp:Label id="Label2" runat="server"
          Text='<%# DataBinder.Eval(Container, _
                    "DataItem.Address") %>'>
        </asp:label>
      </itemtemplate>
    </asp:templatecolumn>
    ...
  </columns>
</asp:datagrid>
```

The important element inside the <asp:TemplateColumn> element is <ItemTemplate>. As you can see, it contains ordinary server controls with binding expressions just like the ones you've seen so far. New concepts, however, are the `Container` and the `DataItem`, both of which are used in the binding expression. The first part of the binding expression evaluation, `Container`, resolves to the context of the binding operation. `DataItem` points, in this case, to the current row in the data table.

At runtime, when the grid finds a templated column, it creates the template, performs the bindings, and adds the controls to the cell, resulting in the rich output you saw.

Paging

You've arranged for the panels to disappear if there's nothing to display, but what happens if there are a lot of records to display? You could end up with a very long page indeed, which wouldn't be a great way to treat your users. Fortunately, there's something you can do about that, too.

The technique known as *paging* divides the total count of items to be displayed by the maximum number of items you want to display simultaneously, and shows only that subset of data. By also providing a means to navigate back and forth among these logical pages, you can allow users to browse through the data a page at a time.

Note Paging is very common for applications that display long lists, such as a list of products for a big company, a list of expenses for the last two years, or a complete set of stock quotes. Although you wouldn't expect such a lengthy list in the sample application (unless the user is really popular!), we will use it here for demonstration purposes.

Try It Out: Add Paging The DataGrid control has intrinsic support for paging, and all that's required to take advantage of it is to set a couple of properties and handle a single event that's fired when the user changes the current page. You'll add this functionality to the grdApproved grid, limiting the visible rows to only one, so that you can see paging in action.

1. Change the grdApproved properties to set AllowPaging to True and the PageSize to 1.

2. Locate the PagerStyle property, and set the following subproperties:

   - Mode: NextPrev
   - NextPageText: Next >
   - PrevPageText: < Previous
   - HorizontalAlign: Left

3. To reconfigure the page when the user moves back and forth through the records, you need to wire up and handle the PageIndexChanged event that's fired by the DataGrid. To do this, go to the code-behind page, select the grdApproved item from the leftmost drop-down list at the top of the code editor, and then select the PageIndexChanged event from the rightmost drop-down list. Now you can modify the handler that is created:

```
Private Sub grdApproved_PageIndexChanged(ByVal source As Object, _
  ByVal e As System.Web.UI.WebControls.DataGridPageChangedEventArgs) _
  Handles grdApproved.PageIndexChanged
  ' Set the new index
  grdApproved.CurrentPageIndex = e.NewPageIndex

  ' Fill approved contacts
  adApproved.SelectCommand.Parameters("@ID").Value = _
    Page.User.Identity.Name
  adApproved.Fill(dsApproved)
  grdApproved.DataBind()
End Sub
```

4. Save and run the page, and voilà, you have paging, as shown in Figure 5-10.

How It Works

You start the process by setting two properties that enable the paging mechanism in the grid: AllowPaging and PageSize. The pager mode and style are set next, where you specify the text the links will have, as well as their placement in the footer. Once the pager links are in place, they raise the PageIndexChanged event when the user clicks them, which you handle in the code-behind page:

```
Private Sub grdApproved_PageIndexChanged(ByVal source As Object, _
 ByVal e As System.Web.UI.WebControls.DataGridPageChangedEventArgs) _
 Handles grdApproved.PageIndexChanged
  ' Set the new index
  grdApproved.CurrentPageIndex = e.NewPageIndex

  ' Fill approved contacts
  adApproved.SelectCommand.Parameters("@ID").Value = _
    Page.User.Identity.Name
  adApproved.Fill(dsApproved)
  grdApproved.DataBind()
End Sub
```

The argument e received by the handler allows you to retrieve the new page index the user selected. You set it to the grid's `CurrentPageIndex` property, and perform the binding again. As a result, the DataGrid will automatically skip the rows that don't fit in the current page, according to the page size you set.

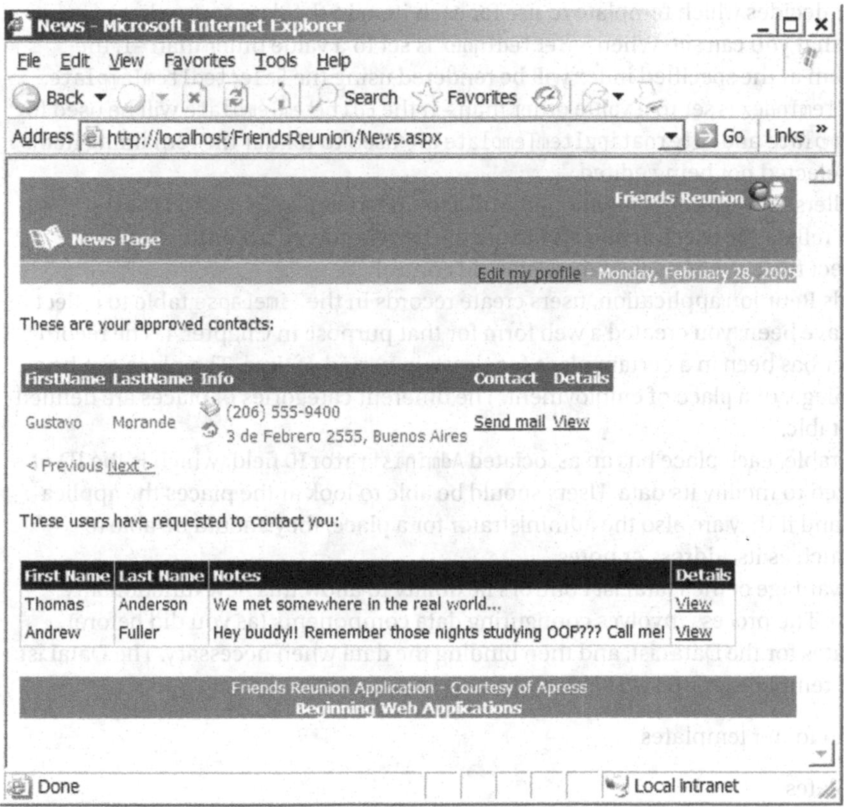

Figure 5-10. *The News page with paging*

Freestyle Data Binding and Editing—The DataList

With all of the features you've seen for the DataGrid control, it is quite a challenge to find a control that's more suitable to your data display needs. However, you might need even more control over presentation than the DataGrid allows. For example, if you want to display rows in some arbitrary, nontabular format, a grid isn't such a good fit. Sure, you could use a complex template and a single cell, but ASP.NET comes with another control that is better suited to this task: the DataList control. With regard to the data-binding process and the design of templates, this control is similar to the DataGrid, but it has no concept of columns.

As a template-only control, the DataList is highly flexible, but crucially, it also supports the concepts of selecting, editing, updating, or canceling the editing of an item. You can use different templates for each of those actions, and react to events fired by the control to perform the actual work against the database. The events fired by the DataList are, not surprisingly, `SelectedIndexChanged`, `EditCommand`, `UpdateCommand`, and `CancelCommand`. But how does the control know when any of these actions has taken place?

To cause these events to be fired, you need to place a Button, LinkButton, or ImageButton control in a template, and set its `CommandName` property to one of the following values, according to the event you want to cause: `Select`, `Edit`, `Update`, or `Cancel`.

The DataList decides which template to use for each item in the data source based on some properties that you can set. When `SelectedIndex` is set to a value other than –1, the corresponding item at the specified index will be rendered using the `SelectedItemTemplate`. Likewise, if `EditItemIndex` is set to a value other than –1, the `EditItemTemplate` will be used for that item. `ItemTemplate` and `AlternatingItemTemplate` are used to render the remaining items that are neither selected nor being edited.

In your handlers for the events mentioned, you can update the `SelectedIndex` or `EditItemIndex` to reflect the user's action and to get the item rendered accordingly, much as you did to reflect the current page in the DataGrid control.

In the Friends Reunion application, users create records in the `TimeLapse` table to reflect the places they have been; you created a web form for that purpose in Chapter 4. The record reflects that a user has been in a certain place for a certain period of time. The place can be a high school, a college, or a place of employment. The different categories of places are defined in the `PlaceType` table.

In the `Place` table, each place has an associated `AdministratorID` field, which is the ID of the user authorized to modify its data. Users should be able to look at the places the application works with, and if they are also the administrator for a place, they should be able to modify its data, such as its address or notes.

Let's take advantage of the DataList control's flexibility to allow this new functionality in the application. The process involves configuring data components (as you did before), designing templates for the DataList, and then binding the data when necessary. The DataList control has three template groups available to edit:

- Header and footer templates
- Item templates
- Separator templates

You can edit the various templates available for the DataList control by right-clicking it and selecting the appropriate menu option under Edit Template.

Try It Out: Show Places in a DataList Control In this example, you'll build a page that displays the list of places registered for the application, showing only their names and an icon to let the user select them. Once selected, complete data about the place will be displayed. Figure 5-11 shows how the View Place page will look, with one place selected after the user clicked the corresponding arrow next to it.

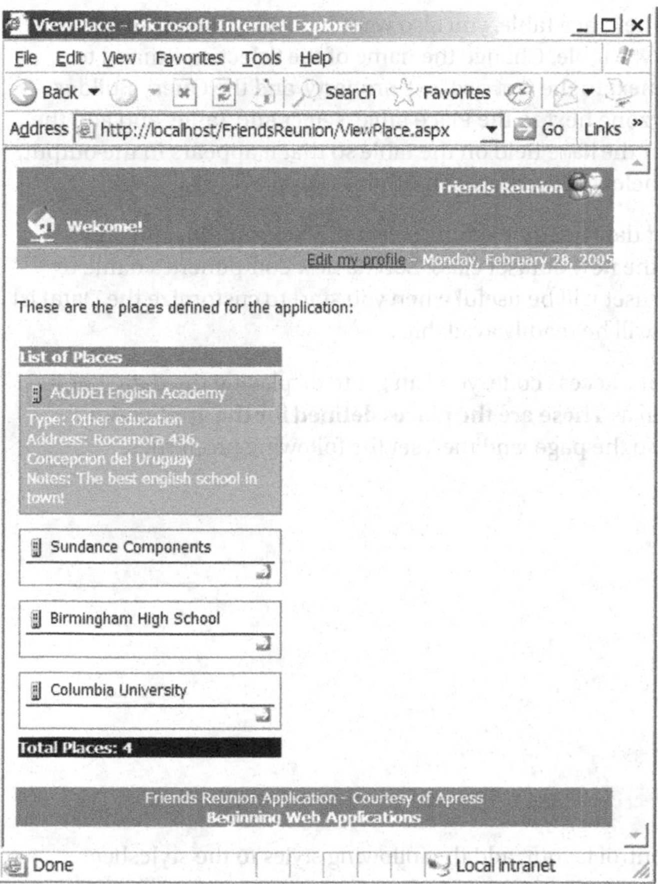

Figure 5-11. *The View Place page with a DataList control*

1. To our burgeoning project, add a new web form named `ViewPlace.aspx`. Add the `iestyle.css` stylesheet to it, and change the code-behind page to inherit from `FriendsBase`.

2. Drop a `SqlDataAdapter` component onto the form and configure it as you did earlier (in the "Try It Out: Retrieve Contacts from the Database" section), setting the SQL statement to `SELECT * FROM Place`. In this same wizard step, click the Advanced Options button and leave only the first option checked. When the wizard has finished, change the name of the adapter to `adPlaces`. Select Don't include password from the dialog box that appears next. (This is irrelevant, as you'll pick the connection string from the `Web.config` file in the next step.)

3. Change the automatically added SqlConnection's name to cnFriends and set its ConnectionString to use the dynamic property value, as you did before.

4. Set the adapter's InsertCommand and DeleteCommand to None in the Properties browser, as you won't allow these operations for the data adapter. Leave UpdateCommand as it is, but change its name to cmUpdate (you'll be using updates later on).

5. As well as the details from the Place table, you also want to display the place type, which resides in the PlaceType table. Change the name of the Select command to cmSelect. Click the ellipsis next to the CommandText property, and the Query Builder will appear. Right-click the zone next to the Place table, select Add Table, and add the PlaceType table. Next, select the Name field on the table so that it appears in the output, and set its alias in the grid below to TypeName. Then click OK.

6. Select the Generate Dataset data adapter action, select the New option, and enter PlaceData as the name for the new dataset class. Set the new component's name to dsPlaces. Using a typed dataset will be useful when you start to customize the DataList control, as the field names will be readily available.

7. At last, having set up the data-access code, you can get to displaying the data. Enter some introductory text such as **These are the places defined for the application:**. Drop a DataList control onto the page, and then set the following properties:

   - ID: dlPlaces
   - DataSource: dsPlaces
   - DataMember: Place
   - DataKeyField: PlaceID
   - BorderStyle: Solid
   - BorderWidth: 1px
   - Width: 220px

8. Before moving on to the control layout, add the following styles to the stylesheet:

```
.Hidden
{
  visibility: hidden;
  display: none;
}
.PlaceHeader
{
  border-bottom: 1px solid;
}
.PlaceItem
{
  border-bottom: #336699 1px solid;
  border-left: #336699 1px solid;
```

```
    border-right: #336699 1px solid;
    border-top: #336699 1px solid;
    padding: 5px 5px 5px 5px;
    margin-top: 5px;
    margin-bottom: 5px;
}
.PlaceTitle
{
    font-weight: bold;
    width: 100%;
    color: white;
    background-color: #336699;
}
.PlaceSummary
{
    font-weight: bold;
    width: 100%;
    color: white;
    background-color: black;
}
```

9. To set up the templates, right-click the DataList control, select Edit Templates, and then choose the Header and Footer Templates submenu option.

10. In the HeaderTemplate section of the template, place a Panel control, set its `CssClass` to `PlaceTitle`, and enter the text **List of Places**. In the FooterTemplate section, drop another Panel control and set its `CssClass` to `PlaceSummary`. Type the text **Total Places:**, and then place a Label control within it. The template should look like this:

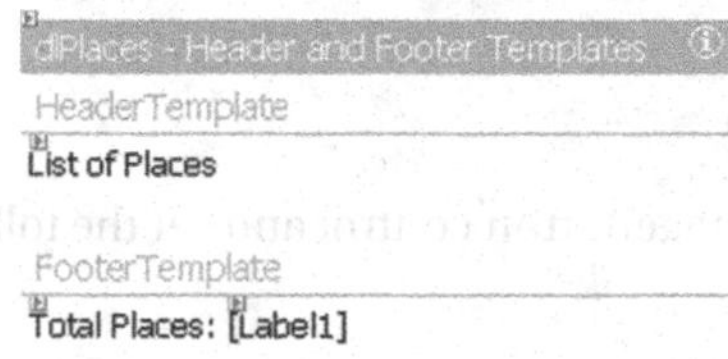

11. With the last label selected, click the ellipsis next to `(DataBindings)` in the Properties browser to open the DataBindings dialog box. Set the following custom binding expression, as shown in Figure 5-12:

```
dsPlaces.Place.Rows.Count
```

12. Right-click the DataList control again, select Edit Templates, and then choose the Item Templates submenu option. You'll see several sections that apply to each kind of item to render: ItemTemplate, AlternatingItemTemplate, SelectedItemTemplate, and EditItemTemplate. Inside the ItemTemplate section, drop an HTML Flow Layout Panel control. Set its `style` properties for a width of 100% and a background color of white. Set its `class` to `PlaceItem`.

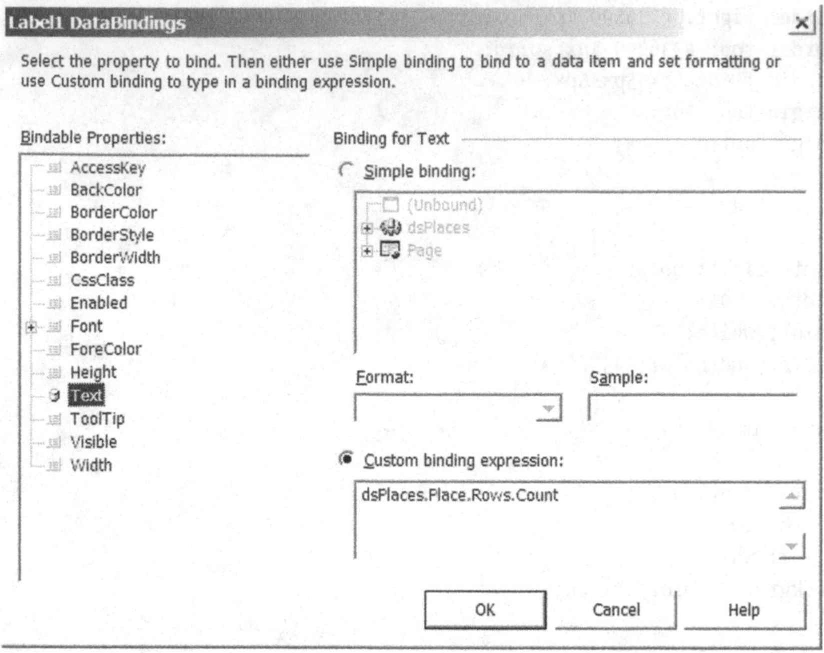

Figure 5-12. *The DataBindings dialog box*

13. Inside the panel, drop a web forms Panel control with `BackColor` set to `Gainsboro` and `CssClass` to `PlaceHeader`. Position the cursor inside it, remove the default text, and drop an Image control with `ImageUrl` set to `Images/building.gif` and `ImageAlign` to `Middle`. Next to it, drop a Label control. Click the ellipsis next to `(DataBindings)` in the Properties browser to open the DataBindings dialog box, and then set the following custom data binding expression:

    ```
    DataBinder.Eval(Container, "DataItem.Name")
    ```

    Finally, below the gray Panel control, drop an ImageButton control and set the following properties for it:

    - AlternateText: **Select**
    - ImageUrl: `Images/bluearrow.gif`
    - CommandName: **Select**
    - ImageAlign: `Right`

    The layout of the ItemTemplate section should look like this:

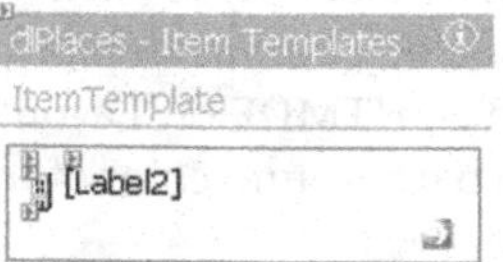

14. For the AlternatingItemTemplate section, you can simply copy the entire Flow Layout Panel control, including its controls from the previous steps, into this section to reuse the code (they are using essentially the same behavior). Then change its `style` property to set the background color to `lightskyblue`, so it looks like this:

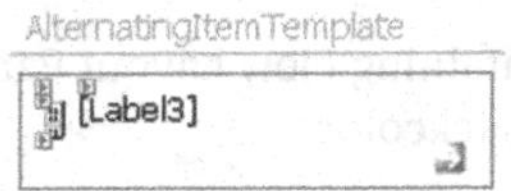

15. Now you need to set up the SelectedItemTemplate, which is a little more complex than the previous templates. To start with, copy the panel you configured for the previous templates. Then change the containing Flow Layout Panel control's `style` property to define `BACKGROUND-COLOR` as `#5d90c3`. Also change the contained web form's Panel control so `BackColor` is `Gray`. Next to the existing Label control, drop another one with `CssClass` set to `Hidden`, and set `ID` to `lblAdministratorID`. Then set the following custom data binding expression:

```
DataBinder.Eval(Container, "DataItem.AdministratorID")
```

This Label control will be used to determine whether the current user can edit the selected row, and set the ImageButton control's `Visible` property accordingly. The style ensures it won't appear in the display, yet it will be rendered (unlike setting `Visible = False`) so you can use it. Change the ImageButton control's properties as follows:

- AlternateText: **Edit**
- ImageUrl: `Images/edit.gif`
- CommandName: **Edit**
- Visible: `False`
- ID: `cmdEdit`

Directly above this button, enter a line break (Shift+Enter). Then add three Label controls with text **Type:**, **Address:**, and **Notes:**, respectively, as shown here:

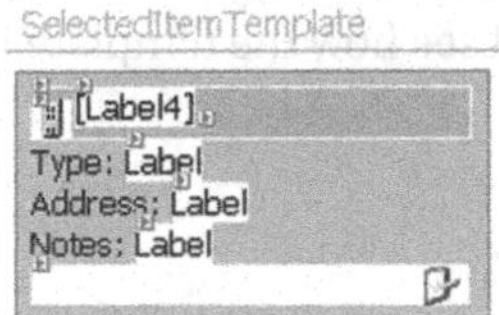

For the Type label, set the following custom data binding expression:

```
DataBinder.Eval(Container, "DataItem.TypeName")
```

For the Address label, set this custom data binding expression:

```
DataBinder.Eval(Container, "DataItem.Address")
```

And for the Notes label, set this custom data binding expression:

```
DataBinder.Eval(Container, "DataItem.Notes")
```

Finally, set `COLOR: white` for the `style` property of the containing Flow Layout Panel control, to make the text stand out against the new blue backcolor.

16. Reopen the code-behind page and add the following code, which performs the binding and additionally prevents the DataList from being displayed if there are no places to display:

```
Private Sub Page_Load(ByVal sender As Object, _
  ByVal e As System.EventArgs)
  If Not Page.IsPostBack Then
    BindPlaces()
  End If
End Sub

Private Sub BindPlaces()
  adPlaces.Fill(dsPlaces)
  If dsPlaces.Place.Rows.Count = 0 Then
    dlPlaces.Visible = False
  Else
    dlPlaces.DataBind()
  End If
End Sub
```

17. In the Design view, end template editing in the DataList control (right-click it and select End Template Editing). Then double-click it to create the handler for the `SelectedIndexChanged` event, adding the following code to it:

```
Private Sub dlPlaces_SelectedIndexChanged(ByVal sender As System.Object, _
  ByVal e As System.EventArgs) Handles dlPlaces.SelectedIndexChanged
  BindPlaces()
End Sub
```

18. Save and run the page. Test the selection mechanism, and see how the template is applied to the selected item to show the complete details.

How It Works

For a DataList control, data binding works just as it does with a DataGrid control. At runtime, the template is instantiated, binding expressions are evaluated, and controls are added to the output for each element in the data source.

The important controls are the ImageButton controls that you placed at the bottom right of each template. The values that you've assigned to the `CommandName` properties of these buttons—`Select` and `Edit`—have special meanings: the DataList uses them to raise the events discussed earlier in this section. When the user clicks the select ImageButton of an item (or an alternating item), the DataList detects the `Select` command name the button contains and raises the `SelectedIndexChanged` event. Inside this event handler, you just rebind the data:

```
Private Sub dlPlaces_SelectedIndexChanged(ByVal sender As System.Object, _
  ByVal e As System.EventArgs) Handles dlPlaces.SelectedIndexChanged
  BindPlaces()
End Sub
```

The DataList control automatically tracks the currently selected element, and as you can see, this rather simple procedure can have a powerful impact.

An interesting point to note here is that you didn't bother to set your own IDs for the controls. This would usually be considered to be bad practice, but the process here results in several controls being created from the same template, making it impossible to predict the ID of a runtime control. (If this didn't happen, there would be naming collisions.) If you cannot predict the ID of a control at runtime, there is little point in setting it to anything special at design-time. Besides that, you can see in the code-behind file that the controls inside the template are not given class-level variables either.

The final step to take in the page setup is to allow the user to edit an item. To enable this feature, you'll add a handler to the code-behind page to receive the `EditCommand` event, which will be fired when the `cmdEdit` button, defined earlier, is clicked. You will need to hide this button if the current user is not the place's administrator.

Try It Out: Enable Editing Capabilities You will create an editing template that uses data binding to load the editable fields. If the user accepts the changes, you will post the changes back to the database, using the configured data adapter. You will build the following layout:

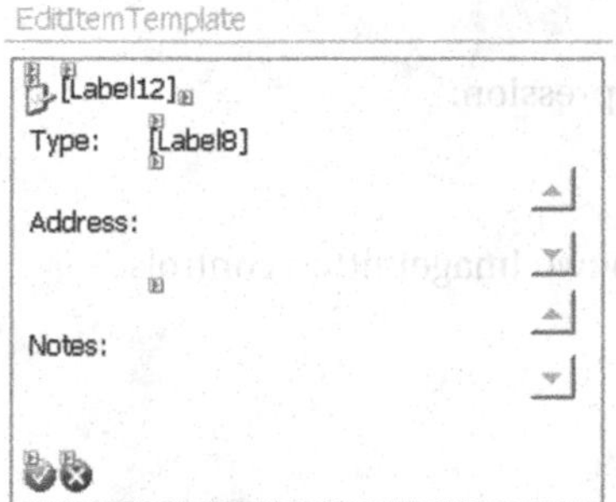

1. Start editing the Item Templates as you did before. Copy the Flow Layout Panel control of the SelectedItemTemplate section and place it in the EditItemTemplate section. Set its `style` property to `width: 100%` and `BACKGROUND-COLOR: lemonchiffon`. Delete all the controls except for the web form's Panel control and its contents at the top, and set its `BackColor` property to `Wheat`. Change the remaining image `ImageUrl` property to `Images/edit.gif`.

2. Insert an HTML Table control with two columns and three rows *outside* the Panel control (as illustrated at the beginning of this exercise), using the Table ➤ Insert ➤ Table menu option, so that you can specify its properties before creating it. Set the `class` property to `TableLines` and its `border` to `0`. Enter the text **Type:**, **Address:**, and **Notes:** in the leftmost cells.

3. Drop a Label control and set its data binding expression as follows:

```
DataBinder.Eval(Container, "DataItem.TypeName")
```

4. Add a TextBox control and set its properties as follows:

   - ID: `txtAddress`
   - CssClass: `TextBox`
   - Rows: 3
   - TextMode: `MultiLine`

   Give the TextBox control the following data binding expression:

```
DataBinder.Eval(Container, "DataItem.Address")
```

5. Add another TextBox control and set its properties as follows:

   - ID: `txtNotes`
   - CssClass: `TextBox`
   - Rows: 3
   - TextMode: `MultiLine`

   Give the TextBox control the following data binding expression:

```
DataBinder.Eval(Container, "DataItem.Notes")
```

6. Below the table, enter a carriage return, and then drop two ImageButton controls. Set the first control's properties as follows:

   - ID: `cmdUpdate`
   - CommandName: **Update**
   - AlternateText: **Save**
   - ImageUrl: `Images/ok.gif`

7. Set the second ImageButton control's properties as follows:

   - ID: `cmdCancel`
   - CommandName: **Cancel**
   - AlternateText: **Cancel**
   - ImageUrl: `Images/cancel.gif`

8. Next to the top Panel control is an existing Label control with the `Hidden` class. You need to change a couple properties for it, but because of its style, you won't be able to select it in the Design view. Switch to HTML view and locate `Label12` by using Edit ➤ Find and Replace ➤ Find (Ctrl+F). The label next to it is the one to modify. Set its `ID` to `lblPlaceID`, and modify the binding expression to this:

```
DataBinder.Eval(Container, "DataItem.PlaceID")
```

You will use the value bound to this label to determine the row that needs to be updated.

9. When you have finished adding the inner controls, you can safely remove the table `width` property value and let its size adjust to its content. Switching to the HTML view causes template editing to end, so you'll need to start it again for the Item Templates. After removing the table `width` value, select End Template Editing from the DataList context menu to return to the page Design view.

10. Now you need to add the appropriate event handlers to the code-behind page. First, let's deal with the `ItemDataBound` event, which is fired when an item is being bound to the template. You receive the current item in the argument to the event, and you want to show the Edit button only for users whose ID matches the current place's `AdministratorID`. Switch to the Code view, select the `dlPlaces` element from the leftmost drop-down list at the top of the window, and then select the `ItemDataBound` event from the rightmost drop-down list. In the new event handler, add the following code:

```
Private Sub dlPlaces_ItemDataBound(ByVal sender As Object, _
  ByVal e As System.Web.UI.WebControls.DataListItemEventArgs) _
  Handles dlPlaces.ItemDataBound
  ' Is the item selected?
  If e.Item.ItemType = ListItemType.SelectedItem Then
    ' Locate the hidden Label containing the AdministratorID
    Dim admin As Label = _
      CType(e.Item.FindControl("lblAdministratorID"), Label)
    ' If it matches the current user, show the Edit button
    If admin.Text = Page.User.Identity.Name Then
      e.Item.FindControl("cmdEdit").Visible = True
    End If
  End If
End Sub
```

11. In all of the event handlers, you call `BindPlaces()` at the end, to re-create the controls in the DataList according to the last changes made. Whenever the Edit button is clicked, you'll also need to update the DataList's `EditItemIndex`, and set it to the `ItemIndex` of the item passed with the arguments to the event. Select the `EditCommand` event from the appropriate drop-down list in the code editor, and then add the following code to the method:

```
Private Sub dlPlaces_EditCommand(ByVal source As Object, _
  ByVal e As System.Web.UI.WebControls.DataListCommandEventArgs) _
  Handles dlPlaces.EditCommand
```

```
    ' Save the edit index
    dlPlaces.EditItemIndex = e.Item.ItemIndex
    BindPlaces()
End Sub
```

12. Of course, users could just change their mind and directly select another item without either canceling or accepting the current item's edit session. In this case, you just need to reset the EditItemIndex by adding the following line to the existing handler:

```
Private Sub dlPlaces_SelectedIndexChanged(ByVal sender As System.Object, _
  ByVal e As System.EventArgs) Handles dlPlaces.SelectedIndexChanged
    ' Remove the edit index just in case we were editing
    dlPlaces.EditItemIndex = -1
    BindPlaces()
End Sub
```

13. Once editing is started, the user can cancel it, which resets the EditItemIndex property. You also set the SelectedIndex property to leave users positioned on the item they were editing. Now select the CancelCommand event to create a handler for it and enter the following code:

```
Private Sub dlPlaces_CancelCommand(ByVal source As Object, _
  ByVal e As System.Web.UI.WebControls.DataListCommandEventArgs) _
  Handles dlPlaces.CancelCommand
    ' Reset the edit index
    dlPlaces.EditItemIndex = -1

    ' Set the selected item to the currently editing item
    dlPlaces.SelectedIndex = e.Item.ItemIndex
    BindPlaces()
End Sub
```

14. Another option is for the user to click the OK button to perform an update. At this time, you will perform the binding inside this method, instead of calling BindPlaces(). That is because you need to work with the dataset before binding, to perform the appropriate update. You will locate the row corresponding to the current PlaceID and issue an Update through the data adapter. Finally, reset the indexes as you did for CancelCommand. Select the UpdateCommand event from the drop-down list and add the following code:

```
Private Sub dlPlaces_UpdateCommand(ByVal source As Object, _
  ByVal e As System.Web.UI.WebControls.DataListCommandEventArgs) _
  Handles dlPlaces.UpdateCommand
    ' Find the updated controls
    Dim addr As TextBox = CType(e.Item.FindControl("txtAddress"), TextBox)
    Dim notes As TextBox = CType(e.Item.FindControl("txtNotes"), TextBox)
    Dim place As Label = CType(e.Item.FindControl("lblPlaceID"), Label)
    ' Reload the dataset and locate the relevant row
    adPlaces.Fill(dsPlaces)
    Dim sql As String = "PlaceID = '" + place.Text + "'"
```

```
    Dim row As PlaceData.PlaceRow = _
      CType(dsPlaces.Place.Select(sql)(0), PlaceData.PlaceRow)
    ' Set the values using the typed properties
    row.Address = addr.Text
    row.Notes = notes.Text

    ' Update the row in the database
    adPlaces.Update(New DataRow() {row})

    ' Reset datalist state and bind
    dlPlaces.EditItemIndex = -1
    dlPlaces.SelectedIndex = e.Item.ItemIndex
    dlPlaces.DataBind()
  End Sub
```

15. Save and run the page. To try it out, edit the ACUDEI English Academy place, adding or changing its comment, for example. (ACUDEI stands for Academia Cultural Uruguayense de Enseñanza de Idiomas, a great place to study English!)

How It Works

Let's start from the beginning. When `BindPlaces()` is first called, the first time the page is run, the DataList control iterates through the data source and binds the corresponding template with each row. At this time, the `ItemDataBound` event is raised. In the handler for that event, the code reacts only to items of type `ListItemType.SelectedItem`, as they are the only ones that have the Edit button you want to show, if it is appropriate to do so.

```
Private Sub dlPlaces_ItemDataBound(ByVal sender As Object, _
  ByVal e As System.Web.UI.WebControls.DataListItemEventArgs) _
  Handles dlPlaces.ItemDataBound
  ' Is the item selected?
  If e.Item.ItemType = ListItemType.SelectedItem Then
    ...
```

Note that even when you have given the control an ID, you need to use the `FindControl()` method (inherited from the base `Control` class) to access the label that contains the `AdministratorID` field value. To understand this, recall that the controls in the corresponding template are created *once for each row*. The e argument passed to this event handler (and to the others, too) has an `Item` property that contains the collection of controls created for the current item. You call `FindControl()` on this collection to retrieve the label:

```
' Locate the hidden Label containing the AdministratorID
Dim admin As Label = CType(e.Item.FindControl("lblAdministratorID"), Label)
```

If the current user ID matches the administrator ID, set the `Visible` property of `cmdEdit` to `True`. Note that you also need to find this command in the collection.

```
If admin.Text = Page.User.Identity.Name Then
  e.Item.FindControl("cmdEdit").Visible = True
End If
```

With the button visible, the user can start editing the item by clicking it, which causes the `EditCommand` event to be fired. In this handler, you save the index received in the DataList's `EditItemIndex` property and rebind the data. Note that the selected index is kept automatically by the DataList component, but the edit index is not, unfortunately. At this stage, the DataList control will render the interface shown in Figure 5-13.

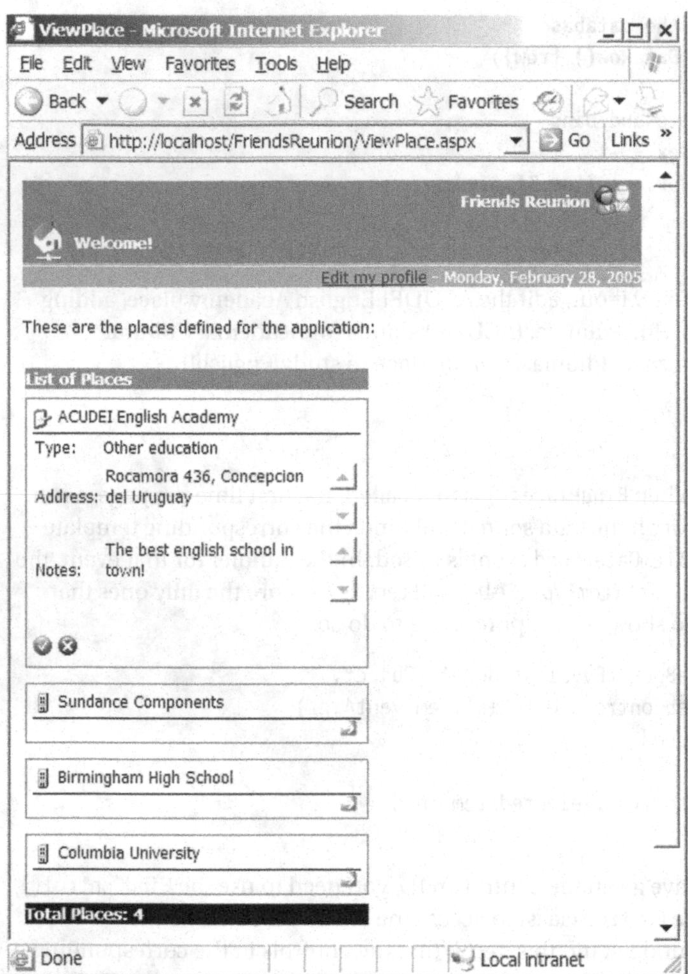

Figure 5-13. *The interface for editing places, with a DataList control*

Now the user can stop editing simply by navigating to another item. This is handled in the `SelectedIndexChanged` event handler, which resets any previous `EditItemIndex` value to -1 and calls `BindPlaces()` to refresh the display.

On the other hand, the user can click the Save or the Cancel button. If the user chooses the latter, the `CancelCommand` event is raised, in response to which you reset the `EditItemIndex` and set the `SelectedIndex` to the current element. The user will then be positioned in the element he or she was just editing.

If the user clicks the Save button, the `UpdateCommand` event is raised. The handler for this event first locates the controls with the data to be used for the update, as in:

```
Dim addr As TextBox = CType(e.Item.FindControl("txtAddress"), TextBox)
```

Then it gets a reference to the original row. To achieve this, first reload the dataset:

```
adPlaces.Fill(dsPlaces)
```

Then build a filtering expression with the `PlaceID` found in the corresponding (hidden) label:

```
Dim sql As String = "PlaceID = '" + place.Text + "'"
```

Then define a `row` variable using the corresponding typed dataset class, `Places.PlaceRow`:

```
  Dim row As PlaceData.PlaceRow = _
    CType(dsPlaces.Place.Select(sql)(0), PlaceData.PlaceRow)
```

Note that you use the `Select()` method of the `Place` table, which receives an expression with the same syntax as the `WHERE` SQL clause and returns an array of `DataRow` objects that match the request. You take the first element in the resulting array (`dsPlaces.Place.Select(sql)(0)`) and perform a type cast to assign the value to the `row` variable.

From this point, you have access to the typed properties of the row, and you use them to set the new values:

```
row.Address = addr.Text
row.Notes = notes.Text
```

Next, submit changes to the adapter:

```
adPlaces.Update(new DataRow[] {row})
```

Here, you use the overload of the `Update()` method that receives an array of `DataRow` objects. You initialize the array in the same method call with the single row edited. Because the adapter has a configured `UpdateCommand`, it will know how to submit changes in the row you passed to it to the database.

Finally, this event handler resets the DataList state and rebinds:

```
dlPlaces.EditItemIndex = -1
dlPlaces.SelectedIndex = e.Item.ItemIndex
dlPlaces.DataBind()
```

You don't call `BindPlaces()` here, because you've already loaded the dataset. And you know that you have at least one row, because you've just edited it!

Summary

Data access is essential for all but the most trivial web applications. However, the data-access code itself should not hinder a programmer's productivity. Easy and intuitive data facilities are crucial in any good development environment, and VS .NET, together with ADO.NET, fulfills both requirements. In this chapter, we looked at ADO.NET components and how they interact with the IDE to enhance our experience. You saw that VS .NET includes some powerful wizards and design-time advantages that have not previously been seen in a Microsoft IDE.

Components and data binding make the process of displaying and editing data a breeze. You learned how it works with simple controls, as well as with the more advanced DataGrid and DataList controls. You saw how the incredibly versatile templates can be used to achieve some real-world goals. Our Friends Reunion sample application became much more useful, and it's a good example of the possibilities of the new platform.

In the next chapter, you will learn about the importance of state in web applications, and you'll find out how ASP.NET overcomes the stateless nature of the HTTP protocol through its impressive state management features.

CHAPTER 6

ASP.NET State Management

Back in Chapter 1, we discussed the particularities of web applications and the *stateless nature* of the HTTP protocol. Every time a page is requested, the server processes it, returns it to the client, and completely forgets about it. The same happens on the client side: every page received is a completely new one, even if it comes from the same URL after a postback, for example. It's immediately evident that if you want to keep some information about the current users while they use the application—login information, selected items in a shopping basket, preferences about the site, filled form fields, selected values, and so on—you need some sort of mechanism from ASP.NET or HTML itself, as HTTP (the protocol) doesn't provide one.

The information we're referring to here is generally called the application *state*. In this chapter, we'll discuss the variety of state-handling features ASP.NET offers, as well as the more traditional approaches provided by HTML and browsers, and when to use each one. We'll build a search engine for the Friends Reunion case study application, taking advantage of all the state-related features to make it fast, resource-conservative, and developer- and user-friendly.

In this chapter, we'll cover the following topics:

- Where the state can be stored
- Different scopes available
- When you should use each one
- How to preserve server resources
- Server state configurations and options

State Storage and Scope

Let's start by saying that *state* is any kind of information that needs to remain active for a period of time. This period can be the entire application life, the time a user spends using it, the page life before the user browses to another page, and so forth. Examples of each are a global visitor counter, items selected while shopping on a site, and values entered in a form field.

You already know the HTTP protocol that drives web applications is *stateless*. With that fact in mind, there are only two places in which to store the state: the server or the client. The application on the server side—that is, ASP.NET—can keep this data in some place and provide the page developer with some way to retrieve and save values there. Alternatively, you can keep data on the client machine, and rely on the browser to submit it to the server each time a new request is performed, so that the application on the server side can use it.

ASP.NET provides mechanisms to save data on both sides, but usually, their categorization takes into account the *scope* of the data—where it can be accessed from and by whom. Table 6-1 shows the available state utilities in ASP.NET for the server, organized by the storage location used by each feature.

Table 6-1. *ASP.NET State Utilities for the Server*

Utility	Description
Application	Data that is accessible by all users during the entire life of the application
Session	Keeps state associated with each user (for example, a shopping basket)
Transient state	Data that lives only during the processing of a single request

Table 6-2 shows the state utilities for the client.

Table 6-2. *ASP.NET State Utilities for the Client*

Utility	Description
Viewstate	Retains data related to a page, such as filled-in form fields
Cookies	Keeps arbitrary data on the client browser
Query string	Passes values between the client and the server in the URL itself
Hidden form fields	Form fields containing data useful to the application but hidden from the user

We'll start by discussing the session state, and then move on to the application state and the rest of the utilities.

Session State

Some applications may need to keep user data while the user is surfing the site or performing some task that takes several steps, such as filling a shopping basket or proceeding to checkout. It would be impossible to get all the data required for those tasks in a single page, so you need a way to store such items. Of course, this data must be *private* to each user; selected items or credit card information must not be accessible to other users performing the same tasks!

The first problem ASP.NET faces here is the HTTP protocol's statelessness nature, as we already mentioned. There's no way the server can identify a returning user (the same user requesting another page, for example) just by looking at the HTTP request itself. So, whenever the session state is needed for a user, ASP.NET creates a random, unique ID called the *session ID*, and, by default, attaches it to the client in the form of a cookie, although you can have the session ID appended to the URL as well. (A *cookie* is a small piece of data, usually 4KB maximum, that is kept by the client browser and handed back to the server on each subsequent request.)

This way, ASP.NET can identify a returning user based on the user's saved session ID. This sort of identity card given to the user is reclaimed when the user leaves the application or the session times out. So the next time that user returns, a new identification will be created.

Note Creating a session ID to identify returning users doesn't imply they have been *authenticated*. Authentication is a different process, related to security, and is discussed in Chapter 10.

Some users may disable cookies in their browsers for security reasons, or they may even be disabled as a general corporate policy. Later, in the "Configuring the Session State" section, we'll describe a way to still gain the benefits of sessions without using cookies.

Based on the session ID, ASP.NET provides a separate store for each user. Once the user is identified, ASP.NET can provide access to it. The session data is accessible through an object of type `HttpSessionState`, which is available through any of the following class properties:

- `Page.Session`
- `Page.Context.Session`
- `HttpContext.Current.Session`

All of these properties point to the same object, which you can use to keep data. This code could be placed in a code-behind page to access the session data:

```
' Save a value to the session state
Session("creditcard") = txtCard.Text

' Retrieve the value later to proceed to checkout
Dim card As String = Session("creditcard")
```

Since all your pages inherit from `Page`, you can use `MyBase.Session`, `Me.Session`, or just `Session` to access this object, as in the example here.

The session object provides methods and properties that deal with the session, such as `Abandon()`, `Clear()`, `Count`, `Keys`, and others. You can refer to the MSDN help for a list of members and what they are used for (most of the member names are fairly self-explanatory).

You'll now use the session state in a new feature you'll add to the Friends Reunion case study application. Up to now, users have been able to log in and see some news related to them, such as requests for contact and approved contacts, but so far, there's no way for them to search for fellow users. You'll add this search facility, and also allow the user to perform searches within previous results, in order to narrow the initial search. This is a good place to use the session state, as the whole dataset can be kept there to perform subsequent narrowing searches against it.

An important consideration to take into account is that the session state is held on the *server*, thus consuming resources. If you allowed users to perform very wide searches, with potentially thousands of records being retrieved from the database (assuming your application is popular enough!) and saved to the session state, the server would be brought to its knees very soon. So, we will use a configurable limit of maximum allowed results for the search engine, through the application configuration file, Web.config. This is common practice in most search engines, even Microsoft's.

Try It Out: Create a Search Engine You'll add a Search page to allow users to search for their missing friends.

1. Add a new web form to the application, called Search.aspx.
2. Add the following new styles to the iestyle.css stylesheet (notice the use of shorthand notation for both the border and padding).

```
.MediumTextBox
{
  border: solid 1px #c7ccdc;
  font-size: 8pt;
  font-family: Tahoma, Verdana, 'Times New Roman';
  width: 140px;
}
.Search
{
  border: solid 1px silver;
  padding: 5px 5px 5px 5px;
  background-color: gainsboro;
  width: 250px;
}
.SearchResults
{
  padding: 5px 5px 5px 5px;
}
```

3. Just as you did in previous chapters, drag-and-drop the stylesheet file on the form to link to it.
4. Import the following namespaces at the top of the code-behind page:

```
Imports System.Configuration
Imports System.Data.SqlClient
Imports System.Text
```

5. Make the page inherit from FriendsBase and add the icon and page header message:

```
 Public Class Search
  Inherits FriendsBase
  Private Sub Page_Load(ByVal sender As System.Object, _
    ByVal e As System.EventArgs) Handles MyBase.Load
    ' Configure the icon and message
    MyBase.HeaderIconImageUrl = "~/Images/search.gif"
    MyBase.HeaderMessage = "Search Users"
  End Sub
End Class
    ...
```

6. Insert an HTML Table control using Table ➤ Insert ➤ Table. Give the table one row and two cells. Make the border 0 and the width 100%. Set the resulting table's id to tbResults and the two cells' valign attribute to top.

7. Switch to the source HTML view and add the following code inside the first <td> element.

```
<td valign="top">
  <asp:panel id="pnlResults" cssclass="SearchResults" runat="server">
    Search results:
    <hr width="100%" size="1">
    <asp:label id="lblLimit" runat="server" /><br><br>
    <asp:datagrid id="grdResults" runat="server" />
  </asp:panel>
</td>
```

This is the panel that will hold the results from the search.

8. Switch to the Design view again. Inside the second cell element, drop a web forms Panel control named pnlSearch, set its CssClass to Search, and type **Search Friends Reunion:** inside it. Drop an HTML Horizontal Rule (<hr> element) next to the text, and insert an HTML Table control below it, with two columns and seven rows. It should have border set to 0 and width to 100%. The last row in the table should have only one cell with its colspan property set to 2.

9. In the table's left-hand cells, type the following text: **First Name:**, **Last Name:**, **Place:**, **Type:**, **Year In:**, and **Year Out:**. Drop four TextBox controls next to the name and year fields. Drop two DropDownList controls (also known as combo boxes) next to the place and type fields. Finally, drop two Button controls in the last table row. The panel should look like the one shown in Figure 6-1.

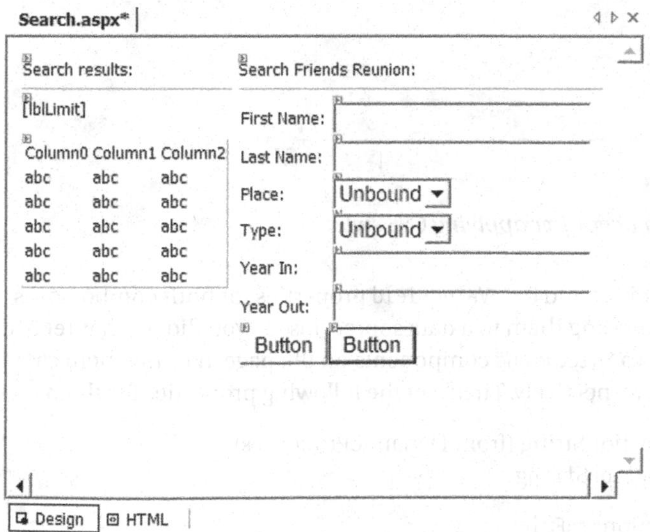

Figure 6-1. *The Search page design*

10. Set the following ID properties for the controls, working down the page through them, and set their properties as shown. When you're finished the form should look like Figure 6-2.

   - txtFirstName: `CssClass` to `MediumTextBox`
   - txtLastName: `CssClass` to `MediumTextBox`
   - cbPlace: `CssClass` to `MediumTextBox`; `DataTextField` to `Name`; `DataValueField` to `PlaceID`
   - cbType: `CssClass` to `MediumTextBox`; `DataTextField` to `Name`; `DataValueField` to `TypeID`
   - txtYearIn: `CssClass` to `SmallTextBox`
   - txtYearOut: `CssClass` to `SmallTextBox`
   - btnSearch: `CssClass` to `Button`; `Text` to **New Search**
   - btnSearchResults: `CssClass` to `Button`; `Text` to **Within Results**

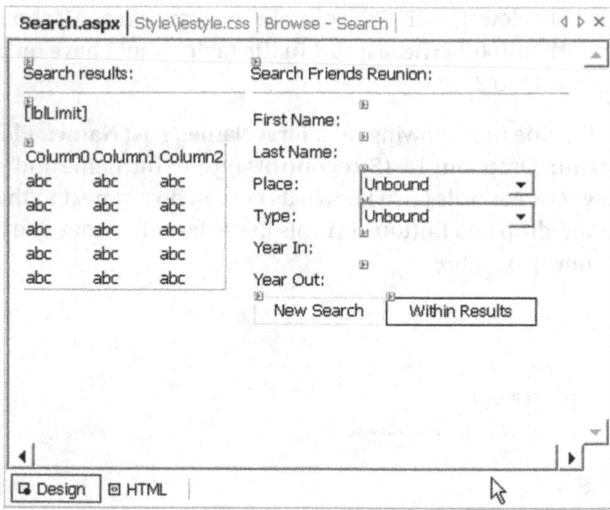

Figure 6-2. *The Search page after applying CSS styles*

11. You set the `DataTextField` and `DataValueField` properties for both combo boxes because you will be binding them to a data source. Just as you did in Chapter 5, drop a `SqlConnection` and two `SqlCommand` components on the page, naming them `cnFriends`, `cmPlace`, and `cmType`, respectively. Then, set the following properties for them:

   - cnFriends.ConnectionString (from DynamicProperties): `cnFriends.ConnectionString`
   - cmPlace.Connection: `cnFriends`

- cmPlace.CommandText: `SELECT PlaceID, Name FROM Place ORDER BY Name`
- cmType.Connection: `cnFriends`
- cmType.CommandText: `SELECT TypeID, Name FROM PlaceType ORDER BY Name`

12. Now load the results of both commands into the combo boxes in the `Page_Load()` method:

```
Private Sub Page_Load(ByVal sender As System.Object,
  ByVal e As System.EventArgs) Handles MyBase.Load
  ' Configure the icon and message
  MyBase.HeaderIconImageUrl = "~/Images/search.gif"
  MyBase.HeaderMessage = "Search Users"

  cnFriends.Open()
  ' Initialize combo boxes
  Try
    Dim reader As SqlDataReader = cmPlace.ExecuteReader()
    Try
      cbPlace.DataSource = reader
      cbPlace.DataBind()
      cbPlace.Items.Add(New ListItem("-- Not selected --", "0"))
      cbPlace.SelectedIndex = cbPlace.Items.Count - 1
    Finally
      reader.Close()
    End Try

    reader = cmType.ExecuteReader()
    Try
      cbType.DataSource = reader
      cbType.DataBind()
      cbType.Items.Add(New ListItem("-- Not selected --", "0"))
      cbType.SelectedIndex = cbType.Items.Count - 1
    Finally
      reader.Close()
    End Try
  Finally
    cnFriends.Close()
  End Try
End Sub
```

You have used data binding before, in Chapter 5, so you already know what's involved, but this time you're binding directly to a `SqlDataReader` object. The `DataTextField` and `DataValueField` properties of the combo boxes define which values to load from the data source. As you learned in previous chapters, a data reader is fast, read-only, and forward-only—everything that's needed to load the data controls. You manually add an item to allow the user to specify that no filter should be applied for that field. You want to make sure to always enclose your accesses to data readers in `Try..Finally` blocks to ensure the underlying database connection is always closed.

13. Drop a `DataSet` on the page and select the Untyped option from the dialog box. You will use it to load the results of the query. Set its name to `dsResults`. You are using a `DataSet` instead of a data reader, because you will need this object later to perform refining searches. A data reader object, being a connected and forward-only cursor, isn't suitable for this purpose.

14. Now you need to prepare the data properties of the DataGrid control you added manually to the page source in step 7 to support data binding to this new dataset. Set the `grdResults.DataMember` property to `User`. Set the `grdResults.DataSource` property to `dsResults`.

15. Double-click the New Search button and add the following code to the handler, which will perform the initial search and save the results to the session state. It's mostly string-manipulation code and command-parameter initialization, as you can see.

```
Private Sub btnSearch_Click(ByVal sender As System.Object, _
  ByVal e As System.EventArgs) Handles btnSearch.Click

  Dim limit As Integer = Convert.ToInt32(
    ConfigurationSettings.AppSettings("searchLimit"))

  Dim sql As New StringBuilder
  ' Limit maximum resultset size
  sql.Append("SELECT TOP ").Append(limit)
  sql.Append(" [User].UserID, [User].FirstName, [User].LastName, ")
  sql.Append(" Place.PlaceID, Place.Name AS PlaceName, ")
  sql.Append(" PlaceType.Name AS PlaceType, PlaceType.TypeID, ")
  sql.Append(" TimeLapse.Name AS LapseName, TimeLapse.YearIn, ")
  sql.Append(" TimeLapse.MonthIn, TimeLapse.YearOut, ")
  sql.Append(" TimeLapse.MonthOut ")
  sql.Append("FROM [User] ")
  sql.Append("LEFT OUTER JOIN TimeLapse ON ")
  sql.Append(" TimeLapse.UserID = [User].UserID ")
  sql.Append("LEFT OUTER JOIN Place ON ")
  sql.Append(" Place.PlaceID = TimeLapse.PlaceID ")
  sql.Append("LEFT OUTER JOIN PlaceType ON ")
  sql.Append(" Place.TypeID = PlaceType.TypeID ")

  ' Build the WHERE clause and accumulate parameter values now
  Dim values As Hashtable = New Hashtable
  Dim qry As StringBuilder = New StringBuilder
  If Not (txtFirstName.Text = String.Empty) Then
    qry.Append("[User].FirstName LIKE @FName AND ")
    values.Add("@FName", "%" & txtFirstName.Text & "%")
  End If
  If Not (txtLastName.Text = String.Empty) Then
    qry.Append("[User].LastName LIKE @LName AND ")
```

```
  values.Add("@LName", "%" & txtLastName.Text & "%")
End If
' All other values can take advantage of ADO.NET parameters
If Not (cbPlace.SelectedValue = "0") Then
  qry.Append("[Place].PlaceID = @PlaceID AND ")
  values.Add("@PlaceID", cbPlace.SelectedValue)
End If
If Not (cbType.SelectedValue = "0") Then
  qry.Append("[PlaceType].TypeID = @TypeID AND ")
  values.Add("@TypeID", cbType.SelectedValue)
End If
If Not (txtYearIn.Text = String.Empty) Then
  qry.Append("TimeLapse.YearIn = @YearIN AND ")
  values.Add("@YearIN", txtYearIn.Text)
End If
If Not (txtYearOut.Text = String.Empty) Then
  qry.Append("TimeLapse.YearOut = @YearOut AND ")
  values.Add("@YearOut", txtYearOut.Text)
End If

Dim filter As String = qry.ToString()
If Not (filter.Length = 0) Then
  ' Add the filter without the trailing AND
  sql.Append(" WHERE ").Append(filter.Remove(filter.Length - 4, 4))
End If

Dim ad As SqlDataAdapter = New SqlDataAdapter(sql.ToString(), cnFriends)
' Now add all parameters to the select command
For Each prm As DictionaryEntry In values
  ad.SelectCommand.Parameters.Add(prm.Key.ToString(), prm.Value)
Next

dsResults = New DataSet
ad.Fill(dsResults, "User")

' Adjust label for results
If dsResults.Tables("User").Rows.Count < limit Then
  lblLimit.Text = "Found " & _
  dsResults.Tables("User").Rows.Count & _
  " users matching your criteria on initial search."
Else
  lblLimit.Text = "You're working with the first " & _
    limit & " results.<br/>" & _
    "If you're looking for someone who's not in this list, " & _
    "please search again with a more precise search criterion."
End If
```

```
  ' Place results in session state
  Session("search") = dsResults
  BindFromSession()
End Sub
```

16. The method called at the end, BindFromSession(), performs the actual binding from the dataset found in the session. Add its code below the previous event handler.

```
Private Sub BindFromSession()
  dsResults = CType(Session("search"), DataSet)
  grdResults.DataBind()
End Sub
```

We created a separate method in order to call the same binding method from the code that narrows search results.

17. Double-click the Within Results button and add the following code to the handler. This handler will filter the previously retrieved dataset with further criteria, using the dataset's Select() method.

```
Private Sub btnSearchResults_Click(ByVal sender As System.Object,
  ByVal e As System.EventArgs) Handles btnSearchResults.Click

  dsResults = CType(Session("search"), DataSet)
  ' If we can't get the previous results, then we lost session
  ' information (failure), or no previous results were available
  ' Default to normal search
  If dsResults Is Nothing Then
    btnSearch_Click(sender, e)
  End If

  ' We can't use parameters as this is a common filter
  ' expression to use with the DataSet
  Dim qry As StringBuilder = New StringBuilder
  If txtFirstName.Text.Length > 0 Then
    qry.Append("FirstName LIKE '%")
    qry.Append(txtFirstName.Text).Append("%' AND ")
  End If
  If txtLastName.Text.Length > 0 Then
    qry.Append("LastName LIKE '%")
    qry.Append(txtLastName.Text).Append("%' AND ")
  End If
  If cbPlace.SelectedItem.Value <> "0" Then
    qry.Append("PlaceID = '")
    qry.Append(cbPlace.SelectedItem.Value).Append("' AND ")
  End If
  If cbType.SelectedItem.Value <> "0" Then
    qry.Append("TypeID = '")
```

```
      qry.Append(cbType.SelectedItem.Value).Append("' AND ")
    End If
    If txtYearIn.Text.Length > 0 Then
      qry.Append("YearIn = ")
      qry.Append(txtYearIn.Text).Append(" AND ")
    End If
    If txtYearOut.Text.Length > 0 Then
      qry.Append("YearOut = ")
      qry.Append(txtYearOut.Text).Append(" AND ")
    End If

    Dim filter As String = qry.ToString()
    If Not (filter.Length = 0) Then
      filter = filter.Remove(filter.Length - 4, 4)
    End If
    Dim rows As DataRow() = dsResults.Tables("User").Select(filter)

    ' Rebuild results with new filtered set of rows,
    ' maintaining structure
    dsResults = dsResults.Clone()
    For Each row As DataRow In rows
      dsResults.Tables("User").ImportRow(row)
    Next

    ' Place results in session state
    Session("search") = dsResults
    BindFromSession()
  End Sub
```

18. As the search results may now be saved to the session state, you could check for that when the page is loaded, and automatically bind the DataGrid control if the data is there. Add the following lines immediately before the end of the `Page_Load()` method:

```
If Not Session("search") Is Nothing Then
  BindFromSession()
End If
```

19. You're almost finished. Recall that in the `btn_Search` handler, you're using a setting from the `Web.config` file that specifies the limit of rows retrieved from a search. Add this setting to the configuration file:

```
<appSettings>
  ...
  <add key="searchLimit" value="10" />
</appSettings>
```

You set it to this very low value in order to see it in action with the small set of test data included with the sample database.

20. Finally, add the link in the Default.aspx page to allow the users to access the search feature. As you learned in Chapter 4, you can do this by placing the following code in the If block of the Page_Load() method:

```
' ----- Search button ----
' Create a new blank table row, this time for Search link
row = New TableRow
' Search link
img = New System.Web.UI.WebControls.Image
img.ImageUrl = "Images/search.gif"
img.ImageAlign = ImageAlign.Middle
img.Width = New Unit(24, UnitType.Pixel)
img.Height = New Unit(24, UnitType.Pixel)

' Create the cell and add the image
cell = New TableCell
cell.Controls.Add(img)
'  Add the cell to the row
row.Cells.Add(cell)

' Set up the Search link
lnk = New HyperLink
lnk.Text = "Search"
lnk.NavigateUrl = "Search.aspx"

'  Create the cell and add the link
cell = New TableCell
cell.Controls.Add(lnk)
' Add the new cell to the row
row.Cells.Add(cell)

' Add the new row to the table
tb.Rows.Add(row)
```

21. You are now ready to test the search engine by setting Search.aspx as the start page and compiling and running the application as usual.

How It Works

If you perform a search with all the fields empty, you should see something like the page shown in Figure 6-3.

We'll improve the DataGrid control as we go, because we surely don't want all those GUIDs being displayed, right? What's important to notice up front is the message being displayed. It states that we're working with the first ten records, because the initial search exceeded that limit. If we set a lower value, the message will change accordingly.

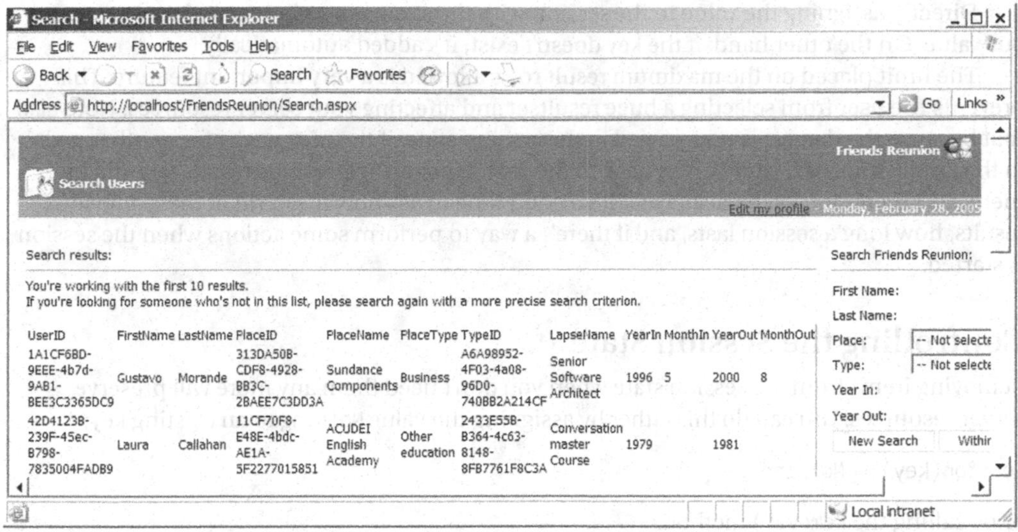

Figure 6-3. *Performing a search without specifying criteria*

Tip In the code that built the query, we used ADO.NET parameters with the query exclusively. This makes for a more secure application, because by using parameters, you avoid the most common types of so-called *SQL injection* attacks. This is an advanced topic, but you should be aware of its existence and take advantage of parameters whenever you can. You can read the article at `http://www.securityfocus.com/infocus/1768` as a starting point, or search Google for more information on the subject.

Now try to narrow the search by specifying 1984 in the Year In field and clicking the Within Results button (filtering through the combo boxes won't work yet, but you will see what's wrong when we get to the "Viewstate" section). This time, instead of hitting the database again, the search is performed in-memory on the server, a feature offered by the `DataSet` class. You're retrieving only the matching rows from the previously saved dataset:

```
Dim rows As DataRow() = dsResults.Tables("User").Select(filter)
```

Note that after you get the rows satisfying the new filter, you clone the structure of the saved dataset and start importing the rows into its `User` table:

```
dsResults = dsResults.Clone()
For Each row As DataRow In rows
  dsResults.Tables("User").ImportRow(row)
Next
```

The code that follows is just like the version that searches against the database. The dataset is saved to the session, and the helper method, `BindFromSession()`, is called:

```
Session("search") = dsResults
BindFromSession()
```

Directly assigning the value to the session with the same key as before replaces any previous value. On the other hand, if the key doesn't exist, it's added automatically.

The limit placed on the maximum result rows allowed is a very important feature. This prevents the user from selecting a huge resultset and affecting your server resources. Note also that because the dataset is now placed in the session state, if the user navigates to other pages in the application and later comes back to the search page, the previous results will still be there, and therefore will be displayed. It's a good time to ask how to get rid of those previous results, how long a session lasts, and if there's a way to perform some actions when the session is started.

Controlling the Session State

Removing items from the session state when you don't need them any more will preserve server resources. You can do this either by assigning the value `Nothing` to an existing key:

```
Session(key) = Nothing
```

or by calling the `Remove()` method:

```
Session.Remove(key)
```

Even though both effectively remove the reference to the item, thus allowing the garbage collector to remove the object from memory, the latter is more appropriate, because it completely removes both the value and the associated key.

You can also use the `Clear()` method, which removes all items and their corresponding keys.

Try It Out: Remove Session State Items Now you'll improve the Search page. The users will be able to perform some actions related to their search results, such as clearing the items, and you'll add other actions as we go.

1. In the `Search.aspx` file, add a panel below `pnlSearch` (which you created in the previous exercise). Insert a line break (press Shift+Enter) immediately after the search panel on the right of the page, and drop a Panel control. Name it `pnlActions` and set its `CssClass` to `Search`.

2. Enter the text **Actions:** inside the panel, and drop an HTML horizontal rule next to it, but still inside the panel.

3. Insert an HTML Table control below the rule, with only one row (you will add more later) and two columns. Set the `border` property to `0`, `cellpadding` to 4, and `width` to 100%.

4. Drop a web server ImageButton control on the leftmost cell, with the following properties:

    - ImageUrl: `Images/results.gif`
    - Tooltip: **Clear all results from the search**
    - (ID): `btnClearResults`

5. Type the text **Clear Results** in the rightmost cell, and set the cell's `width` to 100%. The form should look like Figure 6-4 now.

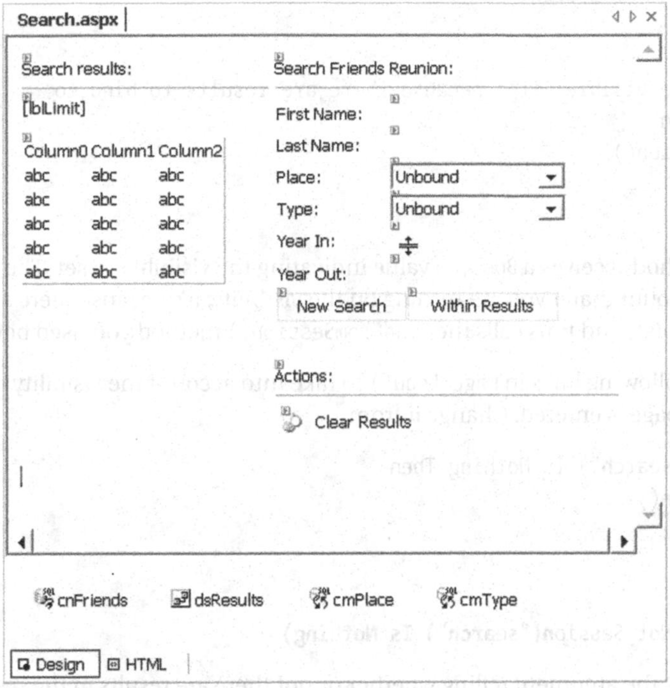

Figure 6-4. *The Search page with a new section for actions*

6. Double-click the ImageButton control to get to the event handler, and then enter the following code:

```
Private Sub btnClearResults_Click(ByVal sender As System.Object, _
  ByVal e As System.Web.UI.ImageClickEventArgs) Handles btnClearResults.Click
  Session.Remove("search")
  SetResultsState(False)
End Sub
```

7. Once the results have been cleared, you don't want the actions panel to display anymore. Also, you want to hide the results panel altogether, leaving just the search panel visible, and hide the button to perform refined searches, too. When a new search is performed though, you want to restore the visibility of all those controls. Additionally, you are setting the `btnSearch` text to something more meaningful, depending on visibility. For that purpose, create the helper `SetResultsState()` method:

```
Private Sub SetResultsState(ByVal visible As Boolean)
  pnlActions.Visible = visible
  pnlResults.Visible = visible
  btnSearchResults.Visible = visible
```

```
    If visible Then
      btnSearch.Text = "New search"
    Else
      btnSearch.Text = "Search"
    End If

    ' If setting to visible, it's because there are results to bind to
    If visible Then
      BindFromSession()
    End If
  End Sub
```

Note that the method receives a `Boolean` value indicating the visibility to set. The last line takes into account that if you are turning on the visibility, it's because there are new results to display, and thus calls the `BindFromSession()` method you used before.

8. Now modify the following lines in `Page_Load()` to take into account the visibility of panels when the page is entered. Change it from:

```
If Not Session("search") Is Nothing Then
  BindFromSession()
End If
```

to:

```
SetResultsState(Not Session("search") Is Nothing)
```

Note that you pass the argument telling whether or not there are results in the session state.

9. To restore this visibility in `btnSearch_Click`, replace the following line:

```
BindFromSession()
```

with:

```
SetResultsState(True)
```

10. Save and run the page.

How It Works

The most important bit of code here is when you remove the object from the session state:

```
Session.Remove("search")
```

Toggling visibility of items depending on the session state presence makes the page shown in Figure 6-5 appear the first time now.

To gain more granular control over the session state, ASP.NET provides two events that are fired at different points during the life of the user session: `Start` and `End`.

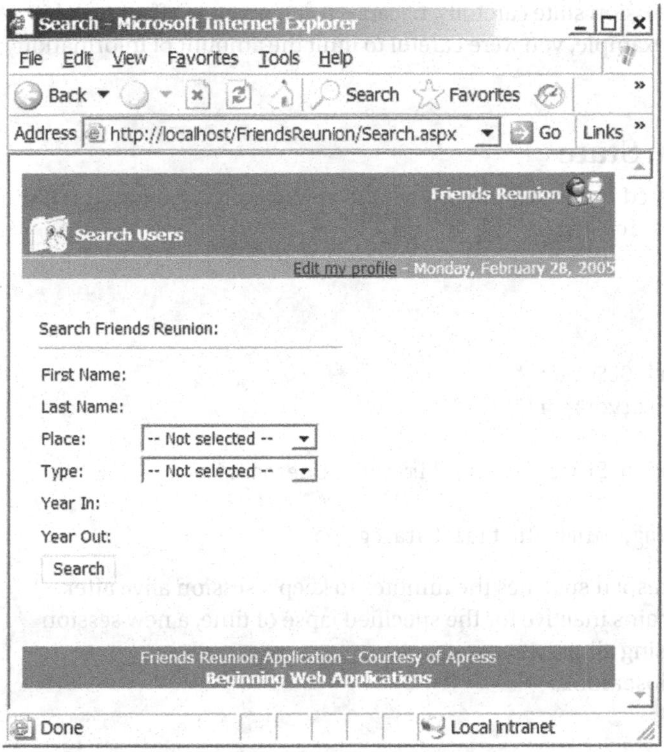

Figure 6-5. *On the Search page, selective controls' visibility depends on the session state items.*

You can attach event handlers for them through the special file `Global.asax`. This file allows you to add handlers to these kinds of events, which are global in the sense that they don't happen inside a single page or control. They belong to the web application as a whole. You'll use other global events later in this chapter. For now, you need to use only the following special syntax in the `Global.asax` code-behind file to handle the session `Start` and `End` events:

```
Sub Session_Start(ByVal sender As Object, ByVal e As EventArgs)
   ' Fires when the session is started
End Sub

Sub Session_End(ByVal sender As Object, ByVal e As EventArgs)
   ' Fires when the session ends
End Sub
```

The empty signatures are already placed there whenever you start a new web application. A good use of such methods would be, for example, to release expensive or locked resources, such as a file or a database connection, if you keep it in the session state (a generally unadvisable practice, given the fact that ADO.NET already provides connection pooling), or to initialize some context related to the user as soon as the session starts, such as reloading a previously saved shopping cart. Note that the `Session_End()` event will be fired only when using `InProc` mode for the `sessionState` configuration element, as explained in the next section.

However, you should use the session state carefully, because it can severely affect scalability if it's used without care. In this example, you were careful to limit the amount of information placed there as a result of a search.

Configuring the Session State

You can tweak several settings related to this feature though the application configuration file, in a section called (guess what) sessionState:

```
<sessionState
  timeout="timeout in minutes"
  cookieless="[true|false]"
  mode="[Off|InProc|StateServer|SQLServer]"
  stateConnectionString="tcpip=server:port"
  stateNetworkTimeout=
      "for network operations with State Server, timeout in seconds"
  sqlConnectionString=
      "valid SqlConnection string, minus Initial Catalog" />
```

The first attribute is easy to grasp; it specifies the minutes to keep a session alive after activity has ceased. If the user remains inactive for the specified lapse of time, a new session will be created afterwards, thus losing all previous state.

The other settings require a closer look.

Session IDs and Cookies

When we introduced the session state, we said the generated session ID is stored by default in a cookie, which is later read by ASP.NET on further requests to determine the session state to associate with the current user. We also said that some users may have disabled cookies in their browsers, so how do you enable the session state for them?

The answer lies in the second setting for the sessionState configuration element:

```
cookieless="[true|false]"
```

When you set the cookieless value to true, ASP.NET will append the session ID to the URL itself, and append it to any *relative* URL existing on the requested page. If you simply change this setting in Web.config, and navigate to Search.aspx (you can click the link in the home page), you will notice the change in the URL shown in the Address box.

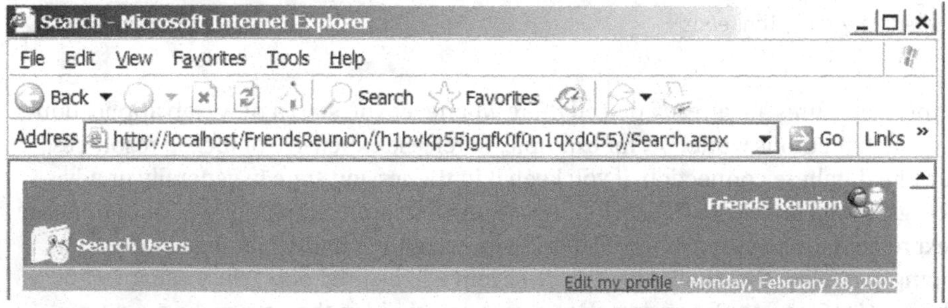

You should be aware that this mechanism adds a processing step. This is because all the links in the page must be rewritten to include the session ID, and further requested URLs must be parsed to extract it and to get the actual resource URL (without the session ID).

Note ASP.NET dynamically adds the session ID to all *relative* links, but not to *fully qualified* links.

You should check that the URLs you add at design-time are always relative if they point to resources in the same application. This way, a migration to cookieless session mode will not affect the application's behavior.

State Modes

Up to now, we never said where the objects you place in the session object are stored. ASP.NET provides three options when it comes to session state storage, configurable through the mode setting and related attributes:

```
mode="[Off|InProc|StateServer|SQLServer]"
```

The following sections explain what the different modes mean.

InProc Mode

`InProc` is the default setting. All the state is kept in-memory, in the same AppDomain that is running the application. This provides maximum performance, but if the application is restarted, or the process hangs for some reason, all the session data associated with your users is lost. This may be acceptable in many scenarios, but you need to keep this possibility in mind.

Note An application domain (or AppDomain) is a new concept in .NET. It's similar to the concept of a process, in that it represents a boundary of application isolation. However, multiple AppDomains can exist in a single operating system process.

StateServer Mode

The `StateServer` mode allows you to separate the state storage from the process that is running your application. It is used in conjunction with the following two attributes:

```
stateConnectionString="tcpip=server:port"
stateNetworkTimeout="for network operations with State Server, timeout in seconds"
```

You can specify the address and port of the machine that will keep the state information in its own process and memory. This isolates the state from your application, protecting it from failures. In the state server machine, you need to start the ASP.NET State service, either from the Services console or from the command prompt with the following command:

```
> net start aspnet_state
```

You can configure this service to be started automatically, too. You can specify that the state server be the same machine holding your application by setting the IP to 127.0.0.1. This will protect the state from application restarts, but not from machine restarts. You should also note that taking the state storage out of the application process imposes a performance impact, especially if the state server is located in another machine on the network, as it not only involves the necessary network traffic, but also serialization of all data that must travel through it. You should carefully determine if retaining your session information justifies this impact.

Note In .NET version 1.1, `SessionState` has been modified to not allow connections from locations other than localhost (127.0.0.1). You must explicitly tweak a Registry setting to allow for this.

SQLServer Mode

If you absolutely *must* preserve the session state at all costs, the `SQLServer` mode setting is for you. This mode saves all the session state in a SQL Server database, so it can survive any failure in your application, server, and even database server (provided the database itself survives!). Setting this mode involves configuring the following attribute of the `sessionState` element:

```
sqlConnectionString="valid SqlConnection string, minus Initial Catalog"
```

You also need to run a script to prepare the required database where the state is stored. It is usually located in the Windows directory at `Microsoft.NET\Framework\[version]\InstallSqlState.sql`. (For ASP.NET version 1.0, the version is `v1.0.3705`; for version 1.1, it's `v1.1.4322`.)

Fortunately, you don't need SQL Server 2000 Query Analyzer to run this script. MSDE comes with a command-line utility called `osql`. The following command will run the script on the server and prepare the database and tables needed to hold state:

```
> osql -S [servername] -U [login] -P [pwd] < InstallSqlState.sql
```

You can use `(local)` as the server name to install in the current machine. You could even have clustered SQL Servers for maximum reliability. This mode is the most robust way to protect critical session state, but it is the most expensive in terms of performance. A round-trip to the database will be needed for each request, which can severely affect the application responsiveness. Also, the processing cost of serialization and the network may become bottlenecks under high load.

The most important impact for application performance is the network hop. If you'll keep the session state in a separate machine, `SQLServer` mode is certainly far more reliable and preferable to `StateServer`, since you'll be paying the network cost anyway.

Application State

Sometimes, you need to keep some data *globally* available to *all* users, who can share it. Of course, you can think of a database record as application-level state: all users can query it as needed. The performance impact would be unacceptable though, especially if it's used very often. Additionally, it involves several steps, such as opening the connection, issuing a query, and managing the results, just as you learned in Chapter 4. What's more, you would be limited to storing records, not arbitrary objects.

Tip You could actually use serialization to store objects. You can find information about object serialization in the MSDN documentation. Search for Serializing Objects in the index of the *.NET Framework Developer's Guide* topics.

To make matters easy, ASP.NET supports the concept of an *application state*. Each web application has its own set of globally available state, which can be accessed and used as easily as the session state. The data is held in an object of type `HttpApplicationState`, which is available through any of the following class properties:

- `Page.Application`
- `Page.Context.Application`
- `HttpContext.Current.Application`

This kind of state is obviously kept on the server side, too. Notice that the storage options available for the session state (state server and SQL Server) are not available for the application state, which will be lost on application or machine restarts.

Usually, the application state is loaded from some permanent store (a database for example) when the application is started, and saved for later use (if it's appropriate) when the application ends. These events, just like their session counterparts, can be handled in the `Global.asax` file:

```
Sub Application_Start(ByVal sender As Object, ByVal e As EventArgs)
  ' Fires when the application is started
End Sub

Sub Application_End(ByVal sender As Object, ByVal e As EventArgs)
  ' Fires when the application ends
End Sub
```

During the application's life, the application state is used anywhere you need it—retrieving it, changing its value, and so on. But because it's available to all users simultaneously, you must take care of *concurrency*. For example, if you implement a global counter of visitors and increment its value any time a new session is started, it's possible that between the retrieval of the current counter and the saving of the new incremented value, another user increments the value, too, so the second write will overwrite the previous value. What you need is to synchronize access to the application value when you are about to change it. The `HttpApplicationState` object provides two methods to do just that:

```
Application.Lock()
' Read and change values
Application.UnLock()
```

The code that accesses the application state between the Lock() and UnLock() method calls is protected from concurrency; that is, it's guaranteed to be executed by only one user at a time. Note that other users trying to access the application state during the lock will be blocked until the lock is released, so you should use locking for the minimum possible time.

Let's now implement all these features in a global counter of visitors to the Friends Reunion application.

Try It Out: Implement a Global Counter You will increment the counter when new sessions start, and display this value in the footer user control you created back in Chapter 3.

1. Open the Global.asax code-behind page and add the following code to the Session_Start() skeleton code:

```
Sub Session_Start(ByVal sender As Object, ByVal e As EventArgs)
  Application.Lock()
  If Application("counter") Is Nothing Then
    Application("counter") = 1
  Else
    Application("counter") = CType(Application("counter"), Integer) + 1
  End If
  Application.UnLock()
End Sub
```

2. Open FriendsFooter.ascx in the Design view. Below the existing content, add the text **This site has had**, followed by a Label control with an ID of lblCounter, followed by the text **visitors**, as shown here.

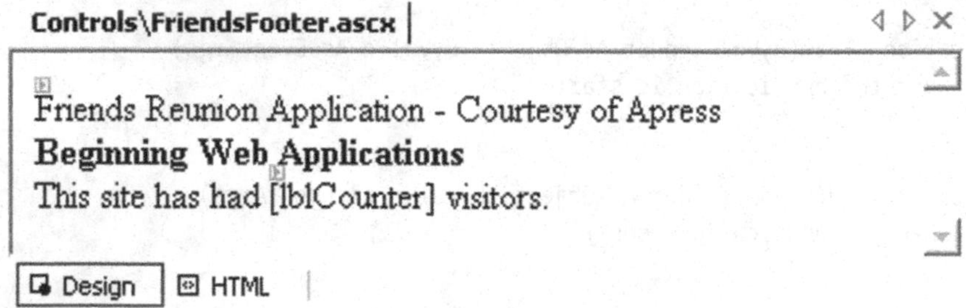

3. Open the code-behind page for this user control and add the following code:

```
Private Sub Page_Load(ByVal sender As System.Object, _
  ByVal e As System.EventArgs) Handles MyBase.Load
  lblCounter.Text = Application("counter").ToString()
End Sub
```

4. Save and run the pages of the application to see the results.

How It Works

When you start the application again, a new session is created. Because the application has just been started, the counter application state value will be Nothing, so the value 1 is assigned directly. The footer then retrieves this value and displays accordingly, as shown in Figure 6-6.

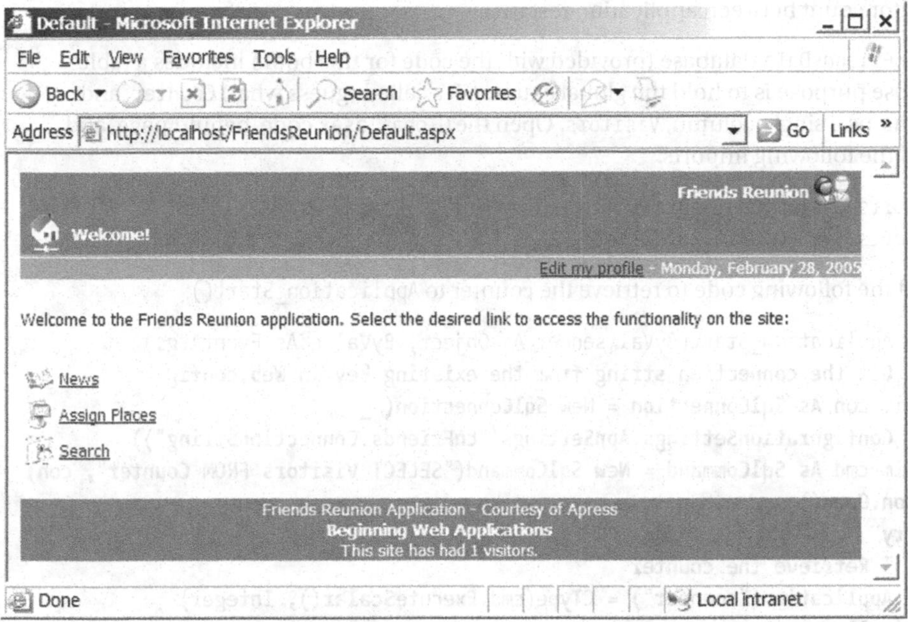

Figure 6-6. *The Welcome page with a counter added to the footer*

As you will remember, session IDs are saved by default as a browser cookie, so to simulate a new user session, you can just browse to the application using another browser, such as Mozilla, Netscape, or Firefox, or restart the current browser and navigate back to the application. ASP.NET will not find the session cookie and will thus believe you're a new user. This time, the handler in `Session_Start()` will find the previous value in the application state, and will increment it.

Notice that you have protected the code that performs the increment using `Lock()` and `UnLock()` methods.

Now try adding a blank line to the application `Web.config` file. Save it and refresh the page. Oops, the counter is again set to 1! What happened is that any change to the application configuration results in an application restart, so that the new settings take effect. The same would happen if the ASP.NET process were stopped and restarted for some reason, such as a failure. Of course, a global counter that resets automatically every time the application is restarted isn't of much use!

Note Any change to `Web.config` (either the root one or anyone in subfolders) or `Global.asax` results in an application restart.

If you want to preserve and later restore the application state from some permanent storage such as a file or a database, you can do so in the global events described earlier in this section.

Try It Out: Preserve and Restore the Application State You will now fix the counter so that it retains the site visitor count between application restarts.

1. The FriendsData database (provided with the code for this book) includes a table whose purpose is to hold the global counter. It's called (guess what) Counter, and contains a single column, Visitors. Open the Global.asax code-behind page, and add the following imports:

```
Imports System.Configuration
Imports System.Data.SqlClient
```

2. Add the following code to retrieve the counter to Application_Start():

```
Sub Application_Start(ByVal sender As Object, ByVal e As EventArgs)
  ' Get the connection string from the existing key in Web.config
  Dim con As SqlConnection = New SqlConnection( _
    ConfigurationSettings.AppSettings("cnFriends.ConnectionString"))
  Dim cmd As SqlCommand = New SqlCommand("SELECT Visitors FROM Counter", con)
  con.Open()
  Try
    ' Retrieve the counter
    Application("counter") = CType(cmd.ExecuteScalar(), Integer)
  Finally
    con.Close()
  End Try
End Sub
```

3. Add the following code to save the counter to Application_End():

```
Sub Application_End(ByVal sender As Object, ByVal e As EventArgs)
  ' Get the connection string from the existing key in Web.config
  Dim con As SqlConnection = New SqlConnection(
    ConfigurationSettings.AppSettings("cnFriends.ConnectionString"))
  Dim cmd As SqlCommand = New SqlCommand(
    "UPDATE Counter SET Visitors=" + Application("counter").ToString(), con)
  con.Open()
  Try
    cmd.ExecuteNonQuery()
  Finally
    con.Close()
  End Try
End Sub
```

4. Let's modify the Session_Start() event, as the counter will always be there now, since it will be initialized by Application_Start():

```
Sub Session_Start(ByVal sender As Object, ByVal e As EventArgs)
  Application.Lock()
  If Application("counter") Is Nothing Then
    Application("counter") = 1
  Else
    Application("counter") = CType(Application("counter"), Integer) + 1
  End If
  Application.UnLock()
End Sub
```

5. From the Server Explorer, set an initial value on the `Visitor` field of the `Counter` table.
6. Save and run the application to see what differences the changes in the code have made.

How It Works

The counter is now kept in the database, thus preserving it across application restarts. Figure 6-7 shows an example of how the application might look after some usage.

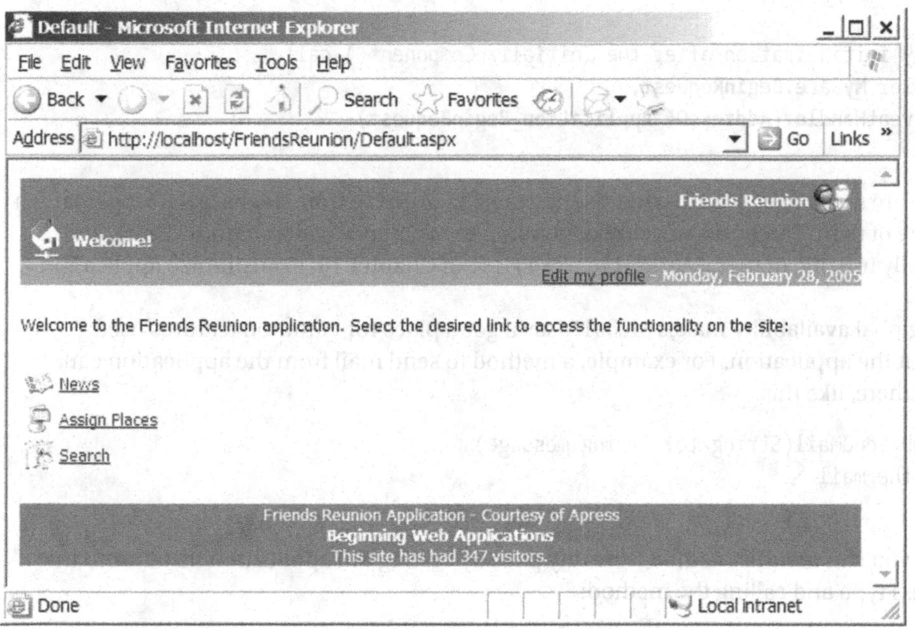

Figure 6-7. *The counter preserved across application restarts*

You can try this by making a small change to `Web.config` and refreshing the page. It won't change unless a new session is started. When you retrieve the counter, you use `ExecuteScalar`, which returns the value of the first column in the first row—just what we need. Note that both `SELECT` and `UPDATE` queries work with the whole table, as you'll always keep a single record, so you don't need to worry much about selecting the appropriate record in the first place.

You're using a database to persist changes across application restarts, but you're paying only the cost of querying it once: at application start time.

Using Application Object and Events

You may have noticed that the `Global` class in the code-behind page of `Global.asax` inherits from `HttpApplication`. This means that this file actually contains the class that defines the *application instance at runtime*. An instance of this class is instantiated when the application is first started by the ASP.NET runtime. You can access this instance through the `HttpContext.Current.ApplicationInstance` property.

So, the various empty event handlers you see in `Global.asax` are actually the events exposed by the base `HttpApplication` class. The special `Application_EventName()` (or `Session_EventName()` event, as you saw earlier in this chapter) event is an easy way to attach to the event, but it's equally possible to do so manually, for example, in the class constructor:

```
Public Sub New()
  MyBase.New()

  'This call is required by the Component Designer
  InitializeComponent()

  'Add any initialization after the InitializeComponent() call
  AddHandler MyBase.BeginRequest,
    New EventHandler(AddressOf Application_BeginRequest)
End Sub
```

There are many events and methods that you can override from the base `HttpApplication` class. Some of them can be very useful, depending on your application requirements, and we'll actually use one of them, `AuthenticateRequest` in Chapter 10, to customize application security.

This global availability makes `Global.asax` a good place for common features used throughout the application. For example, a method to send mail from the application can be placed there, like this:

```
Public Sub SendMail(String to, String message)
  ' Send the mail
End Sub
```

Then you can use this method from any page by casting the application instance to the `Global` class type and calling the method:

```
Dim app As Global = CType(Context.ApplicationInstance, Global)
app.SendMail("user@target.com", "This is a mail from Friends Reunion")
```

We'll let your imagination take over here, since the Friends Reunion application doesn't require global functions.

A Side Note: Modules and Global.asax Method Signatures

In ASP.NET, most of the functionality is implemented by so-called *modules*. These modules are classes that are instantiated when the application starts and participate in the processing of a request. Session state is one such module. You can see the predefined modules in the %WINDIR%\Microsoft.NET\Framework\v1.1.4322\CONFIG\machine.config file, in the <httpModules> section. Here are some of them:

```
<httpModules>
    <add name="OutputCache" type="System.Web.Caching.OutputCacheModule"/>
    <add name="Session" type="System.Web.SessionState.SessionStateModule"/>
    ...
</httpModules>
```

Other modules are included for authorization and security features, and you'll learn about these in Chapter 10. What's important here is that modules are associated with a name, such as Session.

When the application object is created, it looks at all the methods placed in the Global.asax file and splits their name based on the underscore character. If the method name starts with Application, it attaches the method as an event handler of the event on the HttpApplication class with the name and signature that follows the underscore character. If the method name doesn't start with Application, it looks at all configured modules, trying to match a module name with the part before the underscore, and then tries to find an event in the module type with the name and signature matching that part following the underscore. If it finds a match, it creates the corresponding delegate object and appends it to the event. In VB terms, this is what it's doing:

```
AddHandler CType(Me.Modules("Session"), _
  System.Web.SessionState.SessionStateModule).Start, _
  AddressOf Session_Start
```

Note that the method name can also be Session_OnStart(), and it will be attached properly, too.

Viewstate

ASP.NET introduces a new concept to solve one of the most common problems web developers have faced in the past: how to retain HTML form state across postbacks. By *form state*, we mean selected values, filled fields, and so on. This had to be done manually in the past, retrieving the posted values and setting them back again on the fields when the page returned. ASP.NET *viewstate* handles this situation and more, such as remembering not only the selected value in a combo box but also all the values in the list!

Back in Chapter 3, when we analyzed the postback mechanism, you saw that a hidden form field is automatically added by ASP.NET:

```
<body ms_positioning="FlowLayout">
  <form name="Default" method="post" action="Default.aspx" id="Default">
    <input type="hidden" name="__VIEWSTATE"
           value="dDwtOTk4MjU3NjkzOzs+5LhhCG/25vTEDfpObTJAhwkpYFQ=" />
    ...
```

You can see this code by selecting View ➤ Source in your browser when the rendered Default.aspx page is displayed. This information is used to refresh some page state across postbacks, as well as a means to know which controls have changed their state (such as text in a text box or a selected item in a combo box) in order to fire the appropriate events. ASP.NET automatically persists this information to the __VIEWSTATE hidden field, so that it is available on later postbacks. In Chapter 2, we reviewed the overall page lifecycle. Now we can take a closer look at the events happening right after the Init and PreRender events, as shown in Figure 6-8.

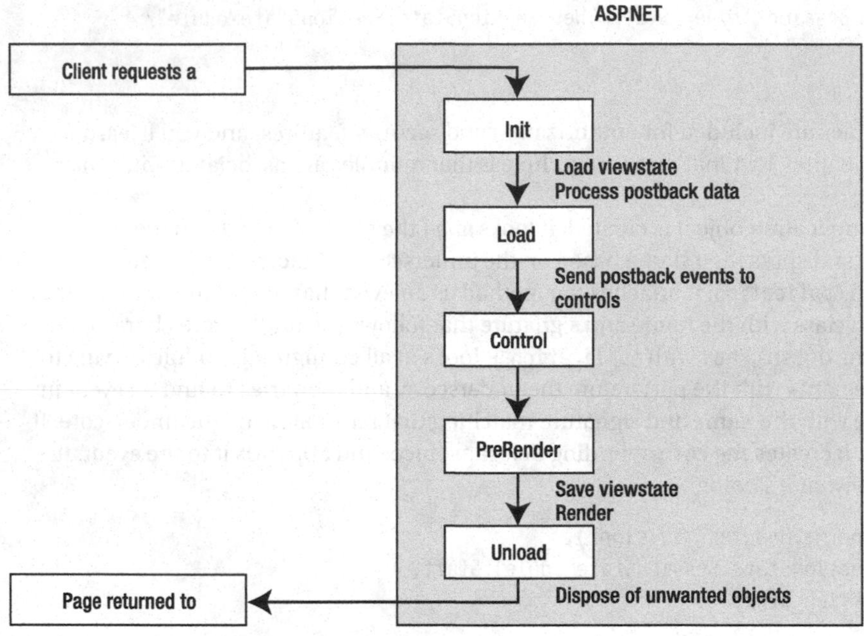

Figure 6-8. *The ASP.NET page lifecyle revisited*

We're now interested in these two stages:

- Load the viewstate (between the Init and Load stages)
- Save the viewstate (between the PreRender and Render stages)

The content of the hidden field is parsed and placed again in the control's properties, immediately after the Init event, through a method called LoadViewState(). The new, posted values are then processed and loaded, and assigned as the values of their corresponding controls. The Control Events stage in the middle is the moment when your event handlers are called.

Now you can understand how a TextBox can know that its Text property has changed and raise the corresponding event, for example. From viewstate, ASP.NET loads the value originally sent to the client, and when processing the posted data, the control can detect that the new value is different from the original value. This mechanism, which is also available to custom control developers, makes it almost unnecessary to use the `Request.Form` collection anymore. As you can see, the viewstate doesn't hold resources on the server side. It's a client-side state feature, as it's kept in a field in the HTML page itself. It's not for free, however; state serialization must be done, as well as optionally hashing and encrypting it for increased security (discussed in Chapter 10).

An interesting case where you can see all these concepts applied is when a value selected in a combo box is changed. When the page is initially submitted to the browser, the viewstate contains the items in the list, with the first one selected (for example). If the user changes the selected element, on postback, `LoadViewState` will load the complete list of items. Next, `LoadPostData` will contain the newly selected item. Based on this information, the new item in the server control will be marked as selected, and ASP.NET will also know it needs to raise the `SelectedIndexChanged` event at the appropriate time (after the `Load` event). This is how the whole event-based structure works.

Inside your handlers, you can set controls' values as usual, and immediately after the `PreRender` event, the `SaveViewState()` method will be called to take care of persisting them to the viewstate for later use. When the page is posted back again, those values will be automatically loaded by ASP.NET. Now you can understand the importance of the moment you use to perform processing. If you change values in the Render phase (overriding the `Render` virtual method), the changes won't be persisted to the viewstate, and thus will be lost on postback. The PreRender stage, on the other hand, or for that matter, any event handler you attach to a control, are good places to make changes that should be persisted in the viewstate.

Because the viewstate is saved to a hidden input field in the rendered HTML, it increases not only the page size, but also the posted form at runtime. It also adds processing on the server, because the server needs to deal with it and perform the steps for handling the viewstate. Thus, you should enable the viewstate only when it's really needed. It can be configured at four levels:

- **Web server control:** All these controls have an `EnableViewState` property to enable/disable this feature.
- **User controls:** These controls also have an `enableViewState` property. It can also be configured through the `@ Control` directive:

  ```
  <%@ Control enableViewState="True|False" %>
  ```

- **Page:** The viewstate can be configured through the `enableViewState` page property, or through the `@ Page` directive:

  ```
  <%@ Page enableViewState="True|False" %>
  ```

- **Web application:** The viewstate can be configured through the `<pages>` element in `Web.config`:

  ```
  <pages enableViewState="true|false" />
  ```

Unfortunately, the viewstate is enabled by default for all pages and controls, so you must manually disable it when you don't need it.

Try It Out: Preserve Processing by Using the Viewstate We will now take advantage of the viewstate to avoid reloading the combo boxes each time the page loads.

1. Change the code in `Page_Load()` of the `Search.aspx` page to match the following:

```
Private Sub Page_Load(ByVal sender As System.Object,
  ByVal e As System.EventArgs) Handles MyBase.Load
  ' Configure the icon and message
  MyBase.HeaderIconImageUrl = "~/Images/search.gif"
  MyBase.HeaderMessage = "Search Users"

  If Not Page.IsPostBack Then
    ' Previous code to load values here...
  End If
  SetResultsState(Not Session("search") Is Nothing)
End Sub
```

2. Run the page and perform a search with all fields blank, and select View ➤ Source. Note the *huge* value in the hidden `__VIEWSTATE` field. This field is bigger than the rest of the page!

3. Copy the entire value of the `__VIEWSTATE` field to the Clipboard, open Notepad, and paste it. Now save the file and take a look at its size.

4. Go back to the page Design view, select the DataGrid control, and set its `EnableViewState` property to `false`.

5. Repeat steps 2 and 3. Notice how the hidden field value has now been dramatically reduced. You'll see that the file size is reduced from approximately 10KB to 1.3KB!

Tip ASP.NET comes with built-in features to debug and test your pages, including analyzing their size, loaded controls, the time it takes to process them, and so on. We'll discuss these features in detail in Chapter 12.

How It Works

The `Page` class exposes an `IsPostBack` property that can be used to determine if the page is being accessed for the first time or not, so you load the values from the database only on the first hit. Note that on further postbacks, you don't load the values, but they are not lost, as the viewstate keeps track of them and reloads them each time. You can see this every time a new search is performed, and the values in the combo boxes remain in place. You can try setting a combo box's `EnableViewState` property to `False` and see how the values are lost afterwards. It's so evident that the values are lost that you'll even get an exception stating that the combo box `SelectedItem` property is `Nothing`.

You can also try filtering by place or type, as it now works as expected. If you take a second look at the sequence of events during the page life (Figure 6-8), you'll notice that the Load phase happens *before* your event handlers are called. As you were data binding the combo boxes at that moment, you were effectively removing the user selection before the handler for the Search button could retrieve the selected value, and that's why it didn't work. Now that the binding is performed only once, selection is preserved, and the event handler can successfully retrieve the filter.

When you disabled the viewstate for the DataGrid control, you prevented ASP.NET from persisting all the information in the grid (including rows and data) to the viewstate, thus preserving a lot of bandwidth your users will appreciate, and also relieved the server from processing all that state about the grid that wasn't used by the code.

Using the Viewstate As a Datastore

The viewstate can also be used much like the session and application state to hold arbitrary data. This opens opportunities to avoid using the session state whenever the data you need to track is relevant to only a single page. It can be accessed from your code using syntax identical to that of the session and application state:

```
' Save a value to viewstate
ViewState("selected") = True

' Retrieve the value later
Dim selected As Boolean = CType(ViewState("selected"), Boolean)
```

Strictly speaking, almost anything can be saved to the viewstate, even a whole `DataSet`, but it is optimized for simple values, such as string, integer, Boolean, array, `ArrayList`, `Hashtable`, `Pair`, and `Triplet` types. Saving objects to the viewstate involves a process known as *serialization*, which converts an object to a string representation, which can later be deserialized back to its original form. The types we mentioned have optimized serializers that produce very compact representations and have almost no performance impact on deserialization, unlike, for example, a dataset, which will be *very* slow to process! It's very important to avoid, as much as possible, serializing any object whose type is not one of the optimized ones.

Caution The viewstate increases the HTML payload (the size of the page sent to the browser, and therefore of the form posted back), so it's not well suited for large amounts of data.

Try It Out: Enable Record Selection with the Viewstate In our Friends Reunion search engine, it would be useful to allow the user to select desired records in order to perform some action with them later, such as sending a request for contact to all of them in one step. You will add the selection feature now, using the viewstate to keep this list.

1. You will use an `ArrayList` object to keep a list of selected items. You need to customize the DataGrid control to enable this functionality, so first set its `EnableViewState` property to `False`. Also, add the following import to the code:

   ```
   Imports System.Collections.Specialized
   ```

2. Apply the Auto Format style Colorful 4 to the DataGrid control and set its AutoGenerateColumns property to False through its Property Builder.

3. Switch to the HTML view. Inside the DataGrid control declaration, directly below the pagerstyle element, add the following column definitions:

```
<asp:datagrid id="grdResults" ...>
  ...
  <pagerstyle horizontalalign="Right" forecolor="#4A3C8C"
              backcolor="#E7E7FF" mode="NumericPages">
  </pagerstyle>
  <columns>
    <asp:templatecolumn headertext="Sel">
      <itemtemplate>
        <asp:imagebutton id="imgSel" runat="server"
                         tooltip="Toggle user selection"
                         commandargument='<%#
          DataBinder.Eval(Container, "DataItem.UserID") %>'
                         commandname="SelectUser"
                         imageurl="Images/unok.gif" />
      </itemtemplate>
    </asp:templatecolumn>
    <asp:boundcolumn datafield="FirstName" headertext="First Name" />
    <asp:boundcolumn datafield="LastName" headertext="Last Name" />
    <asp:boundcolumn datafield="PlaceName" headertext="Place" />
    <asp:boundcolumn datafield="PlaceType" headertext="Type" />
    <asp:boundcolumn datafield="LapseName" headertext="Lapse" />
    <asp:boundcolumn datafield="YearIn" headertext="Year In" />
    <asp:boundcolumn datafield="MonthIn" headertext="Month In" />
    <asp:boundcolumn datafield="YearOut" headertext="Year Out" />
    <asp:boundcolumn datafield="MonthOut" headertext="Month Out" />
  </columns>
  ...
```

You cannot add these bound columns through the Property Builder as you did in Chapter 5, because the DataSet you are using is untyped.

4. Switch to the code-behind view. Select the grdResults element from the leftmost drop-down list at the top of the code editor, and then select the ItemDataBound event from the rightmost one.

5. Add the following code to the event handler that is created for you:

```
Private Sub grdResults_ItemDataBound(ByVal sender As Object,
  ByVal e As System.Web.UI.WebControls.DataGridItemEventArgs)
  Handles grdResults.ItemDataBound
  If ViewState("selected") Is Nothing Then Return
```

```
  Dim sel As StringCollection = CType(ViewState("selected"), StringCollection)
  Dim img As ImageButton = CType(e.Item.FindControl("imgSel"), ImageButton)

  If img Is Nothing Then Return

  If sel.Contains(img.CommandArgument) Then
    img.ImageUrl = "Images/ok.gif"
    img.CommandName = "DeselectUser"
    e.Item.ForeColor = Color.Red
  End If
End Sub
```

This event handler will be called every time a new item (data row) is created and bound to the data source.

6. Select the ItemCommand event from the drop-down list and add the following code to the handler:

```
Private Sub grdResults_ItemCommand(ByVal source As Object, _
  ByVal e As System.Web.UI.WebControls.DataGridCommandEventArgs) _
  Handles grdResults.ItemCommand

  If e.CommandName = "SelectUser" Then
    Dim sel As StringCollection = _
      CType(ViewState("selected"), StringCollection)
    If sel Is Nothing Then
      sel = New StringCollection
      ViewState("selected") = sel
    End If

    If Not sel.Contains(CType(e.CommandArgument, String)) Then
      sel.Add(CType(e.CommandArgument, String))
    End If

    BindFromSession()

  ElseIf e.CommandName = "DeselectUser" Then
    Dim sel As StringCollection =
      CType(ViewState("selected"), StringCollection)
    sel.Remove(CType(e.CommandArgument, String))

    BindFromSession()
  End If
End Sub
```

This handler will be called when the image button is clicked.

7. Finally, in order to show the count of selected items, drop a label below the whole table, but inside the same table cell, named `lblSelected`. Clear its `Text` property, and add the following method to the code-behind page:

```
Protected Overrides Sub OnPreRender(ByVal e As System.EventArgs)
  If Not ViewState("selected") Is Nothing Then
    lblSelected.Text = CType(ViewState("selected"), _
      StringCollection).Count & " users selected."
  End If
  MyBase.OnPreRender(e)
End Sub
```

8. Set the `EnableViewState` property of the `lblSelected` label to `False` (you don't need to track changes to it, and it will probably change in every postback).

9. Clear this viewstate value whenever the Clear Results image button is clicked:

```
Private Sub btnClearResults_Click(ByVal sender As System.Object,
  ByVal e As System.Web.UI.ImageClickEventArgs) Handles btnClearResults.Click
  Session.Remove("search")
  ViewState.Remove("selected")
  SetResultsState(False)
End Sub
```

10. Save and run the page.

How It Works

If you perform a search with a Place filter set to Sundance Components, you will see results similar to those shown in Figure 6-9.

After you select a couple users from the grid, the page will look something like Figure 6-10.

Note that because selection is performed on a per-user basis, if a user appears in more than one row (that user has been in more than one place), all of these instances will be selected/deselected at once.

You used bound columns in the grid and a templated column, something you learned to do in Chapter 5. Whenever you click the selection button, the `ItemCommand` handler is fired. In order for this event handler to receive the user ID of the user in the row, you used a data binding expression:

```
<asp:imagebutton id="imgSel" runat="server" tooltip="Toggle user selection"
  commandargument='<%# DataBinder.Eval(Container, "DataItem.UserID") %>'
  commandname="SelectUser" imageurl="Images/unok.gif" />
```

Note that even if the dataset is not typed, you can successfully retrieve the user ID, which is passed to the handler that saves it to the viewstate:

```
If Not sel.Contains(CType(e.CommandArgument, String)) Then
  sel.Add(CType(e.CommandArgument, String))
End If
```

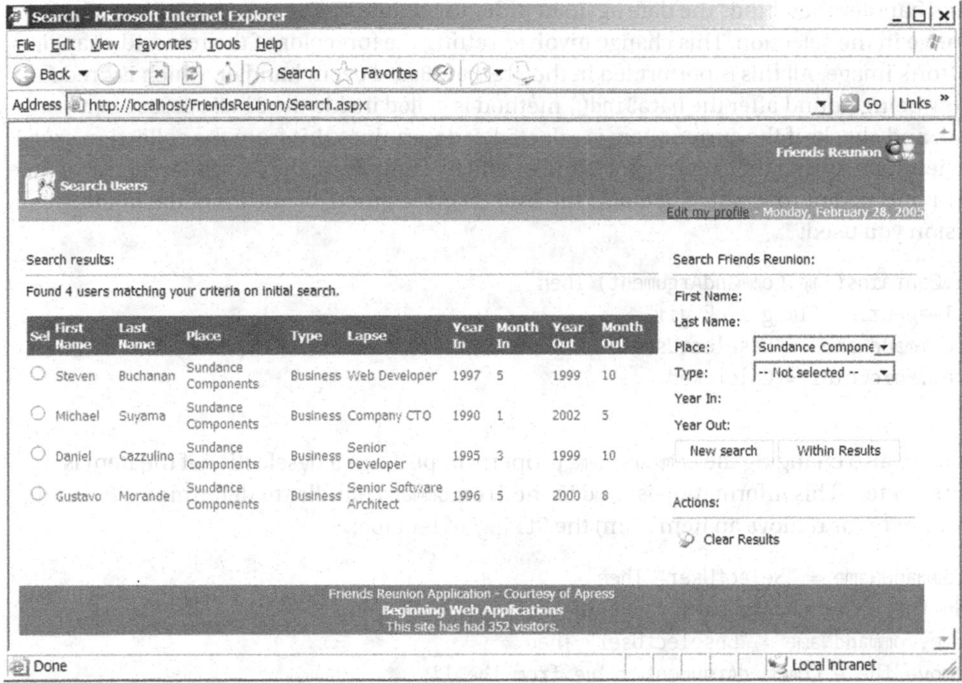

Figure 6-9. *Performing a place search*

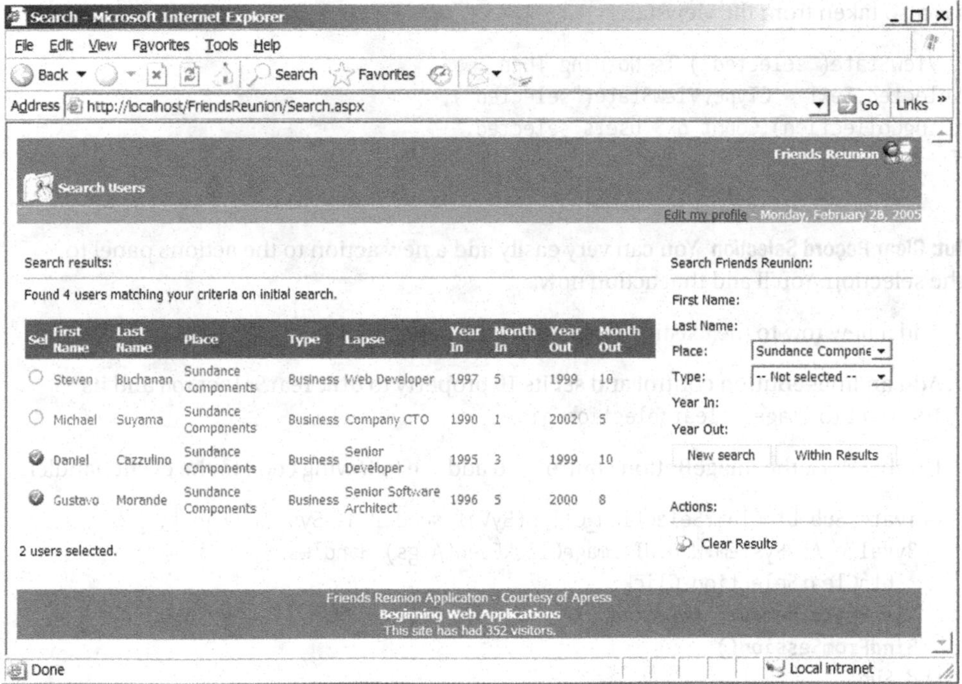

Figure 6-10. *Record selection with viewstate*

This handler then binds the data again in order to let the ItemDataBound handler reflect the change in the selection. This change involves setting the forecolor of the row and changing the button's image. All this is performed in the ItemDataBound event handler, which is fired for each row being bound after the DataBind() method is called inside the BindFromSession() method, and checks if the current item is selected. It determines this from the collection saved to the viewstate during the ItemCommand handler and by comparing the CommandArgument of the image in the current row, which contains the user ID placed there by means of the binding expression you used:

```
If sel.Contains(img.CommandArgument) Then
  img.ImageUrl = "Images/ok.gif"
  img.CommandName = "DeselectUser"
  e.Item.ForeColor = Color.Red
End If
```

You are also changing the CommandName property to perform a deselection if the item is already selected. This information is used in the ItemCommand handler to determine if it should add an item to (or remove an item from) the StringCollection:

```
If e.CommandName = "SelectUser" Then
  ' Add the e.CommandArgument value to the list
ElseIf e.CommandName = "DeselectUser" Then
  ' Remove the e.CommandArgument value from the list
End If
```

Finally, the override in the OnPreRender() method now shows the count of selected users, which is also taken from the viewstate:

```
If Not ViewState("selected") Is Nothing Then
  lblSelected.Text = CType(ViewState("selected"), _
    StringCollection).Count & " users selected."
End If
```

Try It Out: Clear Record Selection You can very easily add a new action to the actions panel to clear the selection. You'll add that action now.

1. Add a new row to the existing table inside the panel.

2. Add an ImageButton control and set its ID property to btnClearSelection and its ImageUrl to Images/clearselection.gif.

3. Double-click the ImageButton control and add the following code to the event handler:

```
Private Sub btnClearSelection_Click(ByVal sender As System.Object, _
  ByVal e As System.Web.UI.ImageClickEventArgs) Handles _
    btnClearSelection.Click
  ViewState.Remove("selected")
  BindFromSession()
End Sub
```

How It Works

Not surprisingly, the syntax is just the same as you used to remove elements from the session and application state, and to the line you added to the `btnClearResults_Click` event handler.

Transient State

Many times, all you need is for the state to last for the duration of the request and be discarded automatically. One such scenario is whenever you need to pass data between pages, or even between controls at different stages of page processing, especially if such controls are contained in separate classes (like the Friends Reunion application header and footer user controls, or our `SubHeader` custom control class). In those cases, you may need a way to pass data between pages or controls, but it needs to last for only the time it takes to process the current page request.

You could use the session state, but that is clearly an overkill solution, because it would waste server resources for a state that doesn't need to last for the whole session duration. Even if you can preserve resources by manually removing the items once you're finished, if the session state is configured to be stored in a separate state server or even SQL Server, you would suffer the corresponding performance impact.

ASP.NET provides a class that represents the context of the current execution, including the request and its response: the `HttpContext` class. You have already seen how you can access the application or session state using properties provided by this class, through its `HttpContext.Current.Session` and `HttpContext.Current.Application` properties. What's more, an instance of this class is readily available as a property of the `Control` class, from which `Page` and all server controls derive: `Context`. We'll call this instance the `Context` object from now on.

In addition to these properties, the `Context` object has an `Items` property that can hold any kind of data. Whatever you place there is automatically discarded as soon as the request finishes processing. That's why we call it *transient*, because it's never persisted across requests, unlike the session state, application state, and viewstate, as well as cookies, as you will see shortly.

The Friends Reunion application can take advantage of this transient state. Suppose that Victor (that old friend from the previous chapter) now has a list of the users he is interested in contacting. You need to provide him with a means to send a request to all of them in one step. For this purpose, you'll send him to another page, where he will enter the desired message and post the request for contact. You'll use the transient state to pass the list of selected users you have been saving in the viewstate (which obviously doesn't live across pages) to the target page.

Try It Out: Pass the List of Selected Users to Another Page Let's now add a function for requesting contact to the Friends Reunion application.

1. Add a new row to the table inside the actions panel. Drop an ImageButton control on the leftmost cell with the ID `btnRequest`, set its `ImageUrl` to `Images/requestcontact.gif`, and type some meaningful text, such as **Request Contact**, in the rightmost cell. The form should look something like Figure 6-11.

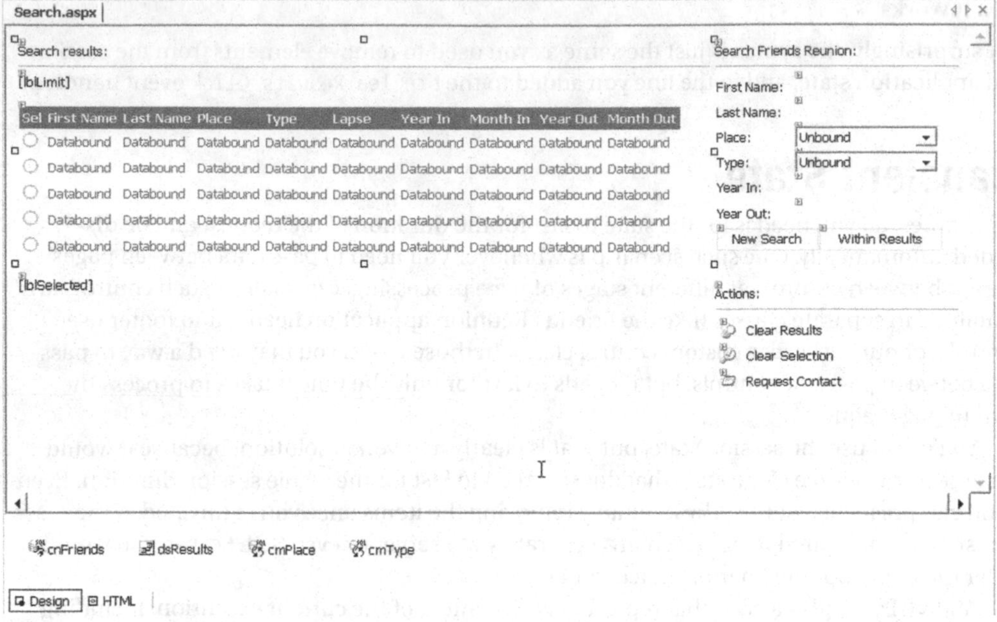

Figure 6-11. *Adding a Request Contact action*

2. Double-click the new button, which should have the ID `btnRequest`, and add the following code to the event handler:

```
Private Sub btnRequest_Click(ByVal sender As System.Object,
  ByVal e As System.Web.UI.ImageClickEventArgs) Handles btnRequest.Click
  Context.Items("selected") = ViewState("selected")
  Server.Transfer("RequestContact.aspx")
End Sub
```

3. Add a new web form called `RequestContact.aspx`. As usual, add the link to the stylesheet and make the page inherit from `FriendsBase`.

4. Add the following `import` statements at the top of the code:

```
Imports System.Collections.Specialized
Imports System.Data.SqlClient
Imports System.Text
```

5. Drop a `SqlConnection` component on the page, name it `cnFriends` and configure its `ConnectionString` through `(DynamicProperties)`, as you have done before.

6. Drop a `SqlCommand` component onto the form and set its `Connection` property to point to the connection component. Name it `cmInsert` and set its `CommandText` property as follows:

```
INSERT INTO Contact (RequestID, IsApproved, Notes, DestinationID)
VALUES (@RequestID, @IsApproved, @Message, @DestinationID)
```

7. Insert some text and drop a TextBox, a Button, a ListBox, and a Label control to match the following UI.

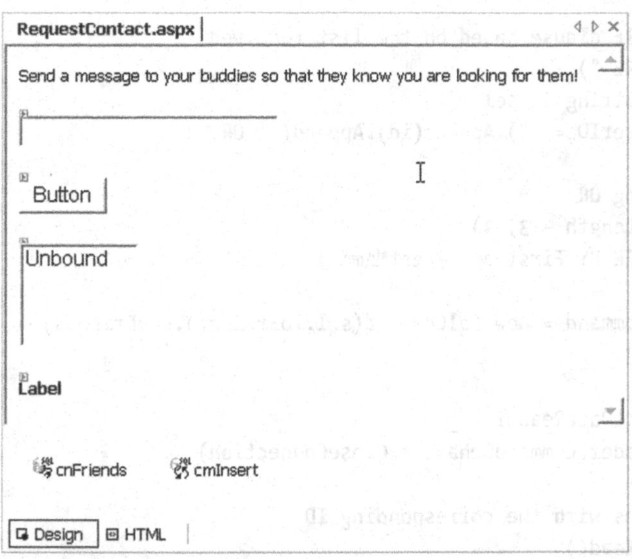

8. Set the controls' ID properties as in this list, from top to bottom, and then set the control properties as shown:

   - txtMessage: CssClass to BigTextBox; MaxLength to 300; TextMode to Multiline; Rows to 5; Width to 424 pixels
   - btnSend: CssClass to Button; Text to **Send**
   - lstUsers: CssClass to Normal; Rows to 5; Width to 224 pixels
   - lblSuccess: Font.Bold to True; ForeColor to #0000C0; Text to (none)

9. Add the following lines to the Page_Load() method:

```
Private Sub Page_Load(ByVal sender As System.Object,
  ByVal e As System.EventArgs) Handles MyBase.Load
  MyBase.HeaderMessage = "Contact your buddies!"
  MyBase.HeaderIconImageUrl = "~/Images/contact.gif"

  ' Initialize the list of users only once
  If Not Page.IsPostBack Then
    Dim sel As StringCollection =
      CType(Context.Items("selected"), StringCollection)
    If sel Is Nothing OrElse sel.Count = 0 Then
      Server.Transfer("Search.aspx")
    End If
```

```
      Dim sql As StringBuilder = New StringBuilder
      sql.Append("SELECT FirstName + ', ' + LastName AS FullName, ")
      sql.Append("UserID FROM [User] ")

      ' Build the WHERE clause based on the list received
      sql.Append("WHERE ")
      For Each id As String In sel
        sql.Append("UserID = '").Append(id).Append("' OR ")
      Next
      ' Remove trailing OR
      sql.Remove(sql.Length - 3, 3)
      sql.Append("ORDER BY FirstName, LastName")

      Dim cmd As SqlCommand = New SqlCommand(sql.ToString(), cnFriends)
      cnFriends.Open()
      ' Using
      Dim reader As SqlDataReader = _
        cmd.ExecuteReader(CommandBehavior.CloseConnection)
      Try
        ' Add the items with the corresponding ID
        While reader.Read()
          lstUsers.Items.Add(New ListItem(
            reader(0).ToString(), _
            reader(1).ToString()))
        End While
      Finally
        reader.Close()
      End Try
    End If
  End Sub
```

10. Double-click the btnSend button and add the following code:

```
Private Sub btnSend_Click(ByVal sender As System.Object,
  ByVal e As System.EventArgs) Handles btnSend.Click
  cmInsert.Parameters("@RequestID").Value =
    Page.User.Identity.Name
  cmInsert.Parameters("@IsApproved").Value = False
  cmInsert.Parameters("@Message").Value = txtMessage.Text

  Try
    cnFriends.Open()
    For Each it As ListItem In lstUsers.Items
      cmInsert.Parameters("@DestinationID").Value = it.Value
      cmInsert.ExecuteNonQuery()
    Next
    lblSuccess.Text = "Message successfully sent!"
  Finally
```

```
        ' Always close the connection
        cnFriends.Close()
      End Try
    End Sub
```

11. Save and run the page.

How It Works

If you now perform a search, select some users, and click the button to request a contact, you will be taken to the RequestContact.aspx page, but just before you get to it, the code in the event handler saves the list you were saving in the viewstate to the transient state:

```
Context.Items("selected") = ViewState("selected")
Server.Transfer("RequestContact.aspx")
```

Note that you use Server.Transfer() instead of Response.Redirect(). By using this method, ASP.NET passes the processing responsibility to the specified page, but doesn't terminate the current execution context, nor the request, which is now transferred to the target page. Because the processing shift takes place on the server side, the client browser doesn't know that it happens, and that's why the URL stays the same after the transfer, as shown in Figure 6-12.

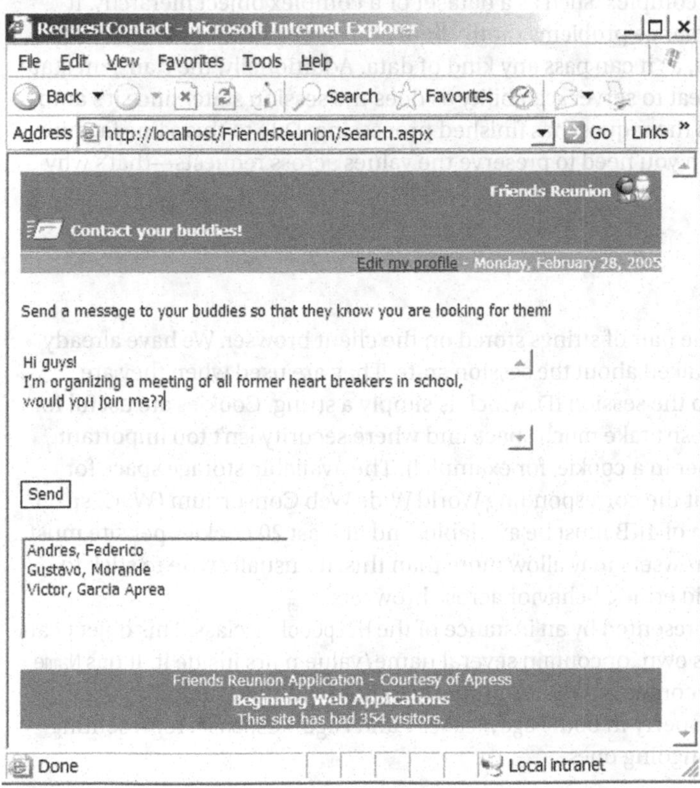

Figure 6-12. *The Request Contact page*

This page takes advantage of both the transient state and viewstate. The first is used to populate the list box when the page is first hit (it's not a postback), right after the transfer:

```
If Not Page.IsPostBack Then
  Dim sel As StringCollection = _
    CType(Context.Items("selected"), StringCollection)
```

Note that if a postback were performed, the `Context.Items` collection would be empty this time, and there would be no way of getting to the user selection again. Here is where the page takes advantage of the viewstate to preserve the values loaded initially. This makes it possible to get the IDs of the selected users directly from the list box loaded the first time the page was hit, as shown by the code in the `btnSend_Click` handler:

```
For Each it As ListItem In lstUsers.Items
  cmInsert.Parameters("@DestinationID").Value = it.Value
  cmInsert.ExecuteNonQuery()
Next
```

As you learned in previous chapters, requests for contact are saved to the `Contact` table, together with the ID of the user requesting the contact (extracted, as usual, from `Page.User.Identity.Name`), so you just need to update the target user ID command parameter in order to perform the insertion for each item in the list.

Although you can appreciate the utility of the transient state here, it's even more useful if the data being passed is more complex, such as a dataset or a complex object hierarchy. It doesn't suffer from the performance problems (both client and server side) of the viewstate regarding complex sets of data, as it can pass any kind of data. Additionally, the transient state doesn't impose a potential threat to server scalability as does the session state, since it's automatically discarded as soon as the request has finished processing. Due to this same fact, it's not suitable for scenarios when you need to preserve the values across requests—that's why we call it *transient*.

Cookies

Basically, a *cookie* is a key/value pair of strings stored on the client browser. We have already mentioned cookies when we talked about the session state. They are used when they are enabled in the browser to keep the session ID, which is simply a string. Cookies are useful for that kind of storage, which doesn't take much space and where security isn't too important (don't save a credit card number in a cookie, for example!). The available storage space for cookies is browser-specific, but the corresponding World Wide Web Consortium (W3C) specification states that a minimum of 4KB must be available, and at least 20 cookies per site must be allowed. So, even if some browsers may allow more than this, it's usually wise to stick to these limits if you want to avoid erratic behavior across browsers.

A cookie in ASP.NET is represented by an instance of the `HttpCookie` class. This object can have a name and a value on its own, or contain several name/value pairs inside it. It has `Name` and `Value` properties, but also contains a `Values` property to hold multiple values.

Also, there is a `Cookies` property in both `Page.Request` and `Page.Response`, representing the received cookies and the ongoing ones.

A very common use for cookies is to keep user preferences regarding site appearance. Let's add a feature to the Friends Reunion application to allow users to change their preferred background color for the site. You'll add a control to the common footer user control to change it. Doing so, however, will imply some modifications to the `FriendsBase` class, which will also be the one in charge of applying the style change based on the cookie value. While we analyze the changes involved, you'll get a deeper understanding of the page lifecycle and how controls (both user and custom controls) need to be aware of it in order to behave properly.

The first thing to analyze is how to trap the event fired when the control you're adding to the footer (a combo box with a list of colors) changes. The answer may seem obvious: double-click the control and add the event handler. However, if you take a look at our current `FriendsBase` class, you will realize that you're actually creating and loading these controls in the `Render()` method override. You did so before, since you didn't need to support postbacks or the viewstate. If you look at the picture of the page lifecycle in Figure 6-8 earlier in this chapter, you'll realize that this method is the last one on the chain. All chances to get the event handlers called have already gone. Therefore, when the control causes a postback as a consequence of a change, the ASP.NET runtime won't be able to find the control to call its handler, because it won't exist yet. The only way to get the event handlers called, then, is to create the controls during a previous stage. The place to do so is the Init phase.

Try It Out: Use Cookies to Keep User Preferences Now, you will add the code to use cookies for preserving user preferences.

1. Open `FriendsFooter.ascx` in HTML view and add the following code:

```
  </strong>This site has had 
<asp:label id="lblCounter" runat="server"></asp:label> visitors. 
<asp:image id="imgShow" runat="server"
           imageurl="../Images/down.gif"
           imagealign="AbsMiddle"
           tooltip="Change preferences">
</asp:image><br>
  <div id="tbPrefs" style="DISPLAY: none; TEXT-ALIGN: center">BackColor:
    <asp:dropdownlist id="cbBackColor" runat="server" cssclass="Normal"
                      autopostback="True"></asp:dropdownlist></div>
</asp:panel>
```

2. Open the code-behind file and add the following `import` statements:

```
Imports System.ComponentModel
Imports System.Collections
```

3. Modify `Page_Load()` as follows:

```
Private Sub Page_Load(ByVal sender As System.Object,
  ByVal e As System.EventArgs) Handles MyBase.Load
  lblCounter.Text = Application("counter").ToString()

  ' Script to show/hide the options and change the image
  Dim script As String =
```

```
  " var table=document.getElementById('tbPrefs'); " +
  " if (table.style.display=='block') { " + _
  "   this.src='%down%'; table.style.display='none'; " +
  " } else { " + _
  "   this.src='%up%'; table.style.display='block'; " +
  " } "

' Resolve images relative to the current context
script = script.Replace("%down%",
  ResolveUrl("../Images/down.gif"))
script = script.Replace("%up%",
  ResolveUrl("../Images/up.gif"))

imgShow.Attributes.Add("onclick", script)
imgShow.Style.Add("cursor", "pointer")

If Not Page.IsPostBack Then
  ' Empty item to clear color preference
  cbBackColor.Items.Add(String.Empty)
  Dim cv As ColorConverter = New ColorConverter

  ' Retrieve current color preference to preselect the item
  Dim selected As Color = Color.Empty
  If Not Request.Cookies("backcolor") Is Nothing AndAlso
    Not Request.Cookies("backcolor").Value Is Nothing AndAlso
    Not Request.Cookies("backcolor").Value = String.Empty Then
    selected = CType(cv.ConvertFromString(
      Request.Cookies("backcolor").Value), Color)
  End If

  ' Get all standard colors
  Dim col As ICollection = cv.GetStandardValues()
  For Each c As Color In col
    ' Convert each color to its HTML equivalent
    Dim li As ListItem = New ListItem(c.Name,
      ColorTranslator.ToHtml(c))
    If c.Equals(selected) Then
      li.Selected = True
    End If
    cbBackColor.Items.Add(li)
  Next
End If
End Sub
```

4. Switch to the Design view to see your new control.

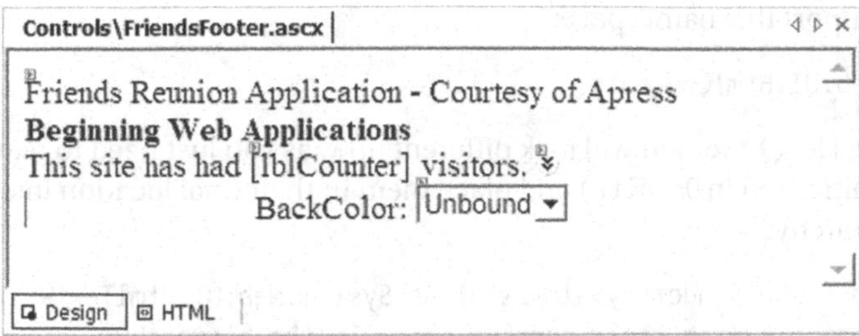

5. Double-click the combo box and add the following code:

```
Private Sub cbBackColor_SelectedIndexChanged(ByVal sender As System.Object,
  ByVal e As System.EventArgs) Handles cbBackColor.SelectedIndexChanged
  Response.Cookies.Add(New HttpCookie("backcolor",
    CType(sender, DropDownList).SelectedItem.Value))
End Sub
```

6. Open the `FriendsBase.vb` file. As we discussed earlier, you need to add the controls to the hierarchy on the Init phase, meaning you will need to override the `OnInit()` method. You'll do this, and also keep a reference to the loaded controls, as you'll work with them further at rendering time. For that purpose, let's modify the class code as follows:

```
Public Class FriendsBase
  Inherits Page

  Protected HeaderMessage As String = ""
  Protected HeaderIconImageUrl As String = ""

  Private _footer As FriendsFooter
  Private _header As FriendsHeader
  Private _subheader As SubHeader

  Protected Overloads Overrides Sub OnInit(ByVal e As EventArgs)
    _header = CType(LoadControl("~/Controls/FriendsHeader.ascx"),
      FriendsHeader)
    _footer = CType(LoadControl("~/Controls/FriendsFooter.ascx"),
      FriendsFooter)
    _subheader = New SubHeader

    ' Add to the Controls hierarchy to get proper
    ' event handling, on rendering we reposition them
    Page.Controls.Add(_header)
    Page.Controls.Add(_subheader)
    Page.Controls.Add(_footer)
    MyBase.OnInit(e)
  End Sub
```

7. You also need to import this namespace:

```
Imports System.Web.UI.HtmlControls
```

8. The code for the Render() method will look different now, as you just need to rearrange the controls you initialized in OnInit() and place them in their final location inside the form Controls hierarchy:

```
Protected Overrides Sub Render(ByVal writer As System.Web.UI.HtmlTextWriter)
  ' Remove the controls from their current place in the hierarchy
  Page.Controls.Remove(_header)
  Page.Controls.Remove(_subheader)
  Page.Controls.Remove(_footer)

  ' Get a reference to the form control
  Dim form As HtmlForm = CType(Page.Controls(1), HtmlForm)

  ' Reposition the controls on the page
  form.Controls.AddAt(0, _header)
  form.Controls.AddAt(1, _subheader)
  form.Controls.AddAt(form.Controls.Count, _footer)

  ' Set current values
  _header.Message = HeaderMessage
  _header.IconImageUrl = HeaderIconImageUrl

  ' New cookies are set to Response by the color selector
  Dim bg As String = Response.Cookies("backcolor").Value

  ' If not, check Request for a previously saved cookie
  If bg Is Nothing AndAlso Not Request.Cookies("backcolor") Is Nothing
    AndAlso Not Request.Cookies("backcolor").Value Is Nothing
    AndAlso Not Request.Cookies("backcolor").Value = String.Empty Then
    bg = Request.Cookies("backcolor").Value
    ' Preserve cookie in the response
    Response.Cookies.Add(Request.Cookies("backcolor"))
  End If

  ' Do we have a value to work with?
  If Not bg Is Nothing AndAlso bg <> String.Empty Then
    ' Enclose form in a DIV to display the backcolor
    Dim div As HtmlGenericControl = New HtmlGenericControl("div")
    div.Style.Add("background-color", bg)

    ' Relocate the form inside the DIV
    Page.Controls.Remove(form)
    Page.Controls.AddAt(1, div)
    div.Controls.Add(form)
  End If
```

```
  ' Render as usual
  MyBase.Render(writer)
End Sub
```

9. That's it! Save and run the page. Try clicking the new icon next to the visitor count and selecting a color from the combo box.

How It Works

To get the list of available colors and to convert to and from HTML representations, you use two classes in the `System.Drawing` namespace: `ColorConverter` and `ColorTranslator`. Those are exactly the same classes VS .NET uses to handle color properties in the Properties browser and Style Builder. You added a little piece of JavaScript to the image `onclick` attribute (actually an event on the client side) to toggle visibility of the panel containing the color selector, and to switch the image to display accordingly.

The important thing to notice in that code is that you're not directly embedding the images' relative URLs in the JavaScript string. Rather, you're using `ResolveUrl()`, a method provided by the base `Control` class, which takes into account the current context. This is important because the user control can be used in pages whose location is different than the control's page. This is, in fact, the case for all our pages. If you didn't use that method, a URL relative to the control may not always work. Here's the code where you use it:

```
' Resolve images relative to the current context
script = script.Replace("%down%", _
  ResolveUrl("../Images/down.gif"))
```

Testing the page, the first thing you will notice is that as soon as you select a color from the list, the change takes place. That is a consequence of the `AutoPostBack` attribute you added to the combo box. The workaround to get the event handler called involves creating and adding the control in the hierarchy during initialization (`OnInit()`):

```
Page.Controls.Add(_footer)
```

and later removing it and adding it to the desired position (last in the `Controls` collection) for rendering purposes:

```
Page.Controls.Remove(_footer)
HtmlForm form = (HtmlForm)Page.Controls(1)
form.Controls.AddAt(form.Controls.Count, _footer )
```

By keeping the controls' instances in class-level private variables, removing them and adding them to the `Controls` collection is very easy, as you don't need to find the controls in the hierarchy previously. This technique allows the event handler for the `SelectedIndexChanged` event to be called after initialization has completed. Inside this handler (in the footer user control's code-behind file), you just save the selected HTML value to a cookie in the `Response.Cookies` collection:

```
Response.Cookies.Add(New HttpCookie("backcolor",
  CType(sender, DropDownList).SelectedItem.Value))
```

Then, as the final step in the page lifecycle, comes the FriendsBase.Render() method, which besides repositioning controls as you've seen, checks the status of the cookies, both from Response and Request. Based on that, it creates an enclosing <div> element, where it places the whole form, to get the background color displayed:

```
Page.Controls.Remove(form)
Page.Controls.AddAt(1, div)
div.Controls.Add(form)
```

The process for relocating the form is exactly the same as you used to position the other controls. Because all this code is placed in the base class for all your pages, they all gain this feature immediately. The home page (Default.aspx) might look like Figure 6-13 after you changed the color preference and expanded the preferences panel at the bottom.

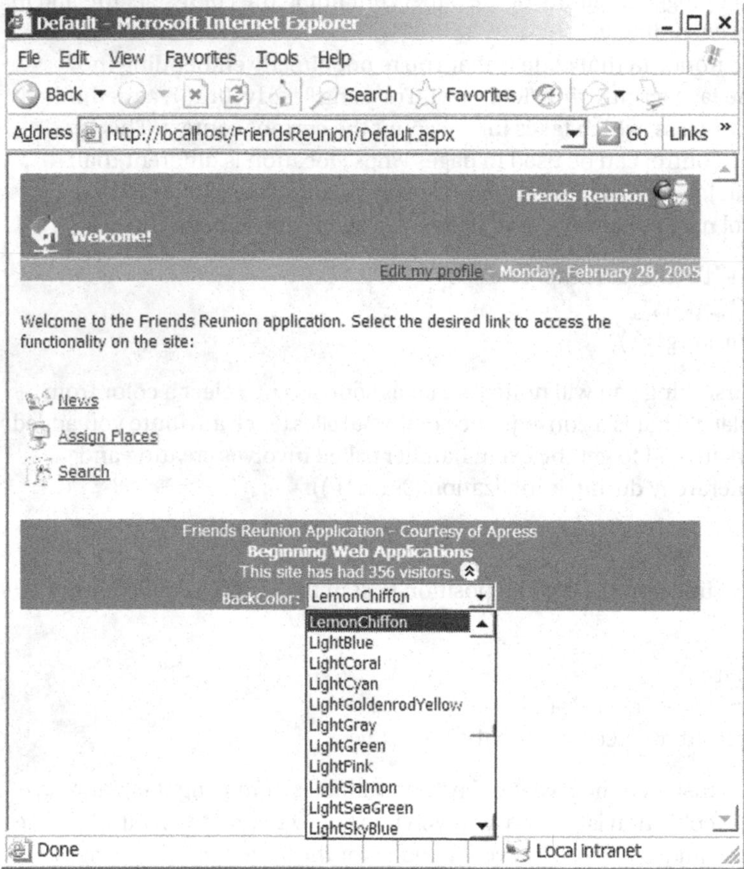

Figure 6-13. *The Default page with color preference choices*

Caution You can reposition controls on the page collection only during the Rendering phase, when the viewstate for all of them has already been saved. If you do so earlier in the page lifecycle, the viewstate may stop working, as well as the firing of events that depend on it.

If you restart your browser right now, you'll lose your preference. That's because the cookie expires with the browser session by default. Let's fix this now.

Try It Out: Survive Browser Restarts In order to change the default behavior, so the cookie is retained after the browser session ends, add the following line to the `FriendsBase.Render()` method:

```
 div.Controls.Add(form)
Response.Cookies("backcolor").Expires = DateTime.Now.AddYears(1)
```

How It Works

You have set the expiration for the cookie that holds the color preference to one year from the current time on the server. You should avoid setting the expiration to a higher value, because some browsers will distrust it and may ignore it altogether.

Passing Data with Query Strings

A query string is everything appended to a URL after the name of the page plus a question mark, such as in the following:

```
http://localhost/ViewUser.aspx?UserID=99
```

Some developers consider that passing data in the query string between pages is a way to keep state, too. You actually have used this form of state in your work with the Friends Reunion application; for example, you used it when you provided a link to view details about a user in `News.aspx`, which rendered very similarly to the preceding example to pass the user ID to the `ViewUser.aspx` page. It comes in especially handy when you use it in conjunction with data binding, as you did. You retrieved this value simply with:

```
userID = Request.QueryString("UserID")
```

Note that the key used is the value before the =, and the value you get is the string following it. The `QueryString` property is of type `NameValueCollection`, containing all the key/value pairs found in the URL. If multiple values are needed, they must be separated by an & sign.

Caution Remember to always check input parameters you receive before using them, to ensure they are valid and within the expected values.

Except for this and similar cases where small sets of data need to be passed, this mechanism is not recommended. HTTP 1.0 web servers usually don't handle more than 255 characters in a query string, nor do older browsers. HTTP 1.1 solved this, but older browsers still won't work.

Passing Data with Hidden Form Fields

Using hidden form fields to pass data between the client and the server, as well as between pages, is also possible. You can simply add an HTML input field to the form, set its type to `hidden`, and then set values on it, either on the client side using a script or on the server. This is an example of a hidden field:

```
<body ms_positioning="FlowLayout">
  <form name="Default" method="post" action="Default.aspx" id="Default">
    <input type="hidden" name="myField" value="myValue" />
```

On the client side, you can easily set the value of the field using JavaScript, ready to be passed to the server:

```
document.getElementById(myField).value = "the value to pass!!";
```

You can get the values in a hidden form field using the `Request.Form` property on the server side:

```
string value = Request.Form("myField")
```

You already know that the viewstate uses this technique, so you can easily imagine your own applications for it, and they don't necessarily need to be simple, as you can see!

This concludes our journey through the exciting ASP.NET state management features.

Summary

Equally important as dynamic features for web applications is the ability to retain state in its different forms. ASP.NET offers a wide range of possibilities, filling all the gaps of the past and creating new and improved state-handling approaches, such as the viewstate and transient state. We have covered each of the features it offers. We also discussed the performance and scalability trade-offs among them, and offered some hints on where to use each one.

We've taken advantage of the session state to allow the user to perform refining searches for fellow users. We have taken into account scalability problems that may arise and placed a limit on maximum search results, and also discussed different storage locations for this state data. We then used the viewstate to further increase our application's responsiveness by reducing the HTML payload as a result of enabling it only when needed. We also reduced server-side processing by avoiding reloading data, letting the viewstate take care of reconstructing UI elements, such as combo boxes.

We then moved to more advanced uses of the viewstate as a store for arbitrary data, and added the possibility to select users from the search results and stored those selections in the viewstate. Next, we learned about a new feature available in ASP.NET, transient state, which allowed us to pass this selection data between pages without consuming server resources.

We discussed the application state, and used it to provide a global count of visitors to our application, and finally used the most traditional client state feature, cookies, to store user preferences for the site's background color.

Our application is becoming more mature, offering the possibility to register, add places, and search for fellow users, and doing so in a user-friendly and responsive way. We have built this functionality by taking advantage of ASP.NET state management features, as well as all the features you learned about in previous chapters: server controls, ADO.NET, and data binding.

It's now time to open up our application to partners and associates, and we will take advantage of XML, XML schemas, and web services to allow them to access our data and interact with our application. You'll learn about these exciting new technologies and the great potential they offer in the upcoming chapters.

CHAPTER 7

Markup Languages and XML

In Chapters 4 and 5, we introduced the concept of working with data. We placed a relational database behind our web application, and used it predominantly for data storage. We also used ADO.NET techniques to manipulate and organize data as it passed between the user and the database. By the end of Chapter 6, the Friends Reunion web application was acting as a "middle man," allowing individuals (on one side) to interact with the data stored within the database (on the other side).

Of course, there is more to data than just storage and manipulation. Internet connectivity is now widespread, and it is often desirable to have disparate applications working together across the Internet. In this type of scenario, you need a way for such applications to *exchange* data. Exchanging data involves formatting the data in a way that is compatible with all of your applications and is easy to transport between applications.

For example, suppose we wanted to extend the Friends Reunion application to allow a subscribing college or other institution to upload or download information about its users and attendees. To achieve this, we would need some agreement about the format of the data and how the data would be transferred. Ideally, we would build on a data format that is standardized and universally understood.

It sounds complex, but *Extensible Markup Language* (*XML*) makes it all much easier. In fact, XML was devised largely in answer to the generic need for a ubiquitous, transportable data format, and as you'll begin to see in this chapter, it's very powerful.

As it happens, Microsoft has subscribed heavily to XML in its implementation of .NET. You have probably already noticed that. XML is becoming increasingly important in a number of ways, and over the course of the next two chapters, we'll touch on only a few of its applications.

In this chapter, we will cover the following topics:

- The concept of markup that underpins XML
- The basic principles of an XML document
- The two properties of XML documents that allow you to read and work with them: well-formedness and validity
- How XML Schemas play an important role in XML-based applications

In Chapter 8, we'll use the preparatory work done in this chapter to extend the Friends Reunion application. We'll create a feature that allows an individual to upload an XML document containing details of many registrants from a single college or institution.

XML is a markup language. To get a good understanding of XML, it helps if you first understand the terms *markup* and *markup language*. Let's start our exploration there.

Markup Languages

Whenever you look at a document, you are looking at an organized set of data. Consider some everyday examples:

- Your salary slip contains data that relates to the amount of money you earned and how much was deducted in tax.
- A recipe for chocolate cake is an organized collection of data, telling you what ingredients you'll need (and how much of each), what method you should use to combine them all, and the cooking time and temperature.
- This book is also an organized collection of data—specifically, an ordered set of headings, paragraphs, and illustrations.

The data in documents such as these is generally arranged visually in such a way that the organization of the data is clear to the human eye, and is therefore easy for humans to read. In a similar way, we often need our computerized applications to be able to read a document and deduce the structure and organization of the data contained within it. To do this, we use *markup*.

Markup consists of tags or markers that exist in the document along with the data, and describe the different elements of data within the document. Let's consider an example:

```
<recipe title="Classic Chocolate Cake">
  <ingredients>
    <ingredient>
      <description>Eggs<description>
      <quantity>2</quantity>
    </ingredient>
    <ingredient>
      <description>Butter<description>
      <quantity unit="oz">4</quantity>
    </ingredient>
    ...etc...
  </ingredients>
  <method>
      Cream the butter and sugar. Add the milk and beaten eggs.
      Sieve in the flour and cocoa, and fold into the mixture.
      Turn into a lined cake tin and place into the oven.
  </method>
  <cookingTime unit="min">25</cookingTime>
  <ovenSetting unit="C">180</ovenSetting>
</recipe>
```

This example clearly describes a recipe for chocolate cake. All the information (or data) relating to the recipe is contained between the opening <recipe> tag and the closing </recipe> tag. Within the recipe, you see an organized list of ingredients, a method, and information about the cooking time and temperature. This document may not look like the attractive glossy cookbooks you see in the bookstores these days, but all the necessary information is presented in a well-organized, well-structured, unambiguous way.

HyperText Markup Language

You've seen markup before—in the HTML that is generated by your web applications and sent to the browser for display. HTML is a *markup language*. It is a set of tags and attributes that allow you to describe (or to mark up) the structure of a particular type of document. (In fact, HTML is specifically designed to describe the structure of web page documents.)

The data in an HTML document is intended for *display* (in a browser window), so the markup in an HTML document is intended specifically to *describe* the way the browser should *display* the data. Here is an example:

```
<html>
  <body>
    <h1>Classic Chocolate Cake</h1>
    <p>
      <b>Ingredients</b><br/>
      2 eggs<br/>
      4oz butter<br/>
      4oz sugar<br/>
      4oz self-raising flour<br/>
      1oz cocoa<br/>
      2tbsp milk<br/>
    </p>
    <p>
      <b>Method</b><br/>
      Cream the butter and sugar. Add the milk and beaten eggs.
      Sieve in the flour and cocoa, and fold into the mixture.
      Turn into a lined cake tin and place into the oven.
    </p>
    <p>
      <b>Cooking Time:</b> 25 minutes<br/>
      <b>Oven Setting:</b> 180C<br/>
    </p>
  </body>
</html>
```

Like the previous example, this HTML document contains all the data required for a chocolate cake recipe. However, the markup in this document structures the data very differently. The data in this document is *not* structured as a recipe (there are no <ingredients> and <method> sections). Instead, it is structured as a web page (with a heading and a sequence of paragraphs).

You can send this HTML document to a browser. Because the browser is programmed to recognize HTML tags, it will be able to work out the structure of the HTML document (the sequence of headings and paragraphs, and so on) by reading the tags, and hence display all the elements of the document in the right places on the page, as shown in Figure 7-1.

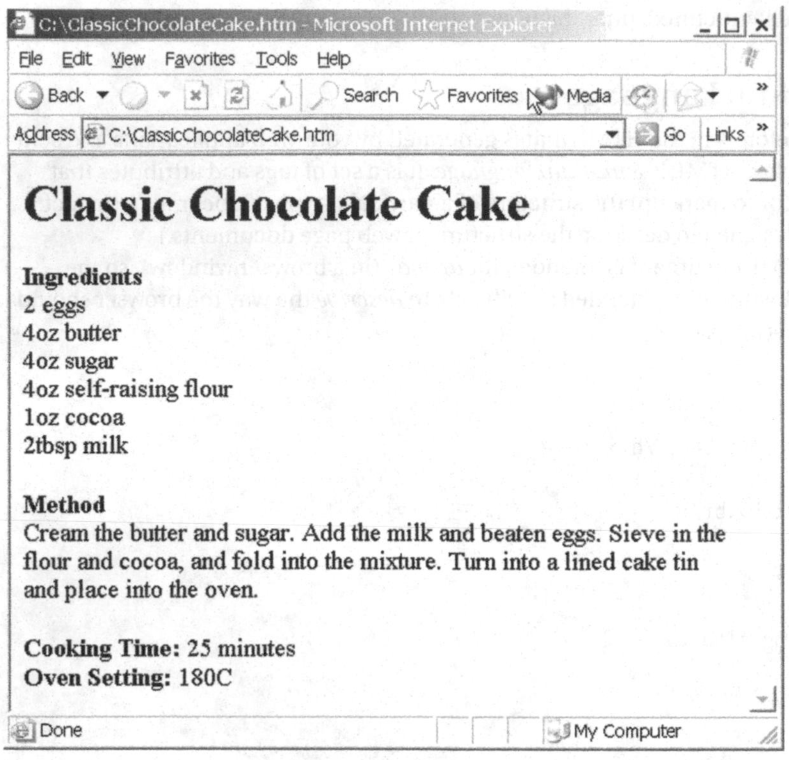

Figure 7-1. *An HTML document viewed in a browser*

Unsurprisingly, browsers are not programmed to recognize the `<recipe>` tag or the `<ingredients>` tag, and so the recipe structure (in our first example) means nothing to them. There would not be much point to sending the recipe markup to a browser. However, the recipe markup would be very useful, say, as part of a custom application that deals with archives of thousands of recipes.

Extensible Markup Language (XML)

So, markup is used to describe the structure and organization of data within a document. We describe the structure of a *web page* document using a markup language called HTML. But not every document is a web page; sometimes we need to describe data using a structure that does not resemble web page structure at all. In that case, HTML will not do the job, so we need a different markup language.

You've already seen a recipe document, which describes the structure of a recipe using special "recipe markup" tags like `<ingredients>` and `<cookingTime>`:

```
<recipe title="Classic Chocolate Cake">
  <ingredients>
    ...etc...
  </ingredients>
  <method>
    ...etc...
   </method>
   <cookingTime unit="min">25</cookingTime>
   <ovenSetting unit="C">180</ovenSetting>
</recipe>
```

Here, everything between the `<recipe>` and `</recipe>` tags is recipe information, and we use other tags to describe the exact nature of each bit of data.

You've also seen other types of markup already in this book, such as in the configuration files used by the Friends Reunion web application:

```
<configuration>
  <appSettings>
    <add key="sqlCon.ConnectionString" value="...etc..." />
  </appSettings>
  <system.web>
    <authentication mode="Forms">
      <forms loginUrl="Secure/Login.aspx" />
    </authentication>
    <customErrors mode="RemoteOnly" />
    ...etc...
  </system.web>
  <location path="Secure/NewUser.aspx">
    <system.web>
      <authorization>
        <allow users="*" />
      </authorization>
    </system.web>
  </location>
</configuration>
```

The principle here is similar: everything between the `<configuration>` and `</configuration>` tags is configuration data, and we use other tags to describe the exact nature of each bit of configuration data. As a result, the configuration data can be interpreted and its structure deduced programmatically, whenever it is required within the application.

These two examples have a common ancestor: they are both examples of *Extensible Markup Language* (*XML*). XML is a little like HTML, in that each is a tag-based and attribute-based text format for describing the structure of the data in a document. The main difference is that HTML is a language of tags and attributes for describing a *specific* structure (a web page), while XML is a more generic language that allows you to use almost *any* names for your tags and attributes.

The Significance of XML

As a data format, XML has a number of important characteristics that are its strengths. In particular, it is a *text-based* data format (this fact should be fairly obvious from the two samples above). In other words, any XML document is a plain-text document that contains both data and the markup that describes its structure. This means that:

- XML data is easy to store. You can store XML in text documents on hard disk.
- XML data is easy to transfer. Sending XML is as easy as transferring a text file or an HTML file.
- XML data is easy for machines to read. Hence, XML is highly compatible with many different types of systems.
- XML data is easy for humans to read. This makes it easy for a human to interpret the data in an XML document, and even makes it possible for humans to write XML documents using a keyboard. (This was one of the requirements that was considered when XML was being developed.)

Equally important is the fact that XML is a standard developed by the World Wide Web Consortium (W3C), an independent organization responsible for developing web standards, and the W3C's XML 1.0 specification is a globally accepted specification. This means that the following apply to XML:

- Any XML document can be expected to obey a standard set of rules, regardless of platform or software vendor.
- Any application that produces XML is expected to produce XML that adheres to the same standard (regardless of the operating system and programming language with which the application is developed or run).
- Any application that reads XML data is expected to be able to read XML that adheres to the same standard (again, regardless of the operating system and programming language, or the origin of the XML document).

In other words, any two applications that need to exchange XML data can do so, regardless of the platform or programming language.

Note The home page for all W3C XML specifications and works in progress can be found at `http://www.w3.org/XML`.

Some Applications of XML

Since the release of XML 1.0 in 1998, XML has found its way into plenty of diverse areas of computing. For example, Microsoft has adopted XML as a cornerstone of the .NET web applications model. This section is not a comprehensive list of its uses, but rather is intended to illustrate the usefulness of XML and how a good grounding in this important technology will help you in many areas.

Web Applications

These are just a few places in which XML is directly relevant in this book:

- **In configuration files:** You have already seen how ASP.NET uses the `Web.config` XML file to contain configuration settings for web applications. In fact, XML-based configuration files are used throughout the .NET Framework. XML's hierarchical and readable format makes it easy to locate and change configuration details.
- **In web forms:** The data contained by web controls on a page is often represented by XML fragments inside HTML and can be seen when the page is opened in HTML view. This information is used by the controls to render themselves appropriately.
- **In web services**: As you'll see in Chapter 9, web services are generally invoked using an XML-based language called *SOAP*, which is also used for returning results.

Data-Access Features

In the area of data access, XML provides a convenient, standard way of passing data between applications and databases. As you'll see, XML is inherently hierarchical in its nature. This hierarchical nature means that XML lends itself very well to representing the structure of the data and relationships between elements of the data. It offers the following features for data-access applications:

- **Interoperability:** XML is platform- and language-neutral, so it is ideal for moving data between disparate database products and operating systems.
- **ADO.NET support:** The `DataSet` object, which we studied in Chapter 4, has extensive support for XML, including the ability to read and save files and streams in this format through its `ReadXml()` and `WriteXml()` methods.
- **Support from major database vendors:** Most major database vendors now build some degree of XML support into their products. For example, many products can return the results of queries in XML format. Some products can natively read and process XML files and XML strings within stored procedures (using functions or types added to their respective languages). SQL Server, Oracle, and IBM's DB2 all offer native XML support.

Also as a platform-neutral standard, XML is the perfect candidate for data representation in e-business, where business partners need their systems and applications to interact and communicate, and where systems range from the latest super-sleek setups to ancient monoliths. In the past, the standard for business intercommunication was Electronic Data Interchange (EDI). Unfortunately, EDI was very difficult to understand and costly to implement. XML, in conjunction with the Internet, makes it much easier for smaller companies to implement e-commerce solutions.

The Nature of an XML Document

The nature of XML as a data format implies that it imposes a set of formatting rules. If a document conforms to these rules, then we say that it is a *well-formed* XML document.

The key rules of XML are simple, and mostly very intuitive:

- **Matching start and end tags**: Any block (or *element*) of data that begins with a start tag (for example, `<myElement>`) should end with a matching end tag (in this case `</myElement>`). For example, the following element is well-formed:

```
<quantity>2</quantity>
```

- **Empty elements:** An element composed of a start tag/end tag pair, but with no data in between them, can be abbreviated by using a single *empty tag*. For example, you can replace the following element:

```
<description></description>
```

  with this empty element (note the position of the / character):

```
<description/>
```

- **Attributes:** If you want to add attributes to an element, you can write them within the element's start tag. The attribute is a name/value pair expressed using the format `att_name="att_value"` (where the value is expressed as a string and enclosed in single or double quotes). For example, the following element is well-formed:

```
<quantity unit="oz">4</quantity>
```

  You can also add attributes to an empty tag:

```
<freezeable duration="3 months" />
```

- **Case-sensitivity of tag and attribute names:** Tag names and attribute names are case-sensitive. In particular, this means the case of an element's end tag must match the case of its start tag. For example, the following element is *not* well-formed:

```
<Quantity>2</quantity>
```

- **Nesting:** Elements must be properly nested. In other words, if an element contains another opening tag, it should also contain its closing tag. For example, the following is well-formed:

```
<player><name>Joe DiMaggio</name></player>
```

  By contrast, the following is *not* well-formed:

```
<player><name>Joe DiMaggio</player></name>
```

- **Top-level element:** There must be one (and only one) top-level element that encloses all other elements in the document.

Any XML document that meets these requirements is said to be well-formed. In fact, the chocolate cake document we presented at the beginning of this chapter is a well-formed XML document. You'll see how to check for well-formedness shortly.

XML Data Exchange

You've seen some examples of XML documents. We've described what makes a well-formed XML document. We also noted that XML is particularly useful when it comes to data exchange. Specifically, XML is a *text*-based, data-formatting mechanism. This means that the XML data format is compatible with any application (regardless of operating systems and languages) and that it is easy to transfer XML documents from one system to another.

Over the remainder of this chapter and during the next two chapters, you'll develop your Friends Reunion application a little further, by adding a couple of data-exchange features that make use of different XML data-exchange techniques. As we go, you'll learn a lot more about XML and how it is used in web applications. We'll begin by describing one of the features that you're going to add.

Suppose that a college or other institution wants to upload information about a number of its students to the Friends Reunion web application, or a social group (such as an Old Classmates' Society) wants to add the details of *all* of its members to the site. In its current form, the application doesn't enable an individual to upload details about a lot of people *at the same time*. Instead, that individual would need to use the existing interface to insert the details of each member manually. If there were more than a few members in the group, this would be a fairly laborious task!

It would be much easier for the individuals concerned if you allowed them to upload the *complete* set of details of their members all at once, as an XML document. The XML document would pass from the individual's web browser to the Friends Reunion web application on the server. Then the application would read and interpret the uploaded XML document, and display the information on the screen. From there, you could extend the feature further and have the application place the uploaded data into your database. The four steps in this procedure are illustrated in Figure 7-2. We'll go only as far as the third step in the book, but you should learn enough in this book to be able to implement the fourth step yourself, if you wish.

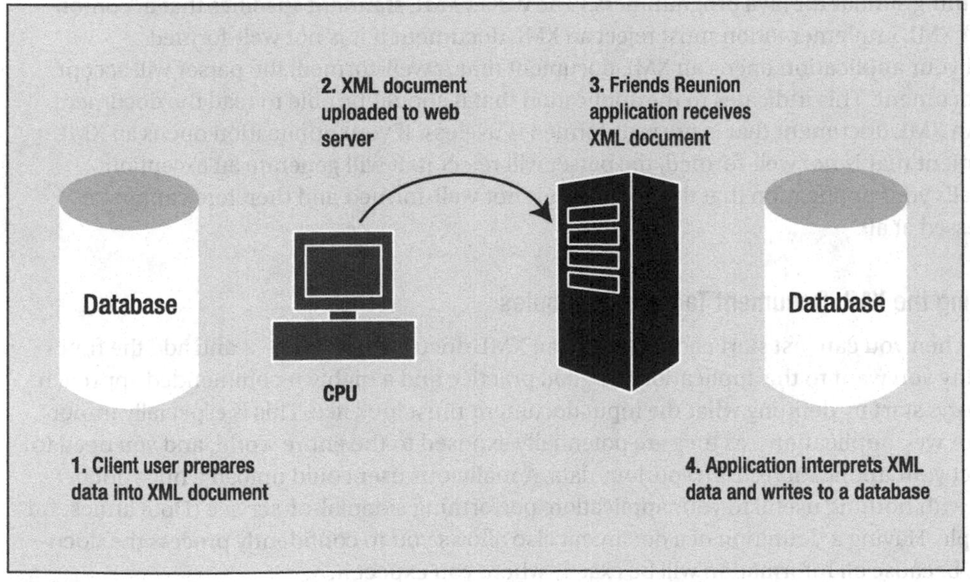

Figure 7-2. *The procedure for XML data exchange*

XML Schemas and Validation

Before you rush in and build the upload tool, you have some preparatory work to do. In particular, it's quite easy to see that, unless you impose some careful checking mechanism, an individual would be able to upload *any* type of document to your web application. You need to develop a mechanism that checks the uploaded document, to confirm that it contains *exactly* the kind of information that the Friends Reunion application expects.

We can break this checking process into two parts:

- First, your application needs to be able to *read* the XML document. In other words, you need to check that the uploaded document *is* an XML document and that it is well-formed.
- Second, your application needs to be able to *interpret* your well-formed XML document. What does this mean? Well, the application's task is to understand the data in the document, extract it, and perform some task with it (in our case, display it on the screen or place it into the database). If the document contains tags and attributes that the application doesn't understand, the application will not be able to extract the data it's looking for, and it will not be able to complete the job.

Let's look at how to perform both of these checks: for well-formedness and to ensure that the XML document contains the expected tags and attributes.

Checking for Well-Formedness

When an application opens an XML document, it uses an *XML parser* to check that the document is well-formed. The parser is part of the XML implementation that your application uses whenever it needs to deal with XML documents. (For example, Microsoft's .NET Framework provides an implementation through the classes in the `System.Xml` namespace, and Sun does something similar for Java programmers.) The W3C's XML standard specifies that a "conformant" XML implementation must reject an XML document if it is not well-formed.

If your application opens an XML document that *is* well-formed, the parser will accept the document. This indicates to the application that it should be able to read the document.

An XML document that is *not* well-formed is useless. If your application opens an XML document that is *not* well-formed, the parser will reject it. It will generate an exception that tells your application that the document is not well-formed and therefore cannot be processed at all.

Defining the XML Document Tags and Attributes

Even when you can just start coding to read an XML document to process and add the functionality you want to the application, it's good practice and a highly recommended approach to *always* start by defining what the input document must look like. This is especially important for web applications, as they are potentially exposed to the entire world, and you need to protect your applications from spurious data. A malicious user could upload a huge document with nothing useful to your application, performing a denial-of-service (DoS) attack, for example. Having a definition of a document also allows you to confidently process the document, because all information will be exactly where you expect it.

The best way to start solving this problem is to work out the tags and attributes that you expect an uploaded XML document to have. Then, as you'll learn in the next section, you can formalize this by writing something called an *XML Schema*. So, let's look at what a typical uploaded XML file should contain for the purposes of the Friends Reunion application.

When the XML file is uploaded, the Friends Reunion application will extract the data from it and use it to populate the TimeLapse and User tables of your database. Here's a reminder of the structure of those tables:

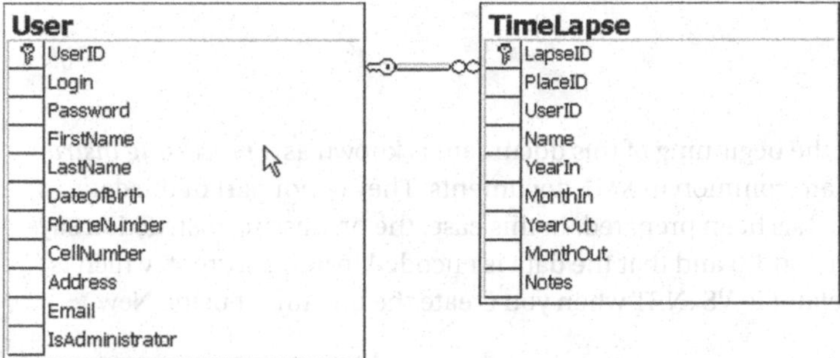

We won't dive into the process of database updates here. The main point is to see the type of attendee-related information that individuals will want to include in their XML document. The TimeLapse table holds data that describes how long a particular individual (or user) spent at a particular institution (or place), while the User table holds more general information about users.

Our XML document will contain data about a collection of users who attended a particular place. For each user, the document will contain data about the individual, and it may also contain data about the attendance details of that user.

So, here's an example XML document that shows the kind of structure we're looking for. It has a single root element (called <Friends>), which specifies the identity of the institution submitting the document in an attribute called PlaceID. The <Friends> element is then allowed to contain <User> elements (one for each user), and this element, in turn, contains <Attended> elements (each element describes the period of attendance of the user it's enclosed by):

```
<?xml version="1.0" encoding="utf-8"?>
<Friends PlaceID="C9796AD1-5A7E-4d9c-9F99-0090E11E5662">
  <User ID="E81A8BCD-47A3-4038-9F7B-2DF25C741833">
    <Login>gmorande</Login>
    <Password>gusygaby</Password>
    <FirstName>Gustavo</FirstName>
    <LastName>Morande</LastName>
    <PhoneNumber>042-700-7007</PhoneNumber>
    <Address>2755 3rd. February Street, Buenos Aires</Address>
    <Email>gmorande@clariusconsulting.com</Email>
    <Attended Name="High School Complete">
      <YearIn>1972</YearIn>
      <MonthIn>3</MonthIn>
```

```
      <YearOut>1977</YearOut>
      <MonthOut>11</MonthOut>
      <Notes>I played cymbals in the school band!</Notes>
    </Attended>
    ...other courses attended by user...
  </User>
  <User>
    ...etc...
  </User>
  ... other users...
</Friends>
```

The `<?xml ... ?>` line at the beginning of this document is known as a *processing instruction*. Processing instructions are common in XML documents. They're not part of the data itself but explain how the data has been prepared. In this case, the processing instruction says that we're using W3C XML version 1.0 and that the data is encoded in `utf-8` format, which is the most common and the default in VS .NET when you create the document using New ➤ Item ➤ XML File.

We've deliberately chosen tags and attributes that match the field names used in the database (like `User`, `UserID`, `YearIn`, and so on). You don't need to do this, but it's helpful if you want to use this feature to extract data from the XML file and insert it into the database.

We've also decided not to use a one-to-one mapping between the elements of the document and the fields in the database tables. Instead, we've tried to give the XML document a more intuitive layout, allowing us to demonstrate the full functionality of .NET's XML objects, which you'll see later on. For example, the place is referred to at the root element as an attribute, because we expect uploads to be performed by a single institution. In the database, however, each `TimeLapse` record contains the `PlaceID`. Likewise, the enclosing `<User>` element defines the `UserID` that is attending to the place; as a consequence, there's no need to repeat this for each `<Attended>` element either. Again, this information *is* present in the database.

How is a document like this created? You could type it into a text editor such as Notepad or create it using a specialized XML editor, like the one included with VS .NET or the new InfoPath application included with Office 2003 Enterprise Edition. Alternatively, it could be generated by a program that extracts the information from the organization's database and places it in a file of this format. However, since XML is a universally adopted standard across platforms, languages, and tools, we don't need to worry about that. We'll leave it to individual institutions and societies to decide how they want to create their XML documents, and we can be sure we'll be able to read it back, irrespective of this process. (However, we'll be able to help them, by supplying them with the XML Schema definition that we'll begin to build shortly.)

Markup Languages, Schemas, and Validation

When you write the application code that interprets the uploaded XML file, that code will assume the XML document has a certain structure (the sample document in the previous section gives you an idea of that structure). But as we said, it's quite dangerous to make that assumption without some kind of explicit verification, because if the XML document has the wrong structure, the application will fail in some unpredictable way.

What you should do is perform a formal *check* that the XML document has the structure that the application expects. This check is usually performed at the same time the application checks that the XML document is well-formed (so you know you can read it), but *before* the application starts interpreting it.

To perform this check, you can use an *XML Schema*. An XML Schema is a way of describing a markup language. More accurately, it describes the structure of a given language formally, as follows:

- It states precisely which element names and attribute names are allowed.
- It can also state the permitted relationships between elements (for example, that a `<User>` element can contain an `<Attended>` element, but not the other way around).
- It can impose restrictions on the values (or types of values) contained in elements or attributes (for example, the ID attributes have a well-defined and known structure, a GUID).

When the application receives an XML document, you can check that it has the appropriate structure by *validating* it against the schema. If the XML document adheres to the rules described in the schema, then we say that the XML document is *valid*—it contains the expected structure. Figure 7-3 illustrates this validation process.

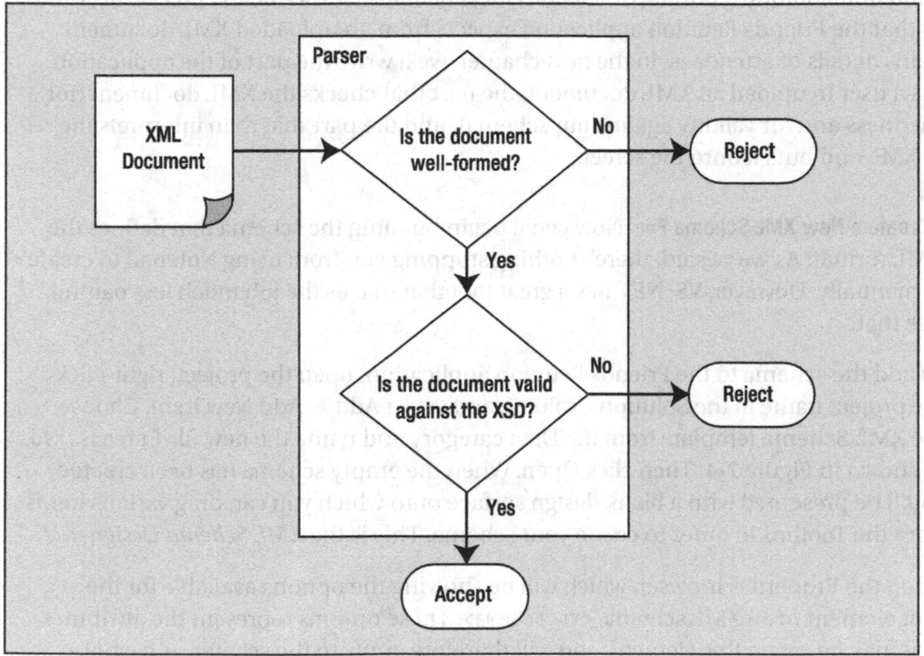

Figure 7-3. *Validating an XML document against the schema*

Thus, as we stated earlier, an XML document usually needs to pass *two* important tests before you can use it. First, it must pass the *well-formed* check (it can actually be read), and then it must pass the *validity* check (and thus you can interpret it).

XML Schema Creation

The way you write an XML Schema is in the form of an *XML Schema Definition* (*XSD*) file. As you'll see, an XSD file is actually just an XML file that uses special tags and attributes designed to describe XML Schemas.

Because the XML Schema can be completely described in a single XSD file, it's easily transportable. This means that not only is it a valuable part of the Friends Reunion application, but also that you can send it to the developers of client applications. These developers can use the XSD file to find out the exact structure of the XML documents that their custom applications should be generating, and even to validate the generated XML before it is uploaded, and thus ensure that their uploaded XML documents are not rejected by the Friends Reunion application.

Moreover, because an XSD file is written in XML, it's language-independent and platform-independent. Therefore, *any* client developer should be able to make use of your XSD, once you've written it.

So, we had better get down to writing it! We'll devote the remainder of this chapter to building and understanding our XML Schema. Our schema will describe the precise tags and attributes that the Friends Reunion application expects from an uploaded XML document that contains details of attendees. In the next chapter, we'll write the part of the application that allows a user to upload an XML document, the part that checks the XML document (for well-formedness and for validity against our schema), and the part that then interprets the uploaded XML and puts it onto the screen.

Try It Out: Create a New XML Schema File Now you'll begin building the schema that defines the chosen XML format. As we've said, there's nothing stopping you from using Notepad to create a schema manually. However, VS .NET has a great tool that makes the job much less painful, so we'll use that.

1. To add the schema to the Friends Reunion application, open the project, right-click the project name in the Solution Explorer, and select Add ➤ Add New Item. Choose the XML Schema template from the Data category and name the new file `Friends.xsd`, as shown in Figure 7-4. Then click Open. When the empty schema has been created, you'll be presented with a blank design surface onto which you can drag various items from the Toolbox in order to create your schema. This is the *XML Schema Designer*.

2. Open the Properties browser, which will be showing the options available for the root element of an XML schema, `<xs:schema>`. These options represent the attributes that may be set on this element, and will therefore apply to the schema as a whole. Locate the `targetNamespace` property. You'll notice that it is set to a default value, `http://tempuri.org/Friends.xsd`. Change it to `http://www.apress.com/schemas/friendsreunion`.

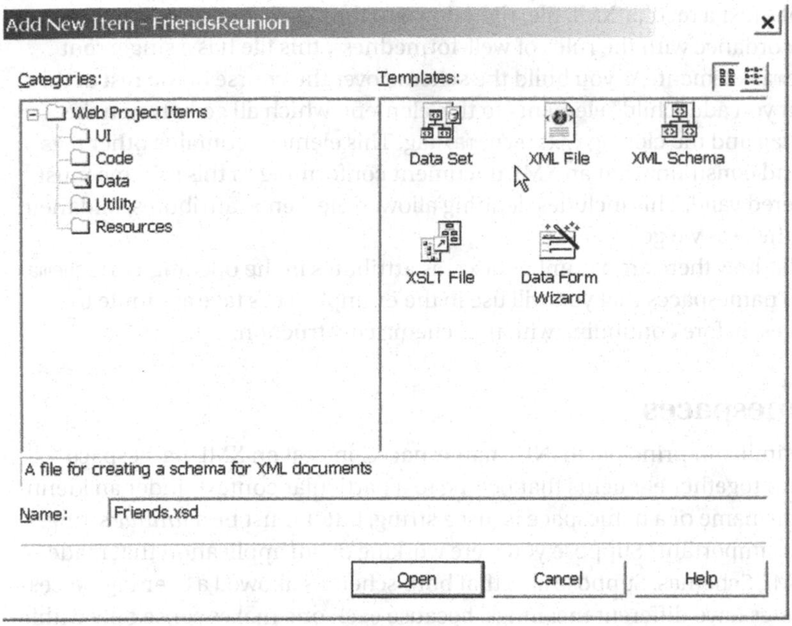

Figure 7-4. *Creating a new XML Schema file*

There's not much to see yet, but let's find out more about what you've done in these steps, and how they contribute to the overall schema.

How It Works

Just like the VS .NET forms designers, the XML Schema Designer is a visual tool that generates code corresponding to the drag-and-drop actions you perform. You can see the code it produces by clicking the XML button at the bottom-left corner of the designer.

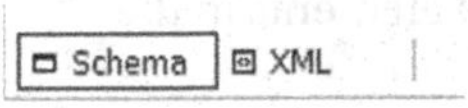

If you do this now, you'll see that your schema currently consists of a single, empty `<xs:schema>` element, which looks like this (formatted a little here to make it more legible):

```
<?xml version="1.0" encoding="utf-8" ?>
<xs:schema id="Friends"
      targetNamespace="http://www.apress.com/schemas/friendsreunion"
      elementFormDefault="qualified"
      xmlns="http://www.apress.com/schemas/friendsreunion"
      xmlns:mstns="http://www.apress.com/schemas/friendsreunion"
      xmlns:xs="http://www.w3.org/2001/XMLSchema">
</xs:schema>
```

You can see that it's just a regular XML file, right down to the `<?xml ?>` processing instruction at the start. In accordance with the rules of well-formedness, this file has a single root element: the `<xs:schema>` element. As you build the schema over the course of the rest of this chapter, you'll see that you add "child" elements to this element, which all go between the opening `<xs:schema>` tag and the closing `</xs:schema>` tag. This element contains other tags that together define and constrain what an XML document conforming to this schema must look like to be considered valid. This includes defining allowed elements, attributes, and their types. You'll see all of these as we go.

Notice in particular how there are a number of `xmlns` attributes in the opening `<xs:schema>` tag. These relate to the namespaces that you will use in the example. Let's take a minute to understand namespaces, before continuing with the schema construction.

Using XML Namespaces

XML namespaces are similar in principle to .NET namespaces, in that an XML namespace provides a way to group together elements that belong to a particular context under an identifying name. In XML, the name of a namespace is just a string, but it must be a *unique* string.

Why is uniqueness important? Suppose you were working on an application that made use of two different XML Schemas. Suppose also that both schemas allowed a `User` tag. Necessarily, these two `User` tags have different meanings, because each one makes sense only within the context of its own schema. So in order for the application to tell them apart, it uses namespaces. Each namespace has a name, and in order to guarantee that the names of different namespaces are different, you use a uniqueness rule for naming them.

The recommendation is that you should identify namespaces using URIs (that is, URLs or URNs), because URIs must, by their nature, be unique. When an organization's developers create schemas for its data, they can place the schemas within namespaces that specify the organization's own URLs (for example, Apress might choose namespace names that begin `http://www.apress.com`, and Microsoft might choose namespace names beginning with `http://www.microsoft.com`). This gives each organization control of the uniqueness of its own namespace names, by guaranteeing that they are different from those of all other organizations. The W3C itself follows this recommendation by using namespaces that start with `http://www.w3.org/`. They take advantage of namespaces to define all XSD elements in the `http://www.w3.org/2001/XMLSchema` namespace.

In order to specify that an element belongs to a certain namespace, you use a *prefix*. A prefix is mapped to a namespace by means of the `xmlns` attribute:

```
<xs:schema xmlns:xs="http://www.w3.org/2001/XMLSchema"
```

Here, the `xs` prefix is mapped to the W3C XML Schema namespace, and the prefix is used to specify that the `schema` element belongs to it (`xs:schema`). Multiple namespace/prefix mappings can be defined.

So, how do we plan to use XML namespaces in the Friends Reunion example? Well, namespace names are used both in the XSD file that contains the schema and in the XML document that contains the data. They are needed in the latter so that the application using the document knows to which namespace the elements in the document belong.

Namespaces in the XSD File

In the schema document you created in the previous exercise, you use a (unique) URI to identify the target namespace of this XML Schema:

```
<?xml version="1.0" encoding="utf-8" ?>
<xs:schema id="Friends"
        targetNamespace="http://www.apress.com/schemas/friendsreunion"
        elementFormDefault="qualified"
        xmlns="http://www.apress.com/schemas/friendsreunion"
        xmlns:mstns="http://www.apress.com/schemas/friendsreunion"
        xmlns:xs="http://www.w3.org/2001/XMLSchema">
</xs:schema>
```

The `targetNamespace` attribute defines which namespace this schema defines. All element, attribute, and type definitions in the schema will belong to this namespace.

The `xmlns` attribute specifies the default namespace of the schema. Here, it is set to the same value that you just set for the `targetNamespace` attribute. The effect of this is that any element appearing inside the schema element without a prefix will be assumed to belong to that namespace.

Note that the value of the `<xs:schema>` element's `elementFormDefault` attribute comes into play here:

```
<xs:schema id="Friends"
           targetNamespace="http://www.apress.com/schemas/friendsreunion"
           elementFormDefault="qualified"
           ... >
```

This attribute is set to `qualified`, which means that in this schema, all elements defined anywhere will belong to the target namespace. The default is that only the elements defined directly under the root `schema` element belong to the namespace (`elementFormDefault="unqualified"`). This is common practice and ensures consistent placement of both top-level and nested elements in the same namespace.

Namespaces in the XML Document

In the XML document itself, you specify that an element belongs to a particular namespace by using the `xmlns` attribute on that element. For example, to associate a whole XML document with one namespace, you would add the `xmlns` attribute (for that namespace) to the root element of the document:

```
<?xml version="1.0" encoding="utf-8"?>
<Friends xmlns="http://www.apress.com/schemas/friendsreunion"
         PlaceID="C9796AD1-5A7E-4d9c-9F99-0090E11E5662">
  <User ID="E81A8BCD-47A3-4038-9F7B-2DF25C741833">
  ...etc...
```

This adds the `http://www.apress.com/schemas/friendsreunion` namespace to the `<Friends>` element. When you add a namespace to an element like this, all of the children *elements* of that element inherit that namespace, too.

What if you have multiple namespaces in use within a single XML document? In that case, you can use a different prefix for each namespace. For example, the following (hypothetical) code states that the prefix `af` is to be equated with the namespace `http://www.apress.com/schemas/friendsreunion`:

```
<?xml version="1.0" encoding="utf-8"?>
<af:Friends xmlns:af="http://www.apress.com/schemas/friendsreunion"
            xmlns:ms="http://www.microsoft.com/Friends"
            af:PlaceID="C9796AD1-5A7E-4d9c-9F99-0090E11E5662">
  <af:User>
  ...etc...
  </af:User>
  <ms:User>
  ...etc...
  </ms:User>
```

Then the `af:User` element is from the `http://www.apress.com/schemas/friendsreunion` namespace, and the `ms:User` element is from the `http://www.microsoft.com/Friends` namespace. An application can distinguish both and, for example, ignore the ones that are not from the Friends Reunion "official" namespace.

Building an XML Schema

Returning to the schema definition for the Friends Reunion application, you have just an empty schema at the moment—it does not contain any rules about tags or attributes. Now you will start adding these rules, so that the XSD begins to take shape.

We will focus on the XSD Designer features, looking at what's generated next. With the designer's XML and Schema views, and an explanation in the "How It Works" section, you'll gain an understanding of the concepts and components that make up an XML Schema.

Try It Out: Add an Element Every XML document must have exactly one root element, and the Friends Reunion XML documents will be no different. You will start by adding the definition for the root `<Friends>` element to your XSD.

1. Switch back to the Schema view of the XSD file by clicking the Schema button at the bottom-left corner of the designer.

2. Open the Toolbox. At the moment, it offers just one tab, called XML Schema, which contains all the items used when designing a schema.

3. In the Toolbox, double-click element, or drag-and-drop it onto the design surface.

4. Change the new element's name from the default `element1` to `Friends`, either through the Properties browser or by clicking inside the element in the designer.

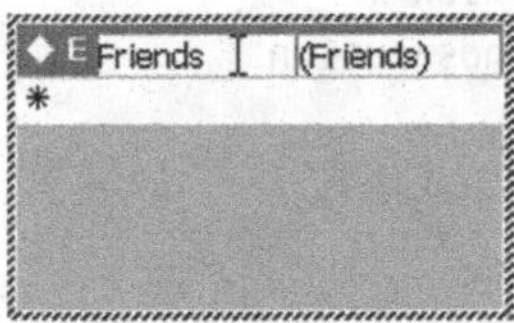

5. Drag an attribute from the Toolbox, and drop it onto the `Friends` element. Change its name to `PlaceID`, and check that string is selected in the right-hand column (either type it or select it from the combo box).

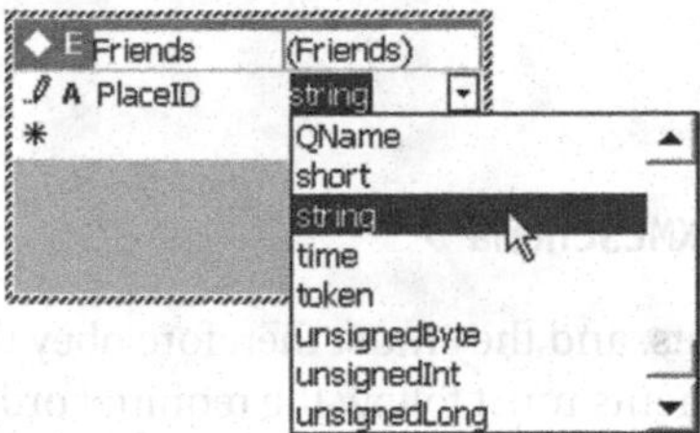

How It Works

The element you have added corresponds to the root <Friends> element of the XML format you are going to use for uploads:

```
<?xml version="1.0" encoding="utf-8"?>
<Friends xmlns="http://www.apress.com/schemas/friendsreunion"
         PlaceID="C9796AD1-5A7E-4d9c-9F99-0090E11E5662">
  ...etc...
</Friends>
```

Your schema now specifies that the root element must have the name Friends. It also says that the Friends element can have a string attribute called PlaceID. (The attribute is not compulsory, however, because attributes are optional by default; see the "Restricting Element Occurrence" section later in this chapter for more information.)

If you switch to the XML view, you can check out the schema markup that VS .NET has generated, based on what you added in the designer:

```
<?xml version="1.0" encoding="utf-8" ?>
<xs:schema id="Friends"
           targetNamespace="http://www.apress.com/schemas/friendsreunion"
           elementFormDefault="qualified"
           xmlns="http://www.apress.com/schemas/friendsreunion"
           xmlns:mstns="http://www.apress.com/schemas/friendsreunion"
           xmlns:xs="http://www.w3.org/2001/XMLSchema">
  <xs:element name="Friends">
    <xs:complexType>
      <xs:sequence />
      <xs:attribute name="PlaceID" type="xs:string" />
    </xs:complexType>
  </xs:element>
</xs:schema>
```

Notice that all of the new elements use the xs prefix. The xs prefix is associated with the XML Schema namespace:

```
<xs:schema id="Friends"
           ...
           xmlns:xs="http://www.w3.org/2001/XMLSchema">
```

This marks these elements as XML Schema elements, and they must therefore obey the rules of validity for XML Schemas. This means that elements must follow the required order and have valid values and attributes, such as the type attribute on the <xs:attribute> element.

According to the validity rules for an XSD, an <xs:element> that is a direct child of the <xs:schema> describes the *root* element of any document that conforms to this schema. The name attribute of the <xs:element> element here defines the name that the root element must have, so it is <Friends>.

Note For details about the validity rules for an XSD, see the W3C's XML Schema specification at http://www.w3.org/XML/Schema.

Once the element is defined, you need to specify what content it may hold. There are two types of content: simple and complex. Simple content consists of direct values, without any nested elements. Complex content, on the other hand, can contain nested elements. These content models are specified through *types*. A type is defined by either a `simpleType` or `complexType` element, which constrains the allowed content. For example, the Friends `xs:element` includes the following `complexType` definition:

```
<xs:element name="Friends">
  <xs:complexType>
    <xs:sequence />
    <xs:attribute name="PlaceID" type="xs:string" />
  </xs:complexType>
</xs:element>
```

This type, being defined inside the containing `xs:element`, is called a *local type*. If a type is to be reused by several elements, you can also define it as a *global type*, and give it a name so you can refer to it:

```
<xs:complexType name="AddressDef>
  ...type content model...
</xs:complexType>

...Somewhere else in the schema, probably inside a Customer, Order, etc...
<xs:element name="Address" type="AddressDef"/>
```

When the element content model is defined in a global type, you just need to specify it as the element type attribute. As you can see, complex types are usually custom ones you create to reflect the content of your elements.

Many simple types, on the other hand, are so common that they are already provided by XSD. For example, you don't need to define what an integer, string, or date looks like, because there are built-in types that already define them. You can see the full list of available built-in simple types in the XML Schema Designer's drop-down list you used to set the `PlaceID` attribute type to `string`.

You can, however, define your own custom simple types, too. For example, you may want to modify one of the basic XSD types to restrict numbers to a given range of values or to specify maximum and minimum lengths for string-based types. But keep in mind that `simpleType` elements cannot contain attributes or child elements; they can represent only a simple value.

Defining a complex type is a bit like defining a new class in a project, in that you define its structure in the abstract, and then all "instances" of it will have that same structure. By "instance" of an XSD element or type, we refer to the element that appears in a concrete document and that must comply with that element's type. The schema that has been produced so far specifies that the `<Friends>` element may have an attribute called `PlaceID`, and this attribute value is of type `xs:string`.

Defining Complex Types

The most common elements that can appear in an `<xs:complexType>` element are `<xs:sequence>`, `<xs:choice>`, and `<xs:attribute>`. You've already seen `<xs:attribute>` in action, and the only thing to add is that its type must be either a built-in XSD simple type or a custom simple type, because an XML attribute cannot contain other elements. For example, it's not valid to have an attribute like the following in an XML document:

```
<Friends PlaceID="<Place>6555</Place>">
```

The `<xs:sequence>` element defines the elements that can appear in instances of the type and the order in which they must appear. Each allowed child element is defined by a nested `<xs:element>` element inside the sequence. By default, each element in the sequence is compulsory, and only one of each element can be present. (This sounds inflexible, but you can use the `minOccurs` and `maxOccurs` attributes to permit multiple occurrences and optional elements, as you'll see later, in the "Restricting Element Occurrence" section later in this chapter.) If a document contains elements in the wrong order, it is said to be an *invalid* instance with regard to the element definition in the schema.

The `<xs:choice>` element, by contrast, defines a set of interchangeable elements. By default, only one member of the set can be present in an XML instance document (again, unless you use `minOccurs` and `maxOccurs`, as we'll discuss later). There's a third `xs` element for describing groups of allowed elements in an instance document: `<xs:all>`. This describes a set of elements that can appear in any order.

The plan that we've devised has a `<User>` element inside the root `<Friends>` element, and an `<Attended>` element inside each `<User>`. Both arrangements can be represented by `<xs:sequence>`.

Try It Out: Define the <User> Element Now you'll build on the schema that you've created so far, and start to define the `<User>` element. This will involve two parts: first, you specify that you want it to be a child of the `<Friends>` element, and then you specify what you want it to contain.

1. If necessary, switch to the visual designer, by clicking the Schema button. You may find it helpful to switch to XML view after each of the following steps, to see the code that is being generated.
2. Drag an element from the Toolbox and drop it onto the `Friends` element that you added earlier, to indicate that the new element is a child of `<Friends>`. This relationship is shown in the designer by a solid line from the `Friends` element to the new element.

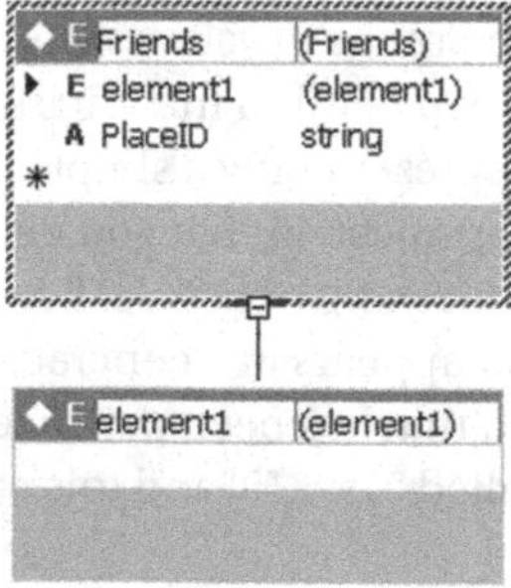

Note that the new element is represented not only by the new graphic below Friends, but also by a new row within the Friends element, currently with the default name of element1.

3. Change the name of this element from element1 to User, by typing either in the new element or in the new row of the Friends element.

4. Drag an attribute from the Toolbox, this time placing it on the new empty element that you just added. Set its name to ID, and ensure its type is string.

5. Drag an element inside below it. Set its name to Login.

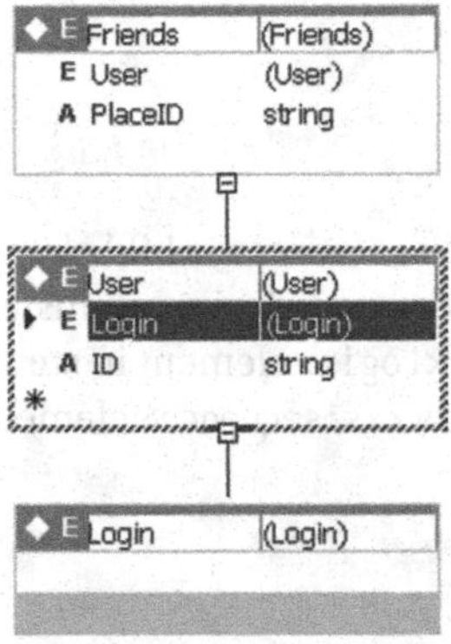

6. Using the drop-down list in the right-hand column of the new element inside User, set the type of the Login element to string. Being simple types, string-typed elements cannot contain any attributes or child content, and so the third box, representing the Login element, disappears from the designer.

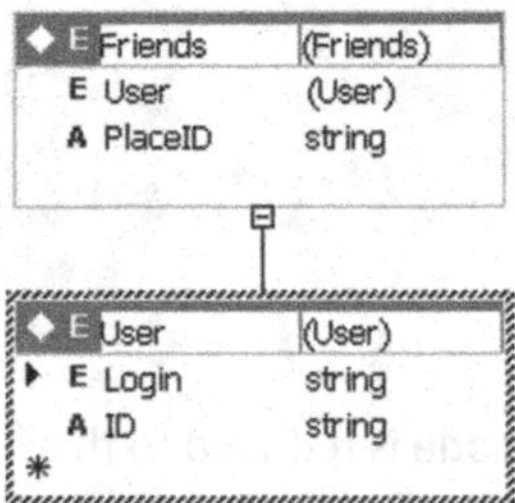

How It Works

When you add the <User> element in steps 2 and 3, the code generated consists of a complex type element with an empty <xs:sequence> inside it, similar to the code created for the <Friends> element:

```
<?xml version="1.0" encoding="utf-8" ?>
<xs:schema id="Friends" ...etc... >
  <xs:element name="Friends">
    <xs:complexType>
      <xs:sequence>
        <xs:element name="User">
          <xs:complexType>
            <xs:sequence />
          </xs:complexType>
        </xs:element>
      </xs:sequence>
      <xs:attribute name="PlaceID" type="xs:string" />
    </xs:complexType>
  </xs:element>
</xs:schema>
```

The new code has been placed inside what was the empty <xs:sequence> child element of <Friends>, as the new <User> element will be a direct child of the root element in instance documents. A similar process takes place when you first add the <Login> element in step 5. By default, VS .NET represents it as a complex type, with an empty <xs:sequence> element:

```
<?xml version="1.0" encoding="utf-8" ?>
<xs:schema id="Friends" ...etc...>
  <xs:element name="Friends">
    <xs:complexType>
      <xs:sequence>
        <xs:element name="User">
          <xs:complexType>
            <xs:sequence>
              <xs:element name="Login">
                <xs:complexType>
                  <xs:sequence />
                </xs:complexType>
              </xs:element>
            </xs:sequence>
    ...etc...
</xs:schema>
```

Once you set the type to string in the designer in step 5, the code is reduced to this:

```
<?xml version="1.0" encoding="utf-8" ?>
<xs:schema id="Friends" ...etc... >
  <xs:element name="Friends">
    <xs:complexType>
      <xs:sequence>
        <xs:element name="User">
          <xs:complexType>
```

```
        <xs:sequence>
          <xs:element name="Login" type="xs:string"></xs:element>
        </xs:sequence>
        <xs:attribute name="ID" type="xs:string" />
      </xs:complexType>
    </xs:element>
  </xs:sequence>
  <xs:attribute name="PlaceID" type="xs:string" />
</xs:complexType>
</xs:element>
</xs:schema>
```

This occurs because the string type is a simple type. Such elements cannot contain child elements, so they don't require the extra information that the `<xs:complexType>` element specifies. Nor is there any need to draw it as a separate element on the design surface.

Try It Out: Complete the <User> Element Definition Now you will define the nine remaining child elements of `<User>`. As you did in steps 5 and 6 of the previous exercise, drag elements into the `User` element and set their types. Add one for each field in the corresponding database table, in the following order and of the type listed:

`Password`	string
`FirstName`	string
`LastName`	string
`DateOfBirth`	date
`PhoneNumber`	string
`CellNumber`	string
`Address`	string
`Email`	string
`ID`	string

	User	(User)
E	Login	string
E	Password	string
E	FirstName	string
E	LastName	string
E	DateOfBirth	date
E	PhoneNumber	string
E	CellNumber	string
E	Address	string
E	Email	string
A	ID	string
*		

How It Works

If you've ever used graphical database design tools such as those included with VS .NET, you may recognize the layout of schema elements within the XML Schema Designer. They appear much like a database table, with a row for each child element.

Note We won't discuss XML data types in detail in this book. If you're curious about the different data types, what they mean, the range of valid values, and so on, take a look at the *XML Schema Part 2: Datatypes* document (`http://www.w3.org/TR/xmlschema-2/`).

Try It Out: Add an Element Directly As well as adding new child elements by dragging-and-dropping them from the Toolbox, you can add them by typing directly into the table. You'll see this in action as you create the definition of the `<Attended>` element.

1. Click the empty row at the bottom of the graphic representing the `User` element, and type `Attended` in the center column. When you press Enter, it will place an `Attended` element, as shown here.

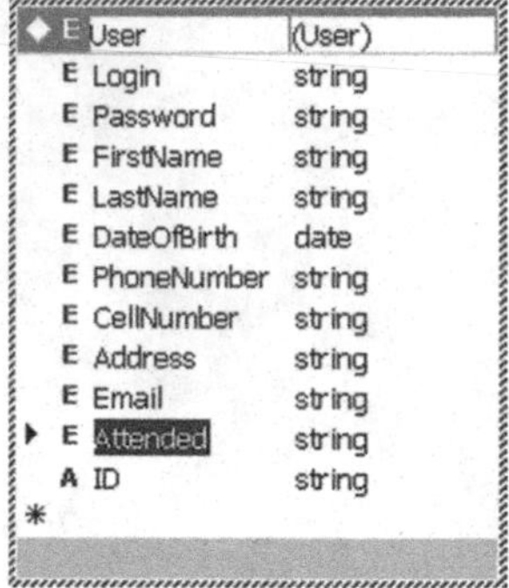

2. Change the type of `Attendee` from the default (string) to Unnamed complexType, which appears at the top of the list. This step creates a new, empty element below the `User` element. This is where content of the `Attended` element can be described.

3. Inside the `Attended` element, add a new row, with the name `YearIn`, and set its type to short.

4. Add four more rows: `MonthIn` (type byte), `YearOut` (type short), `MonthOut` (type byte), and `Notes` (type string).

5. You also need to specify that the `<Attendee>` element will have a `Name` attribute. Add a new row called `Name`, and then click the capital *E* that appears in the left-most column to open a drop-down list. Select attribute.

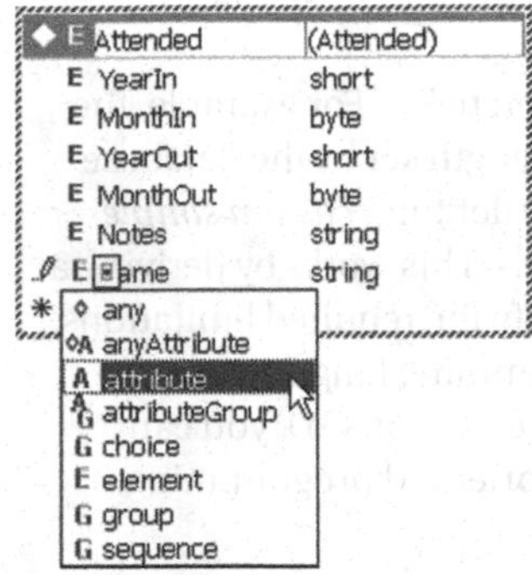

How It Works

When you use the drag-and-drop approach to create a new element, the designer creates a complex type by default. But when you create a new element by typing directly into the designer, the behavior is opposite: it creates a simple type by default. More precisely, this technique creates a string type each time. So, you need to manually change the type of the `<Attended>` element to Unnamed complexType (that is, a local complex type definition). When you do this (in step 2), VS .NET produces exactly the same `<complexType>` definition as it generated when you used the drag-and-drop approach:

```
<?xml version="1.0" encoding="utf-8" ?>
<xs:schema id="Friends" ...etc... >
  <xs:element name="Friends">
    <xs:complexType>
      <xs:sequence>
        <xs:element name="User">
          <xs:complexType>
            <xs:sequence>
              ...etc...
              <xs:element name="Attendee">
                <xs:complexType>
                  <xs:sequence />
                </xs:complexType>
              </xs:element>
```

Notice that the nesting inside `User` is just like that for the `User` inside `Friends`.

For the *child* elements of `<Attended>`, the default behavior is more or less what you want: these elements are all simple types.

The other default when adding new rows to an element is that the new item is itself an element. In the final step, you needed to change the Name row, specifying Name as an attribute using the drop-down list.

Note For a complete list of built-in simple types and their definition, see the W3C *XML Schema Part 0: Primer* document at `http://www.w3.org/TR/xmlschema-0`.

Defining Custom Simple Types

Usually, databases place restrictions on the permitted values for given fields. For example, the SQL Server type called `varchar` is a string, with a certain maximum length set by the database designer. XSD Schemas also allow you to define such restrictions, by defining *custom simple types* that modify intrinsic XSD types according to your specific needs. This works by deriving a new type from a base type—you select the base type, and then specify the required limitations.

In this regard, XSD is similar to the way object-oriented programming languages work: you inherit an existing type and modify its behavior. However, in the case of XSD, you can either extend or *restrict* a base type, which is different from object-oriented programming, where inheritance is mainly a way to extend types.

Try It Out: Define a Custom Simple Type A suitable use of a custom simple type in our example is to restrict valid IDs to strings of exactly 36 characters, which is what our database expects. Let's see how to go about arranging that.

1. From the Toolbox, drop a new simpleType element onto a blank area of the designer surface, and give it the name `KeyDef`. Note that, by default, the new type derives from the string type, as shown in the right-hand column on the top line.

2. On the blank row below the name and type, click the first column of the row and turn it into a facet, indicated by the capital *F*. Now open the drop-down list for the second column and select length. Tab to the next column, and enter **36**.

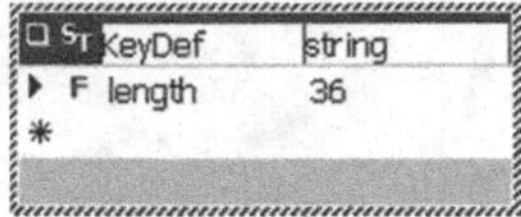

3. Set the "ID" items in the schema to the newly created simple type. There are two of them to change: the `ID` attribute on the `<User>` element and the `PlaceID` attribute of the `<Friends>` element. You'll see the new type shown in the drop-down list for the attribute type.

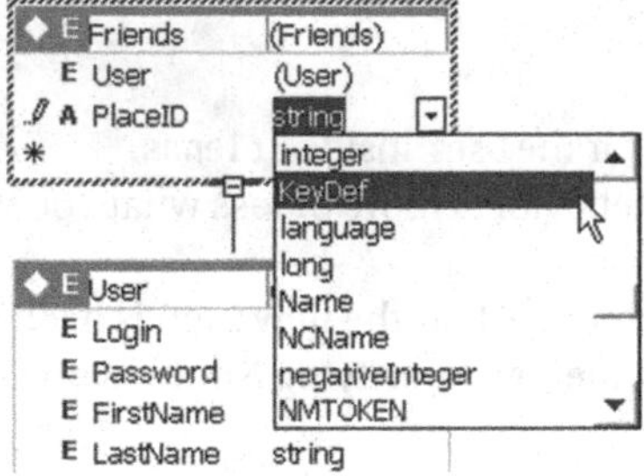

How It Works

VS .NET offers a variety of restrictions, which it calls *facets*, on XSD built-in simple types. The available facets depend on the base type in use, and most are self-explanatory. For the `KeyDef` type, which is derived from the string simple type, you may have noticed that there were options for length and maxLength. Another useful facet is the enumeration, which allows you to define a list of valid string values.

Note For a complete list of base types and available facets, see the W3C XML Schema Part 0: Primer document at `http://www.w3.org/TR/xmlschema-0`.

Try It Out: Use a Regular Expression Pattern By far, the most powerful facet is *pattern*, which allows you to specify a regular expression that must be matched by the value in order to be valid. In the case of the `KeyDef` type you defined, you know the exact format for a GUID string: it's composed of five sections of mixed characters (either uppercase or lowercase) and digits, in groups of 8-4-4-4-12 characters, as in `C9796AD1-5A7E-4d9c-9F99-0090E11E5662`.

1. Add a new facet row to the `KeyDef` simple type definition.
2. Specify that the facet is of type pattern. Set its value to the following regular expression, which defines the format of a GUID string:

```
^[a-fA-F\d]{8}-([a-fA-F\d]{4}-){3}[a-fA-F\d]{12}$
```

How It Works

If you switch to the XML view again, the new facet will look like the following in the XML source:

```
<xs:simpleType name="KeyDef">
  <xs:restriction base="xs:string">
    <xs:length value="36" />
    <xs:pattern value="^[a-fA-F\d]{8}-([a-fA-F\d]{4}-){3}[a-fA-F\d]{12}$" />
  </xs:restriction>
</xs:simpleType>
```

This is the second time you've encountered regular expressions in this book. You saw them in Chapter 3, when we discussed validation controls, and now for XSD simpleType restrictions. By now, you probably realize their importance in data validation.

If you look at the XSD code (by clicking the XML button on the bottom-left side of the pane), you'll see that the `KeyDef` type is defined as a child of the root `<xs:schema>` element. This means that this type definition is available to all other elements in the document; that is, it's a global type. As we mentioned before, a global type must have a name so that other elements can reference it; it is therefore also a *named type*.

It's also possible to define global *complex* types, which you can reuse in several places in a schema (just as we have done here, by using the `KeyDef` type definition in the `UserID` and `PlaceID` items).

Incidentally, this probably helps to explain why an element such as `<User>`, which is local to the `<Friends>` element, is described as an *unnamed* complex type.

Restricting Element Occurrence

By default, each element defined by a schema must appear once (and only once) in the instance document. Clearly, this is not appropriate for all cases. In particular, in our example, we want to allow multiple `<User>` and `<Attended>` elements in a single XML document.

By contrast, some of the fields in our database are optional, and they won't always have values. For instance, the `MonthIn` and `MonthOut` fields of the `TimeLapse` table can be null.

You can cater to requirements like these through the `minOccurs` and `maxOccurs` attributes of XSD elements, as you'll see now.

Try It Out: Set Minimum and Maximum Occurrences We'll use this example to set up the rules we just described: you'll allow multiple instances of the `<User>` and `<Attended>` elements and force the presence of the `PlaceID` and `ID` attributes.

1. We support uploading multiple users in a single document. However, at least one user should be present, or there would be no purpose in the upload! Select the `User` element of the `Friends` element in the designer, and open its Properties browser. Set the `maxOccurs` property to `unbounded`. The `minOccurs` default of 1 is appropriate in this case.

2. Each user may attend any number of courses in a single institution. On the other hand, the user may still be in the middle of a first course (no `YearOut` yet). So, the `Attended` element should be optional and allow multiple occurrences. Select the `Attended` element inside the `User` element in the designer and open its Properties browser. Set the `maxOccurs` property to `unbounded`, and set the `minOccurs` property to 0.

3. Select the `PlaceID` attribute of the `Friends` element. Set its `use` property to `required` (which means that this attribute *must* be set on the `<Friends>` element of instance documents). You will need this attribute to know which institution is uploading users.

4. Repeat step 3 for the `ID` attribute of the `User` element.

5. Select the `DateOfBirth` element of the `User` element. Set its `minOccurs` property to 0. Leave `maxOccurs` at the default setting.

6. Repeat step 3 for the `CellNumber` element of the `User` element.

7. Repeat step 3 for three elements of the `Attendee` element: `MonthIn`, `MonthOut`, and `Notes`.

8. Save the file.

How It Works

The minOccurs and maxOccurs properties determine the lower and upper limits for the number of occurrences of that element allowed in an instance document. Setting minOccurs to zero makes an element optional (it means that there can be no occurrences of that element or any number of occurrences, up to and including the upper limit). Setting maxOccurs to unbounded means that there is no upper limit.

Notice that the <Friends> element itself doesn't have minOccurs and maxOccurs properties available. This is because, as the root element, there must be *exactly one* occurrence present in any instance document, by definition.

In XML, attributes can either appear once (within a given element) or not at all. Accordingly, VS .NET shows you the valid choices for setting them as optional, prohibited, or required, where the first of these is the default. You set this property to required for the PlaceID and user ID attributes, because those must be present for you to be able to make sense of, and process, an XML file that you receive.

Viewing the Entire Schema

We have finished our schema! Maybe this seems like a lot of work before you get to write a single line of code, but you'll soon see the great benefits that this preparatory endeavor can bring. Figure 7-5 shows how the finished schema looks in the XML Schema Designer.

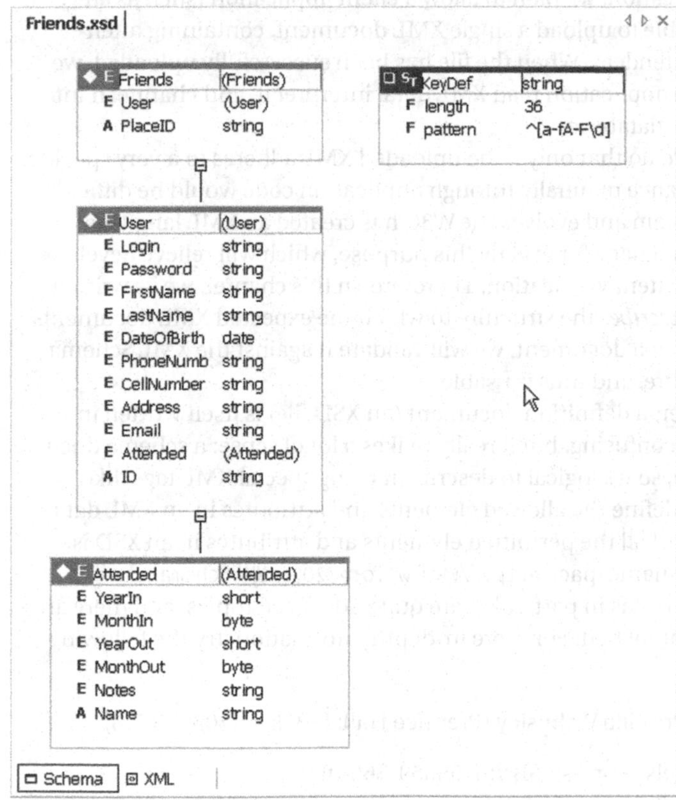

Figure 7-5. *The completed XML Schema*

If you now switch to XML view, VS .NET allows you to validate the schema, and hence double-check that you haven't made a mistake (such as setting an invalid type for an element or attribute, or introducing an error when modifying the file manually). Select Schema ➤ Validate Schema. Any invalid content in the schema will be underlined and added to the Task List. If there are no errors, you'll see a "No validation errors were found" message at the bottom left of the window.

Summary

Markup plays an important role in web applications, because one of the key tasks of such applications is to deliver web pages to client browsers. We use HTML to mark up the information in a web page, and the HTML describes the structure of that page in terms of headings, paragraphs, tables, images, and so on.

HTML is a markup language specifically designed for describing the structure of web pages. XML is also a form of markup, but it is much more generic. We can use XML to describe the structure of any type of data. XML, like HTML, is text-based markup. It uses tags and attributes to describe the different elements of data. Because XML is text-based, it's ubiquitous—you can use XML techniques in any environment or language, and to allow any combination of platforms to communicate with one another. In particular, in .NET, Microsoft has invested heavily in XML.

In our Friends Reunion application, we plan to allow a client application (such as an "Old Classmates Society") to be able to upload a single XML document, containing attendance details of any number of attendees. When the file has been successfully uploaded, we plan to have our Friends Reunion application read XML data, interpret it, and channel it into the correct tables and fields of the database.

The application will be able to do that only if the uploaded XML adheres to a very specific structure. Checking this conformance manually through application code would be difficult, error-prone, and difficult to maintain and evolve. The W3C has created an XML language called XML Schema Definition Language for exactly this purpose, which will relieve developers from the burden of manual content verification. Therefore, in this chapter, we've written the XML Schema that precisely *describes* the structure to which the expected XML documents must adhere. When we receive such a document, we will validate it against the XML Schema to ensure it has the correct structure, and thus is usable.

As you've seen, the XML Schema definition document (an XSD file) is itself written in XML. Perhaps this sounds a little confusing, but it really makes a lot of sense: a schema document is a structured block of data, so it's logical to describe it using special XML tags (like `<element>` and `<attribute>`) that define the allowed elements and attributes in an XML data document. The exact description of all the permitted elements and attributes in an XSD is contained in a schema within the namespace `http://www.w3.org/2001/XMLSchema`.

XML in general, and XML Schemas in particular, are quite advanced topics, and there are many aspects that we have left untouched. For more in-depth information, try the following books:

- *Definite XML Schema*, by Priscilla Walmsley (Prentice Hall; ISBN: 0-13065-567-8)
- *Pro .NET XML*, by Kent Tegels (Apress; ISBN: 1-59059-366-9)

We've covered all the preparatory material for the upload feature of our Friends Reunion application. In the next chapter, we'll take advantage of it by building an XML document that adheres to our XML Schema and writing the feature that uses the XML Schema to validate, interpret, and understand the uploaded XML.

CHAPTER 8

XML and Web Development

The XML Schema that we created in Chapter 7 is a document that describes a certain data structure. Specifically, it describes the XML data structure that a third party must use when it uploads an XML document (containing details of multiple attendees of a college or other institution) to the Friends Reunion web site.

The best way to think of an XML Schema is as a set of rules for the data structure. We (as developers of the Friends Reunion application) will use our schema, our set of rules, when we write the code that interprets an uploaded XML document and processes it. (As you'll see, we'll write code that assumes that any uploaded document contains *only* the tags and attributes that are allowed by the schema.) When a user creates a data document containing attendee details, that document should use the same set of rules. Provided we all adhere to the same rules, as defined in the schema, each uploaded document will be compatible with the application, so the application should be able to process it without any trouble, regardless of the tool used to generate it.

The preparatory work that we did in Chapter 7 to create the schema document, `Friends.xsd`, puts us in good shape to complete the XML upload feature. In this chapter, we'll make use of it as we build the feature, and we'll continue our studies of XML in the process.

In this chapter, we will perform the following tasks:

- Use the VS .NET IDE to create a sample XML document that validates against the XSD.
- Build a feature that allows a user to upload an XML file onto the web server, via a browser interface.
- Build the back-end functionality that reads and interprets the uploaded XML document, extracts the relevant data, and displays it on screen. This will require the following steps:
    - Programmatically validate an XML document against a specified XSD, to ensure it has the expected structure
    - Read the XML data, to analyze the information received
    - Query the XML data, to search for a particular piece of data

Using XML, XML Schemas, and XPath makes all of these tasks easy—and that is part of what makes XML and its satellite technologies such a powerful set of tools. By the end of this chapter, you'll have employed some of the most fundamental XML-related capabilities.

XML Document Creation in VS .NET

With your XSD file complete, you can start building some valid XML documents. Many different tools and techniques are available for writing and generating XML documents. As noted in the previous chapter, because XML is text-based, you could even use a simple text editor such as Notepad to type data and markup into a document. It's occasionally convenient to do that, but usually, you'll want to use one of the more powerful tools around that are specifically designed for XML-based development. The XMLSpy program (`http://www.xmlspy.com`) is one of those tools, and, the VS .NET IDE also contains some nifty features for creating XML documents. In this section, you'll use some of the VS. NET IDE features to create an XML document visually.

Creating XML Documents Visually

As we said, the VS .NET IDE has some very useful features for generating XML documents. These features are useful not only for creating small test files, but also for working with XML configuration files in custom applications, for example.

Try It Out: Create a Valid XML Document First, you need a sample instance document that conforms to the schema (`Friends.xsd`) that you built in Chapter 7. Once you have that XML document, you'll be able to use it to test the XML upload functionality of the web application that you're going to build in this chapter.

1. Right-click the `FriendsReunion` project to add a new item, select the Data category, and choose the XML File template, as shown in Figure 8-1. Name the file `upload.xml`.

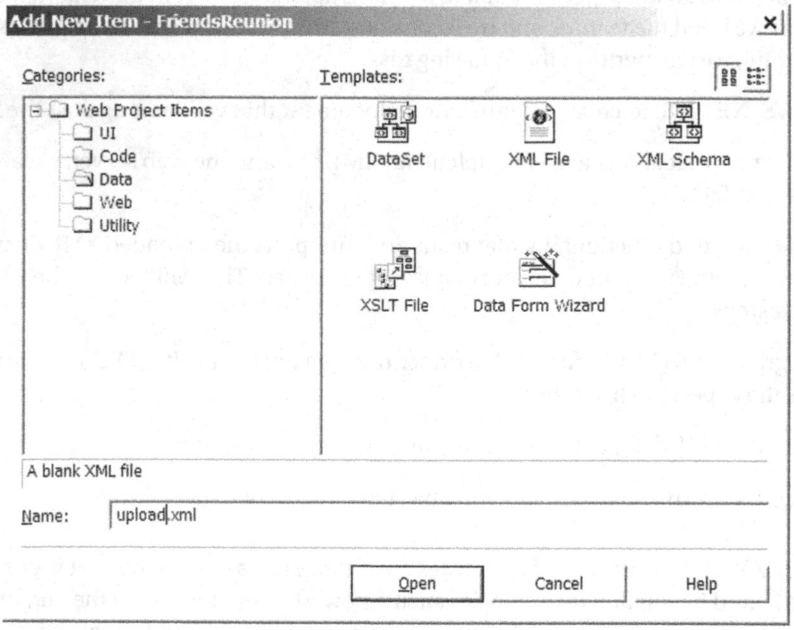

Figure 8-1. *Creating a new XML file*

GENERATING XML DOCUMENTS PROGRAMMATICALLY

There's also the question of how third-party users would generate an XML document ready for upload. It's possible that they might use a development tool such as XMLSpy or VS .NET; however, if they were planning to upload XML documents on a regular basis, taking data from their own database, it would be appropriate for them to spend some effort building an application that used a defined XML Schema and generates XML documents programmatically.

We're not going to build such an application in this book. However, the Friends Reunion application will use programmatic techniques (not to build an XML document, but to extract data from an XML document), as described later in this chapter, so you'll get an idea of how to take advantage of them.

2. The IDE will open an XML editor window, with a single line of code: an XML processing instruction. Below that line, start typing in a new `<Friends>` element. Give it an `xmlns` attribute, to set the `http://www.apress.com/schemas/friendsreunion` namespace as the default one, as shown here.

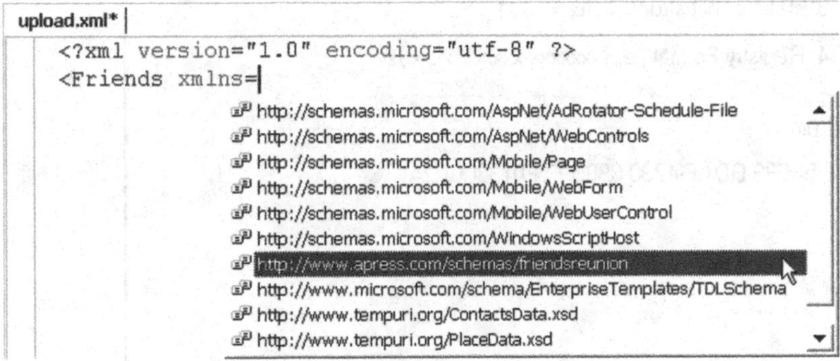

3. Type a right-angle bracket (>) to mark the end of the tag; the closing `</Friends>` tag will automatically appear after the cursor.
4. Now add the `<Friends>` element's required `PlaceID` attribute. To do this, place the cursor just before the > character of the opening `<Friends>` tag and insert a space. IntelliSense will recognize that you want to insert an attribute, and will offer a list of the names of all the valid attributes that you're allowed to put there.

```
<?xml version="1.0" encoding="utf-8" ?>
<Friends xmlns="http://www.apress.com/schemas/friendsreunion" ></Friends>
                                                              PlaceID
```

As it happens, there's only one attribute available: `PlaceID`. Choose that, and type an equal sign (=). This will insert `PlaceID=""`.

5. The value of the `PlaceID` attribute must be a GUID (a globally unique identifier). Choose Tools ➤ Create GUID to create a new GUID. In the Create GUID dialog box, check option 4. Registry Format, as shown in Figure 8-2. Then click the Copy button to copy the new GUID to the Clipboard, and paste the result into the XML document (between the two double quotes). You don't need to exit the Create GUID dialog box; it can be left open in the background until it's needed again. Just remember to click New GUID each time you need a new ID.

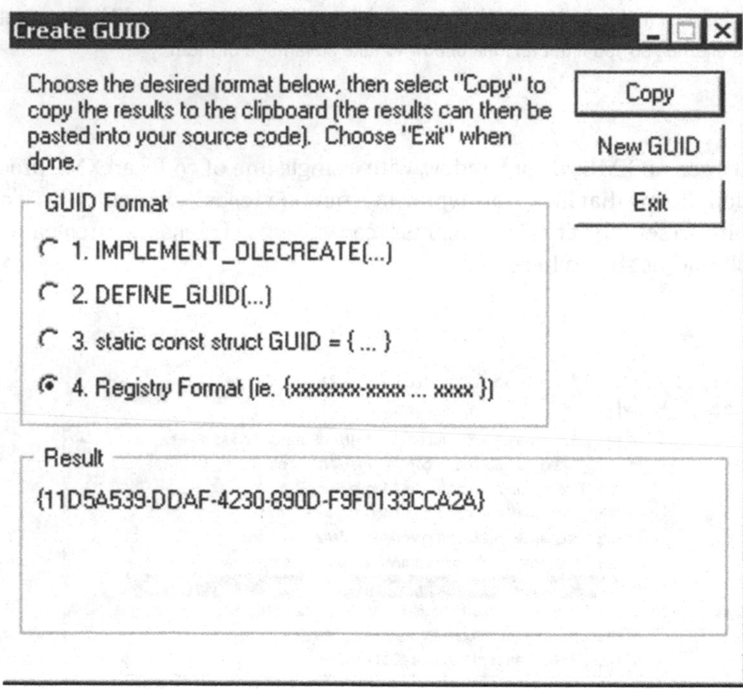

Figure 8-2. *Creating a new GUID*

6. In the XML document, the GUID is enclosed in surrounding braces. Delete those.
7. Add a `<User>` element. Place the cursor between the `<Friends>` and `</Friends>` tags, press Enter, and type a left-angle bracket (`<`). Select User from the drop-down list that appears, and press the spacebar to add it.
8. Inside the opening `<User>` element, you'll see the attributes valid for the element, namely, the `ID` attribute. Its value must also be a GUID. Return to the Create GUID dialog box, click the New GUID button to create a new GUID, and then click the Copy button. Now paste the result into the XML document as the value of the attribute. Again, the GUID is enclosed in surrounding braces, and you need to delete them. Type the > character to complete the `User` element and close it appropriately.

9. Now add the remaining child elements for <User>. Recall that DateOfBirth and CellNumber are optional elements, because we defined them with minOccurs=0; for simplicity, we'll leave them out here. You should end up with something that looks like this:

```
<?xml version="1.0" encoding="utf-8" ?>
<Friends xmlns="http://www.apress.com/schemas/friendsreunion"
         PlaceID="C95FE0A8-D24F-43cf-99CD-AA267BEFB21C">
  <User ID="6F724ACE-4230-42a1-9EE2-EA18C5A251B5">
    <Login>gmorande</Login>
    <Password>gusygaby</Password>
    <FirstName>Gustavo</FirstName>
    <LastName>Morande</LastName>
    <PhoneNumber>0191-700-7007</PhoneNumber>
    <Address>2266 3rd. February Street, Buenos Aires</Address>
    <Email>gmorande@clariusconsulting.net</Email>
  </User>
</Friends>
```

10. Now you can validate the document against the schema, to check that it satisfies its rules. To do that in the VS .NET IDE, choose XML ➤ Validate XML Data. This document should validate successfully. If there are validation errors, they will be underlined with a green, wavy line in the editor ("ala Word"), and listed in the Task List window.

How It Works

As soon as you type the xmlns attribute, IntelliSense starts to do its magic. First, you're offered a list of available namespaces known to VS .NET, which includes a number of built-in ones, plus all the namespaces from schemas in the current project, including the http://www.apress.com/schemas/friendsreunion namespace used by our schema.

Once the namespace is specified, IntelliSense uses the associated XML Schema to make suggestions as you type. VS .NET provides a list of all elements that are valid according to the schema, and this list is context-sensitive. So you see only the <User> element when you're in the process of inserting an element into the <Friends> element, and all the others once you're inside the <User> element. Notice, however, that the list is ordered alphabetically, so it doesn't necessarily reflect the actual schema constraints, particularly when the order of elements can be important. For instance, as soon as you start inserting elements inside <User>, <Address> and <Attended> elements are suggested as valid children, but you know that <Login> and <Password> must appear *before* both of them, as defined by an <xs:sequence> element in the schema.

The validation process that you used at the end, by choosing XML ➤ Validate XML Data, is exactly the same as the one that you'll apply programmatically in a moment, and it demonstrates the value of namespaces. At design-time, namespaces enable the IDE to activate IntelliSense and validation; at runtime, they allow the elements in a file to be matched unambiguously to their definition in the appropriate schema.

Creating XML Documents in the Data View

The VS .NET IDE offers another way to create an XML document visually when you have a schema for it: the *Data view*. Click Data in the lower-left corner of the designer (next to the XML button), to open a two-pane view: Data Tables on the left and Data on the right. In the Data pane, you can add data to an XML file.

If an element is specified as a complex type in the schema, it will be represented in the Data view as a data table. The simple type attributes and elements within that complex type will appear as fields within the table. In our document, the `<Friends>`, `<User>`, and `<Attended>` elements are the complex types; this is why they are listed as tables in the left pane, as shown in Figure 8-3.

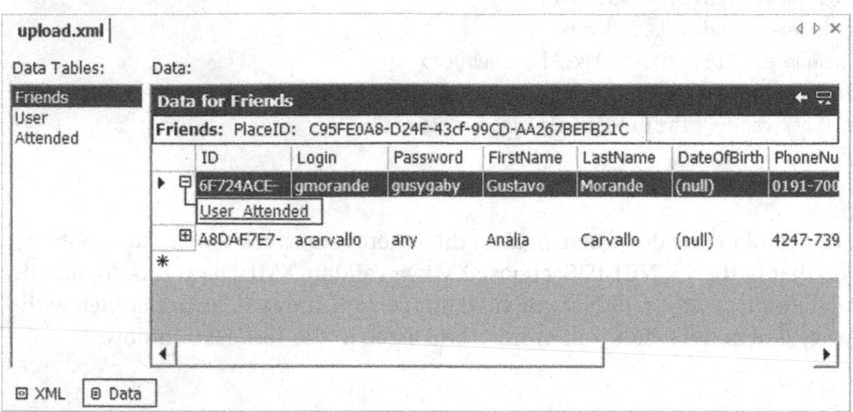

Figure 8-3. *The Data view shows the elements in an XML document and allows you to navigate and modify them.*

When a complex type element is enclosed inside another complex type (such as the `<User>` inside the `<Friends>` root element, and `<Attended>` inside `<User>`), you will be presented with a navigation link in the Data pane that lets you get inside the contained elements to add child ones. Click the plus sign to show the available children. Click the link, and it will expand to list the child elements. In Figure 8-3, we have navigated to the first `User` element. Notice that the UI keeps track of the parent element of the current one and shows it above the table. In Figure 8-3, you see the `PlaceID` attribute of the `Friends` parent. The arrow icon in the top-right corner of the window allows you to navigate back to the parent element.

In order for elements to be put in the *right place* in the XML file, you must *follow the links* through the elements until you get to the level where the new element must be placed. This is important, because the tool doesn't prevent you from selecting the `User` or `Attended` "tables" directly (through the list in the Data Tables panel) and creating elements right there. If you do that, the resulting elements are placed under a *new* root `<Friends>` element (not under the existing `<Friends>` element). The result would contain two nested `<Friends>` elements, and that would be invalid according to our schema.

Caution Not following the links in Data view is very likely to mess up the document.

Try It Out: Add an Element in the Data View Let's see how the Data view works in practice. You'll use it to create a new `<Attended>` element in your `upload.xml` file.

1. Click the Friends User link in the Data pane for the Friends data table (as shown in Figure 8-3).

2. Try adding a new user directly in the grid. It will look something like Figure 8-4.

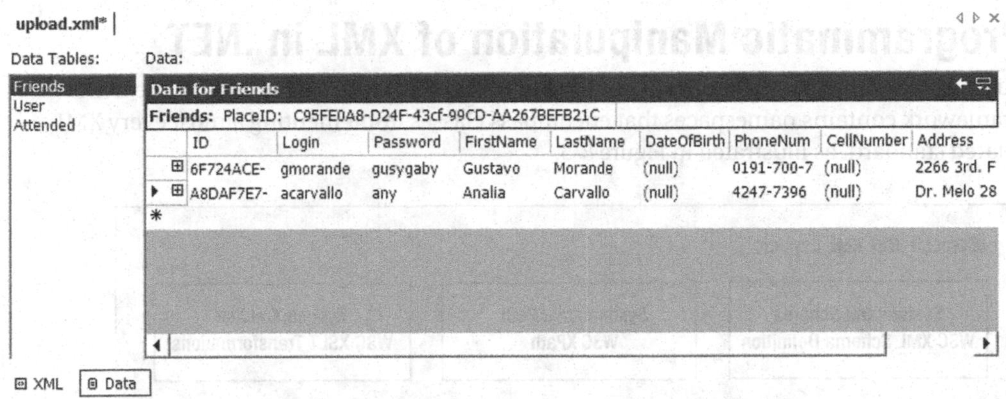

Figure 8-4. *Adding a new user in the Data view*

3. Switch back to the XML view to see the new data that you've generated:

```
<?xml version="1.0" encoding="utf-8" ?>
<Friends xmlns="http://www.apress.com/schemas/friendsreunion"
         PlaceID="C95FE0A8-D24F-43cf-99CD-AA267BEFB21C">
  <User ID="6F724ACE-4230-42a1-9EE2-EA18C5A251B5">
    ...etc...
  </User>
  <User ID="A8DAF7E7-E736-4d54-8797-BB6BA9E07639">
    <Login>acarvallo</Login>
    <Password>any</Password>
    <FirstName>Analia</FirstName>
    <LastName>Carvallo</LastName>
    <PhoneNumber>555-205-9999</PhoneNumber>
    <Address>Dr. Melo 2836</Address>
    <Email>any@clariusconsulting.net</Email>
  </User>
</Friends>
```

Notice that because you navigated inside the `<Friends>` element to the desired child "table," the elements have been added inside the appropriate parent element.

Note The Data view (tables-and-rows) approach is suitable for most XML files, but the IDE does not allow you to use this feature for some schema designs. For example, if you have child elements with the same name but different parent elements—a perfectly valid schema definition—the Data view won't be available.

Programmatic Manipulation of XML in .NET

Microsoft has made a substantial commitment to XML with the .NET platform. The .NET Framework contains namespaces that encompass classes implementing almost every XML-related standard, as illustrated in Figure 8-5.

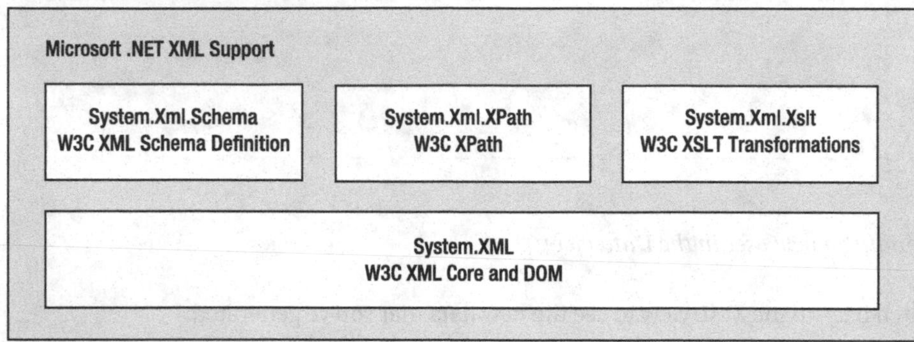

Figure 8-5. *.NET Framework support for XML standards*

In the upcoming examples, you will use classes contained in the `System.Xml` and `System.Xml.Schema` namespaces to load and validate an XML file, ready for use in our web application. After that, you'll be ready to start issuing queries using XPath, and we'll look at the options you have when dealing with in-memory XML documents.

Reading and Validating XML

In .NET, the task of reading an XML document from a file is accomplished in much the same way as reading any other file type. However, the source of the XML does not need to be a file; it can be any form of *stream*, such as an in-memory stream, a file stream, or a network stream.

Throughout the .NET Framework, the process of reading a stream follows the same pattern: a reader object systematically steps through the stream from start to end, through a succession of calls to the `Read()` method. Each method call reads a new portion of the stream and returns a Boolean value; `Read()` returns `true` unless the end of stream has been reached, in which case `Read()` returns `false`. As you progress through the stream, the methods and properties (provided by the specific reader implementation) allow you to retrieve information and data for the current position in it. Figure 8-6 illustrates some of the readers offered by the .NET Framework classes that are relevant to XML handling.

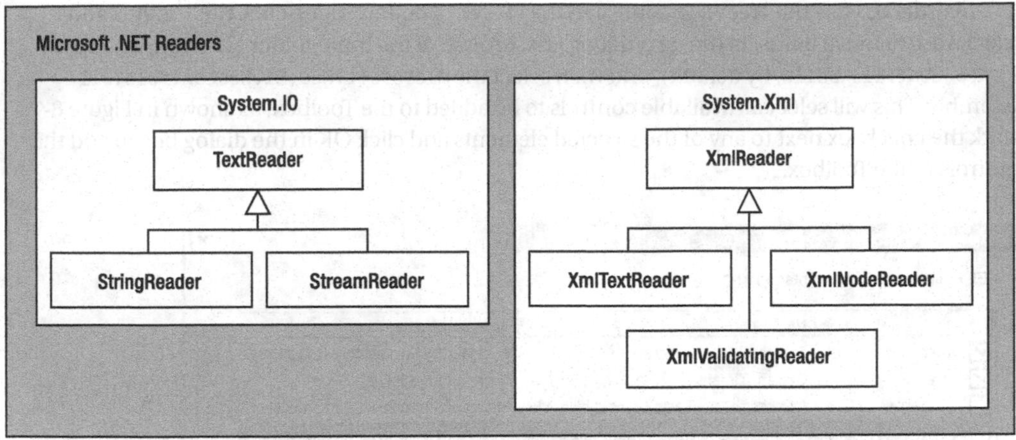

Figure 8-6. *.NET Framework reader approach for general I/O and XML processing*

The readers in the `System.IO` namespace are relevant to us because we can pass them to overloaded constructors of many of the `XmlReader`-derived classes in order to read XML content from them. The `XmlReader` and derived classes take advantage of the features of the `System.IO` readers. You'll see this mechanism in action as you develop the Friends Reunion application in this chapter.

Uploading an XML File

The first step in creating the upload feature for our application requires adding a new web form that will be used to receive a file from the client. To make the web form visually appealing, we will use an ASP.NET server control from Microsoft called TreeView. The TreeView control makes it simple to display hierarchical information, and so it's perfect for showing XML content.

In order to make the TreeView control available in your application, you must download and install the Internet Explorer WebControls server control on the web server. At the time of writing, this download is 361KB, and you can get it from the official ASP.NET web site: `http://www.asp.net/IEWebControls/Download.aspx`. (Even if it was programmed for version 1.0 of .NET, it works flawlessly in version 1.1, too.)

Note The Internet Explorer WebControls server control product doesn't have official support from Microsoft, although the download page points to a quite active forum dedicated to it, where you can get peer support from fellow developers. ASP.NET 2.0 will already include a built-in TreeView control.

The code download contains the source for the controls, which also makes it a good opportunity to take a closer look at production-quality custom server controls. You will need to open a VS .NET Command Prompt window, go to the installation directory (`C:\Program Files\IE Web Controls`, by default) and run `build.bat`. Follow the further instructions in the `Readme.txt` file for deploying the various files it uses, including images.

In order to view the TreeView control in the VS .NET Toolbox, right-click the Toolbox and select Add/Remove Items. In the next dialog box, browse to the build folder (`C:\Program Files\IE Web Controls\build`, by default), and then select the `Microsoft.Web.UI.WebControls.dll` assembly. This will select all available controls to be added to the Toolbox, as shown in Figure 8-7. Mark the checkbox next to any of the selected elements and click OK in the dialog box to add the controls to the Toolbox.

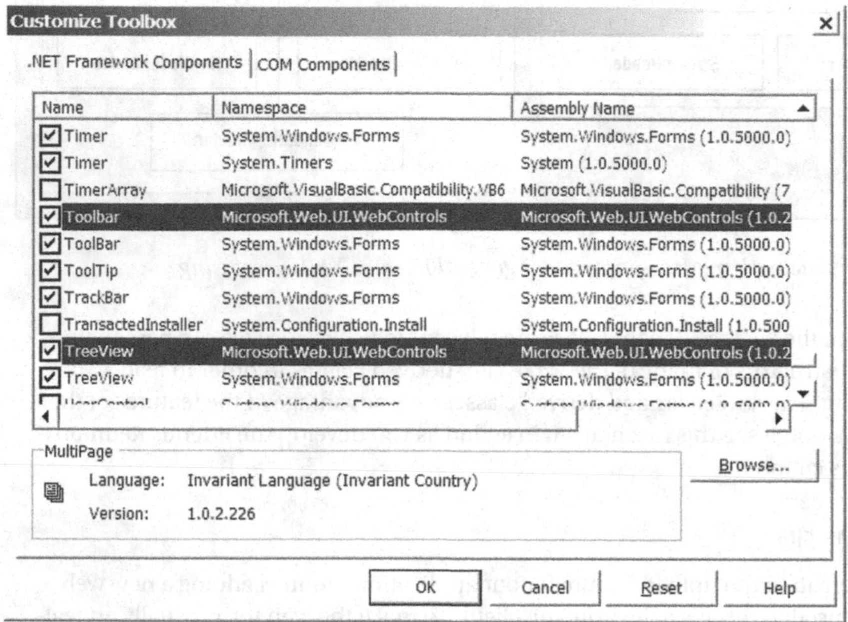

Figure 8-7. *Adding the Internet Explorer WebControls to the VS .NET Toolbox*

Note The TreeView control works in all browsers, but it will be much smoother in Internet Explorer because it takes advantages of Internet Explorer "behaviors," a feature that exploits Dynamic HTML (DHTML).

We're going to build a web form that will receive an XML file posted by the user and perform further processing on it. First, it will show the contents of the uploaded file in the TreeView control, so users can see if the information they're sending is correct. We will also add a link to the schema file that's used to validate the incoming file, and also a link to a sample XML file that users can either view or load in the page for testing purposes.

Try It Out: Create the Upload List Form Now you'll build the form and review key settings in it. You'll add the code for specific features in later sections. Before beginning these steps, you need to have downloaded and installed the TreeView control, as just described.

You'll set up the form's text and controls to give it the layout shown in Figure 8-8.

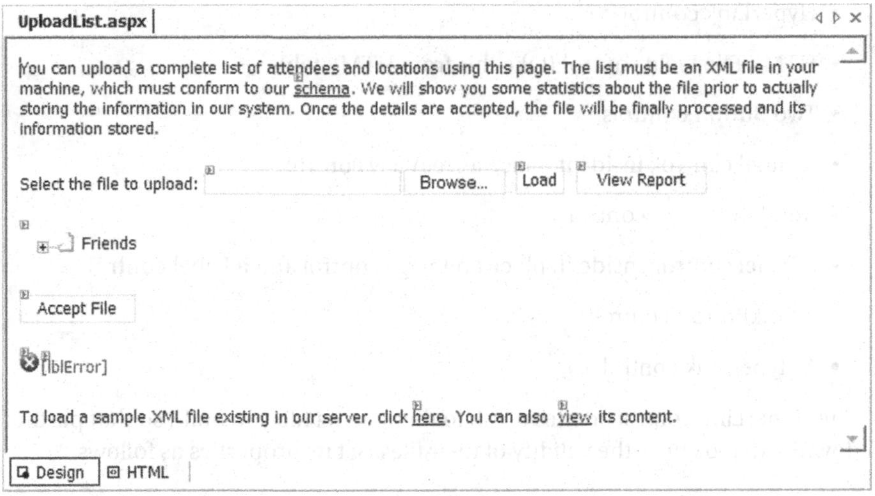

Figure 8-8. *The Upload List page layout*

1. Add a new web form to the `FriendsReunion` project and name it `UploadList.aspx`. Switch to the Code view and import the `System.IO` namespace at the top of the code-behind file (`UploadList.aspx.vb`):

```
Imports System.IO
```

2. Make the page inherit the `FriendsBase` class you built in Chapter 3, to add the site header and footer. To do this, change the class declaration line to:

```
Public Class UploadList
  Inherits FriendsBase
```

3. Drag-and-drop the `iestyle.css` file onto the web form surface to link the stylesheet.

4. Add the following style rule to the stylesheet, which is used to format the TreeView control:

```
.TreeView
{
  border: solid 1px #c7ccdc;
  padding: 5px 15px 5px 5px;
  font-size: 8pt;
  font-family: Tahoma, Verdana, 'Times New Roman';
  background-color: #f0f1f6;
}
```

5. Add the following controls, in order of their appearance on the page, from left to right and top to bottom. Take all these from the Web Forms tab in the Toolbox, except the HTML File Field control. Arrange the controls as shown in Figure 8-8.

- HyperLink control
- HTML File Field control (take this from HTML tab)
- Two Button controls
- A Panel control; inside it, place a TreeView control
- Another Button control
- A Panel control; inside it, place an Image control and a Label control
- A LinkButton control
- A HyperLink control

6. The HyperLink control creates a link to the schema file you built, so that partners can download it to check the validity of their files. Set its properties as follows:
   - ID: `hySchema`
   - Text: **schema**
   - NavigateUrl: `Friends.xsd`
   - Target: `_blank`
7. The HTML File Field control will allow users to upload a file from their machine. The `name` property is important; although you don't use it in the code, the mechanism depends on the existence of a value here. Set this control's properties as follows:
   - id: `fldUpload`
   - class: `Button`
   - style: `WIDTH: 238px`
   - name: `fldUpload`

   Right-click the `fldUpload` control and select Run As Server Control from the context menu.
8. The first Button control will allow users to submit the file selected with the previous control, to upload it from their machine to the web server. Set its properties as follows:
   - ID: `btnLoad`
   - CssClass: `Button`
   - Text: **Load**

9. The next Button control will redirect users to a page showing statistics about the file they posted. Set its properties as follows:

   - ID: `btnReport`
   - CssClass: `Button`
   - Text: **View Report**

10. The TreeView control will show information in the XML file. Set its properties as follows:

   - ID: `tvXmlView`
   - CssClass: `TreeView`
   - ExpandedImageUrl: `Images/opened.gif`
   - ImageUrl: `Images/findfolder.gif`
   - SelectedImageUrl: `Images/selected.gif`
   - Visible: `False`
   - Nodes: Add a root node and two children to it, with the text **Friends** and **User** respectively, using the editor that appears, so that you can have a preview of the layout at design-time.
   - TreeNodeTypes: This is a collection of node type definitions, which can be used to give new nodes a default formatting. Add a new type using the TreeNodeType Collection Editor. Set its `ID` and `Type` to Normal. Set the `DefaultStyle` to `font-size: 8pt; font-family: Tahoma,Verdana,'Times New Roman'`.
   - ChildType: This sets the default style for new nodes. Set it to Normal (created in the previous property).

11. The next Button control will save the posted file to the database. Set its properties as follows:

   - ID: `btnAccept`
   - CssClass: `Button`
   - Text: `Accept File`

12. The Panel control will display any errors found in the incoming file. Set its `ID` to `pnlError` and its `Visible` property to False.

13. Set the panel's Image control's `ImageAlign` property to AbsMiddle and `ImageUrl` property to `Images/error.gif`.

14. Set the panel's Label control's `ID` to `lblError`, `ForeColor` to Red, and `Text` to **Clear this field**.

15. The LinkButton control will allow the user to load a sample file from the server, for testing purposes and to grasp the UI functionality. Set its `ID` to `btnDefaultXml` and `Text` to **here**.

16. The HyperLink control will provide a link to the sample XML file so the user can view it in the browser or download it for testing. Set its properties as follows:

    - ID: `hyXmlFile`
    - Text: **view**
    - NavigateUrl: `upload.xml`
    - Target: `_blank`

17. Add the following code to the `Page_Load()` event handler to configure the header image and text (as described in Chapter 3):

```
Private Sub Page_Load(ByVal sender As System.Object, _
  ByVal e As System.EventArgs) Handles MyBase.Load
  HeaderIconImageUrl = "~/Images/pctransfer.gif"
  HeaderMessage = "Upload Attendees"
End Sub
```

18. Through the Windows Explorer, select the `upload.xml` file you already created and open its Properties dialog box (right-click and select Properties). On the Security tab, add the Everyone group to the list of users allowed to access the file, and leave the default permissions of Read and Read & Execute. This will allow your code to read this file from disk.

19. Double-click the `btnDefaultXml` control and add the following code to its event handler:

```
Private Sub btnDefaultXml_Click(ByVal sender As System.Object, _
  ByVal e As System.EventArgs) Handles btnDefaultXml.Click
  Dim sr As New StreamReader(Server.MapPath("~/upload.xml"))

  Try
    Session("xml") = sr.ReadToEnd()
    Session("file") = "Sample file"
  Finally
    sr.Close()
  End Try
End Sub
```

20. The Upload List page is now complete, so set it as the start page, and compile and run the application by pressing Ctrl+F5. After the usual login process (using `apress` as the user name and password), the page shown in Figure 8-9 should appear in your browser. If you click the Browse button, you'll see the standard Windows dialog box for locating files.

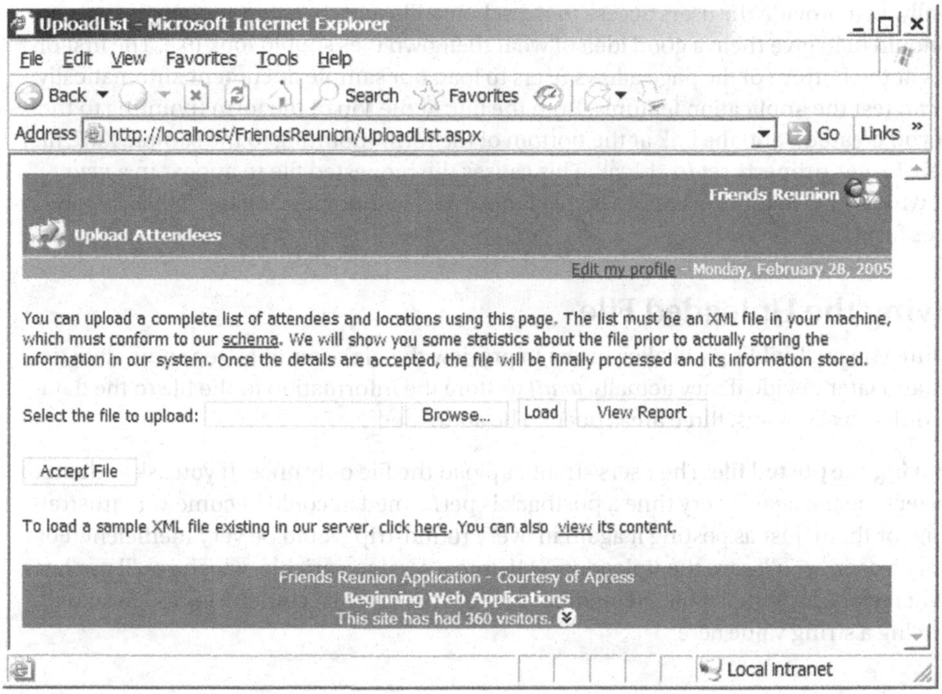

Figure 8-9. *The Upload List page running*

How It Works

As we said, the objective of this form is to allow partner institutions to submit an XML file containing all their users and attendees. In order to specify the file to upload, the user clicks the Browse button. The control that makes this possible is an HTML File Field, which is nothing more than `<input>` control, whose `type` attribute is set to `file`. However, this control allows only for a local file name selection. The form is not posted. Therefore, you placed a Load button control on the form solely for this purpose, but, in fact, any postback caused by any server control will cause the file to be uploaded.

Traditionally, for the file to be sent to the server, the form not only needed to use a `post` method but *also* had to specify an additional attribute called `encType`:

```
<form id="Form1" method="post" encType="multipart/form-data"...
```

Setting the file input field as an HTML *server* control automatically handles this for us.

When the file is uploaded, you will use the values contained in the file to fill the TreeView control. You'll do that in the next section, but there are a couple of things to say about this control right now. The TreeView control is similar to its Windows counterpart. It basically consists of a collection of `TreeNode` elements that can, in turn, contain other `TreeNode` elements, and so on. The server control provides several options to add styles to it, such as defining the style to use to render child nodes. You used the `TreeNodeTypes` property to define a `Normal` node type, and then used it in the `ChildType`.

Finally, you provide the users access to the schema file and to a sample XML document, which should help give them a good idea of what their own files should look like. The first of two links at the bottom of the page allows users to load our sample document automatically, so they can test the application features. Both the link at the top of the form (pointing to the schema you created), and the link at the bottom of the form (pointing to the sample XML file) have their `Target` property set to `_blank`. This causes the requested file to appear in a *new* browser window, so that the users can inspect those files without leaving the main Upload Attendees form.

Receiving the Uploaded File

The feature you are building will allow users to preview the file's contents, see some statistics about it, and later decide if they actually *want* to store the information in the file to the database. In order to allow this, three areas need to be addressed:

- **Saving the posted file:** The users should upload the file only once. If you asked them to select the file again every time a postback is performed, it could become very frustrating for them, just as posting it again in every round-trip would be very inefficient. For this reason, you'll save the uploaded XML into a session variable, which you'll use later when working with the file. Remember that XML is just text content, so you're actually saving a string value here.

Note As this is a testing scenario, we don't pay much attention to size limits, scalability issues, and so on. Some would say it would be better to save the file in the server's file system; while others would complain that the I/O access and security permissions involved would actually turn out to be worse. Such topics would need to be evaluated in a production environment.

- **Setting up the reader**: Configuring an `XmlValidatingReader` object requires several steps, so you'll move all that code into a private function.
- **Using the reader**: You'll create another method that uses the reader to add nodes to the `TreeView` control, to show the XML contents on the web page. This will help the users to preview the file they are about to store, prior to confirmation.

You'll complete these three tasks over the course of the next three "Try It Out" sections.

Saving the Posted XML File

Let's analyze the code for reading and saving the incoming file to the session variable that we'll use later on.

Try It Out: Save the Posted XML File

1. Import the following namespace at the top of the code-behind file, `UploadList.aspx.vb`:

```
Imports System.Text
Imports System.Xml
Imports System.Xml.Schema
Imports Microsoft.Web.UI.WebControls
```

The last of these points to the namespace where the TreeView control and its related classes are located. When you dropped that control onto the page, a reference to the `Microsoft.Web.UI.WebControls.dll` assembly was automatically added to your project. It will come as no surprise that this is the assembly that contains the namespace you imported.

2. Add the following method to the `UploadList` class, in the same file:

```
'Save the input file if appropriate
Private Sub SaveXml()
  If Request.Files(0).FileName.Length > 0 Then
    ' Save the uploaded stream to Session for further postbacks
    Dim stm As New StreamReader(Request.Files(0).InputStream)
    Try
      Session("xml") = stm.ReadToEnd()
      Session("file") = Request.Files(0).FileName
    Finally
      stm.Close()
    End Try
  End If
End Sub
```

3. Double-click the Load button and add the following line:

```
 Private Sub btnLoad_Click(ByVal sender As System.Object, _
  ByVal e As System.EventArgs) Handles btnLoad.Click
  SaveXml()
End Sub
```

4. Grab a copy of the `upload.xml` file that you created earlier and place it somewhere handy on your hard drive (say, `C:\upload.xml`).

5. Set a breakpoint in the line of code in the `btnLoad` button's `Click` event handler that contains the `SaveXml()` method call, so that you can test the new method (you can do that by positioning the cursor on that line and pressing F9). Compile and run the application with Ctrl+F5, and after the usual login process, use the Browse button to select the sample XML file (at `C:\upload.xml` or wherever you put it), and then click the Load button.

How It Works

When you click the Load button (after selecting the XML file), the corresponding handler will be called. Press F11 to step into `SaveXml()`. Inside the routine, you first check whether you received any content from the client:

```
If Request.Files(0).FileName.Length > 0 Then
  ...
```

The Request.Files property contains the list of uploaded files. You can't just use its Count property because of the way the HTML File Field control works: there will always be an item in this collection for each of these controls on a page, and you can know if an actual file was submitted only by checking for the FileName property of each element in this collection. As you know, there will be only one element, so you directly check that against the first element in the collection.

The Files collection itself contains a single HttpPostedFile object (Request.Files(0)) that represents the uploaded file, and it contains a number of useful subproperties that describe the file being uploaded (ContentLength, ContentType, and FileName, for example).

Next, you see one of the reader implementations of the System.IO namespace in action, the StreamReader:

```
Dim stm As New StreamReader(Request.Files(0).InputStream)
```

Its constructor requires an object of type Stream, which you get from the InputStream property of the posted file. This Stream contains the uploaded content. The Imports construct ensures this reader will be properly disposed of as soon as you leave the block.

You put of all the file content returned by the reader into a Session item called xml. You also hold the original file name in a second Session variable, called file:

```
Session("xml") = stm.ReadToEnd()
Session("file") = Request.Files(0).FileName
```

The ReadToEnd() method returns the whole file—the XML document—as a single string.

Validating XML from a Web Application

The XmlValidatingReader class that you will use derives from XmlReader, so it shares many properties and methods with that class. It also adds a set of new properties (that is, it *extends* the base class) to set options required for validation. In this book, we'll use the term *validator* to refer to an instance of this class.

Once the validator is configured, you can start reading an XML file and taking values from it, just as you would with a regular XmlReader object. Behind the scenes, though, the object ensures that the file is valid as it is read, according to the settings you have made and to the schema you have configured. You can configure the validator to react when validation errors are found in the XML source in two ways:

- The validator can throw exceptions. This is the default mode. When an error is found, processing is aborted and an XmlSchemaException is thrown.
- The validator can fire the event handler attached to the ValidationEventHandler event of the XmlValidatingReader class. When a handler is specified for this event, the validator won't throw an exception when an error appears; instead, it will call the handler. It is up to the developer to collect information inside the handler and respond accordingly.

Clearly, the second approach allows more complete reporting of any failures found in an XML file, and it also allows you to continue through the document and process all elements, whenever it makes sense.

Try It Out: Set Up Validation You're now ready to handle the second step for receiving the uploaded file: setting up the reader. You'll write the code to set up the `XmlValidatingReader` object.

1. Declare the following private member at class level, before the `Page_Load()` event handler:

```
Dim _errors As New StringBuilder
```

Note As a naming convention, we prefix class-level variables with an underscore so that we can easily differentiate them from local variables inside a method.

---

2. Add the handler for the validation event. It needs to have exactly the signature specified here, and you'll be using it later when you configure validation:

```
Private Sub OnValidation(ByVal sender As Object, _
  ByVal e As ValidationEventArgs)
  _errors.AppendFormat("<b>{0}</b>: {1}<br/>", _
    e.Severity.ToString(), e.Message)
End Sub
```

3. Using the Windows Explorer, open the properties for the `Friends.xsd` file. In the Security tab, add the Everyone group to the list of members allowed to access the file, and leave the default permissions of Read and Read & Execute. You need to add this permission so the web application can read the schema from disk.

4. The procedure responsible for reading and displaying the XML content doesn't need to know that it's using an `XmlValidatingReader` instance or how it has to be configured. It only cares about the reading methods. You'll isolate it from the initialization code for the validator in a function that returns a generic `XmlReader` object type:

```
Private Function GetReader() As XmlReader
  If Not Session("xml") Is Nothing Then
    Throw New InvalidOperationException( _
      "No XML file has been uploaded yet.")
  End If

  ' Build the XmlTextReader from the in-memory string saved before
  Dim xmlinput As New StringReader(CType(Session("xml"), String))
  Dim reader = New XmlTextReader(xmlinput)

  ' Configure the validating reader
  Dim validator As New XmlValidatingReader(reader)
  AddHandler validator.ValidationEventHandler, AddressOf OnValidation

  Dim schema As XmlSchema
  Dim fs As FileStream = File.OpenRead( _
```

```
        Server.MapPath("~/Friends.xsd"))
      Try
        schema = XmlSchema.Read(fs, Nothing)
      Finally
        fs.Close()
      End Try

      validator.Schemas.Add(schema)
      validator.ValidationType = ValidationType.Schema
      Return validator
    End Function
```

How It Works

The XML processing code (which you'll build in the next "Try It Out" section) will call the `GetReader()` method to get the object it will use to process the XML file. Notice that you return a generic `XmlReader` object from the method:

```
Private Function GetReader() As XmlReader
  ...
```

In this way, the act of getting an object for reading the file is independent of the actual `XmlReader` implementation being used to work through it. This makes it easy to turn off validation just by returning an `XmlTextReader` instead of an `XmlValidatingReader`.

You first check to see if there is actual content in the `Session` variable you saved earlier. The first time the page loads, or if an error on the server causes session information to be lost, you raise an exception. You use an `InvalidOperationException`, already defined in the .NET Framework, since it seems to be an appropriate exception to throw if you're trying to read an XML file when none has been actually found:

```
  If Session("xml") Is Nothing Then
    Throw New InvalidOperationException( _
      "No XML file has been uploaded yet.")
  End If
```

Next, you set up a `StringReader` from the `System.IO` namespace, which you will use as the source when you create the XML reader. In effect, the `StringReader` class applies a `TextReader` implementation to a simple string, which you can then pass to an `XmlTextReader` constructor:

```
  Dim xmlinput As New StringReader(CType(Session("xml"), String))
  Dim reader As New XmlTextReader(xmlinput)
```

You could have avoided declaring the `xmlinput` variable altogether (and constructed it directly inside the `XmlTextReader` constructor), but this way, the code is a bit clearer. At this point, if you wished to disable validation, you could just add the following line:

```
Return reader
```

But instead, as you *do* want to validate, you use the `XmlTextReader` to create an instance of the `XmlValidatingReader` class. You also set the validator's `ValidationEventHandler` property, to tell it what method it should use to handle events (such as encountering errors) that occur during the validation process. In this case, it will be the OnValidation() method:

```
Dim validator As New XmlValidatingReader(reader)
AddHandler validator.ValidationEventHandler, AddressOf OnValidation
```

We'll look at the OnValidation() method in a moment, to see how that works.

The validator needs a reference to the schema that it should validate against, through its property called Schemas, which is a collection of XmlSchema objects. You read your schema using the static Read() method of the XmlSchema class, which loads and returns the specified schema. Because you added permissions to Everyone to read the schema, the ASP.NET application can load it directly from disk. You get a reference to the physical file using Server.MapPath and read the schema from the stream:

```
Dim schema As XmlSchema
Dim fs As FileStream = File.OpenRead( _
  Server.MapPath("~/Friends.xsd"))
Try
  schema = XmlSchema.Read(fs, Nothing)
Finally
  fs.Close()
End Try
```

The second parameter to the Read() method is a validation handler to deal with any errors that are found in the schema itself. In this case, we'll assume the schema is valid (since we created it). Once you've loaded the schema, adding it to the collection of schemas for the validator is simple:

```
validator.Schemas.Add(schema)
```

Finally, you return the initialized XmlValidatingReader object:

```
validator.ValidationType = ValidationType.Schema
Return validator
```

Now let's return to look at how errors are handled during the validation process. You have created a class-level variable, _errors, that will help to handle the errors that can occur during the reading phase. It is initialized to a new StringBuilder object and will accumulate error messages:

```
Dim _errors As New StringBuilder
```

If an error is found during the reading phase, this is considered as an event, so it is handled by the nominated event handler: the OnValidation() method.

```
Private Sub OnValidation(ByVal sender As Object, _
  ByVal e As ValidationEventArgs)
  ...
```

If the validator finds an error, it calls this method, passing in information about the event in the e parameter, which is of type ValidationEventArgs. This parameter supplies details about the error that you append to the _errors variable for later use. You want to know the severity of the validation failure (which will be either an Error or a Warning) and the error message itself, with some formatting to display nicely in the page:

```
_errors.AppendFormat("<b>{0}</b>: {1}<br/>", _
  e.Severity.ToString(), e.Message)
```

Should you need it, the Exception property of the ValidationEventArgs class holds the actual exception that was caught. This property is of type XmlSchemaException, and it can be queried to obtain comprehensive information about the error, including the line number and position where the error occurred, the schema object causing the exception, and so on. For short files though, the Message property contains just about everything you need to locate the problem. For example, a PlaceID with a length other than the 36 characters and the pattern required by the schema will generate a message string something like this:

```
The 'http://www.apress.com/schemas/friendsreunion:PlaceID' element has an invalid
value according to its data type. An error occurred at (2, 72).
```

Processing the Uploaded XML Data

The XmlSchema class is Microsoft's implementation of the W3C XML Schema Definition Language standard, and it performs validation while the XML stream is being read. There is no need for a special validation method. Remember that these readers are read-only and forward-only, which makes them fast and light, but also means that you need to process the XML while you are still validating it. You will not know whether the *entire* XML file meets the requirements of your schema until you have finished processing it.

As you examine the following example, notice that the code for retrieving data from the validator (that is, the XmlValidatingReader object) always refers to *nodes* in the first instance (through its NodeType property), rather than to elements, or attributes, or text. This is due to the way that the reader perceives the XML: as it moves through the document, one by one it comes across the entities that document contains. The next item that it comes across could be an element, an attribute of an element, or the content of an element. We use the generic term *node* to refer to all of these items. When each entity arrives in your code, you need to find out what it is.

Try It Out: Display XML Data It's time for us to implement the steps that process the XML file. You're going to read the elements and display them in the TreeView control.

1. Place the reading and processing code in a method called BuildTreeView():

```
Private Sub BuildTreeView()
  ' Keep the current node and its parents
  Dim hierarchy As New Stack(5)
  Dim node As TreeNode
  Dim reader As XmlReader

  pnlError.Visible = False
  ' Save the incoming file if appropriate
  SaveXml()
```

```
Try
  reader = GetReader()
  ' Clear the tree view
  tvXmlView.Nodes.Clear()

  Do While reader.Read()
    ' We create new nodes for all elements
    If reader.NodeType = XmlNodeType.Element Then
      'Create the new node
      node = New TreeNode
      node.Text = reader.LocalName
      AddAttributes(reader, node)

      ' Anchor to its parent
      If hierarchy.Count > 0 Then
        CType(hierarchy.Peek(), TreeNode).Nodes.Add(node)
      End If

      ' Set it as the last node in the stack
      hierarchy.Push(node)
    ElseIf reader.NodeType = XmlNodeType.Text Then
      ' If it's a text, set the text value of the last node
      CType(hierarchy.Peek(), TreeNode).Text &= _
        ": " & reader.Value
    ElseIf reader.NodeType = XmlNodeType.EndElement Then
      ' Remove the element as we're done with it
      node = hierarchy.Pop()
    End If
  Loop

  ' Last node will be the root one, with the whole
  ' hierarchy properly built. Append the file name to it.
  node.Text &= " (" & Session("file").ToString() & ")"

  tvXmlView.Nodes.Add(node)
  tvXmlView.Visible = True

  ' Check for errors accumulated during XSD validation
  Dim msg As String = _errors.ToString()
  If (msg.Length > 0) Then
    pnlError.Visible = True
    lblError.Text = msg
    ' Remove invalid document from session
    Session.Remove("xml")
  Else
    pnlError.Visible = False
  End If
```

```
  Catch ex As Exception
    pnlError.Visible = True
    lblError.Text = ex.Message
    ' Remove invalid document from session
    Session.Remove("xml")
  End Try
End Sub
```

2. Add the AddAttributes() helper method next:

```
' Helper method of BuildTreeView that adds attributes found as
' child nodes of the passed node, using a different icon
Private Sub AddAttributes(ByVal reader As XmlReader, _
  ByVal node As TreeNode)
  If Not reader.HasAttributes Then
    Return
  End If

  Dim child As TreeNode
  Dim attrs As New TreeNode
  ' Define the node that will contain all attributes
  attrs.Text = "Attributes (" & reader.AttributeCount & ")"
  attrs.ImageUrl = "Images/attributes.gif"
  attrs.ExpandedImageUrl = "Images/attributes.gif"

  For i As Integer = 0 To reader.AttributeCount - 1
    child = New TreeNode
    ' Move to the appropriate attribute
    reader.MoveToAttribute(i)
    ' Configure the node and add it to the list of attributes
    child.Text = reader.Name & ": " & reader.Value
    child.ImageUrl = "Images/emptyfile.gif"
    attrs.Nodes.Add(child)
  Next

  node.Nodes.Add(attrs)
  ' Reposition the reader on the element
  reader.MoveToElement()
End Sub
```

3. Now you need to remove the call to SaveXml() in the Load button handler, and put in its place a call to BuildTreeView(). This is because you want to reload the contents of this control. As you see from the code in the first step, the call to SaveXml() is performed inside that method already:

```
private void btnLoad_Click(object sender, System.EventArgs e)
{
  BuildTreeView();
}
```

4. You need to call `BuildTreeView()` after uploading the `btnDefaultXml` button (the one that loads a sample document). Add the call to the method after the current event-handling code:

```
Private Sub btnDefaultXml_Click(ByVal sender As System.Object, _
  ByVal e As System.EventArgs) Handles btnDefaultXml.Click
  ...
  BuildTreeView()
End Sub
```

5. Save the solution and run the page. After the usual login process, load the `upload.xml` file, just as you did before. This time, the XML file will be represented in a tree view, as shown in Figure 8-10.

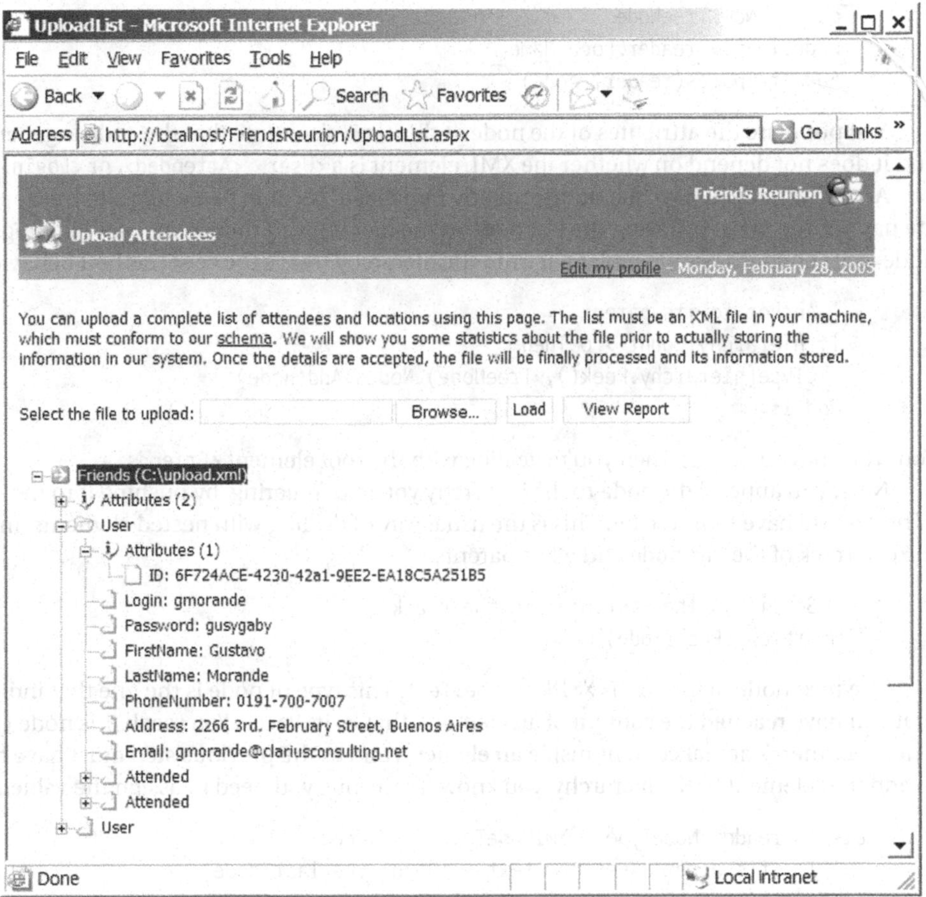

Figure 8-10. *The XML file in tree view*

How It Works

Clicking the Load button causes a postback. The code in the button event handler calls the BuildTreeView() method, where you save the incoming XML file and then uses an XmlReader to create nodes and add them to the tree view. You also append any attributes that may be found, by calling the helper AddAttributes() method.

The processing code using the XmlReader is typical when dealing with XML in a streaming fashion, and you basically read until you reach the end, testing in the loop for the occurrence of nodes you're interested in. In this case, you care about three types of nodes: XmlNodeType.Element, XmlNoteType.Text, and XmlNoteType.EndElement.

XmlNodeType.Element signals the start of a new element. For each element, you will add a child TreeNode to the tree, therefore, you create a new one here:

```
If reader.NodeType = XmlNodeType.Element Then
  'Create the new node
  node = New TreeNode
  node.Text = reader.LocalName
  AddAttributes(reader, node)
```

You populate the attributes of the node at this time also. Note that the code is generic, and it does not depend on whether the XML element is a <User>, <Attended>, or <Login> one.

At this point, you have the node properly initialized. It's time to anchor it to the appropriate parent. You do so by taking the last node in the hierarchy (if there's one), and adding this node as its child, without removing it from the hierarchy (that's the Peek method behavior):

```
  ' Anchor to its parent
  If hierarchy.Count > 0 Then
    CType(hierarchy.Peek(), TreeNode).Nodes.Add(node)
  End If
```

You won't have a parent when you're dealing with the root element <Friends>.

Next, you append the node to the hierarchy you're populating, by pushing it to the stack of nodes you have found so far. This is the usual way of dealing with nested elements, in order to keep track of the last node and all its parents.

```
  ' Set it as the last node in the stack
  hierarchy.Push(node)
```

The next node of interest is XmlNoteType.Text. This type of node is the one that indicates that you have reached the content of an element; that is, its Value. You reach this node type whenever there's actual content inside an element, and as the previous step must have been to add that element to the hierarchy, you know it's the one you need to assign the value to:

```
ElseIf reader.NodeType = XmlNodeType.Text Then
  ' If it's a text, set the text value of the last node
  CType(hierarchy.Peek(), TreeNode).Text &= _
    ": " & reader.Value
```

As noted, we retrieve the node through the Peek method, because we only need to assign its value, *not* actually remove it. If we wanted to remove it on retrieval, we would use the Pop method instead.

The third node of interest is XmlNoteType.EndElement. This one comes where the closing tag is reached for an element. At this point, you're finished processing the current element (the one at the top of the stack), so you can safely remove it.

```
ElseIf reader.NodeType = XmlNodeType.EndElement Then
  ' Remove the element as we're done with it
  node = hierarchy.Pop()
End If
```

If a validation error occurs while the tree view is being built, the handler you created in the previous section will be called, and the error will be appended to the _errors variable. The code will continue processing and adding nodes, until finally you check whether this variable contains any error messages and show the error panel if appropriate:

```
' Check for errors accumulated during XSD validation
Dim msg As String = _errors.ToString()
If (msg.Length > 0) Then
  pnlError.Visible = True
  lblError.Text = msg
  ' Remove invalid document from session
  Session.Remove("xml")
Else
  pnlError.Visible = False
End If
```

Just in case other unexpected exceptions happen during processing, you handle them through a common catch section (we'll discuss exceptions in detail in Chapter 11):

```
Catch ex As Exception
  pnlError.Visible = True
  lblError.Text = ex.Message
  ' Remove invalid document from session
  Session.Remove("xml")
End Try
```

In both cases, you remove the invalid document from the Session object, to force the user to load a valid one.

To finish off this section, let's take a look at what happens to a file that contains some validation errors. This time, add the uploadBad.xml file that's available in the code download for this chapter, which contains an invalid ID (shorter than it should be), and an invalid <Institution> element (not expected according to the schema). You can also append this kind of invalid content to your current upload.xml file. Click the Load button, and you should see the page shown in Figure 8-11.

XML Schema validation provides our system with a watertight seal against invalid data. As it's an external text file, you can modify your schema if your business requirements change, without necessarily recompiling or even stopping the web application. And the processing code is drastically simplified, because you simply rely on the schema for validating content. We don't need to check anything else.

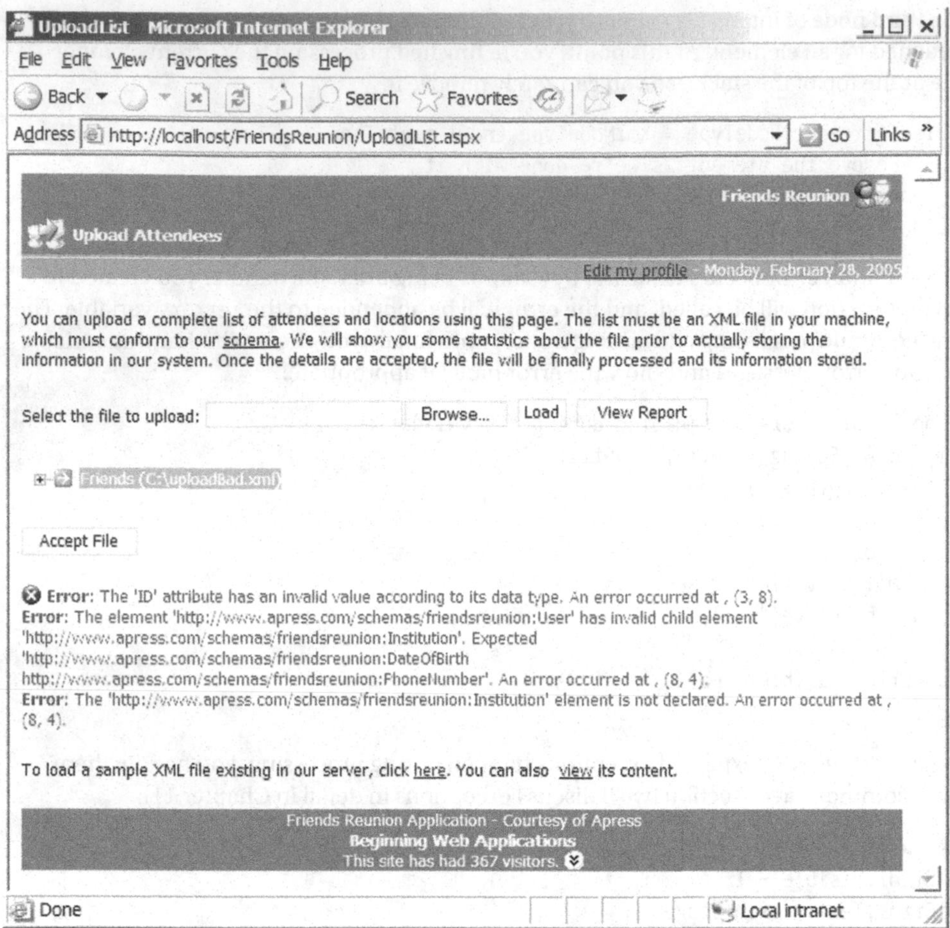

Figure 8-11. *The Upload List page after trying to load an invalid XML file*

Note that, in practice, schemas are usually loaded only once per application. So far, we have loaded it every time the page is posted back. This isn't good for performance. Typically, you would define a static variable for the schema and a property to access it, which loads and initializes it on first use, such as:

```
Shared _schema As XmlSchema

Private ReadOnly Property SchemaInstance() As XmlSchema
  Get
    If _schema Is Nothing Then
      Dim fs As Stream = File.OpenRead(Server.MapPath("~/Friends.xsd"))
      Try
        _schema = XmlSchema.Read(fs, Nothing)
```

```
    Finally
      fs.Close()
    End Try
  End If
  Return _schema
 End Get
End Property
```

Now, the validating reader would just need to add this cached version of the schema to its collection:

```
validator.Schemas.Add(SchemaInstance)
```

XML Queries with XPath

XML represents a powerful and increasingly popular way of storing and manipulating data, so it would be a huge shortcoming if there were no way to perform queries against that data. Now, we know that the de facto standard for querying relational data stores is SQL, so why can't we just use that to extract data from our XML documents?

The answer lies in the differences between the relational model of tables and rows, and the hierarchical structure of XML documents, where elements can be arbitrarily nested to any depth. This is why the W3C came to the rescue again with *XPath*, which is, as the specification says, "a language for addressing parts of an XML document."

XPath will be immediately familiar if you have an understanding of the file structure of a modern operating system, and particularly if you remember the days of the DOS command prompt. This is because XPath is based on the same slash-based syntax to locate items. The following XPath expression, for example, would locate all of the `<User>` elements in our sample XML document:

```
/Friends/User
```

The first slash indicates that the search should start from the root node of the document. The following elements compose a path, called a *location path*, that leads to the elements you want to be included in the result. When an XPath expression like this is executed, the result is a *node set* (or collection of nodes). The slash after `<Friends>` is the *axis* for the next element, `<User>`. It means that the next node is a child of `<Friends>`. XPath defines many other axes, such as parent and sibling.

We could refine this query by adding some further constraints on the results we wanted returned:

```
/Friends/User[LastName="Brown"]
```

This revised expression would return only those `<User>` elements for which the `<LastName>` child element has the text value `Brown`. The constraint is called the *predicate*. Let's dissect this expression:

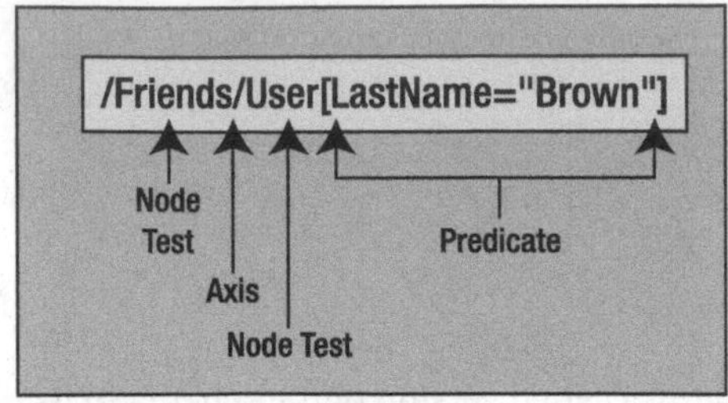

A set consisting of an axis (optional) plus a node test and an optional predicate is referred to as a *location step*. The example has two location steps: `/Friends`, and `/User[LastName="Brown"]`. The *axis* determines the direction in which to move down the location path. You can move to child nodes, as in this example, with the forward slash, which means that the next step is evaluated against the children of the previously evaluated step. Other possibilities include moving to the parent node (`../`), staying in the current node (`.`), or moving to an attribute (`/@`).

Another important feature of XPath is its numeric, string, and Boolean functions, which include `count()`, `sum()`, `string-length()`, `starts-width()`, `contains()`, and some others.

Tip For more information about XPath, visit `http://www.w3c.org/TR/xpath`. You can find the complete list of functions, axes, and other features of XPath in the specification itself at `http://www.w3.org/TR/1999/REC-xpath-19991116.html`. Additionally, you can refer to *Pro .NET XML*, by Kent Tegels (Apress 2005; ISBN: 1-59059-366-9).

Try It Out: Build the Reports Form In our application, we want to provide some statistical information about the uploaded file, such as a report of users and their Attended information. You can achieve this without needing to traverse the file laboriously, by using the features of XPath.

You'll set up the report form as shown in Figure 8-12.

UploadListReport.aspx*

Read from the submitted file:

Query Value

Query course name and attendee from year to Execute

Course Name Year In Year Out User ID

Back to Upload

[lblError]

Design HTML

Figure 8-12. *The Upload List Report page*

1. Add a new web form to the application and name it `UploadListReport.aspx`. As usual, make the class defined in the code-behind page inherit the `FriendsBase` class:

```
Public Class UploadListReport
  Inherits FriendsBase
```

2. Drag-and-drop the `iestyle.css` file onto the form surface to link the stylesheet.

3. Add two HTML Table controls from the HTML tab of the Toolbox, and two TextBox controls, two LinkButton controls, and an ImageButton control from the Web Forms tab, arranged as shown in Figure 8-12. Copy and paste at the bottom the `pnlError` panel from the `UploadList.aspx` form.

4. The first Table control will contain some fixed statistics values retrieved using XPath queries against the file. Set its properties as follows:

   - ID: `tbReport`
   - CssClass: `TableLines`
   - GridLines: `Both`
   - CellPadding: `0`
   - CellSpacing: `0`
   - Rows: Add a new row, with its `BackColor` set to #D3E5FA. Use the `Cells` property to add the two cells shown on the page (you'll just need to insert the `Text` property of each cell).

5. The TextBox control will show the starting year for the XPath query to filter attendees. Set its properties as follows:

   - ID: `txtYearFrom`
   - CssClass: `SmallTextBox`
   - MaxLength: `4`
   - Width: `36px`

6. The next TextBox control will show the ending year for the XPath query to filter attendees. Give it the `ID` `txtYearTo` and set the other properties the same as for the previous TextBox control.

7. The LinkButton control will perform the query with the range of years specified. Set its `ID` to `btnExecute` and its `Text` to **Execute**.

8. The Table control below the LinkButton control holds the results from the previous query execution. Set its properties as follows:

   - ID: `tbDates`
   - CssClass: `TableLines`
   - GridLines: `Both`

- CellPadding: `0`
- CellSpacing: `0`
- Rows: Add a new row, with its `BackColor` set to #D3E5FA. Use the `Cells` property to add the four cells shown on the page (you'll just need to insert the `Text` property of each cell).
- Visible: `False`

9. The ImageButton control will redirect the user back to the upload page. Set its properties as follows:
   - ID: `btnBackImg`
   - AlternateText: **Back to Upload**
   - ImageUrl: `Images/back.gif`
   - ImageAlign: `Middle`
10. The bottom LinkButton control links to the upload page. Set its `ID` to `btnBackLink` and its `Text` to **Back to Upload**.

The error panel and its controls will be already properly configured, as you use the same approach to handling errors as in the `UploadList.aspx` form.

How It Works

This form will show the statistics that you'll add in the code-behind page. The table at the top of the page will be populated with the results of some predefined queries, while the second table will execute a custom XPath query built from the value in the text boxes above it. It will allow the user to select the `<Attendee>` elements whose child elements' `<YearIn>` and `<YearOut>` text values match the desired range.

Before moving on to perform the queries, however, we need to introduce one last XML-related standard: the Document Object Model.

Querying Document Object Model (DOM) Documents

`XmlReader`-based objects provide forward-only access to the underlying XML data, which means that as soon as you move forward, you lose all information pertaining to the previous element. Clearly, such an approach is unsuited to querying a document, because you would end up reading the entire file for every query you perform. Even if the element you were looking for was the first one in the document, there would be no way to know that for sure, and you would need to read it in its entirety to be certain.

To perform queries effectively, you really need the complete document in memory, so that you can perform all the queries without needing to reparse the file. The W3C again has an answer: the *Document Object Model* (or *DOM*).

The DOM defines the way an XML document is stored in memory, and how its nodes are loaded, accessed, and changed using a "collection" approach: each node contains other nodes as children, and these, in turn, can contain other nodes, and so on. The DOM allows you to navigate back and forth between child and parent elements, too, tinkering with them as you go. It is neither forward-only nor read-only.

The DOM is built on several key building blocks. The fundamental one is the concept of the `Document`, which is to DOM what the `Schema` element is for XSD. This important object is implemented by the .NET Framework in the `System.Xml.XmlDocument` class.

Try It Out: Query a DOM Document With the information about the DOM in mind, you're ready to build the code for performing XPath queries, as we outlined in the previous section.

1. Open the code-behind page for the `UploadListReport.aspx` web form and import the following namespaces at the top of the file:

```
Imports System.IO
Imports System.Xml
Imports System.Xml.XPath
Imports System.Text
```

2. Add the `GetReader()` helper method to the `UploadListReport` class. This method will serve the same purpose as the function by the same name in the `UploadList.aspx` page:

```
  Private Function GetReader() As XmlReader
  If Session("xml") Is Nothing Then
    Throw New InvalidOperationException( _
      "No XML file has been uploaded yet.")
  End If

  ' Build the XmlTextReader from the in-memory string saved before
  Dim xmlinput As New StringReader(CType(Session("xml"), String))
  Return New XmlTextReader(xmlinput)
End Function
```

3. Locate the `Page_Load()` method and place the following code inside it:

```
 Private Sub Page_Load(ByVal sender As System.Object, _
  ByVal e As System.EventArgs) Handles MyBase.Load
  ' Configure header
  MyBase.HeaderIconImageUrl = "~/Images/print.gif"
  MyBase.HeaderMessage = "Upload Attendees - Report"

  Dim ns As String = "http://www.apress.com/schemas/friendsreunion"
  Try
    ' Retrieve the reader object and initialize the DOM document
    Dim reader As XmlReader = GetReader()
    Dim doc As New XmlDocument
    doc.Load(reader)
```

```
    ' Initialize the namespace manager for the document
    Dim mgr As New XmlNamespaceManager(doc.NameTable)
    mgr.AddNamespace("af", ns)

    ' List of new users
    Dim nodes As XmlNodeList = doc.SelectNodes("/af:Friends/af:User", mgr)
    Dim row As TableRow = New TableRow
    Dim cell As TableCell = New TableCell
    cell.Text = "Users: " + nodes.Count.ToString()
    row.Cells.Add(cell)

    Dim sb As StringBuilder = New StringBuilder
    For Each node As XmlNode In nodes
      sb.AppendFormat("{0}, {1} ({2})<br/>", _
        node("LastName", ns).InnerText, _
        node("FirstName", ns).InnerText, _
        node("Email", ns).InnerText)
    Next

    ' Add the cell with the accumulated list
    cell = New TableCell
    cell.Text = sb.ToString()
    row.Cells.Add(cell)
    tbReport.Rows.Add(row)
  Catch ex As Exception
    lblError.Text = ex.Message
    pnlError.Visible = True
  End Try

  If tbReport.Rows.Count = 1 Then
    tbReport.Visible = False
  End If
End Sub
```

4. Double-click the btnBackImg and btnBackLink controls in the designer to create Click event handlers for each of these. Add the following line of code to each handler to allow the user to navigate back to the UploadList form:

```
Private Sub btnBackImg_Click(ByVal sender As System.Object, _
  ByVal e As System.Web.UI.ImageClickEventArgs) Handles btnBackImg.Click
  Response.Redirect("UploadList.aspx")
End Sub

Private Sub btnBackLink_Click(ByVal sender As System.Object, _
  ByVal e As System.EventArgs) Handles btnBackLink.Click
  Response.Redirect("UploadList.aspx")
End Sub
```

5. Leave this page, and open the UploadList.aspx web form in the designer. Double-click the View Report button, and add the following code to the event handler that is created:

```
Private Sub btnReport_Click(ByVal sender As System.Object, _
  ByVal e As System.EventArgs) Handles btnReport.Click
  SaveXml()
  Response.Redirect("UploadListReport.aspx")
End Sub
```

6. With the UploadList.aspx page set as the startup page, run the project by pressing Ctrl+F5.

7. Select the sample XML file to upload and click View Report. You should see a summary that looks something like Figure 8-13.

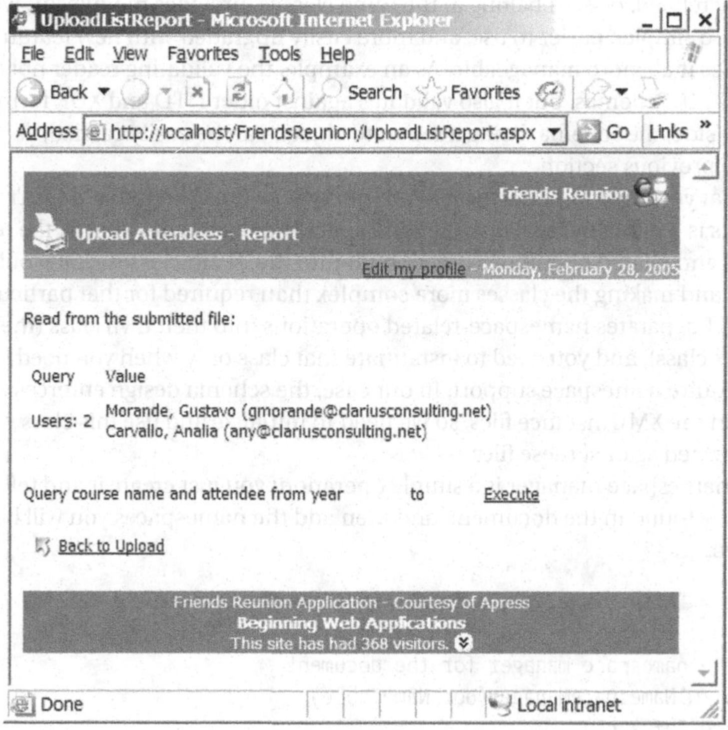

Figure 8-13. *Viewing a report*

How It Works

When you click the View Report button in the previous page, this page takes up the XML you saved in the session variable and produces the report you see in the table at the top of the page. In order to achieve this, you load an XmlDocument from it and perform the queries you need.

Loading the document involves retrieving an XmlReader that points to the XML string in the session variable, just as you did in the previous section, and passing it to the Load() method of the XmlDocument class:

```
' Retrieve the reader object and initialize the DOM document
Dim reader As XmlReader = GetReader()
Dim doc As New XmlDocument
doc.Load(reader)
```

You use a class called XmlNamespaceManager when you perform the queries. To understand why this class even exists, you need to understand the great effort Microsoft made to separate out functionality and make individual objects more manageable, lighter, and faster.

You saw how XmlValidatingReader builds on the XmlTextReader. You also learned how to pass XML Schemas to it. Why was the schema a separate object and not an intrinsic part of the validating reader? The answer lies in modularization and performance. Separating functionality that, while closely related, doesn't belong to the same classes, provides modularity, which allows each class to be simpler, easier to use, and more easily upgraded with new features. That effectively makes it all more manageable. As an example, the validating reader not only works with the new XML Schemas, but it also validates against older DTD and XDR formats. On the performance side, the schema, being a separate object, can be easily cached, as demonstrated in the previous section.

Now imagine that you need to perform an XPath query on a document that doesn't use namespaces (this is a perfectly legal task). If namespace management—that is, the resolution of XML prefixes and related operations—were built into the XPath classes, you would be wasting memory and making the classes more complex than required for that particular scenario. Hence, .NET separates namespace-related operations into their own class (the XmlNamespaceManager class), and you need to instantiate that class only when you need to issue queries that require namespace support. In our case, the schema design enforces the use of namespaces in the XML instance files, so we need to initialize and use this class whenever a query is performed against these files.

Initializing the namespace manager is a simple operation: you just create it and tell it to use the names already found in the document, and then add the namespaces you will be using in your queries:

```
Dim ns As String = "http://www.apress.com/schemas/friendsreunion"
..
  ' Initialize the namespace manager for the document
  Dim mgr As New XmlNamespaceManager(doc.NameTable)
  mgr.AddNamespace("af", ns)
```

Once loaded, the document will be completely available, from top to bottom.

Note Here, we focus on the methods that the XmlDocument class provides to perform queries against data. It contains many more methods and properties to work with, and they can be found in the MSDN documentation simply by typing "XmlDocument" in the Help Index window.

In the example, you execute a query to retrieve the list of new users in the file; that is, all <User> elements that are present in the document and children of the <Friends> element:

```
Dim nodes As XmlNodeList = doc.SelectNodes("/af:Friends/af:User", mgr)
```

It really is that easy to get the results! Note that you need to include the namespace prefixes on both element names in the XPath expression, because the document uses a namespace. Prefixes allow you to locate elements that belong to different namespaces, and the namespace manager is responsible for resolving them. Of course, you can still use documents without a namespace, and execute queries without using this class at all, but it's strongly recommended that you make namespaces part of your regular XML handling. Note that the specific prefix you use is irrelevant, as long as the manager is able to map it to a namespace. Also note that even when the namespace was applied to the root <Friends> element, all its children (including <User>) are also in that namespace, so they need the prefix, too.

Once you get the results, displaying them in the table is just a question of creating the appropriate TableRow and TableCell objects to contain the information about it. To build the result string containing all the users in the file, use the StringBuilder class:

```
Dim sb As StringBuilder = New StringBuilder
For Each node As XmlNode In nodes
  sb.AppendFormat("{0}, {1} ({2})<br/>", _
    node("LastName", ns).InnerText, _
    node("FirstName", ns).InnerText, _
    node("Email", ns).InnerText)
Next
```

As you iterate through the nodes found, the StringBuilder accumulates a sort of summary about new users, containing their full name and e-mail address (between parentheses). Each node offers some accessors to get at its content. Here, you've used the InnerText property to extract that content as a string value.

Understanding the XPath Data Model

The XPath specification defines four basic types that can result from executing expressions: node set, Boolean, number (floating point), or string. These are the only types in XPath. As you saw in the previous section, the XmlDocument provides basic support for querying and working with the results of XPath expressions. This support is limited to expressions returning node sets. The XmlDocument.SelectSingleNode is just a helper method that returns the first of such a node set.

XPath itself is independent of the DOM. Actually, there are many concepts in DOM that don't have an equivalent in XPath. So, instead of merging two different things into the XmlDocument implementation, Microsoft did the modularization work and completely separated the XPath processing from the underlying document implementation, such as the XmlDocument.

The fundamental class for XPath evaluation is the XPathNavigator that resides in the System.Xml.XPath namespace. This is an abstract class that implements a cursor-like interface to the underlying data. Most methods are navigation methods such as MoveToAttribute, MoveToFirstChild, MoveToNext, and so on. The XPath evaluation engine uses these methods to move through the data as it executes an XPath expression. In order to avoid the limitations of XmlDocument with regard to XPath native types (other than node set), you need to move to the XPathNavigator. For example, if you want to use some of the built-in XPath functions such as sum(), count(), substring(), and so on, you simply can't use XmlDocument's methods.

But since the XPathNavigator is an abstract class, how do you get at it? Here's where the System.Xml.XPath.IXPathNavigable interface comes into play. This interface is implemented by those classes that support the XPathNavigator. It has a single method, CreateNavigator(), which returns the instance you need to execute XPath expressions. The XmlDocument inherits the implementation of this interface from its base XmlNode class, and therefore you can get the navigator as follows:

```
Dim doc As New XmlDocument()
' Load it somehow

Dim nav As XPathNavigator = doc.CreateNavigator()
```

From now on, you can use the navigator to select nodes:

```
Dim it As XPathNodeIterator = nav.Select(expression)
```

Or to get scalar values resulting from a query:

```
Dim value As Object = nav.Evaluate(expression)
```

Note that instead of the DOM-related XmlNodeList class you get from the XmlDocument, you receive an XPathNodeIterator, which implements the usual iterator pattern:

```
Do While it.MoveNext()
  Response.Write(it.Current.Value)
Loop
```

After each call to MoveNext(), the internal cursor in the iterator is placed on the next element that matched the expression. If no more results are available, the method returns false.

The picture is completed by the XPathExpression class. This class represents a parsed XPath expression, and it is used to execute queries involving namespaces. Additionally, it offers the very convenient AddSort() method, and it gives you a chance to also cache these expressions for improved performance, much as you did for the XmlSchema. Basically, you must compile the expression with the navigator and assign the XmlNamespaceManager that is going to resolve namespaces before you use it:

```
Dim expr As XPathExpression = nav.Compile( "/af:Friends/af:User" )
' mgr is the configured XmlNamespaceManager
expr.SetContext( mgr )
```

Next, just pass the expression instead of a string to the navigator Evaluate() or Select() methods:

```
Dim it As XPathNodeIterator = nav.Select(expr)
```

Let's apply these concepts to our reporting application.

Try It Out: Query with XPathNavigator You will add a couple more queries that return scalar values: the count of <Attended> elements and the last user ID in the file. Because they are simple values, you need to use the XPathNavigator. Given your document uses namespaces, you need to use XPathExpression.

1. Add the following code to the Page_Load() event handler in UploadListReport.aspx:

```
Private Sub Page_Load(ByVal sender As System.Object, _
  ByVal e As System.EventArgs) Handles MyBase.Load
  ...etc.
  Try
    ...previous code...
    ' Create a navigator over the document
    Dim nav As XPathNavigator = doc.CreateNavigator()

    ' Total number of attendees anywhere in the document
    Dim expr As XPathExpression = nav.Compile("count(//af:Attended)")
    ' Set the manager to resolve namespace
    expr.SetContext(mgr)
    ' Execute expression
    Dim count As Object = nav.Evaluate(expr)

    ' Build the cell and row that shows the result
    row = New TableRow
    cell = New TableCell
    cell.Text = "Global count of attendees: " & count
    cell.ColumnSpan = 2
    row.Cells.Add(cell)
    tbReport.Rows.Add(row)

    ' The last attendee in the file, in document order
    expr = nav.Compile("string(/af:Friends/af:User[position() = last()]/@ID)")
    expr.SetContext(mgr)
    Dim last As Object = nav.Evaluate(expr)

    ' Build the cell and row that shows the result
    row = New TableRow
    cell = New TableCell
    cell.Text = "Last attendee ID in file: " & last
    cell.ColumnSpan = 2
    row.Cells.Add(cell)
    tbReport.Rows.Add(row)
  Catch ex As Exception
    Me.lblError.Text = ex.Message
    Me.pnlError.Visible = True
  End Try
```

```
    If tbReport.Rows.Count = 1 Then
      tbReport.Visible = False
    End If
  End Sub
```

2. With the UploadList.aspx page set as the startup page, run the project by pressing Ctrl+F5.

3. Select the sample XML file to upload and click View Report. The summary should look something like Figure 8-14 now.

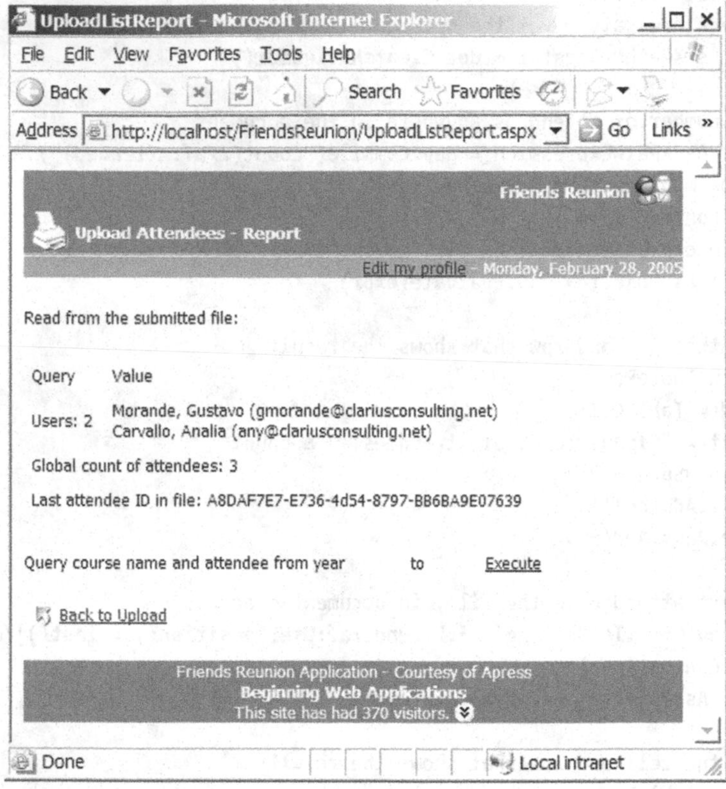

Figure 8-14. *The report with queries that return scalar values*

How It Works

As we said, when you use the XmlDocument's SelectNodes() method (or for that matter, the SelectNode() method, which returns the first node in the results), the XPath expression issued *must* evaluate to a node set (although this might contain only one node). For example, the following query is a valid XPath expression that returns a number, representing the count of <Attendee> elements found in the entire document:

```
count(//af:Attended)
```

This query would fail if you used it for the SelectNodes() method. Note that the double slash (//) at the beginning of the expression means that you're looking for *all* <Attended> elements *anywhere* in the document, starting from the root.

You use the IXPathNavigable.CreateNavigator() method implemented by the XmlDocument to get a navigator suitable for this kind of expression evaluation:

```
Dim nav As XPathNavigator = doc.CreateNavigator()
```

As your document uses a namespace (xmlns="http://www.apress.com/schemas/friendsreunion" attribute on the root <Friends> element), you must use an XPathExpression that allows for namespace resolution:

```
Dim expr As XPathExpression = nav.Compile("count(//af:Attended)")
```

This XPathExpression object can be used to precompile commonly used queries, in a similar way to stored procedures in database systems. This can speed up execution, because it allows you to reuse the expression and avoid repetition of the string-parsing step that interprets the query. You can also find the return type of the expression dynamically, through its ReturnType property.

In order for the expression to resolve the namespace used, it needs an associated XmlNamespaceManager, which is performed by calling the SetContext() method:

```
expr.SetContext(mgr)
```

Recall that the mgr variable was already initialized at the beginning of this method.

Finally, you evaluate the expression:

```
Dim count As Object = nav.Evaluate(expr)
```

The rest of the code just deals with adding the cells and row to show the result, exactly as you did before.

The second expression used is more complex:

```
// The last attendee in the file, in document order
expr = nav.Compile("string(/af:Friends/af:User[position() = last()]/@ID)");
```

As the comment indicates, this query returns the ID attribute (/@ID) of the last <User> element found in the document, for the user's verification purposes. More important though, this expression illustrates a number of useful XPath functions:

- string(), in this case, converts the ID attribute node to its string value.
- position() returns the position of the context element (in this case, each <User> being evaluated).
- last() returns the position of the last element in the context node (the context being the result of the previous location step evaluation; that is, the root <Friends> element).

Note that a predicate (the part of an XPath expression appearing in square brackets) can appear in any or all location steps. Here, a predicate selects the last <User> element so that you can access its ID attribute. This element is converted to a string and shown in the results table. This query isn't particularly useful in the context of our application, but it does show the power behind XPath expressions and the flexibility available for performing complex queries.

Building XPath Expressions Dynamically

As a final feature for our site, we are going to let the user enter a range of years, and query the uploaded file for matching nodes. For this feature, instead of using `XmlDocument` class, you will use another class that implements a read-only in-memory representation of the document and that is highly optimized for XPath querying: `XPathDocument`.

When we introduced `XmlDocument`, we said it is an implementation of the W3C DOM standard. As such, it's built around the concepts laid out in that specification. Microsoft developers realized that the DOM is not particularly efficient at executing XPath queries because of the way it stores its information as collections of nodes containing child nodes, and so on. They also discovered that many scenarios don't actually require a read/write representation, especially for query processing. We have such a scenario in our application already: reporting doesn't require any editing features.

As a result, the `XPathDocument` class was created. It's a really simple class that contains nothing but a `CreateNavigator()` method (the implementation of `IXPathNavigable.CreateNavigator()`). Once you have a navigator, you deal with queries and results in the same way as you did with an underlying `XmlDocument`. That's the beauty of `XPathNavigator` and the modularization achieved in `System.Xml`!

Try It Out: Query Based on User Input To allow execution based on user input, your code will build an XPath expression based on what's contained in the text boxes on the `UploadListReport` page when the Execute button is clicked. It will use the values to filter the matching nodes and show them in the second (currently invisible) table on the page.

1. Open the `UploadListReport` page in the designer, double-click the Execute button (`btnExecute`), and add the following code:

```
Private Sub btnExecute_Click(ByVal sender As System.Object, _
  ByVal e As System.EventArgs) Handles btnExecute.Click

  Dim ns As String = "http://www.apress.com/schemas/friendsreunion"

  Try
    ' Clear any previous state
    Dim row As TableRow = tbDates.Rows(0)
    tbDates.Rows.Clear()
    tbDates.Rows.Add(row)

    ' Set up the document
    Dim doc As New XPathDocument(GetReader())
    ' Get the navigator over the document
    Dim nav As XPathNavigator = doc.CreateNavigator()
    ' Set up the manager
    Dim mgr As New XmlNamespaceManager(nav.NameTable)
    mgr.AddNamespace("af", ns)
    ' Build the expression to execute
    Dim path As String = String.Format("/af:Friends/af:User/" + _
      "af:Attended[af:YearIn>={0} and af:YearOut<={1}]", _
```

```
      txtYearFrom.Text, txtYearTo.Text)
    Dim expr As XPathExpression = nav.Compile(path)
    expr.SetContext(mgr)

    Dim it As XPathNodeIterator = nav.Select(expr)
    Do While it.MoveNext()
      ' Create the empty row and cells
      row = New TableRow
      row.Cells.Add(New TableCell)
      row.Cells.Add(New TableCell)
      row.Cells.Add(New TableCell)
      row.Cells.Add(New TableCell)
      ' Grab the current navigator
      Dim attended As XPathNavigator = it.Current
      row.Cells(0).Text = attended.GetAttribute("Name", String.Empty)

      ' Iterate children of current Attended element
      attended.MoveToFirstChild()
      Do
        If attended.LocalName = "YearIn" AndAlso _
          attended.NamespaceURI = ns Then
          row.Cells(1).Text = attended.Value
        ElseIf attended.LocalName = "YearOut" AndAlso _
          attended.NamespaceURI = ns Then
          row.Cells(2).Text = attended.Value
        End If
      Loop While attended.MoveToNext()

      ' We have moved to Attended children
      ' Reposition to Attended node
      attended.MoveToParent()
      ' Get the parent (User) ID attribute
      attended.MoveToParent()
      row.Cells(3).Text = attended.GetAttribute("ID", String.Empty)

      ' Finally, add the new row
      tbDates.Rows.Add(row)
    Loop
    tbDates.Visible = True
  Catch ex As Exception
    lblError.Text = ex.Message
    pnlError.Visible = True
  End Try
End Sub
```

2. Press Ctrl+F5, leaving UploadList.aspx as the start page. Select the sample XML document and click View Report.

3. Insert a range of years in the boxes on the `UploadListReport` page, and click Execute to view the results. Figure 8-15 shows an example of the output when the years 1980 and 1990 are inserted into the text boxes.

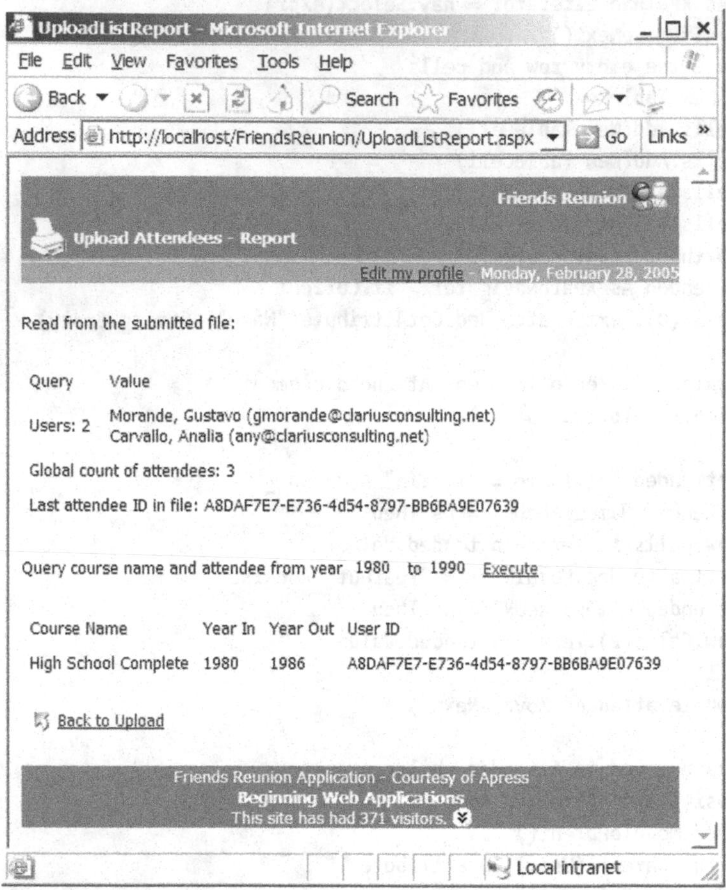

Figure 8-15. *Executing a query based on user input*

How It Works

When you click the Execute button, you load an `XPathDocument` constructed with the reader returned by the method you have used so far:

```
' Set up the document
Dim doc As New XPathDocument(GetReader())
```

You create the navigator and set up the namespace manager as you did before:

```
' Get the navigator over the document
Dim nav As XPathNavigator = doc.CreateNavigator()
```

```
' Set up the manager
Dim mgr As New XmlNamespaceManager(nav.NameTable)
mgr.AddNamespace("af", ns)
```

The XPath expression is built using the values in the text boxes. For this purpose, you use `String.Format()` to replace the dynamic values and compile the expression with the navigator:

```
Dim path As String = String.Format("/af:Friends/af:User/" + _
  "af:Attended[af:YearIn>={0} and af:YearOut<={1}]", _
  txtYearFrom.Text, txtYearTo.Text)

Dim expr As XPathExpression = nav.Compile(path)
```

Setting the expression context to the namespace manager and executing the `Select()` method is straightforward:

```
expr.SetContext(mgr)
Dim it As XPathNodeIterator = nav.Select(expr)
```

You will notice the differences in the way attribute and child elements are accessed from an `XPathNavigator` inside the `while` loop. First, an attribute value is retrieved directly through the `GetAttribute()` method:

```
row.Cells(0).Text = attended.GetAttribute("Name", String.Empty)
```

The first argument to the method is the name of the attribute to retrieve, and the second is its namespace. The attributes don't use namespaces, which is the default behavior in both XML and the XML Schema, as you saw in the previous chapter.

To process the child `YearIn` and `YearOut` elements, you need to move the navigator cursor into the children of the current `Attended` node. This is achieved by the following method call:

```
' Iterate children of current Attended element
attended.MoveToFirstChild()
```

At this point, it's important to remark that you are *sure* there are children, thanks to our schema. You *know* the document is valid, because you uploaded it with an `XmlValidatingReader`. You can now appreciate the simplification in code that derives from that fact. The method in this code returns a Boolean indicating whether or not it could move to the first child. You know it will always succeed; otherwise, the document would have been invalid in the first place. If you had not used an XML Schema, you would have needed to add checks everywhere to ensure that the structure conformed to that expected by your code.

The code to access children values is a little more complicated than with `XmlNodes`, but once you get used to it, it's fairly easy. Basically, you iterate until you run out of children (`Loop While attended.MoveToNext()`), checking the information in the current position to see if it's a node you're interested in:

```
Do
  If attended.LocalName = "YearIn" AndAlso _
    attended.NamespaceURI = ns Then
    row.Cells(1).Text = attended.Value
  ElseIf attended.LocalName = "YearOut" AndAlso _
```

```
        attended.NamespaceURI = ns Then
        row.Cells(2).Text = attended.Value
      End If
    Loop While attended.MoveToNext()
```

Retrieving the parent User element's ID requires moving the cursor upwards. As you have already moved into Attended's children, you need to move twice in that direction, and finally retrieve the attribute with the GetAttribute() method you used before:

```
attended.MoveToParent()
attended.MoveToParent()
row.Cells(3).Text = attended.GetAttribute("ID", String.Empty)
```

Once you have the results loaded in the table, you can change the values and click the Execute button again, to reload the table with the new values

XML APIs Comparison

As you've learned in this chapter, there are three basic approaches available when accessing an XML file; the XmlReader, the DOM through XmlDocument, and the XPath-optimized XPathDocument. In this section, we'll sum up what differentiates each of them, to help you make the correct decision when choosing which one to use in your own applications.

What mainly differentiates XmlReader from the other two approaches is that these readers provide forward-only, read-only access to documents, with no caching, while the other approaches cache an entire document in memory. The main difference between the XmlDocument and XPathDocument approaches is the editing capability: the latter is read-only. These differences give rise to a range of pros and cons for each one, as noted in Table 8-1. This table presents an analysis of the key features of all three approaches and compares implementations.

Table 8-1. *Comparing XmlReader, XmlDocument, and XPathDocument*

XmlReader	XmlDocument	XPathDocument
Context		
The reader doesn't persist any information about the file. Once the cursor has moved on, there is no access at all to the previous element. To preserve information, you must set up your own mechanisms and variables. **Con**	The document is completely loaded in memory when opened, and it stays there until you are finished with it. This means you can move freely from the current element to its parent, siblings, and children. The complete document is available to provide any context information you may require. It's tied to the W3C specification with regard to how the data is accessed and stored. **Pro**	Like XmlDocument, the XML document is completely loaded in memory when opened, and it stays there until you are finished with it. Therefore, you can freely navigate it and have full context information for queries and the like. Unlike XmlDocument, it's not tied to any specific in-memory storage or object model. Therefore, it was specifically optimized for XPath query executions. **Pro**

XmlReader	XmlDocument	XPathDocument
Resources Consumed		
Stemming from the previous "con," the reader gets its most important "pro": it consumes minimal resources because of the fact that only the current element is held in memory. As soon as the position is changed, the previous element is discarded, and its resources are freed. **Pro**	Loading a complete document in memory can become a serious hindrance, especially for applications that work with large files. For smaller files, the impact is less noticeable, although even then, several concurrent users of a web application can quickly consume significant resources. **Con**	Same problems as `XmlDocument`. **Con**
Random Access		
These readers provide only sequential access. To find a particular element, you must start at the beginning and work your way through. This can be a real problem if you need to access elements scattered through the XML "tree." **Con**	Nodes can be accessed using indexes or names, even queried using XPath. This complete random access support makes the DOM ideal for storing configuration files or offline data files. **Pro**	Full flexibility in navigating and accessing the document, but through a different navigation approach, implemented as a cursor over the underlying data. XPath queries are fully supported, and it's the foundation for fast XSLT transformations in .NET, too. **Pro**
Read-Write Access		
As the name implies, `XmlReader` and family can only read. **Con**	`XmlDocument` provides complete control over elements in a file. You can add, remove, and change them. This makes it very suitable for data storage (from a form, for example) and for offline client-side functionality (where you send intermittent batch updates to the server). **Pro**	No editing supported. **Con**
Speed		
The reader can be considerably faster, because it is so lightweight. If read-only access is suitable for a scenario, these classes are well worth consideration. **Pro**	Due to the comprehensive features it offers, DOM can take much longer than a reader to load and read a document from top to bottom. Improvements can be made through caching, but this will only increase the already high level of resources consumed. **Con**	Compared to `XmlReader`, `XPathDocument` is certainly slower, as the entire document needs to be loaded. But the added functionality and ease of use may be worth the price. Compared to `XmlDocument`, it's faster if you're doing intensive XPath querying. **Depends**

Continued

Table 8-1. *Continued*

XmlReader	XmlDocument	XPathDocument
Ease of Use		
The reader has several methods, and the fact that it simultaneously represents the reader object and the current element makes the interface somewhat clumsy. For example, some methods will be useful when the current element is of some specific type, but not when it is positioned over another type. You must work harder with readers. For instance, to retrieve the value of an element (with the `Value` property), you must first check the `HasValue` property to determine whether or not the current element can have a value. **Con**	The DOM has a more structured specification. There is an inheritance tree of classes, which starts from a general node type and adds specialization for other node types. The base `XmlNode` class is easy to master, and it is inherited by all the other disparate node types, greatly helping your learning curve. **Pro**	The cursor model of `XPathNavigator` (the main way to interact with an `XPathDocument`) resembles that of the reader, but with navigation methods. It is harder to learn if you come from the DOM world, but in the long term, it offers only a slightly more difficult API. **Pro**

This list is by no means a definitive comparison, but aims to provide some guidance. As with almost everything in programming, there is no guaranteed formula for successfully choosing one technique over another, and you must weigh the particular needs of each application.

Finally, keep in mind that in .NET version 2, the `XPathNavigator` cursor model will be the recommended way to handle XML data. So, unless you really need the DOM or write access to the document, we suggest that you stick to the `XPathDocument` approach.

Summary

In this and the previous chapter, you learned some important concepts about the use of XML in web applications. We looked at several standards that are regulated by the W3C and have a crucial role to play in the evolution of the Web.

When you use XML files, you need to understand the difference between well-formed XML and valid XML. Looking at valid XML led us to the W3C's XML Schema Definition Language (XSD) specification. We looked at some of the most important elements for defining the structure of XML instance documents, such as simple types, complex types, sequences, and attributes. We added occurrence constraints and learned how to restrict a base type to meet our needs. We added validation to our application using the schema we built, and it proved to be simple yet highly flexible and powerful. Storing validation logic for incoming data separate from business logic by the use of schemas helps maintenance and minimizes the coding required should your validation requirements change.

We exploited the full power of the XML support built into VS .NET, to visually create both schemas and instance documents. We saw how a schema enables IntelliSense during the creation of an XML document, and also played with the visual designers provided for drag-and-drop authoring.

A closer look at .NET's XML classes shed some light on the close relation between disparate namespaces, such as `System.IO` and `System.Xml`, as we used them in conjunction when building a useful upload feature for our application. On the way, we tried out a third-party custom control, in this case, the TreeView from Microsoft.

While reading XML may suffice for some applications, you usually need to perform queries against XML data. XPath is designed to fulfill this goal, and we applied it to generate statistical information about the file being uploaded to our web page.

Finally, we examined the W3C's DOM standard and its implementation in the .NET Framework: the `XmlDocument` class. We learned that it was not the only way to query documents and discussed the new and innovative `XPathDocument` and its companion, the `XPathNavigator`. These two are the foundation of the future of XML handling in .NET. We contrasted both the `XmlDocument` and `XPathDocument` with the `XmlReader` alternative, to determine for which situations each is most suited.

These chapters should provide the groundwork that we hope will be useful as you work through the next chapter, which is about the very important emerging XML technology of web services.

CHAPTER 9

Web Services in Web Applications

We've looked at the creation of web applications, connecting these applications to data sources, and then adding XML functionality to them. In this chapter, you'll make use of what you've learned from the previous chapters, applying that knowledge to a different aspect of web development that opens up a wealth of new functionality: *web services*.

Web services are seen by many as critical to the future of Internet-connected applications. Such a bold claim can be made for two main reasons. First, web services allow remote applications to be connected together over the standard Internet network. Second, they allow systems developed on other platforms and in different languages, such as Linux and Java, to integrate with functionality developed in .NET.

In this chapter, we'll explain what is unique about web services and why they are so lauded, and cover everything you need to know in order to create and use them. This chapter will cover the following topics:

- What a web service is
- How to create a web service
- How to consume a web service
- Error handling in web services
- Web service optimization
- Third-party web services

Overview of Web Services

Before you roll up your sleeves and start writing web services, it's a good idea to understand how they work. Here, we'll look at what web services are, how they came to be, and how they compare to the browser client/server application model that we described in Chapter 1.

Web services are parts of a system that are externally exposed (like web pages) via a new, open-standard wire format. This allows disparate applications to communicate with one another and share information. The web services standard itself is built on other standards such as HTTP (for transport) and XML (for message format). By making use of such widely accepted technologies, web services do not rely on any proprietary system or vendor. This allows support for them to be freely developed for any platform and language: .NET, Java, Perl, and so forth.

A web service itself (as implemented in .NET) is a collection of methods that can be called from a remote location. These methods accept parameters and optionally return a value, just as normal methods can, allowing for the vast majority of (appropriate) functionality that is used internally in an application to be exposed to a wider public.

Although web services themselves are fairly new, the concept behind them isn't. There has long been the need for disparate applications to communicate with each other in order to share information and functionality; this is called *distributed services*. Historically, tying these applications together was done on an ad hoc basis, with only the parties involved in the integration deciding on the structure and format of the data. As it became clear that a standardized specification would shorten development time and lower costs, several options were put forward; DCOM and CORBA are two examples. These options were based on proprietary formats, however, slowing their acceptance by developers and creating barriers to their use. They also imposed further technical issues, such as requiring the use of TCP/IP ports that are regularly blocked by firewalls. An alternative approach was needed that wasn't vendor- or platform-specific. Enter web services.

Having such a flexible mechanism available provides two main features to web application developers:

- You can draw on all of the custom functionality and information of a separate application, just as easily as you would use functionality provided by the .NET Framework or your own application code. For example, you could retrieve a company's current stock price, or get news in the relevant industry sector for display on the site, providing more information to the end user.
- You can publish information, allowing other applications to consume it. For example, you could publish a company's product catalog in a format that allows other sites to use the information, potentially increasing sales.

In the case of our Friends Reunion application, web services can be used to aid in the creation of affiliate sites, allowing people to sign up for the system from the web site of their old high schools, for instance.

Web Services Relationship to the Browser/Server Model

A simple way of visualizing a web service would be to think of it as a web page, which, rather than returning information that is useful to an end user, returns information that can be consumed by another application. In the simplest form, requests for information are made in a similar manner: calling a URL and passing any required information either on the URL (a `GET` verb), or as the body of the request (a `POST` verb). More complex mechanisms such as *SOAP* are also available (we'll look at SOAP later in this chapter). Requests for these URLs are then handled by IIS and the .NET runtime, just as they would be for a web request for a web form, for example. Any processing necessary is performed by code written by the developer, and the results are returned as the body of the HTTP response. However, rather than the response being an HTML document containing markup for display, it is made up of an XML document that contains data.

Figure 9-1 shows the process of making a request for a web service. From this logical point of view, it is the same as that of a web browser requesting a page.

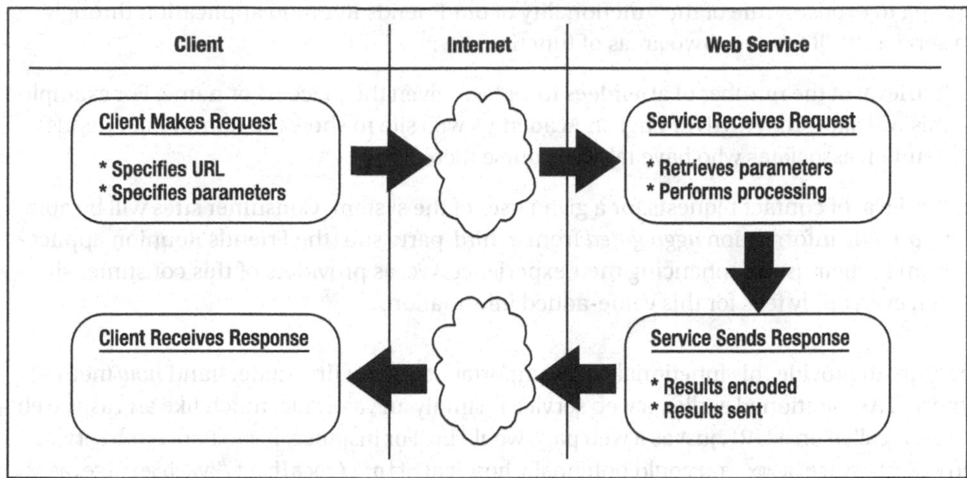

Figure 9-1. *Making a request for a web service*

Although web services and web pages are similar in nature, the fundamental purpose of them is different. Web services are intended as a standard way of exchanging information between two computers. This leads to a couple key differences:

- **Interface:** A web page has a user interface. A web service does not have a user interface. (Although it's not part of the standard, Microsoft does provide a simple way of testing your web services using an auto-generated interface.)
- **Interaction:** A web page is designed to interact with users. A web service is designed to interact with other applications.

To cater to these differences, and other technical differences, web services are created distinctly in VS .NET, and they have a different file extension from web pages: `.asmx`, rather than `.aspx`. This allows the ASP.NET runtime to process them differently and to provide extra functionality.

VS .NET Support for Web Services

Prior to the release of .NET, Microsoft's main offering for the creation of web services was in the form of a simple command-line tool, the SOAP Toolkit. Although this did a lot of the hard work for you, it certainly wasn't the easiest way of getting an introduction to the topic. As with many other new areas (such as XML, which we've looked at in Chapters 7 and 8), VS .NET has tightly integrated the creation of web services into the IDE.

To the developer, creating a web service is now almost identical to writing a user control or the code-behind page for a web form. Other features that we'll look at later in the chapter allow for the automatic creation of a UI for testing web services and treating web service methods just like normal methods when they're called from within your code.

Web Service Implementation

To get a good understanding of what constitutes a web service and how one is developed, we're going to expose some of the functionality of our Friends Reunion application through such a service. We'll focus on two areas of functionality:

- Retrieval of the number of attendees to a place, given the place ID or name. For example, this will allow the ACUDEI English Academy's web site to show the number of Friends Reunion associates who have taken a course there.
- Retrieval of contact requests for a given user of the system. Consumer sites will be able to provide information *aggregated* from a third-party site (the Friends Reunion application) to their users, enhancing their experience. We, as providers of this consumer site, can even apply fees for this value-added information.

In order to provide this functionality, it's important that you first understand *how* methods are exposed. As mentioned earlier, a web service is simply an `.asmx` file, much like an `.aspx` web form. This is called on a URL, just as a web page would be. For instance, if you had a web service named `MyWebService.asmx`, you could potentially host it at `http://localhost/MyWebService.asmx`.

To add such functionality to your solution and to ensure that it works correctly, several steps are involved:

- Create a new ASP.NET Web Service project to contain the service functionality.
- Create an `.asmx` file that will provide the web methods that can be called.
- Add the methods that are needed for the service to the code-behind class for the `.asmx` file.
- Enable anonymous access for third parties (our whole site is secured right now).
- Build the project.
- Test the project.

To start with, we'll implement the simpler of the two functions we mentioned: retrieving the count of attendees to a place. This will allow us to focus on the web service, rather than getting too involved in the logic of the application.

Implementing Web Methods

Within each web service, you add *web methods*. If a web service is thought of as a class (which it technically is), then a web method is akin to marking a method as `public` on a class, making it available externally. For our application, we'll create the `Partners.asmx` service and add web methods called `GetAttendees()` and `GetContactRequests()`, which actually implement the functionality we're trying to expose. Although the way in which these methods are called depends on the format used—`HTTP-GET`, `HTTP-POST`, and so on—the methods are always accessed from the containing service URL.

Try it Out: Create a Web Service You will now add a web service to your Friends Reunion project. Note, however, that you could instead create a completely separate application for this purpose. Doing so would allow for some more independent control over authentication, permissions, and so on. In our example, building a separate web service application isn't necessary.

1. Add a new folder to the application, called `Services`. This will allow you to set different authentication and authorization policies than the ones in effect for the main site.
2. Right-click the folder, select Add ➤ Add Web Service, and name the new item `Partners.asmx`, as shown in Figure 9-2.

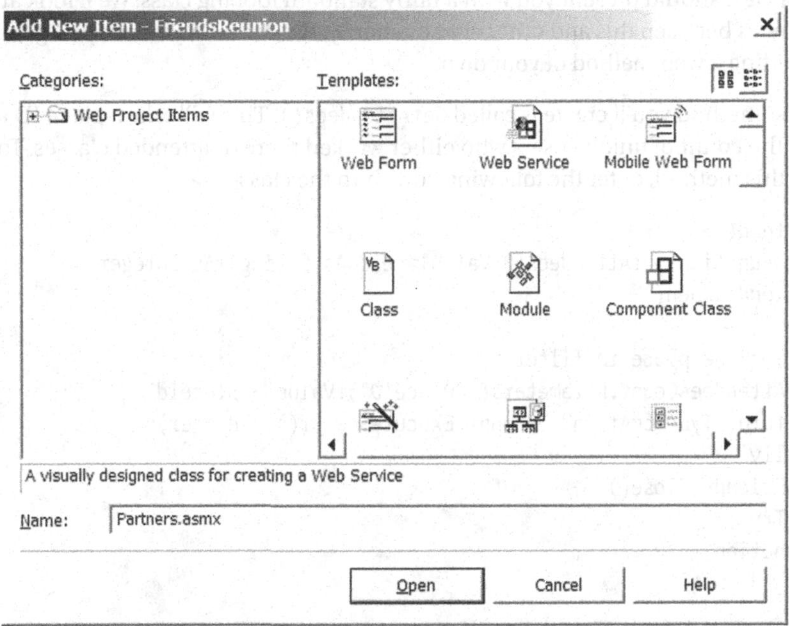

Figure 9-2. *Creating a new Web Service*

3. Next, you need to create `SqlConnection` and `SqlCommand` components to interact with the database. To do this, return to the new `Partners.asmx` file, in the Design view. In this view, you'll be able to drag-and-drop the database components that you need onto the design surface, just as you have done in earlier chapters.
4. From the Data tab of the Toolbox, drag-and-drop a `SqlConnection` component onto the design surface. Set the `Name` property of this to `cnFriends` and select the `ConnectionString` property from the `DynamicProperties` section, mapping it to the suggested default key of `cnFriends.ConnectionString` that we have been using since Chapter 4.
5. Once the connection has been created, drag-and-drop a `SqlCommand` component onto the design surface, and rename it to `cmAttendeesCount`. Next, set the `Connection` property to the existing connection, `cnFriends`. Set the `CommandText` required to retrieve the count of unique users for the requesting place in the `TimeLapse` table to the following SQL query:

```
SELECT COUNT(0) AS Attendees, @PlaceID
FROM
    (SELECT UserID FROM TimeLapse
      WHERE PlaceID = @PlaceID GROUP BY UserID) Users
```

If you set it directly in the Properties browser, enter the query without line breaks. Accept the suggestion to regenerate command parameters. You need to place the @PlaceID parameter in the outside query in order to get the appropriate command parameter to be generated and added automatically.

6. Switch to the code-behind view to start developing your web methods. The code-behind view should present you with a fairly standard looking class. We'll look at the differences between this and other classes shortly, but for now, you can just get on with adding a web method of your own.

7. The first method you'll create is called GetAttendees(). This will take a place ID and return the count of unique users who either worked there or attended classes. To create this method, enter the following code into the class:

```
<WebMethod()> _
Public Function GetAttendees(ByVal placeId As String) As Integer
  cnFriends.Open()
  Try
    ' Set the place to filter by
    cmAttendeesCount.Parameters("@PlaceID").Value = placeId
    Return CType(cmAttendeesCount.ExecuteScalar(), Integer)
  Finally
    cnFriends.Close()
  End Try
End Function
```

Tip When the web service was originally created, the IDE would have placed a short HelloWorld() web method example in it for you to see how the functionality works. This is a sample web service that simply returns the string "Hello World" to anyone who calls it. It is provided as a template for the creation of your own web services and as a means for testing. We won't be showing you how to get it running here, as all you need to know is explained in the method's comments, so you can delete it without causing any concerns. If you leave it there, it can always be uncommented and run to help you diagnose any problems you may encounter.

---

8. In order to make the services publicly available, you must allow Anonymous access to them. To do this, add the following location element to the Web.config file, just as you did back in Chapter 3 for the NewUser.aspx page. This time, however, you simply specify the folder. Remember this element must be under the root <configuration> element.

```
<location path="Services">
  <system.web>
    <authorization>
      <allow users="*" />
    </authorization>
  </system.web>
</location>
```

How It Works

Creating a web method within a web service really is that simple, because VS .NET takes care of all the low-level XML and HTTP plumbing required to make this work. It knows how to deal with your class and method in a web service fashion because of the slight differences in their definition. The first thing to note is the declaration of the class itself:

```
Public Class Partners
    Inherits System.Web.Services.WebService
```

As you can see, this class inherits from the `WebService` base class, instead of the `System.Web.UI.Page` class you're used to. This means that it automatically takes on all of the characteristics of a `WebService`, leaving you with little to do to implement the functionality that you need.

The second thing to note is the attribute that you place at the top of your method declaration:

```
<WebMethod()> _
Public Function GetAttendees(ByVal placeId As String) As Integer
```

This attribute informs the ASP.NET runtime to perform all of the actions necessary to expose your methods as part of the web service. The `WebMethodAttribute` attribute effectively adds the method to the public interface of your web service. If you wanted, you could also write other methods in this class that are made simply `Public` and can be consumed from within your application. Unless they are marked with this attribute, however, they would not form part of the publicly visible web service.

Finally, you added a new `<location>` to make your services freely accessible.

Testing the Web Service

Now that you've implemented a web method, you'll want to test it. Testing this method is similar to testing a web application; it can be done using a web browser. In some ways, it is far simpler, however, due to the fact that the functionality is contained within discrete methods that take and return specific parameters, rather than the verbose, UI-driven nature of web pages.

In order to test any service methods that you create, you must do the following:

- Set the web service file (`.asmx`) as the start page.
- Build and run the project.
- Select the web method to test.
- Enter the parameters and execute the method.

Try it Out: Test a Web Service You will now test your new `GetAttendees()` web method to check that it works correctly.

1. Right-click the `Partners.asmx` file, and set this as the start page. This has the same effect as in a web application: it informs the environment that when the solution is built and run, it should navigate to this location by default.

2. Compile and run the solution by pressing Ctrl+F5. You should see the results shown in Figure 9-3. Keep in mind that this page is intended only for testing purposes, not as a public interface to the web service. Whenever you create a web service using VS .NET, this is always available to you and to other users as a way to discover what the web service offers and to test it. The main point of interest to us on the page is the list of hyperlinked methods that are displayed near the top of the screen. This list takes you to a definition of every method that was marked as a web method in your code. The pages that are displayed when you select the hyperlinked method names provide the means to test your web service.

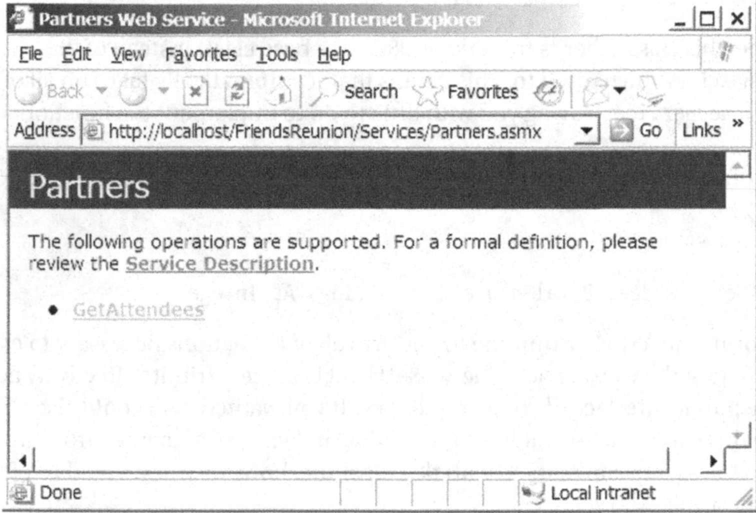

Figure 9-3. *Running the web service test page*

3. Click the one entry in the list, `GetAttendees`. This will take you to a second page that is again generated by .NET, as shown in Figure 9-4. This page allows you to test the individual method using the `HTTP-POST` verb and provides other details, such as the SOAP requests and responses that are used beneath the hood to make the necessary calls. (You can ignore this information for now; we'll discuss it shortly.)

4. Enter any valid `PlaceID`, such as `11CF70F8-E48E-4bdc-AE1A-5F2277015851`, and then click the Invoke button. This will create a new window in which the method is called. The method should return the following XML, containing the count of unique users that attended that place:

```
<?xml version="1.0" encoding="utf-8" ?>
<int xmlns="http://tempuri.org/FriendsReunion/Partners">2</int>
```

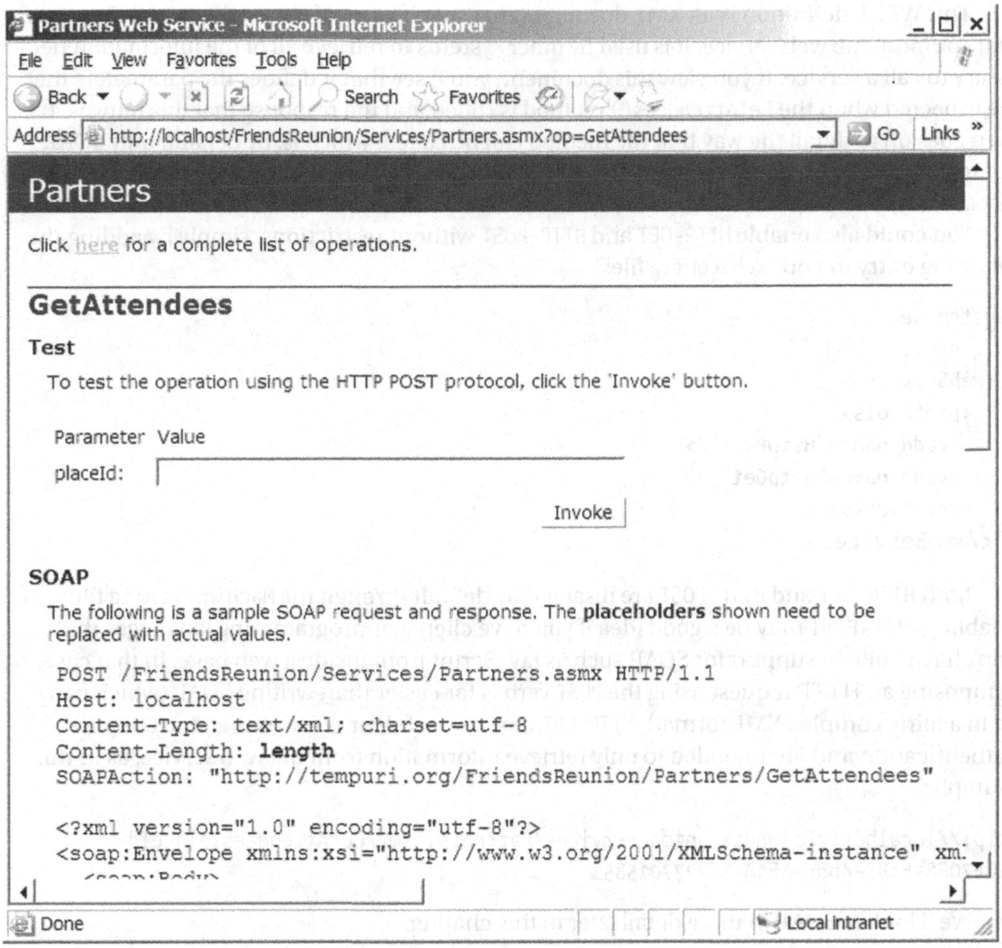

Partners Web Service - Microsoft Internet Explorer

File Edit View Favorites Tools Help

Address http://localhost/FriendsReunion/Services/Partners.asmx?op=GetAttendees

Partners

Click here for a complete list of operations.

GetAttendees

Test

To test the operation using the HTTP POST protocol, click the 'Invoke' button.

Parameter Value

placeId:

Invoke

SOAP

The following is a sample SOAP request and response. The **placeholders** shown need to be replaced with actual values.

```
POST /FriendsReunion/Services/Partners.asmx HTTP/1.1
Host: localhost
Content-Type: text/xml; charset=utf-8
Content-Length: length
SOAPAction: "http://tempuri.org/FriendsReunion/Partners/GetAttendees"

<?xml version="1.0" encoding="utf-8"?>
<soap:Envelope xmlns:xsi="http://www.w3.org/2001/XMLSchema-instance" xml
```

Done Local intranet

Figure 9-4. *The page for testing the GetAttendees() web method*

How It Works

If you look at the URL after clicking the Invoke button, you can see the actual URL of the web method you called:

```
http://localhost/FriendsReunion/Services/Partners.asmx/GetAttendees
```

Notice that the URL is built by appending the method name after the URL to the `.asmx` file.

These web pages provide us, as developers, with a great means of viewing and testing web services, but the textual descriptions, text boxes, and so on are not of the structured nature used by other applications when interfacing with web services. If you select the Service Description link from the `Partners.asmx` page (Figure 9-3), you are taken to a page with the query string parameter of `?WSDL`. This parameter can be added to any `.asmx` URL, and it provides the Web Service Description Language (WSDL) definition of the service.

This WSDL definition is an XML document that specifies all of the methods and data types that compose the web service. It is used by other systems to retrieve all of the information necessary to call a service. If you view this document, you'll see that it defines the parameters that are expected when the `GetAttendees()` method is called and the response that this returns. It then goes on to detail the way that the method can be called, which is, by default, only SOAP. For testing and debugging purposes, the `HTTP-POST` verb is allowed only on the local machine (`localhost`), but is not reflected on the WSDL, as it's not accessible from the outside world.

You could also enable `HTTP-GET` and `HTTP-POST` without restrictions, simply by adding the following entry in your `Web.config` file:

```
<system.web>
  ...etc...
  <webServices>
    <protocols>
      <add name="HttpPost"/>
      <add name="HttpGet"/>
    </protocols>
  </webServices>
```

Both `HTTP-GET` and `HTTP-POST` are disabled by default through the `Machine.config` file. Enabling `HTTP-POST` may be a good idea if you have clients or programming languages that don't have built-in support for SOAP, such as JavaScript from inside a web page. In that case, composing an HTTP request using the `POST` verb is far easier than writing SOAP (which can be in a fairly complex XML format). `HTTP-GET` may be useful for services that don't require authentication and are intended to only retrieve information from the web service, as in this example:

```
http://localhost/FriendsReunion/Services/Partners.asmx/GetAttendees?placeId=
11CF70F8-E48E-4bdc-AE1A-5F2277015851
```

We'll look at SOAP in more detail later in this chapter.

Using Complex Data Types

The web method that you created in the previous section returns an integer. As we mentioned, applications making use of the functionality that you expose determine this by examining the WSDL definition of your services. While returning simple data such as strings and integers will work fine this way, what happens when you want to return something more complicated, such as an object containing all of the requests for contact for a person?

When retrieving this information from the database, and passing it around internally using normal methods, you could use a `DataSet`. This same approach works with a web method, and that's how we'll handle the other functionality we're adding to the Friends Reunion database, which is the retrieval of contact requests for a given user of the system.

To implement this functionality, you'll need to create a new method within the service that takes in a user name and password and returns a `DataSet`. The information returned will include complete information about all the users who requested to contact the individual performing the query, based on the user's login data. In our simple implementation, entering the wrong user name or password will simply cause no results to be returned, instead of a failure.

Try It Out: Return Complex Data Types Now, you will add another web method, called `GetContactRequests()`, which will return complex data.

1. Open the `Partners.asmx` file in the Design view and drop a new `SqlCommand` component on the design surface. Name it `cmContacts` and set its `CommandText` to the following query, through the Query Builder (so that you can enter the comments and line breaks):

```
SELECT
  /* Return fields we're interested in */
  ContactUser.FirstName, ContactUser.LastName, ContactUser.Email,
  ContactUser.Notes, ContactUser.IsApproved
FROM
  [User] INNER JOIN
  /* Join with the contact information to get
       the one for the user matching the login and pwd */
  (SELECT
    [User].FirstName, [User].LastName, [User].Email,
    Contact.Notes, Contact.IsApproved, Contact.DestinationID
  FROM
    /* Another join to retrieve the requester name */
    Contact INNER JOIN [User] ON [User].UserID = Contact.RequestID)
  AS ContactUser
  /* Filter contact information for the current destination user */
  ON [User].UserID = ContactUser.DestinationID
WHERE
/* This is the filter that restricts the inner contact results */
[User].Login = @Login AND [User].Password = @Password
```

2. Import the following namespace at the top of the web service code-behind `Partners` class:

```
Imports System.Data.SqlClient
```

3. Add the following new web method to the class:

```
  <WebMethod()> _
  Public Function GetContactRequests(ByVal login As String, _
    ByVal password As String) As DataSet
    cnFriends.Open()
    Try
      cmContacts.Parameters("@Login").Value = login
      cmContacts.Parameters("@Password").Value = password

      Dim contacts As New DataSet
      Dim ad As New SqlDataAdapter(cmContacts)
      ad.Fill(contacts)
      Return contacts
    Finally
      cnFriends.Close()
    End Try
  End Function
```

4. Finally, let's use our own namespace for the web service messages:

```
<System.Web.Services.WebService( _
  Namespace:="http://www.apress.com/services/friendsreunion")> _
Public Class Partners
```

5. Save and run the application. You'll see that there are now two methods listed on the page that is displayed, as shown in Figure 9-5, since you now have two web methods in the code-behind page.

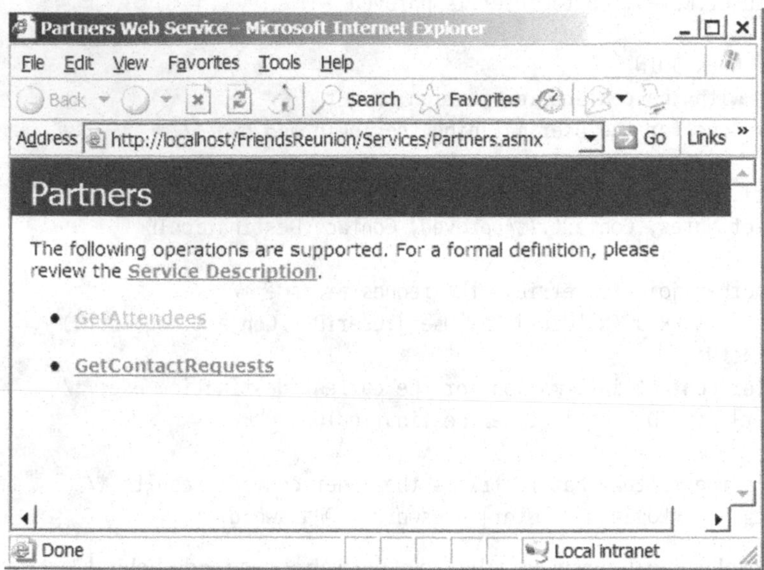

Figure 9-5. *The web service now has two methods.*

6. Click the `GetContactRequests` link to bring up the test page for this method. Enter **apress** as the user name and password and click the Invoke button. This will generate a new browser window, containing the XML that the .NET Framework generates from the `DataSet`. The output should be similar to Figure 9-6. As you can see, it's a rather large XML document.

How It Works

Up front, we must say that passing a user name and password over an unencrypted URL should not be done in production systems. In addition to using unencrypted HTTP, web services can also use HTTPS. This could then be combined with methods of calling web services other than an `HTTP-GET`, ensuring that parameters aren't placed on the URL and that all of the data is encrypted.

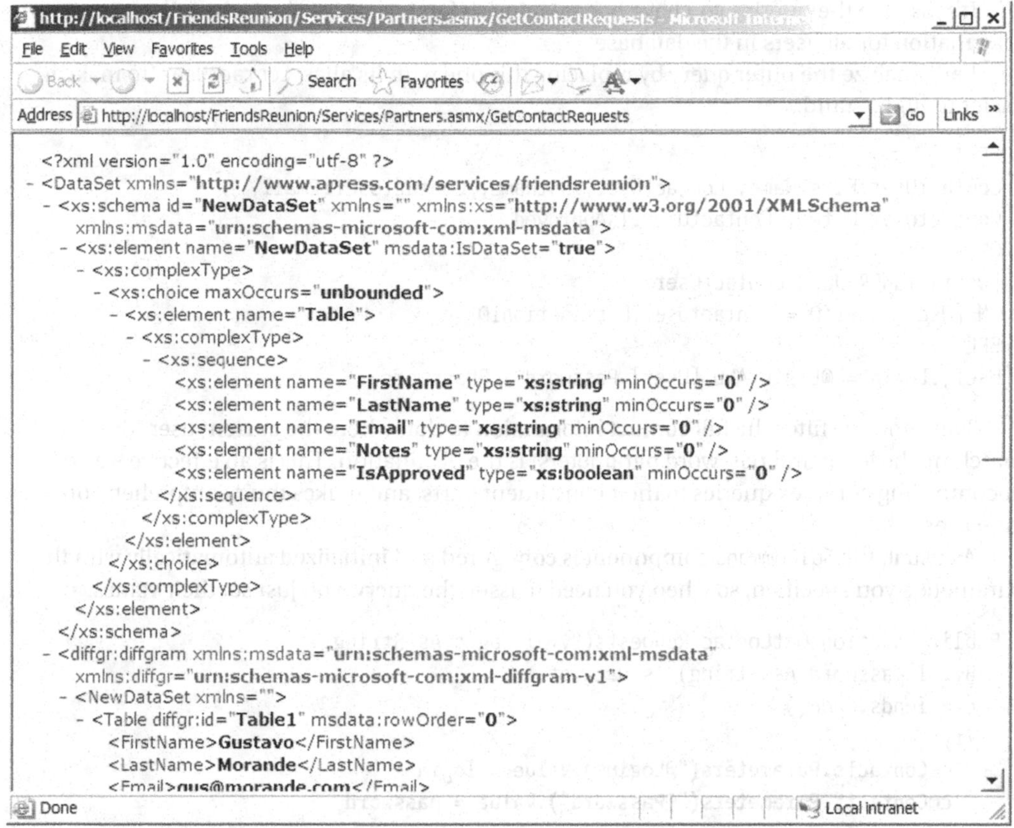

Figure 9-6. *The XML for the DataSet*

Tip In the future, securing web services will also be available at the message level, instead of the transport level, as in HTTPS. That means you will be able to encrypt and sign the communication with your service without the need for SSL. This is the WS-Security specification, headed by OASIS (`http://www.oasis-open.org/`) with the support of major industry players such as Microsoft, IBM, and BEA.

The query to retrieve contact information is a bit complex. It's actually made of two queries: one selecting all requests for contact (including joining this information with the User table), and another one selecting only the user that matches the login and password received, filtering the previous result. The former query is nested in the latter. Let's look at the nested query:

```
SELECT
  [User].FirstName, [User].LastName, [User].Email,
  Contact.Notes, Contact.IsApproved, Contact.DestinationID
FROM
  Contact INNER JOIN [User] ON [User].UserID = Contact.RequestID
```

It's just like the queries you have been issuing so far. It simply selects the full contact information for all users in the database.

Let's analyze the outer query by replacing this one with its alias, ContactUser, to make it easier to understand:

```
SELECT
  ContactUser.FirstName, ContactUser.LastName, ContactUser.Email,
  ContactUser.Notes, ContactUser.IsApproved
FROM
  [User] INNER JOIN ContactUser
  ON [User].UserID = ContactUser.DestinationID
WHERE
 [User].Login = @Login AND [User].Password = @Password
```

This time, we filter the full contact information to that where the current user (the one matching the login and password parameters) is the destination. This is an effective way of decomposing complex queries to their constituent parts, and makes their comprehension far easier.

As usual, the SqlCommand component is configured and initialized automatically with the parameters you specified, so when you need to issue the query, you just set their values:

```
  Public Function GetContactRequests(ByVal login As String, _
    ByVal password As String) As DataSet
    cnFriends.Open()
    Try
      cmContacts.Parameters("@Login").Value = login
      cmContacts.Parameters("@Password").Value = password
```

Next, you simply initialize an adapter and fill the DataSet you are about to return:

```
      Dim contacts As New DataSet
      Dim ad As New SqlDataAdapter(cmContacts)
      ad.Fill(contacts)
      Return contacts
```

When you return a complex data type, such as a DataSet from a web method, it undergoes a process known as *XML serialization*, whereby an object is converted to an XML string that represents it. XML is a good technology for doing this, as it allows for arbitrarily large and complex data structures, making it possible to store almost any type of data in a convenient and portable format. DataSet objects have better support than most objects for converting to this string-based representation, but almost all data types can be serialized automatically, whether they are structs, arrays, or some other type.

Serialization is only half of the story, though. Once another application has retrieved the data in this format, it can deserialize it back into an object. *Deserialization* is the reverse process to serialization: it takes the XML string that was built during serialization and creates an object of the correct type, populated with the data contained within the XML document (and hence representing the original object).

Thankfully, rather than needing to implement the serialization and deserialization process yourself in the consuming application, when you add a reference to a web service,

.NET creates a wrapper for you, allowing all of this processing to happen behind the scenes—and you can just get on with writing your applications. You'll see this deserialization in action shortly.

Realize that, in allowing VS .NET to take care of all this for you, you can no longer return this data to a non-.NET application without writing a lot of wrapper code yourself. But even if it's harder, non-.NET applications can still get the relevant information out of the data returned, since it's just plain XML in the end, with all the advantages we discussed in previous chapters.

Web Service Consumption

As well as implementing web services in your applications, you may also need your applications to use, or *consume*, another application's web services. The process of consuming a web service from .NET is exactly the same, regardless of the nature of the application: it can be a web application, a Windows forms application, a command-line utility, or even a Windows service!

To use a web service from an application, you reference that web service. Adding a *web reference* performs a similar function to adding a reference to a .NET assembly: it allows the IDE to know the location of the external classes you're using and methods available on them.

As a demonstration of how to consume a web services, we'll create a test application that, rather than displaying the XML that is produced when you test a method using an Internet browser, uses the web services we've implemented in the Friends Reunion application as though they were functionality local to the application.

Try it Out: Consume a Web Service For this example, you'll need to create a new project for an institution associated with the Friends Reunion community, and therefore with full permissions to upload lists of users (as discussed in the previous chapter). The home page of this institution, ACUDEI English Academy, will welcome users and show how many Friends Reunion members have attended the school, and will allow users to enter their login and password to retrieve their list of contacts.

1. Add a new Web Application project to the solution and call it `Acudei`. Once the IDE has finished creating the application, it will present you with the usual blank form named `WebForm1.aspx`. Let's remove it.

2. Add a new Web Form, named `Default.aspx`, and set its `pageLayout` property to `FlowLayout`. Add some text and a Label control that will hold results of the web service execution, reflecting the following layout.

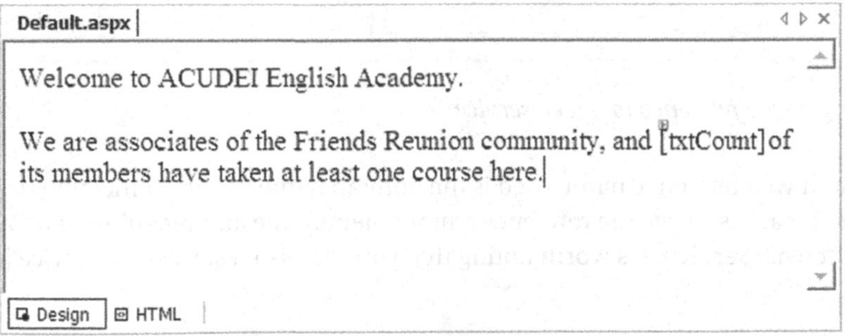

3. To add a web reference, right-click the project name and select the Add Web Reference option from the context menu. This will bring up the Add Web Reference dialog box, which allows you to locate web services being hosted, either locally or at any publicly visible URL. It also allows you to view details about them and test them (where supported) before they're added to the project.

4. In the URL field at the top of the dialog box, enter the location of your web service: `http://localhost/FriendsReunion/Services/Partners.asmx`. Then click the Go button (the little green arrow next to the Address box) or press Enter. The IDE will retrieve the URL specified and display details about the service in the two panes. The left-hand pane will contain the same web page that you saw when you browsed to the web service in your browser. The right-hand pane displays details of the actual web services that are available at that URL. If there is an error retrieving web service information from the specified URL, it will be displayed in this right-hand pane. Once the URL has been located, and the page has been loaded, the dialog box should look like Figure 9-7.

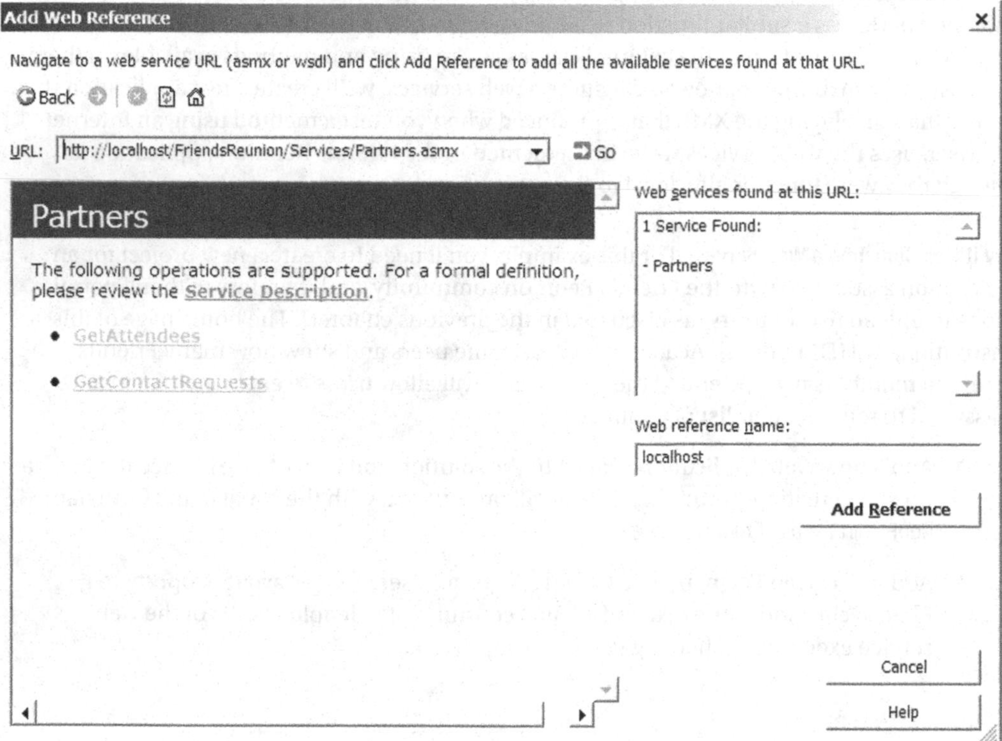

Figure 9-7. *Adding a web reference to a web service*

5. The default web reference name used is the domain name you're connecting to—in this case, `localhost`. Give the reference a more memorable and meaningful name, such as `FriendsService`. It's worth noting that you can also test the web service just as

you did earlier, but directly from this window, before adding the reference. If you are making use of a third-party web service, you should ensure that service is functioning as expected before trying to consume it. To complete the addition of the web reference, click the Add Reference button. If you click Show All Files in the Solution Explorer at this point, you'll see the IDE has added several files to the Acudei project.

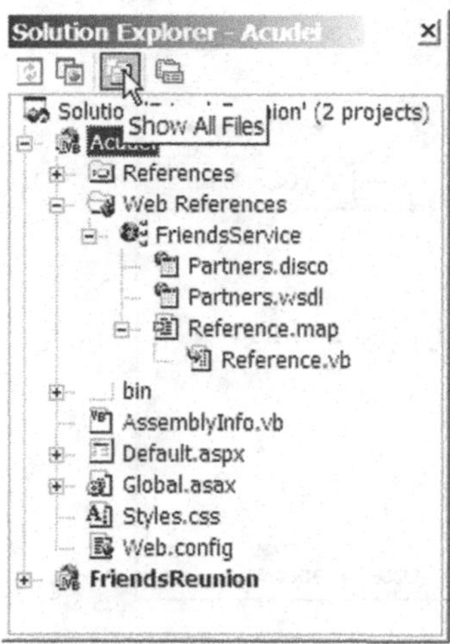

6. You will need to pass a PlaceID to the web service. Let's make it configurable by adding a key to the <appSettings> section in the Web.config file:

```
<configuration>
  <appSettings>
    <add key="PlaceID" value="11CF70F8-E48E-4bdc-AE1A-5F2277015851" />
  </appSettings>
```

7. Next, import the following namespace on the code-behind page:

```
Imports System.Configuration
```

8. Now you can start adding code that makes use of the web methods, just as though they were in a built-in class, such as a SqlCommand. The runtime will take care of calling the remote service and handling the data marshaling. This code will be called when the page loads, to fill the blank with the count of Friends Reunion users in the associate institution. Therefore, add the following code fragment to Page_Load():

```
 Private Sub Page_Load(ByVal sender As System.Object, _
  ByVal e As System.EventArgs) Handles MyBase.Load
  Dim friends = New Acudei.FriendsService.Partners
  Dim count As Integer = friends.GetAttendees( _
    ConfigurationSettings.AppSettings("PlaceID"))
  txtCount.Text = count.ToString()
End Sub
```

9. That completes the implementation of the simple consumer application, so you can save, compile, and run it. In order to run this project, you'll need to set it as the startup project for the solution (by right-clicking on the project and selecting Set as Startup Project, as in previous examples). Next, set the `Default.aspx` page as the start page. The page should render the count of users for the place entered, as shown in Figure 9-8.

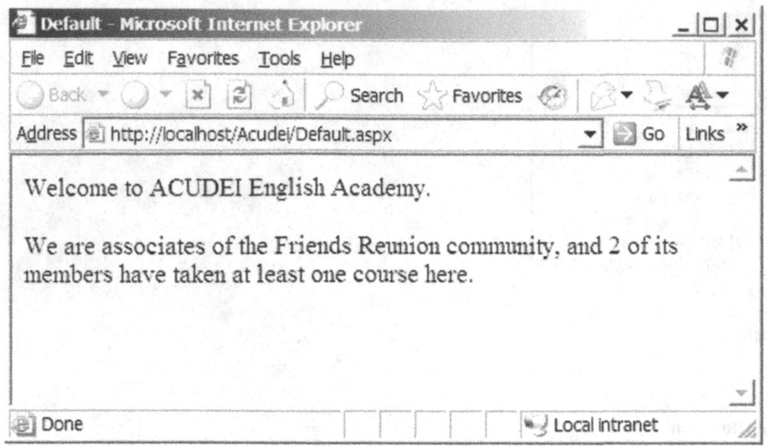

Figure 9-8. *The consumer application*

How It Works

When you add a web reference, VS .NET asks for the service WSDL formal description. You looked at such a description earlier, by appending the `?WSDL` parameter to the service URL, in our case, `http://localhost/FriendsReunion/Services/Partners.asmx?WSDL`. With this description at hand, the IDE generates a class to represent this service, with a method for each web method exposed by it, and places it in a namespace that matches the name you used for the web reference. In the Solution Explorer, you can see this WSDL file is actually downloaded and stored as part of the web reference.

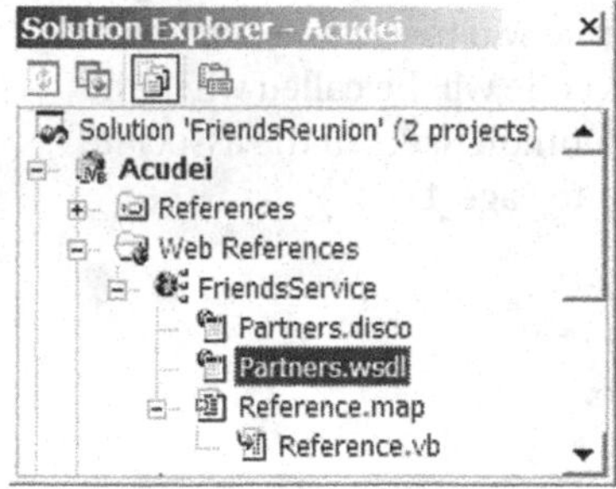

The class generated from this file is located below the `Reference.map` file. You can dig into it to discover how the remote web service invocation is done when you call the `GetAttendees()` method.

The code in `Page_Load()` uses this class as any other regular class, initializing an instance of it and calling the method. Notice how the call to this method looks identical to calls to any other regular class method. There's nothing in the code that indicates this is a web service call. You also get a typed result, the integer you are expecting.

As mentioned earlier, the so-called *proxy class* and the .NET runtime deal with the nuts and bolts of passing requests to the service, serializing parameters being passed in to the method, deserializing return values, initiating the connection, and so on. By generating the proxy class at design-time, you get strong typing and IntelliSense right away.

Try It Out: Retrieve Contact Requests Now that you've seen how our `GetAttendees()` method can be called from within an application, let's extend the consumer application to retrieve the contact requests for users. To do this, you'll need to call the `GetContactRequests()` method, passing in the user login name and password, and add a DataGrid control to the form in order to present the `DataSet` of results that are returned. Figure 9-9 shows the layout you'll set up for the Default page.

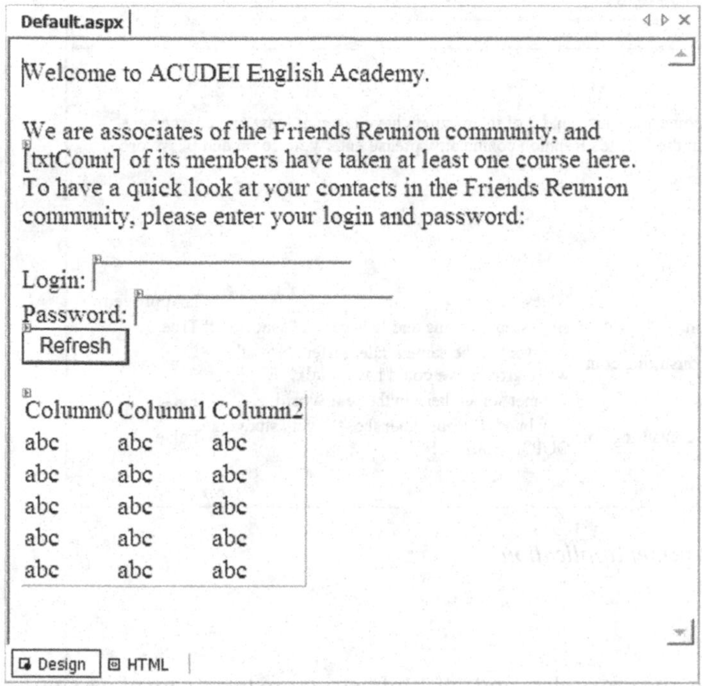

Figure 9-9. *The Acudei project's Default page layout*

1. Add text, two TextBox controls, a Button control, and a DataGrid control to the `Default.aspx` form of the `Acudei` test application, as shown in Figure 9-9.
2. Set the TextBox `ID` properties to `txtLogin` and `txtPassword`, the button's to `btnRefresh`, and the DataGrid's to `grdContacts`. Set the button's `Text` property to **Refresh**.

3. Double-click the button to get to the `Click` event handler. Add the following code to it:

```
Private Sub btnRefresh_Click(ByVal sender As System.Object, _
  ByVal e As System.EventArgs) Handles btnRefresh.Click
  Dim friends = New Acudei.FriendsService.Partners
  Dim ds As DataSet = friends.GetContactRequests( _
    txtLogin.Text, txtPassword.Text)
  grdContacts.DataSource = ds
  grdContacts.DataBind()
End Sub
```

4. Start the application again, and then fill the text boxes with the usual **apress** login and password. You'll see a page like the one shown in Figure 9-10.

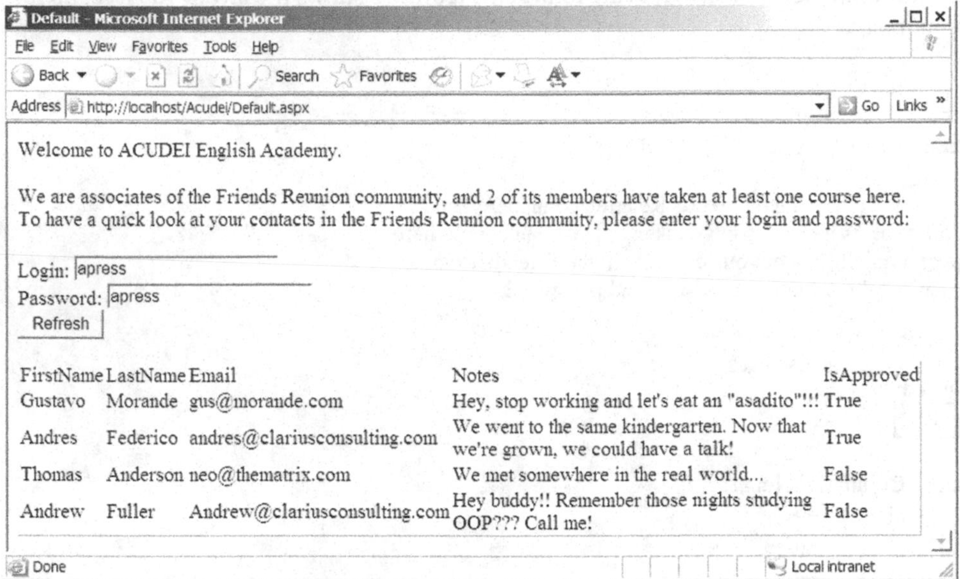

Figure 9-10. *The web service consumer application*

How It Works

Just as in the previous example, the proxy class and .NET infrastructure takes care of passing the information to the remote web method and handing results back. In this case, you receive a complex `DataSet` object back, which can be readily used to fill your DataGrid control. You take advantage of data binding, as discussed in Chapter 5.

Having both the consumer application and the web service inside the Friends Reunion project makes it extremely easy to follow the execution flow. If you place breakpoints in your web methods' code before starting the `Acudei` consumer site project, you can step into the code easily. Note that we don't handle errors that could happen, such as connectivity problems, service malfunctioning, and so on. We will introduce some error handling that is particular to web services in the "Error Handling in Web Services" section later in this chapter. General debugging and exception-handling techniques are covered in Chapter 11.

An Introduction to SOAP

Although there's no need for us to go deep into the gory details (as .NET takes care of it all for us), it's useful to know where SOAP comes in to all of this, as it plays a fundamental behind-the-scenes role in web services. SOAP is a means of sending a message to an endpoint (URL), and it offers an alternative to the `HTTP-POST` options that we've already discussed. It is used in .NET as the default method for accessing web services. This is due to the richer functionality that it offers, namely a more structured way of alerting the calling application to errors (which we'll cover shortly), support for return parameters (reference parameters), and other such features.

Note SOAP originally stood for Simple Object Access Protocol, although we doubt anyone can call it *simple* anymore.

SOAP is not just yet another Remote Procedure Call (RPC) mechanism. It certainly can be used as such, but SOAP is more message-oriented, and it's exclusively based on XML.

The SOAP specification consists of the following parts:

- The message format, required elements, and processing model
- An optional set of rules for encoding application data and method parameters for performing RPC-style calls between web services
- SOAP message transmission through HTTP

The latter two belong to low-level support from libraries, and they are already handled for you in .NET infrastructure. The first, the message format itself, defines an open structure that allows for easy and structured extensibility, and is worth looking at further, as it's at the core of web services.

Understanding the SOAP Message Format

SOAP uses XML to send information between applications as messages. This usage of XML supports sending the data in a well-structured format. This allows you to provide more robust systems than would be possible if the only way of accessing web services was by passing parameters on a URL—imagine trying to pass an entire dataset around using only a query string!

When used for request/response message exchange, there will be two types of messages:

- **SOAP request:** This is sent to a SOAP-compliant application (such as IIS and ASP.NET) for processing, usually over HTTP. This processing can be (and usually is) an invocation of an application method exposed as a web service. In this case, the request includes information such as the arguments required by the method.
- **SOAP response:** This is returned from a SOAP-compliant application and contains the results of processing a SOAP request, if it completed successfully.

In this usage scenario, we can draw a direct parallel with the standard HTTP request and response. In the case of web services, each of the SOAP messages maps directly to the underlying HTTP messages.

If an error occurs during processing that is not handled, or the developer code throws an exception, a special type of message, called a *SOAP Fault*, is sent in place of the SOAP response. This message contains details of the exception that was thrown, and allows you to provide information about errors in a standardized format that can be interpreted by a system easily, as opposed to the error pages that are displayed to alert users to errors in web applications.

A SOAP message is transmitted within an *envelope*, just like sending a letter. This allows extra information to be transmitted along with the message data itself. Figure 9-11 shows the basic structure of a SOAP message, whether it's a request or a response.

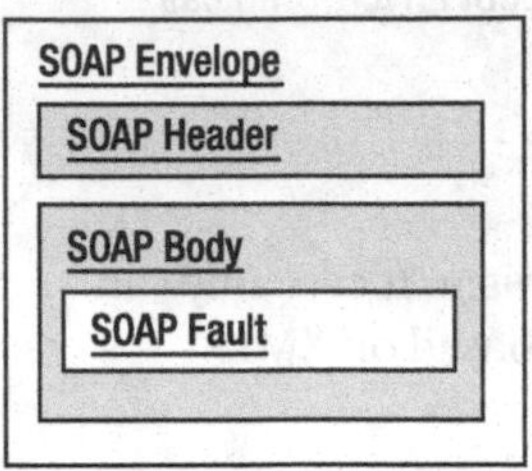

Figure 9-11. *The basic structure of a SOAP message*

As you can see in the diagram in Figure 9-11, a SOAP message has the following structure:

- The SOAP envelope contains the entire SOAP message.
- The SOAP header contains arbitrary and extensible information, such as details about transactions, security, login information, the source of a request, and so on. These are similar in functionality to HTTP headers, but far more extensible.
- The SOAP body contains either a SOAP Fault or the actual XML payload of the message, which could be the bulk of the request message (the name of the method to call and the parameters that are to be passed to it) or the response generated after the call.
- The optional SOAP Fault contains details of errors that occurred. This is available only if an untrapped exception is raised, and it is available only as part of a SOAP response message.

Other than when you're testing your methods through a browser, or when you implement a lot of the nuts and bolts work of creating web services yourself rather than relying on VS .NET, you are not actually exposed to the underlying SOAP messages. If you're developing an application that must integrate with a platform other than .NET, then such messages become far more important, as they may not be directly compatible with the output generated by the IDE. In most cases, however, XML serialization in .NET, combined with the built-in proxy class generation, is sufficient.

Viewing a SOAP Request and Response

You can see an example of a SOAP request and response by browsing to the URL `http://localhost/FriendsReunion/Services/Partners.asmx?op=GetContactRequests`.

Beneath the input boxes that allow you to enter the login and password information, you can see a sample SOAP request and response for the method that you are examining (`GetContactRequests()`). The first block of code details the request. This can be split into two parts: the XML document (the data you're interested in sending) and all of the information that is required to send this document via HTTP. The headers merely ensure that the HTTP request being sent is well-formed and complies with standards. Beneath this is the SOAP message that we're interested in:

```
<?xml version="1.0" encoding="utf-8"?>
<soap:Envelope xmlns:xsi="http://www.w3.org/2001/XMLSchema-instance"
              xmlns:xsd="http://www.w3.org/2001/XMLSchema"
              xmlns:soap="http://schemas.xmlsoap.org/soap/envelope/">
  <soap:Body>
    <GetContactRequests
              xmlns="http://www.apress.com/services/friendsreunion">
      <login>string</login>
      <password>string</password>
    </GetContactRequests>
  </soap:Body>
</soap:Envelope>
```

You can see that the structure of the XML follows the diagram in Figure 9-11. The root node in the document is the `soap:Envelope`, which, in turn, contains a `soap:Body`. This body then details the name of the method to be called, along with the parameters to pass to it. The occurrences of `string` within the `login` and `password` tags are where you would insert the values for these parameters, such as apress.

The response shows the complex information contained in a dataset. Both the schema for the data being returned and the actual information are included in the body:

```
<?xml version="1.0" encoding="utf-8"?>
<soap:Envelope ...etc...>
  <soap:Body>
    <GetContactRequestsResponse
              xmlns="http://www.apress.com/services/friendsreunion">
      <GetContactRequestsResult>
        <xsd:schema>schema</xsd:schema>xml</GetContactRequestsResult>
    </GetContactRequestsResponse>
  </soap:Body>
</soap:Envelope>
```

The schema is included as a W3C XML Schema, immediately preceding the actual data (the `xml` word before the closing `</GetContactRequestsResult>`). Other non- .NET platforms can therefore handle even this complex .NET object, as it's represented by standard XSD and XML data.

Error Handling in Web Services

As with any piece of code, there is the potential for an error to occur during the processing of a web service. This may be either through a mistake in the original implementation or because an external error has occurred, such as losing a database connection on the service side. In the .NET projects we've looked at so far, this is handled through the throwing of *exceptions*. Such exceptions aren't used only when an unexpected error occurs; they can also be thrown within code whenever you want to abort processing and signify to the caller that a special (usually undesired) state has been reached. This technique is also available to you when you're developing web services.

The main caveat here has to do with the details that are returned to you when you allow VS .NET to create the proxies around services for you. Every exception that is thrown is wrapped up within another `SOAPException` error, which doesn't store all of the details of your original .NET exceptions, making handling them a little more difficult. This does not prevent you from handling errors in a manageable fashion, however, as you'll see in the next example.

Looking at the `GetAttendees()` method in our web service, it should be clear that if an invalid place ID is passed into the system, it will simply return zero as the count of attendees. Rather than have the calling application determine that this value means that no match was found (and which may be an incorrect assumption, anyway), you can throw an exception that informs the application of the result if no match was found.

To add such a mechanism to the service, you will modify the query sent to the database to include a check for the `PlaceID` before issuing the count of attendees. If the `PlaceID` is not found in the `Place` table, it will return `-1`.

Try It Out: Handle Web Service Errors To handle web service errors, you'll need to update both the web service and the consumer application. The service needs to throw exceptions when an error occurs, and the consumer needs to trap them.

1. Open the `Partners.asmx` code-behind file, locate the `InitializeComponent` method, and change the line that sets the `cmAttendeesCount.CommandText` property to match the following:

```
Private Sub InitializeComponent()
  ...etc...
  '
  'cmAttendeesCount
  '
  Me.cmAttendeesCount.CommandText = _
    "IF EXISTS(SELECT PlaceID FROM Place WHERE PlaceID = @PlaceID)" & _
    " SELECT COUNT(*) AS Attendees, @PlaceID " & _
    " FROM  (SELECT UserID" & _
    "        FROM   TimeLapse" & _
    "        WHERE PlaceID = @PlaceID" & _
    "        GROUP BY UserID) Users" & _
    "ELSE" & _
    " SELECT -1"
  Me.cmAttendeesCount.Connection = Me.cnFriends
  ...etc...
End Sub
```

You can't set the property to this value through the Properties browser or the Query Builder because the designer does not support `IF` statements (and many other valid SQL statements). Therefore, it will fail to set it. Once you set it this way, however, it will be properly reflected in both and preserved when you make changes to other properties.

2. Import the following namespace at the top of the code-behind class:

```
Imports System.Web.Services.Protocols
```

3. Go to the `GetAttendees()` method and modify the code as follows:

```
 <WebMethod()>
Public Function GetAttendees(ByVal placeId As String) As Integer
  cnFriends.Open()
  Try
    ' Set the place to filter by
    cmAttendeesCount.Parameters("@PlaceID").Value = placeId
    Dim count As Integer = CType(cmAttendeesCount.ExecuteScalar(), Integer)
    If count = -1 Then
      Throw New SoapException("Invalid Place identifier!", _
        SoapException.ClientFaultCode, Context.Request.Url.AbsoluteUri)
    End If
    Return count
  Finally
    cnFriends.Close()
  End Try
End Function
```

Now, whenever the user passes in a place ID that doesn't exist, the application will throw a `SoapException`, which inherits from the standard `Exception` class.

4. Now that you've altered this method so that it specifically throws exceptions, you must update your consumer application to ensure that it doesn't fall over when the exception is thrown. In other words, you need to make use of this exception, by catching it whenever it is thrown. To do this, drop a new Label control at the bottom of the `Default.aspx` page in the Acudei project and set the following properties for it:

   - ID: `lblError`
   - Visible: `False`
   - EnableViewState: `False`
   - ForeColor: `Red`

5. Locate the `Page_Load()` event handler in the code-behind code. Add the following `try...catch` block:

```
 Private Sub Page_Load(ByVal sender As System.Object, _
  ByVal e As System.EventArgs) Handles MyBase.Load
  Dim friends = New Acudei.FriendsService.Partners
```

```
    Try
      Dim count As Integer = friends.GetAttendees( _
        ConfigurationSettings.AppSettings("PlaceID"))
      txtCount.Text = count.ToString()
    Catch se As SoapException
      lblError.Text = String.Format( _
        "<h2>An error happened connecting to Friends Reunion service.</h2>" & _
        "<h3>Service location: {0}</h3>" & _
        "Error: <br/>{1}", se.Actor, se.Message)
      lblError.Visible = True
    End Try

  End Sub
```

6. Since you are catching a SoapException, you need to import the following namespace at the top of the code in this file:

```
Imports System.Web.Services.Protocols
```

7. Modify the Web.config file in the test application, adding some characters at the end of the PlaceID in <appSettings>, to make it an invalid GUID.

8. Start the project. You should now get the message stating the error occurred. However, it doesn't simply contain the text that you would expect: "Error: Invalid Place identifier!" Rather, you'll be presented with something like this:

```
Error:
System.Web.Services.Protocols.SoapException: Invalid Place identifier!
at FriendsReunion.Partners.GetAttendees(String placeId) in C:\Apress\
Code Download\Chapter09\FriendsReunion\Services\Partners.asmx.vb:line 91
```

   This is due to the way SOAP faults are serialized and deserialized by .NET, and unfortunately, there's little you can do to resolve the issue.

9. You might not be able to stop the errors from being formatted in this manner when they're returned, but you can write a bit of code to retrieve solely the original message using string manipulation, as long as you always return a single-line error message from your web service. To do this, amend the catch block as follows:

```
    Catch se As SoapException
      lblError.Text = String.Format( _
        "<h2>An error happened connecting to Friends Reunion service.</h2>" & _
        "<h3>Service location: {0}</h3>" & _
        "Error: <br/>{1}", se.Actor, _
        se.Message.Substring(45, se.Message.IndexOf(vbLf) - 45))
      lblError.Visible = True
    End Try
```

10. Now run the application again. You will be presented with a different, more user-friendly message, as shown in Figure 9-12.

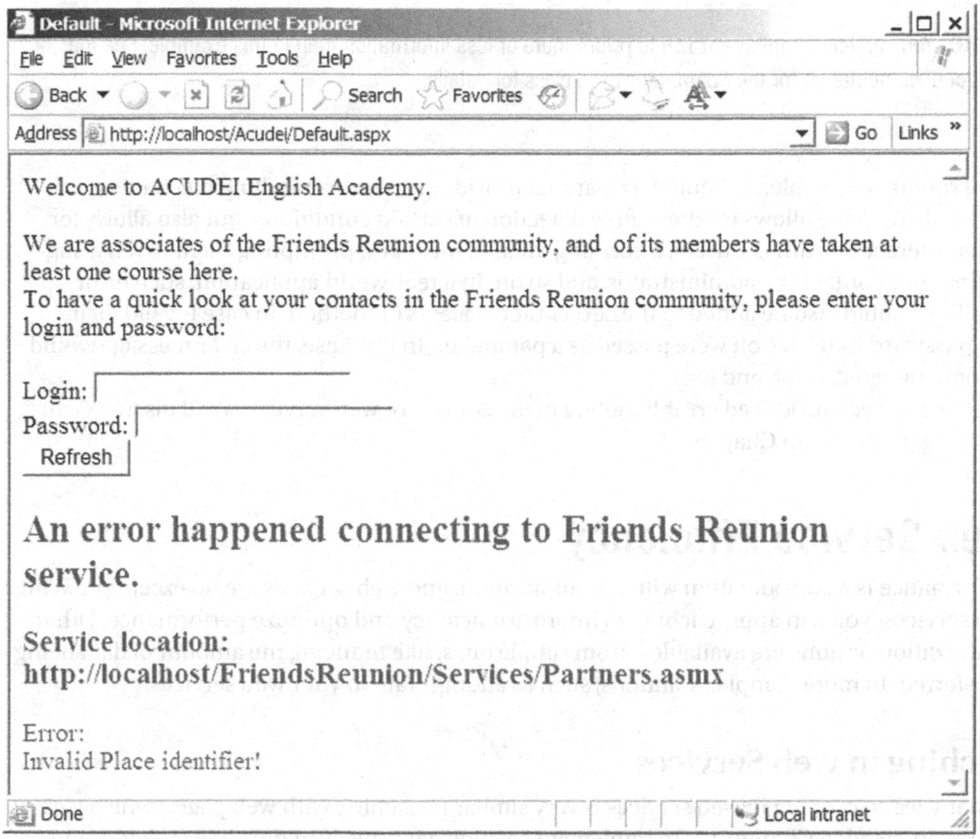

Default - Microsoft Internet Explorer

File Edit View Favorites Tools Help

Back Search Favorites

Address http://localhost/Acudei/Default.aspx Go Links

Welcome to ACUDEI English Academy.

We are associates of the Friends Reunion community, and of its members have taken at least one course here.
To have a quick look at your contacts in the Friends Reunion community, please enter your login and password:

Login:
Password:
Refresh

An error happened connecting to Friends Reunion service.

Service location: http://localhost/FriendsReunion/Services/Partners.asmx

Error:
Invalid Place identifier!

Done Local intranet

Figure 9-12. *By using string-manipulation, you can present a user-friendly error message related to a web service problem.*

How It Works

Within your code, you can throw exceptions, just as in any other code. These could technically be any exception supported by the CLR, such as an `ArgumentException`, an `ApplicationException`, and so on. However, rather than use these, you can throw a special type of exception: the `SoapException`. This provides a structure within which you can store more appropriate and detailed information than with more generic exceptions. Such information includes the URL at which the error occurred and details of what caused the error. In this example, you used this information to show the error message.

You determined the information for the error message from two values:

- `SoapException.ClientFaultCode` specifies that the error was due to the values that were passed in to the function.
- `Context.Request.Url.AbsoluteUri` returns the location at which the code is running.

When you passed these values to the constructor of the `SoapException`, you used one of the six overloaded methods.

Note You can use `SoapException` to return more or less information than in this example. See the product documentation for the `SoapException` class for details.

From this example, it should be clear that providing an error-handling mechanism in your code not only allows for the simple detection of certain conditions, but also allows for richer interaction with the users, informing them of mistakes, prompting them to retry, suggesting they contact the administrator, and so on. In a real-world application, such error handling should also be added to the `GetContactRequests()` method, in case invalid login and password information were passed as a parameter. In this case, the error message would be more targeted at the end user.

Here, we've introduced error handling in the context of web services. We'll discuss error handling in general in Chapter 11.

Web Service Efficiency

Performance is a consideration with any application, and web services are no exception. With web services, you can apply caching to improve efficiency and optimize performance. Other optimization options are available—from simple ones, like reducing the amount of data being transferred, to more complex solutions, such as adding state to your web services.

Caching in Web Services

In many ways, caching in web services is very similar to caching with web pages, which we'll discuss in detail in Chapter 12. To implement caching, you specify a *duration* to determine how long to cache a response. After the request has been processed for the first time (with a given set of input parameters), this version will be cached until the specified duration has expired. Adding caching to web services is done on a per-method basis. Each method can have its own caching settings applied.

Although caching can greatly improve performance, you should always cache information judiciously. Caching should be added only to methods that don't need to return the most current information. This makes them very useful for caching results of intensive processing, such as weather reports, but not for more dynamic data, such as current stock market prices for trading systems or account balance information.

The data being returned by one of the Friends Reunion web methods, `GetContactRequests()`, is fairly static in nature. Although a new contact request may be made, it is more than likely not imperative that the recipient of this request sees it immediately. So, this information is suitable for caching, especially given this scenario applies for third-party consumers of the web service.

Try It Out: Cache Information Now, you will add the caching functionality to the `GetContactRequests()` web method.

1. Open the Code view of the `Partners.asmx` file in the `FriendsService` project. In this file, locate the `GetContactRequests()` web method. The method's definition is already prefixed with the attribute `[WebMethod]`. To implement caching, just amend this attribute so that it reads as follows:

```
<WebMethod(CacheDuration:=600)>
```

This specifies, in seconds, how long the item should be cached. In this case, you've set this to 600 seconds, or 10 minutes.

Note When you enable the `CacheDuration` setting, the method response is managed by ASP.NET *output caching*. We'll discuss this in depth in Chapter 12.

---

2. You haven't changed the signature of any of the methods in the service, so there is no need to update the reference from within your consumer. You just need to recompile the application to ensure that this change is applied. Then you're ready to test the application again to see that this caching is working. Press F5 (the compile and debug shortcut) to do both.
3. Within the test application main page, enter the **apress** login and password, and then click the Refresh button. This will show all the requests for contact that this user has made so far.
4. Switch to the Friends Reunion web site, log in with a different user credentials, such as login vga and password vga, and make a *new* request for contact with Daniel Cazzulino (the one with the apress login and password), using the `Search.aspx` facility you created in Chapter 6.
5. Return to the consumer application and click the Refresh button again. If less than 10 minutes have passed since the last time you clicked the Refresh button (more precisely, since the server-side method was executed, and therefore, its output entered the cache), the test application's grid will show the cached version of the data again, so you won't see the new request for contact you just added via the web site. However, the speed boost with your `GetContactRequests()` method should be noticeable. After a 10-minute period, a fresh output will be generated, as the data in the cache will have expired, so the grid will include the new request for contact.

Reducing the Amount of Data Involved

The tasks in servicing a request for a web method can be split into three parts:

- Requesting information
- Performing processing
- Returning results

We've just covered how to lower the processing overhead using caching, but this still leaves the time taken to request data and retrieve results. This part of the overall round-trip time is governed by two factors: the amount of data and the speed at which it can be transmitted. There is little that you can do to improve transmission speed without paying for faster Internet connections, leaving you with the option of reducing the amount of data transferred.

When you're making simple calls, such as to the `GetAttendees()` method, not much can be done to decrease the amount of data, since there is very little data there to start with. However, in the case of retrieving a list of contact requests, you can apply optimizations, ranging from better serialization of the `DataSet` itself to completely replacing it with more efficient and resource-conservative representations.

You've seen the amount of data generated by a `DataSet` when used as the response of a web service (as shown in Figure 9-6, earlier in this chapter). You can have another look at it by navigating to the `http://localhost/FriendsReunion/Services/Partners.asmx?op=GetContactRequests` URL and invoking the service with the apress user name and password. You will notice that the generated output contains both the data and its schema information, in the form of an XML Schema embedded in the response.

Sometimes, just as in our case for a few contact requests, the schema is actually bigger than the data itself! While this schema may be useful to .NET consumers, as it helps to re-create the `DataSet` structure on the client side, it's mostly useless otherwise. The `DataSet` supports another serialization format, called a *diffgram* of its internal data, but it's equally unsuited for easy portability to other programming languages. (Look for the index entry "DiffGrams" in the product documentation for more information about the diffgram format.)

Given that datasets serialize in such a heavyweight format, there are several options available to us when trying to optimize the `GetContactRequests()` method. The first thing we'll do is simplify the returned data by delivering only the contact information, without schema and with the following format:

```
<?xml version="1.0" encoding="utf-8"?>
<Contacts>
  <Contact>
    <FirstName>Gustavo</FirstName>
    <LastName>Morande</LastName>
    <Email>gus@morande.com</Email>
    <Notes>Hey, stop working and let's eat an "asadito"!!!</Notes>
    <IsApproved>true</IsApproved>
  </Contact>
  ...etc...
</Contacts>
```

We'll then update the consumer to make use of this amended data format. Once that's done, we'll take a look at ways of returning even less data for situations where high performance is critical.

Try it Out: Return Less Data Now, you'll implement a different way to return XML to the consumer application.

1. In the Partners.asmx.vb file, locate the GetContactRequests() method, and update it to match the following code, causing an XML document, rather than a DataSet, to be returned:

```
Public Function GetContactRequests(ByVal login As String, _
  ByVal password As String) As XmlDocument
  cnFriends.Open()
  Try
    cmContacts.Parameters("@Login").Value = login
    cmContacts.Parameters("@Password").Value = password

    Dim contacts As New DataSet("Contacts")
    Dim ad As New SqlDataAdapter(cmContacts)
    ad.Fill(contacts, "Contact")
    Return New XmlDataDocument(contacts)
  Finally
    cnFriends.Close()
  End Try
End Function
```

2. The XmlDataDocument and XmlDocument classes you're using here come from the System.Xml namespace, so let's import the corresponding namespace:

```
Imports System.Xml
```

3. Because you've altered the *signature* of the web method, it no longer accepts or returns the same number or type of parameters that it did previously. As the web reference could technically be a link to functionality on the other side of the world that is unavailable for long periods of time, .NET doesn't automatically update the details of these references; as far as the test application is concerned, you haven't changed the web service. Before synchronizing it with the latest version of the service, you must first rebuild the project. Select Build ➤ Rebuild Solution to do this.

4. Switch to the Acudei project. Right-click the FriendsService entry under Web References in the Solution Explorer for the project, and then select the Update Web Reference option.

5. Open the Default.aspx form and import the following namespace, so that you can use the XmlNode and XmlNodeReader classes in the next step:

```
Imports System.Xml
```

6. With the references updated, you can tweak the code to make use of the amended method. Within the btnRefresh_Click() method in the Default.aspx form, modify the following code:

```
Private Sub btnRefresh_Click(ByVal sender As System.Object, _
  ByVal e As System.EventArgs) Handles btnRefresh.Click
  Dim friends = New Acudei.FriendsService.Partners
```

```
  ' We now retrieve a bare XML representation
  Dim contacts As XmlNode = friends.GetContactRequests( _
    txtLogin.Text, txtPassword.Text)

  Dim ds As New DataSet
  ' Read from the node
  ds.ReadXml(New XmlNodeReader(contacts))

  grdContacts.DataSource = ds
  grdContacts.DataBind()
End Sub
```

This will create a new DataSet, and then read the information into it from the XML that is now returned from your web service. Note that the proxy generated a method returning an XmlNode instance, which is the base class for the XmlDocument. This is due to the very nature of SOAP: the whole message is an XML document, so the contents of the body can be only a node inside it, instead of a separate document. Once the DataSet is populated, you data bind the DataGrid control with this source, just as before.

7. If you like, you can start the project and test this functionality. What is more interesting, though, is testing the GetContactRequests() method in a browser. To do this, type http://localhost/FriendsReunion/Services/Partners.asmx?op=GetContactRequests into the browser, and type in the **apress** login and password as usual. The window showing the returned XML will look similar to Figure 9-13. If you compare this with Figure 9-6, you'll see that there is far less data present.

How It Works

Usually, retrieving information from the database into the web application isn't an excessively expensive operation, because the connection to the database server from the web server is probably of high bandwidth. However, returning that data from the web server to the client can be a major bottleneck that causes poor performance in applications, because it's usually a low-bandwidth connection, such as a dial-up connection or wide area network (WAN) access. So, you must ensure that you send only the necessary information, and in the most compact format possible.

We have already discussed how the DataSet serializes to a heavy XML representation. To solve this problem, you can take this DataSet and serialize it in a more lightweight structure. In this case, you simply contained data as a clean XML document, within the business logic of the service. You can then return this simpler data instead, resulting in a far lower data overhead.

XmlDataDocument is an XmlDocument-derived class that presents a DataSet as an XmlDocument, hiding all the non-XML relevant information, such as row IDs and type. It simply wraps the DataSet, and you can directly return it from the web service:

```
Dim contacts As New DataSet("Contacts")
Dim ad As New SqlDataAdapter(cmContacts)
ad.Fill(contacts, "Contact")
Return New XmlDataDocument(contacts)
```

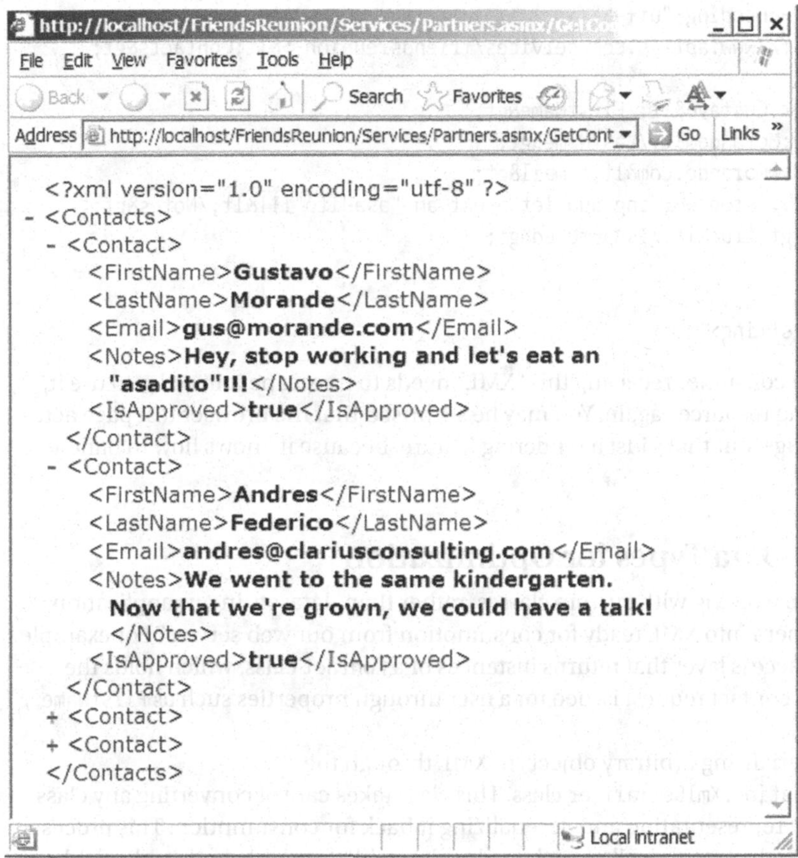
http://localhost/FriendsReunion/Services/Partners.asmx/GetCo
File Edit View Favorites Tools Help
Back Search Favorites
Address http://localhost/FriendsReunion/Services/Partners.asmx/GetCont Go Links
<?xml version="1.0" encoding="utf-8" ?>
- <Contacts>
- <Contact>
<FirstName>Gustavo</FirstName>
<LastName>Morande</LastName>
<Email>gus@morande.com</Email>
<Notes>Hey, stop working and let's eat an "asadito"!!!</Notes>
<IsApproved>true</IsApproved>
</Contact>
- <Contact>
<FirstName>Andres</FirstName>
<LastName>Federico</LastName>
<Email>andres@clariusconsulting.com</Email>
<Notes>We went to the same kindergarten. Now that we're grown, we could have a talk!</Notes>
<IsApproved>true</IsApproved>
</Contact>
+ <Contact>
+ <Contact>
</Contacts>
Local intranet

Figure 9-13. *The XML after reducing the amount of data returned*

This is, together with the base `XmlDocument`, the preferred way of returning XML to the consumer application. By looking at the result of the web service execution through the auto-generated test page with a browser, you can see that it's the actual XML data that is returned—no wrapping elements. A client can directly pass this data to the tool of choice, knowing it can be processed as-is.

You should resist the temptation of simply returning a string by calling the `DataSet.GetXml()` method:

```
Return contacts.GetXml()
```

Such "XML" is actually nothing more than a raw string to the ASP.NET Web Services infrastructure, and as such, it must be escaped in order to avoid invalid characters that could make for a non-well-formed document. For example, if your web service returned the string `12 < 83`, the infrastructure must escape the < character and replace it with `<`. This is to maintain the document well-formedness inside the SOAP body. Multiply that by the number of opening and closing tags in your data document, and you'll get an idea of how much harder it is. And after all the escaping is done, you end up with something like the following as a response from the service:

```
<?xml version="1.0" encoding="utf-8"?>
<string xmlns="http://www.apress.com/services/friendsreunion">&lt;Contacts&gt;
  &lt;Contact&gt;
    &lt;FirstName&gt;Gustavo&lt;/FirstName&gt;
    &lt;LastName&gt;Morande&lt;/LastName&gt;
    &lt;Email&gt;gus@morande.com&lt;/Email&gt;
    &lt;Notes&gt;Hey, stop working and let's eat an "asadito"!!!&lt;/Notes&gt;
    &lt;IsApproved&gt;true&lt;/IsApproved&gt;
  &lt;/Contact&gt;
  ...etc...
&lt;/Contacts&gt;</string>
```

What's more, the consumer receiving this "XML" needs to unescape it in order to use it, consuming processing resources again. You may be surprised that the browser test page actually shows the XML tags, but that's just a rendering feature, because it knows how to handle escaped characters.

Using Custom Data Types for Optimization

Suppose that we were working with custom classes, rather than datasets in our application. How could we turn them into XML ready for consumption from our web service? For example, we may have a data-access layer that returns instances of a `Contact` class, which holds the information for each contact request issued for a user through properties such as `FirstName`, `LastName`, and so on.

.NET supports serializing arbitrary objects to XML through the `System.Xml.Serialization.XmlSerializer` class. This class takes care of converting any class to an equivalent XML representation and deserializing it back for consumption. This process, by default, converts each class, as well as each read/write public property and public field, to an XML element. You can control this formatting through the use of *XML serialization attributes.*

Note For more information about serialization attributes and the XML serialization process, see the product documentation for the `XmlSerializer` class or online at `http://msdn.microsoft.com/library/default.asp?url=/library/en-us/cpref/html/frlrfSystemXmlSerializationXmlSerializerClassTopic.asp`. You can also read Dare Obasanjo's (former Program Manager of the XML WebData team, now part of the MSN team) excellent article about .NET XML serialization at `http://msdn.microsoft.com/library/default.asp?url=/library/en-us/dnexxml/html/xml01202003.asp`.

Let's take a look at the powerful support for custom types serialization by adding such a feature to our web service.

Try It Out: Return Custom Data Types To demonstrate the use of custom data types, you'll create a new method that returns the same data as the `GetContactRequests()` method, but with a different name. By implementing it this way, you can compare the output of the methods side by side, as well as compare the consumer-side code and how it changes in this case.

1. Within the Partners.asmx code-behind file, in the SQL statement, you can see that you are returning five fields: FirstName, LastName, Email, Notes, and IsApproved. To represent this, you can add a class called Contact alongside the Partners class in the Partners.asmx.vb file, as follows:

```
Public Class Contact
    Public FirstName As String
    Public LastName As String
    Public Email As String
    Public Notes As String
    Public IsApproved As Boolean
End Class
```

2. Next, add a new web method, called GetContactRequestsCustom(), to the Partners class. This new method is very similar to the existing GetContactRequests() method, except that you use the SqlDataReader to initialize the Contact objects:

```
<WebMethod(CacheDuration:=600)> _
Public Function GetContactRequestsCustom(ByVal login As String, _
  ByVal password As String) As Contact()
  cnFriends.Open()
  Try
    cmContacts.Parameters("@Login").Value = login
    cmContacts.Parameters("@Password").Value = password

    Dim reader As SqlDataReader = cmContacts.ExecuteReader()

    Dim contacts As New ArrayList
    While reader.Read()
      Dim ct As New Contact
      ct.FirstName = CStr(reader("FirstName"))
      ct.LastName = CStr(reader("LastName"))
      ct.Email = CStr(reader("Email"))
      ct.Notes = CStr(reader("Notes"))
      ct.IsApproved = CBool(reader("IsApproved"))
      contacts.Add(ct)
    End While

    Return CType(contacts.ToArray(GetType(Contact)), Contact())
  Finally
    cnFriends.Close()
  End Try

End Function
```

As you can see, you've simply changed the return type, and replaced the dataset handling and filling code with a block of lines that move the data into an ArrayList containing Contacts initialized with the SqlDataReader data. Finally, you simply convert this list to an array and return that array instead of the XML.

3. Rebuild the solution with these changes, browse to the `Partners.asmx` file with a browser, and run the `GetContactRequestsCustom()` web method. You'll be presented with an XML document similar to the one shown in Figure 9-14.

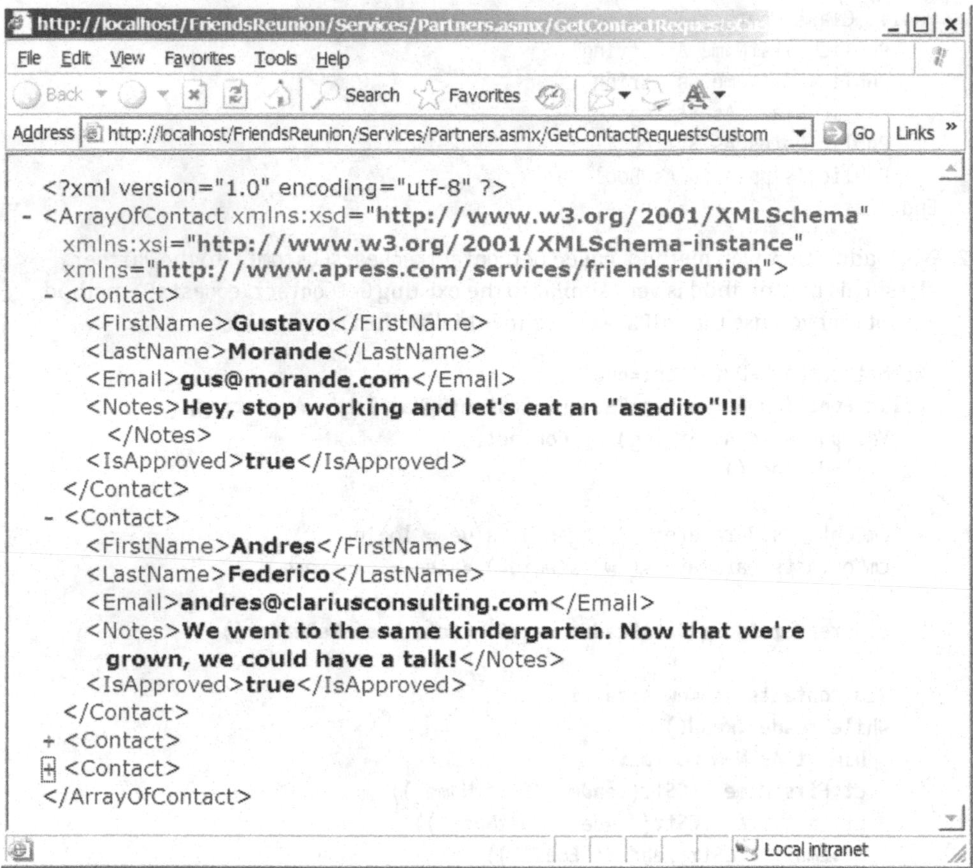
http://localhost/FriendsReunion/Services/Partners.asmx/GetContactReques
File Edit View Favorites Tools Help
Back Search Favorites
Address http://localhost/FriendsReunion/Services/Partners.asmx/GetContactRequestsCustom Go Links
<?xml version="1.0" encoding="utf-8" ?>
- <ArrayOfContact xmlns:xsd="http://www.w3.org/2001/XMLSchema"
xmlns:xsi="http://www.w3.org/2001/XMLSchema-instance"
xmlns="http://www.apress.com/services/friendsreunion">
- <Contact>
<FirstName>Gustavo</FirstName>
<LastName>Morande</LastName>
<Email>gus@morande.com</Email>
<Notes>Hey, stop working and let's eat an "asadito"!!!
</Notes>
<IsApproved>true</IsApproved>
</Contact>
- <Contact>
<FirstName>Andres</FirstName>
<LastName>Federico</LastName>
<Email>andres@clariusconsulting.com</Email>
<Notes>We went to the same kindergarten. Now that we're
grown, we could have a talk!</Notes>
<IsApproved>true</IsApproved>
</Contact>
+ <Contact>
+ <Contact>
</ArrayOfContact>
Local intranet

Figure 9-14. *The XML for the new web method*

4. Having the root `<ArrayOfContact>` element is not ideal, however. You can take advantage of the XML serialization attributes we mentioned before. Specifically, you can modify the root element generated for the array returned, by adding the following line directly above the method declaration:

```
<WebMethod(CacheDuration:=600)> _
Public Function GetContactRequestsCustom(ByVal login As String, _
  ByVal password As String) As _
  <System.Xml.Serialization.XmlRoot("Contacts")> Contact()
```

5. Recompile and execute the web method again, and you'll see the new `<Contacts>` root element.

6. Finally, you can make the output even more compact by turning all child elements of <Contact> (its properties) into attributes. This is done through another serialization attribute, this time applied to the Contact class members:

```
Public Class Contact
  <System.Xml.Serialization.XmlAttribute()> _
   Public FirstName As String
  <System.Xml.Serialization.XmlAttribute()> _
  Public LastName As String
  <System.Xml.Serialization.XmlAttribute()> _
  Public Email As String
  <System.Xml.Serialization.XmlAttribute()> _
  Public Notes As String
  <System.Xml.Serialization.XmlAttribute()> _
  Public IsApproved As Boolean
End Class
```

7. Recompile again and execute the web method. You will see a much more compact format this time, as shown in Figure 9-15.

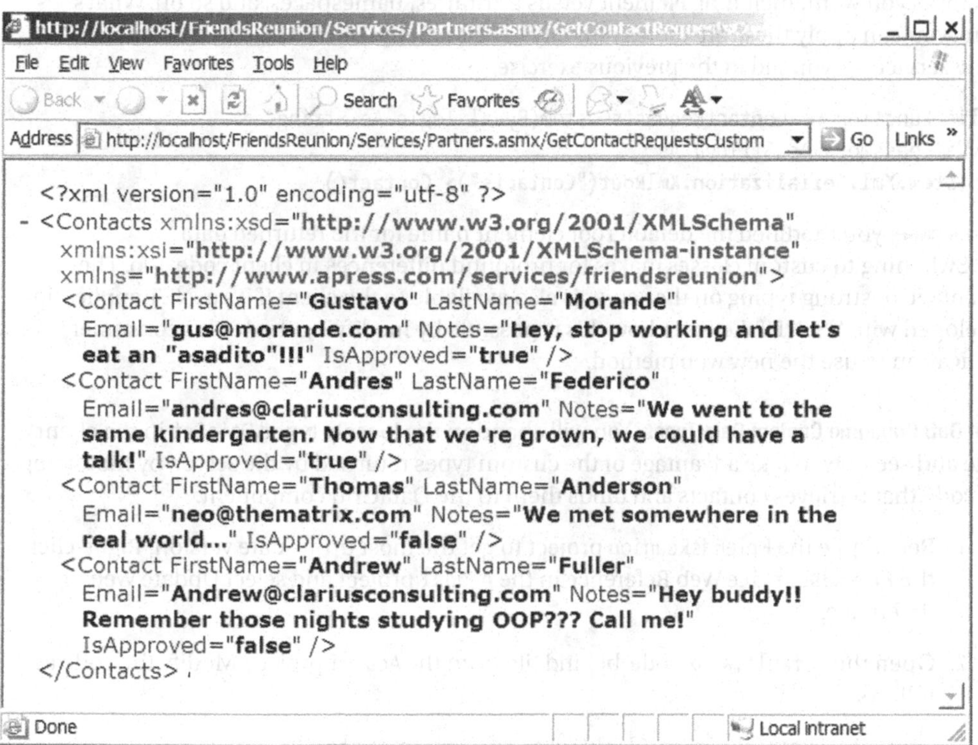

Figure 9-15. *The new method with child elements converted to attributes*

How It Works

As you learned earlier in the chapter, objects are converted into a string representation of themselves via a process of serialization. Serialization into XML is a special kind of serialization where the `XmlSerializer` class enters the scene. By default, this process results in a structure consisting of the following:

- One root tag to contain the results if it's an array (`ArrayOfContact`)
- One tag (`Contact`) to denote the start and end of each `Contact` instance
- One tag for each property of the `Contact` (`FirstName`, `LastName`, and so on)

When you use this type of serialization, rather than the `GetXml()` method on a `DataSet` object, you not only return XML containing the data, but also have a definition of the structure of this XML provided in the WSDL for the service, automatically. You can test this by asking for the WSDL using the URL `http://localhost/FriendsReunion/Services/Partners.asmx?wsdl`. This will be extremely useful in the next section, where we look at the changes in the consumer .NET application.

The attributes in `System.Xml.Serialization` namespace control the `XmlSerializer` class that is used for object serialization under the hood, and help to accommodate the format exactly as you want, including element versus attributes, namespaces, and so on. What's more, you can apply these attributes not only to class members, but also to the return value of the service, as you did in the previous exercise:

```
Public Function GetContactRequestsCustom(ByVal login As String, _
  ByVal password As String) As _
  <System.Xml.Serialization.XmlRoot("Contacts")> Contact()
```

In this case, you modified the default root element name for the returned data.

Switching to custom classes makes for profound differences in client code, too. The advantage of strong typing on the server is also available to the client if it's a .NET application developed with VS .NET. Let's see how this is possible by modifying the `Acudei` consumer application to use the new web method.

Try It Out: Consume Custom Data Types You will abandon the loosely typed `DataSet` in the client code and see how to take advantage of the custom types returned by the server, by modifying the code that retrieves contacts and binds them to the DataGrid component.

1. Recompile the `FriendsReunion` project to get the most up-to-date version. Right-click the `FriendsService` Web Reference in the `Acudei` project and select Update Web Reference.

2. Open the `Default.aspx` code-behind file from the `Acudei` project. Modify the code as follows:

```
Private Sub btnRefresh_Click(ByVal sender As System.Object, _
  ByVal e As System.EventArgs) Handles btnRefresh.Click
  Dim friends = New Acudei.FriendsService.Partners
```

```
    Dim contacts As FriendsService.Contact() = _
      friends.GetContactRequestsCustom( _
      txtLogin.Text, txtPassword.Text)

    grdContacts.DataSource = contacts
    grdContacts.DataBind()
End Sub
```

Note that you're simply using the data binding facility, but you could actually iterate and work with the typed collection of contacts and query for their properties.

3. In order for data binding to work, the custom type must have public properties. By default, however, these classes are generated with public fields in this specific case, just as in the server-side version. You can confirm this by looking at the `Reference.vb` class under the `FriendsService` web reference.

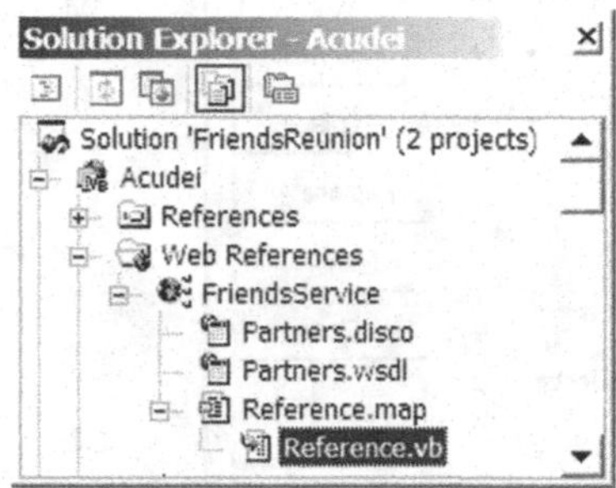

The relevant piece of code looks like the following:

```
'<remarks/>
<System.Xml.Serialization.XmlTypeAttribute( _
  [Namespace]:="http://www.apress.com/services/friendsreunion")> _
Public Class Contact

    '<remarks/>
    <System.Xml.Serialization.XmlAttributeAttribute()> _
    Public FirstName As String

    '<remarks/>
    <System.Xml.Serialization.XmlAttributeAttribute()> _
    Public LastName As String

    ...etc...
End Class
```

4. In order to convert all public fields into their property equivalents, you can simply perform a search and replace on this file. Open the Replace dialog box and specify the following settings, as shown in Figure 9-16 (type all values in a single line):

- **Find what:** `Public {[^ ]+} As {[^ ]+}`
- **Replace with:**

  ```
  Public Property \1() As \2
  \n\t\t\tGet
  \n\t\t\t\tReturn \1field
  \n\t\t\tEnd Get
  \n\t\t\tSet(ByVal Value As \2)
  \n\t\t\t\t\1field = Value
  \n\t\t\tEnd Set
  \n\t\tEnd Property
  \n\t\tDim \1field As \2
  ```

- **Use:** Regular expressions

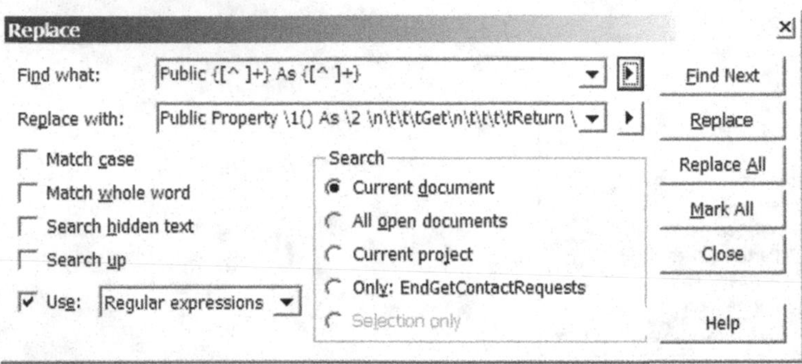

Figure 9-16. *The Replace dialog box settings for converting public fields into their property equivalents*

5. Click Replace All, and that will do the trick, converting the previous class to the following:

```
Public Class Contact

  '<remarks/>
  <System.Xml.Serialization.XmlAttributeAttribute()> _
  Public Property FirstName() As String
    Get
      Return FirstNamefield
    End Get
    Set(ByVal Value As String)
      FirstNamefield = Value
    End Set
  End Property
  Dim FirstNamefield As String
```

```
    '<remarks/>
    <System.Xml.Serialization.XmlAttributeAttribute()> _
    Public Property LastName() As String
      Get
        Return LastNamefield
      End Get
      Set(ByVal Value As String)
        LastNamefield = Value
      End Set
    End Property
    Dim LastNamefield As String

    ...etc...
  End Class
```

6. Run the application, and you should see the same rendering as you saw with the `DataSet` examples in the preceding sections.

How It Works

The consumer application, if developed with VS .NET, benefits from the switch to custom classes because it gains IntelliSense and strong typing for each item value. A `DataSet` regenerated without schema information, on the other hand, will necessarily treat all values as strings. With custom types, you avoid polluting the message response with schema information, but you don't lose the advantages of strong typing. What's more, you gain in validation, as the information being deserialized must forcibly match the data type of its destination class and members. Having similar functionality with datasets either requires you to send the schema with the data or reparse the service output with an `XmlValidatingReader` to ensure conformance with a locally cached schema. In the former case, you can't be certain of preventing unexpected application behavior anyway, as the embedded schema could have been tampered with, too.

Leveraging data binding is straightforward, and the code looks much the same as with the dataset: get the results, set it as the `DataSource`, and call `DataBind()`:

```
Dim contacts As FriendsService.Contact() = _
  friends.GetContactRequestsCustom( _
  txtLogin.Text, txtPassword.Text)

grdContacts.DataSource = contacts
```

The only issue you needed to deal with was the requirement that the custom class have public properties instead of fields. Let's go through the find and replace expressions.

Note For more information, refer to the documentation of the regular expressions support available for VS .NET search and replace operations (this differs slightly from in the .NET Framework).

The find expression looks like this:

```
Public {[^ ]+} As {[^ ]+}
```

This means to find the string Public, followed by a space and one or more characters *except* a space, specified by [^]+. The curly braces around the expression mean that you want the engine to capture this value, so that you can use it in the Replace dialog box by referring to its position. This would be capture \1, indicating the type of the field. Immediately after the field name capture, we match the As keyword, and then match again any character except a space, which signals the end of a field declaration in this case. You also use curly braces here, and this will become capture \2. For a field like Public FirstName As String, the find captures \1 = FirstName, \2 = String. You use these captures to build the replace expression.

The replace expression starts with the property declaration:

```
Public Property \1() As \2
```

Here, you just redeclare the same line that has been matched, but as a property: the string Public, followed by the member name, followed by the type.

Next, you add new lines (\n) and tabs (\t) for pretty formatting:

```
\n\t\t\t
```

We'll omit these characters in the analysis that follows for clarity, and replace them with a couple whitespaces.

Next comes the property Get accessor declaration, which returns the first capture (FirstName) with a field suffix, which will be the format of the private field backing the new property:

```
Get  Return \1field  End Get
```

You then define the property Set accessor, which assigns the value of the same variable to the incoming value:

```
Set(ByVal Value As \2)  \1field = Value  End Set
```

Finally, you add the closing End Property statement. Then declare the private variable, which is the Dim followed by the first capture, which is the member name, suffixed with the field word; followed by the second capture, which is the type:

```
Dim \1field As \2
```

So, for the example FirstName field, you get:

```
Public Property FirstName() As String
  Get
    Return FirstNamefield
  End Get
  Set(ByVal Value As String)
    FirstNamefield = Value
  End Set
End Property
Dim FirstNamefield As String
```

This is yet another example of where regular expressions come to the rescue, and they're not for validation in this case.

Adding State to Web Services

If you take a look at the web methods you have developed, you can see that they are all *stateless*, just like the protocol supporting them, HTTP. That is to say that the application doesn't remember the previous calls that have come in to it or store any information based on them.

For example, in our Friends Reunion application, by default, you couldn't call one method that specified what place you are interested in, and then make subsequent calls related to that place, as you would be able to do with many other objects, such as a `SqlConnection`.

The following is an example of how state could be useful in our Friends Reunion application:

```
Dim place As New FriendsService.Place()
place.Name = "ACUDEI English Academy"
Response.Write(place.GetAddress())
place.UpdateNotes("There are no notes for this place")
```

Here, we're assuming the `Place.Name` property will be "remembered" by the remote web service as the value we used in a previous interaction, such as `GetAddress()`. This is the same issue that web developers came up against with traditional web application development, and one of its possible solutions is also the same: the use of the `Session` object. This is the same `Session` that is used for web sites, and works in the same way: by storing a cookie on the calling machine to identify it to .NET. Therefore, it must be used with great care, as not all service consumers may support this feature. Cookieless sessions, described in Chapter 6, are *not* supported by web services.

Adding such support for stateful web services is largely handled for you by the .NET Framework. From the point of view of the creation of a web service, all you need to do is update the attributes of the web method in a similar way to setting the `CacheDuration`:

```
<WebMethod(EnabledSession:="true")>
```

The way to consume this web service is slightly more interesting. Since you're writing an application to use web services, rather than an Internet browser, the cookie that is used to track your requests is stored only as long as you have the same instance of an object. As an example of this, once `place` is set to `Nothing`, or goes out of scope in the block of code shown earlier in this section, the cookie is lost, and the session is ended. This can be seen as the web service equivalent of closing a browser window.

Due to this limitation, and because of the added overhead for using session information and cookies, you should be careful about adding state with web services. It's also worth considering that stateful services may not be supported by other platforms, and that a service-oriented approach is mostly stateless, by definition.

As there is no real use for state in our web services, and the subject of session state was covered thoroughly in Chapter 6, we won't delve into an example here. It really is as simple as updating the attribute, if both ends are .NET applications!

Third-Party Web Services

It is very gratifying to create your own web services and publish them so that they can be used by other applications you develop and by other people you tell about them. But how can you share your web service functionality with all of the other developers who may be interested? And how do you find out about the web services offered by others—services that may improve or speed up the development of your own applications?

The solution to this is quite elegant: a web service to let developers know about other web services. This is known as *UDDI* (for Universal Description, Discovery, and Integration). Using these directories, you can look up the functionality that other developers have made available to the public, and inform others of your own services easily. These listings are maintained not only by Microsoft, but also by several other major companies including IBM. The simplest way to access these listings is by using Microsoft's own UDDI directory, though. You can browse `http://uddi.microsoft.com/` and search for published services and maybe even publish your own. The UDDI is one of the main reasons why web services are succeeding where previous technologies have failed!

Other than the services listed at the UDDI location, many of the more popular (and useful) web sites on the Internet are beginning to make their functionality available via web services. The following are some of the most interesting ones to try out with the Friends Reunion application:

- **Google's search service:** `http://www.google.com/apis`
- **Microsoft's services, such as MapPoint.NET:** `http://msdn.microsoft.com/webservices/building/livewebservices/`
- **Amazon:** `http://www.amazon.com/gp/aws/landing.html`

You can use these services in your applications in an identical manner to those you create yourself: by adding a web reference in the same way you did for your test consumer web application. The only differences with commercial services are the requirements for information such as login information to be passed in to method calls to allow usage statistics, billing data, and so on to be maintained by the provider. Using these services, you could, for example, click a personal details link and see all matches for the person returned from a search engine, display a map of a place next to that person's address, or show that person's wish list in Amazon.

Tip You can find a good overview of Microsoft Web Services and how they can be used to enhance your applications at `http://msdn.microsoft.com/msdnmag/issues/03/12/XMLFiles/default.aspx`. You can also read the book *Google, Amazon, and Beyond: Creating and Consuming Web Services*, by Tom Myers and Alexander Nakhimovsky (Apress, 2003; ISBN: 1-59059-131-3).

Summary

In this chapter, we provided an introduction to web services, showing how they're not only an open standard in themselves, but are built up from other open standards such as HTTP and XML. You've seen that by making use of web services, you have a method for allowing disparate applications to interact with one another very simply, where it would have taken a great deal of painstaking integration work in the past.

These features and ease of use were put into action in the development of web service functionality for our Friends Reunion application. By creating a test application, we showed how this functionality can be used (consumed) as simply as any other object in .NET, once a reference has been added within the project.

After we created and used our own web services, we took a look at one of the key underlying technologies of web services, SOAP, which allows information to be passed around in a structured XML format. We then went on to look at exception handling, and saw how this tied in to SOAP with the `SoapException` object.

We then discussed the performance of web services. You saw how you can improve performance by retrieving less data by using built-in mechanisms and by creating your own mechanisms, as well as by taking advantage of and controlling XML serialization support in .NET.

Finally, we looked at how you can publish your web services so that others can use them, and how you can find third-party services to use in your own applications, including a few examples of currently available services that can be used to add further functionality to the Friends Reunion application.

CHAPTER 10

ASP.NET Authentication, Authorization, and Security

The role of security in an application is related to the need to restrict the ability of a user to access certain resources or to perform certain actions. For example, a web application may offer administrative tools that should be accessible only to authorized users, or it may have information that's restricted to registered users. (In fact, you've already seen this kind of restriction in our Friends Reunion application.) It's also possible to apply different security-related settings at the web-server level.

In this chapter, we'll focus on ASP.NET and how to take advantage of the security features it offers. ASP.NET works closely with IIS to provide the infrastructure available, so we'll look at their interaction, too.

This chapter will cover the following topics:

- Authentication and authorization—what are they and how they interact with each other
- The ASP.NET security infrastructure
- Interaction between ASP.NET, IIS, and the operating system
- ASP.NET security settings
- Authentication options and how to use them

You've already seen some of these concepts in action, but we haven't said much about how they actually work. We will take a closer look at the mechanics during this chapter, and you will gain a much better understanding of what is going on behind the scenes.

Security Overview

Security is a long-standing concern that pervades all kinds of software:

- Operating systems (think of the Windows NT/2000/XP login process)
- Web servers (think of the IIS management console's Application Settings and Directory Security settings)

- Database servers (remember the login process to add a connection to MSDE in Chapter 4)
- Desktop applications (you should know several examples)
- Web sites (such as e-commerce sites and sites like Hotmail.com)

In each of these cases, the main purpose is to prohibit unauthorized users from accessing sensitive information or performing certain tasks and actions. For example, you may want to prevent a user from posting comments on a site unless that user is logged in; or you may want to prohibit a developer from deleting records in a table or creating a new database in a server, unless that user is properly authorized.

With Internet connectivity available almost everywhere, this becomes increasingly important, because the information in your application has the potential to be exposed to the entire world. If an application isn't secure (that is, if unauthorized access is allowed), you run the risk that users will be unwilling to trust it to keep any critical information.

Security Architecture

Whether you configure it carefully or not, your ASP.NET web applications will always have some kind of security in place. This is a consequence of the security architecture itself, which can be divided into three layers:

- **The operating system:** Unless you are using DOS or Windows 9*x*, there will always be some built-in security. Windows NT, 2000, and XP use domains to keep users' information and to ensure that they have permission to access resources such as files and folders, printers, network shares, and so on. Users must always log in before using the system, and every request made by a user is checked for the necessary permission before it is allowed.
- **The web server:** A web server runs in the operating system, and as such, also uses the security infrastructure built into it. Even when Anonymous access is enabled for an application, it will actually be bound to the account specified for the anonymous user; by default, the `IUSR_MACHINENAME` account.
- **The web application:** When an ASP.NET application is run on IIS (there are alternatives, as there's a public ASP.NET hosting API), the security available in the previous two levels is always in effect, whether or not you explicitly decide to use it. At this level, you have some additional configuration options and features that ASP.NET offers over plain IIS settings, as you'll learn in this chapter.

Essential Terminology

Because they crop up so frequently in discussions about security, we need to clearly define two key terms: *authentication* and *authorization*. We'll also explain credential stores, security tokens, role-based security, principal, and identity. These refer to essential security concepts that you'll learn how to apply in this chapter.

Authentication and Authorization

In order for users to get access to a resource with restricted access, they must first be *identified* and *authenticated*. This means that they must provide some sort of identifier (such as a login name) and credentials (such as a password). Here, the login name allows them to say who they are, and the password allows them to *prove* that they are who they say they are. The way these credentials are validated depends on the authentication scheme you choose. ASP.NET offers several, and we'll discuss them in this chapter.

Once users have been identified and their identification has been authenticated, another step known as *authorization* takes place. Here, the process consists of checking whether authenticated users have permission to access the resource they requested. For example, an ordinary user may not be allowed to access certain administrative features of a web application.

As a side effect of authentication, an application may also provide customized content that's tailored to the current user accessing the resource. In fact, some applications will use security concepts with the sole aim of offering users an improved experience through *personalization*— supplying content filtered according to their needs.

Credential Stores and Security Tokens

As we've said, authentication is the process of positive identification of a user based on the credentials they supply. In order to perform this process, the credentials supplied by the user are compared to those existing in a *credential store*. Once again, the nature of the credential store depends on the type of authentication. For example, Windows authentication compares the credentials against a Windows domain. Passport sites such as Hotmail, MSN, McAfee, and others use the Microsoft-owned Passport credential store, which is in charge of the authentication. The credential store could also be a database, an XML file, or any other media that developers decide to use for this purpose. Later in this chapter, you'll learn which types of authentication are available for your ASP.NET applications.

In order to allow a security-aware application to detect that the current user has already been authenticated, a *security token* is attached to that user. The security token is used to keep information about the user; again, its format and manner of use depend on the application. In a Windows environment, for example, this token is directly associated with the user while the user's session remains open. It is later used as a sort of key when the user performs an action such as opening a folder or printing a document; security settings on any of these objects may bar that user from accessing the resource. In a web environment, things are somewhat different, because of the disconnected and stateless nature of the HTTP protocol. Later in this chapter, we'll discuss how ASP.NET solves this problem.

Once the user has been authenticated and the user's security token is in place, authorization happens. Once more, the association between a resource and the list of users allowed to access it depends on the specific application type or environment. For example, restrictions on access to files and folders in Windows are kept in *access control lists* (ACLs). These ACLs are set through the Security tab of the Properties window corresponding to the file or folder. Figure 10-1 shows an example of the security settings of a folder called `MyArchive`.

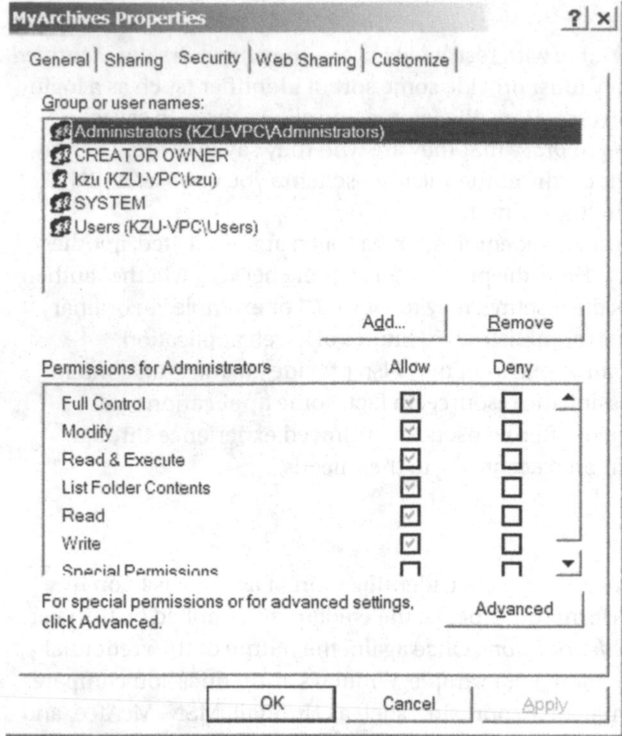

Figure 10-1. *Security settings on a folder in Windows*

As another example, you may have used the Component Services MMC snap-in to assign permissions to COM+ applications. Like file and folder ACLs (Figure 10-1), this approach also uses the credentials in the Windows domain credential store, but assigns access permissions to components based on them. Figure 10-2 shows an example of a component that can be accessed only by managers.

For ASP.NET applications, you have other options for assigning permissions to resources, as described in this chapter.

In Figure 10-1, you can see that Windows allows you to assign permissions to an individual user or to a Windows *group*. Figure 10-2 shows a similar way to assign permissions: through *roles*, such as Employees and Managers. This leads us to the next key concept: *role-based security*.

Role-Based Security

You can easily imagine the administrative nightmare it would be to assign permissions to resources to one user at a time, especially if you have a large number of users. Furthermore, each new user created would need to be manually added to all of the resources that the user is supposed to be able to access. To avoid this, a higher-level construct is available, in which users are assigned to groups or roles according to application requirements. For example, a project administration and tracking system may define groups such as Administrators, Developers, Testers, and Users.

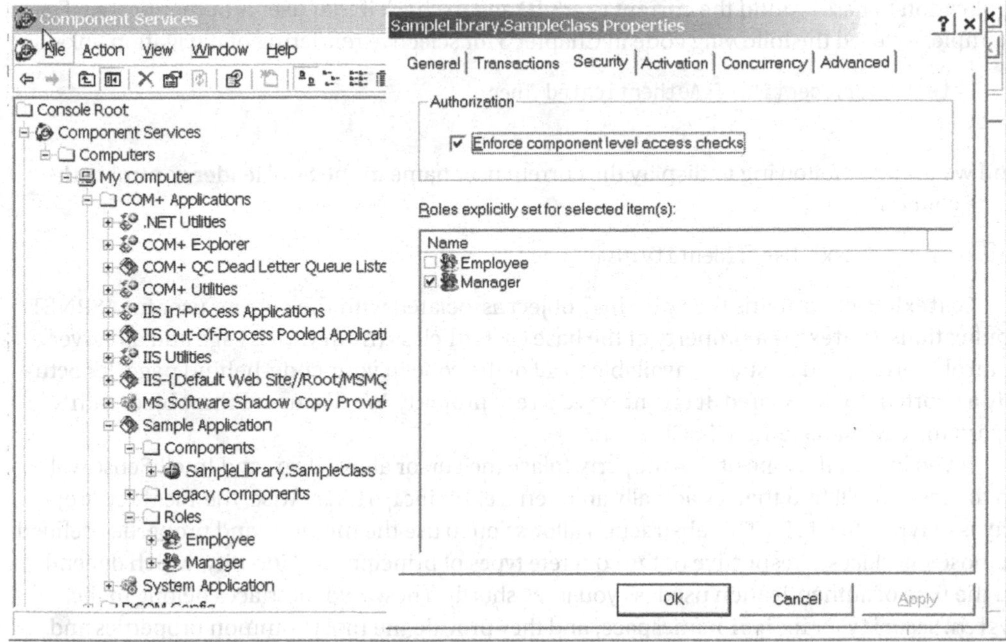

Figure 10-2. *Security settings on a component in COM+*

This generalization allows you to apply permissions according to roles, as well as (or even instead of) according to individual users. New users can then be included in certain roles. The most obvious advantage to this is that once a particular permission has been assigned to a role, new users with that role will automatically gain that permission. For example, if there is a resource that allows developers to upload the code they have developed, and which is obviously restricted to users who are included in the Developers' role, a new programmer hired by the company will be able to access it automatically, provided she is included in the Developers role when the system administrator creates her account.

A user can be included in more than one role simultaneously. For example, a user may be added to the Developers and Testers roles, if that user performs tasks related to both roles simultaneously. (Although some would say, with good reason, that it's not a good idea to be the only tester of your own code!)

Principal and Identity

In order for an application to use role-based security, it needs a way to access the information. For example, it must be able to check that the current user is included in a certain role, and to act accordingly. The .NET Framework supports and exposes this scheme through the concepts of *principal* and *identity*.

A principal is an object that contains the roles associated with a user. It also contains an identity object that holds information about that user. Together, they map onto the access controls provided by the Windows and COM+ security we discussed earlier. In fact, though you may not have noticed it at the time, you have already used these objects in the Friends Reunion application to pass around the current user's ID and to check if that user is authenticated. For example, we used the following code in Chapter 3 for selective rendering of navigation links:

```
If Context.User.Identity.IsAuthenticated Then
  ...
```

And we used the following to display the current user name in the SubHeader control in the same chapter:

```
lbl.Text = Context.User.Identity.Name
```

`Context.User` contains the `Principal` object associated with the current user for ASP.NET applications. `Context` is a property of the base `Control` class (from which `Page` and all server controls derive), and as such is available to all of the code in your code-behind page. It's actually a shortcut to the Shared `HttpContext.Current` property. We discussed this object with regard to state management in Chapter 6.

If you look at the type of this property (place the cursor above `User`, and IntelliSense will do the rest), you'll find that it's actually an interface, `IPrincipal`. Likewise, the `Identity` property is of type `IIdentity`. This abstraction allows you to use the methods and properties defined in those interfaces, irrespective of the concrete types of principal and identity, which depend on the type of authentication used, as you'll see shortly. These two interfaces belong to the `System.Security.Principal` namespace, and they provide the most common properties and methods you may need when working with role-based security, as illustrated in Figure 10-3.

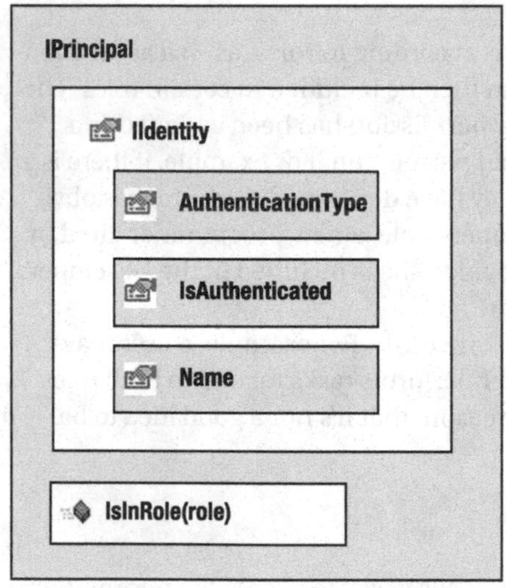

Figure 10-3. *Role-based security properties and methods*

The `Page` object provides access to the `Principal` object through a `User` property, too, which actually points to the same value in `Context.User`.

The ASP.NET Security Infrastructure

In Chapter 1, you saw that when a request for an ASP.NET resource (such as an .aspx page) is received by IIS, it is handed to the ASP.NET worker process (an ISAPI extension), which passes execution to the ASP.NET engine (.NET-managed code) to continue processing the request. In order to understand how the security context is initialized, we need to take a closer look at what happens beyond that point, as illustrated in Figure 10-4.

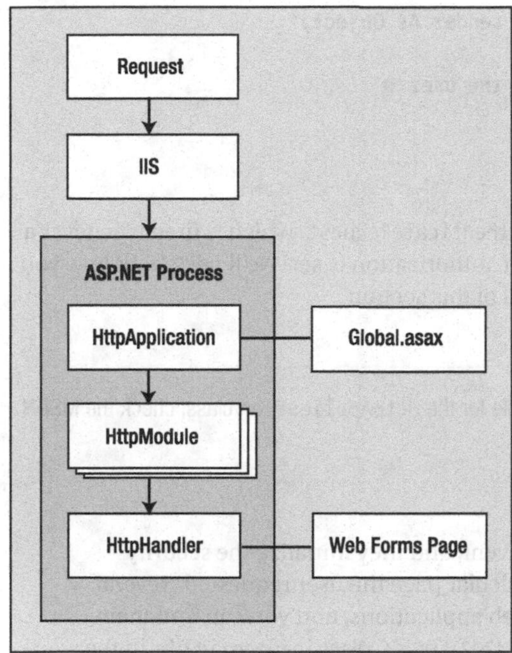

Figure 10-4. *ASP.NET processing*

When the ASP.NET engine (implemented by a class called HttpRuntime) receives the request from IIS, it hands it to an instance of the application corresponding to the page requested. As you saw in Chapter 6, the HttpApplication object is defined in the Global.asax code-behind file of your web application, hence the line in Figure 10-4 showing that relationship:

```
Public class Global
  Inherits System.Web.HttpApplication
  ...
```

The ASP.NET engine, after initializing the HttpApplication object, initializes any configured module for it. The HttpApplication raises a number of events at different stages of processing, such as AuthenticateRequest, BeginRequest, and EndRequest, which any HttpModule that's configured in the application can listen to. These events can also be handled in the Global.asax.vb code-behind file itself. You can see empty skeletons for those event handlers in the code-behind file:

```
Public Class Global
    Inherits System.Web.HttpApplication

  Sub Application_BeginRequest(ByVal sender As Object, _
    ByVal e As EventArgs)
    ' Fires at the beginning of each request
  End Sub

  Sub Application_AuthenticateRequest(ByVal sender As Object, _
    ByVal e As EventArgs)
    ' Fires upon attempting to authenticate the user
  End Sub
  ...
End Class
```

The key event for security initialization is AuthenticateRequest, which is fired whenever a client requests a resource for which some kind of authorization is set. We'll talk about how you can configure this for your application at the end of this section.

Note If you want to know about other events available for the HttpApplication class, check the MSDN documentation.

Security-related modules subscribe to this event, and they initialize the security context before the request is handled by the particular page the user requested. Several modules are configured by default for all your web applications, and you can find them in the %WinDir%\Microsoft.NET\Framework\v1.1.4322\CONFIG\Machine.config file, in the <httpModules> section (as you saw back in Chapter 6). Here are the ones we're interested in right now:

```
<httpModules>
  ...
    <add name="WindowsAuthentication"
         type="System.Web.Security.WindowsAuthenticationModule"/>
    <add name="FormsAuthentication"
         type="System.Web.Security.FormsAuthenticationModule"/>
    <add name="PassportAuthentication"
         type="System.Web.Security.PassportAuthenticationModule"/>
  ...
</httpModules>
```

Depending on the authentication scheme you choose for your application, the appropriate module loads and then sets the current Principal and Identity objects:

Windows authentication: If you choose Windows authentication, the module will use the information passed by IIS (which must be configured to use the same type of authentication) to create a WindowsIdentity object with the user's Windows account name, such as MYCOMPANY\Daniel. It will then use this object, together with the list of Windows groups to which the user belongs, to initialize a WindowsPrincipal object. The new Principal object is then set to the Context.User property.

Passport authentication: If you choose Passport authentication, the user will be redirected to the Microsoft Passport login page. When the user is redirected back to your application from this page, the module will use the information passed back to create a PassportIdentity object. As roles can't be configured in Passport (because it is intended to only authenticate users), a GenericPrincipal object must be initialized with the newly created identity. Finally, the object must be set to the Context.User property. All this needs to be done manually for Passport, as the PassportIdentity object itself contains the methods to perform the checks.

Forms authentication: If you choose Forms authentication, the module will rely on a cookie-based mechanism. (We described how cookies work in Chapter 6.) Forms authentication settings include a loginUrl setting that points to a web form page to be used for authentication purposes. The Forms authentication module will check for the presence of an *authentication cookie* (also called an *authentication ticket*) in the current request. If it finds one, it will use the information in it to create a FormsIdentity object. This module doesn't support roles either, so this identity object is used to create a GenericPrincipal, which is set to the Context.User property. If the cookie is *not* present, the user is redirected to the login page. A utility method that we've been using already, FormsAuthentication.RedirectFromLoginPage(), allows the module to create the authentication cookie and save it to the client browser's cookie collection. Once this process finishes, the user is redirected to the page originally requested, this time with the cookie in place.

With all of this new information, we can complete the picture of ASP.NET processing, as shown in Figure 10-5.

If this infrastructure is not enough for your particular security requirements, you can extend it by creating a handler for the AuthenticateRequest event in the Global.asax file. The .NET Framework provides another generic object that you can employ for custom security, GenericIdentity, which you can use as-is or extend to suit your needs. In the "Implementing Custom Authentication" section later in this chapter, you'll see how to do this and discover why it might be necessary.

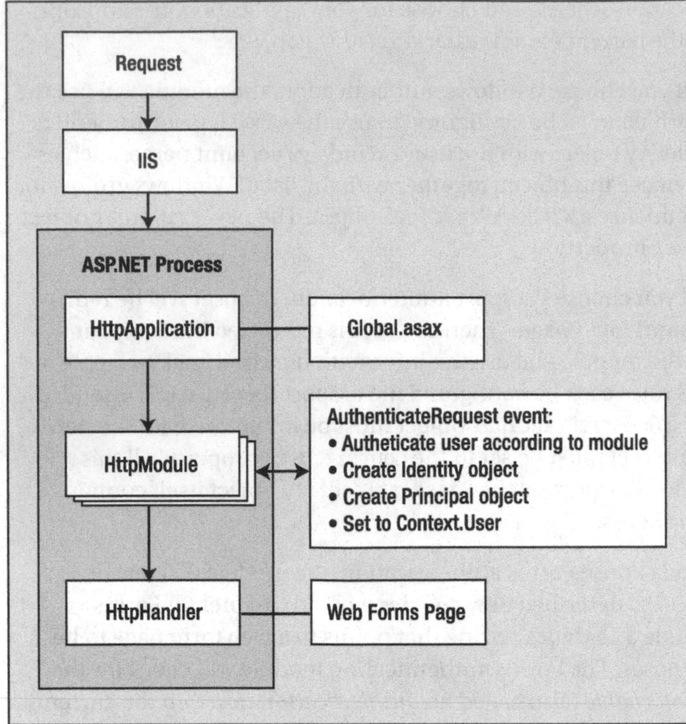

Figure 10-5. *ASP.NET security initialization*

Application Security Configuration

A repeated refrain in this chapter is that the security behavior will largely depend on application configuration. As you already know, all web application-wide settings are configured in a file called `Web.config` under the application root folder. You have already used some of the security settings in developing the Friends Reunion application, but let's now take a look at all the options available.

In the configuration file, security-related settings are divided into three elements: `<authentication>`, `<authorization>`, and `<location>`. In the following sections, we'll examine the purpose of each of these three elements.

Authentication Configuration

The `<authentication>` element defines the type of authentication that will be enforced, and it can contain child elements like `<forms>` and `<passport>` for those two types of authentication options. The element's syntax is as follows:

```
<authentication mode="Windows|Forms|Passport|None">
  <forms name="name"
         loginUrl="url"
         protection="All|None|Encryption|Validation"
```

```
        timeout="30" path="/" >
    <credentials passwordFormat="Clear|SHA1|MD5">
      <user name="username" password="password" />
    </credentials>
  </forms>
  <passport redirectUrl="internal"/>
</authentication>
```

When the authentication mode is set to `Windows`, all other tags will be ignored. For `Forms` authentication, all of the `<forms>` element's attributes have preconfigured default values, which are also found in the `Machine.config` file shown in the previous section:

```
<forms name=".ASPXAUTH"
       loginUrl="login.aspx"
       protection="All"
       timeout="30" path="/">
```

So, if you configure Forms authentication only with the following syntax, you will need to provide a `login.aspx` page under the application root:

```
<authentication mode="Forms" />
```

Note The other `<authentication>` element attributes, valid child nodes, and their meanings are explained in depth in the MSDN help.

So far, you've used these configuration settings in `Web.config`:

```
<authentication mode="Forms">
  <forms loginUrl="Secure/Login.aspx"/>
</authentication>
```

For the Friends Reunion application, you let the default values take effect, and only overrode the `loginUrl` attribute to point to the location of your login form.

Authorization Configuration

The `<authorization>` element is the one used in ASP.NET to assign permissions to resources. The process of creating this element and its child elements and attributes is therefore comparable to the process of assigning file or folder security in Windows, or to that of defining the application roles allowed in COM+, as you saw earlier in the chapter (Figures 10-1 and 10-2).

The `<authorization>` element has the following syntax:

```
<authorization>
  <allow users="comma-separated list of users|?|*"
         roles="comma-separated list of roles"
         verbs="comma-separated list of verbs" />
  <deny users="comma-separated list of users|?|*"
```

```
        roles="comma-separated list of roles"
        verbs="comma-separated list of verbs" />
</authorization>
```

The ? and * (which don't actually appear in the documentation) represent the anonymous user (that is, an unauthenticated user) and any users (authenticated or not), respectively. The following is the default setting for this element in Machine.config:

```
<authorization>
  <allow users="*" />
</authorization>
```

In other words, all users are allowed to access the resources, unless otherwise specified in your application configuration file. This is the authorization setting you've been using for the Friends Reunion application (in Web.config):

```
<authorization>
  <deny users="?"/>
</authorization>
```

This means that you don't allow unauthenticated users to access any resource in the application.

Location Configuration

The <location> element can be used to specify <authorization> elements with regard to a certain path in the application. This is useful for setting exceptions to the rules defined for the whole application. You used it in Chapter 4 to explicitly allow Anonymous access to the NewUser.aspx form (which wouldn't be available according to the authorization setting shown in the previous section):

```
<location path="Secure/NewUser.aspx">
  <system.web>
    <authorization>
      <allow users="*"/>
    </authorization>
  </system.web>
</location>
```

If you didn't set this rule, unregistered users wouldn't be able to register themselves, since the NewUser.aspx page wouldn't be available unless they were previously authenticated!

The path can also be a folder instead of a specific file, so the following setting would work equally well:

```
<location path="Secure">
  <system.web>
    <authorization>
      <allow users="*"/>
    </authorization>
  </system.web>
</location>
```

In fact, using a `<location>` element with a path to a folder instead of a file (as in the example here) is equivalent to adding a `Web.config` file in that folder with the same authorization settings. So, you could achieve the same configuration as the `<location>` setting in the code you have just seen by adding a `Web.config` file to the `Secure` folder and adding the following elements to it:

```
<configuration>
  <system.web>
    <authorization>
      <allow users="*" />
    </authorization>
  </system.web>
</configuration>
```

It's worth noting how the process of authorization takes place here. There is another module, called `UrlAuthorizationModule`, that is registered by default to *all* web applications and performs the checks. It is called after the other security modules have processed the request, so it uses the `Principal` that was associated with the current user by the appropriate authentication module. This way, these checks are independent of the authentication mode selected. This means that you can use authorization elements to deny or allow access to certain roles, for example, and leave the settings intact, even if you later decide to change the authentication mode, as long as the role names remain the same.

The settings in a configuration file apply to the current folder and all its child folders, except for the `<location>` element, which applies only to the element specified in its `path` attribute. Application configuration files are hierarchical, which means that you can place multiple configuration files in different folders under the root application path, overriding the appropriate elements whenever necessary. These overrides can either broaden or tighten the settings in the parent folders. For example, you might deny Anonymous access to an application in general, just as we did for our Friends Reunion application, but make available a subfolder that contains items such as registration information or help pages.

Authentication Modes

Let's now move on and see how we can use the three authentication modes: Windows, Passport, and Forms. In the following sections, we'll explain how these modes work and examine their advantages and drawbacks.

Windows Authentication

Windows authentication works closely with IIS and the operating system. In fact, ASP.NET doesn't do much more than receive what IIS passes it, and then map it to .NET `Principal` and `Identity` objects. All of the business of exchanging credentials and authentication is handled at the IIS side, where Integrated Windows authentication (and optionally Basic authentication) should be used, with Anonymous access disabled. This is most suitable for intranet and extranet scenarios, where the users are a part of your organization and already have a Windows account in the company domain.

If you use Integrated Windows authentication, this will be the most secure method, as everything will be handled inside the Windows domain. In addition, access to pages can be set directly using file-access permissions (such as the ones shown in Figure 10-1), which makes for the lowest impact on your pages' design with regard to security. The user experience will also be improved, because users will not even need to log in to the application—the security token will automatically be passed to ASP.NET whenever the user opens the browser and points to a page.

Recall that in Chapter 4, we alternated between Integrated Windows authentication and Anonymous access settings. Now you can fully understand what was going on. The `Web.config` file was left with the default authentication mode of Windows, so when Integrated Windows authentication was turned on, the user automatically became authenticated; the token was received by ASP.NET behind the scenes. When you turned on Anonymous access, ASP.NET no longer received the Windows user's security token, so the user became unauthenticated.

If you select the Windows authentication mode in ASP.NET, and set the IIS security settings to use any method other than Anonymous access, you won't see the Windows login form, unless you try to access the application through the Internet from another machine. Machines on your local area network will get the effect we achieved in Chapter 4: the credentials will be passed automatically, and you become authenticated to the application without needing to do anything. On the other hand, if you tried to access the application through the Internet, you would see the dialog box shown in Figure 10-6.

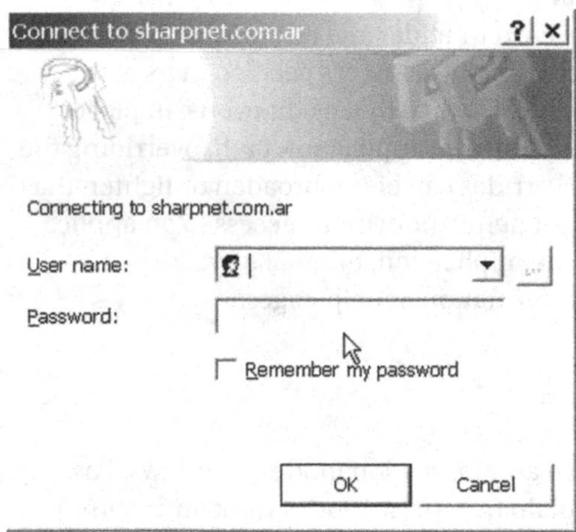

Figure 10-6. *Accessing a Windows authenticated application from the Internet*

The Connect to *application* dialog box replaces the Forms login page that you've been using so far. The information entered in this dialog box is encoded/encrypted according to the specific setting used in IIS. This dialog box is the same as the one that appears when you try to access a network share for which you haven't been authenticated, such as a share from a computer outside your domain.

Passport Authentication

Passport is a paid authentication service provided by Microsoft. It is the authentication service backing up Hotmail, MSN, and MSN Messenger, so you could say that it's a well-tested, streamlined, production-quality, high-volume service. However, setting it up for use in your web application is not as easy as setting up Windows or Forms authentication, and the actual authentication process is not as automatic.

For more information about Passport authentication, you can download the Software Developers Kit (SDK) from `http://msdn.microsoft.com/library/default.asp?url=/downloads/list/websrvpass.asp` and read the product documentation.

Forms Authentication

Forms authentication has been the mode of choice for our Friends Reunion web application, for two reasons:

- It is easily implemented.
- It is the most likely to be used for web applications, as it allows for administration of users outside Windows accounts, which is paramount for the Internet. However, as we noted earlier, for intranet/extranet scenarios, Windows authentication is a better choice.

The processing sequence that has been taking place in our Friends Reunion application is a typical Forms authentication interaction, which can be represented as shown in Figure 10-7 (the numbers in the diagram reflect the request processing order of execution).

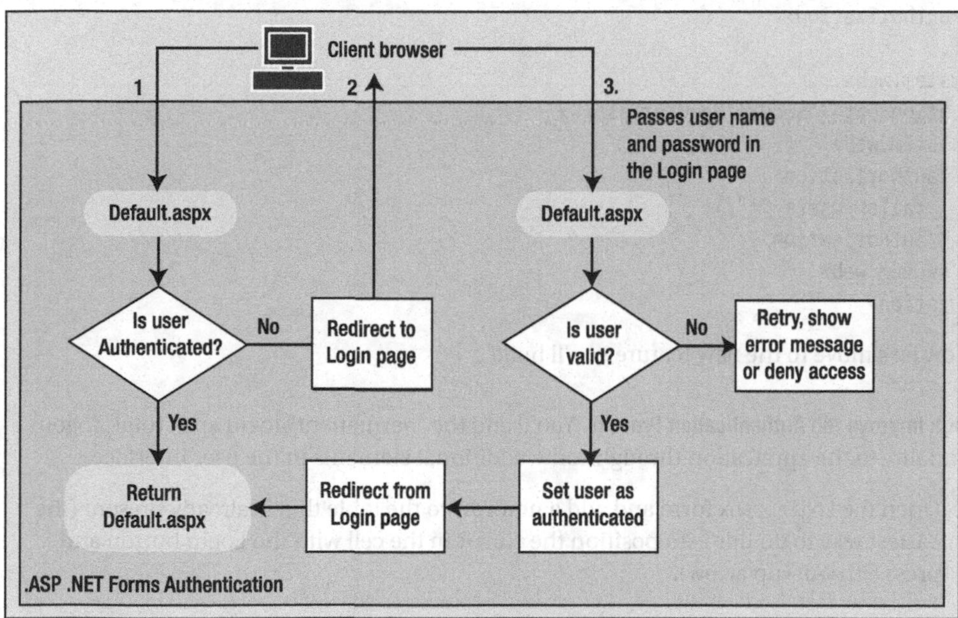

Figure 10-7. *The Forms authentication processing sequence*

The figure shows a user requesting a page that requires authentication (Default.aspx). If the user hasn't been authenticated previously with the application, that user is redirected to the login page. After the user has entered a user name and password, and these credentials have been successfully validated, the user is set as being authenticated. As you've learned, this involves the creation of an authentication cookie that is saved with the request and later passed back to the server on every subsequent request. Using the built-in infrastructure will suffice for most applications, such as our Friends Reunion example.

In the next example, we'll extend the functionality of the login form we've been using so far. We will improve it by giving the user the ability to "persist" login information; that is, to save the cookie in order to survive browser restarts. This will allow users to avoid the inconvenience of needing to enter the same information again when they return to the site. Most sites that offer this feature also allow users to sign out of the application explicitly, so that any authentication cookies are removed from their machine. This is very important for users who access your application from shared machines.

Let's first recap the security-related settings the application is using (in Web.config) so far:

```
<?xml version="1.0" encoding="utf-8" ?>
<configuration>
  ...
  <system.web>
    ...
    <authentication mode="Forms">
      <forms loginUrl="Secure/Login.aspx" />
    </authentication>
    <authorization>
      <deny users="?" />
    </authorization>
    ...
  </system.web>
  <location path="Secure/NewUser.aspx">
    <system.web>
      <authorization>
        <allow users="*"/>
      </authorization>
    </system.web>
  </location>
```

Now let's move to the new feature you'll build.

Try It Out: Improve the Authentication Process You'll add the "permanent" login and "total" logout functionality to the application through some additional elements in the user interface.

1. Open the Login.aspx form and add a new row to the table that is already present (the easiest way to do this is to position the cursor in the cell with the Login button and press Ctrl+Alt+up arrow).

2. Drop in a CheckBox web server control named chkPersist, and set its Text property to **Remember me on this machine**, as shown in Figure 10-8.

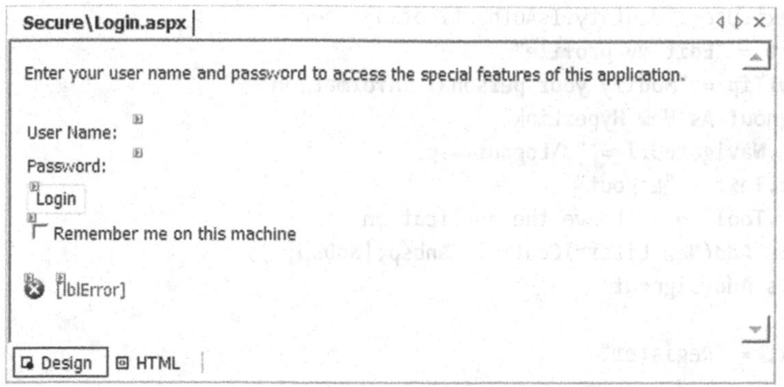

Figure 10-8. *Adding an option for a persistent login to the Login page*

3. Add the code to persist the cookie according to the user's selection in the new check box (a change to just one line!):

```
Private Sub btnLogin_ServerClick(ByVal sender As System.Object,
  ByVal e As System.EventArgs) Handles btnLogin.ServerClick
  ...
  If Not id Is Nothing Then
    ' Set the user as authenticated and send him to the
    ' page originally requested
    FormsAuthentication.RedirectFromLoginPage(id, chkPersist.Checked)
  Else
    pnlError.Visible = True
    lblError.Text = "Invalid user name or password!"
  End If
End Sub
```

4. Now let's add the logout feature. The natural place to put this is as a link next to Edit my profile, in the SubHeader control you created in Chapter 3. Open `SubHeader.vb` and add the code to create and add the new link next to the old one:

```
Protected Overrides Sub CreateChildControls()
  Dim lbl As Label

  ' Always render a link to the registration/edit profile page
  Dim reg As New HyperLink

  ' If a URL isn't provided, use a default URL to the
  ' registration page
  If _register = "" Then
    reg.NavigateUrl = "~\Secure\NewUser.aspx"
  Else
    reg.NavigateUrl = _register
  End If
```

```
  If (Context.User.Identity.IsAuthenticated) Then
    reg.Text = "Edit my profile"
    reg.ToolTip = "Modify your personal information"
    Dim signout As New HyperLink
    signout.NavigateUrl = "~\Logout.aspx"
    signout.Text = "Logout"
    signout.ToolTip = "Leave the application"
    Controls.Add(New LiteralControl(" | "))
    Controls.Add(signout)
  Else
    reg.Text = "Register"
  End If

  ' Add the newly created link to our
  ' collection of child controls
  Controls.AddAt(0, reg)

  ' Add a couple of blank spaces and a separator character
  Controls.Add(New LiteralControl(" - "))

  ' Add a label with the current data
  lbl = New Label
  lbl.Text = DateTime.Now.ToLongDateString()
  Controls.Add(lbl)
End Sub
```

Note that you will actually redirect the users to a confirmation page, just as Passport does.

5. Let's now create the logout confirmation page. Add a new web form called `Logout.aspx`. Drag-and-drop the CSS stylesheet we've been using so far on the design surface. Also, change the code-behind page to inherit the class from the `FriendsBase` class.

6. Inside a new paragraph, add a table with a row and two columns. Set its border to `0` and its width to 100%. Set the first cell's `valign` attribute to `top`. Put an image (`images/question.gif`) on the first column and the following text on the second:

   You are about to leave the application. After this process, you will have to enter your user name and password in order to use the application.

   Do you want to proceed?

   Add a new paragraph below the table and drop a button to perform the actual logout operation. Set its `ID` property to `btnLogout`, its `CssClass` to `Button`, and its `Text` to **Logout**. The Logout form should look like Figure 10-9.

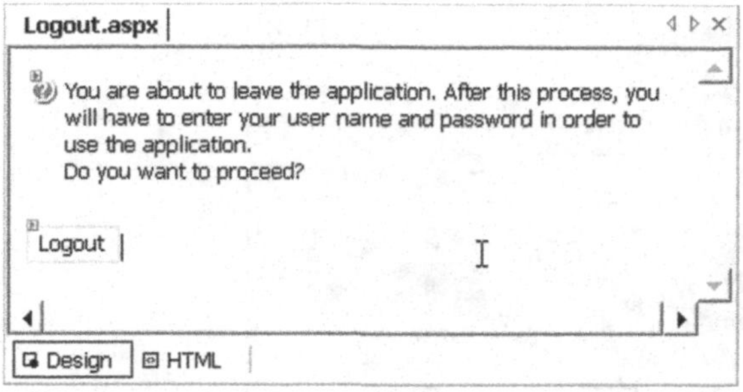

Figure 10-9. *The layout of the Logout form*

7. Add the following event handler to the Logout button:

```
Private Sub btnLogout_Click(ByVal sender As System.Object,
  ByVal e As System.EventArgs) Handles btnLogout.Click
  ' Remove the authentication ticket
  System.Web.Security.FormsAuthentication.SignOut()

  ' Redirect the user to the root application path
  Response.Redirect(Request.ApplicationPath)
End Sub
```

8. Add the following code to `Page_Load()` to set up the message and icon for the page:

```
Private Sub Page_Load(ByVal sender As System.Object, _
  ByVal e As System.EventArgs) Handles MyBase.Load
  MyBase.HeaderMessage = "Leave the Application"
  MyBase.HeaderIconImageUrl = "~\images\back.gif"
End Sub
```

9. Run the application with `Default.aspx` as the start page, and log in (select the Remember me on this machine check box if you like). After a successful login, the default page with the new Logout link looks like Figure 10-10.

10. Close the browser window directly (don't log out). Now run the application again. What you see depends on whether you checked the Remember me on this machine check box. If you did, the cookie (which is caching your identity) will be sent along with the request, so you won't need to log in, and you'll go directly to the Welcome page. If you didn't check that option, you'll need to log in again.

11. Once you're at the Welcome page, you can formally log out (and destroy the cookie) by clicking the Logout link. This will take you to the confirmation page, as shown in Figure 10-11. If you now confirm the logout, you'll be sent back to the application's login page. The next time you start the application, you'll need to log in again.

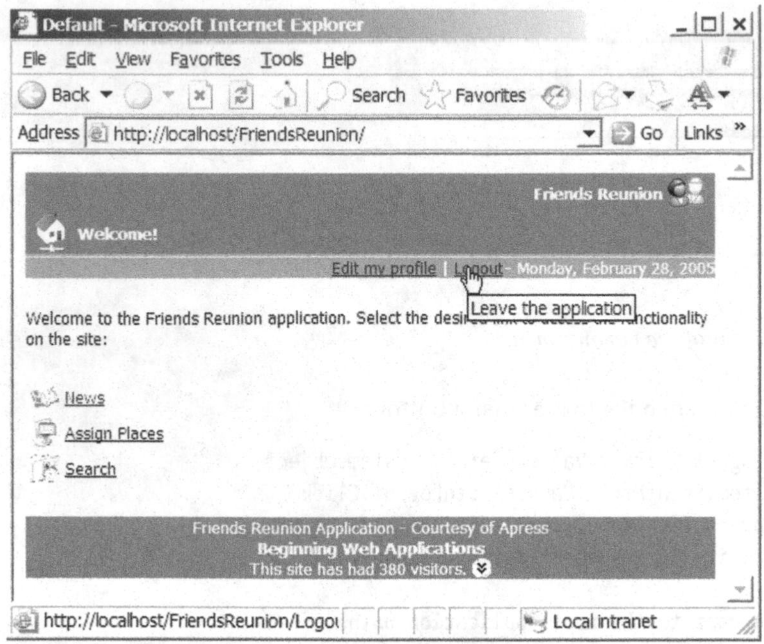

Figure 10-10. *The new Logout link on the Default page*

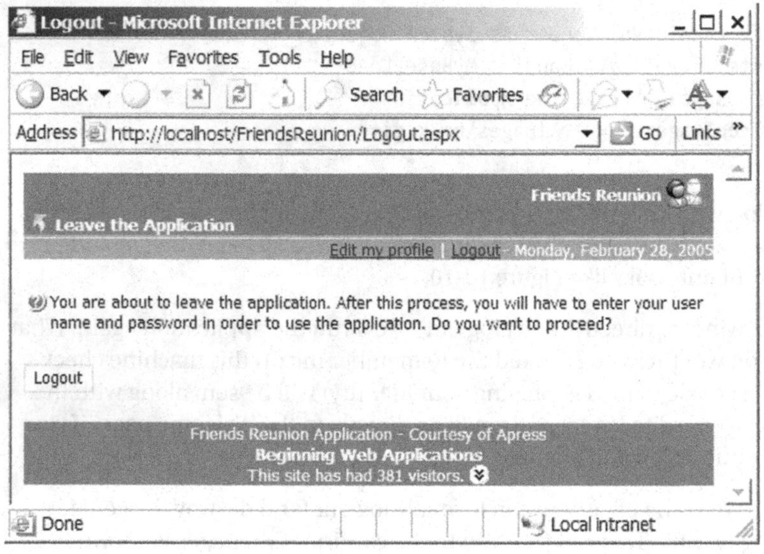

Figure 10-11. *Confirming logout*

How It Works

The login form uses the following method to set authentication:

```
FormsAuthentication.RedirectFromLoginPage(id, chkPersist.Checked)
```

This method takes care of creating the authentication cookie and saving it for subsequent requests. You pass the UserID, just as you did before, which is used to perform queries across the application. The new parameter you pass now is the Checked state of the check box, which tells the method to create a persistent cookie that will be preserved in the client machine even across browser and machine restarts.

The other new feature is the logout link in the SubHeader control. The process for creating this new link is similar to what you already did for the existing link in the SubHeader control: add the control to the Controls collection, and then add the existing link at the first position, so that it appears at the left of the new one:

```
Controls.AddAt(0, reg)
```

As you can see, the biggest advantage of Forms authentication is its flexibility. You can authenticate against a database store of credentials, using the infrastructure absolutely as-is, and achieve some very acceptable results! You were able to query the database, customize content tailored to the current user, and secure the whole application to require authentication. (You could even have used authorization on a per-user basis, although it wasn't necessary for this application.) Not bad for a sample project!

Tip Putting the Login and NewUser forms in a separate folder from the rest of the application makes it easier to increase security for these two especially sensitive forms. One way to do this would be to set SSL security for that folder, forcing the web server and client browser to encrypt the entire conversation between them, making it harder for hackers to get in the middle. This is an advanced topic that's treated in greater depth in *Building Secure Microsoft ASP.NET Applications* (Microsoft Press, 2003; ISBN: 0735618909), which can also be downloaded as a PDF from www.microsoft.com/practices.

Customized Authentication and Role-Based Security

Forms authentication is great, but it doesn't use the role-based features we talked about at the beginning of the chapter. As you saw, it will simply create an empty GenericPrincipal object, containing only the initialized FormsIdentity object. If we were to build an administration section in our application, and we wanted to restrict access only to administrator users, we would need to deny access to everyone, and then add the administrator users one by one.

To take advantage of role-based authentication, you need to customize the process. In the "The ASP.NET Security Infrastructure" section earlier in this chapter, you saw that the various authentication modules actually hook into the same events that you can use, particularly AuthenticateRequest, an event to which you can attach a handler in your Global.asax file.

You also learned that the infrastructure is prepared to work with any role-based scheme, as long as it works around the concepts of principal and identity (represented by the `IPrincipal` and `IIdentity` interfaces). So far, however, you've let the default modules take charge. Your only intervention in Forms authentication was to check a user name and password in the login form. You didn't need to bother about the cookies, encryption/decryption (yes, the cookie *is* encrypted), creation of the `Principal` and `Identity` objects, or anything else. Some things are going to have to change.

Implementing Custom Authentication

For our implementation of custom authentication, we will start by using the `GenericPrincipal` and `GenericIdentity` objects, which provide a reasonable and simple implementation. In case they are not enough, we can always inherit and extend them, or even implement `IPrincipal` and `IIdentity` directly in a custom class.

You already know the processing that takes place in order to make the default modules work. You can now apply that knowledge to build custom authentication. As we stated, the key event to handle in the process is `AuthenticateRequest`. During the handler for this event, you can perform some actions, and then set the `Context.User` property to your custom `Principal` and `Identity` objects. As with any other authentication scheme, this security context will follow the user through pages, user controls, code-behind pages, and so on. You'll be able to access these objects from any point in running code.

To customize authentication, you need to intercept the process at some point. In this instance, we'll leave the code as it is in the `Login.aspx` page, and let the Forms authentication module perform all the work it has been doing so far, until a certain point. Let's look again at the steps for a typical request in our application, and see where to override the default behavior:

1. User requests `Default.aspx` (this is the initial request to enter the application).
2. The `Application_AuthenticateRequest` event is fired; `IsAuthenticated = false`, so Forms module redirects to `Login.aspx?ReturnUrl=....`
3. The redirect causes a new request to another page (namely `Login.aspx`).
4. The `Application_AuthenticateRequest` event is fired again, this time by the access to `Login.aspx`. The module realizes that this is the login page, so it doesn't redirect to itself again.
5. The user enters credentials and submits. Posting the form to itself is actually another new request.
6. The code checks against database and returns OK. The module saves `UserID` with the authentication cookie, and performs a redirect to `ReturnUrl` (`Default.aspx`).
7. As a result of the redirect, a new request is made for `Default.aspx`. This time, the authentication cookie is set.
8. The `Application_AuthenticateRequest` event fires; this is the first time you get `IsAuthenticated = true`. The application picks up processing from here, and rebuilds customized versions of `GenericPrincipal` and `GenericIdentity`, based on the information retrieved from the database using the `UserID` attached to the authentication cookie. It replaces the `Context.User` with the new complete `Principal`.

In this sequence, note that the last `AuthenticateRequest` is the first one for which the `IsAuthenticated` property returns `true`. From now on, this is the only response that will be issued to an authenticate request, because the authorization cookie will be present and the Forms authentication module will take care of recovering the `UserID` from it. You will actually customize the authentication mechanism after the Forms authentication module has handled it.

We can refer to `Default.aspx` more generally as a "restricted page," which can be any protected resource in the application. Graphically, the interaction is as shown in Figure 10-12.

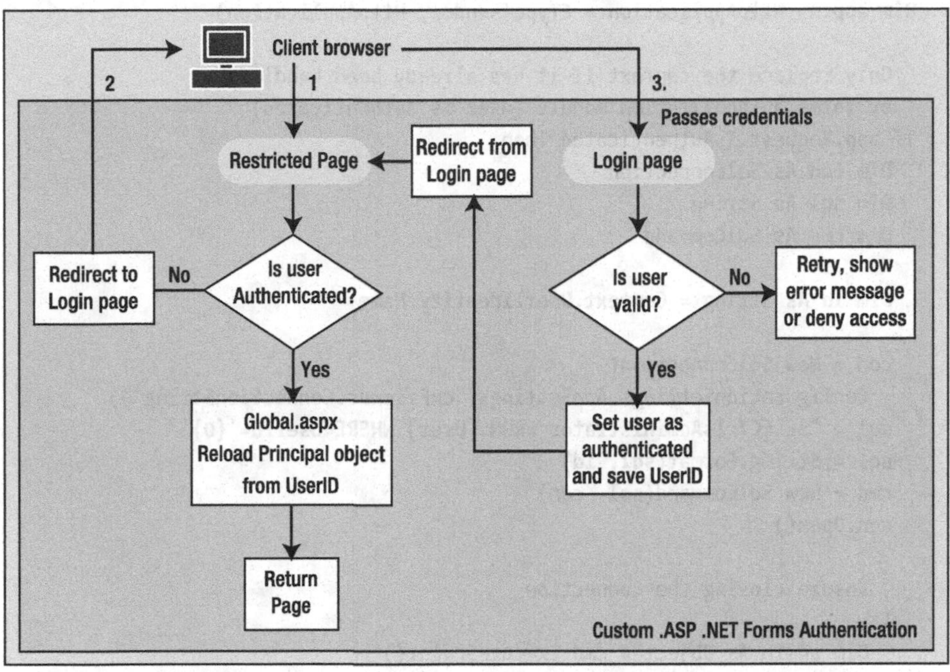

Figure 10-12. *Custom ASP.NET Forms authentication*

After you use the `FormsAuthentication.RedirectFromLoginPage()` method, the restricted page is actually requested again, but this time, with the security token (or authentication ticket) set. At this time, you have a chance to override the default behavior implemented by Forms authentication, and you can set the `Context.User` property to an object that better represents your needs. For our example, this will be a `GenericPrincipal` that contains the roles associated with the current user.

Try It Out: Use and Replace the Principal Object In our database, there are only two roles: Users and Administrators. These roles aren't actually defined anywhere, but Administrators are distinguished by the `IsAdministrator` flag in each record in the `User` table. This is the information you will use to create a `GenericPrincipal` containing the Users role, or both the Users and Administrators roles (an administrator will always be a user, too).

1. Open the Global.asax.vb code-behind file, and import the following namespace:

   ```
   Imports System.Security.Principal
   ```

2. Find the Application_AuthenticateRequest() event handler, and add the following code to it:

```
Sub Application_AuthenticateRequest(ByVal sender As Object, _
  ByVal e As EventArgs)
  ' Cast the sender to the application type
  Dim app As HttpApplication = CType(sender, HttpApplication)

  ' Only replace the context if it has already been handled
  ' by forms authentication module (user is authenticated)
  If app.Request.IsAuthenticated Then
    Dim con As SqlConnection
    Dim sql As String
    Dim cmd As SqlCommand

    Dim id As String = Context.User.Identity.Name

    con = New SqlConnection(
      ConfigurationSettings.AppSettings("cnFriends.ConnectionString"))
    sql = "SELECT IsAdministrator FROM [User] WHERE UserId='{0}'"
    sql = String.Format(sql, id)
    cmd = New SqlCommand(sql, con)
    con.Open()

    ' Ensure closing the connection
    Try
      Dim admin As Object = cmd.ExecuteScalar()

      ' Was it a valid UserID?
      If Not (admin Is Nothing) Then
        Dim ppal As GenericPrincipal
        Dim roles() As String

        ' If IsAdministrator field is true, add both roles
        If CBool(admin) = True Then
          roles = New String() {"User", "Admin"}
        Else
          roles = New String() {"User"}
        End If

        ppal = New GenericPrincipal(Context.User.Identity, roles)
        Context.User = ppal
      Else
```

```
            ' If UserID was invalid, clear the context so they log on again
            Context.User = Nothing
          End If
        Finally
          con.Close()
        End Try
      End If
    End Sub
```

3. Create a new folder named `Admin`, and add a new web form called `Users.aspx` to it. As always, add the stylesheet reference to it, and change the code-behind page so that it inherits from the `FriendsBase` class.

4. On the Users page, drop a DataGrid control. Set its `ID` to `grdUsers`, and set its width to 100%. Right-click the DataGrid control, select Auto Format, and select Colorful 4. Just above the DataGrid control, add this text: **Welcome to the Users Administration page. This is the complete list of users:**. The `Users.aspx` page should look something like Figure 10-13.

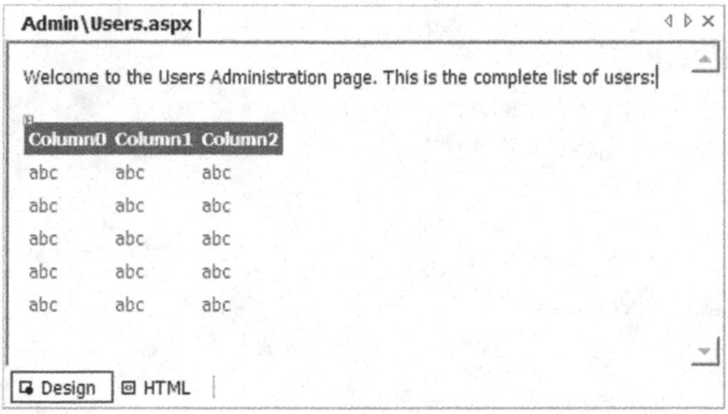

Figure 10-13. *The beginning layout of the Users page*

5. Drop a `SqlDataAdapter` component onto the form, and follow the wizard as you did in Chapter 5: first select the appropriate connection string, then select that you want to use SQL statements, and then set the SQL statement to `SELECT * FROM [User]`. Finally, select Finish to complete the wizard.

6. Change the name of the `SqlDataAdapter` object to `adUsers`. Change the name of the connection to `cnFriends`.

7. Check the properties of the `SqlDataAdapter` component (`adUsers`). Its `SelectCommand` property should be `cmUsers` (change the `Name` property of `SelectCommand` if necessary). Also, if you haven't unchecked the Generate insert... advanced option, remember to set the `UpdateCommand`, `InsertCommand`, and `DeleteCommand` properties to (`none`).

8. Set the cnFriends connection string property to use the dynamic configuration you used before. (Select the Dynamic Configuration property called ConnectionString, and use the button there to map the property to the key cnFriends.ConnectionString in the configuration file.)

9. Right-click the SqlDataAdapter component (adUsers) and select Generate Dataset. Select the New option button, and give it the name UserData. Click OK in the dialog box, and rename the new dataset to dsData.

10. Bind the DataGrid control to this new dataset (by setting its DataSource property to dsData). The form will look something like Figure 10-14 now.

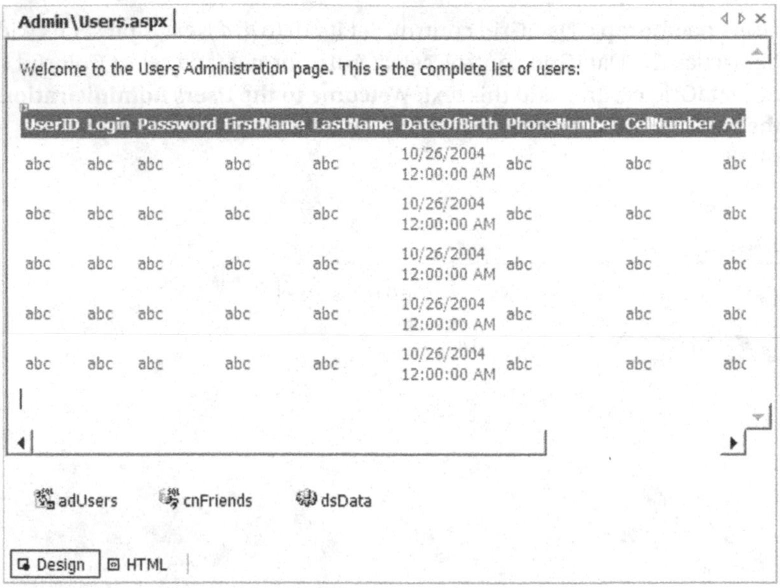

Figure 10-14. *The User page with data components*

11. Let's add the code to load the dataset and bind the grid to display the data. Add the following code to the Page_Load() method of this page:

```
Private Sub Page_Load(ByVal sender As System.Object, _
  ByVal e As System.EventArgs) Handles MyBase.Load
  MyBase.HeaderIconImageUrl = "~/images/padlock.gif"
  MyBase.HeaderMessage = "Administer Users"

  If Not IsPostBack Then
    Me.adUsers.Fill(Me.dsData)
    Me.grdUsers.DataBind()
  End If
End Sub
```

12. Add a link to this new page in the Default.aspx page, so that administrators have easy access to it. Open the Default.aspx page, and add the following code to the bottom:

```
<form id="Default" method="post" runat="server">
  ...
  <p class="Normal">
    <asp:placeholder id="phNav" runat="server"></asp:placeholder>
  </p>
  <p>
    <asp:hyperlink id="lnkUsers" runat="server"
                                    navigateurl="Admin/Users.aspx">
      Users Administration Page
    </asp:hyperlink>
  </p>
</form>
```

13. Finally, make the link visible only if the current user is an administrator. Open the code-behind page for Default.aspx and add the following code at the bottom of the method:

```
Private Sub Page_Load(ByVal sender As System.Object, _
  ByVal e As System.EventArgs) Handles MyBase.Load
  ...
  ' Show the Admin link only to administrators
  lnkUsers.Visible = User.IsInRole("Admin")
End Sub
```

14. Save the project, and then run it with Default.aspx as the start page.

How It Works

As you can see from step 13, the purpose of the code you added is to be able to control application behavior (in this case, showing a link) based on the current user's role, instead of the particular user name or ID. This allows you to take advantage of the benefits of the role-based approach.

You're handling the AuthenticateRequest event in the Global.asax file in order to replace the default principal that's associated by Forms authentication with a custom one. This will allow you to add roles to the current user, based on the information in the database. Note that you used the application request's IsAuthenticated property, instead of the Context.User.Identity.IsAuthenticated property you've used before:

```
If app.Request.IsAuthenticated Then
  ...
```

You had to do this because the first time the page is accessed, the Context.User property isn't initialized yet, and you would have caused an exception. To take this into account, you could have replaced the previous code with the following:

```
If (Not (Context.User Is Nothing) AndAlso
  (Context.User.Identity.IsAuthenticated)) Then
```

If you pass the IsAuthenticated check, it will mean that Forms authentication has already done its work, and the UserID is placed where you're used to finding it: in the Context.User.Identity.Name property. This is the work that's already achieved in the Login.aspx page, and it's what you've been doing since Chapter 4.

In the remainder of the handler, you replace the empty GenericPrincipal object that's created by the Forms authentication module with one containing the actual roles the user belongs to. So, in the Application_AuthenticateRequest() handler, you retrieve the UserID and use it to issue a database query to discover whether it corresponds to an administrator. You use ExecuteScalar(), because you expect a single Boolean value to be returned. As usual, you placed the code in a Try...Finally block to ensure the connection is always closed.

The GenericPrincipal constructor receives an identity and a string array containing the roles it belongs to. You reuse the identity created by Forms authentication, which is attached to the Context.User.Identity property you have been using; you don't need to change anything about it:

```
ppal = new GenericPrincipal(Context.User.Identity, roles)
```

Finally, you assign the newly created principal to the Context.User property:

```
Context.User = ppal
```

If you go look at the diagram shown earlier in Figure 10-12, you'll notice that the next page to be processed is the page that was originally requested. So, when execution reaches your code for the page, it will have access to the new role-aware principal you attached. You use this in the Page_Load() method of the Default.aspx page to display a link to the user's administration page:

```
lnkUsers.Visible = User.IsInRole("Admin")
```

User is a property of the Page class that provides a shortcut to Context.User, and its IsInRole() method allows you to check whether it pertains to a specific role. Figure 10-15 shows the page when an administrator user logs in.

Securing Folders

You have used your new, custom, roles-aware principal to display information on the page selectively. However, merely hiding or showing a link is not enough security. If a non-administrator user knows the administration page's location and name, he could type the address into the browser's Address box and gain access to a resource that is supposed to be restricted! To solve this problem, you will add a configuration file inside the Admin folder, to secure all the items in that folder.

Tip If you were to add more administration tools later, the configuration file would automatically protect them, too. Organizing an application into separate folders according to resource features makes it extremely easy to administer its security settings and ensures that future growth won't become a maintenance nightmare.

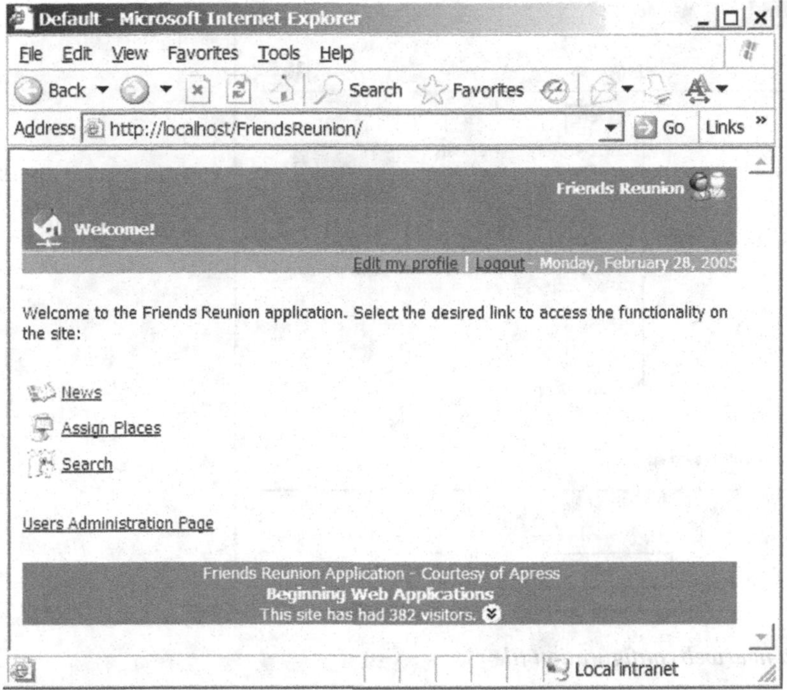

Figure 10-15. *The page an administrator sees after logging in*

Try It Out: Take Advantage of Roles for Authorization To secure the items in your new `Admin` folder, you just need to provide it with a new web configuration file, as you're about to do.

1. Right-click the `Admin` folder and select Add ➤ Add New Item. Choose Web Configuration File from the Utility folder, as shown in Figure 10-16.

2. Open the `Admin/Web.config` file that you've just created. Remove all of this file's content, and replace it with the following:

```
<?xml version="1.0" encoding="utf-8" ?>
<configuration>
  <system.web>
    <authorization>
      <allow roles="Admin" />
      <deny roles="User" />
    </authorization>
  </system.web>
</configuration>
```

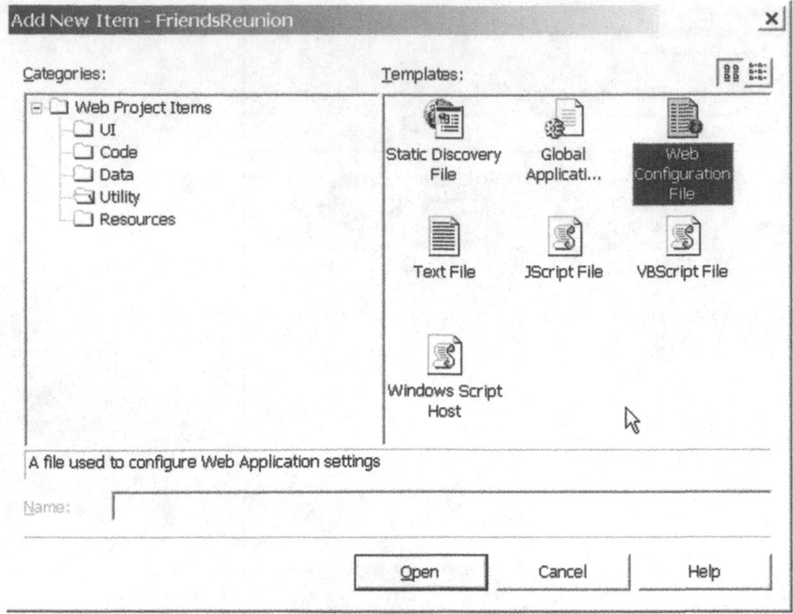

Figure 10-16. *Creating a new web configuration file*

How It Works

If a user who is not an administrator is logged in, that user won't see the link to the administration page, because the page's code (added in the previous example) hides it. But now, if the user tries to type the page's address directly into the browser's Address box, that user *still* won't be allowed to access it, thanks to the configuration file you just placed in the folder. Instead, the user will be redirected to the Login page again, to provide appropriate credentials.

Up to now, you have been using user-related information to restrict access to resources, such as denying anonymous users or granting all users. Now, you are taking advantage of role-based security to set permissions. This means that new administrator users registered with the application later on will automatically gain access to these resources, without any further changes to the application's configuration. If you had used user-related information, you could have granted the apress user access to this folder, but you would then need to add any new administrators manually.

Having logged on as a *non*-administrator user, try typing the URL directly into the browser's Address box to see what happens. You should be redirected to the Login page, to provide new credentials with appropriate permissions. Only users belonging to the Administrators role will be able to see the administration page, regardless of how they try to access it. Needless to say, an unauthenticated user will be redirected to the Login page, too.

Summary

Security in web applications is very important, because of the exposure to the entire Web (of hackers!). In this chapter, we looked at some general security concepts, as well as modern role-based security.

We examined the various authentication options available in ASP.NET, and provided some guidance that should allow you to choose among them. We discussed application configuration files in the context of security settings, and we used authentication and authorization to secure an application. We also used custom authentication to meet application requirements, showing the level of extensibility available in the general security infrastructure.

In order to describe the close relationship between IIS and ASP.NET, we provided an overview of the modular and extensible architecture that exists to process web requests, and how the various authentication options are implemented internally, as well as their interaction with the main web application.

Now our Friends Reunion application has become much more secure, through the use of the concepts you've learned in this chapter. However, we certainly haven't covered every possible security-related feature available in .NET, as that is a subject for a whole book. As noted earlier, one such book is *Building Secure Microsoft ASP.NET Applications*, which can also be downloaded as a PDF from `www.microsoft.com/practices`.

CHAPTER 11

Debugging and Exception Handling

In the previous chapters, we've written and generated a lot of code in our Friends Reunion application. In this chapter, we have two aims:

- To explain techniques that will help you to ensure the code you've written is free of bugs
- To look at how to include exception-handling code that is designed to deal with unexpected runtime errors

These two topics are often bundled together and confused with one another. That's because, although they are different, they are related. If you can get a good understanding of exception handling, it will help you to write robust code that is capable of dealing with unexpected occurrences. Then, if your application does have a bug, that bug is less likely to cause a horrible failure at runtime, because the exception-handling code will be designed to deal with it gracefully.

We'll devote the first part of the chapter to the subject of debugging:

- The different types of errors and which tools are most suitable for finding and fixing them
- Alternative techniques for debugging applications without the aid of a debugger (useful when you move your application from the test environment into a live environment)
- How to use the VS .NET debugger to debug an application

In the second part of the chapter, we'll introduce you to the subject of error handling using exceptions:

- How to catch, throw, and rethrow exceptions
- How to define your own custom exceptions
- How to recover gracefully from an unhandled exception
- How to log exceptions to the System event log

By the end of the chapter, you should have a good understanding of what is offered by the .NET Framework in general, and ASP.NET in particular, in the battle against bugs. You'll also know how the exception-handling mechanism works and how to integrate it with some specific ASP.NET features.

Types of Errors

If you have any experience developing applications, you already know that it's very difficult to rid an application of errors entirely. It doesn't matter how much effort you put into writing error-free code—developers are human, and humans make mistakes. Therefore, we must accept that we won't write perfect code the first time; it's as simple as that.

After accepting that we're not all as infallible as we would like to think we are, the next thing to realize is that we should at least try to *minimize* the number of coding errors and the effect that those errors can have on our application's behavior. To do this, we need to understand a little about the different *types* of errors that we may encounter.

We can classify errors into three distinct types: syntax errors, semantic errors, and input errors. As you'll see, these three types are different in nature, and thus you need different tools and techniques to find and fix them.

Syntax Errors

A *syntax error* occurs when you write code that violates the rules of grammar of the programming language. A debugger will not be of any help in detecting and correcting syntax errors! The compiler is the main tool here. If the compiler detects a syntax error, it will refuse to complete compilation of the code, and so there will be no program to debug.

Syntax errors are said to be caught at *compile-time* (because it is the compiler that catches and reports them). When you're building your VB .NET web application in VS .NET, the VB.NET compiler will check the code for syntax errors and output its results to the Output window. (To view the Output window, select View ➤ Other Windows ➤ Output or press Ctrl+Alt+O.) The Output window will contain a short description of each error, along with the file and line number in which it was found.

Generally, the compiler will be able to tell you the location of a syntax error with reasonable accuracy. If there isn't a syntax error at the exact line reported by the compiler, then the error is usually located somewhere above the specified line (and probably within just a few lines). For example, consider this code fragment from `SubHeader.vb` shown in Figure 11-1.

The code in Figure 11-1 contains a simple syntax error: the closing `End Sub` for the constructor is missing at line 10. If you tried to compile this code, the compiler would detect this syntax error and report it to the Output window, as shown in Figure 11-2. However, it doesn't detect the error at line 10, but it does detect that there's something at line 13 that isn't as it should be.

The compiler works from the top down, so in this case, it finds the `Public Property` statement as part of the constructor, which is not valid in that context, and highlights the error there. Although the exact location of the error is not quite right, the information is enough for you to work out what's wrong in the code.

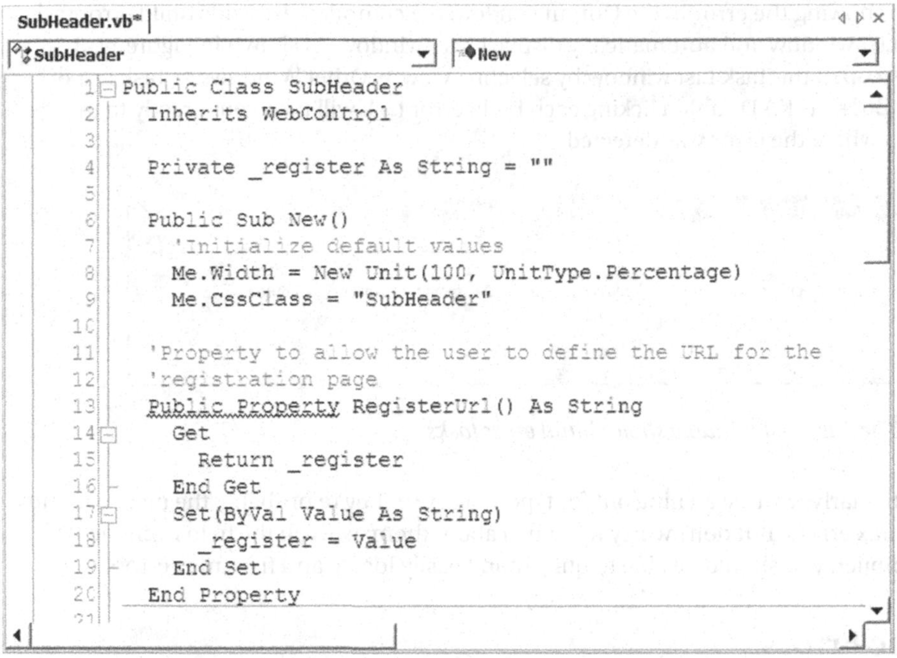

SubHeader.vb*

SubHeader | New

```
1  Public Class SubHeader
2    Inherits WebControl
3
4    Private _register As String = ""
5
6    Public Sub New()
7      'Initialize default values
8      Me.Width = New Unit(100, UnitType.Percentage)
9      Me.CssClass = "SubHeader"
10
11   'Property to allow the user to define the URL for the
12   'registration page
13   Public Property RegisterUrl() As String
14     Get
15       Return _register
16     End Get
17     Set(ByVal Value As String)
18       _register = Value
19     End Set
20   End Property
```

Figure 11-1. *Code with a syntax error*

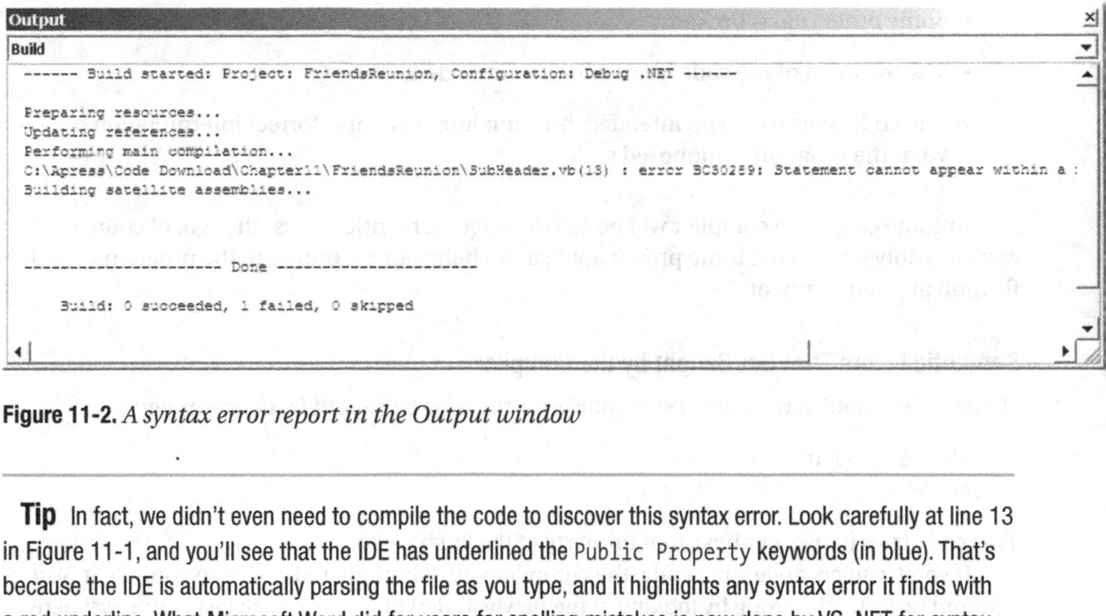

Output

Build

```
------ Build started: Project: FriendsReunion, Configuration: Debug .NET ------

Preparing resources...
Updating references...
Performing main compilation...
C:\Apress\Code Download\Chapter11\FriendsReunion\SubHeader.vb(13) : error BC30289: Statement cannot appear within a :
Building satellite assemblies...



---------------------- Done ----------------------

    Build: 0 succeeded, 1 failed, 0 skipped
```

Figure 11-2. *A syntax error report in the Output window*

Tip In fact, we didn't even need to compile the code to discover this syntax error. Look carefully at line 13 in Figure 11-1, and you'll see that the IDE has underlined the `Public Property` keywords (in blue). That's because the IDE is automatically parsing the file as you type, and it highlights any syntax error it finds with a red underline. What Microsoft Word did for years for spelling mistakes is now done by VS .NET for syntax errors!

Besides showing the error in the Output window, the compiler also adds build error tasks to the Task List window and automatically displays that window, as shown in Figure 11-3. (You can also open the Task List window by selecting View ➤ Other Windows ➤ Task List or by pressing Ctrl+Alt+K.) Double-clicking each build error task will take you directly to the file and position where the error was detected.

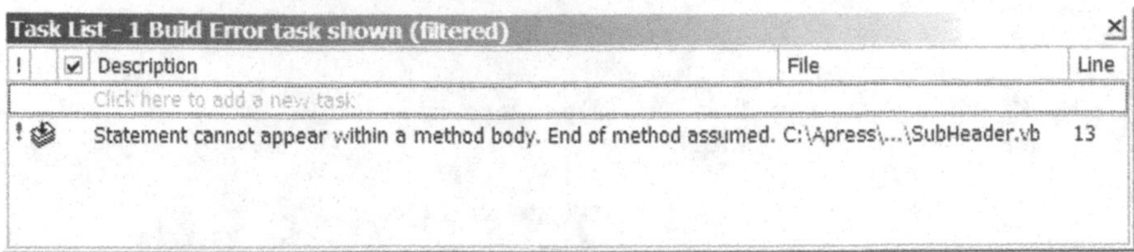

Figure 11-3. *The Task List window shows build error tasks.*

It's particularly worth watching out for typos, because they're probably the most common cause of syntax errors. But don't worry too much about them; with all the help from the IDE and the compiler, you should be able to quickly and easily locate and fix syntax errors.

Semantic Errors

A semantic error occurs when the syntax of your code is correct but one of the following occurs:

- Some other rule is broken.
- The meaning of the code is not what you intended.
- The code does what you intended, but your intent is not a correct interpretation of what the program is supposed to do.

In some cases, the compiler will be able to detect semantic errors (though, of course, it can't possibly know what is the proper application behavior according to the program's specification and requirements!).

Semantic Errors That Get Caught by the Compiler

Here's an example of the type of semantic error that *can* be caught by the compiler:

```
Dim btn As New Button
btn.Age = 32
```

This code tries to use a nonexistent property of the `Button` class.

If you try to compile such code, the compiler will complain and refuse to compile it. You can find out what is wrong by looking at the newly added task in the Task List window, where the compiler correctly tells you that the `Button` class doesn't have a definition for `Age`, as shown in Figure 11-4.

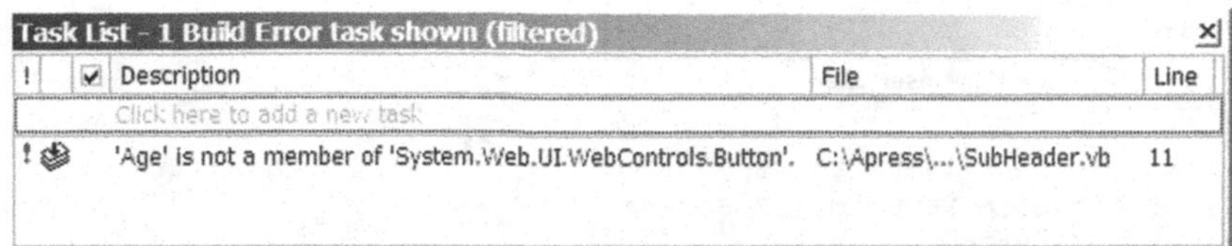

Figure 11-4. *The compiler can catch some semantic errors.*

This kind of semantic error is easy to fix. You just need to browse the Output window or check the Task List window to locate the error, and then fix the code to satisfy the compiler's complaints.

Semantic Errors That Don't Get Caught by the Compiler

The other kind of semantic error is what we usually call a *bug*. Bugs get through the compilation stage and become part of a compiled application.

A bug cannot be caught by the compiler because it is not a problem that can be identified by rigorous systematic application of a set of rules. Rather, a bug is a problem with the meaning of the code or the developer's interpretation of the requirements. The only way to find bugs is by testing the application. Many bugs are found by the programmer or tester during the test cycle or by the end user when the application is actually being used.

The following code contains an example of such an error:

```
Dim btn As Button
btn.Text = "OK"
```

The developer who wrote these lines of code forgot to instantiate `btn` before using it. Therefore, the expression `btn.Text` (in the second line) evaluates to `Nothing.Text`, which is nonsensical. But the compiler will not find this error, because the compiler doesn't run all the code. This error will be found only at runtime. When these two lines of code are executed, an exception will be thrown and the application will halt execution, usually showing the user the exception that happened.

However, not all semantic errors manifest themselves in such an obvious way as to raise an exception and cause a termination. Sometimes, a program will continue to run after a semantic error has occurred, even though the logic it executes is in error (for example, if the flow of execution takes an inappropriate path or a variable contains an invalid value). Consider the code excerpt from the `InsertUser()` method of the `NewUser.aspx.vb` file (in the `Secure` folder) shown in Figure 11-5.

If we swap the order of lines 132 and 133, the application will still appear to run smoothly, but it will contain a logic error that causes the first and last names of the newly registered user to be added to the wrong fields in the database.

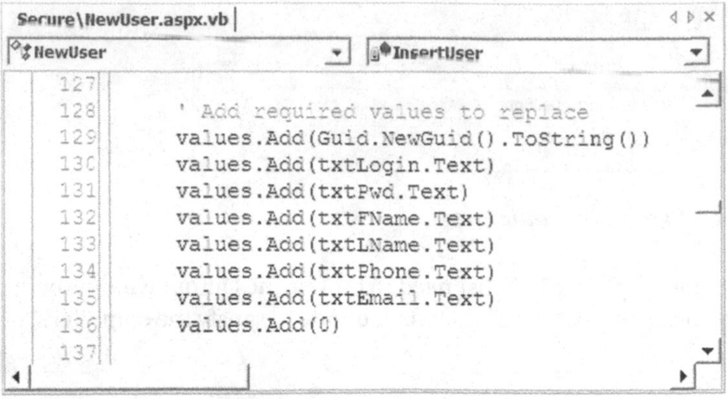

Secure\NewUser.aspx.vb

NewUser | InsertUser

```
    ' Add required values to replace
    values.Add(Guid.NewGuid().ToString())
    values.Add(txtLogin.Text)
    values.Add(txtPwd.Text)
    values.Add(txtFName.Text)
    values.Add(txtLName.Text)
    values.Add(txtPhone.Text)
    values.Add(txtEmail.Text)
    values.Add(0)
```

Figure 11-5. *A code excerpt from the NewUser.aspx.vb file*

Input Errors

An *input error* occurs when input into your application (from an external source) is not of the expected form. For example, suppose the application is required to open a file that it expects to be in JPG format, but it finds the file to be in a different format. Alternatively, consider when the application has a web form that invites the user to enter a date of birth, but the user types a meaningless value instead. These are input errors.

Input errors can and do happen. Moreover, input errors occur at *runtime*, so no compiler will be able to help find them. You can deal with input errors only by anticipating the type of input errors that might happen and preparing your code to be able to handle them. As you will see in this chapter, the .NET Framework provides an *exception*-based mechanism that allows you to code your applications to handle input errors properly and recover from them gracefully.

An effective way to detect potential input errors, as well as many of the semantic errors that cannot be detected by a compiler, is to test the application. (Testing is discussed in Chapter 12.) However, the testing process is only half the story. You can test an application to confirm that it is not working as you expected. But testing, in itself, doesn't tell you much about where the error is and or how to fix it. That's why you also need *debugging*.

Debugging Web Applications

Debugging is the process of finding and fixing errors that can't be caught by the compiler. It's very common to associate the debugging process with the use of a *debugger*—a piece of software designed to help you find and fix bugs—but there are other ways to debug applications.

In this section, we'll look at some alternative debugging techniques that .NET provides through the classes in the `System.Diagnostics` namespace and through the more specific ASP.NET tracing features. We'll also perform a useful debugging demonstration that doesn't use any debugger software at all. Finally, we'll introduce the powerful VS .NET debugger, and we'll do some debugging of the Friends Reunion application.

ASP.NET Tracing

When developing an application, a useful technique is to include lines of code that print messages, which are specifically intended to help the developer determine the path of execution that the application takes and the values of key variables at any given point in the application. This is what we call *tracing* the execution of an application.

If you have done much development work, it's very likely that you're used to tracing code. In the development of traditional Windows applications, tracing messages are often output to the screen or logged to a file. In ASP web applications (written before ASP.NET), the most common tracing method was to use `Response.Write` to output the tracing messages to the browser, along with the output of the rendered page.

When you're developing your ASP.NET web applications, there is nothing wrong with including your own tracing code (using `Response.Write` or your favorite technique) to help you fix bugs without resorting to a debugger. However, there are significant drawbacks to this approach:

- It's likely that while you're looking for the error, your tracing output will be mixed in with the actual content of your page, and that makes it harder to read the original format of the page (this is a particular weakness of the `Response.Write` technique).
- After you've fixed the bug, you need to go back over your code and remove all the tracing code that helped you to trace the error in the first place!
- There is a chance, in some cases, that the added tracing code has its own effect on the behavior of the application, and actually makes it harder to locate the problem.

Until now, web application developers had to reinvent the wheel, creating their own tracing mechanism and facing these problems. But now, ASP.NET introduces a new tracing facility, intended to free the developer from such chores.

This new functionality, designed from the ground up to avoid all the previously mentioned drawbacks, is implemented by the `TraceContext` class that is exposed via the public `Trace` property of the `Page` class. This makes the tracing feature easily available in every place where you deal with a page. When you use the methods of the `TraceContext` class to output tracing messages to the browser, ASP.NET arranges for these messages to be rendered at the bottom of the page, after the proper content of the page, so that the two different types of information being rendered don't get mixed. Apart from printing custom messages, ASP.NET will also output key data for your page and application, such as the items of the `Form` collection, the items of the `QueryString` collection, the `Application` state, and the `Session` state.

Enabling Tracing in ASP.NET

You can easily enable tracing for a page by setting the `Trace` attribute to `true` in the `Page` directive for your page:

```
<%@ Page Trace="true"
        Language="vb" AutoEventWireup="false"
        Codebehind="NewUser.aspx.vb"
        Inherits="FriendsReunionSec.NewUser" %>
```

Try It Out: Enable Trace Information for a Page Let's enable trace information for the News page of our Friends Reunion application, and take a look at the type of information it shows.

1. Using VS .NET, browse the Friends Reunion files and open `News.aspx`. Switch to the HTML view and add the `Trace` attribute to the `Page` directive, like this:

```
<%@ Page Trace="true"
    language="vb" Codebehind="News.aspx.vb"
    AutoEventWireup="false" Inherits="FriendsReunion.News" %>
```

   If you prefer a visual approach, you can do this from the Design view. Click anywhere on the form (but not over a control!) so that the Properties browser shows the properties of the page. Then find the `Trace` property and set it to `True`.

2. Set this form as the start page, press Ctrl+F5 (the shortcut for the Debug ➤ Start Without Debugging menu option) and log in to Friends Reunion. After that, you will be redirected to `News.aspx`. Notice that the tracing information has been appended after the regular output of the page, as shown in Figure 11-6.

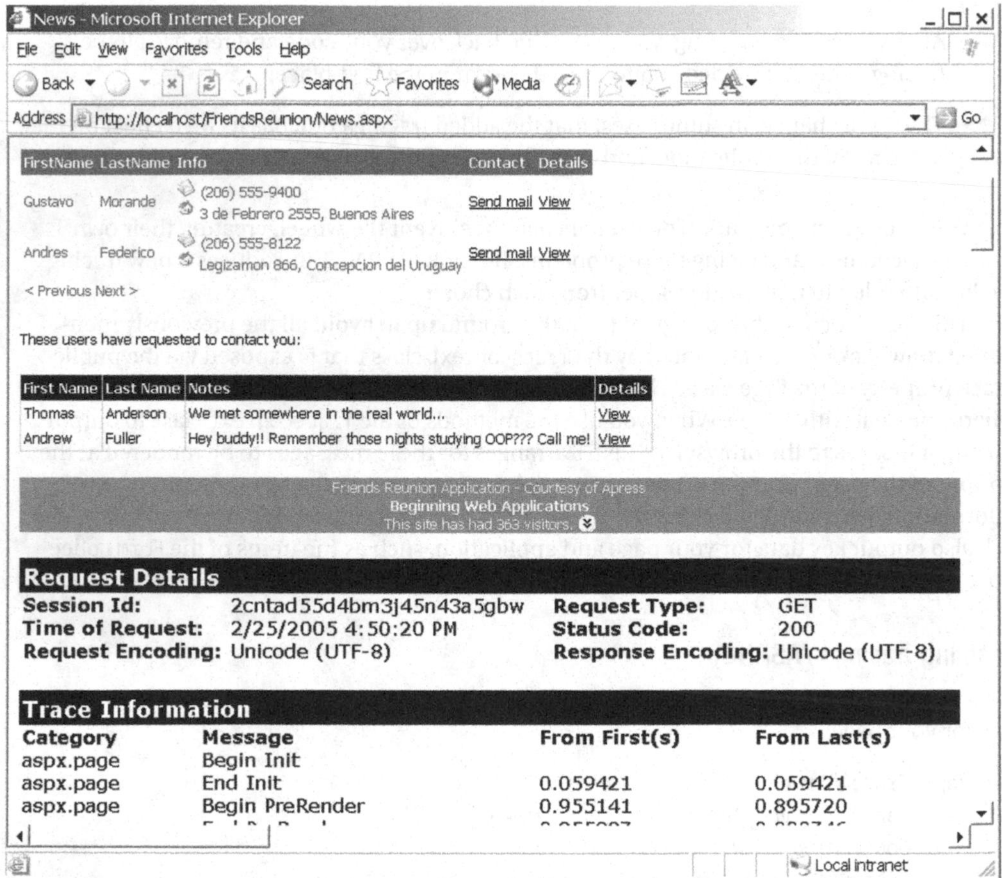

Figure 11-6. *The News page after enabling tracing*

3. Scroll down through the tracing information. You'll see that it's divided into several different sections.

How It Works

As part of its normal processing, the `Page` class checks to see if tracing is enabled for the page before and after performing any major task (loading viewstate, processing events, rendering its content, and so on). If tracing *is* enabled, the `Page` class will output corresponding tracing messages by using the `TraceContext` class's `Write` method.

The trace is broken down into ten sections:

- **Request Details:** Summary information with the details of the request just made, including the following fields:
    - Session ID is the session ID for the specified request.
    - Request Type is the HTTP method used (`POST` or `GET`).
    - Time of Request is the date and time the request was made.
    - Status Code is the status code of the response (see `http://www.w3c.org`, RFC 2616, Section 6.1.1, for a list of possible status codes).
    - Request Encoding and Response Encoding are the character encoding for the request and response, respectively (for example, UTF-8, ASCII, and so on).
- **Trace Information:** Includes all the trace messages that are generated automatically by ASP.NET and your application. The following information will be shown for each message:
    - Category is the category to which the message belongs.
    - Message is the text of the message itself.
    - From First (s) is the time (in seconds) since the first trace message was generated.
    - From Last (s) is the time (in seconds) since the most recent previous trace message was generated.
- **Control Tree:** Lists all the controls available in the page in an indented, hierarchical fashion, which allows you to differentiate between parent and child controls. This is very useful, for example, when inserting controls dynamically to check that they are being added to the correct parent. Also, it shows the render size and viewstate size of each control, so you can check that neither of these values goes too high.
- **Session State:** Lists the name, type, and value of all objects stored in the current `Session` collection. This will show up only if there are actual values stored in it.
- **Application State:** Lists the name, type, and value of all objects stored in the `Application` collection. This will also show up only if there are values in it.
- **Cookies Collection:** Lists the name and value of each cookie in the request and response.

- **Headers Collection:** Lists the names and values of the HTTP headers that the client sent to the server.
- **Form Collection:** Displays the names and values of all form elements, along with the built-in `__VIEWSTATE` form field. These values should provide a brief representation of the state of each one of the controls contained in the page. Note that data for this section will not be displayed if your page doesn't contain a form (obviously!) or if it is your first request for the page; it will be displayed only on postbacks.
- **Querystring Collection:** Displays values passed to the page after the ? character. This comes in handy when you need to check whether the page is really receiving a specific parameter via the query string and to find out what value has been set. This will contain information only if parameters are specified.
- **Server Variables:** Provides a dump of all predetermined server environment variables.

In the next example, you'll see how to add your own custom trace messages to the trace information output.

Adding Custom Tracing Statements

The information you get by default by enabling tracing in a page is very useful, and in many cases, it provides enough information to allow you to isolate and solve a particular problem. However, tracing is more powerful than that.

You can add your own tracing statements that tell the application to output specific information that you need about the state of the application at any particular point. The `TraceContext` class provides two methods that provide this capability: the `Write()` and `Warn()` methods. The only difference between these two methods is that the `Warn()` method marks its messages as warnings. Any message you output using this method will be rendered in red type. This is useful when you're scanning the trace information, because it makes it easy to differentiate between regular trace messages and warning messages.

Both the `Write()` and `Warn()` methods write a message to the *trace log* (the log of all trace information generated by the application). Each of these methods has three overloads. In the example that follows, we'll use the overload that takes two string arguments. The first argument corresponds to the *category* of the message you want to output, and the second argument is the *text* of the message itself. The ability to specify a category is useful because you can define your own categories and have the trace output sorted alphabetically by category.

Try It Out: Add Custom Trace Statements In order to exploit the capabilities of the ASP.NET tracing feature, you'll output some trace messages of your own during the process where you insert new users. This will allow you to examine the path the code takes and to check that everything is running as expected.

1. Using VS .NET, open the `NewUser.aspx` file (in the `Secure` folder). Add a `Trace` attribute to the `Page` directive as you did in the previous example:

```
<%@ Page Trace="true"
         language="vb" Codebehind="NewUser.aspx.vb"
         AutoEventWireup="false"
         Inherits="FriendsReunion.Secure.NewUser" %>
```

2. Switch to the Code view (NewUser.aspx.vb) and make the following changes to the btnAccept_Click() method:

```
Private Sub btnAccept_Click(ByVal sender As System.Object, _
  ByVal e As System.EventArgs) Handles btnAccept.Click
  If Page.IsValid Then
    Trace.Write("FriendsReunion", "Page data was validated ok")
  ...etc...
  End If
End Sub
```

3. Modify the InsertUser() method as follows:

```
Private Sub InsertUser()
  Trace.Write("FriendsReunion", _
    "We're entering the InsertUser() method")

  ' Build SQL statement
  ...etc...

  ' Connect and execute the query
  Dim con As New SqlConnection( _
   "data source=.;initial catalog=FriendsData;" + _
   "user id=apress;pwd=apress")
  Dim cmd As New SqlCommand(sql, con)
  con.Open()

  Trace.Write("FriendsReunion", _
    "Connection string in use: " + con.ConnectionString)

  Dim doredirect As Boolean = True

  Try
    cmd.ExecuteNonQuery()
  Catch ex As SqlException
    Trace.Warn("FriendsReunion", _
      "An exception was thrown: " + ex.Message)
    doredirect = False
    lblMessage.Visible = True
    lblMessage.Text = _
     "Insert couldn't be performed. User name may be already taken."
  Finally
    ' Ensure connection is closed always
    con.Close()
  End Try

  'If (doredirect) Then Response.Redirect("Login.aspx")
  Trace.Write("FriendsReunion", _
    "We're leaving the InsertUser() method")

End Sub
```

As well as adding four trace statements here, you've done two other things. First, you've used the ex variable mapped to the `SqlException` trapped in the `Catch` block on the `Trace.Warn()` method, where you report its `Message` property to the trace log. Second, you have commented out the `Response.Redirect()` call. This prevents the page from being redirected to `Login.aspx` and gives you a chance to look at the trace information for the `NewUser.aspx` page.

Note If your code still uses the hard-coded connection string, recall that back in Chapter 5, in the "Try It Out: Configure a Dynamic Connection String" section, you learned how to use the `ConfigurationSettings` class from the `System.Configuration` namespace, and we suggested changing all hard-coded connection strings with it. If you change that now, make sure there's an `Imports` statement for this namespace at the top of the `NewUser.aspx.vb` file: `Imports System.Configuration`.

---

4. Press Ctrl+F5 to start the application without debugging. Click the Register link. Then fill in the registration form and click the Accept button. After the page postback, scroll down a bit and look at the Trace Information section, which should look something like Figure 11-7.

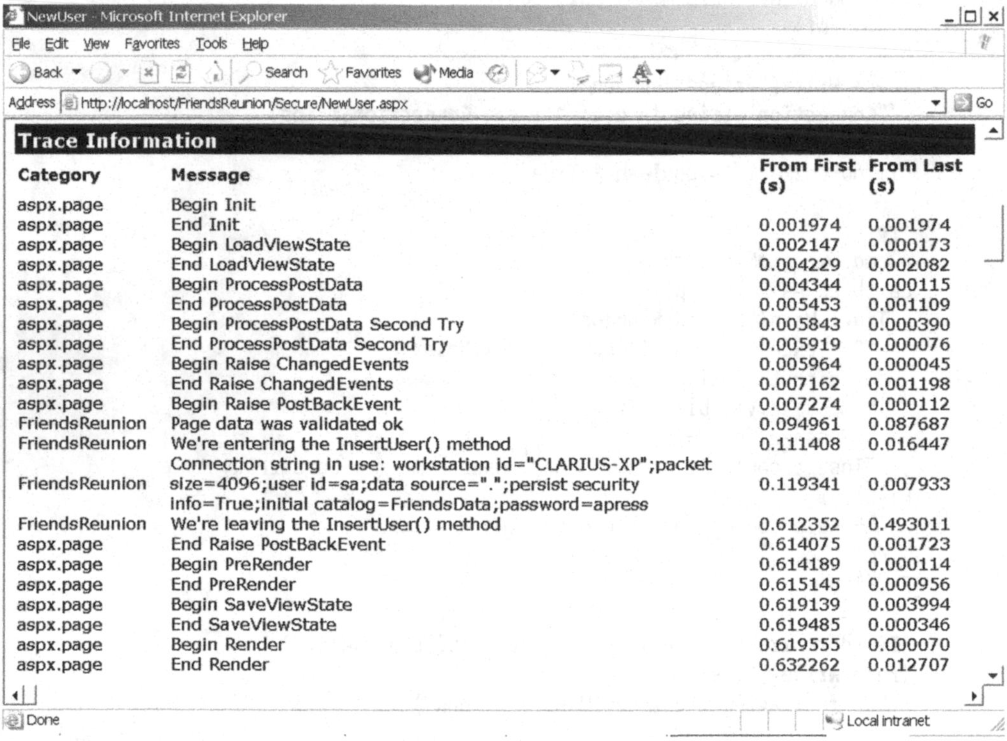

NewUser - Microsoft Internet Explorer

File Edit View Favorites Tools Help

Back Search Favorites Media

Address http://localhost/FriendsReunion/Secure/NewUser.aspx Go

Trace Information

Category	Message	From First (s)	From Last (s)
aspx.page	Begin Init		
aspx.page	End Init	0.001974	0.001974
aspx.page	Begin LoadViewState	0.002147	0.000173
aspx.page	End LoadViewState	0.004229	0.002082
aspx.page	Begin ProcessPostData	0.004344	0.000115
aspx.page	End ProcessPostData	0.005453	0.001109
aspx.page	Begin ProcessPostData Second Try	0.005843	0.000390
aspx.page	End ProcessPostData Second Try	0.005919	0.000076
aspx.page	Begin Raise ChangedEvents	0.005964	0.000045
aspx.page	End Raise ChangedEvents	0.007162	0.001198
aspx.page	Begin Raise PostBackEvent	0.007274	0.000112
FriendsReunion	Page data was validated ok	0.094961	0.087687
FriendsReunion	We're entering the InsertUser() method	0.111408	0.016447
FriendsReunion	Connection string in use: workstation id="CLARIUS-XP";packet size=4096;user id=sa;data source=".";persist security info=True;initial catalog=FriendsData;password=apress	0.119341	0.007933
FriendsReunion	We're leaving the InsertUser() method	0.612352	0.493011
aspx.page	End Raise PostBackEvent	0.614075	0.001723
aspx.page	Begin PreRender	0.614189	0.000114
aspx.page	End PreRender	0.615145	0.000956
aspx.page	Begin SaveViewState	0.619139	0.003994
aspx.page	End SaveViewState	0.619485	0.000346
aspx.page	Begin Render	0.619555	0.000070
aspx.page	End Render	0.632262	0.012707

Done Local intranet

Figure 11-7. *Custom trace statements for the News page*

5. Fill in the registration form again, this time using the same user name that you provided before. Click the Accept button and look at the Trace Information again. You should see something like Figure 11-8.

NewUser - Microsoft Internet Explorer

File Edit View Favorites Tools Help

Address http://localhost/FriendsReunion/Secure/NewUser.aspx

Trace Information

Category	Message	From First (s)	From Last (s)
aspx.page	Begin Init		
aspx.page	End Init	0.001005	0.001005
aspx.page	Begin LoadViewState	0.001108	0.000103
aspx.page	End LoadViewState	0.004960	0.003852
aspx.page	Begin ProcessPostData	0.005075	0.000115
aspx.page	End ProcessPostData	0.005316	0.000241
aspx.page	Begin ProcessPostData Second Try	0.005818	0.000502
aspx.page	End ProcessPostData Second Try	0.005916	0.000098
aspx.page	Begin Raise ChangedEvents	0.005960	0.000044
aspx.page	End Raise ChangedEvents	0.006007	0.000047
aspx.page	Begin Raise PostBackEvent	0.006048	0.000041
FriendsReunion	Page data was validated ok	0.007055	0.001007
FriendsReunion	We're entering the InsertUser() method	0.007156	0.000101
FriendsReunion	Connection string in use: workstation id="CLARIUS-XP";packet size=4096;user id=sa;data source=".";persist security info=True;initial catalog=FriendsData;password=apress	0.008047	0.000891
FriendsReunion	An exception was thrown: Violation of UNIQUE KEY constraint 'IX_Login'. Cannot insert duplicate key in object 'User'. The statement has been terminated.	0.355825	0.347778
FriendsReunion	We're leaving the InsertUser() method	0.356241	0.000416
aspx.page	End Raise PostBackEvent	0.356335	0.000094
aspx.page	Begin PreRender	0.356385	0.000050
aspx.page	End PreRender	0.357078	0.000693
aspx.page	Begin SaveViewState	0.384656	0.027578

Done · Local intranet

Figure 11-8. *The Trace Information section with a custom trace warning statement*

This time, there is one extra trace message in the FriendsReunion category. The extra one is actually displayed in red, because it's a warning (generated by the `Warn()` method), which says that the user is trying to take a user name that already exists in the database.

How It Works

The new custom tracing code outputs messages to the Trace Information section in the same way as the `Page` class does. In this simple example, you've used the trace to check the execution path that the application takes. You expect the data to be validated first and the `InsertUser()` method to run next, and you expect to see the four regular trace messages that you've placed in that method.

You don't expect any of those messages to be missing from the trace output, and you don't expect any of the messages to appear more than once. If they did, you could deduce that there is a problem with the application's flow, and then you would take further steps to pinpoint the exact problem and fix it.

You used the Trace.Warn() method in the Catch block, because it helps you to see when the execution path leads to an exception being thrown. Finally, the From First (s) and From Last (s) columns tell you how much time has passed since the first message in the trace and the current one, and the same interval relative to the previous message.

Enabling and Disabling Tracing at the Application Level

You've seen how to enable tracing for a particular page. But if you're developing an application that contains a lot of pages, it is potentially more convenient to enable tracing across the whole application in one step.

You can control this in the application's Web.config file, through the <trace> element, which belongs under the <system.web> element. If there is no <trace> element, you need to add one like the one shown here; if there's one there already, just change its enabled attribute to true:

```
<configuration>
  ...
  <system.web>
    <trace enabled="true" requestLimit="10" pageOutput="true"
           traceMode="SortByTime" localOnly="true" />
    ...
  </system.web>
  ...
</configuration>
```

With this set, all your pages will contain trace information. It's then possible to *disable* tracing on an individual page, if you wish, by setting Trace="false" in the Page directive of that page.

As you can see, the <trace> element in Web.config has quite a number of other attributes, and it's worth a quick look to see how they work:

- The enabled attribute allows you to enable or disable tracing for the application (its default is false).
- The requestLimit attribute is the maximum number of trace requests to be stored on the server (the default is 10). You'll see this in action in the next example, when you use the trace viewer.
- The pageOutput attribute allows you to force the tracing information to be appended to the application's pages (in the way you've seen in Figures 11-6, 11-7, and 11-8). This defaults to false.
- The traceMode attribute sets the mode used to display trace information. It can be SortByTime, which sorts them in the order they were processed, or SortByCategory, which sorts them by category. The default is SortByTime.
- The localOnly attribute allows you to specify where the tracing information is available. If it's set to true (the default), tracing information will be available only on the host server. For viewing trace information from a browser running on a PC *other* than the host machine, set this to false.

Caution Be sure to specify the exact casing shown here when setting the `<trace>` element attributes in the `Web.config` file, because attributes are case-sensitive. If you specify any with the wrong case, you will get an error.

Using the Trace Viewer

You have seen how to enable tracing for a single page or an entire application and how to add your own tracing statements. Although all that may seem to be sufficient ASP.NET tracing capability, one more important feature needs to be covered: `trace.axd`, or the *trace viewer*.

The server stores the tracing information for a specified number of the most recently requested pages. (By default, this number is 10, but you can use the `requestLimit` attribute of the `<trace>` element in `Web.config` to change this value, as described in the previous section.) You can use the trace viewer to access all that trace information. This means that you can step through a number of different pages in the course of testing the application, and then review the trace for all those pages at your leisure when you're finished.

Try It Out: Use the Trace Viewer In this example, you'll use the trace viewer to access the tracing information recorded by the server for the last ten pages requested. You'll see summary and detailed views of the tracing information—all with just a browser and a few clicks!

1. Enable tracing at the application level. Do this by locating the `<trace>` element in the `<system.web>` section of the `Web.config` file and changing its `enabled` attribute to `true` (as described in the previous section).

2. Point your browser to Friends Reunion, log in, and start surfing to different pages (News, Assign Places, Search, and so on).

3. Browse to the `trace.axd` file in the application directory of Friends Reunion (`http://localhost/FriendsReunion/trace.axd`). Your output should look like Figure 11-9.

   As you can see, `trace.axd` presents a summary list of the last ten pages for which you have tracing information recorded. For each entry, you have a link named View Details, which will take you to a details page. Note that in the example in Figure 11-9, we only navigated through seven pages, so the Remaining label at the right of the table heading indicates we have three more pages we could view.

4. Click any of the View Details links, and you will see the details page for that particular page. Figure 11-10 shows the details page for `Default.aspx`.

   Note that you're just getting the tracing information for a particular page; you're not getting regular content. That's because you're not actually requesting the pages now. You're just looking at the trace information that was generated at the time the page was requested.

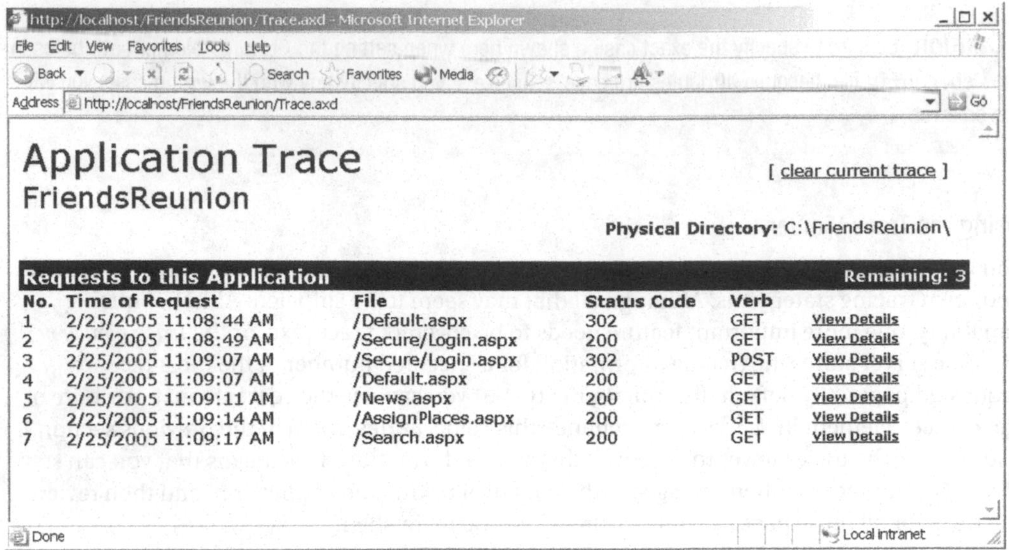

Figure 11-9. *Viewing trace information in the trace viewer*

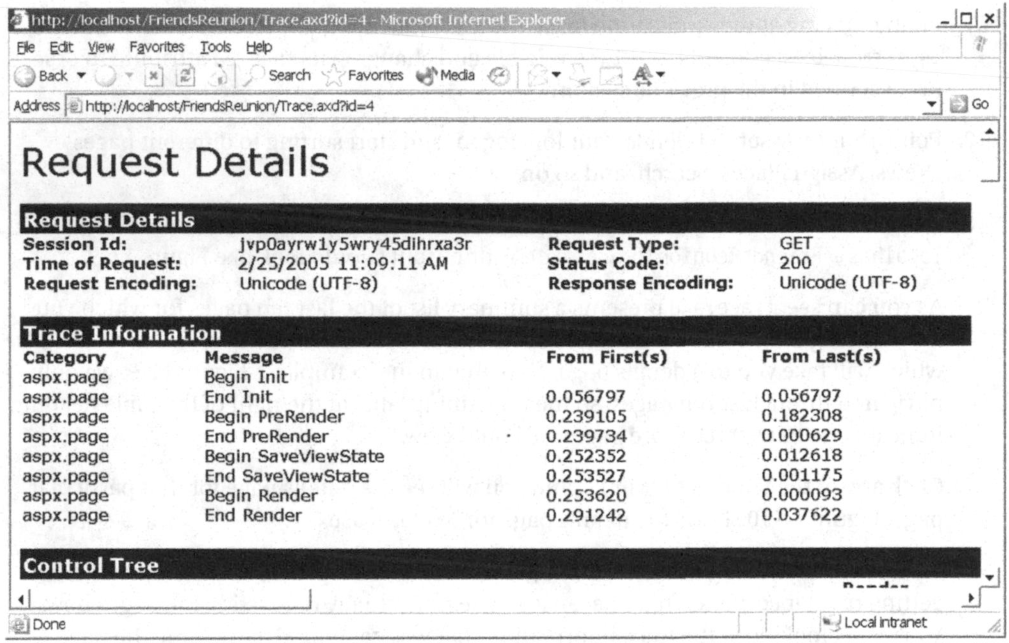

Figure 11-10. *Viewing details of the Default.aspx page tracing information*

How It Works

When tracing is enabled at the application level, the server records the tracing information for pages most recently visited. The trace viewer makes this trace information available after the event.

This trace recording is totally transparent and doesn't require any special intervention by the user; it just happens as users request pages. When you want to take a look at the tracing information captured by the server, just open a browser and navigate to `trace.axd`. In fact, you can actually access the trace viewer by using any URL that begins with the application directory and ends with the filename `trace.axd`, so something as random as `http://localhost/FriendsReunion/f1/f2/trace.axd` will also do the job.

Note that there's no such file as `trace.axd` in your application. What happens here is that the request is intercepted by a specialized HTTP Handler that responds by showing the recorded tracing information, instead of going to disk to look for the specified file name.

Note An *HTTP Handler* is a piece of code that gets a chance to work with HTTP requests at a basic level. To learn more about the topic, refer to *Pro ASP.NET 1.1 in VB .NET*, by Steven Livingstone and John Timney (Apress; ISBN: 1-59059-352-9) or the MSDN article at `http://msdn.microsoft.com/msdnmag/issues/02/09/HTTPPipelines/`.

Tracing and Assertions in .NET

In a chapter about debugging, we really should take a look at some of the other features (aside from the ASP.NET-specific ones) in the .NET Framework that can help you to debug your applications. In this section, we'll describe how you can benefit by using *assertions* in your code.

An assertion is a statement in the programming code that enables you to test your assumptions about your application. Each assertion contains a Boolean expression that you believe to be true when the assertion executes:

- If the expression evaluates to `true`, your assumption about the behavior of your application is confirmed, increasing your confidence that the application is free from errors.
- If the expression evaluates to `false`, an error will be thrown, and you will need to check what went wrong and made your assumption fail.

For example, if you write a method that calculates the age of a person, you might assert that the result is greater than 0 and less than 120.

If you include additional code to use assertions, will that added code have an impact on the performance and code size of your application? No, because all assertion code is compiled only when you create a debug build; for release builds, it is automatically discarded. This means you can use assertions to write robust code, without affecting the performance and code size of your final application.

Using Assertions in .NET Code

The .NET Framework provides an entire namespace, called `System.Diagnostics`, which is dedicated to diagnosing applications. The tracing and assertion mechanisms are implemented by the `Trace` and `Debug` classes, respectively. The two classes are almost identical, providing the same properties, methods, and method overloads. The only difference is that any code that uses the `Debug` class is compiled only for debug builds, while code written using the `Trace` class is compiled for both debug *and* release builds.

Tip The `System.Diagnostics` namespace contains very powerful classes that will allow you to manage system processes, performance counters, and event logs. We recommend that you browse the documentation for these classes at `http://msdn.microsoft.com/library`. They'll come in handy very often.

The `Trace` class works in a similar way to the `TraceContext` class you used in the previous example. One significant difference is that, by default, the `Trace` class will send its output to the Output window, instead of directing it to the rendered page. Also, an important (and slightly inconvenient) difference between the `Trace.Write()` and `Debug.Write()` methods and the `TraceContext.Write()` method is that the order of arguments is inverted! The former methods expect the message text to be provided before the category name, while the latter expects the category to come first.

Where could we use assertions in Friends Reunion? Let's take a look at the first lines for the `Render()` method of the `FriendsBase.vb` file:

```
Protected Overrides Sub Render(ByVal writer As System.Web.UI.HtmlTextWriter)
  ...
  ' Get a reference to the form control
  Dim form As HtmlForm = CType(Page.Controls(1), HtmlForm)
```

Note that this code grabs a reference to the control at index `(1)` in the `Page.Controls` collection and assigns it to the `form` variable, but it does so without checking that it really is a reference to the type of control we need there. The rest of the code in that method depends on the assumption that the variable `form` really *does* refer to a control of type `HtmlForm`.

How could the form fail to be there? It should be there for a page newly created in VS .NET, but a developer might delete it in the course of editing the `.aspx` page (perhaps because the developer didn't need an HtmlForm control at all) or include some other controls before it (which would cause the desired HtmlForm control to be at an index higher than 1 in the collection).

One way to solve this would be to modify the code so it doesn't depend on the HtmlForm control being positioned at an exact index. However, if we do that, it could affect the rest of our logic. So, we'll preserve the current code and instead use an assertion to ensure that the expression `Page.Controls(1)` really does refer to a control of type `HtmlForm`.

Try It Out: Add an Assertion You'll use an assertion in the Friends Reunion application to ensure you always have an `HtmlForm` control exactly at index `(1)` in the `Page.Controls` collection, so the rest of the logic will work as expected. You will add a new page to display legal information about the use of the application.

1. Using VS .NET, add a new web form and name it `LegalStuff.aspx`. Then edit its code-behind file to make it inherit from the custom `FriendsBase` class instead of `System.Web.UI.Page`:

```
Public Class LegalStuff
  Inherits FriendsBase
```

2. Now you need to alter the default HTML created by VS .NET for your page. Open `LegalStuff.aspx` in the HTML view and delete the entire `<form>` element (you won't need it in this page). Then add the following code:

```
<html>
  <head>
    <title>LegalStuff</title>
    <link href="Style/iestyle.css" type="text/css" rel="stylesheet">
  </head>
  <body ms_positioning="FlowLayout">
    <asp:label runat="server" id="Label1">Legal Stuff</asp:label>
    <br/><br/>
    <asp:label runat="server" id="Label2">
      If you notice this notice you will notice
      that the notice is not worth noticing.
    </asp:label>
  </body>
</html>
```

3. Open `FriendsBase.vb` and add the following `Imports` statement:

```
Imports System.Diagnostics
```

4. Still in `FriendsBase.vb`, edit the `Render()` method of the `FriendsBase` class to add the assertion code:

```
Protected Overrides Sub Render(ByVal writer As System.Web.UI.HtmlTextWriter)
  ' Remove the controls from their current place in the hierarchy
  Page.Controls.Remove(_header)
  Page.Controls.Remove(_subheader)
  Page.Controls.Remove(_footer)

  Debug.Assert( _
     TypeOf Page.Controls(1) Is HtmlForm, _
     "Form control not found", _
     "Any FriendsReunion page requires that a form tag be " + _
     "the first child of the page body.")

  ' Get a reference to the form control
  Dim form As HtmlForm = CType(Page.Controls(1), HtmlForm)
  ...
```

5. Check the solution configuration drop-down list in the toolbar (or select Project ➤ Properties) to make sure that your project's configuration is set to Debug.

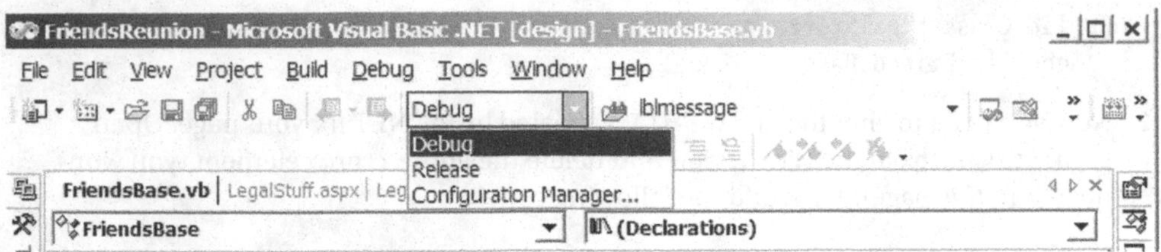

6. Set `LegalStuff.aspx` as the start page and press F5 to start the application in the debugger. A new instance of Internet Explorer will open, showing the Login page for Friends Reunion. Log in to the application, and you will be automatically redirected to the `LegalStuff.aspx` page. However, the page will fail, and you'll see an unpleasant error message, as shown in Figure 11-11.

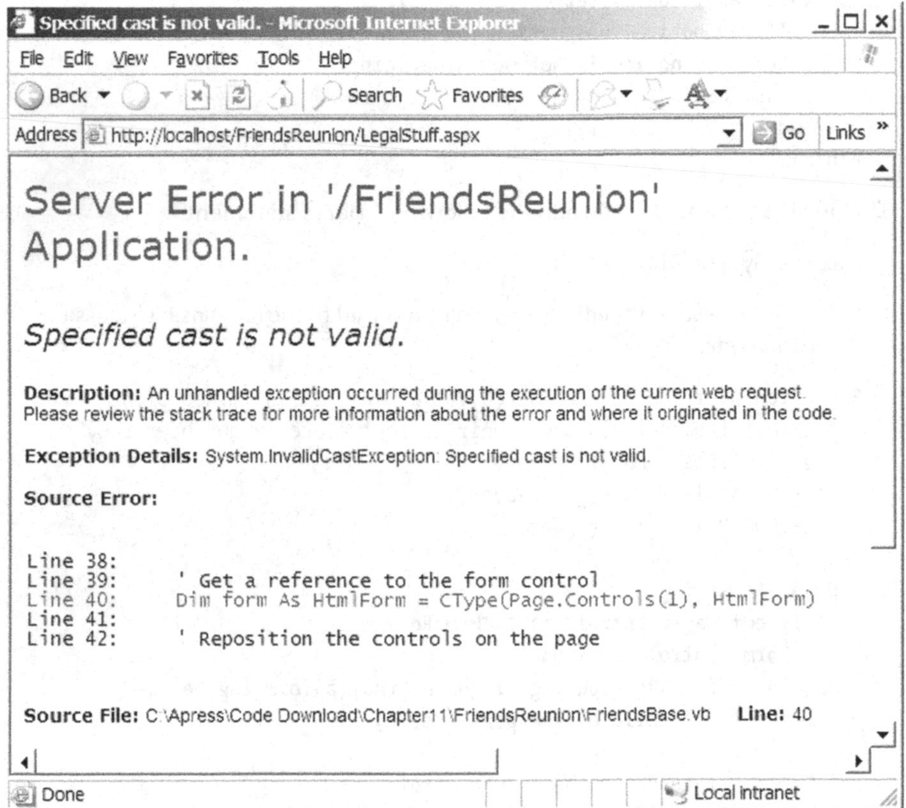

Figure 11-11. *The Legal Stuff page fails.*

7. In VS .NET, look at the Output window (press Ctrl+Alt+O to open it, if necessary). It should look like Figure 11-12.

```
Output
Debug
---- DEBUG ASSERTION FAILED ----
---- Assert Short Message ----
Form control not found
---- Assert Long Message ----
Any FriendsReunion page requires that a form tag be the first child of the page body.

    at FriendsBase.Render(HtmlTextWriter writer)  C:\Apress\Code Download\Chapter11\FriendsReunion\FriendsBase.vb(33)
    at Control.RenderControl(HtmlTextWriter writer)
    at Page.ProcessRequestMain()
    at Page.ProcessRequest()
    at Page.ProcessRequest(HttpContext context)
    at CallHandlerExecutionStep.System.Web.HttpApplication+IExecutionStep.Execute()
    at HttpApplication.ExecuteStep(IExecutionStep step, Boolean& completedSynchronously)
    at HttpApplication.ResumeSteps(Exception error)
    at HttpApplication.System.Web.IHttpAsyncHandler.BeginProcessRequest(HttpContext context, AsyncCallback cb, Object
    at HttpRuntime.ProcessRequestInternal(HttpWorkerRequest wr)
    at HttpRuntime.ProcessRequest(HttpWorkerRequest wr)
    at ISAPIRuntime.ProcessRequest(IntPtr ecb, Int32 iWRType)
```

Figure 11-12. *The Output window with debug information about the assertion*

How It Works

Using the `Debug.Assert()` method, you have asserted that the control at index `[1]` of the `Page.Controls` collection should always be of type `HtmlForm`:

```
Debug.Assert(
   TypeOf Page.Controls(1) Is HtmlForm, _
   "Form control not found", _
   "Any FriendsReunion page requires that a form tag be " + _
   "the first child of the page body.")
```

In the first argument, you specify the Boolean condition you expect to evaluate to `True` at runtime if everything is working correctly. The `Is` operator does exactly that by checking the type of the object at the left and comparing it with the one at the right (`HtmlForm`).

This assumption should be `True` in order for the application to continue to run, because subsequent code expects it to be that way. If this assertion is not `True`, you can't guarantee how your application will perform—at best, you might get some strange rendering; at worst, there's the rude possibility of exceptions being thrown and your application terminating abruptly (as in this case).

When you started debugging Friends Reunion and requested the `LegalStuff.aspx` page (which doesn't include a `<form>` element), your assertion code was eventually executed, and the Boolean expression evaluated to `False`. This caused the message text to be output to the debugger's Output window.

The VS .NET Debugger

We've looked at a number of different methods for debugging applications, but we haven't yet looked at any debugging software. Let's round off this section with a look at the VS .NET debugger.

The VS .NET debugger takes many web developers into new territory. It's the first tool that enables you to debug a web application using techniques similar to those you would use when debugging a traditional (Windows) application. In VS .NET, all you need to do in order to start the debugger is press F5.

One of the most tedious problems found with previous versions of the debugger was its inability to detach from a running process without killing it. For a web application, if the debugger kills the process used to run the application, any state information will be lost. Now, thanks to the Common Language Runtime (CLR), the debugger can *detach* from a process without killing it. All you need to do is select Debug ➤ Stop Debugging or click the Stop Debugging button in the Debug toolbar.

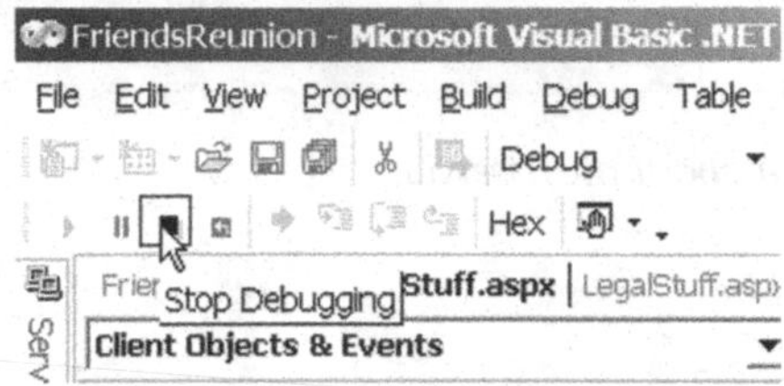

The VS .NET debugger allows you to debug across different languages, as well as to debug multiple processes across machines. Besides these new features, there is more good news: many of the features that have been previously available only when debugging traditional applications can be used now for debugging web applications!

The VS. NET debugger offers several useful windows: Breakpoints, This, Locals, Autos, Watch, and Call Stack. In the following sections, you'll see how these windows help you debug your applications.

Managing Breakpoints

In the VS .NET debugger, you can mark any line of code with a *breakpoint*. When the application runs in the debugger and reaches a line that has a breakpoint, it causes the execution to pause. When the application has paused like this, it is said to be in *break mode*. With the application in break mode, you can perform a number of activities. For example, you can examine the values of variables and object properties, and you can even change these values.

You can also ask the debugger to continue execution one line at a time, stepping through or over subroutines as you desire. Stepping through the code like this is a particularly useful technique, because it allows you to watch the code, observing the values contained in variables' object properties, in "slow motion," and use this analysis to spot semantic coding errors.

To set a breakpoint in the code, click in the gray margin to the left of the line where you want execution to pause, or position the cursor over the line you're interested in and press F9. You'll notice that a red filled circle appears, giving a clear indication that a breakpoint has been set and is enabled at that point, as shown in Figure 11-13.

Global.asax.vb

Global | Application_AuthenticateRequest

```
' If IsAdministrator field is true, add both roles
If CBool(admin) = True Then
  roles = New String() {"User", "Admin"}
Else
  roles = New String() {"User"}
End If
```

Figure 11-13. *A breakpoint set in code*

It's often useful to have a few breakpoints in different places in your code. To allow you to manage your breakpoints, the VS .NET debugger provides the Breakpoints window, shown in Figure 11-14. To view the Breakpoints window, select Debug ➤ Windows ➤ Breakpoints or press Ctrl+Alt+B. Using this window, you can perform the following tasks:

- Add and remove breakpoints.
- Enable and disable breakpoints. (A disabled breakpoint will keep its place in the code, but won't pause execution when execution reaches that line of code.)
- Set the properties of a breakpoint.

Tip To remove all your breakpoints in a single step, press Ctrl+Shift+F9.

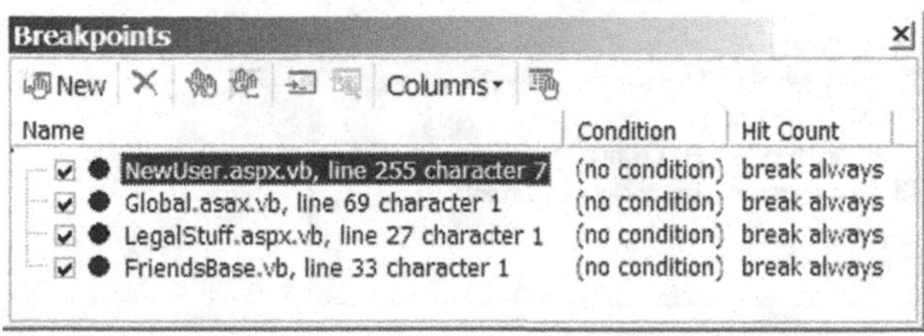

Figure 11-14. *The VS .NET debugger's Breakpoints window*

In the next few examples, you will get some hands-on experience using the VS .NET debugger to set breakpoints in the Friends Reunion application.

Try It Out: Set a Breakpoint in the VS .NET Debugger You'll start by creating a breakpoint that causes the application to pause whenever a request for an already authenticated user is about to be processed.

1. Open the code-behind file for `Global.asax`. Find the following line in the `Application_AuthenticateRequest()` method:

```
con = New SqlConnection( _
  ConfigurationSettings.AppSettings("cnFriends.ConnectionString"))
```

2. Set a breakpoint at this line, by clicking the gray margin to the left of the code (adjacent to that line), or by placing your cursor on the line and pressing F9. You should see the breakpoint indicator, as shown in Figure 11-15.

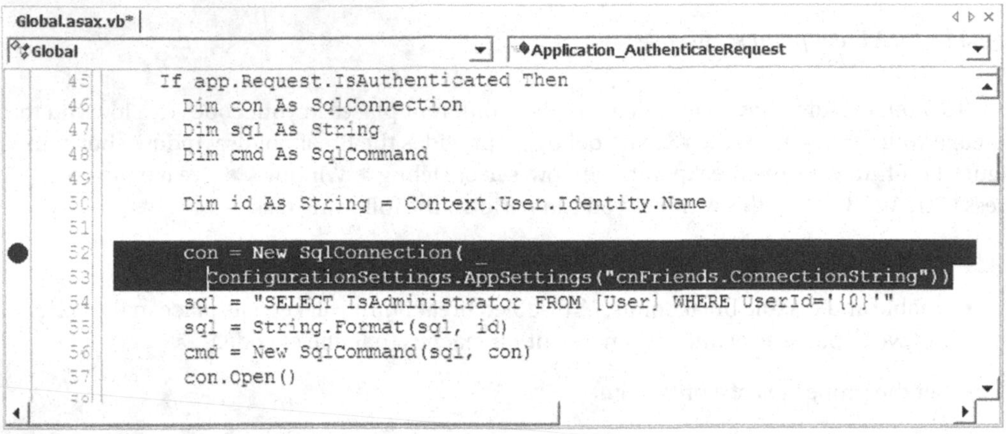

Global.asax.vb*

Global | Application_AuthenticateRequest

```
    If app.Request.IsAuthenticated Then
      Dim con As SqlConnection
      Dim sql As String
      Dim cmd As SqlCommand

      Dim id As String = Context.User.Identity.Name

      con = New SqlConnection( _
        ConfigurationSettings.AppSettings("cnFriends.ConnectionString"))
      sql = "SELECT IsAdministrator FROM [User] WHERE UserId='{0}'"
      sql = String.Format(sql, id)
      cmd = New SqlCommand(sql, con)
      con.Open()
```

Figure 11-15. *Setting a breakpoint in the Application_AuthenticateRequest() method*

3. Press Ctrl+Alt+B to view the details about this breakpoint in the Breakpoints window.

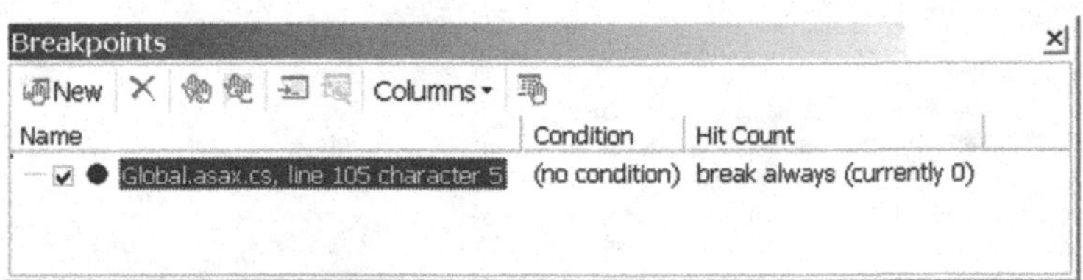

4. In the Solution Explorer, right-click `Default.aspx` and select Set As Start Page.

5. To run the application in the debugger, press F5. A new browser instance will open, pointing to the Friends Reunion Login page. Enter the usual credentials (user name and password apress).

6. Click the Login button to submit the login request to the application. This will cause focus to switch to the VS .NET debugger, and you will see that yellow highlighting is used to show the line with the breakpoint on it.

Don't stop the application yet; we'll continue from here in the next exercise. But first, let's see what has happened so far.

How It Works

Because you chose to run the application in the debugger, execution will pause whenever it reaches any line that has an enabled breakpoint. That's exactly what happens here: when the application receives the login credentials, it begins to process them. As part of that process, the application needs to execute the line on which you placed the breakpoint. When the application reaches that line, it does not execute it; instead, it pauses, as shown in Figure 11-16.

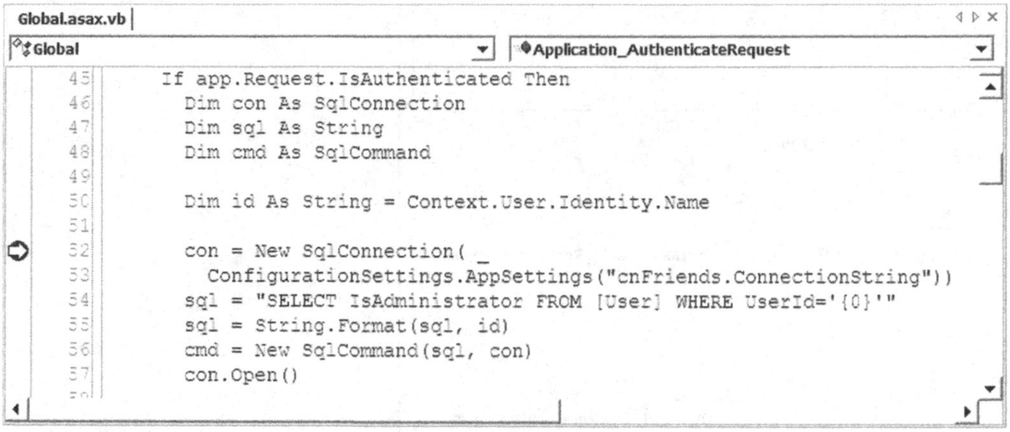

Global.asax.vb

Global | Application_AuthenticateRequest

```
      If app.Request.IsAuthenticated Then
        Dim con As SqlConnection
        Dim sql As String
        Dim cmd As SqlCommand

        Dim id As String = Context.User.Identity.Name

        con = New SqlConnection( _
          ConfigurationSettings.AppSettings("cnFriends.ConnectionString"))
        sql = "SELECT IsAdministrator FROM [User] WHERE UserId='{0}'"
        sql = String.Format(sql, id)
        cmd = New SqlCommand(sql, con)
        con.Open()
```

Figure 11-16. *Execution paused at a breakpoint*

The debugger highlights the progress it has made by using yellow highlighting (in the code) and a yellow arrow (in the gray area to the left). At this point, the application is in break mode, and the debugger is awaiting further instructions.

Note that you can do a lot with a breakpoint by changing its behavior. To view the properties of a breakpoint, select it in the Breakpoints window and click the Properties button in the Breakpoints window, or right-click the line with the breakpoint set and select Breakpoint Properties. You'll see the Breakpoint Properties dialog box, as shown in Figure 11-17. Of particular interest are the Condition and Hit Count buttons at the bottom of this dialog box. Clicking the Condition button allows you to specify a *condition* that will be evaluated when the breakpoint is hit, and whose result will determine whether or not the execution is paused at that breakpoint. For example, you may want the Friends Reunion application to halt only when a user belonging to the Admin group is logged in. Clicking the Hit Count button allows you to specify the number of times a breakpoint must be hit before it pauses the application.

Inspecting Application State

One of the most important features a debugger has to offer is the ability to examine the internals of the application being debugged. The VS .NET debugger includes several windows that show this information (accessible through the Debug ➤ Windows menu):

- **Me window:** Displays the values of the current object being debugged. Figure 11-18 shows an example of the Me window opened at the breakpoint set in the previous exercise.

Breakpoint Properties
Function File Address
Break execution when the program reaches this location in a file.
File: ess\Code Download\Chapter11\FriendsReunion\Global.asax.vb
Line: 52
Character: 7
Condition... (no condition)
Hit Count... break always
Program: [2212] aspnet_wp.exe: /LM/W3SVC/1/Root/FriendsReunion-2·
OK Cancel Help

Figure 11-17. *Viewing a breakpoint's properties*

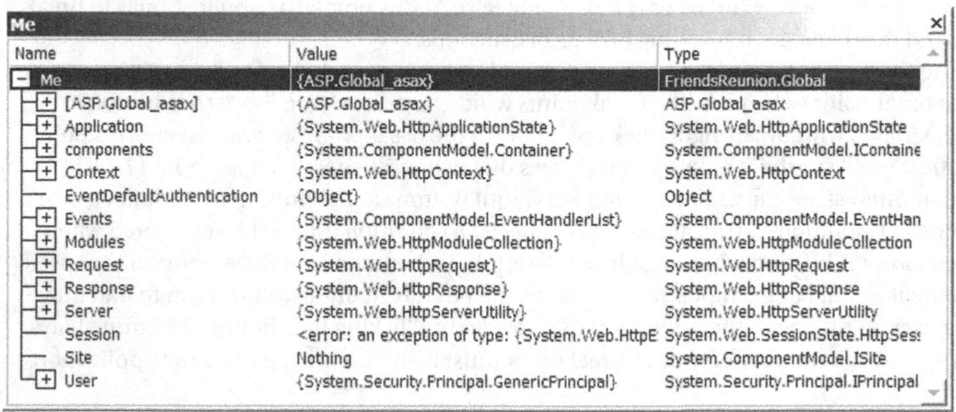

Me

Name	Value	Type
Me	{ASP.Global_asax}	FriendsReunion.Global
[ASP.Global_asax]	{ASP.Global_asax}	ASP.Global_asax
Application	{System.Web.HttpApplicationState}	System.Web.HttpApplicationState
components	{System.ComponentModel.Container}	System.ComponentModel.IContaine
Context	{System.Web.HttpContext}	System.Web.HttpContext
EventDefaultAuthentication	{Object}	Object
Events	{System.ComponentModel.EventHandlerList}	System.ComponentModel.EventHan
Modules	{System.Web.HttpModuleCollection}	System.Web.HttpModuleCollection
Request	{System.Web.HttpRequest}	System.Web.HttpRequest
Response	{System.Web.HttpResponse}	System.Web.HttpResponse
Server	{System.Web.HttpServerUtility}	System.Web.HttpServerUtility
Session	<error: an exception of type: {System.Web.HttpE	System.Web.SessionState.HttpSess
Site	Nothing	System.ComponentModel.ISite
User	{System.Security.Principal.GenericPrincipal}	System.Security.Principal.IPrincipal

Figure 11-18. *The VS .NET debugger's Me window*

- **Locals window:** Shows all variables declared and available in the current execution context, including the `Me` reference. Figure 11-19 shows an example of the Locals window opened at the breakpoint set in the previous exercise.

Locals

Name	Value	Type
+ Me	{ASP.Global_asax}	FriendsReunion.Global
+ app	{ASP.Global_asax}	System.Web.HttpApplication
cmd	Nothing	System.Data.SqlClient.SqlCommand
con	Nothing	System.Data.SqlClient.SqlConnection
+ e	{System.EventArgs}	System.EventArgs
id	"436EA455-BABD-4ca2-9D30-7B4F4608A068"	String
+ sender	{ASP.Global_asax}	Object
sql	Nothing	String

Figure 11-19. *The VS .NET debugger's Locals window*

- **Autos window:** Shows only those values *and* properties actually used in your code. This is a good way to have an overview of the values your code will be working with, and the Autos window, shown in Figure 11-20, is generally more useful than the Locals window.

Autos

Name	Value	Type
+ ConfigurationSettings.AppSettings	{System.Configuration.ReadOnlyNameValueCollection}	System.Collections.S
Context.User.Identity.Name	"436EA455-BABD-4ca2-9D30-7B4F4608A068"	String
cmd	Nothing	System.Data.SqlClien
con	Nothing	System.Data.SqlClien
id	"436EA455-BABD-4ca2-9D30-7B4F4608A068"	String
sql	Nothing	String

Figure 11-20. *The VS .NET debugger's Autos window*

- **Watch window:** Allows you to add any expression you want and watch its value as you debug. This is by far the most flexible window for debugging. The debugger offers *four* Watch windows, named Watch 1, Watch 2, and so on. These are provided to make it easier to debug large applications, so you can group related variables into different windows and focus on the variables you need at a given time. Figure 11-21 shows the Watch 1 window, which is empty when you first open it. The Name column is where you type the expression you want to evaluate. When you do that, its value and output type appear in the Value and Type columns.

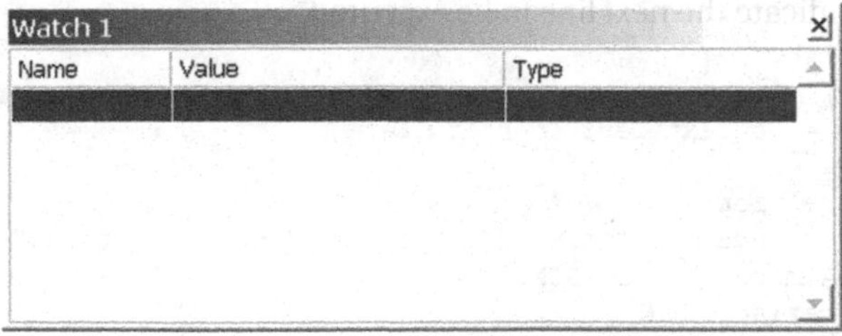

Figure 11-21. *The VS .NET debugger's Watch 1 window*

You can use the Watch window while debugging to check the current value and output type of any variable or expression. More important, the Watch window is the only one that also allows you to *modify* a variable's value. This is a very powerful technique to use when debugging. It allows you to try different values for a variable and watch the execution path to see how the application responds, without repeatedly restarting the application. In this chapter, we'll use the Watch 1 window (and we'll refer to it as just the Watch window).

Note The features of the other debugger windows are similar to those of the Watch window, but they have fixed items. Although we'll focus on the Watch window here, keep in mind that, except for the ability to add your own expressions, the other debugger windows offer mostly the same features.

Try It Out: Step Through an Application with the Watch Window Open Remember how we left the Friends Reunion application in break mode at the end of the previous exercise? Well, we'll pick it up from there, and use the Watch window to check the current values of some variables in the application.

1. Open a Watch window (select Debug ➤ Windows ➤ Watch ➤ Watch 1 or press Ctrl+Alt+W, then 1). You'll use it to watch the connection string for the `SqlConnection` object.

2. Type the name of the variable as well as the property to show in the Name column: `con.ConnectionString`. The Watch window will show an error because the line declaring the variable (where you're paused right now) hasn't been executed yet. Therefore, the variable and its property don't exist yet.

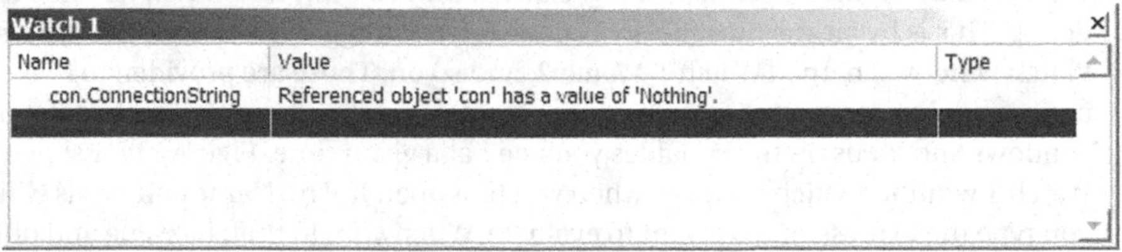

3. Return to the code window. The VS.NET debugger should show yellow highlighting and the yellow arrow to indicate the next line to be executed.

```
    Dim id As String = Context.User.Identity.Name

    con = New SqlConnection( _
      ConfigurationSettings.AppSettings("cnFriends.ConnectionString"))
    sql = "SELECT IsAdministrator FROM [User] WHERE UserId='{0}'"
    sql = String.Format(sql, id)
    cmd = New SqlCommand(sql, con)
    con.Open()
```

4. Let's run the next few lines of code step by step. You can select Debug ➤ Step Over for each step, but it's easier to use the shortcut, F10. So, press F10 once. This causes the highlighted line to be executed. VS .NET now pauses the execution before the next line (and the yellow highlighting and arrow have moved to reflect that).

5. Return to the Watch window. It is updated automatically to reflect the fact that the value of the `con.ConnectionString` property is now valid, as the `SqlConnection` constructor set it with the value passed in.

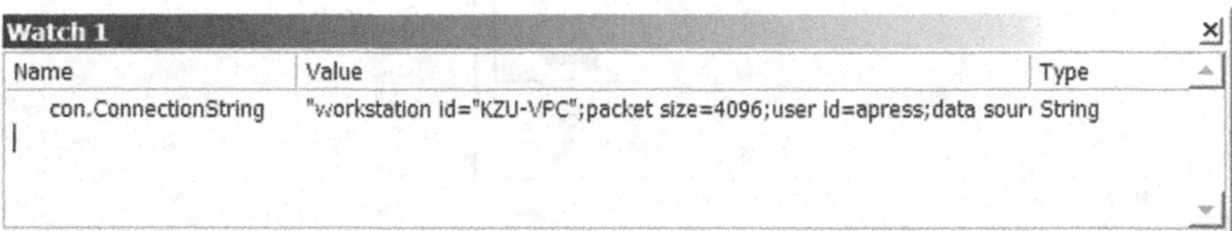

6. Now let's add a watch for the `roles` variable. Find a place where the `roles` variable is used in the code (look within the `Try` block of the method), right-click the variable, and select Add Watch. This will place a new entry in the Watch window. In the Value column, you can see an error indicating that `roles` is not declared. That's okay; in fact, it's what you would expect, because you're watching a variable that hasn't been defined yet! You'll be using it in the next example.

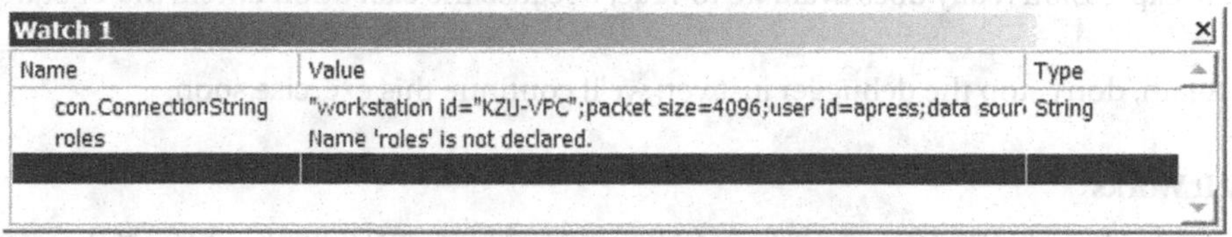

7. Press F10 a few more times, but stop before the following `If` clause is executed.

```
    ' Was it a valid UserID?
  If Not (admin Is Nothing) Then
    Dim ppal As GenericPrincipal
    Dim roles() As String

    ' If IsAdministrator field is true, add both roles
    If CBool(admin) = True Then
      roles = New String() {"User", "Admin"}
    Else
      roles = New String() {"User"}
    End If
```

8. It would be really handy if you could tell whether the expression `CBool(admin) = True` is going to evaluate to `True` or `False` *before* you executed the line. You can do this quickly, using the QuickWatch window. Select the full expression for the condition (*just* the

expression and *not* the brackets that enclose it), right-click it, and select QuickWatch. This will cause the QuickWatch window to open, as shown in Figure 11-22. This window works similarly to the Watch window, showing the expression you've selected and what the expression evaluates to.

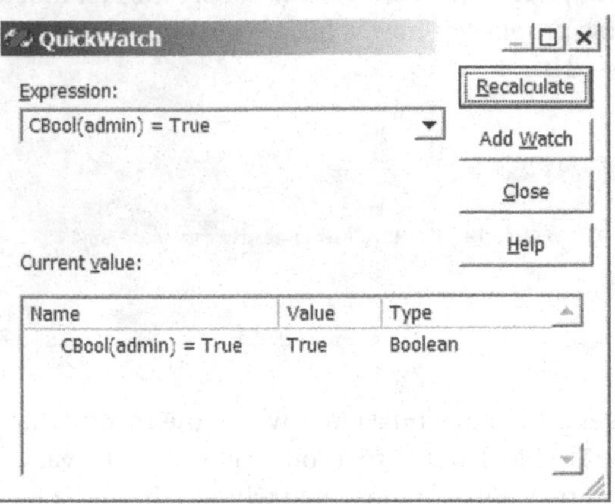

Figure 11-22. *The QuickWatch window*

9. Close the QuickWatch window, and then press F10 one more time. You'll see that the expression really does evaluate to `True`, because the execution enters the `If` statement.

Again, don't stop the debugger just yet; we'll continue this exercise soon.

How It Works

You can see how the Watch window can help you to get information about what's happening inside the application. It can stay open all the time, so you can watch variables and expressions to see how their values change as the execution progresses. A value will be shown in red if it was changed as a result of the last executed step.

The QuickWatch window works in roughly the same way as the Watch window, but it's modal. This means that you can step through the application with the Watch window open, but not with the QuickWatch window open.

The `roles` variable is not a simple object; in fact, it's an array of objects. How does the Watch window cope with things like complex objects and arrays? You'll find out in the next example, in which you'll also see how to use the Watch window to *change* the value of a variable during the debugging process.

Try It Out: Change a Variable Value in the Watch Window You left the Friends Reunion application in break mode at the end of the previous example, so you'll pick it up from there again and do some more tasks with the Watch window.

1. Find the following line in the `Application_AuthenticateRequest()` method, a few lines down from the `If` block discussed in the previous example:

```
ppal = New GenericPrincipal(Context.User.Identity, roles)
```

2. Right-click this line and select Run to Cursor. This will cause the application to execute a few steps further, as far as this line.

3. Check the value of `roles` in the Watch window. You have just stepped over the line that assigns the `roles` variable, so you should now be able to see that `roles` is of type `String()` (an array of strings) with two strings. There's a + icon at the left of the variable name, which indicates that the type being watched is not a simple type. You can watch the values contained within `roles` by clicking the + icon.

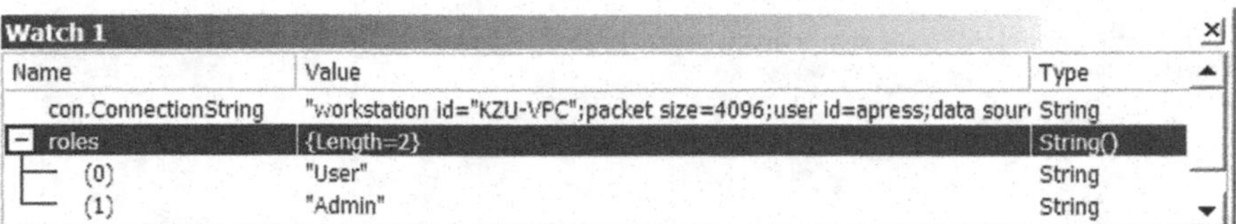

What does this show? Well, you logged in as the user named apress, and this user is an administrator user. Thus, it belongs to both the User and Admin groups, and hence has two roles. These are the two roles shown here.

4. Now let's edit the value of the `roles` variable. In the Watch window, change the value of `roles(1)` (the string at index `(1)` in the array) from Admin to Guest (keep the enclosing quotation marks), and then press Enter. Look at the Watch window.

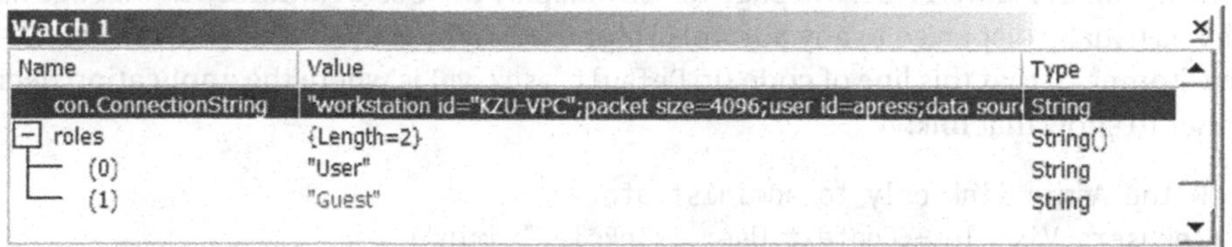

5. Press F5. This will cause the application to continue its execution from the point where you just left off, using any new values you inserted in the Watch window in the previous step. Notice the absence of the link to the Users Administration page, as shown in Figure 11-23.

How It Works

In break mode, the Run to Cursor option in the context menu is a handy way of getting the application to execute as far as a certain point. It's particularly useful when the only other way of reaching the desired point is by pressing F10 repeatedly.

Of particular interest is the way in which values changed in the Watch window can alter the way the application behaves halfway through its execution. You can see evidence of this by looking at the way the application uses the value of `roles(1)`. First, the process in the exercise will log you in as an administrator user. That's because when the application is stepped through the lines of code that oversee the login process, the value of `roles(1)` is `Admin`.

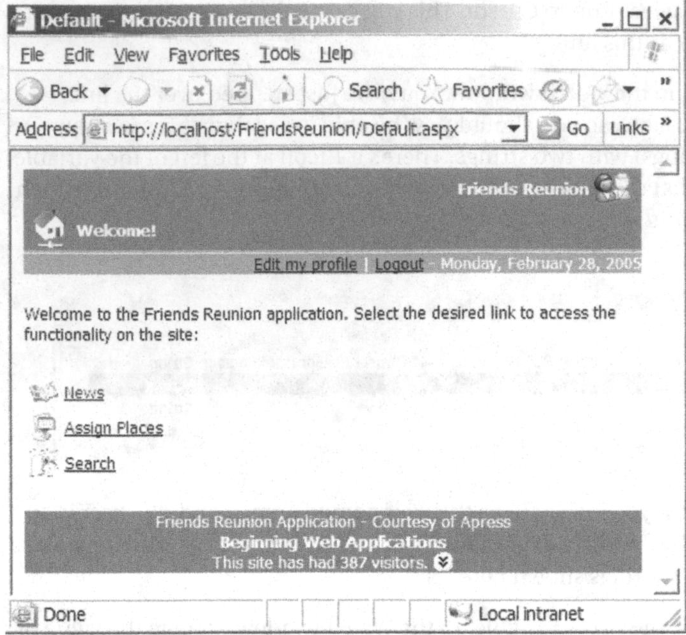

Figure 11-23. *The link to the Users Administration page is gone.*

However, in Figure 11-23, the page doesn't display the Users Administration Page link (which is usually displayed to any administrator user). Why is that? Well, you may recall from Chapter 10 that this line of code (in `Default.aspx.vb`) is where the application decides whether to show that link:

```
' Show the Admin link only to administrators
this.lnkUsers.Visible = Context.User.IsInRole("Admin")
```

However, you changed the value of `roles(1)` (in step 4) *before* the application executed that line. When this line is executed, the expression `User.IsInRole("Admin")` returns `False`, and so the link remains invisible.

Seeing the Call Stack

When you call a method that calls another method, which in turns calls another method, and so on, a *call stack* is created. It's very useful to be able to see the call stack, which is what the VS. NET debugger's Call Stack window shows. This window has information about each method: its name, parameter types, and parameter values. As well as giving you a good idea of the path your code has taken, it also allows you to navigate forward and backward in the stack to debug at any place.

The Call Stack window is available only while the application being debugged is in break mode. To see it, select Debug ➤ Windows ➤ Call Stack or press Ctrl+Alt+C.

Try It Out: Use the Call Stack Window Let's see the Call Stack window in action while debugging Friends Reunion.

1. Open the `NewUser.aspx.vb` file (in the `Secure` folder). Add a breakpoint at the first line of the `InsertUser()` method, by clicking on the gray margin to the left of the code (adjacent to that line), or by placing your cursor on the line and pressing F9.

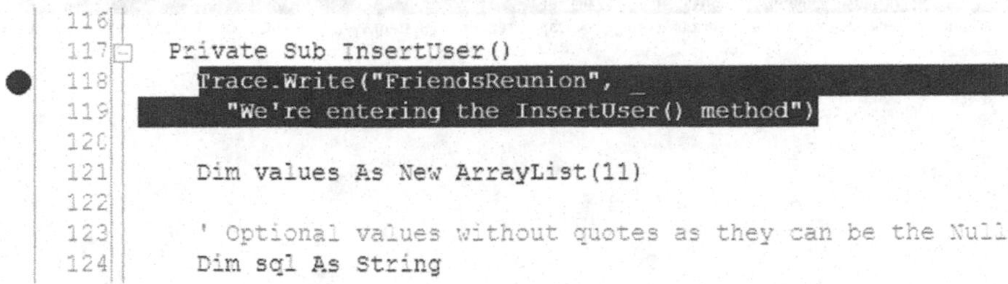

Notice a red dot is added to that line indicating the active breakpoint. There's no need to remove the trace statements you added in previous examples, because they will not affect this example.

2. Set `Secure/NewUser.aspx` as the start page and press F5 to launch the application. A new browser will open with the `Secure/NewUser.aspx` page showing.

3. Fill in the registration form and click the Accept button. The focus should switch to the VS .NET debugger.

4. Open the Call Stack window by pressing Ctrl+Alt+C. Notice that the first line shows that execution is stopped at the `InsertUser()` method, as expected. The previous line in the Call Stack window shows what path the code took to finally get to this method, as well as the method parameters.

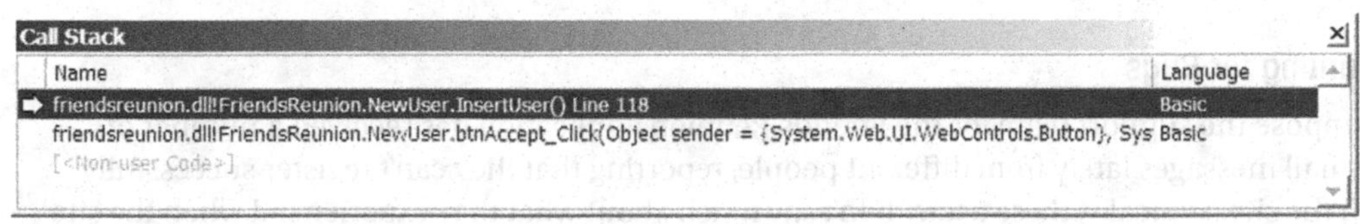

How It Works

The breakpoint that you placed at the start of the `InsertUser()` method causes the application to pause at that point when you're running it using a debugger. After requesting the registration form, filling in the required data, and clicking the Accept button, the application's path of execution eventually leads to the `InsertUser()` method, hits the breakpoint, and pauses.

At this point, the application is in break mode, so you can access the Call Stack window. The Call Stack window reveals how the application got to the `InsertUser()` method: the second line in the Call Stack window shows that the `btnAccept_Click()` method was executed just previously and is the method that called the `InsertUser()` method.

Furthermore, the `btnAccept_Click()` method itself must have been called by some other method. In order dig into that <Non-user Code> line, you can right-click anywhere in the window (except its title) and check the Show Non-user Codc option. This will show you the entire code path, right back to the beginning of it all, as shown in Figure 11-24.

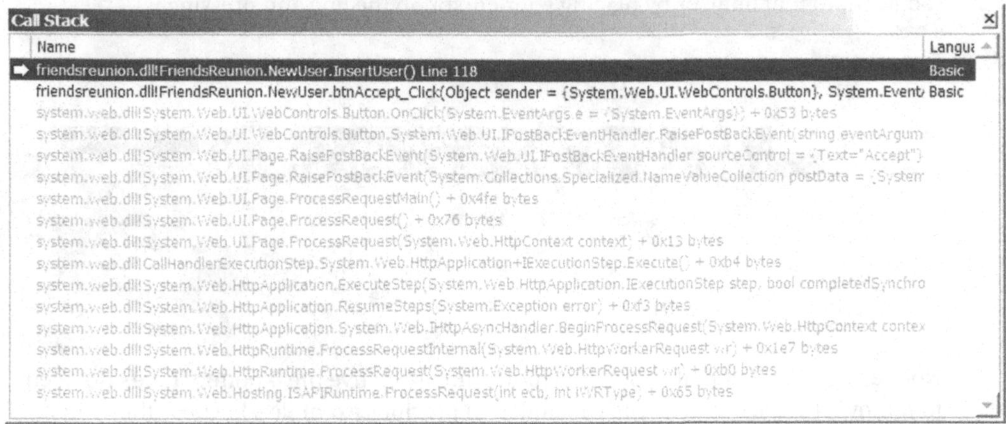

Figure 11-24. *When the Show Non-user Code option is selected, the Call Stack window shows the entire code path.*

As shown in Figure 11-24, you can see that the method responsible for calling `btnAccept_Click()` is a method named `Button.OnClick()`, which is the dispatcher for `Click` events of the Accept button you clicked after filling in the form. You can see this method named on the third line of the Call Stack window, after `btnAccept_Click()`. You can also check that `Button.OnClick()` was called by `RaisePostBackEvent()`, which is the method called by .NET on noticing that this Button control has an event to process.

Armed with these few pieces of debugging functionality, you're in a good position to go hunting for *bugs*, and that's what we'll talk about next.

Hunting for Bugs

Suppose the support team for the Friends Reunion application has received a number of e-mail messages lately from different people, reporting that they can't register successfully on the site. Typically, these users didn't say much about what they experienced when the site failed on them. The only information they provided when contacting support was that they accessed the site, clicked the Register link, filled in the registration form, and clicked the Accept button—and the next thing they saw on the browser was a custom error page.

Using the VS .NET debugger, we can perform a debug session and try to reproduce the error and locate the problem.

Try It Out: Locate Bugs in an Application We need to know what is happening in Friends Reunion to be able to respond to the e-mail enquiries of people who can't register successfully. Our strategy will be to reproduce (as closely as possible) the actions taken by one of the users who couldn't register.

1. Open the NewUser.aspx.vb file (in the Secure folder). Press Ctrl+Shift+F9 to clear all breakpoints at once.

2. In the InsertUser() method, which is the method that controls the addition of new users, set a breakpoint on the line just before the con.Open() method call.

```
Dim con As New SqlConnection( _
 "data source=.;initial catalog=FriendsData;" + _
 "user id=apress;pwd=apress")
Dim cmd As New SqlCommand(sql, con)
con.Open()
```

   This breakpoint will allow you to pause execution of the application just before the database code executes, and hence step through that code and see whether it's causing a problem. This should help you to determine what may be wrong, or at least eliminate some possibilities.

3. Set Default.aspx as the start page. Press F5 to start debugging the application. A new browser instance should open, pointing to the Friends Reunion home page.

4. Click the Register link to navigate to the registration form. Fill out the form, using *exactly* the same data used by one of the users who contacted us:

   - User Name: pjenkins
   - Password: tucker
   - First Name: Peter
   - Last Name: Jenkins
   - Address: 3768 Georgetown's Way
   - Phone Number: 345-449-9481
   - Mobile Number: 459-498-2031
   - E-Mail: peterjenkins@apress.com
   - Birth Date: 1/5/64

5. After completing all the fields, click the Accept button to submit the information. Execution of the application will pause at the line where you placed the breakpoint, and the focus will automatically shift to the VS .NET debugger.

6. Let's start by looking at what the variables are holding, just to check that everything is as you expect. Place the cursor over the values variable, right-click, and select QuickWatch. The QuickWatch window should open, as shown in Figure 11-25. Here, you can check that the data you entered in the registration form is the same data that that application is handling now. This is as expected.

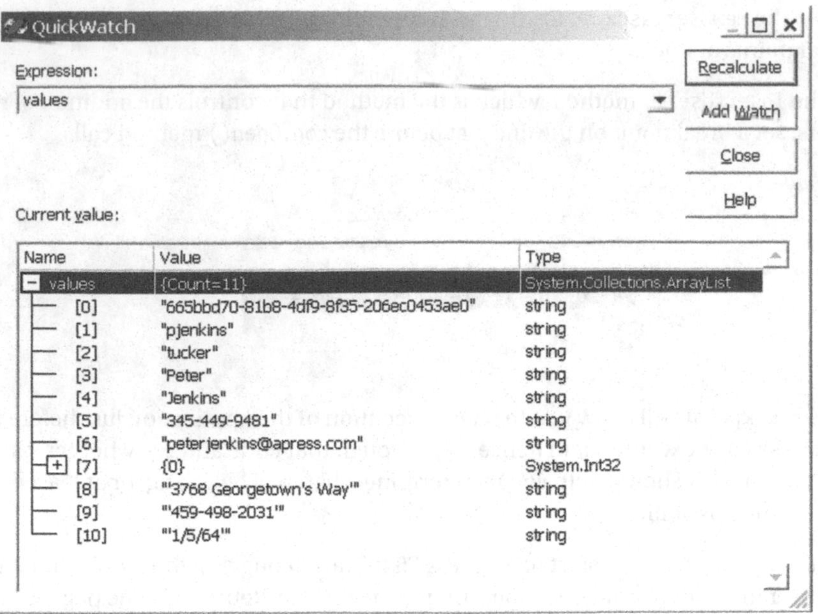

Figure 11-25. *The QuickWatch window showing variable values*

7. In the Expression field of the QuickWatch window, type `sql`, and then click the Recalculate button. The QuickWatch window will now show the value for the `sql` variable. You can check it quickly, but you shouldn't find anything wrong. Everything continues to be as expected.

8. Type `con.ConnectionString` in the Expression field of the QuickWatch window and click the Recalculate button. Again, the results are as expected. It was worth examining all these things, because even though they didn't reveal a problem, each one eliminates another possibility. Close the QuickWatch window for now.

9. Press F10 a few times to get to the `cmd.ExecuteNonQuery()` method call. In this line, you are calling the code that accesses the database.

```
    Dim doredirect As Boolean = True

    Try
      cmd.ExecuteNonQuery()
    Catch ex As SqlException
      Trace.Warn("FriendsReunion", _
        "An exception was thrown: " + ex.Message)
      doredirect = False
```

This line is in a `Try` block, so if anything goes wrong within this method, the code will jump to the `Catch` block just below it. (We'll look at `Try` and `Catch` blocks and exceptions in the next section of this chapter.)

10. Press F10. This causes the `cmd.ExecuteNonQuery()` call to be executed, and the execution pointer *does* move to the `Catch` block! So, something *does* go wrong during the `ExecuteNonQuery()` method call.

11. Press F10 one more time to enter the `Catch` block and examine the e variable, which holds the exception that has been raised. Move the cursor next to the e variable, right-click, and select QuickWatch. Your output should look like Figure 11-26. A quick look at the `Exception` object's `Message` property will reveal a clue: SQL Server is not happy with the SQL text near the character *s*, and it says that you haven't provided a closing quotation mark.

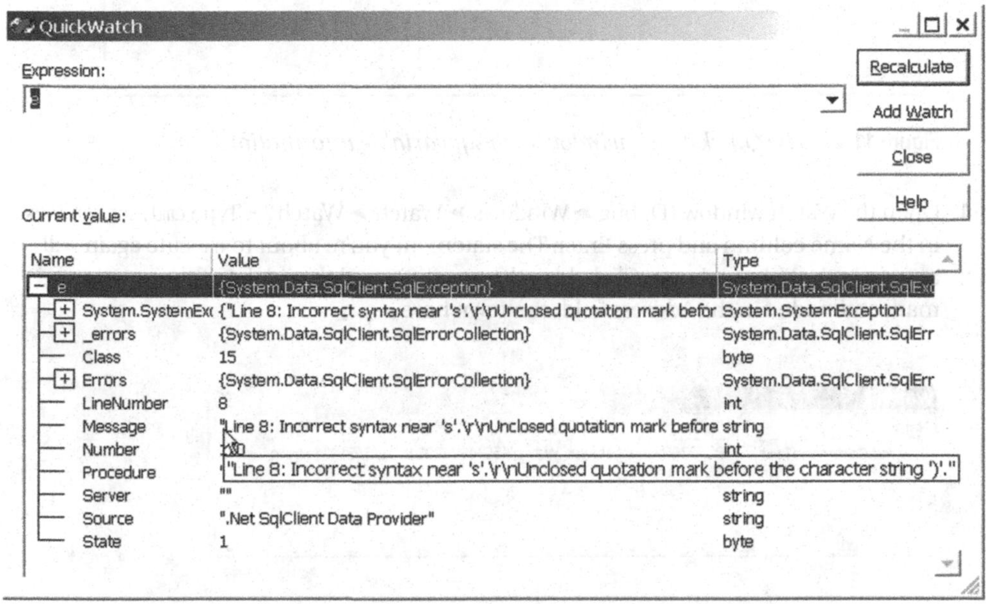

Figure 11-26. *Using the QuickWatch window to inspect the exception Message property*

12. Let's check the value of `sql` again. Type `sql` into the Expression field and press Enter to examine it more closely, as shown in Figure 11-27. In fact, there *is* a syntax error in the SQL here! The problem arises because the value of the `Address` field contains a single quotation mark, and you are not properly escaping it. Thus, the string has an odd number of quotation marks. The syntax of this SQL is incorrect, and so SQL Server is unable to parse it.

13. Let's test if this diagnosis of the problem is correct. Place the cursor in the line that caused the exception: the `cmd.ExecuteNonQuery()` method call. Right-click it and select Set Next Statement from the context menu. This will cause the execution to return to this point. The yellow arrow will move accordingly. (You can also grab the yellow arrow and drag it with the mouse to the line you want to execute next.)

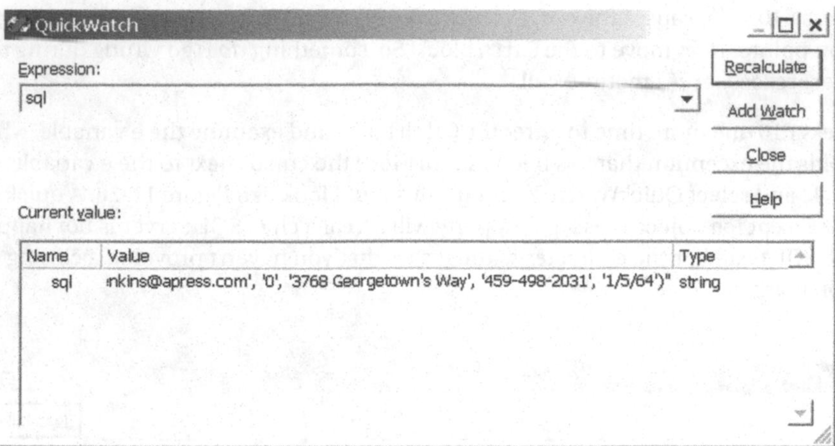

Figure 11-27. *The QuickWatch window with sql variable information*

14. Open the Watch window (Debug ➤ Windows ➤ Watch ➤ Watch 1). Type `cmd.CommandText` in the Name column and press Enter. The statement you're about to execute again will appear in the Value column. Click this value to edit it, and then delete the quotation mark embedded in the Address field, as shown here.

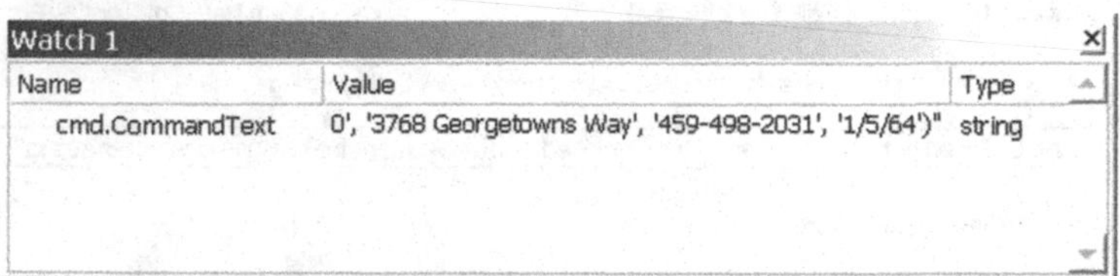

15. After getting rid of the suspicious quotation mark, press Enter to save the new edited value. It will change to a red font.

16. Press F10. This time, the `Catch` block is not executed and you go directly to the `Finally` block, which is normal, to close the connection. This means you have caught the bug! Now you need to code a fix for it.

17. Stop the debugging of the application by selecting Debug ➤ Stop Debugging (or by clicking the Stop Debugging button in the Debug toolbar).

18. Edit the `NewUser.aspx.vb` file to use the `Replace()` method to escape any quotation mark that may be entered by the user filling in the form:

```
' Save new user to the database
Dim values As New ArrayList(11)

' Escape any quotation mark entered by the user
txtLogin.Text = txtLogin.Text.Replace("'","''")
```

```
txtPwd.Text = txtPwd.Text.Replace("'","''")
txtFName.Text = txtFName.Text.Replace("'","''")
txtLName.Text = txtLName.Text.Replace("'","''")
txtPhone.Text = txtPhone.Text.Replace("'","''")
txtMobile.Text = txtMobile.Text.Replace("'","''")
txtEmail.Text = txtEmail.Text.Replace("'","''")
txtAddress.Text = txtAddress.Text.Replace("'","''")
txtBirth.Text = txtBirth.Text.Replace("'","''")

' Optional values without quotes as they can be the Null value
...etc...
```

19. Save this code and run the application again. You should find that single quotation marks in any of the fields no longer cause a problem.

How It Works

By having the chance to run the suspect code one step at the time while checking the status of key variables, you were able to determine exactly what was going on. The QuickWatch window proved very useful in allowing you to examine the value of any variable. Meanwhile, the Watch window allowed you to make a change to one of your variables and see how the application continued to run with the changed value. You also used the ability to move the execution point back in order to test fixes, which was essential to determine if your understanding of the problem was accurate, as well as if the solution worked.

Once you had identified the bug, it was easy to write a few lines of code to fix it.

Exceptions

An *exception* is a violation of an implicit assumption made by your code. For example, suppose that your application contains code to open a file that it depends on, but it doesn't first check that it *can actually* open the file. Here, your application is making an implicit assumption that the file will always be accessible. What happens if, when the code executes, it *cannot* access that file (for example, because it's missing or because the application doesn't have enough privileges to access it)? The underlying .NET Framework class responsible for opening the file recognizes the reason why it *can't* open the file, and it *throws* an exception.

When an exception is thrown, the exception dictates the application's subsequent execution path:

- If the application is able to *catch* the exception, then it will. For this to happen, the application must contain special *exception-handling code*. This kind of code is generally designed both to catch the exception and to handle it in a controlled way.
- If the application is unable to catch the exception, then it will bubble it up and eventually be caught by the CLR. This will result in an unfriendly exception message appearing on the page in the browser. This is the most undesirable result, and the one you want to avoid.

Of course, in the example of the code that opens a file, you could code the application to check that the file is accessible before it tries to open it, and to take an alternative execution path if the file is inaccessible. Then a missing file would no longer be an unexpected occurrence, and no exception would be thrown. But realistically, it's impossible to code for all of the many things that can go wrong. Your code should also be ready to catch general exceptions thrown as a result of unexpected situations.

So, in fact, the example above tells us two things:

- When it's possible, we should avoid implicit assumptions in our applications, by writing code in our applications to anticipate places where things can go wrong and check for them.
- We should also include exception-handling code in our applications, in order to deal with those exceptions that we cannot anticipate.

It's clear from the discussion so far that exceptions are a good way to deal with unexpected situations and errors (in particular, input errors) such as missing files, unexpected user input, and network failures. However, it's also worth noting that not all exceptions are thrown in this way. In fact, .NET also allows you to throw exceptions deliberately, so you can force the application to throw an exception in reaction to an expected problem.

In the remainder of this chapter, we'll talk about exceptions: throwing them, catching them, and handling them.

Exception Handling

We've talked a little about throwing and catching errors, and in this section, you'll see some examples in code. The ideas of throwing and catching are simple:

- When the application *throws* an exception, it's saying, "Hey! Something is up. Maybe some rule was violated here. Someone needs to deal with this right away!"
- When the application *catches* the exception, it's saying, "Okay, I'm ready to handle this violation right now. Let me deal with it."

In VB .NET, four keywords are used when dealing with exception handling: `Try`, `Catch`, `Finally`, and `Throw`.

Throwing Exceptions

From the point of view of the application code, there are two ways an exception can be thrown. The first is illustrated by the example described earlier, in which your application charges a .NET Framework class object with a task (such as opening a file), but the object cannot complete the task. It then tries to inform the calling application of the problem by throwing an exception.

EXCEPTIONS AND RESULT CODES: A COMPARISON

To appreciate the power of exceptions, it's useful to look at them in the light of older error-handling techniques. A common technique used in the absence of exceptions is that of the result code. The concept of a *result code* is quite simple. Method A calls Method B, and when Method B finishes executing, its return value (the result code) is a coded value (usually an integer) that indicates what happened during its execution. Then Method A must interpret the coded return value and act accordingly. For years, developers have used this technique for their error handling. If you have some experience in programming in the Windows environment, you're probably familiar with the idea of watching for functions that return `FALSE`, calling the `GetLastError` function, and dealing with `HRESULT` codes.

The result code technique suffers from two major limitations. One is that *a result code is not descriptive.* A result code is commonly expressed using a simple type (such as an integer). So, for example, a result code that represents an error generally doesn't provide any detailed information about the error. If a client method receives an *invalid argument* error result code, all you can say for sure is that an argument is invalid; there's no way to tell *which* of the arguments was invalid or *at what point* the error happened.

The other problem is that *it's easy to ignore a result code.* If Method A calls Method B, it's Method A's responsibility to check the return code returned by Method B, and to act on it. So, it's the responsibility of the developer who writes Method A to ensure that it tests the result code of every method it calls. This is really tedious; moreover, it produces code that is hard to read (because it becomes bloated with condition-checking statements all over the place). It's very easy for developers to become undisciplined, and that undermines the purpose of result codes. In short, result code methodology produces code that is hard to maintain and limited in capability.

By embracing exceptions and exception handling, the .NET Framework tackles the limitations of result codes head-on. The following are the key characteristics that make exceptions a far superior methodology for handling errors for your applications:

- **Exceptions contain detailed information.** An exception contains a lot of useful information that can be used at runtime to judge how best to handle situation that caused it. This information is also helpful at development/testing time: it includes information about the source of the exception, a stack trace, and the exact source line at which the exception was thrown. With all this information, you should be able to easily identify and fix bugs.
- **Exceptions cannot be ignored.** If your application throws an exception and doesn't handle it, the exception will ultimately be caught by the CLR. There's no room for undisciplined coding, because the exception methodology is far less forgiving, and consequently your code will be more robust.
- **Exception-handling code is more manageable.** With result codes, you dealt with the result of each method immediately after the method call, which meant you had result-handling code all over your code files. In contrast, you can collect *all* exception-handling code for a page in one place in the file. If something goes wrong, the CLR will catch up and direct execution to the handling code. That makes the code faster and easier to maintain.
- **Cleanup code is more manageable.** Just like the exception-handling code, the cleanup code can go in a single place in the file. Moreover, you can rely on it always being executed.

If you're used to using result codes, it means a change of habit. However, exceptions are such a powerful technique that the effort required to learn a little about exceptions and exception handling will be effort well spent. The benefits you will see in your code are quite significant.

Alternatively, the application itself can throw an exception. To do this, use the Throw keyword. For example, suppose you have a method called CalculateDiscount() that expects a parameter of type Double, which must be a nonnegative value. You can write code in this method to check the value passed, and throw an exception if the value is negative:

```
Public Sub CalculateDiscount(ByVal money As Double)
  If money < 0
    Throw new ArgumentException("money", _
      "The money parameter can't be less than zero")
  ...
End Sub
```

Catching Exceptions

How do you catch an exception once it has been thrown? First, the exception must be thrown from within a Try block, or it won't get caught at all. If the exception is thrown from within a Try block, it will be caught if there is an associated Catch block that recognizes the type of exception thrown.

For example, you can call the CalculateDiscount() discount method from within a Try block like this, and include a Catch block that is ready to catch exceptions of type ArgumentException:

```
Try
  CalculateDiscount(a)
  CalculateTax(a)
Catch e As ArgumentException
  ' here we handle the exception...
End Try
```

The Try block is used to enclose all the code that may throw exceptions. Note that there are just two lines in the Try block in this example, but you can add as many lines of code as you want.

The Try block is used to enclose all the code that may throw exceptions. In this example, there are two method calls in the Try block. If either method call results in an exception of type ArgumentException, the execution will immediately switch to the associated Catch block, which will catch and handle the exception. This is the way in which you collect exception-handling code into a single location in the file, and hence improve the maintainability of your code.

Cleaning Up

The Finally keyword allows you to specify a block of code that will always execute, whether or not an exception is thrown. The Finally block, if you include one, goes just after the Catch blocks.

Usually, you will place your cleanup code in this block, so you can be sure that the proper cleanup is done and the state of your application continues to be consistent, even when an exception is thrown.

Try It Out: Improve a Simple Exception-Handling Block Let's take a look at an exception-handling block already coded into Friends Reunion. Armed with your new knowledge about exceptions, you will try to improve it.

1. Open the NewUser.aspx.vb file and look at the Try and Catch blocks in the InsertUser() method:

```
Try
  cmd.ExecuteNonQuery()
Catch ex As SqlException
  Trace.Warn("FriendsReunion", _
    "An exception was thrown: " + ex.Message)
  doredirect = False
  lblMessage.Visible = True
  lblMessage.Text = _
Finally
  ' Ensure connection is closed always.
  con.Close()
End Try
```

2. Add two more Catch blocks *after* the existing one, as follows:

```
Catch ex As SqlException
  Trace.Warn("FriendsReunion", _
    "An exception was thrown: " + ex.Message)
  doredirect = False
  lblMessage.Visible = True
  lblMessage.Text = _
   "Insert couldn't be performed. User name may be already taken."
Catch ex As OutOfMemoryException
  doredirect = False
  lblMessage.Visible = True
  lblMessage.Text = "We just run of out memory, " + _
    "please restart the application!"
Catch ex As Exception
  doredirect = False
  lblMessage.Visible = True
  lblMessage.Text = "Couldn't update your profile!"
Finally
```

How It Works

First, let's take a look at how the code worked *before* you made the change. The Try block shown contains any lines of code that may throw an exception. In this case, there's just one line of code, which contains a call to the ExecuteNonQuery() method:

```
Try
  cmd.ExecuteNonQuery()
```

When the application is executing and reaches the Try block, it just steps into the Try block and executes whatever code it finds within.

If an exception is thrown at any point, execution immediately jumps out of the Try block, and the CLR starts to look for a way for the exception to be handled. In this case, there is a Catch block that accepts an exception of type SqlException. This is a specific exception thrown by SQL Server. So, this Catch block will be used to handle only that type of exception:

```
Catch ex As SqlException
  ...
```

Any other kind of exception will be propagated back to the caller; that is, it will be an *unhandled* exception. Regardless of whether or not an exception is thrown, the database connection that was opened earlier in the page must be closed. This is your cleanup code:

```
Finally
  con.Close()
End Try
```

In this code, you have just a single Catch block, which will catch SQL execution exceptions. The problem is that different types of exceptions require different handling, and you must be prepared for them. Right now, you're simply ignoring them. What you need is to further identify the *type* of exception that is thrown and have different Catch blocks to handle these different types of exception in different ways. That's what you've started to do here. Instead of one Catch block, you now have three:

```
Catch ex As SqlException
  ...
  lblMessage.Text = _
   "Insert couldn't be performed. User name may be already taken."
Catch ex As OutOfMemoryException
  ...
  lblMessage.Text = "We just run of out memory, " + _
    "please restart the application!"
Catch ex As Exception
  ...
  lblMessage.Text = "Couldn't update your profile!"
Finally
```

The first Catch block handles *only* exceptions of type SqlException. The SqlException class inherits from the base class for all exceptions, the Exception class. SqlException is a special type of Exception that is created when the SQL Server .NET data provider comes across an error generated by the database. Within this Catch block, you can write special exception-handling code for this type of exception. (In this case, to keep it simple, we just customized the error message to reflect what we've detected.)

The next Catch block handles *only* exceptions of type OutOfMemoryException. This type of exception occurs when the application server doesn't have enough memory left to continue executing the application. Again, you have special code within this Catch block to handle this type of exception; this code is different from the code in the first Catch block.

You've written exception-handling code in anticipation of a database error or out-of-memory error, but what if the Try block code throws a different type of error? You've added a final generic Catch block to catch those, as every exception will inherit from the Exception class. This Catch block needs to contain more generic exception-handling code, because you cannot be sure exactly what the problem is.

Note You could omit the final Catch block. In that case, exceptions of types other than SqlException and OutOfMemoryException would not be caught here, but would be passed up the call stack to the method that called InsertUser(). If that method couldn't handle the exception, it would be passed to the next level of the call stack, and so on. If it is not caught when it reaches the top of the call stack, it is passed to the CLR. In that case, the user gets an unfriendly message on the browser page, and your application ends!

When an exception is thrown, at most one of these Catch blocks will be used to handle it. The order of these three Catch blocks is important because it acts as a filter. An exception of type SqlException will be caught by the top Catch block, not the bottom one.

Tip You could make more improvements here. In the first Catch block, you could examine the properties of the SQLException object, ex, to find out more about what error occurred within the database, and you could handle different types of database errors in different ways within that Catch block.

Defining Custom Exceptions

The exception types you've seen so far are classes provided by the .NET Framework. When you're writing a complex application like Friends Reunion, it can be useful to devise your own system of *custom exceptions* that contain detailed information about the kinds of errors that are specific to the domain of your application.

Try It Out: Create Custom Exceptions You'll create a couple of custom exception classes here, to see how it's done, and then in subsequent examples in this chapter, you'll use them to good effect.

1. Create a new class file to the project (using Add ➤ Add Class), and call it FriendsReunionException.vb. Change the code so that the class inherits from ApplicationException, and so that it has two constructors, like this:

```
Public Class FriendsReunionException
  Inherits ApplicationException

  Public Sub New()
  End Sub
```

```
    Public Sub New(ByVal message As String, ByVal inner As Exception)
      MyBase.New(message, inner)
    End Sub

  End Class
```

2. Add another new class file to the project, and call this one `DuplicateUsernameException.vb`. Change the code in this class so that it inherits from `FriendsReunionException` and has two constructors, like this:

```
  Public Class DuplicateUsernameException
    Inherits FriendsReunionException

    Public Sub New()
    End Sub

    Public Sub New(ByVal message As String, ByVal inner As Exception)
      MyBase.New(message, inner)
    End Sub

  End Class
```

How It Works

The `FriendsReunionException` class will serve as the base class for any custom exceptions you define for the application. Having such a class will allow you to write a generic `Catch` block to catch *any* custom exception type defined by your application (and thus differentiate them from exceptions thrown by the .NET Framework). It inherits from the .NET Framework class called `ApplicationException`, a generic exception thrown when a nonfatal application error occurs, which itself inherits from the more generic `Exception` class.

The `DuplicateUsernameException` class is an application-specific exception class that you'll use to handle errors caused when a user tries to register using a user name that already exists in the database. It inherits from the `FriendsReunionException` class you just created.

Each of these classes contains two constructors. The more interesting one in each case is the one that contains two arguments. Its purpose will become clear in the next example.

You've used Microsoft's recommendation by appending the word `Exception` to each of your exception classes, and by deriving them from the `ApplicationException` class.

Now it's time to see these classes in action.

Rethrowing Exceptions

When handling an exception within a `Catch` block, it is sometimes useful to be able to perform a few important handling tasks within *that* `Catch` block and then *rethrow* the exception so that it may be caught and handled by a different `Catch` block (which then performs its own exception-handling tasks). It can even be advantageous to catch one type of exception, perform your handling tasks, and then rethrow it as a *different* type of exception—usually a more specific one that will provide additional information about the type of exception being thrown.

Custom (application-specific) exception types can have a big part to play in this. You may catch a generic exception, identify how it relates to the application, and then rethrow it as an application-specific exception so that it can be handled appropriately.

Try It Out: Rethrow Exceptions Let's see how this works with a custom exception type.

1. Modify the exception-handling code of the `InsertUser()` method in `NewUser.aspx.vb` as follows:

```
Try
  cmd.ExecuteNonQuery()
Catch ex As SqlException
  If ex.Number = 2627 Then
    Throw New DuplicateUsernameException("Can't insert record", ex)
  Else
    doredirect = False
    Me.lblMessage.Visible = True
    Me.lblMessage.Text = "Insert couldn't be performed. "
  End If
Catch ex As OutOfMemoryException
...
```

2. Add the following code to the `btnAccept_Click()` method, in the same file:

```
Private Sub btnAccept_Click(ByVal sender As System.Object, _
  ByVal e As System.EventArgs) Handles btnAccept.Click
  If Page.IsValid Then
    Trace.Write("FriendsReunion", "Page data was validated ok")
    If Context.User.Identity.IsAuthenticated Then
      UpdateUser()
    Else
      Try
        InsertUser()
      Catch ex As DuplicateUsernameException
        lblMessage.Visible = True
        lblMessage.Text = _
          "You are trying to register using a user name that has " + _
          "already been taken by someone else. " + _
          "Please choose a different user name. "
      End Try
    End If
  Else
    lblMessage.Text = "Fix the following errors and retry:"
  End If
End Sub
```

How It Works

In the `btnAccept_Click()` method, you've placed the `InsertUser()` method call into a `Try` block. Now if the `InsertUser()` method throws an error, the associated `Catch` block stands a chance of catching it. You're looking in particular for exceptions of type `DuplicateUsernameException` here:

```
Try
  InsertUser()
Catch ex As DuplicateUsernameException
  ... etc ...
End Try
```

Within the `InsertUser()` method, you've changed the first `Catch` block so that it examines the properties of the `SqlException` exception before deciding what to do next:

```
    Catch ex As SqlException
      If ex.Number = 2627 Then
        Throw New DuplicateUsernameException("Can't insert record", ex)
      Else
        doredirect = False
        Me.lblMessage.Visible = True
        Me.lblMessage.Text = "Insert couldn't be performed. "
      End If
```

Here, you're checking the type of error generated in the database. If the error number is 2627, it means that the "unique index" constraint in the database has been violated. In this case, that means that the user is trying to register with an existing user name. You have a custom, application-specific exception class for this situation: the `DuplicateUsernameException` class. You rethrow the exception as this new type, so that up the call stack, the `btnAccept_Click()` method can catch it and handle it accordingly. If the error number is not 2627, then some other database-related error has taken place, and you report a more generic error.

Note that you use the `DuplicateUsernameException` constructor with two arguments. The first argument is a string that contains a message relating to the exception, and the second is the exception object that was caught by this `Catch` block. This allows information from the original exception to be available in the place where the rethrown exception is handled.

Back in the `btnAccept_Click()` method, the `DuplicateUsernameException` is caught and handled using exception-handling code designed specifically for that type of exception

```
Catch ex As DuplicateUsernameException
  lblMessage.Visible = True
  lblMessage.Text = _
    "You are trying to register using a user name that has " + _
    "already been taken by someone else. " + _
    "Please choose a different user name. "
End Try
```

Unhandled Exceptions

What happens when an exception is not handled in the hierarchy of calling methods or by some .NET Framework code? In this case, the exception is said to go *unhandled* and will be caught by ASP.NET, which will deal with the unhandled error by rendering a page that displays details of the unhandled exception.

Displaying a Custom Error Page

Ideally, you should try to write exception-handling code so that every exception is handled within the application. But just in case an exception does bubble all the way up the call stack to the CLR, it would be better to show a friendly error page to your users than the default one provided by ASP.NET. For this purpose, ASP.NET provides two events that will be called when an exception is unhandled:

- The `Page_Error` event provides a way to trap errors occurring at the `Page` level.
- The `Application_Error` event provides a way to trap errors occurring within your code. The application-wide scope of this event also makes it an ideal place for adding logging code.

If you provide handlers for both events, they both will be executed: first `Page_Error` and then `Application_Error`. But in some circumstances (depending on how your application is coded), it may be appropriate that errors handled in `Page_Error` don't get to `Application_Error`. In such cases, you can use the `Server.ClearError` method after handling the error in `Page_Error`, thus causing the last error to be cleared and avoiding the `Application_Event` call.

Try It Out: Create a Custom Error Page In this example, you will use an ASP.NET error-handling feature to redirect to a friendly page in the situation when an exception goes unhandled.

1. Create a new web form and name it `CustomError.aspx`. Edit its code-behind file (`CustomError.aspx.vb`) to make the `CustomError` class inherit from `FriendsBase` instead of `Page`:

```
Public Class CustomError
  Inherits FriendsBase
```

2. While you're still in `CustomError.aspx.vb`, add the following lines to the `Page_Load()` method:

```
Private Sub Page_Load(ByVal sender As System.Object, _
  ByVal e As System.EventArgs) Handles MyBase.Load
  MyBase.HeaderMessage = "An error has been found!"
  MyBase.HeaderIconImageUrl = "~/Images/error.gif"
End Sub
```

3. Drag-and-drop the stylesheet used in your application onto the web form designer surface to link to it.

4. Switch to the HTML view of CustomError.aspx and add some friendly error message within the <form> element:

```
<form id="CustomError" method="post" runat="server">
  <p>
    <font size="5" color="red">
      <img src="~/Images/sad.gif"> 
      <b>An error has been found...</b>
    </font>
  </p>
  <p>
  We have detected an error in the Friends Reunion website. <br/>
  If this error persists, please contact our support team...
  </p>
</form>
```

5. After creating the custom error page, you need to tell ASP.NET to show that error page instead of the default error page. To do this, edit the <customErrors> element of the Web.config file for the application like this:

```
<configuration>
  <system.web>
    ...
    <customErrors defaultRedirect="CustomError.aspx" mode="On" />
    ...
  </system.web>
</configuration>
```

6. Now you need some code that explicitly throws an exception, so you can test that the custom error page works properly. To do this, edit LegalStuff.aspx.vb by adding this code to the Page_Load() method:

```
Private Sub Page_Load(ByVal sender As System.Object, _
  ByVal e As System.EventArgs) Handles MyBase.Load
  Throw New NullReferenceException
End Sub
```

7. Set LegalStuff.aspx as the start page and press Ctrl+F5. A new browser instance will open with the Login page for Friends Reunion. Log in, and you will be automatically redirected to LegalStuff.aspx. You should see the page shown in Figure 11-28.

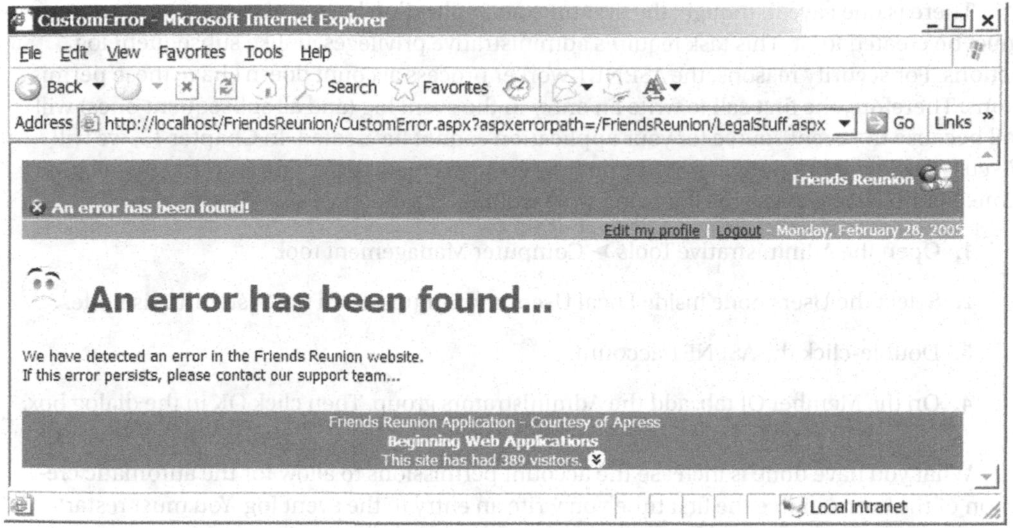

Figure 11-28. *The custom error page*

How It Works

When an exception is neither handled by the exception-handling code in the application nor cleared in the `Page_Error()` or `Application_Error()` event handlers, ASP.NET will check the `<customErrors>` element of the `Web.config` file to see whether a default error page has been specified for your application, through the `defaultRedirect` attribute. If it finds one, it will transfer execution to that page; if not, it will transfer execution to the default error page, which displays all the information about the unhandled exception.

Note that you also changed the `mode` attribute from `RemoteOnly` to `On`, so that you can see the custom error page, even when executing on the local machine. With that new value, the custom page is always shown. If you wanted to still get the detailed, default error page showing the complete exception when running the application locally, you would leave the previous `RemoteOnly` value.

Logging Exceptions to the System Event Log

You have successfully shown the user a customized message. However, in order for your support team (that may be you!) to diagnose the error and determine its cause, you need a way to permanently store the error information for later analysis. Windows provides the event log for that purpose. The event log is a central location, which can also be accessed remotely, that stores logs for all applications that wish to write to it. ASP.NET applications can also do so, by using the `System.Diagnostics.EventLog` class.

There is one caveat, though: the first time an application logs an event, an *event source* must be created for it. This task requires administrative privileges, unlike subsequent log actions. For security reasons, the ASP.NET worker process account doesn't have these permissions. Therefore, the first call to write an entry in the event log (and all subsequent ones) will fail because the event source for your application cannot be created. In Chapter 13, we will discuss deployment options in .NET and how you can create this event source at installation time. For now, we can use the following workaround:

1. Open the Administrative Tools ➤ Computer Management tool.
2. Select the Users node inside Local Users and Groups, from the System Tools node.
3. Double-click the ASPNET account.
4. On the Member Of tab, add the Administrators group. Then click OK in the dialog box.

What you have done is increase the account permissions to allow for the automatic creation of the event source the first time you write an entry to the event log. You must restart IIS in order for this change to have effect. You can do so by running the `iisreset` command (either by using Start ➤ Run or the command line).

Needless to say, you must remove this permission after you've completed the next "Try It Out"!

Now let's see the code to actually write to the event log.

Try It Out: Log Exceptions to the System Event Log We mentioned earlier that the `Application_Error()` event handler is an ideal place for adding application-wide logging of errors. It's ideal because it receives unhandled exceptions raised anywhere in your code, not just on a specific page. Let's see how to code this.

1. Open the `Global.asax.vb` file, and edit the `Application_Error()` method as follows:

```
Public Class Global
  Inherits System.Web.HttpApplication
  ...
  Sub Application_Error(ByVal sender As Object, ByVal e As EventArgs)
    System.Diagnostics.EventLog.WriteEntry("FriendsReunion", _
      Server.GetLastError().InnerException.ToString(), _
      System.Diagnostics.EventLogEntryType.Error)
  End Sub
  ...
End Class
```

2. That's all the code required! Press F5 to run Friends Reunion. Log in to the application, and then navigate to `LegalStuff.aspx` (which still has the code to throw a `NullReferenceException` in its `Page_Load()` method).

3. Open the Event Viewer (Control Panel ➤ Administrative Tools ➤ Event Viewer) and click the Application log. A list of the last application events recorded should be displayed. Locate the one whose Source column shows FriendsReunion and double-click it. You'll see the log shown in Figure 11-29.

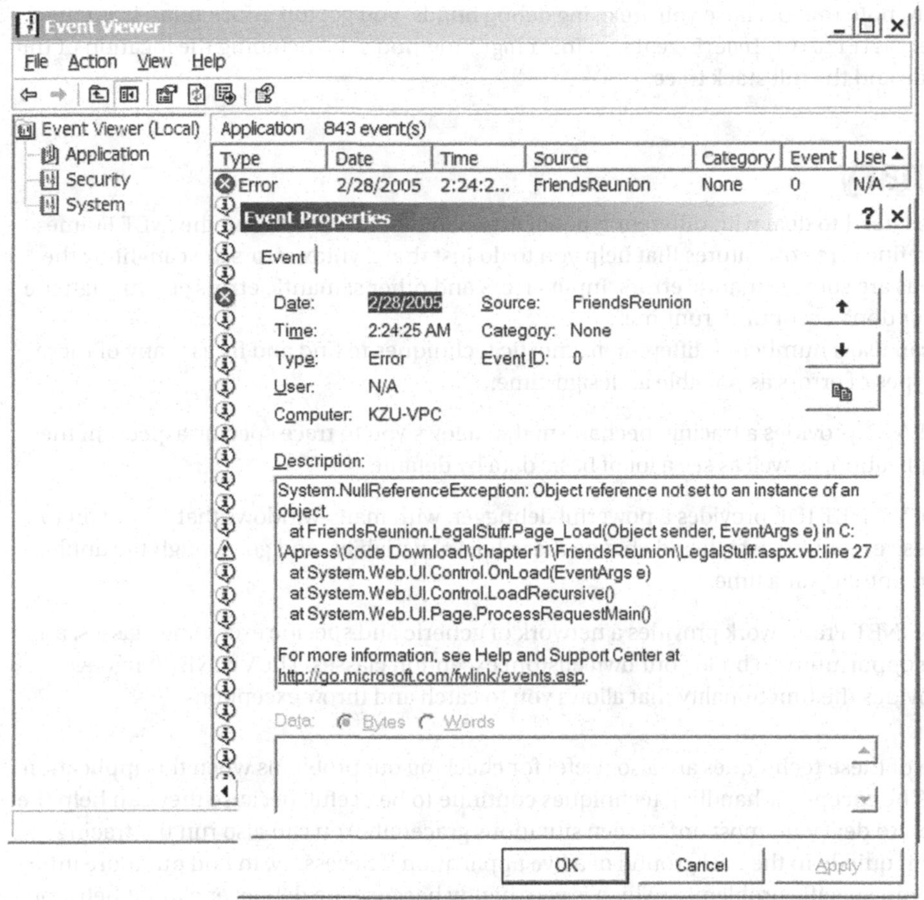

Figure 11-29. *Writing to the System event log*

How It Works

You are handling the `Application_Error` event, which is called by ASP.NET when an exception goes unhandled. Thanks to the great `EventLog` class provided in the `System.Diagnostics` namespace, you need just one line of code to write to the System event log. Note that you're not clearing the exception (there's no call to `Server.ClearError`), so ASP.NET will then check `Web.config` for information about a default error page, and if it finds one, it will transfer execution to it.

Because you granted increased permissions to the ASP.NET account, you get the `FriendsReunion` event source (the fourth column in the Event Viewer right pane) automatically. The elevated permissions are needed only for the first entry written.

Caution Do not forget to remove the Administrators group you added to the ASPNET account!

Finally, note that because you are using debug builds, you get full information from the `Server.GetLastError().InnerException.ToString()` method call, including the location of the failing code and the full stack trace.

Summary

Developers need to deal with different types of errors in different ways, and the .NET Framework has a fine array of features that help you to do just that. Syntax errors are caught by the compiler, as are some semantic errors. Input errors and other semantic errors get through the compiler or don't occur until runtime.

You can use a number of different diagnostic techniques to find and fix as many of these runtime types of errors as possible at design-time:

- ASP.NET provides a tracing mechanism that allows you to trace specific aspects of the application, as well as see a lot of basic data by default.
- The VS .NET IDE provides a powerful debugger, with many windows that allow you to pause execution, watch and change the values of variables, and go through the application one step at a time.
- The .NET Framework provides a network of generic and specific exception classes, and the opportunity to build your own custom exception classes. The VB .NET language provides the functionality that allows you to catch and throw exceptions.

Some of these techniques are also useful for checking out problems when the application goes live. The exception-handling techniques continue to be useful, because they can help the application to deal with most unforeseen situations gracefully. You can also run the tracing mechanism quietly in the background of a live application if necessary, to find out more information about specific problems—which is very handy because the debugger cannot help you in a live situation.

You are armed with a good understanding of the different types of errors and how to deal with them at design-time and runtime, and you should be able to write a bug-free application. When it's written, you'll need to put it through some heavy testing in order to measure how it's performing and what areas can be improved. And that's exactly what we're going to cover in the next chapter.

CHAPTER 12

Caching and Performance Tuning

Since Chapter 3 of this book, we've been building a realistic web application from scratch. In the course of developing the Friends Reunion application, you've had hands-on experience dealing with web forms, user controls, database access, XML Schemas, state, authentication, and so on. You now have a complete web application working on your desktop PC. You can test it over and over again, and it will work as expected.

In this chapter, you'll prepare to take your Friends Reunion application out of the relatively safe confines of your desktop PC and into some real-world scenarios. You'll put it under some stress to see how well it is likely to perform in a live environment with many concurrent users, and you'll look for areas that you can enhance in order to make it perform even better. If you're thinking that we've already tested this application and wondering what needs improvement, read on—there's always room for improvement!

In this chapter, we'll cover the following topics:

- What it means to "improve an application's performance"
- Performance monitoring tools and some useful load-testing techniques
- How different types of caches (in different locations) can be used to get different effects
- How to use ASP.NET output caching and data caching to get some performance improvements
- How to control viewstate
- Other tips for improving resource usage, including using server-side transfers, avoiding unnecessary web controls, disabling session state, and improving database access

What Is Good Performance?

What do we mean when we say that an application "has good performance"? Ultimately, it comes down to the experience of the user. If your application is capable of supporting the requisite number of concurrent users, and each user experiences acceptable response times, then your application is performing adequately.

So, any definition of "good performance" is *relative*, because it depends on the requirements of the system (in terms of number of concurrent users, the activities they perform, and expected response times). An application that performs well under a regular load of 20 concurrent users may not perform well when the load increases to 100 users, and the application's resources are more stretched.

Since this chapter is about *performance tuning* (or essentially, improving the performance of an application), we need to address what it means to "improve" an application's performance. Given what we've already said, it follows that any performance improvement is about changing the application so that it can support greater numbers of concurrent users, and/or so that each user experiences improved response times.

So *how* do you improve an application's performance? Well, performance is restricted only by the available resources and the way the application uses them, so there are two obvious ways to improve performance:

- Increase the resources available to the application (more memory, broader network connections, and so on).
- Find the places in the application that make inefficient use of existing resources (or *bottlenecks*) and improve resource usage in those places.

Obviously, the second of these options is the most interesting one from our perspective. As we said, we know that Friends Reunion performs fine on a local machine with a single user, but to discover its weaknesses, we need to examine how our system's resources cope when the application runs under more stressful conditions. So, much of this chapter will be about monitoring aspects of our application's performance, locating bottlenecks, and doing something about them. Of course, we cannot examine the whole application in one chapter. We'll focus on a few places, identify some optimizations, and demonstrate some important techniques along the way.

You can think of performance as a *characteristic* of your application. A good understanding of performance-optimization techniques in ASP.NET is useful knowledge to apply right from the time you start designing your application. It's often easier and more effective to apply such techniques to the design than to try to fit them retrospectively. But there are usually improvements that can be made, even when you've finished the build, and with a little judicious stress testing, you'll be able to find out just how well the application really does perform under stress.

Performance Monitoring

In order to make judgments about the performance levels of your application, you'll need to do some monitoring, and for that, you'll need some tools. Windows XP, Windows 2000, and later versions provide two tools that help you to monitor the resource usage of the system: the Task Manager and the Performance Console.

The Task Manager (opened by pressing Ctrl+Alt+Del and clicking the Task Manager button) is most commonly used to provide a list of the applications running on your machine, and the processes and memory used by those applications. It also provides readings on CPU, page file usage, and other characteristics of resource usage. Most readers will already be familiar with the Task Manager—it's what you turn to whenever you need to kill a nonresponding application.

Although it provides some useful statistics on how different areas of the system are performing, it is designed more for managing the applications on your system. It's not really intended to be used for serious performance-measurement purposes.

So let's turn our attention to the second of these tools. The *Performance console*, usually referred to as PerfMon, is actually composed of two tools: the System Monitor and the Performance Logs and Alerts. Together, they provide detailed data about the resources used by specific components of the operating system and by programs that were developed with the collection of performance data in mind.

The System Monitor is of particular interest to us here. It allows you to monitor many different aspects of the system, providing different real-time views (graphs, histograms, and reports) that help you to see how your system is performing.

Configuring the System Monitor in PerfMon

To start up the System Monitor, select Start ➤ Control Panel ➤ Administrative Tools ➤ Performance (or just select Start ➤ Run and type **perfmon**). The Performance console should appear immediately, as shown in Figure 12-1.

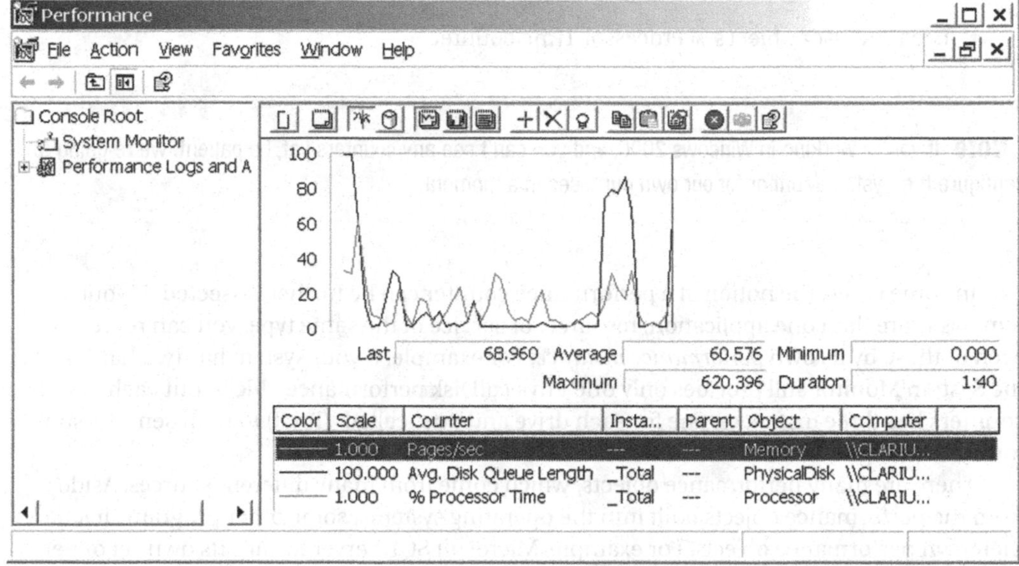

Figure 12-1. *The Performance console*

Note If you're running Windows XP or Windows 2003, the Performance console will look similar to Figure 12-1. If you're running Windows 2000, it will look similar except that the Windows 2000 version doesn't automatically set up the three different-colored graphs in the area on the right side of the window.

The System Monitor monitors use of resources as they change over time. The display shown in Figure 12-1 shows the System Monitor taking readings of three metrics (called *performance counters*) and plotting those readings against time on the graph.

Performance data is defined in terms of *objects, counters,* and *instances.* A *performance object* is any resource, service, or application that can be measured in some way. The processor and paging file on your system are two examples of such a resource; they are various aspects of the processor's activity and the paging file's activity that you can monitor over time.

Any given performance object has a number of different aspects that could be of interest. Each of these aspects is called a *performance counter.* Every performance object has its own collection of performance counters. For example, the processor object includes ten different counters that represent different aspects of its activity, including one for measuring the proportion of time the processor spends working (% Processor Time), and another for measuring the proportion of time it spends dealing with deferred procedure calls (% DPC Time). Figure 12-1 shows the three performance counters that you get by default if you're using Windows XP or 2003:

- The Memory object's Pages/sec counter
- The PhysicalDisk object's Avg. Disk Queue Length counter
- The Processor object's % Processor Time counter

Note If you're working in Windows 2000, and you can't see any counters yet, be patient: we're going to configure the System Monitor for our own purposes in a moment.

In some cases, the notion of a performance counter can be further dissected. If your system has more than one application, resource, or service of the same type, you can represent each of these by its own *performance instance.* For example, if your system has two hard disks, the System Monitor still provides only one PhysicalDisk performance object, but each of the counters has three instances: one for each drive and one (called _Total) to represent the sum total drive usage over both the drives.

There are many performance objects, which come from many different sources. Aside from the performance objects built into the operating systems, some other programs install their own performance objects. For example, Microsoft SQL Server installs its own set of performance objects, each of which comprises a collection of performance counters that you can use to monitor the internals of the database engine. So, it may come as no surprise that when you install the .NET Framework, you also install performance objects for the CLR and for ASP.NET. These allow you to monitor various aspects of the activity of the CLR and ASP.NET, to see what's going on while your ASP.NET application is running.

Adding Counters

To set up the System Monitor to show performance counters and instances, right-click anywhere in the right-pane of the System Monitor and select Add Counters. You'll see the Add Counters dialog box, as shown in Figure 12-2. Select an object from the Performance object list. Then select one of the counters from the counters list, and (if there is an option) select one (or all) of the instances in the instances list. In Figure 12-2, we've chosen the % Disk Time counter of the PhysicalDisk object and selected to watch the C: drive instance.

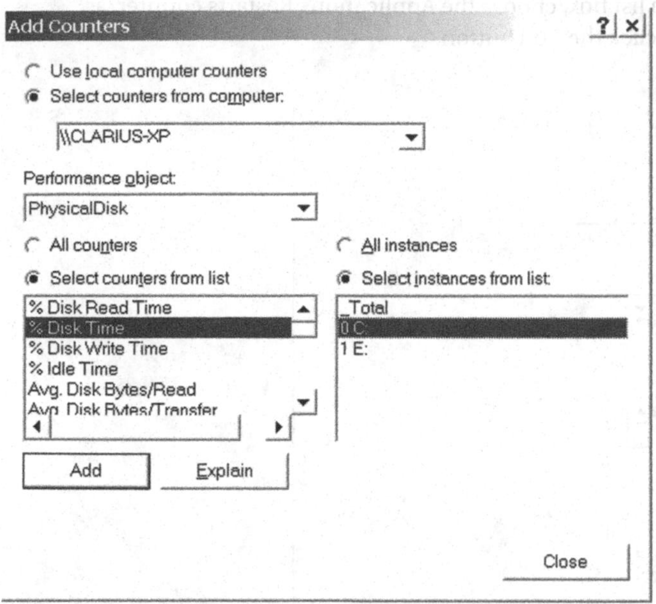

Figure 12-2. *Adding a counter in the System Monitor*

In this chapter, we'll focus on using seven performance counters: five of these relate to ASP.NET, one relates to CLR, and one relates to the processor.

Try It Out: Configure the System Monitor for Key Performance Counters Let's configure PerfMon so that it shows all seven performance counters. Then you'll be able to use it to monitor the Friends Reunion application as it executes.

1. If you haven't done so already, open PerfMon (select Start ➤ Run and type **perfmon**) on the machine that's running the Friends Reunion application. Make sure the System Monitor details pane is shown on the right; if not, click the System Monitor item under Console Root in the left pane.

2. If there are any counters already showing, remove them, so you can start with a clean slate. To do this, select one of the items in the table under the graph, and click the Delete button in the toolbar (the one with an *X*) to delete it. Repeat this for each of the items in the table.

3. Now you're ready to add the counters of interest. Click the Add Counters button (the one with a plus sign), or right-click and select Add Counters, to open the Add Counters dialog box (see Figure 12-2). Select the Use local computer counters radio button.

4. In the Performance object drop-down list, select ASP.NET. When you do this, the contents of the Select counters from list box (immediately below) will change accordingly, so that it shows all the counters that are made available by the ASP.NET performance object.

5. In the Select counters from list box, choose the Applications Restarts counter, as shown in Figure 12-3, and click the Add button.

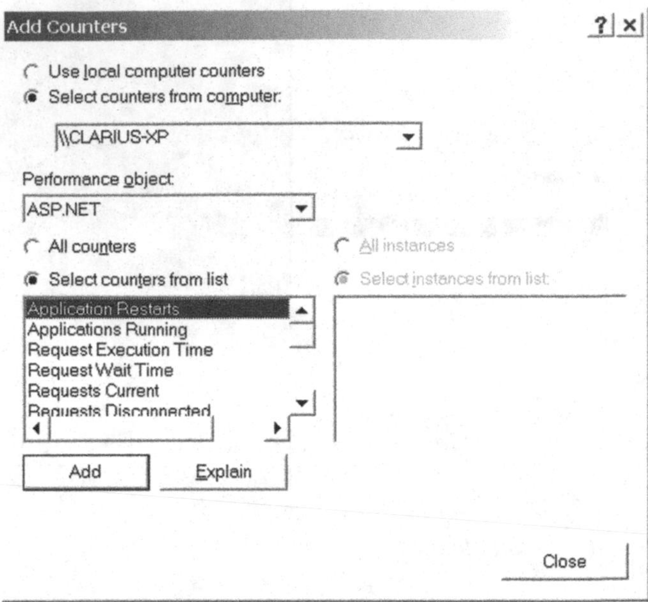

Figure 12-3. *The ASP.NET performance object counters*

6. Repeat the procedure to add the following six counters (shown in *performance object\counter\instance* format, where applicable):

   - ASP.NET\Requests Queued
   - ASP.NET\Worker Process Restarts
   - ASP.NET Applications\Errors Total_LM_W3SVC_1_Root_FriendsReunion (or similar)
   - ASP.NET Applications\Requests/sec_LM_W3SVC_1_Root_FriendsReunion (or similar)
   - Processor\% Processor Time\Total
   - .NET CLR Exceptions\# of Exceps Thrown\aspnet_wp

Note In order to see the _LM_W3SVC_1_Root_FriendsReunion instance, the site must be running. If it's not, just navigate to the `http://localhost/FriendsReunion` site.

7. Close the Add Counter dialog box. You should be able to see all the selected counters at the bottom of the right pane. Each counter is represented by a different colored line.

8. Open your browser and start surfing Friends Reunion. Browse the pages and generate load on the server. Perform some different activities within the application (registering a new user, logging in, accessing different pages, logging out, and so on). The System Monitor will show how your seven monitored counters perform, as in the example in Figure 12-4.

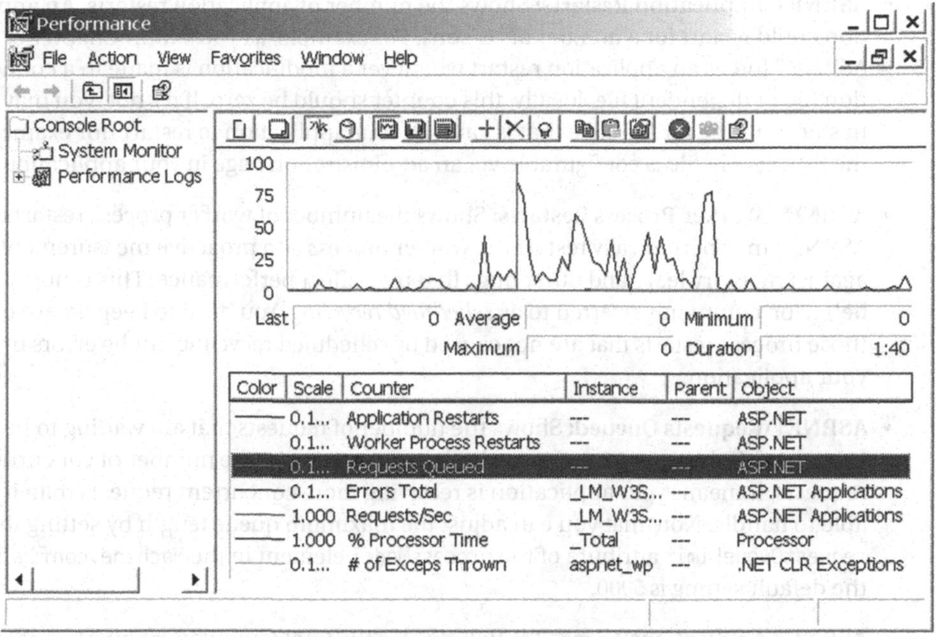

Figure 12-4. *The seven counters added to the System Monitor*

Note You'll probably find that your counters don't give exactly the same results as those shown in Figure 12-4. But the results shown at the moment are really not what we're concerned with right now. They will become more interesting when you start to generate a heavier load on the server (that is, more than just one user!).

---

9. Save these settings by selecting File ➤ Save As. This way, you can easily reload this set of counters at a later time.

How It Works

The ASP.NET performance object contains global-only counters that are not related to applications but to the ASP.NET engine itself. The ASP.NET Applications performance object includes per-application counters. When you select one of these counters, you can monitor the entire server, or select which instance of the counter you're interested in (there is one instance for each application). It was not possible to get this level of granularity in pre-.NET versions of ASP, because the counters available related to the activity of the entire server.

Here are the seven counters we've chosen to monitor:

- **ASP.NET\Application Restarts:** Shows the number of application restarts. An application could restart for a number of reasons. For example, as you saw in Chapter 6, ASP.NET forces an application restart whenever a modification is made to a configuration file or dependent file. Ideally, this counter should be zero. If it's not, you may need to start hunting for the code that is causing your application to restart (for example, if the `Web.config` file is configurable via an administration page in your application).

- **ASP.NET\Worker Process Restarts:** Shows the number of worker process restarts. ASP.NET may periodically restart the worker process as a proactive measurement against memory leaks and other bugs that may affect performance. This is normal behavior, commonly referred to as *scheduled recycling*. You need to keep an eye on those process restarts that are not caused by scheduled recycling but by errors in your application.

- **ASP.NET\Requests Queued:** Shows the number of requests that are waiting to be processed. If this counter starts to climb in proportion to the number of concurrent requests, it means your application is receiving more concurrent requests than it is able to handle. Note that you can adjust the maximum queue length by setting the `requestQueueLimit` attribute of the `processModel` element in the `Machine.config` file; the default setting is 5000.

- **ASP.NET Applications\Errors Total:** Indicates the total (cumulative) number of errors that the application has generated. The output value for this counter should be zero. If it isn't, you should identify and fix the errors before you continue testing.

- **ASP.NET Applications\Requests/sec:** Shows how many requests the application is serving per second. This counter should remain fairly constant and within a "safe" range in relation to a constant load. If this counter shows regular troughs, it may be because the server is also required to perform other tasks (such as garbage collection) or because some other software running on the server is affecting performance. To correct this behavior, you will need to investigate what tasks your server is performing and try to minimize them.

- **Processor\% Processor Time:** Shows how much processor time is being consumed by the application. You can expect this counter to increase with load. If it doesn't, your application is probably using multithreading features of some kind and suffering from a problem called *contention*.

- **.NET CLR Exceptions\# of Exceps Thrown:** Shows the number of exceptions that are being thrown by the application. In terms of resources, exceptions are expensive. It's helpful to know where (and why) your application throws exceptions, and this counter helps you to be aware of them. Although the output for this counter is not *necessarily* supposed to be zero, you need to keep an eye on it, just to make sure it doesn't go too high.

Although the last two counters are not ASP.NET-specific, they are still very important in helping you to measure your application's performance.

There is an abundance of performance counters available. The seven counters listed here constitute some of the key counters that can help you to measure a web application's performance, but they are just a small subset of the many counters available. For example, the two performance objects provided by ASP.NET alone provide more than 60 counters. The CLR alone already provides 10 performance objects (with a total of more than 80 counters!).

In the Add Counters dialog box, you may have noticed at least two extra performance objects whose names contain the .NET version number:

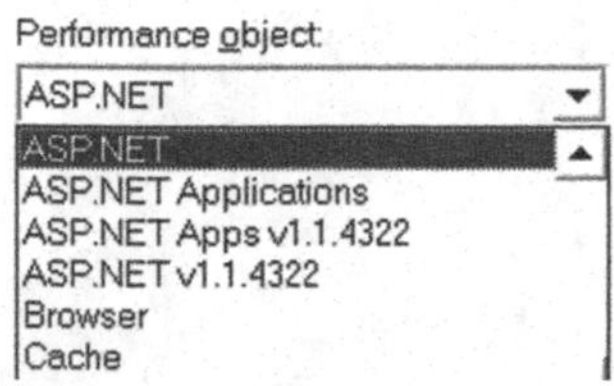

These are intended to support the side-by-side execution features of the CLR and ASP.NET. These objects contain counters that will apply only to that particular ASP.NET version. The unique set that *doesn't* contain any version information in its name will apply to the highest version installed.

It's well worth spending some time with PerfMon to familiarize yourself with some of the other counters. PerfMon provides a handy explanation of each counter (you can view the explanation by clicking the Explain button in the Add Counters dialog box). Of course, the more counters you learn about, the better armed you will be when it comes to the performance-testing process.

Tip Just as other programs provide their own custom performance objects and counters, it's also possible to write custom performance objects for your own applications. This is a potentially powerful way to create tools to measure details that are specific to your application. For example, if you're particularly interested in monitoring the number of users registered per minute, you can do that using a custom performance counter. To learn more about developing and monitoring your own custom performance objects and counters, refer to *Performance Tuning and Optimizing ASP.NET Applications*, by Jeffrey Hasan and Kenneth Tu (Apress, 2003; ISBN: 1-59059-072-4).

Avoiding External Overhead

Although it may be nice to have a real time graph that shows how aspects of your system are performing, you need to be aware that the process of collecting and displaying this information is *itself* a process that consumes server resources! Of course, you should try to keep monitoring overhead to a minimum. The whole idea is to not overload your system with external tools like monitoring, screensavers, and the like, which affect the accuracy of the readings.

One way to reduce the load is to control the frequency with which the System Monitor takes sample ratings. To do this, display the System Monitor Properties dialog box (by clicking the Properties button in the toolbar) and select the General tab. Near the bottom of the dialog box, you'll see the Sample (or Update) automatically every *x* seconds option, as shown in Figure 12-5. The higher you set this value, the longer the System Monitor will wait between samples. This will reduce the amount of processing work that the System Monitor has to do, which may be necessary if your current hardware cannot cope with the required processor power.

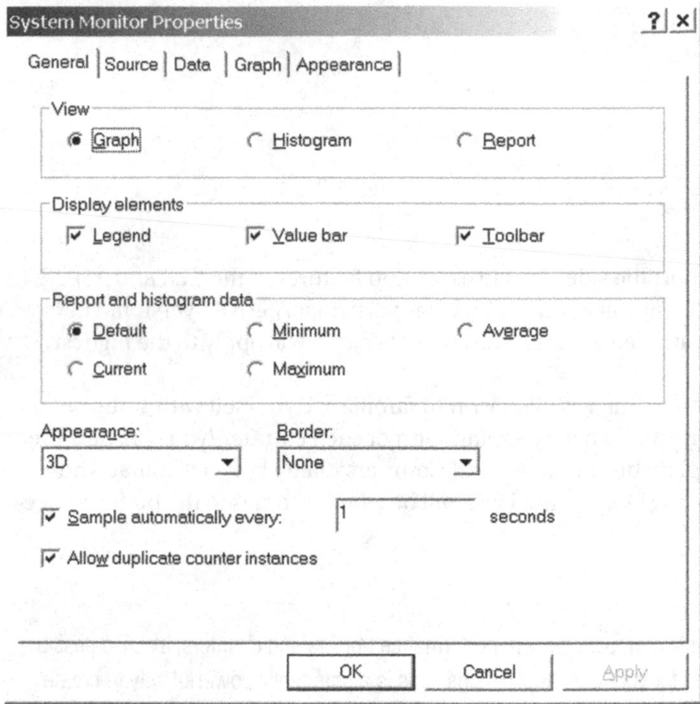

Figure 12-5. *You can adjust the frequency of System Monitoring sampling through the Properties dialog box.*

Another slimmer approach, which will consume even fewer resources, is to avoid using the System Monitor at all, and to use the *counter logs* instead. You'll find the counter logs under the Performance Logs and Alerts node of the Performance console. Here, you can still specify all the counters you want to measure, and their performance data will be recorded silently (no fancy graphics this time!) to a log file from which you can later generate various reports (for example, in Microsoft Excel, using the comma-separated value output format).

So, now you've set up the System Monitor to monitor the resources your application is using. To get some useful results, you need to monitor the resources in a realistic testing scenario. This is the subject of the next section.

Performance Testing an Application

It's important to think of your ASP.NET application as a real piece of software, just like any other software you've ever written, and to test it in all the same ways. Of course, there are a lot of different types of testing processes you can (and should) apply to a piece of software during the course of its development. For example, two main types of software testing are functional testing and load testing.

Functional testing is about checking that the application conforms to the design specifications. You want to verify that each module performs its tasks correctly, that there are no broken or missing links, that client-side scripts run smoothly, that web pages look fine on every different browser you intend to support, and so on.

Load testing is about simulating the amount of load that the application needs to be able to support, and checking that the server can handle that load properly (and without implications such as memory leaks). As you'll see, you can use special tools to simulate large amounts of user activity, and hence reproduce the necessary load. Load testing falls fairly naturally into two areas:

- **Performance testing:** This involves *incrementally* increasing the load on the server while it can properly handle it, with the objective of finding out the maximum number of requests per second your server can handle without degradation.

- **Stress testing:** This is about subjecting the server to a *greater* amount of load than it is capable of handling. The objective here is to make the server break, so that you can find out how it behaves in such a situation. Although you are not expecting the server to *handle* the overload, you do want the server to *behave in a decent manner* (for example, without any data loss or corruption).

In this chapter, we're particularly interested in performance testing. We'll place reasonable levels of load on the server to see how well it copes with that load and to identify bottlenecks, with a view toward improving the overall resource usage of our application. To do this, you'll use the performance objects you've configured in the System Monitor. You'll also need a way to simulate a number of end users browsing the Friends Reunion application simultaneously. That is the purpose of the Web Application Stress tool.

Installing the Web Application Stress Tool

In order to generate amounts of load on your server that you could not generate by other means, you can use a tool that is specifically designed for that job. In this chapter, we will use Microsoft's Web Application Stress (WAS) tool. There are two reasons for choosing WAS here: it is simple to use, and it is available for free. You can use this tool to simulate a specified number of users, to specify the pages these simulated users will be surfing, and so on. At the time of writing, WAS is freely available from `http://www.microsoft.com/downloads/details.aspx?FamilyID=e2c0585a-062a-439e-a67d-75a89aa36495`. It's about 9.5MB in size.

Before you install WAS, it's worth considering on which machine you should put this tool. If you don't have a couple of networked PCs, then you *can* follow the exercises in this chapter by running WAS, the Friends Reunion web application, and the database server on the same machine. However, when you run WAS, it will take up most of the resources of the machine that it runs on, so you should be aware that your results will be skewed by the fact that WAS is using resources that would usually be available to the web application.

If you *do* have access to a couple of machines, and you can take advantage of this, you'll get much more realistic results. Keep one machine for the Friends Reunion web application and database server, and install WAS on the other one. (In this case, it makes sense to think of the former as the *server* machine and the latter as the *client* machine.)

The installation process is straightforward. The download consists of a single file, called `setup.exe`. Just run this file and follow the on-screen instructions of the installer.

Although WAS is not officially supported by Microsoft, the product comes with a very complete online help that should aid you in getting started using it. You can also read the guide at `http://www.microsoft.com/technet/itsolutions/ecommerce/maintain/optimize/d5wast_2.mspx` to learn more about it.

Tip Microsoft also has a more recent tool, called Application Center Test (ACT), which supersedes WAS. ACT is supported by Microsoft, but it's not free. It does come bundled with VS .NET (but only the Enterprise Architect and Enterprise Developer editions). It provides enhanced features, such as a complete reporting capability and integration with the VS .NET IDE. You can learn more about ACT at `http://www.microsoft.com/applicationcenter/`.

Generating a Realistic Set of Data

To get an even greater approximation of reality, you should expand the amount of data in the database you're using. It currently holds just a few users, but once it gets established, you would expect it to hold information about hundreds of people. To do this, you'll run a little script to insert some extra data into the database.

Try It Out: Insert Sample Data into the Database You'll run a SQL script that performs 1,000 loop iterations, adding one new user into the `User` table each time. You'll find this script in the downloadable code for this book (available from the Downloads section of `www.apress.com`), within the folder that contains this chapter's code.

1. Get the file `sp_Fill_User.sql` and place it in a folder somewhere handy on your hard disk (say, `C:\temp`).

2. Start up a command window and navigate to the folder where you placed `sp_User_Fill.sql`. Now run the following command:

   ```
   C:\temp>osql -S server -d FriendsData -E -i sp_Fill_User.sql
   ```

   So, if your database server is called `CLARIUS`, then you should type:

   ```
   C:\temp>osql -S CLARIUS -d FriendsData -E -i sp_Fill_User.sql
   ```

You can also use (local) as the server name if you're running it locally.

3. In VS .NET, open the Server Explorer, browse to your FriendsData database, and check the content of the User database table. You should find 1,000 new rows.

How It Works

The .sql file contains a simple SQL script that runs through a loop 1,000 times, adding a new user to the database table with each iteration:

```
DECLARE @cnt int
SELECT @cnt = 0
DECLARE @u varchar(15)

WHILE @cnt<1000 BEGIN
  SELECT @cnt = @cnt + 1
  SELECT @u = 'user' + CAST(@cnt as varchar)

  INSERT INTO [User]
    VALUES(NEWID(), @u, 'mypassword', 'Carlos', 'Garcia Saccone', GETDATE(),
           '(999) 999-9999', '(999) 999-9999', '7th. Avenue 1234, NY, USA',
           'cgs@clariusconsulting.net', 0)
END
```

Admittedly, all of the new users will have the same personal details, but each user does have a unique ID, so this data should be sufficient for our purposes.

Preparing a Performance Test with a Simulated Load

Over the next few pages, we'll set up and perform a performance test. Specifically, we'll simulate a situation in which a number of Friends Reunion administrator users perform a couple of simple tasks: logging in to the application, and then browsing to the Users Administration page to manage the list of current users.

First, we'll need to write the *test script*. This is a document that describes the requests that each simulated user will perform. Then we'll set up the monitoring criterion in WAS. Finally, we'll run the test.

Try It Out: Create the Test Script To begin, you'll write the test script using the WAS script-writing tool. You should have already installed WAS on your "client" machine, as described earlier in the "Installing the Web Application Stress Tool" section.

1. Open WAS (on your "client" machine) by selecting Start ➤ Programs ➤ Microsoft Web Application Stress Tool.
2. You'll see a dialog box that asks you what you want to do, as shown in Figure 12-6. Select Record (this option allows you to navigate to the site while WAS records your actions and generates a script to reproduce them).

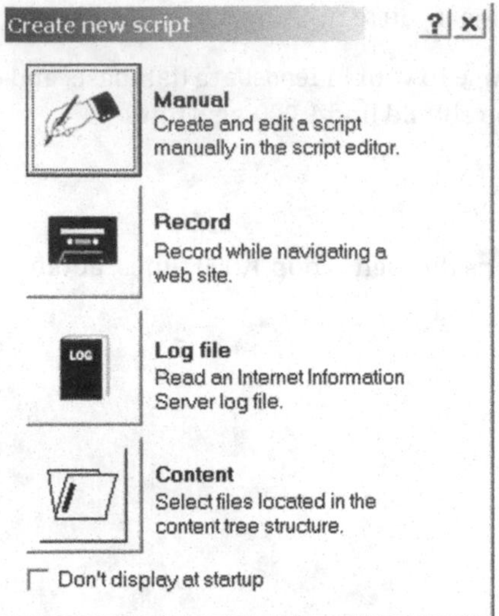

Figure 12-6. *The WAS Create New Script dialog box*

3. Next, you will be prompted with a dialog box that allows you to customize the creation of the script, as shown in Figure 12-7. We won't use any of these options in this example (although we'll examine these options in the following "How It Works" section). For now, just click the Next button to continue.

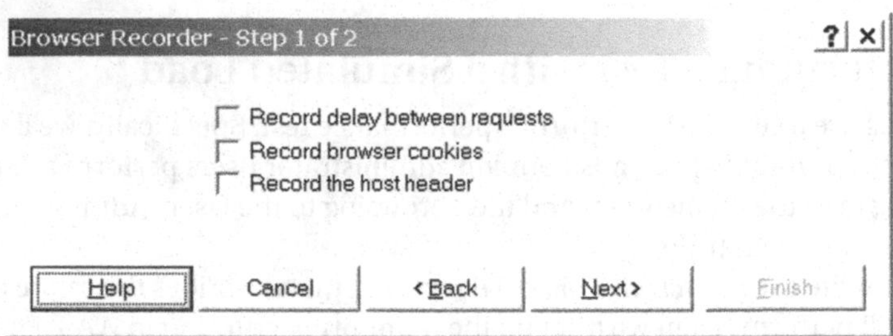

Figure 12-7. *WAS options for customizing your script*

4. Next, you'll see a preparation dialog box. If you're ready to start recording the test script, click Finish.
5. Immediately, a new browser instance will open. You've started recording! Go to the browser and enter the URL for your Friends Reunion application (the `Default.aspx` page). Log in as usual (using the user name and password apress), so that you get to the home page.
6. Click the Users Administration Page link. You should see a grid of current users.
7. Click in the WAS window (but don't close the browser window just yet). Your WAS window should look something like Figure 12-8.

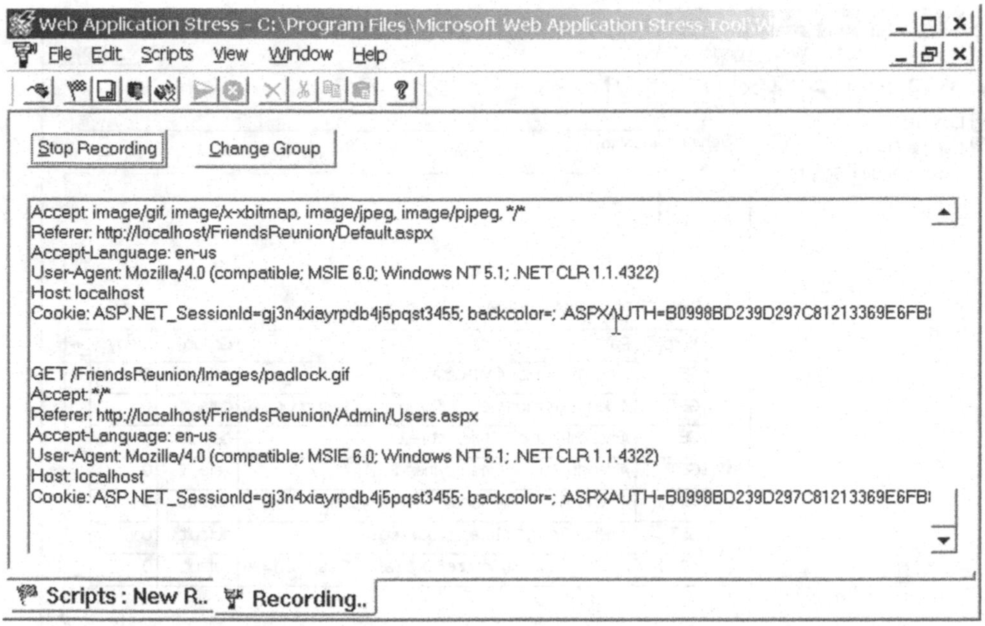

Figure 12-8. *The WAS window with the recorded script*

8. Click the Stop Recording button. The Recording window will close (although it won't cause the opened browser instance to close automatically).
9. The WAS tool will display the Scripts window. In it, you will see a new item named New Recorded Script. It's a good idea to change its name to something more meaningful. Change the script's name to `FRSimpleAdminScript`, as shown in Figure 12-9.
10. Set the Server field to the one hosting your Friends Reunion application. If you're hosting Friends Reunion on the same machine that is running WAS, you don't need to make a change here (`localhost` is the default). If you have different machines for the application and for WAS, type the application server name in the Server field.
11. Now you can clean up the script generated by WAS, so that it does not include any static content. You can do this by clicking the leftmost column of the desired row and then pressing the Delete key. For this test, you should delete all `.gif` and `.css` files, so that your list will end up looking similar to this (with just five items in it):

	Verb	Path	Group	Delay
	GET	/FriendsReunion/Default.aspx	default	0
	GET	/FriendsReunion/Secure/Login.aspx?ReturnUrl=%2fF	default	0
	POST	/FriendsReunion/Secure/Login.aspx?ReturnUrl=%2fF	default	0
	GET	/FriendsReunion/Default.aspx	default	0
	GET	/FriendsReunion/Admin/Users.aspx	default	0
>				

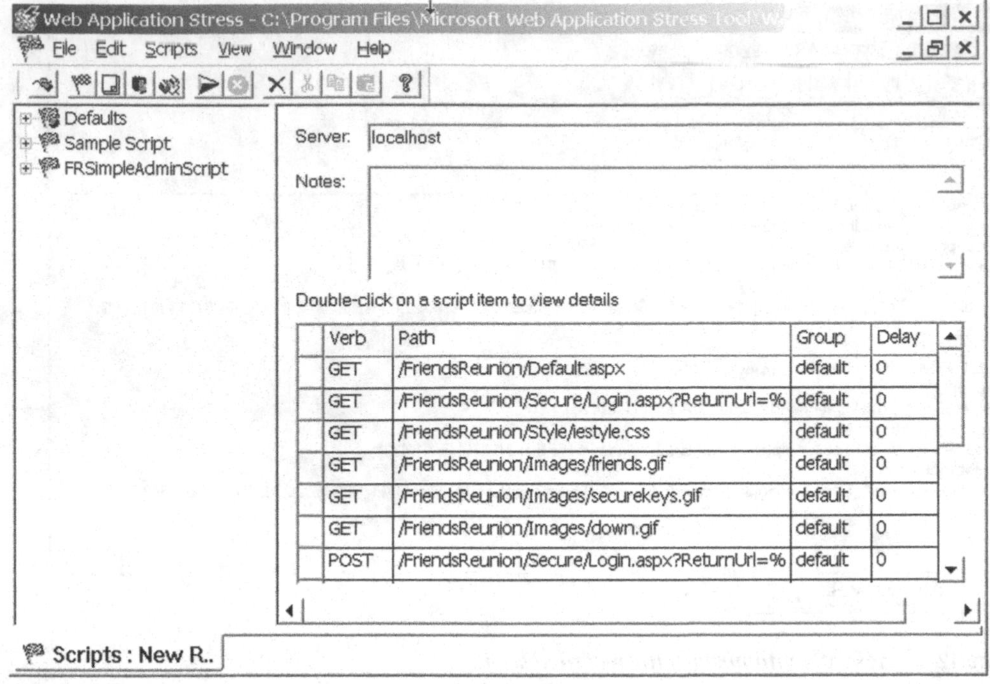

Figure 12-9. *Your new script added to the WAS Scripts window*

12. While still at the Scripts window, adjust a setting of your newly created script. Expand the script node and click the Settings child. Change the default Warmup time from 0 to 10 seconds, as shown in Figure 12-10. This will cause WAS to load-test your server 10 seconds before considering the test started, which will give your server some time to initialize itself in preparation for the test. So, for example, if the server needs to precompile any `.aspx` files, this one-time precompilation will not skew the test results.

How It Works

You have just created your first WAS test script. It will play a crucial part in the Friends Reunion performance test you'll run in the next section.

The script itself follows the steps that an administrator user of the application would usually perform at the beginning of a session: browsing to the home page, logging in, and then browsing to the Users Administrators page.

To create the script, you simply followed the steps that an administrator would follow, but you did it using a browser window that is being spied on by your WAS session. The WAS tool watches what you do in the browser, and records each request and the server's responses into the test script. This cool feature saves you from needing to write the script by hand.

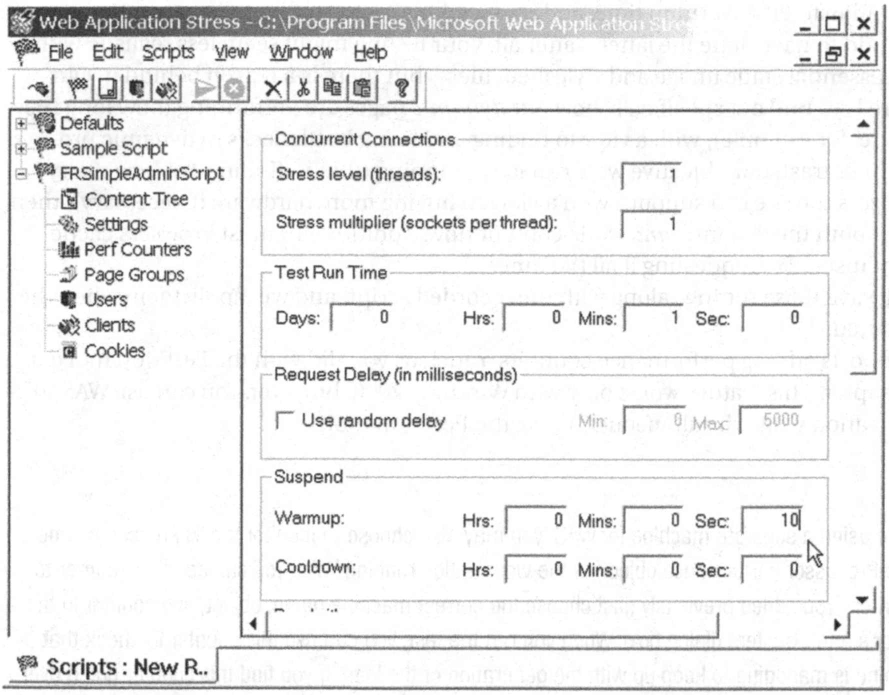

Figure 12-10. *Adjusting WAS script settings*

You've also specified a number of different settings that will affect the execution of the script when you use it in the performance test. In particular, there were three check box options at the beginning of the process (see Figure 12-7). In this case, we opted not to use any of them, but it's worth knowing their purposes:

- **Record time delay between requests:** Controls whether the script records the *pauses* you make while surfing the different pages of the application (this is known as *think time*, because it reflects the time that a user reads the content of a page and thinks about it before making the next request).
- **Record browser cookies:** Controls whether or not the cookies sent to the browser will be recorded into the script.
- **Record the host header:** Allows the recording of host header information.

There's another "think time" control in the Settings dialog box (see Figure 12-10): the Use random delay check box adds further variety to the amount of time between requests, by introducing a random interval of time.

You also adjusted the Warmup time, and removed the requests for static pages. It may seem a little odd to have done the latter—after all, your testing might seem less realistic without all those essential static image and stylesheet files—but there is a reason behind it. Our objective here is to find out specifically how our *dynamic* pages are performing (how long they take to execute, for example), with a view to finding and fixing bottlenecks in dynamic processing. If, by contrast, our objective were capacity planning (that is, finding out how many concurrent users the site can support, with a view to buying more hardware if necessary), then we would test both the dynamic *and* static content now. Additionally, most browsers cache static content instead of requesting it all the time.

WAS will save these settings along with the recorded script, and will apply them when the script is executed.

WAS supports adding performance counters, much as you did with the PerfMon tool earlier in this chapter. This feature works only with Windows 2000, however. You can use WAS to test the application while simultaneously using the PerfMon tool.

Tip If you're using a separate machine for WAS, you may also choose to monitor the % Processor Time counter (in the Processor performance object) of the workstation running WAS. You can add this counter to the seven counters you added previously (just choose the correct machine name, object, and counter in the System Monitor's Add Counters dialog box). When you run the test, you can use this counter to check that the WAS machine is managing to keep up with the generation of the load. If you find this counter going over 80%, it may be a signal that WAS is failing to generate all the specified load; if that's the case, your results will be skewed.

When you execute the test (in a moment), the WAS client will *simulate* many users performing various actions simultaneously, using the test script you've just recorded, while the System Monitor will observe and report whatever the server is doing at any given time.

Running the Performance Test

Now you've created your test script and specified what things you want to keep an eye on while performing the test. You're ready to run the performance test on your web server and collect the results on the WAS client, as well as with the System Monitor. In addition to the results from the performance counters you've set up, you'll also be able to make use of a number of *performance metrics* that WAS collects. The following metrics will be of particular interest:

- **Machine Throughput:** This is the maximum number of requests per second that an application is able to serve.
- **Time to First Byte (TTFB):** This is the number of milliseconds that pass between the time the request is sent and the time the *first* byte of the response is received.
- **Time To Last Byte (TTLB):** This is the number of milliseconds that pass between the time the request is sent and the time the *last* byte of the response is received.

Try It Out: Perform the Test You've done most of the hard work. There are just a few short steps left, and then you'll have some results to analyze.

1. Make sure the `FRSimpleAdminScript` node is selected in the left pane. Then run the script by selecting Script ➤ Run. (Alternatively, click the Run Script icon.) The test will begin, and you'll see a dialog box showing the test's progress.

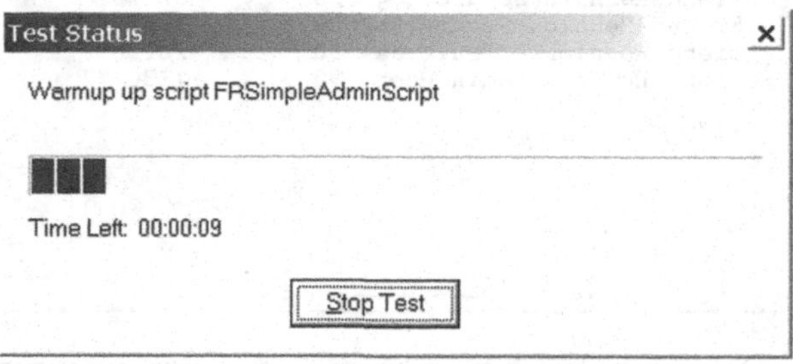

2. When the test completes, the WAS tool should automatically display the Scripts window again. At this point, you should stop the System Monitor so that you keep the last measurements taken.
3. To view the results, select View ➤ Reports, or just click the Reports icon.
4. In the left pane of the Reports window, you'll see a list of all the scripts that have been run (there's just one here). Expand the node. You will find more nodes beneath, one for each occasion the script was run (these nodes are labeled with the date and time of execution; again, there's just one in this example).
5. Beneath each dated node is the result data for that test. Click the Page Summary node. This will show a short description of how each page involved in the test has performed (in terms of numbers of hits, TTFB Average, TTLB Average, and so on), as shown in Figure 12-11. WAS calculates these performance metrics automatically, based on the load it generates and the response it receives from the server. We'll examine and interpret these results in a moment.
6. Now take a look at the performance counters in the PerfMon application. You'll see the results of the server's seven performance counters during the test.

How It Works

You have just run your first load test against your server! After recording the scripts, eliminating unwanted requests for static content, modifying some default values to fit your needs, and setting up key performance counters, you now have your first test results.

For my testing, I used two machines. This is the best approach, because WAS stresses the client machine quite a lot, but what you're really interested in measuring is the *server* load. When I checked the System Monitor after running the test, I found that my server handled 6.50 requests/sec, which is sufficiently low to cause concern. The question is: Why do I get such a low number?

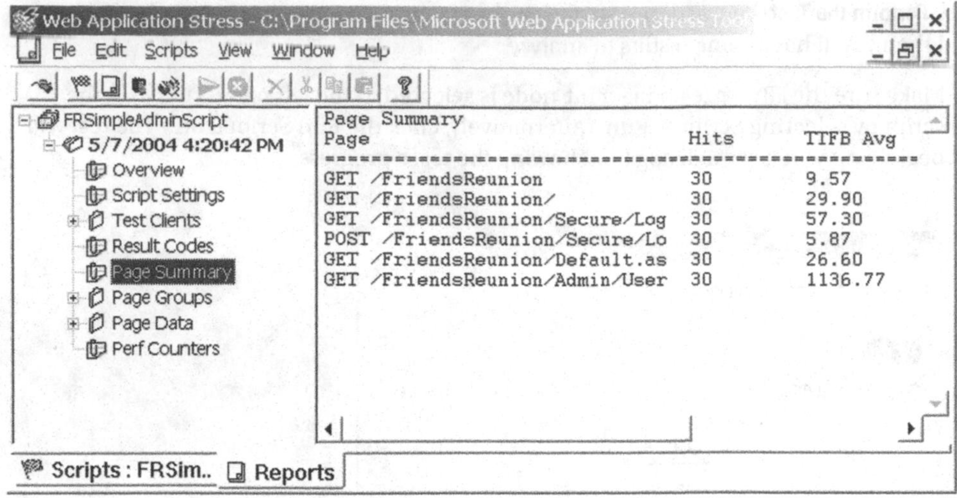

Figure 12-11. *The WAS report after running the script*

Next, you can have a closer look at how each individual page performed, by examining the Page Data node of your report. By briefly examining the data for each page, you may find that the results for `Users.aspx` differ significantly from the rest. Here are the figures that I got in my test:

Page	Average TTFB (milliseconds)	Average TTLB (milliseconds)	Downloaded Content Length (bytes)
`Default.aspx`	7.03	7.27	2360
`Login.aspx`	7.22	8.19	3040
`Users.aspx`	490.84	833.67	1054113

For some reason, my server is taking about 0.5 second in serving the first byte of that page, and then almost another 0.35 second (TTLB minus TTFB) to finish serving it up. Moreover, the output of `Users.aspx` is 1MB long! These two results probably help to explain why the server is handling so few requests per second (6.50 requests/sec) on average.

Why is `Users.aspx` causing that much work on the server? It's probably because the page contains a full-fledged DataGrid control, loaded with the details of 1,000 users, just for display purposes. In the next section, you will make use of *caching* techniques to save your server the immense work of needing to process this DataGrid control on every request, and see how you can tweak it to produce smaller-sized pages.

Caching

A *cache* is an area of memory that stores recently accessed data and resources, so that subsequent requests can reuse them without having them regenerated. When a web page is requested for the very first time, the page must be completely generated from scratch by the server and sent back to that user in the HTTP response. But at the same time, the server can also arrange for the freshly generated material in that page to be put aside into cache areas, so that it can be used to serve subsequent requests from the same user or other users.

So, how does a web application benefit from caching? One benefit from caching is that you can eliminate the need to regenerate the same content many times (because you can generate it once, and then cache it in the appropriate location). Also, depending on the nature of the content, you can try to cache it as close to the client as possible. These two benefits manifest themselves in three immediately obvious ways:

- If content is cached close to the client, you achieve a *reduction in latency* (that is, apparent inactivity) and hence improve the user experience.
- If content is cached close to the client, you also achieve a *saving in bandwidth* (because the route from the client to the cache is shorter than the route from the client to the web server). In particular, if a resource is cached on the browser itself, network resources are eliminated altogether for that resource!
- By reusing generated content many times, you can vastly *reduce the workload* on your server, which can now just generate the material once and cache it (instead of regenerating it for each page request). The reduced demand on the server's resources will improve the server's overall performance.

Caching Overview

If you understand the implications of caching correctly, you can use it in your web applications to gain significant performance improvements. In particular, you need to consider *what* content you can cache, *where* you can cache it, and for *how long*. While the first consideration is application-specific, the other two are not.

Cache Content Expiration and Priority

Most items of content have a natural lifetime. In other words, at the time the content is generated, it's usually possible to specify a date and time at which that freshly generated content will become out-of-date. For example, on a site that publishes stock market shares, much of the data changes every few minutes, so you would not want cached data to last for more than a few minutes (otherwise users will almost always be looking at outdated stock prices). By contrast, you can safely cache the pages of a web site that shows the results of sports events, because those results don't change once they've happened.

You don't want cached data to hang around in the cache after it has become out-of-date. Therefore, any cached item has a *expiry date* that determines its life span—that is, for how long it will stay cached before it is considered invalidated and taken out of the cache. There are essentially two ways to set the expiry date:

- *Absolute expiration* allows you to set the exact date and time when the cached content will expire.
- *Sliding expiration* is a time interval, and it dictates for how long the cached item is permitted to live in the cache *after* the time it was last accessed.

There is another way that items are removed from a cache. Because a cache is just a block of memory (and therefore not infinite in size), there is a *cache management* mechanism that prevents the cache from filling up with nonexpired items. The way it does this is to examine the *priority* of all the items in the cache and remove those with the lowest priority to make way for new items. An item's priority is set at the same time as its expiration, at the time the item is generated and cached. The expiration setting and priority chosen depend very much on the type of data and the context (you'll see an example later in this chapter, in the "Data Caching" section).

Cache Locations

In the web architecture, a cache can reside in a number of different places, and it makes sense to cache different types of content in different places. To be more specific, consider that, in general, a request/response is generally made either directly between the web client (the browser) and the web server, or indirectly via a proxy server, as shown in Figure 12-12.

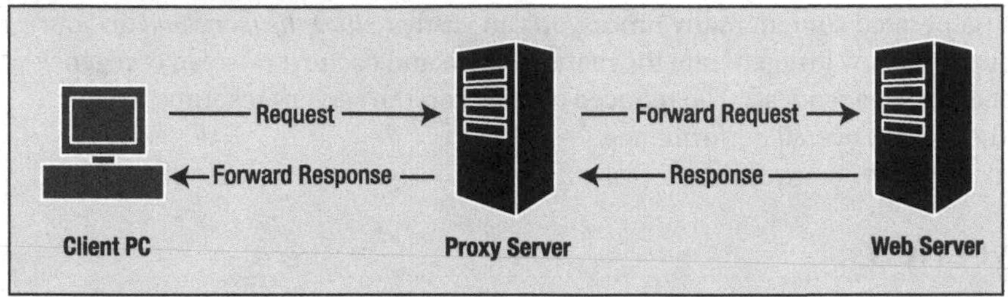

Figure 12-12. *A request/reponse may go through a proxy server.*

This, in fact, gives you three different places where you can cache content: the *client* (browser), the *proxy server*, and the *web server*. The implications of storing content in a cache depend on which cache location is used. Let's examine each one in turn.

Caching at the Client (Browser)

Any browser has a *local cache*, which it can use for temporary storage of any received resources that are marked as cacheable by the content author. When a user requests the same resource a second time, the browser will check the local cache. If the resource is still there (that is, it has not expired or been removed), the browser will fetch the resource from the local cache, rather than fetching it from the server.

The obvious advantage of this situation is that it provides zero latency, because the cached resource can be displayed immediately by the browser without the need to establish a connection and wait for a response. This is as fast as it gets! It also reduces the overall number of necessary transmissions of requests and responses over the network, and hence saves bandwidth. Finally, if the original resource required server resources to generate it, it saves the server the trouble of repeating that work, so there's an overall reduction in demand on the server.

These are compelling benefits, and it's easy to conclude that browser caching seems like an ideal option. But it's not ideal in all situations. One reason is that some browsers choose not to honor the caching attributes specified by the page's author. Another is that if the user has specified any different settings on their browser, these settings will override the default behavior. (For example, users of Internet Explorer can control the browser's internal cache by selecting Tools ➤ Internet Options, and then clicking the Settings button.)

It's important to realize that "caching a page at the browser" means that there's a copy of the cached item stored on the user's local machine. There are potential security and privacy implications here, because it's possible for other users of the same machine to access these resources. In particular, it would be irresponsible to code your application to cache sensitive information such as bank account information at the browser (or, indeed, at the proxy server, as you'll see in the next section).

Caching at the Proxy Server

As illustrated in Figure 12-12, a *proxy server* is a machine that sits between the web application server and the client machines, acting as an intermediary. It receives requests from client machines and forwards these requests to the origin server. It also receives the responses from the origin server and passes them back to clients.

When a proxy server receives a resource from a server, it checks to see whether the page author has deemed the resource to be "cacheable at the proxy server" (something we'll look at when we discuss ASP.NET page caching in the next section). If so, the proxy server can store the page in its own local cache.

The benefits of caching at the proxy are similar to those for caching at the browser. In particular, if the same resource is requested again (either by the same user or by another user via the same proxy server), the proxy server is able to deliver the resource from its own cache, rather than by passing the request on to the server. This saves on the server's resources and bandwidth, and reduces response time in much the same way. Note that the saving is less significant; for example, you get reduced latency but not zero latency. To reduce latency of the cached request to a minimum, the proxy server is usually located close to the client machine. On the other hand, a resource cached on a proxy server can be used to serve the requests of the hundreds (or thousands) of users whose requests are handled by that proxy server, regardless of the identity of the user who requested it first.

Proxy servers are usually put in place by ISPs and corporations with many users. As a consequence, you (as an application developer) generally don't have any control over the existence (or otherwise) of a proxy server. Therefore, while it's useful to take advantage of the possibility of proxy server caching, it is not something you can depend on.

Caching at the Origin Server

Of course, caching content on the server doesn't get the content any closer to the client. If the web server chooses to use its own cache to serve a request, the content still needs to be transmitted back across the network, just as if it were freshly generated. Therefore, there are no savings in latency and bandwidth to be made from caching at the server. However, caching at the server still allows you to reuse resources, avoiding unnecessary regeneration of those resources, and hence reducing the server's workload. While caching at the server doesn't look as attractive as caching at the client or proxy server, it is sometimes your only option, particularly when security and privacy issues are involved.

Ultimately, these three types of caching can help you save resources and get better performance. How much bandwidth and workload can you save? How much is latency reduced?

The answers to these questions depend on where the content is cached, how often it is reused, and when it expires. But there's no doubt that, when used well, caching can help improve your site's performance significantly.

For this reason, ASP.NET has been designed with caching techniques in mind, so let's look at those techniques now.

ASP.NET Caching

ASP.NET has its own *cache*. This cache is an area of memory (on the web server) that it uses to store the output of web pages. ASP.NET stores this output to use it to serve subsequent requests from that memory, and hence avoid executing the page each time the page is requested. As we explained in the previous sections, this reduces the overall amount of processing work required of the server, and the reduction in resources used results in improved performance.

The Microsoft ASP.NET team has given us two APIs that allow us to access the cache:

- A high-level API, which uses a very simple declarative syntax that takes the form of a directive that can be applied to a page or user control
- A low-level API, consisting of a single class (the `Cache` class, which belongs to the `System.Web.Caching` namespace) that can be used in code, allowing us to manage the cache programmatically

The high-level API will save you some typing, while the low-level API requires some coding and a greater understanding of what's going on beneath the surface. Naturally, the latter is the one that gives you more control.

ASP.NET's implementation of caching provides for two different types of caching that relate to the different types of content that can be cached. The first, *output caching*, is about caching the output generated by executing a page or a fragment of a page (a user control). You can use both the high-level and low-level APIs with this type of caching. However, the ASP.NET cache is not limited to storing the output of pages. It's often effective to use *data caching* to cache data whose generation may be expensive in terms of resources (for example, a large dataset is the sort of thing you might cache using this technique). ASP.NET allows you to cache your own data by using the low-level cache API.

Let's look at both of these types of caching in more detail.

Output Caching

As we've said, *output caching* is about caching the output (or results) obtained when a page (or user control) is executed. It's clear from this definition that you're not obliged to cache whole pages; you can cache just a fragment of a page if that's appropriate. In principle, *page caching* and *fragment caching* work in the same way, but there are a few subtle differences that we'll explain in a moment.

Let's look at the principle first. When an `.aspx` page or `.ascx` page fragment is requested, the server checks to see whether the page has been marked as cacheable (using the `OutputCache` directive that you'll meet shortly). Whether the output cache is enabled influences the process at two different stages, as shown as shaded decision items in the flowchart in Figure 12-13.

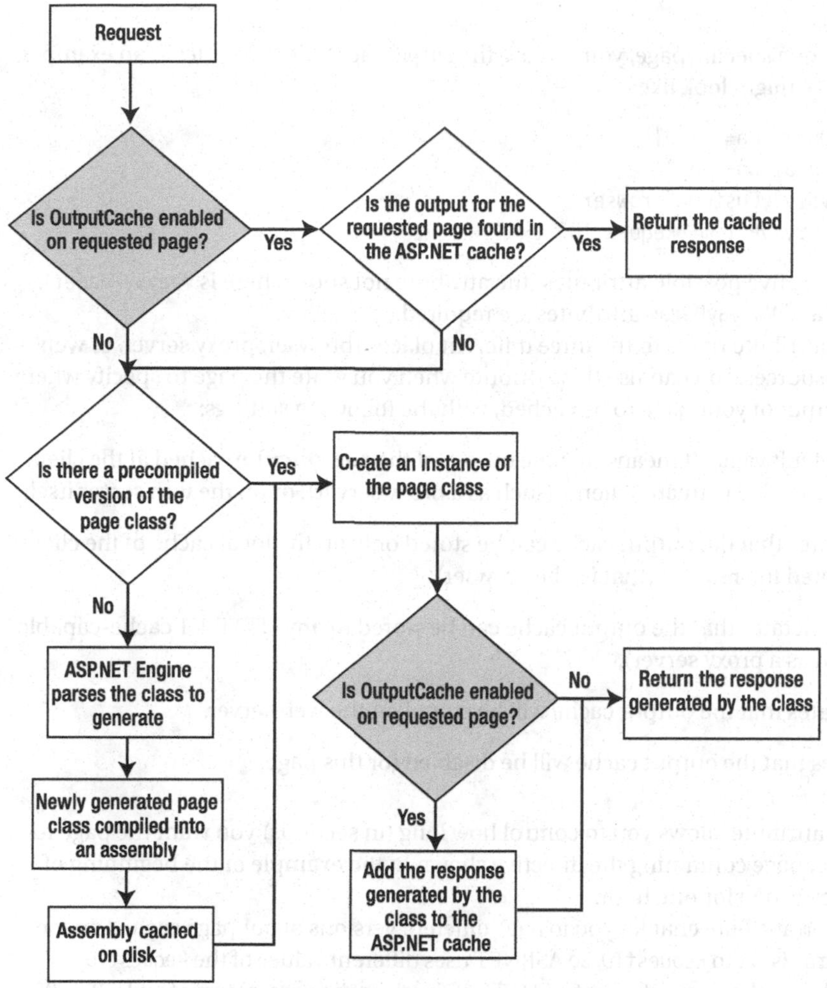

Figure 12-13. *Checking whether output caching is enabled*

The server first checks for the `OutputCache` directive right at the beginning of the process. If it finds that the page (or page fragment) is cacheable, it checks for an existing cached instance of the page, and returns that instance, thus avoiding the subsequent parsing and compilation steps and saving server resources.

If the page is not cacheable, or if there is no cached instance, the parsing and compilation steps occur as usual. Then if the page is cacheable, the newly generated page is placed in the ASP.NET cache so it can be used for subsequent page requests.

The basic process described here applies to both page caching and fragment caching. Now let's look at the practicalities and note the differences between the two.

Page Caching

To enable caching for a specific page, you can use the OutputCache directive. Here's an example of what this directive might look like:

```
<%@ OutputCache Duration="3600"
                Location="Any"
                VaryByCustom="browser"
                VaryByParam="RequestID" %>
```

The directive has five possible attributes (the attribute not shown here is VaryByHeader). Only the Duration and VaryByParam attributes are required.

The Location attribute refers to the three different places (browser, proxy server, or web server) to cache resources. You can use this attribute when you write the page to specify where you'll *allow* the output of your page to be cached, with the following settings:

- Any is the default value. It means that the output of the page *may* be cached at the client browser, at any "downstream" clients (such as a proxy server), or on the web server itself.
- Client dictates that the output cache can be stored only on the local cache of the client who originated the request (that is, the browser).
- Downstream dictates that the output cache can be stored in any HTTP 1.1 cache-capable device (such as a proxy server).
- Server dictates that the output cache will be stored on the web server.
- None dictates that the output cache will be disabled for this page.

The Duration attribute allows you to control how long (in seconds) you want the page to exist in the cache. A page containing the directive shown in the example at the beginning of this section will be cached for one hour.

The VaryByParam attribute enables you to have different versions of our page cached. In the example, VaryByParam is set to RequestID, so ASP.NET uses different values of the RequestID parameter sent either in the query string of an HTTP GET verb or the parameters of an HTTP POST verb. This is useful for pages like ViewUser.aspx in the Friends Reunion application. The exact content of this page varies from user to user, and so there would be no value in caching a single version of the page for all users. So, you can have the application differentiate between individual users by checking the value of the RequestID parameter; and by placing VaryByParam="RequestID" in the OutputCache directive of the page, you can have ASP.NET cache a different version of the page for each user. If you don't want to cache different versions of the page based on the value of a parameter, just set VaryByParam to none:

```
<%@ OutputCache Duration="3600" VaryByParam="none" %>
```

You can also ask ASP.NET to cache a version of the page for *every* possible combination of parameters. To do this, set VaryByParam to *; like this:

```
<%@ OutputCache Duration="3600" VaryByParam="*" %>
```

Caution It's tempting to set VaryByParam to *, and hence to cache every possible version of the page. At first glance, this seems like a good idea for improving overall performance. However, the cache is itself just a memory store of finite size, so the more output you choose to cache, the sooner the cache will fill up. Generally, a more selective approach is required; it's really only worth caching pages that are frequently accessed or whose generation is expensive. There is little sense in caching pages that are almost never accessed or simple pages that don't require any computation.

The VaryByHeader and VaryByCustom attributes work like VaryByParam, in that they allow you to specify when new cached versions of your page should be created. The VaryByHeader attribute allows you to vary the cached versions of a page based on the semicolon-separated list of HTTP headers provided. The VaryByCustom attribute, when set to browser, allows you to vary the cached versions depending on the browser name and major version information. Alternatively, you can set it to the name of a *custom* method, in which you can implement your own logic that controls the versions to cache.

You can use output caching to improve the performance results for the Users.aspx page you saw earlier in the chapter.

Try It Out: Apply Output Caching Generating the dataset of user information displayed in Users.aspx seems to be a real bottleneck, because it uses such a large amount of resources to generate the dataset, and you're asking the application to regenerate the dataset each time the page is requested. One way around this is to cache the entire generated page in the ASP.NET cache, so that the page itself (and hence the dataset that contributes to it) is regenerated less often.

1. Open Users.aspx, and add an OutputCache directive just after the Page directive:

```
<%@ Page Language="vb" AutoEventWireup="false"
         Codebehind="Users.aspx.vb"
         Inherits="FriendsReunionSec.Admin.Users" %>
<%@ OutputCache Duration="300" VaryByParam="none" %>
<!DOCTYPE HTML PUBLIC "-//W3C//DTD HTML 4.0 Transitional//EN">
<html>
  <head>
    ...
```

2. Save the file. If you wish, use the WAS client machine to rerun the FRSimpleAdminScript you tested the application with earlier in the chapter, and examine the results to see whether there's a noticeable improvement. Remember to start collecting information in the System Monitor also.

How It Works

The first time the page is requested, the application must generate the dataset in order to deliver the page, but subsequent requests for Users.aspx are served directly from the ASP.NET cache, and they should be much faster because they require far less processing.

When I tested this using the FRSimpleAdminScript script on my WAS client machine, I got 22 requests per second now, a great improvement over the earlier result of 6.5!

Tip This isn't the only way to deal with the dataset-generation bottleneck in Users.aspx. Instead of caching the entire page, you could have simply cached the dataset itself. The "Caching Data" section later in this section is all about that technique, and for comparison, demonstrates using it with AssignPlaces.aspx.

Fragment Caching

What if some fragment of the page is very dynamic in nature, while the remainder of the page changes very rarely? For example, what if you tried to cache a page that shows live stock quotes (which change every few minutes) along with daily news headlines (which change only every few hours). A high-valued Duration attribute means that the stock quotes are lasting far too long in the cache and becoming outdated; a low-valued Duration attribute means that the less dynamic news headlines are being regenerated too often to be effective. If you really want the stock values to be *live*, you should generate them from scratch for each request, based on the current values at the moment the request is made. Page caching is not really suitable here; you can use *fragment caching* instead.

Fragment caching is a new concept introduced by ASP.NET. It is implemented in practice by using the user controls you learned about in Chapter 3. The idea is that you employ user controls (like the FriendsHeader.ascx and FriendsFooter.ascx controls) to separate different kinds of content in the page. Then you apply an OutputCache directive in the same way as shown earlier, except that you add the directive to the appropriate .ascx files, rather than to the .aspx file. The result is that ASP.NET caches the output for *only* the fragments (that is, the user controls) whose .ascx file contains an OutputCache directive.

Another way of programmatically controlling caching for a user control is to apply the PartialCachingAttribute attribute to its code-behind file:

```
<PartialCaching(7200)> _
Public Class MyControl
    Inherits System.Web.UI.UserControl
```

How would you use this solution to solve the problem of a page containing live stock quotes and news headlines? First, you would implement a user control to show the daily news, and have that user control cache for, say, two hours. So that .ascx file would contain a directive like this:

```
<%@ OutputCache Duration="7200" VaryByParam="none" %>
```

Then you could implement the stock quotes listing in a *separate* user control (which would also allow you to reuse it in a number of different pages), but *this* .ascx page would not contain any OutputCache directive, and it would therefore be regenerated at each request.

Fragment caching works in roughly the same way as page caching, although there are a couple of differences. First, fragment caching does not support the Location attribute; the only valid place to cache a page fragment is the web server. This is because fragment caching is new in ASP.NET, and it is consequently not supported by browsers and proxy servers.

Additionally, fragment caching makes available an extra attribute—VaryByControl—which is not relevant in page caching. The VaryByControl attribute allows you to specify a semicolon-separated list of strings, representing the IDs of controls used inside the user control. ASP.NET will generate one cached version of your user control for each different combination of values. Following the example of a news/stocks page, suppose you added a DropDownList control to the news-headlines user control, with the intention of filtering by company name the displayed news:

```
<asp:dropdownlist id="Company" runat="server" Width="120px">
  <asp:ListItem Value="apress">Apress</asp:ListItem>
  <asp:ListItem Value="msft">Microsoft</asp:ListItem>
  <asp:ListItem Value="amex">American Express</asp:ListItem>
</asp:dropdownlist>
```

Then you can tell ASP.NET to cache different versions of your user control based on the value of the DropDownList control. For that, you modify the OutputCache directive accordingly:

```
<%@ OutputCache Duration="7200" VaryByControl="Company" %>
```

Note that it's not possible to programmatically handle a cached user control like a non-cached one. This is because once the user control is cached, ASP.NET is not creating an instance of your own control, but instead makes a simpler one whose only purpose will be to fetch the cached output. This has an implication for us in the Friends Reunion application. Specifically, we cannot use fragment caching for our FriendsHeader.ascx and FriendsFooter.ascx user controls, because they are manipulated programmatically each time we call them (for example, setting the message in the header and the user count in the footer) in a way that is not allowed for cached controls.

Finally, if a user control is used in several pages (such as a footer control in all your website pages), you can avoid caching the fragment for every page by using the Shared attribute on the OutputCache directive:

```
<%@ OutputCache Duration="7200" VaryByParam="none" Shared="true" %>
```

Or programmatically through the following attribute:

```
<PartialCaching(7200, Shared:=True)> _
Public Class MyControl
    Inherits System.Web.UI.UserControl
```

If you don't specify the Shared value as true, output will be cached for each instance of the control in every page that uses it.

Data Caching

The lower-level API we mentioned earlier is the Cache class, which is contained in the System.Web.Caching namespace in ASP.NET. You can use this API for caching data that is costly to generate. The Cache class is as simple to use as the Session and Application objects you met back in Chapter 6.

There is only one Cache instance per application, which means that the data stored in the cache using it is application-level data. To simplify things further, the Page class's Cache property makes the application's Cache object instance easily available in code.

The data cached through the Cache object is stored in memory within the application. That means that this data will not survive an application restart. (In fact, this is the same as for the data stored in the Application and Session objects, unless you've arranged to store your Session data using the State Service or SQL State session modes, as you saw in Chapter 6.)

The easiest way to add an object to the Cache is by using the index syntax, and specifying a key/value pair like this:

```
Cache("CheckEffectOn") = False
Cache("MembersDataSet") = dsMyDataSet
```

The first of these assigns a Boolean value to the cached flag item called CheckEffectOn. The second assigns a dataset to the item called MembersDataSet. To use these cached values in code, you would access them like this:

```
Dim CheckEffectValue As Boolean = CType(Cache("CheckEffectOn"), Boolean)
Dim dsMembers As DataSet = CType(Cache("MembersDataSet"), DataSet)
```

In each case, you need to cast the retrieved object explicitly. This is because the Cache object handles only references to the System.Object type (which allows it to store objects of any type).

This is not the only way of adding items to the ASP.NET cache. There are two methods of the Cache object that are considerably more flexible: the Insert() method and the Add() method. These methods are very similar in usage, but subtly different:

- The Insert() method should be used to overwrite existing items in the ASP.NET cache.
- The Add() method should be used *only* to add new items to the ASP.NET cache. (If you try to use Add() to overwrite an existing item, it will fail.)

Each of these methods has the same seven arguments (though Insert() has some overloads that allow you to specify fewer than all seven). Using them is so similar that we'll only show you some examples of the Add() method now. You'll see how to use the Insert() method when we apply some data-caching techniques to the Friends Reunion application in the next "Try It Out" section.

Dependencies and Priorities

To appreciate what you can do with Insert() and Add(), you need to know a little about dependencies and priorities. By specifying a *dependency* for an item when you insert it into the cache, you're telling ASP.NET that the item should remain cached until a certain event occurs. The Add() and Insert() methods allow you to specify the dependency of a cached item at the time the item is cached, using these values:

- CacheDependency allows you to specify a file or cache key. If the file changes, your object is removed. If the cache key changes or becomes invalidated, the object is also removed.
- DateTime is a DateTime value that dictates the time at which the cached data expires (as we said earlier in the chapter, we use the term *absolute expiration* for this type of expiration).

- TimeSpan is an interval of time that dictates how long the cached data can remain cached *after* the last time it was accessed (we use the term *sliding expiration* for this type of expiration).

As you add more and more data to the cache, it becomes fuller and fuller. If the data expires at a reasonable rate, there will always be room for more data to be added as the older cached data expires. But if not, the cache will eventually fill up.

If the cache *does* fill up, ASP.NET needs a way to start removing some of the less important items in the cache to allow new items to be cached. To decide which cached items it can delete, ASP.NET rates the importance of all the different items in the cache according to the *priority* of each item. The priority of an item to be stored in the ASP.NET cache can be specified at the time the data is cached (using the Add() or Insert() method). These are the different priority levels, as classified in the CacheItemPriority enumeration:

- High priority items are the least likely to be removed when memory is low.
- AboveNormal priority items prevail over items with a priority of Normal or less.
- Normal priority items will prevail over BelowNormal and Low priorities. The default value for a cached item's priority is Normal.
- BelowNormal priority items use the second lowest priority available. Items with this priority set will prevail over only items whose priority is set to Low.
- Low priority items will be the most likely to be removed when memory is low.
- NotRemovable as a priority level for an item means that ASP.NET should not remove it from the cache, even if memory is low.

When you're assigning the priority of an item, you should base the assignment on the resource cost needed to produce the item: the higher the cost, the higher the priority level.

So, to use the Add() method to add a DataSet object to the ASP.NET cache, you might write the method call like this:

```
Dim dt As New DateTime(DateTime.Now.Year,12,31)
Cache.Add("MembersDataSet", dsMembers, Nothing, _
        dt, TimeSpan.Zero,
        CacheItemPriority.Normal, Nothing)
```

The first and second arguments are the keys by which you reference the cached object and the object to be cached. The third argument is null (signifying no dependency).

The fourth and fifth parameters are the absolute and sliding expirations. Here, we're saying that the cache should expire on the last day of the current year (dt). We want to specify that there is no sliding expiration, so we put TimeSpan.Zero into the fifth argument. The sixth parameter sets the priority to be Normal, using a value from the System.Web.Caching.CacheItemPriority enumeration.

The following example is similar, but it specifies a sliding expiration of 5 minutes instead of an absolute expiration:

```
Cache.Add("MembersDataSet", dsMembers, Nothing, _
          DateTime.MaxValue, TimeSpan.FromMinutes(5), _
          CacheItemPriority.Normal, Nothing)
```

So, if you want to set no absolute expiration, use `DateTime.MaxValue`. If you want to specify no sliding expiration, use `TimeSpan.Zero`. (It's not valid to provide values for both absolute expiration *and* sliding expiration at the same time; if you do, ASP.NET will throw an exception.)

We could add a dependency. In this example, the expiration is also dependent on the modification of a file, `friendsreunion.xml`:

```
Dim dep As New CacheDependency("C:\\data\\friendsreunion.xml")
Cache.Add("MembersDataSet", dsMembers, dep, _
         DateTime.MaxValue, TimeSpan.Zero, _
         Normal, Nothing);
```

In the next example, the expiration is dependent on the modification of another item in the cache:

```
Dim dependencyKeys() As String = {"MembersChanged"}
Dim dependency As new CacheDependency(Nothing, dependencyKeys)
Cache.Add("MembersDataSet", dsMembers, dep, _
         DateTime.MaxValue, TimeSpan.Zero, _
         CacheItemPriority.Normal, Nothing)
```

If you don't want to specify a `CacheDependency` object for your item, you can pass `Nothing` to that argument, as in the first example.

Tip In ASP.NET version 2.0, the `CacheDependency` class is no longer defined as `NotInheritable`, so it's possible to create your own dependency classes with custom logic to determine cache item removal. In fact, the new `SqlCacheDependency` class that is available in version 2.0, for invalidating cache items based on changes on a database, is implemented exactly that way—by deriving from `CacheDependency`.

In case you're wondering, the final argument is of type `CacheItemRemovedCallback`, and it allows you to ask for notification whenever the cached item is evicted from the cache. You can write a custom method (like the `ItemRemovedCallback()` method here), and then specify that method in the seventh argument, as follows:

```
Public Sub ItemRemovedCallback(ByVal key As String, ByVal value As Object, _
   ByVal reason As CacheItemRemovedReason)
   ' This method will be called when the our item expires
End Sub
... other code ...
Cache.Add("MembersDataSet", dsMembers, Nothing, _
         DateTime.MaxValue, TimeSpan.FromMinutes(5), _
         Normal, _
         New CacheItemRemovedCallback(Me.ItemRemovedCallback))
```

Note that the ItemRemovedCallback() method (which is called whenever the cached item expires) has three arguments. The first is the key we used when we stored the item in the cache, the second is the stored object itself, and the third is the reason the item was evicted. There are four possible reasons listed in the CacheItemRemovedReason enumeration: DependencyChanged, Expired, Removed, and Underused.

At least a couple of places in the Friends Reunion application would benefit from some careful application of data caching. In particular, every time we perform an expensive query to the database and then hold the results in a DataSet, we can take the opportunity to cache the DataSet and avoid regenerating it unnecessarily for each request.

Try It Out: Cache Places-Related Data In this example, you'll use data caching in the pages that deal with all the places available to the application. You use this data in different pages and hit the database to get it each time. If you cache the data, and then use the *cached* data in any page that needs it, the resulting reduction in the demands on the server and network should give an overall performance boost.

In particular, AssignPlaces.aspx includes a drop-down list that shows a list of available places. Let's use our new data-caching skills there.

1. Open AssignPlaces.aspx.vb. Change the LoadDataSet() method by removing all the code used to get the Places data from the database. To do this, you just need to remove (or comment out) the following lines:

```
Private Sub LoadDataSet()

  Dim con As New SqlConnection( _
   "data source=.;initial catalog=FriendsData;" + _
   "user id=apress;pwd=apress")

  ' Select the place's timelapse records, descriptions, and type
  Dim sql As String
  sql = "SELECT " + _
   "TimeLapse.*, Place.Name AS Place, " + _
   "PlaceType.Name AS Type " + _
   "FROM " + _
   "TimeLapse, Place, PlaceType " + _
   "WHERE " + _
   "TimeLapse.PlaceID = Place.PlaceID AND " + _
   "Place.TypeID = PlaceType.TypeID AND " + _
   "TimeLapse.UserID = '" + _
   Context.User.Identity.Name + "'"

  ' Initialize the adapters
  Dim adExisting As New SqlDataAdapter(sql, con)
  'Dim adPlaces As New SqlDataAdapter( _
  ' "SELECT * FROM Place ORDER BY TypeID", con)
  Dim adPlaceTypes As New SqlDataAdapter( _
   "SELECT * FROM PlaceType", con)
```

```
    con.Open()
    ds = New DataSet

    Try
      ' Proceed to fill the dataset
      adExisting.Fill(ds, "Existing")
      'adPlaces.Fill(ds, "Places")
      adPlaceTypes.Fill(ds, "Types")
    Finally
      con.Close()
    End Try
  End Sub
```

Note that you've deleted only the code that creates and initializes the SqlDataAdapter component for the Places data, and the code that fills the dataset with its contents.

2. You need to create a dataset for the Places data *somewhere*. You'll implement this functionally in a method called GetPlacesDataSet(). You'll create this method as a Protected method of the FriendsBase class, so that it will be available to AssignPlaces.aspx and any other page that needs to use the cached data. So, open FriendsBase.vb and add the following method to the FriendsBase class:

```
Protected Function GetPlacesDataSet() As DataSet
  ' If it's already cached, return it
  Dim ds As DataSet = CType(Cache("Places"), DataSet)
  If Not (ds Is Nothing) Then
    Return ds
  End If
  ' Generate the new dataset
  Dim con As New SqlConnection( _
    ConfigurationSettings.AppSettings("cnFriends.ConnectionString"))

  Dim adPlaces As SqlDataAdapter
  adPlaces = New SqlDataAdapter("SELECT * FROM Place ORDER BY TypeID", con)
  adPlaces.Fill(ds, "Places")

  ' Reset the dependency flag.
  Cache("PlacesChanged") = False

  ' Create a dependency based on the "PlacesChanged" cache key
  Dim dependencyKeys() As String = {"PlacesChanged"}
  Dim dependency As New CacheDependency(Nothing, dependencyKeys)

  ' Insert the dataset into the cache,
  ' with a dependency to the "PlacesChanged" key
  Cache.Insert("Places", ds, dependency)

  Return ds
End Function
```

3. Import the following namespaces at the top of the FriendsBase.vb file:

```
Imports System.Data
Imports System.Data.SqlClient
Imports System.Configuration
Imports System.Web.Caching
```

4. Now return to AssignPlaces.aspx.vb, and modify the InitForm() method so that it uses the *cached* dataset when populating the drop-down list:

```
Private Sub InitForm()
  ' Initialize combo box
  If Not Page.IsPostBack Then
    ' Retrieve the dataset.
    ' If it's not already cached,
    ' it will be generated automatically and cached.
    Dim cachedDs As DataSet = MyBase.GetPlacesDataSet()

    ' Access the table by index
    Dim row As DataRow
    For Each row In ds.Tables(0).Rows
      ...
    Next
  End If
End Sub
```

5. Finally, you need to invalidate the cached dataset when someone uses ViewPlace.aspx to edit the places-related information in the database. You must do this to ensure that no part of the application (such as AssignPlaces.aspx) uses outdated data. Open ViewPlace.aspx.vb and add the following lines to the end of the dlPlaces_UpdateCommand method:

```
Private Sub dlPlaces_UpdateCommand(ByVal source As Object, _
  ByVal e As System.Web.UI.WebControls.DataListCommandEventArgs) _
  Handles dlPlaces.UpdateCommand
  ...etc...
   ' Invalidate the cached dataset
  Cache("PlacesChanged") = True
End Sub
```

This will ensure that, whenever the list of places is modified, the cached dataset will expire.

How It Works

The lines that you removed from the LoadDataSet() method are the lines that created, initialized, and filled the old dataset with its contents. After these changes, those lines of code reemerge in the GetPlacesDataSet() method, which is the place that now has the responsibility for setting up the new cached dataset:

```
Protected Function GetPlacesDataSet() As DataSet
  ' If it's already cached, return it
  Dim ds As DataSet = CType(Cache("Places"), DataSet)
  If Not (ds Is Nothing) Then
    Return ds
  End If
  ' Generate the new dataset
  Dim con As New SqlConnection( _
    ConfigurationSettings.AppSettings("cnFriends.ConnectionString"))

  Dim adPlaces As SqlDataAdapter
  adPlaces = New SqlDataAdapter("SELECT * FROM Place ORDER BY TypeID", con)
  adPlaces.Fill(ds, "Places")
  ...
```

Note that the method first checks for the existence of the DataSet, returning it if it's already cached.

In the same method, you then create a dummy cache entry called PlacesChanged, which you will use for dependency purposes (essentially it acts like a flag; you change its value to True whenever the data in the database is changed, as you'll see in a moment):

```
Cache("PlacesChanged") = True
```

Then you create a dependency to tie the life of your dataset to the modification of the dummy key:

```
Dim dependencyKeys() As String = {"PlacesChanged"}
Dim dependency As New CacheDependency(Nothing, dependencyKeys)
```

Finally, you use the Insert() method to insert the dataset in the cache. The Insert() method works in a similar way to the Add() method we discussed earlier, but also allows you to overwrite existing cache entries:

```
Cache.Insert("Places", ds, dependency)
```

You made just two changes to the InitForm() method, which is the one that populates the drop-down list. First, you *added* code to retrieve the cached dataset using the GetPlacesDataSet() method:

```
Dim cachedDs As DataSet = MyBase.GetPlacesDataSet()
```

Second, you *changed* the next bit of code so that it uses the cached dataset, rather than a freshly generated one as before:

```
For Each row In ds.Tables(0).Rows
  ...
```

The cached dataset should be regenerated when the database is updated (rendering the existing cached dataset outdated). So, you've added a line of code to ViewPlace.aspx, to flag changes to the database. This line of code changes the value of the dummy "flag" cache item, `Cache("PlacesChanged")`, which is the subject of the cached dataset's dependency:

```
Cache("PlacesChanged") = True
```

The result of all this is that whenever a user requests `AssignPlaces.aspx`, the application will check for a cached version of the dataset first. If one exists, it will build the page using the cached dataset. If not (either because no dataset has been generated yet or because the dataset has expired), the application generates the dataset from scratch, places that dataset in the cache, and then uses that newly cached dataset to generate the page. Invalidating the existing cached dataset is performed in another, entirely different page: the one administering places and their information.

Using this approach, I measured an increase from 10.88 to 19.63 requests per second for the `AssignPlaces.aspx` page when I retested the page with WAS!

Caching at Application Startup

Notice that there is no cached dataset when the application first starts. The dataset will not be generated and cached until the first time someone requests `AssignPlaces.aspx`. This means that the first ever visitor to `AssignPlaces.aspx` will not be served as fast as subsequent visitors to the page; the first user will need to wait slightly longer while the application generates and caches the dataset.

There is a way to eliminate this delay for the `AssignPlaces.aspx` page's first visitor. You could arrange for the dataset to be generated and cached at the time the application *starts*, by adding code to the `Application_Start()` event handler (in `Global.asax`). This process requires identical code to that contained in the `GetPlacesDataSet()` method. Therefore, the best way to do this would be as follows:

1. Create a `Friend` *utility class*, which is accessible from anywhere in the current application and import the following namespaces in it:

```
Imports System.Data
Imports System.Data.SqlClient
Imports System.Configuration
Imports System.Web.Caching
```

2. Move the `GetPlacesDataSet()` method code to a `Public Shared` method of this utility class:

```
Public Class FriendsUtility
  Public Shared Function GetPlacesDataSet() As DataSet
     ... almost same code as before ...
  End Function
End Class
```

Note that because the code is no longer applied to a class derived from the `Page` class, you no longer have access to the `Cache` property. Therefore, you need to replace it with `HttpContext.Current.Cache`, which is the way of getting to the same cache but from anywhere in the application.

3. Replace the `GetPlacesDataSet()` call in `AssignPlaces.aspx.vb` so it calls the new `FriendsUtility.GetPlacesDataSet()` instead:

```
Dim cachedDs As DataSet = FriendsUtility.GetPlacesDataSet()
```

4. Finally, add a call to `FriendsUtility.GetPlacesDataSet()` in `Application_Start()` to force its loading at startup.

Monitoring the Cache API

We've mentioned the dangers of caching too many items. The dilemma is simple. It's tempting to cache everything you generate, because it seems sensible to avoid the resource cost of regenerating items if possible. However, the main cost of caching is memory utilization, since the items must be stored somewhere.

Ultimately, you need to avoid wasting your server's cache memory on an item if caching the item offers no benefit. If an item is not expensive to generate or is rarely accessed, it's generally better to regenerate it each time it is needed.

With this in mind, it's helpful to have some way of monitoring the activities of the cache. There are a number of PerfMon performance counters designed specifically for this purpose, particularly the counters available for the ASP.NET Applications performance object. A key counter to watch here is the Cache Total Turnover Rate counter. If this counter gives high-valued readings, it means that there are many items entering and leaving the cache per second. This could have a negative impact on performance, because of the resources involved in expiring items from the cache (particularly in terms of cleanup). If there is a consistently high volume of material being added to and deleted from the cache, any benefits of the caching process are likely to be outweighed by the additional processing power required to handle the high cache turnover rate.

If you use a lot of short expiration times, your application will be particularly vulnerable to a high cache turnover rate. Of course, some items require short expiration by their very nature; if you need to use short expiration times, be aware that this could have an effect and use them carefully.

Controlling the Viewstate

As you've learned in previous chapters, the viewstate is enabled by default. You can control the viewstate in several ways to improve your application's performance.

Disabling the Viewstate for Controls

In the WAS tests that we performed earlier in the chapter, we noticed a couple of things about the `Users.aspx` page. First, it was taking a long time to generate the page. We identified that this was due to the fact that the server was required to generate a huge dataset (containing data about 1,000 users), and we dealt with that problem by arranging for a *cached* version of the page (from the ASP.NET cache) to be used if possible.

But there was another issue: the size of the response itself (the number of bytes passed from server to client in the page response) is also very large. These were the results I generated in my test, and you probably got something similar:

```
Downloaded Content Length (in bytes)
--------------------------------------------------------
Min:                               1054113
25th Percentile:                   1054113
50th Percentile:                   1054113
75th Percentile:                   1054113
Max:                               1054113
```

Why is the response so large? Admittedly, we need to pass all the data (about the 1,000 users) in the dataset to the client; otherwise, the browser will be unable to display the data in the page. But in addition to that, these bytes *also* contain a hidden __VIEWSTATE form field, which will at least double the size of rest of the page. You can verify this by selecting View Source from the page context menu in the browser.

But is there any reason why the viewstate should be enabled for this DataGrid control? The page has no facility for the user to post back the user data to the server for handling; it contains no code for events on the DataGrid control. In fact, there is nothing in the page that requires the viewstate to be enabled. Therefore, you are free to reduce the response size for this page by *disabling the viewstate* for the DataGrid control.

Try It Out: Disable the Viewstate on a DataGrid Control Since the viewstate is unnecessary on the DataGrid control in Users.aspx, you'll disable it for that control. Then you'll find out whether it has a noticeable effect on the overall response size of the page.

1. Open Users.aspx, select the DataGrid control, and view its properties by pressing F4. Find its EnableViewState property, and set it to False. Save the file.

2. You can check in the HTML view that VS .NET has correctly changed the enableviewstate attribute in the code:

```
<asp:datagrid ...other attributes...
                enableviewstate="False">
  ...
</asp:datagrid>
```

3. Now go back to the WAS client and run the FRSimpleAdminScript test one more time. After the test, check the Downloaded Content Length readings for Users.aspx to see if the download size of the page has been reduced. (You'll find this reading in the Page Data node in the results.)

How It Works

Well, first let's check that it does work! Here are the results that I got for Users.aspx after disabling the viewstate on the DataGrid control:

```
Downloaded Content Length (in bytes)
------------------------------------------------------------
Min:                                 337317
25th Percentile:                     337317
50th Percentile:                     337317
75th Percentile:                     337317
Max:                                 337317
```

The simple act of disabling the viewstate has reduced the download size by two-thirds. It's also worth checking how much impact this has on the server's performance overall. In my results, I found that my server is now able to handle 42 requests per second—that's about twice what I had before, and almost seven times what I had when we started the chapter!

So, what's happening? When the DataGrid's viewstate was enabled, it simply allowed the state to be persisted across postbacks. For this, the state was being included in the page in encoded form, within the `__VIEWSTATE` field of the page. This inflated the page size from a relatively acceptable 0.337MB (in my case) to a massive 1.05MB.

We simply identified that the page doesn't use the DataGrid's `viewstate` data for anything useful on the server and was therefore an unnecessary burden. By explicitly setting the DataGrid's `enableViewState` property to `false`, you tell the DataGrid not to persist any value into the viewstate (the default for this property here is `true`). As a result, the `__VIEWSTATE` hidden field is much shorter, which improves things in two ways:

- Most obviously, there's a significant reduction in page size (as you've seen in the results of your testing).
- There's a saving on the server's resources, because the server now has far less viewstate to encode or decode and process.

The viewstate is enabled by default. It's worth considering each of the controls used in each page to check whether it really depends on having the viewstate enabled. If a particular control does *not* use its viewstate, then simply disable it by setting the control's `enableViewState` property to `false`.

Disabling the Viewstate at the Page and Application Levels

In light of the previous discussion, you might start looking at the Label controls used in the `ViewUser.aspx` page of Friends Reunion. None of these Label controls make use of its viewstate, so they can all be disabled. In fact, in `ViewUser.aspx`, you can go one step further. If you consider the controls in that page, you'll notice that *none* of them need to keep their state between postbacks! So, you could deal with them all in one go by disabling the viewstate for the whole page. To do that, you could just set the `EnableViewState` attribute to `false` within the `Page` directive:

```
<%@ Page language="vb" Codebehind="ViewUser.aspx.vb"
        AutoEventWireup="false" Inherits="FriendsReunion.ViewUser"
        EnableViewState="false" %>
```

If you're writing an application that doesn't use viewstate at all, you could disable the viewstate at the application level by making a simple change to the application's `Web.config` file. Simply find the `<pages>` element and set its `EnableViewState` attribute to `false`:

```
<configuration>
  ...
  <system.web>
    <pages ...
      EnableViewState="false"
    />
```

```
    ...
  </system.web>
  ...
</configuration>
```

Don't do this in the Friends Reunion application, because there are some parts of that application that do rely on the viewstate!

Checking the Viewstate Encryption Features

It is also important to check that the tamper-proofing and encryption features of the viewstate are not enabled in your application if you don't really need the extra security that these features provide. This level of security will certainly impact the performance of your application, so disable it if you don't need it.

The tamper-proofing mechanism can be specified by setting the `EnableViewStateMAC` attribute in the `Page` directive:

```
<%@Page ... other attributes ...
        EnableViewStateMAC="false" %>
```

There is no need to explicitly disable encryption, because it depends on `EnableViewStateMAC` being set to `true`.

Note that the value of the `EnableViewStateMAC` attribute *doesn't* affect your ability to use the viewstate for individual controls. In contrast, if the value of the `EnableViewState` attribute is `false`, then it disables the viewstate-related security settings.

Deciding What to Put in Viewstate

Finally, we recommend that you are selective about what data types you store in the viewstate. Integers, Booleans, hash tables, strings, arrays, and array lists containing any of the former, as well as Pair and Triplet types, are okay, because the viewstate serializer is optimized to work with these types. Other data types should be avoided if possible, because saving other serializable types into the viewstate is a slower process.

More ASP.NET Performance Tips

You have already learned plenty in this chapter about how to examine and improve the performance of specific pages, and you've seen a couple of demonstrations in which carefully chosen caching techniques and controlling the viewstate enhance the overall performance of the page and the application.

In the remainder of the chapter, we'll take a look at some other ASP.NET performance tips. Not all of them are immediately applicable to the Friends Reunion application, but you will surely find them useful when developing your own applications.

Server-Side Redirection Using Server.Transfer

When the user is redirected between pages of an application using `Response.Redirect()`, the server sends an HTTP 302 Redirect response to the client passing the target URL. The 302

Redirect response tells the browser to issue a new request with the new URL. Effectively, the redirection is handled by this extra round-trip between the client and server, to finally get the user to the desired page, as illustrated in Figure 12-14.

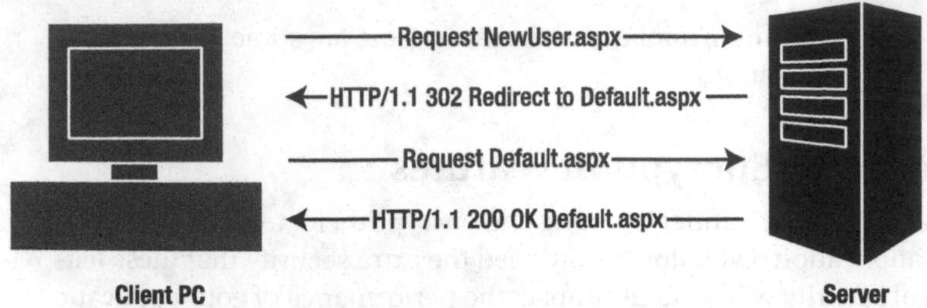

Figure 12-14. *Redirection involves an extra round-trip.*

You can avoid this extra round-trip by employing `Server.Transfer()` instead of `Response.Redirect()`. `Server.Transfer()` transfers the execution to a different page within your application. It's a sort of "server-side redirect," in which the client doesn't notice that a redirect occurs.

Try It Out: Use Server.Transfer for Server-Side Redirection You can quickly apply this improvement to the Friends Reunion application.

1. Perform a search (Ctrl+Shift+F) on the files in the Friends Reunion application to find occurrences of the `Response.Redirect()` method call in the application. There are quite a few; for example, you'll find them in `Logout.aspx.vb`, `NewUser.aspx.vb`, and `ViewUser.aspx.vb`.
2. Go to each one in turn (or perform a global Find and Replace in Files) and replace the `Response.Redirect()` with a `Server.Transfer()` method call. The new method will take the same single parameter as the old one. For example, here's the change in the `UpdateUser()` method in `NewUser.aspx.vb`:

```
If doredirect Then Server.Transfer("../Default.aspx")
```

How It Works

Replacing the `Response.Redirect()` method call with a `Server.Transfer()` method call simply means that the redirection is managed on the server, without a round-trip to the client, as illustrated in Figure 12-15.

The performance improvement from this change manifests itself in two ways:

- The server now needs to handle just one request, instead of two.
- There are only two messages sent (one request and one response) instead of four, and that reduces the delay perceived by the end users as they wait for a response to appear on the browser.

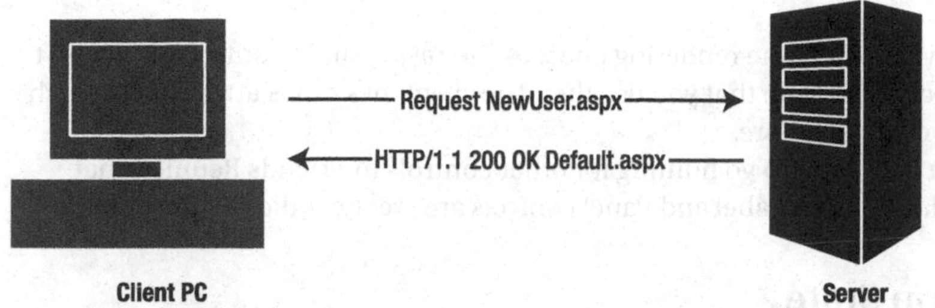

Figure 12-15. *Managing redirection on the server*

When you run the code to test this, you may also notice that the URL shown in the Address box of the browser is the address of the original request (`NewUser.aspx`), even though the page returned to the browser is clearly `Login.aspx`. That's because the server transferred execution to `Default.aspx` without telling the browser about the transfer. This may make things difficult for users if they want to bookmark pages, for example. You'll need to evaluate whether this drawback is an acceptable trade-off for the reduced network traffic.

Using Web Controls Conservatively

You learned about the power of web controls back in Chapter 3. When you're using web controls, you need to be aware that they can involve a lot of processing work for the server, because these controls must be initialized, their properties set, their events handled, and so on. So, you should take a look at each web control in your application and consider whether you really need to use a web control for that function.

For example, take a look at the code in the `ViewPlace.aspx` file. In particular, note the following `<asp:panel>` control there:

```
<headertemplate>
  <asp:panel id="Panel1" runat="server" cssclass="PlaceTitle">
    List of Places
  </asp:panel>
</headertemplate>
```

The `<asp:panel>` control here is not manipulated anywhere in `ViewPlace.aspx.vb` or in any other code. It's just used to hold three words of text, styled using the `PlaceTitle` CSS class. However, it's still a web control and consequently demands server processing time. Since this control isn't manipulated at all, this just wastes processing time.

Try It Out: Avoid Unnecessary Web Controls Now you'll rewrite `ViewPlace.aspx` to demonstrate how to use web controls conservatively, and get a slight performance gain in this case.

Simply open `ViewPlace.aspx` and replace the `<asp:panel>` control with an HTML `<div>` tag, as follows:

```
<headertemplate>
  <div class="PlaceTitle">
    List of Places
  </div>
</headertemplate>
```

How It Works

The <div> element provides the same rendering effect as the <asp:panel> control, but doesn't require server-side processing. Note that you use the <div> element's class attribute to attach the same CSS class as you used before.

As an exercise, you may want to go hunting for other controls in Friends Reunion that may be converted to plain HTML. Label and Panel controls are great candidates for this!

Disabling Session State

It's very convenient that you can just throw objects into session state and use them later, but this convenience comes at a cost. By default, session state is enabled, which means that ASP.NET does all the work involved in making the session state feature available, even if you don't use it. Therefore, it's worth overriding the default value for those pages that do not perform any session handling.

You disable session state by setting the EnableSessionState attribute to false in the Page directive:

```
<%@ Page Language="vb" ...
        EnableSessionState="false" %>
```

If you have a page that *reads* values from session state (but does not *write* new values or *modify* existing ones), then it uses session state in a sort of *read-only* mode. In these cases, you can set the EnableSessionState attribute to ReadOnly, which will provide the page with access to session state but with less overhead (because it omits the writing capabilities).

If you don't use session state anywhere in your application, you can simply turn it off at the application level by setting the <sessionState> element's mode attribute to Off in Web.config:

```
<sessionState mode="Off"
        stateConnectionString="tcpip=127.0.0.1:42424"
        sqlConnectionString="data source=127.0.0.1;user id=sa;password="
        cookieless="false" timeout="20" />
```

Caution Be careful to use an uppercase letter *O* when setting the value, because it is case-sensitive!

Finally, be aware that in State Service and SQL State session modes, session data must be serialized and deserialized to get it in and out of storage, and the cost of this processing will directly depend on the complexity of your objects.

Improving Database Access

A number of factors affect the efficiency of database access. Here are some ways for improving database access to consider for your applications:

Use stored procedures. The first (and perhaps most obvious) consideration is the way you write your queries. In the Friends Reunion application, you have used SQL text queries throughout. You've done this for one reason only: to simplify the code. You can give your application an instant performance boost by converting that code into *stored procedures*. Stored procedures are precompiled and highly optimized, and reside within the database. That means you don't need to transmit and compile the entire query each time you use it. As a result, you benefit from reduced traffic between your web server and the database server, and a significant reduction in the database server workload (especially for complex queries).

Code the DataAdapter component manually. The automatically generated commands that a `DataAdapter` component can produce are not optimized, and not as powerful as coding your own commands.

Choose a managed provider carefully. Use a data provider that is specifically written for the database engine you're targeting, instead of a generic one. If you're targeting Microsoft SQL Server, you should use the classes found in the `System.Data.SqlClient` namespace, rather than the more generic classes found in the `System.Data.Odbc` namespace. This will avoid an extra level of indirection and, better yet, your code will be speaking SQL native language, and thus dramatically improve performance.

Use DataReaders instead of DataSets. What about the relative costs of `DataReader` and `DataSet` objects? You should use a `DataReader` in preference to a `DataSet` wherever possible. Remember that the disconnected nature of a `DataSet` is achieved by storing all the data in memory, so if you don't need to cache the data, you should be using a `DataReader` instead.

Set up connection pooling correctly. Remember that the useful *connection pooling* offered by ASP.NET (which manages open connections and allows them to be reused, thus avoiding some of the overhead of connection opening and closing) will work only if you use identical connection strings for identical datastores. If you have two connection strings that differ by even a single character, the connection-pooling mechanism will consider them as different.

Summary

Performance is a feature of your application, which you should consider even before starting to write your very first line of code. As it happens, in this chapter, you've considered and applied some retrospective changes to the Friends Reunion application:

- Caching expensive pages, page fragments, and data objects
- Disabling viewstate where appropriate
- Replacing `Response.Redirect()` with `Server.Transfer()`
- Replacing web controls with HTML elements where possible
- Disabling session state where possible

You managed to apply all these changes without too much effort, but it would have been a lot easier if you had applied some of the practices here at the time you wrote the application. Certainly, at the time you design an application, it's often possible to pick out places where you have things like large, frequently generated datasets. In those cases, you should plan your cache usage as part of the application design, establish the expiration of the cached object, and convince yourself that there will be enough cache memory to contain it.

The main cache area we've examined in this chapter is the ASP.NET cache. This is an area of memory on the web server that is provided by ASP.NET for output caching and for data caching. You've also seen that some items can also be cached further downstream, in areas of cache at the proxy server or in the browser itself.

Caching is undoubtedly one of the most powerful techniques available for improving web application performance. New ASP.NET caching features, such as the ability to cache the whole or a fragment of a page, are very well suited to their task.

It's clear that you don't need to resort to tricky code. You can write clean and maintainable code that uses the different features you have learned about in this chapter to effectively improve your application's performance.

Our intention has been to demonstrate how to test your application and to suggest some of the options ASP.NET has on offer. There is much to explore, and we hope we've given you some ideas! As we noted earlier, there is much more information on these subjects in *Performance Tuning and Optimizing ASP.NET Applications*, by Jeffrey Hasan and Kenneth Tu (Apress, 2003; ISBN: 1-59059-072-4). Also, see the Microsoft Patterns and Practices site (`www.microsoft.com/practices`), particularly the guide "Improving .NET Application Performance and Scalability" (`http://msdn.microsoft.com/library/en-us/dnpag/html/ScaleNet.asp`).

In the next chapter, we'll turn our attention to the task of preparing the Friends Reunion application for deployment on production servers.

CHAPTER 13

Publishing Web Applications in .NET

Throughout this book, we've examined how to make the best use of VS .NET for developing applications. Once you've finished developing the application, there are just a few final hurdles to overcome before it can be used by the world at large. These hurdles all relate to *publishing* and *maintaining* this application. In particular, you need to select and group the files required for an installation into a *deployment package*, and then *install* the deployment package on production servers. You also need to find a way to *configure* an application for the target system.

The time and complexities involved in the deployment of a project are often overlooked. Once an application has been proved to function, to be reliable, and to fulfill the requirements set out for it, developers may want to relax and assume that there is nothing more to do. But we still need to organize all the elements that make up the application—web pages, compiled components, databases, and so on—and move them from the place where they were developed/built/tested (maybe in the developer environment itself for small teams, or on the build, testing, or preproduction staging servers in larger ones) to the production hosting environment in a controlled way.

This chapter examines the functionality provided by the .NET Framework and VS .NET that comes into play when development of an application finishes and deployment is required. It covers the following topics:

- Installing an application by hand
- Creating a simple deployment project to do the same task, automating a lot of the effort involved
- Adding more complex functionality, such as user interaction to the deployment project, and allowing changes to the configuration to be made during deployment
- Adding custom actions to the installation of applications (including installation of external parts of a system, such as databases)

Methods for Deploying .NET Applications

Historically, the manner of deploying an application has been largely dependent on how the application was composed (that is, what was in it). Traditional ASP files could simply be copied to a folder on the target machine, and as long as a site or virtual directory was configured in IIS, the application would run. If the application made use of COM components, things became much more complicated. You could register COM components by writing a batch file (a script with a `.bat` extension). You could even create a proper installation package that either registered the DLLs or placed them in COM+. Such installation packages could be created either by using third-party applications or by using Microsoft's Packaging and Deployment Wizard, included with Visual Studio 6.0. Other methods were available for different platforms, such as Java. The existence and popularity of such third-party applications for the creation of installation packages demonstrated the commonly held opinion that Microsoft's offering didn't provide the functionality required, and left much to the developer.

When Microsoft announced that it was planning to incorporate a full-featured deployment manager into VS .NET, many were skeptical due to its track record. However, consider that an installation package just goes through the motions that are required when installing by hand. It's now much simpler to deploy an application by hand than it used to be (as you'll see in the next section). So, the simpler this process, the more easily such functionality can be implemented by an installation builder. VS. NET's deployment projects provide an efficient and professional way to manage application deployment. We'll look at the functionality they offer in a moment, after we look at another method for deploying .NET projects: XCOPY.

XCOPY Deployment

Possibly the most talked about aspect of installing .NET applications in general, and web applications in particular, is *XCOPY deployment.* This refers to the old MS-DOS tool XCOPY, which allows files and folders to be copied between locations with a wealth of options.

XCOPY can be used on its own. It can copy subfolders, validate the actions it has performed, ignore errors, select the files to copy based on attributes (such as Last Modified Date), and so on. This is a huge leap forward in comparison to the deployment of projects developed in older technologies such as ASP with COM DLLs, where, once all of the files had been copied, DLLs had to be registered and unregistered, entered into COM+, and so on.

Such a simple method of deployment is possible due to the self-describing nature of assemblies in .NET. Each assembly contains within itself all of the information required for other applications to make use of it (which means that you don't need to store metadata about the assembly in the Registry). This feature, when combined with the fact that .NET applications check specific folders (such as the current one) for libraries to be used with applications, means that the deployment of applications really can be as simple as copying files to the target machine.

Deployment Projects

With the solution to installation as simple as copying files, it may seem that there is little need for the inclusion of deployment packagers with VS .NET. However, there are many secondary questions that need answering for each application, such as the following:

- Where do the files need to be installed?
- How do you provide the files in a manageable format (such as a compressed archive) to those installing the application?
- How do you create an entry in IIS that guarantees that the entry's settings are the same as on the development machines?

- What if the individuals installing the application aren't experienced with file manipulation? (Keep in mind that most of the time administrators, not experienced developers, have the responsibility of installing the application.)
- What if the user makes a mistake while performing a manual installation?
- How much time will be spent copying the files by hand (particularly if the system must be deployed to many machines or is being updated on a regular basis)?
- What if certain parts of the application can be installed and updated separately from others?
- What if you need to provide further functionality, such as the installation of a database or notification of a successful installation for auditing purposes?
- Is your application going to be presented to end users as a commercial product (that they'll expect to install in a similar manner to all of their other software)?
- How do you provide late-breaking information and tips to users installing your applications?

By using *deployment projects* in .NET, you can deal with all of these issues. These projects provide a wizard-style interface that guides users through the installation process, allowing them to make choices at the appropriate times.

Manual Web Application Deployment

Before we look at how to go about creating a deployment project using VS .NET, we'll run through the process of installing an ASP.NET application by hand. This way, you'll gain a better understanding of the underlying architecture and installation process involved in deployment.

If you look at any web application in the Solution Explorer, you'll see that it consists of a large number of files and folders. Here's an example from our Friends Reunion application:

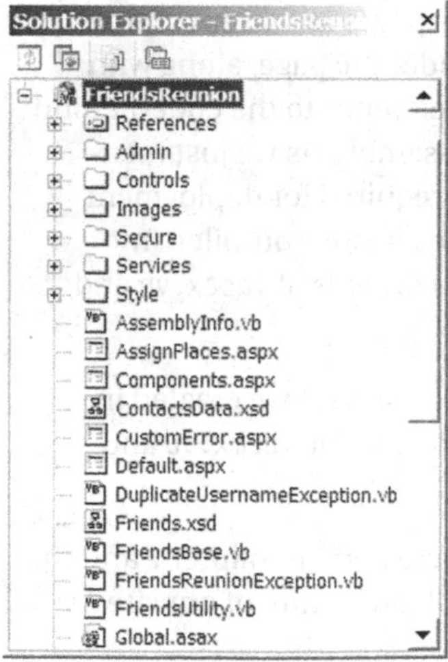

However, this is only half of the story. If you click the Show All Files button on the toolbar of the Solution Explorer, you'll see that several more files and folders are shown with a "ghosted" appearance, along with + symbols next to many of the files.

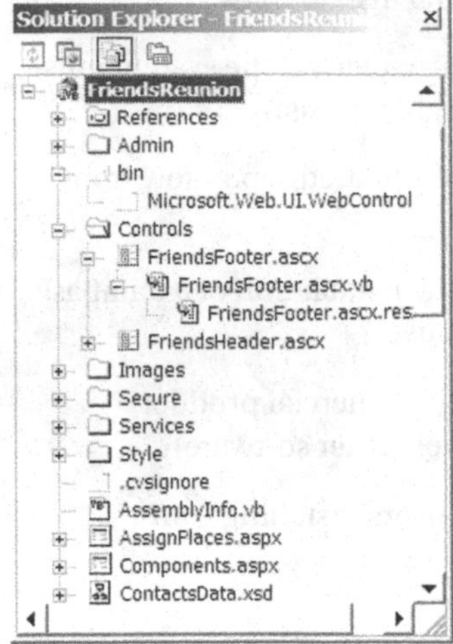

Many of these files are not required when deploying the project to another machine. For instance, all of the files with a `.vb` extension are merely source code for the application. This source code will not be required at runtime, because it will have been compiled.

In order for the Friends Reunion the application to run, the following files *are* required:

- `bin\FriendsReunion.dll`: This is the application's DLL file, which contains the compiled code of the project's classes, methods, declarations, and so on. There is a class for each of the web pages that was created as part of the project.

- `bin\Microsoft.Web.UI.WebControls.dll`: This is the assembly that contains the controls we used for some functionality on our site, such as populating a TreeView control with information from an XML file in Chapter 8.

- `*.aspx` and `*.ascx`: These files represent the individual web pages and user controls in the application. They contain any HTML required to render the page, along with controls that are used (such as `<asp:textbox>` tags) and a reference to the code-behind file that has been compiled into the `FriendsReunion.dll` assembly. As we just mentioned, the `.aspx.vb` (and also the `.aspx.resx`) files are not required for deployment because the code and resources contained in those files are already compiled into the `FriendsReunion.dll` assembly. The same is true for the contents of `.ascx.vb` and `.ascx.resx` files.

- `Services\Partners.asmx`: This is the file that exposes the web service we created in Chapter 9. Just as in the case of the web pages and user controls, the `.asmx.vb` and `.asmx.resx` files don't need to be deployed.

- `Friends.xsd` and `upload.xml`: These are the schema file we created in Chapter 7 and the sample XML file used in Chapter 8. They are used in the upload feature of our site.

- `Global.asax`: This file links to the `Global.asax.vb` code-behind class, which is compiled into `FriendsReunion.dll`. That's where we added the `Application_AuthenticateRequest()` functionality, back in Chapter 10. This is the code that checks to see if a user has logged in, for example. Again, source files that are compiled (those with a `.vb` and `.resx` extension) can be ignored.
- `Web.config`: This is the XML file that contains ASP.NET configuration information for the web application. We can change the values in this file without the need to recompile the entire project. This means that after installation, we can alter the `Web.config` file without affecting the other files we need to deploy.

Obviously, for our site to appear to users as we intend, the files contained in the `Images` and `Style` folders will also need to be included for deployment. If we used any script files, we would need to deploy them, too.

Note The Microsoft IE WebControls package we used in Chapter 8 will need to be installed with its own Microsoft Installer (MSI) file, too, as some scripts need to be deployed to the IIS root application folder.

In addition to the `.vb` source files, there are several other files that are not required for deployment. These include some files shown in the Solution Explorer, such as `.pdb` (program database) files that are created for each project when it is compiled in Debug mode and other files that aren't shown, such as `.vbproj` files that contain information about the project. Also, we don't need the XSD files we used to generate typed datasets in Chapter 5, such as `PlaceData.xsd` or `ContactsData.xsd`. These files were used to generate a class that is already compiled into the application assembly.

Now that you know exactly which files are actually required by an ASP.NET web application, let's try out the process of manual installation.

Try It Out: Deploy by Hand We'll assume here that the destination server already has IIS installed, but does not yet have the .NET Framework installed. After all, it could be that this is the first .NET application to be deployed to your servers.

1. Install the .NET Framework runtime files so that IIS can recognize and process ASP.NET file types such as `.asmx`, `.aspx`, and so on. The Microsoft .NET Framework Redistributable installs the files required to run *any* .NET application, including web applications. This file is called `dotnetfx.exe`, and it can be found on the Microsoft Windows Component Update CD that came with VS .NET. It is located in a subdirectory named `dotNetFramework`. Alternatively, you can download it from Microsoft's web site, at `http://msdn.microsoft.com/netframework/downloads/redist.aspx`. By executing this file, you install all of the essential runtime libraries (files such as `System.dll`, `System.Data.dll`, and so on), as well as the runtime itself, which executes the assemblies that form the compiled application. If it weren't for this runtime, the applications created by .NET projects could not be run at all, as they don't contain *native code*; that is, the code must first be processed by the runtime, converting it to the physical instructions that execute on the machine.

Caution To ensure correct execution, the version of the .NET Framework Redistributable run on the target machine should be the same as the version of the .NET Framework installed on the machine that compiled the original project. A newer version may work, but it's highly recommended to recompile the application against the version used for deployment.

2. Copy the necessary files into a new folder somewhere on the target server's hard disk. By default, IIS uses the `C:\Inetpub\wwwroot` as the folder where individual applications place their subfolders, but you're free to put it anywhere that seems appropriate; after all, that's why they are called *virtual* folders! Throughout this example, it will be assumed that the folder chosen is `C:\Inetpub\wwwroot\FriendsReunion`. Here are the files to copy (an asterisk denotes either all files in a given folder or all files with a specific extension):

   - `Admin\Users.aspx`
   - `Admin\Web.config`
   - `bin\FriendsReunion.dll`
   - `Controls\*.ascx`
   - `Images\*`
   - `Secure\*.aspx`
   - `Services\*.asmx`
   - `Style\*`
   - `*.aspx`
   - `Global.asax`
   - `Web.config`
   - `Friends.xsd`
   - `upload.xml`

   When copying the files across, you should ensure that the exact folder structure is re-created on the target server (in other words, the `FriendsReunion.dll` file is located in the `bin` folder, and so on). There is no need to register the DLL file itself.

3. Depending on the location of these files, you may need to create a virtual directory for them in IIS, set an alias for the folder, and set the physical folder directory as an application. (Refer to Chapter 1 and Appendix B to see how to create and set up virtual directories in IIS.) Or, if you have placed the files under `C:\Inetpub\wwwroot`, you simply need to tell IIS that the directory is an application folder, by clicking the Create button on the Directory tab of the Properties dialog box for it.

4. Set special file and folder permissions if necessary. For example, you need to allow Read permissions on both `Friends.xsd` and `upload.xml` files used by the application and discussed in Chapter 8.

5. Before verifying that the web site is installed properly, let's check the version number of the .NET Framework on the server (to ensure that it matches with that of the development machine). In the Internet Services Manager MMC snap-in (select Start ➤ Settings ➤ Control Panel ➤ Administrative Tools ➤ Internet Services Manager or select Start ➤ Run and type **inetmgr**), right-click the `FriendsReunion` (virtual) directory and select Properties. Then click the Configuration button that appears in the lower-right area of the Properties dialog box. This brings up another dialog box that shows all the file types and their mapping with an executable that handles them. Scroll down a little to the `.asmx` and `.aspx` extensions. Files of this type are run using the `aspnet_isapi.dll`, which will be located in a folder named after the version of the .NET Framework to which it belongs. In Figure 13-1, you can see that the Framework version is 1.1.4322.

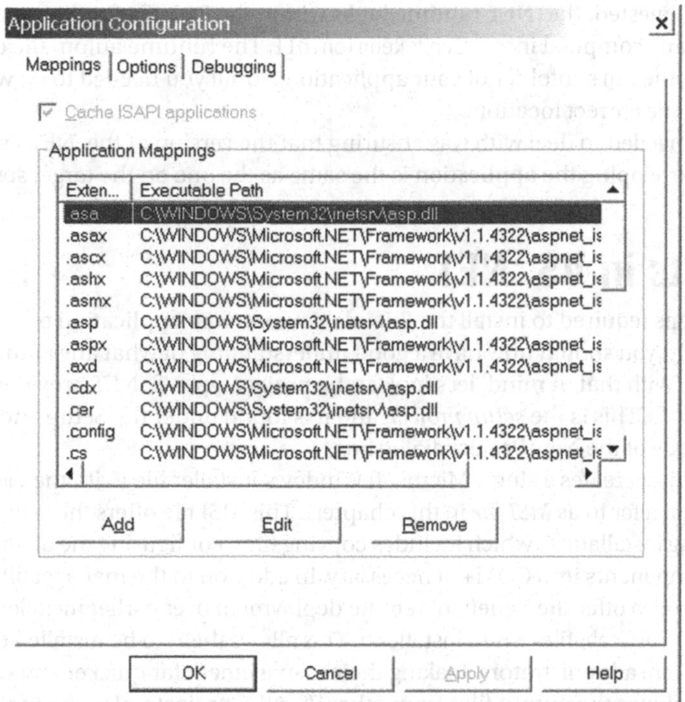

Figure 13-1. *Checking the version number of the .NET Framework*

6. Now you're ready to test the installation. Open a web browser and navigate to the URL http://<servername>/FriendsReunion, where *<servername>* is the name of the server to which the application has been deployed or its IP address. The web application's default page should appear, allowing you to log in or register, as appropriate.

Note If you're getting exceptions when you run an application on the server, but it runs fine on the development machine, it's worth checking that both machines have the same version number installed. Problems with .NET Framework versioning will become more common as additional releases of the Framework are made available by Microsoft. At the time of writing, version 1.1.4322 is the latest released version available. The good news is that ASP.NET version 2.0 adds an option to the virtual directory Properties dialog box that allows you to easily change the version you want to use.

How It Works

You have taken the minimum number of files produced by VS .NET for an ASP.NET web application project and copied them to a folder on our server. You then created a virtual folder that acts as an alias for this location and allows users to view the site through a web browser.

Each of the `.aspx`, `.asmx`, and `.ascx` files (and `Global.asax`, too) contains a line of markup that specifies which class in your project contains the code-behind functionality for that file. When that resource is requested, the .NET runtime looks within the DLL file for the necessary class, which will be already compiled into `FriendsReunion.dll`. The runtime automatically looks for this DLL file in the `bin` subfolder of your application. So, all you needed to do was copy each of the files to the correct location.

The only issue you needed to deal with was ensuring that the version of the .NET Framework that you used in developing the application is the same as the one on the target server.

Setup Projects in VS .NET

Having looked at the steps required to install the Friends Reunion web application onto a different machine manually, you should now have a good understanding of what any automated installer will need to do. With that in mind, let's look at the project type VS .NET provides for installing web applications. This is the *setup project,* and it is found under the Setup and Deployment Projects node of the New Project dialog box.

A VS .NET setup project creates a single Microsoft Windows Installer file (with the `.msi` file extension, which we'll refer to as *MSI file* in this chapter). This MSI file offers the user a friendly GUI for directing installation, which includes copying files, configuring the environment, and installing components into COM+, if necessary. In addition to the manageability of a single file, such MSI files also offer the benefit of remote deployment over earlier installer technologies (such as cabinet, or `.cab`, file-based installers). This allows them to be installed on remote machines by system administrators, making their management far quicker and easier.

A setup project combines the output files from other VS .NET projects, along with any other necessary files, to create an installation file that can be copied and run on the system that is to host the application. Just for reference, Table 13-1 describes the types of VS .NET projects you can use for deployment.

Table 13-1. *VS .NET Deployment Projects*

Project Type	Description
Setup Project	Used to create installers for Windows Forms applications, as opposed to web applications. This is the only option available with the Standard Edition of VS .NET. In order to use the other project types, you need either the Professional Edition or one of the Enterprise Editions.
Web Setup Project	Similar to a standard Setup Project, but it is aimed to the deployment of web applications. It does this by tailoring the installation process to include the creation of a virtual directory in IIS automatically.
Merge Module Project	Can be reused in several installations. If certain groups of components or files are common to many applications, then instead of copying such files one by one into each setup project, you can create a merge module containing a group of files. You can then use the merge module in your setup project to include the common files that it contains automatically. Microsoft itself makes such merge modules available, for the .NET runtime, for example. One difference between merge modules and other setup projects is that they cannot be run on their own. They must be added to other setup projects in order for the files they contain to be deployed. Creating merge modules for common tasks follows a very similar procedure to regular setup projects.
Setup Wizard	Not really a setup type in its own right; it simply asks a series of questions in order to determine the setup project type to use. It also sets certain options within the setup configuration.
Cab Project	Used to create cabinet files that can be downloaded to a web browser or platform. This project type lets you package ActiveX components so that they can be downloaded and installed onto a client's machine from a web site with a single click.

In VS .NET, setting up Web Setup Projects (or any of the other setup project types) is very simple. VS .NET provides a series of editors to alter each stage of the installation. These editors allow you to specify changes that should be made to the Registry, any extra files that are required, the look of the installation interface, and so on. When you select a setup project in the Solution Explorer, the mini-toolbar at the top changes to display an icon for each of the editors available for the project, as listed in Table 13-2.

Table 13-2. *VS .NET Editors*

Icon	Editor Type	Description
	File System Editor	Allows creating, updating, and property setting for all physical files, assemblies, and folders of the project to be installed.
	Registry Editor	For creating or modifying values in the Registry of the machine where the application is being installed.
	File Types Editor	Can create specialized file type commands that assign processes to specific file extensions. Particularly useful if the installed project uses a unique file name extension.

Continued

Table 13-2. *Continued*

Icon	Editor Type	Description
	User Interface Editor	The install process comprises a series of dialog boxes that are displayed to the user. This editor allows you to change or delete any of the default dialog boxes and to create new custom dialog boxes.
	Custom Actions Editor	Allows you to specify additional processes that should be performed on a target computer during installation. The process can take the form of a DLL, an executable, a script file, or an Installer class file within the solution. For instance, you could create a Visual Basic script that creates a new administrator or a SQL script that creates a database.
	Launch Conditions Editor	The installer uses conditions specified in this editor to determine whether the installation can proceed or if dependent components need to be installed first.

Creating Web Setup Projects

The only project type available in the Standard Edition of VS .NET is the Setup Project. In order to try out the creation of a Web Setup Project, you need to have the Professional Edition or one of the Enterprise Editions of VS .NET. Even if you don't have one of the versions, you should still read the steps in the next "Try It Out." The main difference between the Setup Project and Web Setup Project types is that the latter creates a virtual directory in IIS to host the application. You can add this functionality by using custom actions, described later in this chapter, in the "Customized Deployment" section.

Try It Out: Create a Web Setup Project You'll now create a VS .NET Web Setup Project that installs the Friends Reunion application.

1. Within the `Friends Reunion` solution, add a Web Setup Project from the Setup and Deployment Projects node of the Add New Project dialog box, as shown in Figure 13-2. Name this project `FriendsReunionSetup` (this project can be created in any convenient location) and click OK. Once the `FriendsReunionSetup` project has been created by the IDE, it will show up in the Solution Explorer, along with the `FriendsReunion` project that you have created.

2. You now need to add to the deployment package the files that constitute the web site. To do this, click the File System Editor button on the toolbar at the top of the Solution Explorer pane (see Table 13-2). The editor appears, as shown in Figure 13-3.

3. Using the File System Editor, you can add all of the files that are required by your web application in order to function. To do this, right-click Web Application Folder in the tree view on the left and select the Add ➤ Project Output option. This brings up the dialog box shown in Figure 13-4.

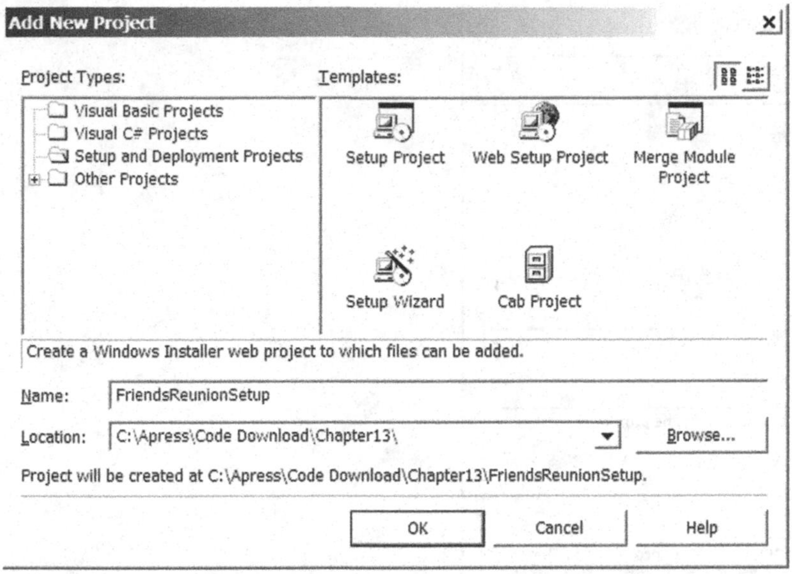

Figure 13-2. *Creating a Web Setup Project*

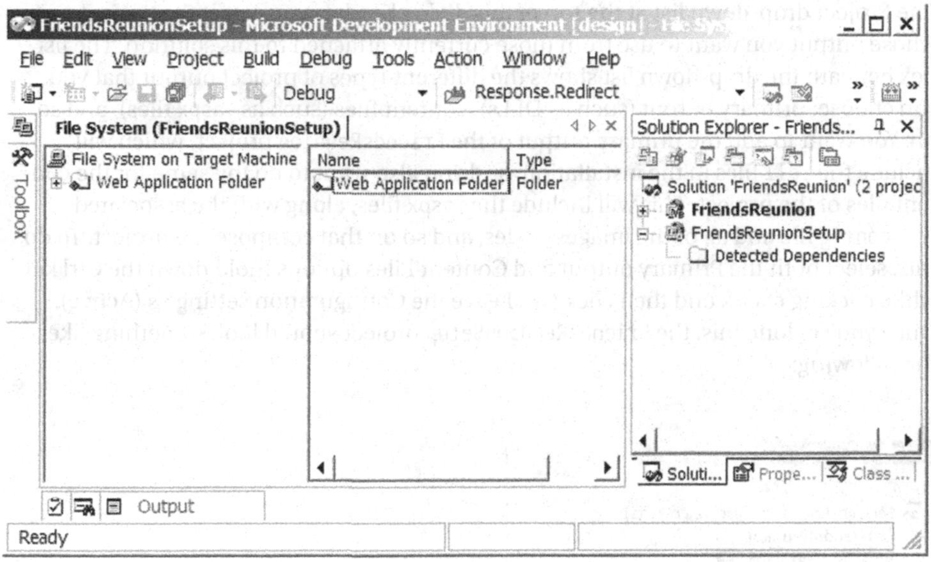

Figure 13-3. *The VS .NET File System Editor*

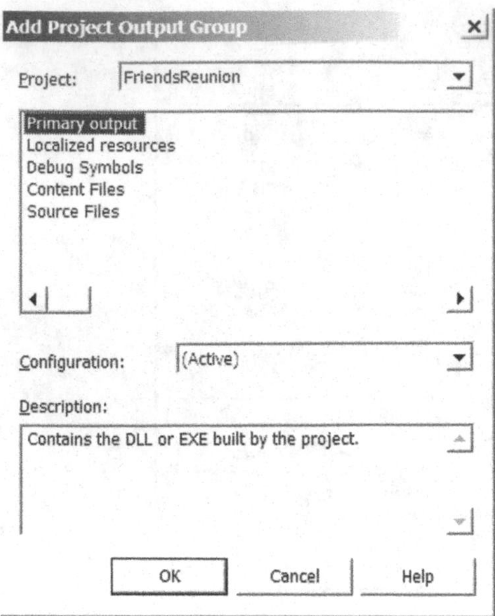

Figure 13-4. *Adding a project's primary output to the setup project*

4. The Project drop-down list at the top of this dialog box lets you select the project whose output you want to use from those currently attached to this solution. The list box beneath the drop-down list shows the different types of project output that you can choose: primary output (such as DLLs), content files (such as `.aspx` files), and so on. You want to add the primary output of the `FriendsReunion` project, which will include the `.dll` files in the installation, and you also want to do the same for the content files of the project. This will include the `.aspx` files, along with the associated `Web.config` file and all of the images, styles, and so on that compose the project. To do this, select both the Primary output and Content Files options (hold down the Ctrl key while clicking each), and then click OK. Leave the Configuration setting as (Active). Once you've done this, the `FriendsReunionSetup` project should look something like the following:

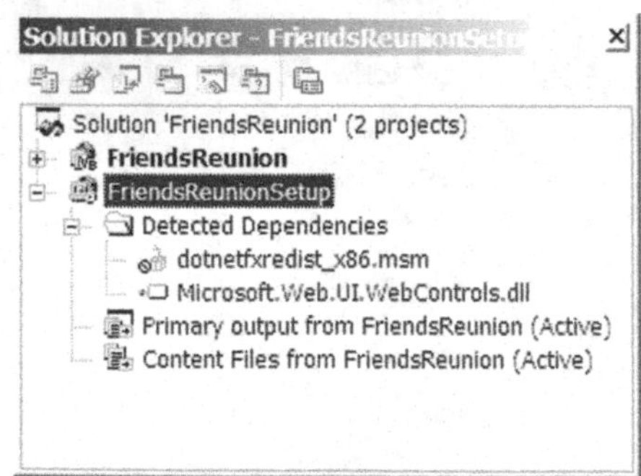

5. That's all you need to do to create a simple installer for your projects in VS .NET. To build the setup package, right-click the `FriendsReunionSetup` project in the Solution Explorer and choose the Build option from the menu.

As it now stands, the deployment package won't work, so don't attempt to install it just yet. We'll look at how this deployment package works first, before trying it out.

How It Works

To add the files that you want to include for installation, you use the File System Editor. This editor uses a layout similar to Windows Explorer, with a tree view on the left and a detail pane on the right showing the contents of the selected folder. To include a file in the installation process, you just need to place it into the appropriate folder in this editor. By default, the `bin` folder is already created, ready for you to place your executables and DLLs.

When VS .NET builds a setup project after you've added such files, it creates all of the installation packages that you might need to distribute in order for your users to install your .NET application. You can see what these are by browsing to the folder that you specified when the `FriendsReunion` project was created. This folder will contain two subfolders, called `Debug` and `Release`, respectively. The compiled code for the installation will be in one of these folders, depending on your project configuration. The default location is the `Debug` folder. The following files are created:

- `Setup.exe` and `Setup.ini`: This program, and its configuration file, will examine the system to determine whether the Microsoft Installer technology itself needs to be installed, and let the user do it if necessary. It will then install your application, using the file described next.

- `FriendsReunionSetup.msi`: This is the package that contains all files for installing your application with the Microsoft Installer. If you are certain that the required version of the Microsoft Installer is already installed on the target machine, this is the only file that you need to distribute.

Using the Microsoft Installer software is the default method of installing any Windows application, and Microsoft and other third-party software vendors throughout the industry use it.

When you selected the Primary output option from the Add Project Output Group dialog box, the `FriendsReunion.dll` file in the `bin` folder was added to the deployment package. This file contains all of the compiled code-behind files for the project. By selecting the Content Files option too, you ensured that all of the other files required (as listed in the previous section) were also included. Table 13-3 describes the output types available from the Add Project Output Group dialog box.

Each of the entries for the content files and primary output is really just a shortcut to the project output files themselves; it's a sort of list of what files are to be included, rather than a copy of each individual file. This means that the setup package adjusts itself to use the latest version of the included files at the time the installation project is built, and hence reduces the danger of producing a setup package that installs an outdated application.

Table 13-3. *The Output Types Available for Setup Projects*

Output Type	Description
Documentation Files	The documentation that has been produced for a project.
Primary output	The compiled executables and libraries (files with an `.exe` or a `.dll` extension). This does not include any DLL or EXE files that have simply been copied into the selected project; only those that are created by the project are included. Libraries that are referenced by the primary output are, however, automatically added to the `bin` folder of the File System Editor.
Localized resources	The locale- or culture-specific resources for a project.
Debug Symbols	The debugging files produced for the project, with either a `.dbg` or `.pdb` extension. These files are required for debugging the project remotely; they are not required if you are deploying a live system.
Content Files	Files such as `.asmx`, `.aspx`, `.ascx`, `.asax`, `.htm`, `.css`, `.xml`, `.xsd`, and images.
Source Files	These comprise the code-behind files for `.aspx`, `.asmx`, and `.ascx` solution items, as well as other code files such as classes and interfaces. Similarly to the Debug Symbols, if the project is to be deployed to a live environment, these are not required.

Tip The files to be included in the Content Files category are those that have the Build Action set to `Content` in the Properties browser. You can set it to `None` to avoid deploying them.

In addition to selecting project outputs, the File System Editor also allows you to drag any files and folders located on your system directly into the desired output folder, either from Windows Explorer or from VS .NET's Solution Explorer pane.

The Configuration drop-down list in the Add Project Output Group dialog box offers the following choices for the selected project:

- **(Active):** Uses whichever one of the following two configurations has been set as the default configuration for the project you're attaching to this installation.
- **Debug .NET:** Includes debug information, making it possible to easily step through code, trace errors, and so on. This produces slightly more of a performance hit than Release .NET builds.
- **Release .NET:** Strips out all code that uses the `DEBUG` command and also omits all debug information from compiled code.

It is also possible to select different code for different configurations at compile-time, on a conditional basis. Look at this simple example as an illustration:

```
#If DEBUG Then
    Response.Write("Test code...")
#Else
    Response.Write("Live code...")
#End If
```

This preprocessor directive (as denoted by a leading hash character, #) is similar to a regular `If` statement, except that it controls the behavior of the compiler itself, rather than the compiled code. So in this simple example, if you were to select Debug .NET as the active configuration for a project, the command would write out the text "Test code..."; otherwise, the text "Live code..." would be displayed.

The value `DEBUG` that is used for testing can be found in the Property Pages of your web application, which are displayed when you select the Properties option from its context menu in the Solution Explorer. If you select the Build node inside the Configuration Properties node from the list on the left side of the window, and you switch to the Release configuration using the drop-down list at the left top of this window, you will see the `DEBUG` value disappears from the Conditional Compilation Constants field, as shown in Figure 13-5. If you change the Configuration drop-down list to Debug, you'll see that this value reappears.

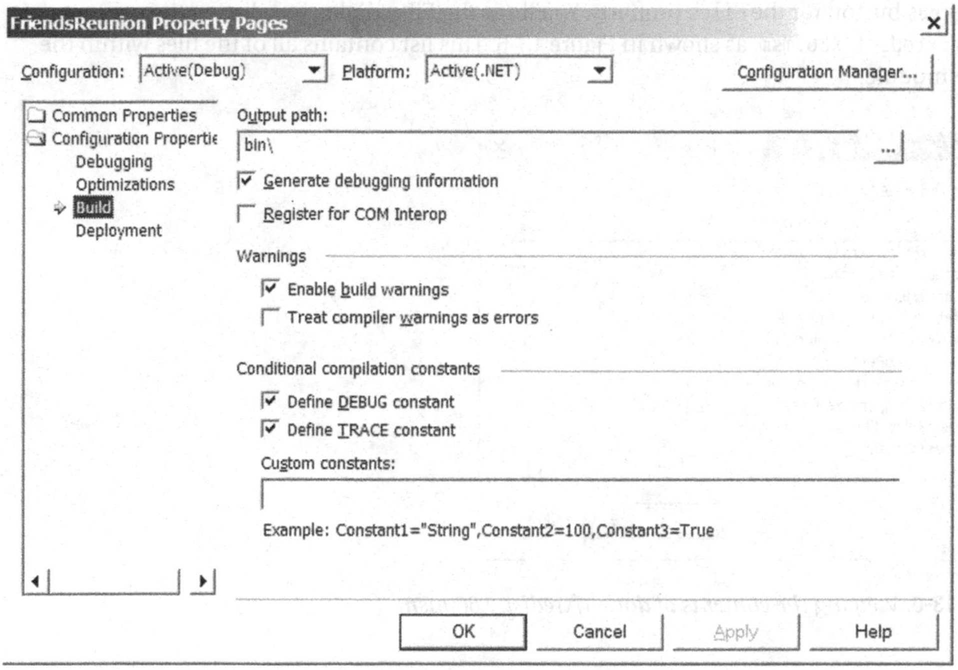

Figure 13-5. *Viewing configuration properties of a web application*

Including the dotnetfx.exe File with Your Installation

Needless to say, your application depends on the .NET Framework being installed on the target machine. When you went through the process for installing the application manually, you dealt with this issue by manually copying the `dotnetfx.exe` file to the target machine and running it to install the .NET Framework. Now that you're having the MSI file do the work for you, you can (if you wish) include the `dotnetfx.exe` file in the installation package. But this comes at a cost: `dotnetfx.exe` is 40MB in size. It needs to be installed only once, so it's probably better to install it *manually* on the target machine, rather than as part of our application's installation. Also, it's worth noting again the importance of being careful about versioning. You must ensure that the correct .NET Framework version is installed to deployment machines.

That said, however, it is extremely easy to include the `dotnetfx.exe` file with your installation. If you were watching closely earlier, you may have seen a file with a similar name, `dotnetfxredist_x86.msm`, under the detected dependencies of your setup project in the Solution Explorer. To include this file in all subsequent installation packages generated from your project, just right-click this entry and uncheck Exclude.

This file has an `.msm` extension because it is a *merge module*. This means that it contains one or more files required for a specific and common installation process. If you're interested, you can view the files it contains by choosing Properties from the context menu and clicking the ellipsis button for the `Files` property. You'll see the Files dialog box, listing the contents of `dotnetfxredist_x86.msm`, as shown in Figure 13-6. This list contains all of the files within the merge module.

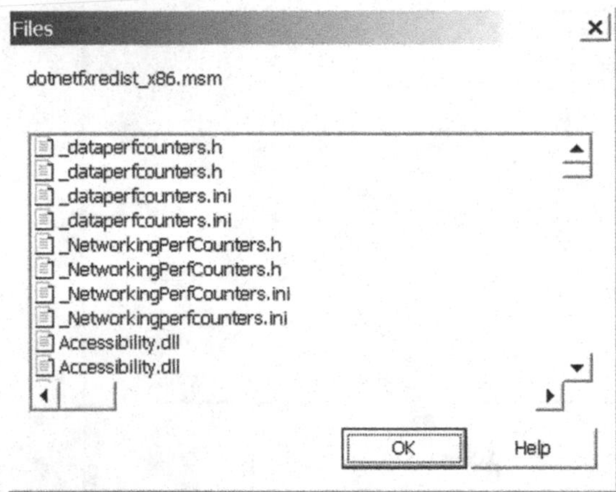

Figure 13-6. *Viewing the contents of dotnetfxredist_x86.msm*

Viewing Application Dependencies and Outputs

At this point, you may be wondering how VS .NET knows that components like `dotnetfx.exe` should be included in the first place. Some files need other files to be installed already if they are to work correctly, and these other files are called *dependencies* of the files requiring them.

To view the dependencies for the files in your install list, right-click either the appropriate item in the right-hand pane of the File System Editor or the Primary output option in the Solution Explorer, and choose Dependencies. Figure 13-7 shows the list for the primary output of `FriendsReunion`.

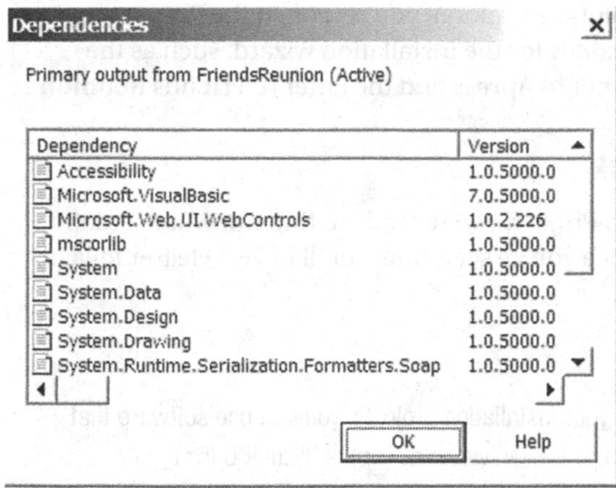

Figure 13-7. *The primary output dependencies for the FriendsReunion project*

The Dependencies dialog box shows the components (and the component's versions) that this file or package is dependent on, and which must, therefore, be included in the installation for it to operate correctly. All of the dependencies shown here are installed with the .NET Framework (by running `dotnetfx.exe`), except for the `Microsoft.Web.UI.WebControls` assembly.

Often, it's also useful to know exactly *which* files are being included with the installation, especially in the case of these shortcuts to project outputs. To see a list of the files being installed, right-click an item listed in the right-hand pane of the File System Editor and choose Outputs. Figure 13-8 shows the outputs for the content files of the `FriendsReunion` project.

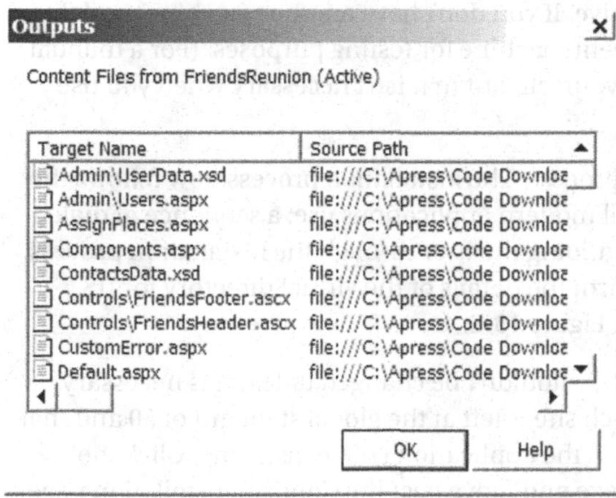

Figure 13-8. *The outputs for the content files of the FriendsReunion project*

Being able to see the outputs and dependencies for files is invaluable when creating an installation project for a web application. It prevents needless hours of hunting for missing files that were assumed to be present.

With the setup project selected in the Solution Explorer, you can open the Properties browser (press F4) and modify some global values for the installation wizard, such as the Manufacturer and ProductName. Set the former to **Apress** and the latter to **Friends Reunion**.

Using the Setup Project

Now that you've created a VS .NET Web Setup Project, you're ready to find out what actually happens when you use the files it creates. Once you've seen that, you'll have a clearer idea of the aspects that you might want to change.

Tip If you don't have a separate machine to test your installation projects, you can use software that simulates a separate machine, such as VMware (`http://www.vmware.com`) or VirtualPC (`http://www.microsoft.com/windowsxp/virtualpc/`). It's a good idea to test not only your setup packages, but also your entire application on other platforms and operating systems. You can do this easily using these products, without needing to have a separate physical machine.

Try It Out: Run the Installation Package In this example, you will deploy the installation files to another folder, ideally on a remote machine, to see how they behave. As the last step in the previous exercise, you built the solution, so you're ready to run it.

1. Navigate to the folder on your local machine that contains the MSI file. This is the folder that was created when you built the deployment project. Its location is specified in the Output window, just as the project build begins. You need only the file with the `.msi` extension to test the installation. If you can, use another machine, because then the demonstration will be more effective. If you don't have another machine available, you can use a folder on the development machine for testing purposes. (For a manual setup process, you need to set up IIS yourself, but that isn't necessary when you use a setup project.)

2. Double-click the MSI file to start the process. The installation process now follows the standard wizard format that almost all modern applications use: a sequence of dialog boxes that asks a series of questions, guiding the user through the installation process. In this case, all you need to do is confirm the details of the virtual directory for IIS, including the port to use, as shown in Figure 13-9.

3. The values of the settings in Figure 13-9 shouldn't be changed unless it is necessary, ensuring that the port to access the web site is left at the global standard of 80 and that the virtual directory name is relevant to the application you're installing. Click the Next button twice, to complete this page and move past the Confirm Installation page, which informs the user that all the required information has been gathered.

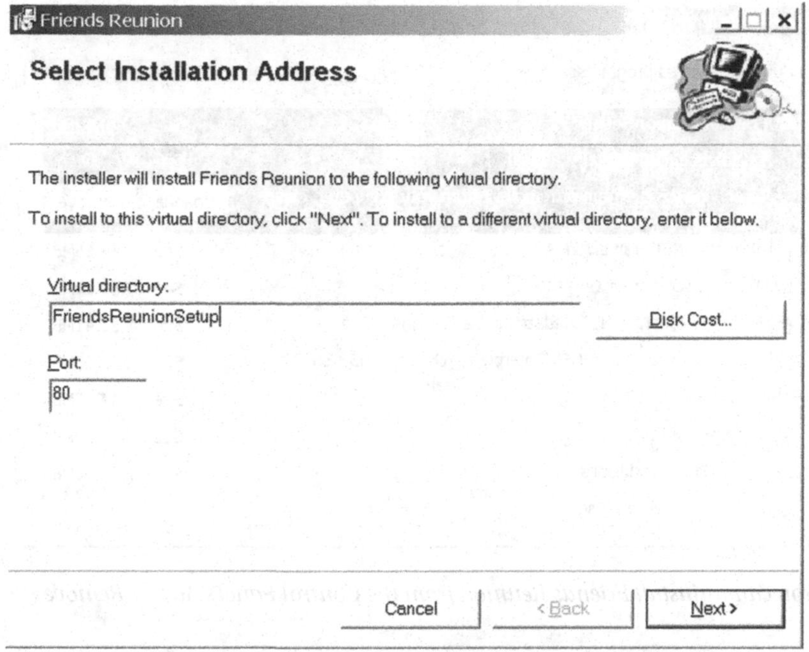

Figure 13-9. *Installing the Friends Reunion application*

4. When you reach the page with the Finish button, the installation is complete, and you can test it. To do this, run Internet Explorer on the machine and enter the URL `http://localhost/FriendsReunionSetup`. This should show the home page of your site, just as when you installed the application manually.

How It Works

The installation process simply creates a folder with the same name as the setup project in the `Inetpub\wwwroot` folder and specifies it as an application in IIS. If you browse to this directory, you'll see that all of the files here are those that you selected using the File System Editor: the primary output and content files from your project. The installer also knows to place the DLLs into the `bin` subfolder.

Uninstalling a Project

Although the deployment packages that you create within VS .NET can automatically remove previous versions of software you've installed before proceeding, there are also times that you may wish to remove the projects manually yourself. You can do this in the same way that you install any other application: using Add or Remove Programs in the Control Panel, as shown in Figure 13-10.

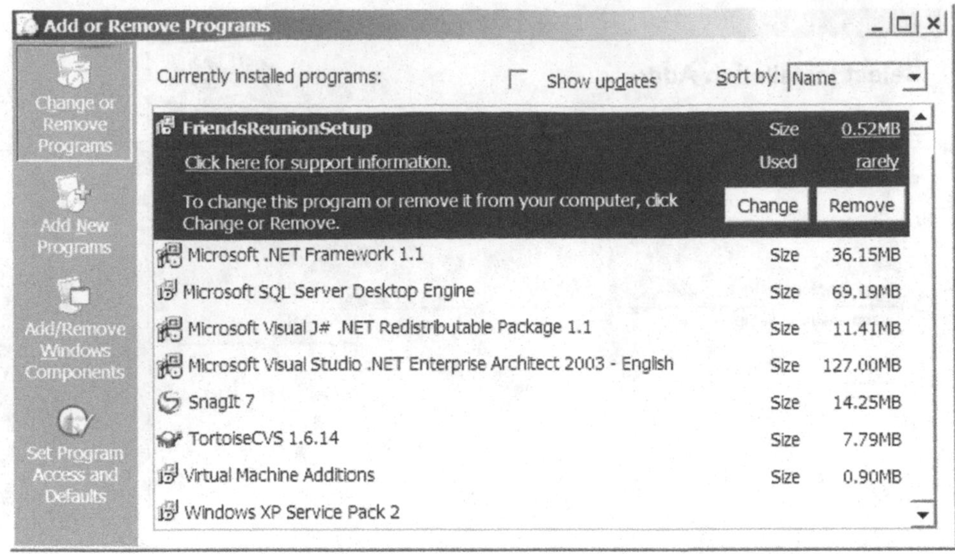

Figure 13-10. *You can uninstall Friends Reunion from the Control Panel's Add or Remove Programs*

Customized Deployment

You've managed to install the web application successfully. The next step is to add your other dependencies to the deployment package, producing an installer that's customized to your particular application. In our case, this means deploying the database. The fundamental method of installing the database is based on using a *custom action* in the setup project to perform the work and using the User Interface Editor to obtain any user input you need during the process.

One option if you have SQL Server Enterprise Manager installed is to generate a SQL script that will re-create the entire database on the target machine, solely based on SQL statements. You can, however, deploy the database files themselves and avoid this step altogether (including the need to install the Enterprise Manager or SQL Query Analyzer to be able to generate the scripts in the first place). This comes in handy if all you have is MSDE on your development machine. For this example, we'll demonstrate this alternative.

Adding a Custom File

Before you can use the more advanced features that will allow you to install the database, you need to add the database files themselves to the installation project. You do this through the File System Editor.

Try It Out: Add Custom Files You've already seen how you can place files in the Web Application Folder that is present in the File System Editor, adding them to the install package. You follow a similar procedure to add other files, namely the database.

1. In the File System Editor, right-click the File System on Target Machine node and select Add Special Folder ➤ Custom Folder. Rename the folder that is created to `Database`.
2. Switch to the Properties browser for this folder and set the `Property` property to `DBPATH`. This will allow you to modify this installation folder by linking its name to the user interface you're going to create shortly.

3. Use Windows Explorer to navigate to the database files. These files are `Friends_Data.mdf` and `Friends_Log.ldf`, and they will be located wherever you uncompressed them after downloading them from the Apress web site. Drag-and-drop the files into the `Database` folder in VS .NET.

Note If warnings about not being able to find the source file are issued by VS .NET at this point, you can probably ignore them. We'll cover correcting this shortly.

That's it. Adding custom files is that easy!

Editing the User Interface

Now that the database will also be installed with the project, you want to allow the user to be able to specify the location of the database server on which this file will be installed. You've seen the user interface that VS .NET creates for the installation process by default, but you can change it to insert new dialog boxes or delete existing ones that appear during the deployment process. To do this, you use the User Interface Editor. Click the User Interface Editor button on the toolbar at the top of the Solution Explorer (see Table 13-2) to open the editor, as shown in Figure 13-11.

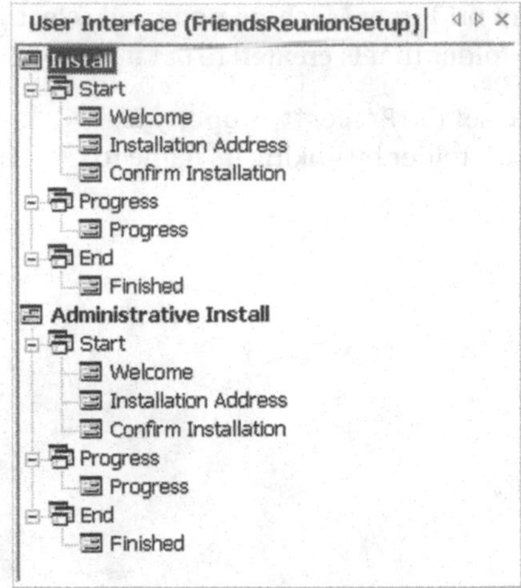

Figure 13-11. *The VS .NET User Interface Editor*

This editor is split into two sections:

- **Install:** This section, the top one in the User Interface Editor, details the user interface for installing from either the MSI file or a network-ready installation. (A *network-ready installation* is one that has been installed to a network drive using the `msiexe.exe` Microsoft Installer command that we'll look at shortly.) This section is used in almost all situations.

- **Administrative Install:** This section pertains to the interface to use when a system administrator uses the `msiexe.exe` command to install the application to a network drive, ready for other users to install from via a standard install later. You can alter the user interface to suit the requirements of the administrator. For example, you may wish to allow the administrator to install to any network location, but to restrict the users' installation to a specific path. In such a case, you would disable the Installation Address dialog box in the Install section, but leave it intact under Administrative Install. This section is only for installations onto a network or shared folders.

Each of these two sections is itself split into three subsections:

- **Start:** This subsection contains dialog boxes that will be displayed before installation takes place. It includes welcome screens, validation screens, folder browsing, custom actions, and so on.

- **Progress:** This subsection contains dialog boxes that will appear during installation, such as a progress bar. Only the Progress dialog box may be placed within this section, and it may appear only once.

- **End:** This subsection contains dialog boxes that will be shown once the installation has completed; for example, to display a simple "Finished" message, details of documentation, or where to check for updates.

As you can see in Figure 13-11, five dialog boxes are included by default when you create a Web Setup Project: Welcome, Installation Address, Confirm Installation, Progress, and Finished.

Before you get too enthusiastic about the possibility of adding dialog boxes to various stages of the installation process, you should know that, as with other third-party installers, the functionality these dialog boxes allow is very limited. In the case of VS .NET, such dialog boxes perform a specific task and/or simply pass on user-entered values for use during the installation. These might be used to make crucial decisions related to the installation or to provide values to place in the Registry for retrieval by the application once it has been installed.

There are 14 basic types of dialog boxes that VS .NET will allow you to add to the installation sequence, as shown in Table 13-4. You may have only *one* of each type within a given installation. To reduce the effect that this restriction may have, the dialog box types that are used most frequently (Checkboxes and Textboxes) have three dialog boxes (A, B, and C), each identical in design. So, if you have already added a Checkboxes A dialog box and you want to add another Checkbox dialog box, you could use Checkboxes B.

Table 13-4. *Types of Dialog Boxes Available for an Installation's User Interface*

Dialog Box Type	Description
Checkboxes (A, B, or C)	Presents up to four choices using check boxes. Check boxes can be used to set conditional values that are used throughout the installation process.
Confirm Installation	Allows the user to confirm settings such as installation location before the installation starts.
Customer Information	Prompts the user for information that may include name, company, and product serial number. Serial information can be checked immediately against a specified template. The Customer Information dialog box, like many of the dialog boxes here, is built on a template and therefore offers little in the way of customization.
Finished	Notifies the user when installation is complete.
Installation Address	Allows the user to choose the IIS virtual directory where the application files will be placed.
Installation Folder	Allows the user to choose the folder where application files will be installed. This option is not available when you create a Web Setup Project (it is intended for standard Setup Projects).
License Agreement	Presents a license agreement for the user to read and acknowledge. You, as the developer, can set up the license.
Progress	Updates the user on the progress of the installation. This is the only dialog box type that can be used in the Progress section of the installation.
RadioButtons (2, 3, or 4 buttons)	Presents a dialog box containing radio buttons that allows the user to choose between two, three, or four mutually exclusive options.
Read Me	Displays a file written in rich-text format.

Continued

Table 13-4. *Continued*

Dialog Box Type	Description
Register User	Allows the user to submit registration details by running an executable that you supply. This executable can display a dialog box of its own, capture the registration, and save it to disk, the Registry, or the Internet. This executable will most likely need the .NET runtime in order to work, and therefore it's better to place it at the end of the installation, once the runtime has been installed. Placing it at the end of the installation also lets you pass in values (using arguments) that have been collected from the user by the installer.
Splash	Presents a bitmap to the user, generally representing a logo for the company or product.
Textboxes (A, B, or C)	Prompts the user for custom information using one to three text boxes. The A, B, and C options work in the same way as the Checkboxes dialog boxes.
Welcome	Presents introductory text and copyright information to the user.

Now that you have a basic idea of the kind of functionality that can be added to an installer by adding dialog boxes, let's try it out.

Try It Out: Modify the Installation User Interface You'll present the users with a text box that allows them to specify a location for the database installation.

1. Select the `FriendsReunionSetup` project in the Solution Explorer and click the User Interface Editor button on the toolbar (see Table 13-2, earlier in this chapter).

2. In the User Interface Editor, right-click the Start node of the Install section of the tree (see Figure 13-11). From the menu that appears, select the Add Dialog option. You'll see the dialog box shown in Figure 13-12. Select the Textboxes (A) option and click OK.

3. The dialog box you've just added will appear at the bottom of the Start node, and the Start node itself will be highlighted with a blue, wavy line. This is to indicate that the Textboxes (A) option has been placed at an invalid location in the tree. In fact, it must appear *before* the Installation Address dialog box. To move it, simply drag it up to beneath the Welcome node.

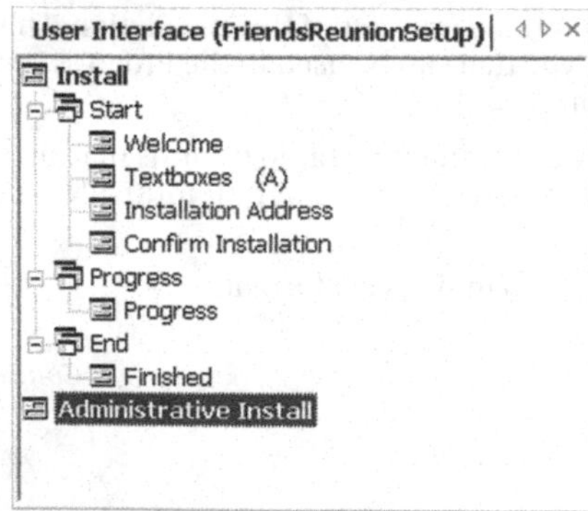

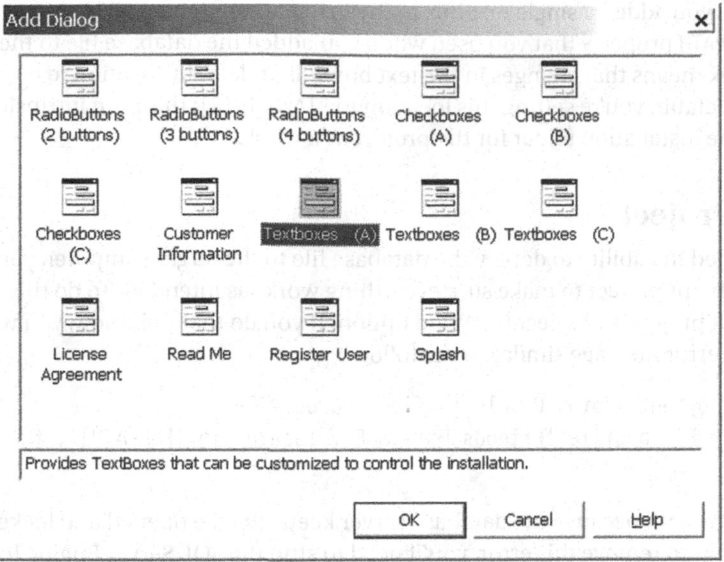

Figure 13-12. *Adding a Textboxes dialog box to the installation*

4. Next, you need to change the details that are displayed in this dialog box when it is presented to the user. For one thing, you need only one text box (rather than the three that are supported). To achieve this and render the correct information, update the values of the following properties:
   - Banner Text: **Database Location**
   - Body Text: **Choose a location to install the database**
   - Edit1Label: **Database Location:**
   - Edit1Property: `DBPATH`
   - Edit1Value: `[TARGETDIR]`
   - Edit2Visible: `False`
   - Edit3Visible: `False`
   - Edit4Visible: `False`

How It Works

When the user runs the MSI file, it processes the dialog boxes in the order in which they appear in the tree in the User Interface Editor. Following the Welcome dialog box, all of the custom dialog boxes that you define (such as the Textboxes dialog box in this example) will be presented before the installation continues with the standard dialog boxes. These dialog boxes can capture data, display information, or both. Such data can then be used during the installation process by referencing the names of the items specified.

In this example, you added a single text box to the installation process, the value of which you linked to the DBPATH property that you used when you added the database file to the project. Creating this link means that changes in the text box will update the location to which the file is deployed. By default, you're setting this location to [TARGETDIR]; this is an intrinsic property that specifies the installation folder for the project as a whole.

Building the Project

Now that you've added the ability to deploy the database file to the target computer, you can rebuild your deployment project to make sure everything works as intended. To do this, right-click the deployment project and select the Build option. If you do that right now, you will probably receive an error message similar to the following:

```
FriendsReunion Deployment.vdproj Unable to find source file
'...\Friends_Data.MDF' for file 'Friends_Data.MDF', located in '[DBPATH]', the file
*
```

If you get this error, it's because the database server keeps the file opened and locked whenever it's running. To remove this error, you'll need to stop the SQL Server Engine for a few seconds while you perform the build.

Try It Out: Manage the MSDE Service The SQL Server Engine doesn't run as an application, so to speak, which means that you cannot simply "close it down." Instead, it runs as a *service*, or task, in the background. You need to stop this service in order to perform the build.

1. To view all of the services running on your machine, select Start ➤ Settings ➤ Control Panel ➤ Administrative Tools ➤ Services. You'll see the Services window, which should look similar to Figure 13-13.

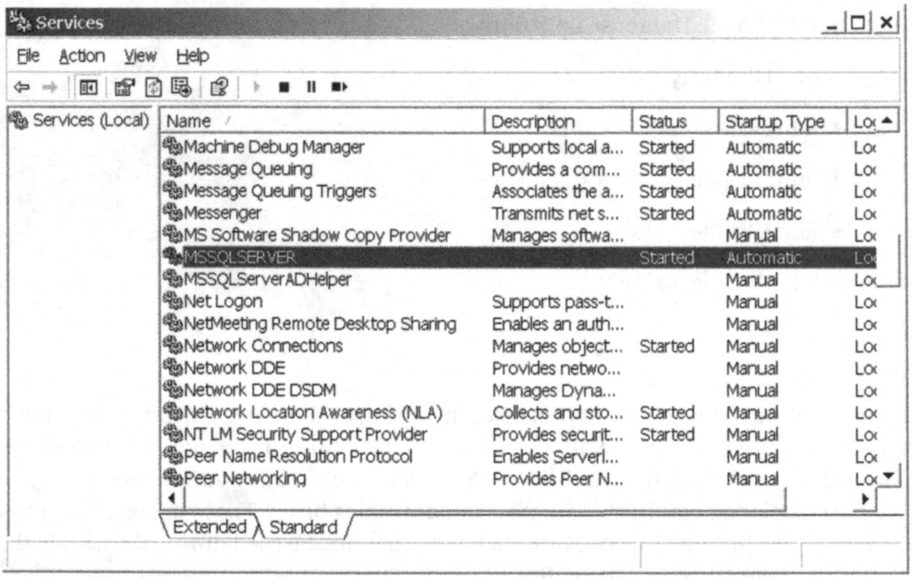

Figure 13-13. *The Services window lists all services installed on your machine.*

2. The entry you want begins with *MSSQL*, and is probably named MSSQL$NetSDK or MSSQLSERVER. Locate this item, right-click it to bring up the context menu, and then select the Stop option. This stops the database server engine.
3. With the SQL Server Engine service temporarily disabled, switch back to VS .NET, right-click the deployment project, and select Build. It should complete successfully.
4. Once the build has finished, the SQL Server Engine can be restarted. To do this, right-click it in the Services window and select the Start option that should now be enabled.
5. Now run your installation package to install the application. You'll find that it includes an extra screen, which prompts you for the desired database location, as shown in Figure 13-14.

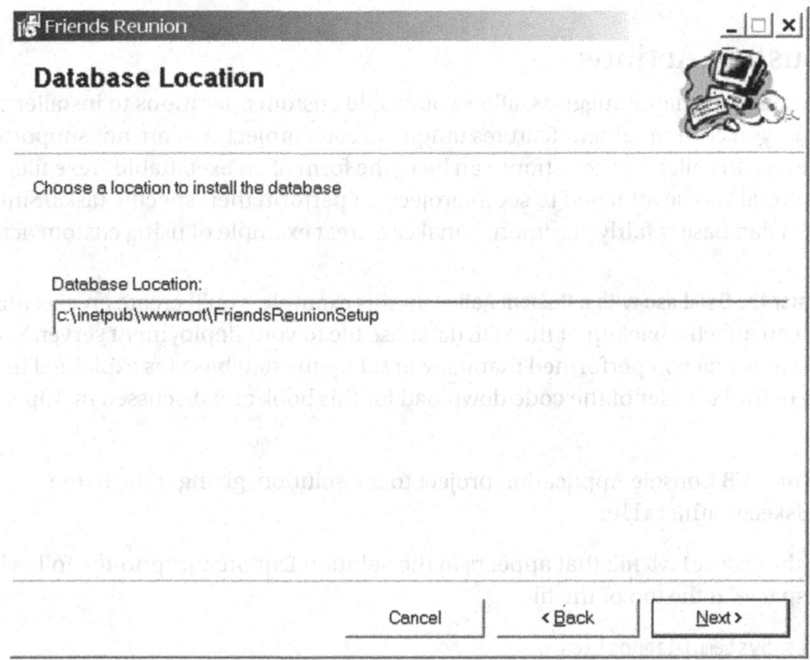

Figure 13-14. *The new Database Location dialog box added to the installation*

How It Works

While SQL Server is running, it maintains connections with all of the files it uses for storing database information, allowing it to have fast access and greater control over them. The cost of this is that it stops such files from being manipulated in the ways necessary to create installation packages. By stopping the SQL Server Engine service, you force SQL Server to shut down, releasing all of its locks on these files in the process. With this done, any operations that need to be performed on these files, such as copying, can be carried out. Once the build has been completed, SQL Server can be restarted, at which point it will reestablish its locks on the files.

Try It Out: Restrict Access to Database Files As a security precaution, you will forbid access from clients to the database files, just in case the user installs them in the same folder as the web application.

Add the following code to the `Web.config` file:

```
<configuration>
  <system.web>
    <httpHandlers>
      <add verb="*" path="*.mdf" type="System.Web.HttpForbiddenHandler" />
      <add verb="*" path="*.ldf" type="System.Web.HttpForbiddenHandler" />
    </httpHandlers>
```

This configuration tells the ASP.NET engine that all files with extensions `.mdf` and `.ldf` cannot be downloaded by a client.

Adding Custom Actions

Custom actions, as their name suggests, allow you to add custom operations to installers. With custom actions, you can implement features unique to each project that are not supported by the out-of-the-box installer. These actions can be in the form of an executable (`.exe` file), a `.dll`, or a script that can be attached to setup projects to perform their specific tasks. Since the installation of a database is fairly common, it makes a great example of using custom actions.

Try It Out: Register the Database with a Custom Action In this example, you'll create an executable program that can attach a backup of the SQL database file to your deployment server. You'll automate the steps that you performed manually to set up the database (as explained in the `Setup.txt` file in the `Db` folder of the code download for this book and discussed in Appendixes A and B).

1. Add a new VB Console Application project to the solution, giving it the name `FriendsReunionInstaller`.

2. Open the `Module1.vb` file that appears in the Solution Explorer. Import the following namespaces at the top of the file:

   ```
   Imports System.Diagnostics
   Imports System.IO
   ```

3. Add the following code to the `Main` method:

   ```
    Sub Main(ByVal args As String())

     Dim patharg As String = args(0)
     Dim cmd As String = String.Format( _
       "-S (local) -E -Q ""sp_attach_db N'FriendsData', N'{0}', N'{1}'", _
       Path.Combine(patharg, "Friends_Data.mdf"), _
       Path.Combine(patharg, "Friends_Log.ldf"))

     ' Execute the attach DB command
     Dim p As Process = Process.Start("osql", cmd)
     p.WaitForExit()
   ```

```
    ' Create the apress user
    p = Process.Start("osql", _
      "-S (local) -E -Q ""sp_addlogin @loginame='apress', " + _
      "@passwd='apress', @defdb='FriendsData'""")
    p.WaitForExit()

    ' Set the apress user as owner of the database
    p = Process.Start("osql", _
      "-S (local) -E -d ""FriendsData"" -Q ""sp_adduser 'apress', " + _
      "null, 'db_owner'""")
    p.WaitForExit()
End Sub
```

You'll pass the [DBPath] property collected from the user through the installer into this method. It basically calls the osql command-line utility to attach the two database files you deployed and configure the apress user login. This utility is guaranteed to exist if either SQL Server or MSDE is installed on the machine. This is a check that will be performed up front when the installer is started, which you'll add later in the chapter, in the "Using Launch Conditions" section.

4. With your code in place to attach the database, you now need to hook it up to the installer. The first step in accomplishing this is to add to your deployment project the primary output from the project you just created. To achieve this, right-click the Database folder and select Add ➤ Project Output. In the Add Project Output Group dialog box, select the FriendsReunionInstaller project, and highlight the Primary output option, as shown in Figure 13-15. Then click OK.

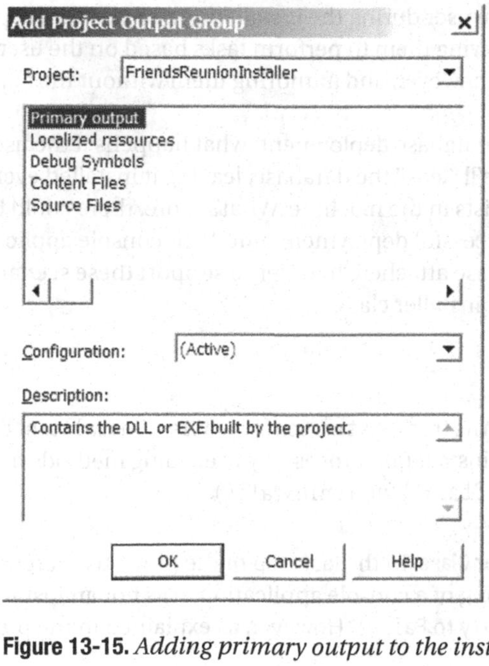

Figure 13-15. *Adding primary output to the installer project*

5. You now need to change the settings for this output to ensure that it is not left on the system after installation. To do this, view its properties and change the `Exclude` setting to `True`.

6. To arrange for the project to be called during the installation process, you use the Custom Actions Editor. Select the Custom Actions Editor button from the toolbar at the top of the Solution Explorer (see Table 13-2 earlier in this chapter) to open this editor.

7. Right-click the Install node on the left side of the editor window and select the Add Custom Action option. In the Select Item in Project dialog box that appears, select the Database element in the Look in list, and then choose the Primary output from `FriendsReunionInstaller`. Click the OK button to add the item to the Install folder.

8. Rename the item to `FriendsReunionInstaller`. Select this item and view its properties. There are two properties that you need to change here. First, the application you've created is a standard executable, rather than an `InstallerClass` (a special type of application that adheres to certain standards, which we'll discuss in the next section), so set that property to `False`. Second, you need to pass in the `DBPath` property to this program, so that it can use it when attaching the database. To do this, set the `Arguments` parameter to `[DBPath]`.

How It Works

Following the installation of all of the files specified in the File System Editor, the installer runs any tasks that have been specified in the Install folder of the Custom Actions Editor. These tasks can be executables (such as command-line applications), Windows form-based applications, DLLs, and so on. Other useful files for custom actions are VBScript and JavaScript files, which are simple and easy to create; they don't require separate projects. The values that have been captured through interaction with the user during the installation process can be passed as arguments to these custom actions, allowing them to perform tasks based on the user's input. Debugging script files is quite hard, however, and authoring them without the aid of IntelliSense is even harder!

We now face a problem regarding the database deployment: what happens if the user uninstalls our product? As things stand, we'll "leak" the database, leaving it installed even when the product that uses it no longer exists in the machine! What's more, there could be an error in the installation that impedes a successful deployment, but if our console application has already run, it will also leave the database attached. In order to support these scenarios, setup projects introduce the concept of an installer class.

Using Installer Classes

An *installer class* is a special class that inherits from `System.Configuration.Install.Installer`. Installer classes can participate in the MSI installation process, by overriding methods from the base class, such as `Install()`, `Commit()`, `Rollback()`, and `Uninstall()`.

Try It Out: Register the Database with an Installer Class In the last step of the previous exercise, you specified that your custom action, consisting of a console application, was not an installer class (by setting the `InstallerClass` property to `False`). However, as explained in the previous section, using a console application for the database deployment presents some problems. In order to support uninstallation of the database and account for errors that may happen during installation, you'll now transform your console application into a class library assembly with an installer class.

1. Open the `FriendsReunionInstaller` project properties and change the Output Type from Console Application to Class Library, in the Common ➤ General node, as shown in Figure 13-16. You can safely clear the Application Icon value, too.

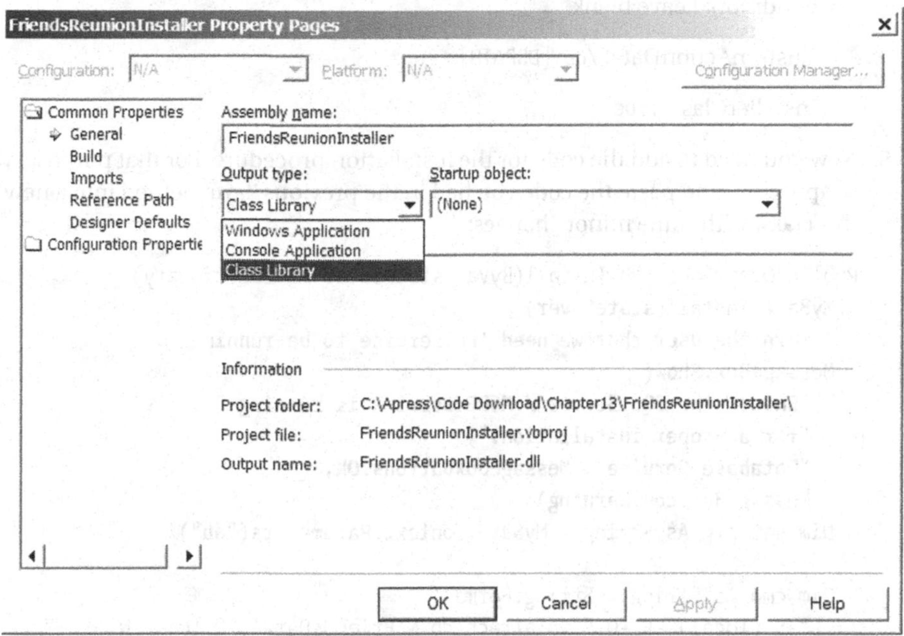

Figure 13-16. *Changing the custom installer project to a class library*

2. Add references to `System.Configuration.Install` and `System.Windows.Forms` assemblies to the project.

3. Add a new class named `DbInstaller`, and modify it as follows:

```
Imports System.Configuration.Install
Imports System.Collections
Imports System.Diagnostics
Imports System.IO
Imports System.Windows.Forms

<System.ComponentModel.RunInstaller(True)> _
Public Class DbInstaller
  Inherits Installer
End Class
```

4. In order to pass arguments to the installer classes, instead of using the Arguments property you used for the console application, you must use the CustomActionData property. Switch to the Custom Actions Editor for the setup project, select the FriendsReunionInstaller item inside the Install folder, and set the following properties on it:

   - (Name): FriendsReunionInstaller
   - Arguments: Leave blank
   - Condition: Leave blank
   - CustomActionData: /db=[DBPATH]
   - InstallerClass: True

5. Now you need to add the code for the installation procedure. For that purpose, you will simply copy and paste the code you had in the previous Main method into a new one in this class, with some minor changes:

```
Public Overrides Sub Install(ByVal stateSaver As IDictionary)
  MyBase.Install(stateSaver)
  ' Warn the user that we need the service to be running
  MessageBox.Show( _
    "Ensure the SQL Server / MSDE service is running " + _
    "for a proper installation.", _
    "Database Service", MessageBoxButtons.OK, _
    MessageBoxIcon.Warning)
  Dim patharg As String = MyBase.Context.Parameters("db")

  Dim cmd As String = String.Format( _
    "-S (local) -E -Q ""sp_attach_db N'FriendsData', N'{0}', N'{1}'", _
    Path.Combine(patharg, "Friends_Data.mdf"), _
    Path.Combine(patharg, "Friends_Log.ldf"))

  ' Execute the attach DB command
  Dim p As Process = Process.Start("osql", cmd)
  p.WaitForExit()

  ' Create the apress user
  p = Process.Start("osql", _
    "-S (local) -E -Q ""sp_addlogin @loginame='apress', " + _
    "@passwd='apress', @defdb='FriendsData'""")
  p.WaitForExit()

  ' Set the apress user as owner of the database
  p = Process.Start("osql", _
    "-S (local) -E -d ""FriendsData"" -Q ""sp_adduser 'apress', " + _
    "null, 'db_owner'""")
  p.WaitForExit()
End Sub
```

6. You can now delete the `Module1.vb` file, since you are not using it anymore.
7. Now add the `Uninstall` method:

```
Public Overrides Sub Uninstall(ByVal savedState As IDictionary)
  ' Warn the user that we need the service to be running
  MessageBox.Show( _
    "Ensure the SQL Server / MSDE service is running " + _
    "for a proper uninstallation.", _
    "Database Service", MessageBoxButtons.OK, _
    MessageBoxIcon.Warning)
  Process.Start("osql", _
    "-S (local) -E -Q ""sp_detach_db N'FriendsData'""")
  MyBase.Uninstall(savedState)
End Sub
```

   Here, you are simply calling another command that detaches a database from the server.

8. In order to make the procedure bullet-proof, you'll also implement the `Rollback()` method:

```
Public Overrides Sub Rollback(ByVal savedState As IDictionary)
  MyBase.Uninstall(savedState)
End Sub
```

9. Installer classes need to be deployed to the target machine in order to be executed. Therefore, you must set the `FriendsReunionInstall` project output `Exclude` property to `False`. Do this by selecting the project output item in the setup project, opening the Properties browser for it, and changing the `Exclude` property setting.
10. Now you must add the project output to the Rollback and Uninstall nodes in the Custom Action Editor. Right-click the Rollback node and select Add Custom Action. In the editor, select the `Database` folder in the Look in drop-down list and select the Primary output from `FriendsReunionInstaller` (Active) item. Rename the custom action to `FriendsReunionInstaller`.
11. Repeat step 10 for the Uninstall node.
12. Compile the setup project and install it.

How It Works

Installer classes allow more structured control over the installation process, and they give you a chance to react to certain stages during installation, such as `Install`, `Uninstall`, and `Rollback`. You did so by overriding methods of the base `Installer` class. The attribute you used on the class definition tells the MSI file that it must always run your installer class:

```
<System.ComponentModel.RunInstaller(True)>
Public Class DbInstaller
  Inherits Installer
```

Without this attribute, the methods are not called, and your installer class is simply ignored.

You also needed to pass arguments to your class, namely the folder to which the user chose to install the database. Instead of using the `Arguments` property as you did for the console application, you use the `CustomActionData` property. It's a simple string with the following format:

```
/name1=value1 /name2=value2 ... /nameN=valueN
```

For the values, you can use the usual notation for referring to properties collected by the installation wizard—that is, the property name enclosed in square brackets: `/db=[DBPATH]`. These values are converted to a collection of key/value pairs that is accessible through the `Context.Parameters` property of the base `Installer` class:

```
Public Overrides Sub Install(ByVal stateSaver As IDictionary)
  ...
  Dim patharg As String = MyBase.Context.Parameters("db")
```

One thing to note here is that the pair name (which becomes the key into the `Parameters` collection) is always converted to lowercase.

There's one caveat to the uninstallation process implemented this way. All file copying (and subsequent deleting) is done prior to custom actions execution. This means that when the MSI file tries to remove the database files, they will be locked if the database is in use, because the custom action that detaches it hasn't run yet. Therefore, the service must be stopped in order for file removal to succeed. However, in order to detach the database (the custom action that executes after file deletion), you need the service running, so the user will need to first stop the service to initiate uninstallation, and restart it when you warn the user about it through your custom action (the `MessageBox.Show()` call in the code). You could avoid this inconvenience by starting the service yourself, but it's not a trivial task, because the SQL Server/MSDE service may have different names, and you may need to use a technology called WMI (Windows Management Instrumentation) to achieve it in a reliable way. You can read more about WMI at `http://msdn.microsoft.com/library/en-us/ wmisdk/wmi/wmi_start_page.asp`.

Creating an Event Source to Initiate Windows Event Logging

Back in Chapter 11, you set up the logging of application errors in the Windows System event log. You learned that each application that logs events in the event log has its own event source, and that this event source must exist prior to the first log request from an ASP.NET application. This is due to security permissions related to creating a new event source. We used a workaround, but we said we would solve that at installation time. Now is the time to create the event source. We'll also need to arrange for it to be deleted if the application is uninstalled.

Try It Out: Manage Event Sources You'll add a new installer class that will handle the event source creation and deletion.

1. Add a new class to the `FriendsReunionInstaller` project called `EventLogInstaller`, and then add the following using statements:

   ```
   Imports System.Collection
   Imports System.Configuration.Install
   Imports System.Diagnostics
   ```

2. Add the RunInstaller attribute to the class and make it inherit from Installer:

```
<System.ComponentModel.RunInstaller(True)> _
Public Class EventLogInstaller
  Inherits Installer
```

3. Add the following method overrides:

```
Public Overrides Sub Install(ByVal stateSaver As IDictionary)
  MyBase.Install(stateSaver)
  Try
    EventLog.CreateEventSource("FriendsReunion", "Application")
  Catch ex As ArgumentException
    Context.LogMessage(ex.Message)
  End Try
End Sub

Public Overrides Sub Uninstall(ByVal savedState As IDictionary)
  EventLog.DeleteEventSource("FriendsReunion")
  MyBase.Uninstall(savedState)
End Sub
```

How It Works

This simple installer class creates the event source named FriendsReunion you use in the Global.asax.vb error handler:

```
Sub Application_Error(ByVal sender As Object, ByVal e As EventArgs)
  System.Diagnostics.EventLog.WriteEntry("FriendsReunion", _
    Server.GetLastError().InnerException.ToString(), _
    System.Diagnostics.EventLogEntryType.Error)
End Sub
```

This time, the event source will already exist when an error is logged. Notice that you also chose the Application log. This is one of the standard logs supported in the Event Viewer. You can also pick Security, System, or a log with a custom name.

Additionally, we catch ArgumentException exceptions and log them, which will be thrown if the event source already exists (which is the case in your machine now).

Debugging an Installer Class

An important part of any component development is how to debug it. So, since the custom installer classes are not regular executable code, how can you debug them? To demonstrate how to do this, we'll set up debugging for the final custom action we need to develop: one that sets Read permission to the Everyone built-in group on the two files that are read directly from disk in the application. These are the upload.xml and Friends.xsd files, which were introduced in Chapter 8.

Try It Out: Set ACLs and Debug an Installer Class You need to set the Read permission for the `upload.xml` and `Friends.xsd` files in order for the code to work as expected; otherwise, a security exception will be thrown. As noted in Chapter 10, these permissions are controlled by access control lists (ACLs).

1. Add a new class to the `FriendsReunionInstaller` project called `AclInstaller`, and add the following using statements:

```
Imports System.Collections
Imports System.Configuration.Install
Imports System.Diagnostics
Imports System.IO
```

2. Add the `RunInstaller` attribute to the class and make it inherit from `Installer`:

```
<System.ComponentModel.RunInstaller(True)> _
Public Class AclInstaller
  Inherits Installer
```

3. Add the following `Install` method override:

```
 Public Overrides Sub Install(ByVal stateSaver As IDictionary)
  MyBase.Install(stateSaver)
  System.Diagnostics.Debugger.Break()
  Dim patharg As String = MyBase.Context.Parameters("path")
  Dim files As String() = MyBase.Context.Parameters("files").Split(","c)

  Dim info As New ProcessStartInfo("cacls")
  info.CreateNoWindow = True
  info.WindowStyle = ProcessWindowStyle.Hidden
  Dim file As String
  For Each file In files
    ' Assign permissions to everyone to read the file
    info.Arguments = Path.Combine(patharg, file) + " /E /G Everyone:R"
    Process.Start(info)
  Next
End Sub
```

4. Edit the `FriendsReunionInstaller` custom action properties under the Install node. Set the `CustomActionData` property to the following value:

```
/db=[DBPATH] /path=[TARGETDIR] /files=upload.xml,Friends.xsd
```

5. Compile the setup project, and then run the installation project again.

How It Works

You created another new installer class. You can have as many installer classes as you want, and they are all executed as part of the custom action. If you compile the setup project in Debug mode, at a certain point while running the installation, the Just-In-Time Debugging dialog box will appear, as shown in Figure 13-17.

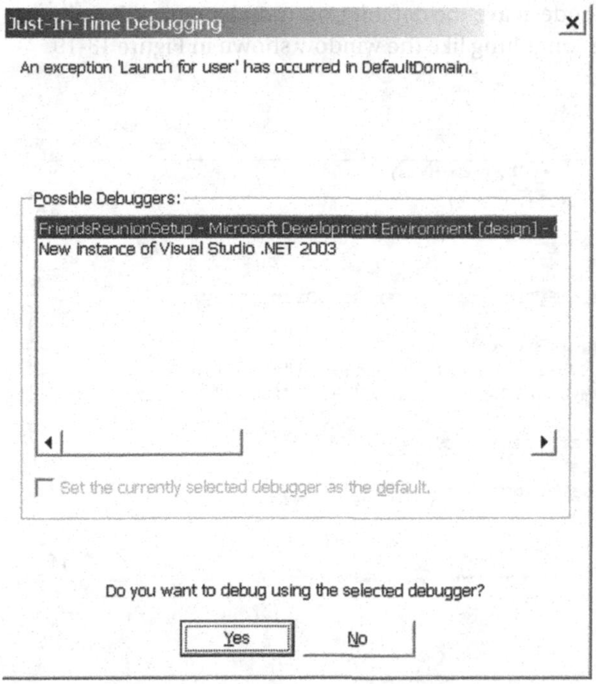

Figure 13-17. *You can choose to debug the setup project.*

If you choose Yes with the existing instance of the Microsoft Development Environment (that is, VS .NET) selected, you'll be offered the choice to attach to the process, as shown in Figure 13-18.

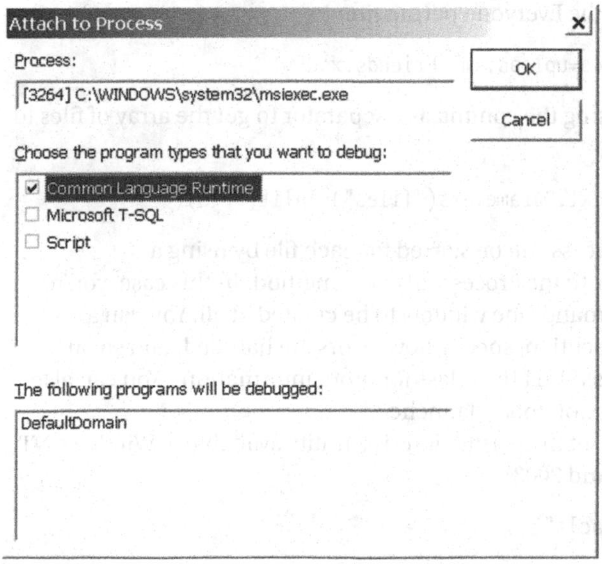

Figure 13-18. *Attaching to a process*

Since you want to debug only .NET code, leave the default Common Language Runtime option checked and select OK. You'll see something like the window shown in Figure 13-19 after the debugger runs.

```
AclInstaller.vb
AclInstaller                                    (Declarations)

<System.ComponentModel.RunInstaller(True)> _
Public Class AclInstaller
  Inherits Installer

  Public Overrides Sub Install(ByVal stateSaver As IDictionary)
    MyBase.Install(stateSaver)
    System.Diagnostics.Debugger.Break()
    Dim patharg As String = MyBase.Context.Parameters("path")
    Dim files As String() = MyBase.Context.Parameters("files").Split(","c)

    Dim info As New ProcessStartInfo("cacls")
    info.CreateNoWindow = True
    info.WindowStyle = ProcessWindowStyle.Hidden
    Dim file As String
    For Each file In files
```

Figure 13-19. *Debugging the installer*

At this point, you can press F10 (or select Debug ➤ Step Over) and start executing your code step by step. You can also inspect variables and use all the debugging techniques you learned about in Chapter 11.

The `Debugger.Break()` method launches the dialog box to attach a debugger whenever it's executed. In order to access variables, you must first press either F10 or F11, so that the debugger actually enters the line you're being shown with a green background color.

Note that you changed the `CustomActionData` property to pass both the installation folder (`[TARGETDIR]`) and the list of files to set the Everyone permission to:

```
/db=[DBPATH] /path=[TARGETDIR] /files=upload.xml,Friends.xsd
```

You simply split the `files` parameter using the comma as a separator to get the array of files to process:

```
Dim files As String() = MyBase.Context.Parameters("files").Split(","c)
```

You also customize the way the process will be started for each file by using a `ProcessStartInfo` object as a parameter to the `Process.Start()` method. In this case, you're specifying that you don't want the command-line window to be created at all. You can also retrieve the output of the command execution, specify how errors are handled, and so on. (Read the documentation for the `ProcessStartInfo` class for more information.) You can also customize the way the database installation tool is launched.

The command you execute next to set the permissions is a utility available in Windows NT and later versions (including 2000, XP, and 2003).

```
Dim info As New ProcessStartInfo("cacls")
```

SOME CUSTOM ACTION CAVEATS

It's quite tempting to start doing everything through custom actions and installer classes. You should resist this temptation. They were created to accommodate exceptional scenarios, and they do not integrate well with the Microsoft Installer infrastructure.

For example, let's say you use a custom action to create some Registry keys instead of using the Registry Editor (we didn't need this editor for our application, but it's a simple editor that allows entering values into the Registry at installation time). If the user (or another application) deletes those keys, your application may stop working, unless you explicitly check for that error. If you used the built-in Registry Editor instead, the Microsoft Installer would automatically pop up and reinstall those keys, without requiring any further actions, either on your part through application code or taken by the user.

The same concept applies to file copying. Using the File System Editor allows you to configure the files you want to add to the target machine. If another installation tries to copy the same files, the latest versions will be preserved—something you would need to do by hand in a custom action. Furthermore, you would need to do the work of checking if no other applications need those files before deleting them upon uninstallation. You can save yourself all those headaches by using the built-in features in setup projects. However, for advanced functionality, such as the one we needed for this example, it's okay to use custom actions.

Note You can learn more about the CACLS tool at `www.microsoft.com/resources/documentation/windows/xp/all/proddocs/en-us/cacls.mspx`.

Once you have all the files passed in by the installer, you execute that tool with the appropriate parameters to set the read permission to Everyone:

```
For Each file In files
  ' Assign permissions to everyone to read the file
  info.Arguments = Path.Combine(patharg, file) + " /E /G Everyone:R"
  Process.Start(info)
Next
```

Whenever you compile the solution as a Release build, the break you specified does *not* cause the debug dialog box to appear. However, it's a good idea to get rid of that line when you're finished debugging the installer class.

Deploying Application Configuration Settings

One further complication with the deployment of an application is the *application configuration,* controlled by the values stored in `appSettings` section of the `Web.config` file. In our Friends Reunion application, we use this to store the connection string for making database calls. When deployed to a live environment, settings such as this need to be changed in order to make them relevant to the target system.

In our solution, there is little need to make changes, as we've developed the system pointing to a database on our local machine (`localhost`) and are deploying it in this configuration, too. If this weren't the case, we would have three options:

- Specify a different `Web.config` file in the deployment package.
- Configure the installation package to edit `Web.config` based on user input.
- Have the user edit the `Web.config` file manually once the application has been installed.

The first two options can be implemented using techniques similar to those described earlier in the chapter. In the first case, you can simply add the new `Web.config` file to the Web Application Folder in the File System Editor. If you want to edit the `Web.config` file via the installation package, you have a more complicated task on your hands; this would require a custom action and a dialog box. This dialog box could ask the users for the connection string that they wish to use. After the installation wizard captured this information, you could pass it in as a parameter to the output of a project that you added as a custom action. This project could then read in the `Web.config` file as an XML document, update the correct setting, and write it back out to disk.

The option of having the user edit the `Web.config` file is not desirable, because it removes the automated end-to-end installation of the application, exposing the user to the underlying nuts and bolts. It is, however, the simplest of the three options.

Using Launch Conditions

Launch conditions allow you to specify certain environmental conditions that must be satisfied before an installation can continue, or to locate a specific value that can subsequently be used within the installation process. For instance, you could vary the installation procedure according to the value of a particular Registry key already set on the destination computer, or you could change the installation process (or stop it altogether) if a certain file is missing.

You can add or modify launch conditions using—unsurprisingly—the Launch Conditions Editor, shown in Figure 13-20.

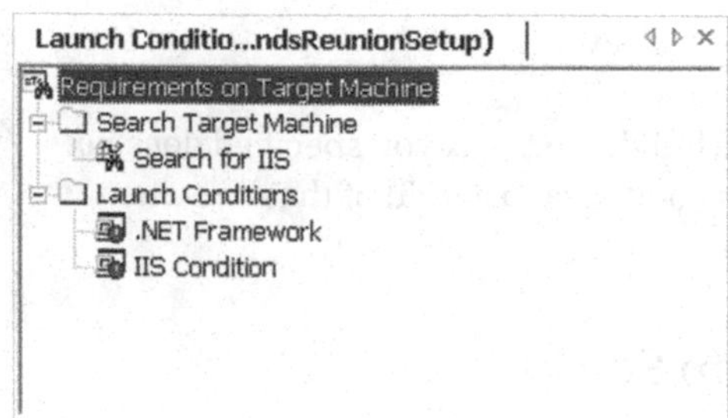

Figure 13-20. *The Launch Conditions Editor*

The Launch Conditions Editor is divided into two sections: Search Target Machine and Launch Conditions, which work together to ensure that a given launch condition is met. The default conditions for Web Setup Projects is to check for the presence of IIS version 4 or higher and to check for the .NET runtime.

Setting Up a Search

Using the Search Target Machine section, you can set up a search for a Registry entry, a file, or a Windows component. The result of the search can then be used in two ways:

- As a value to be used elsewhere in the installation
- In a test that must be satisfied in order for the installation to continue

Figure 13-21 shows the properties for the Search for IIS entry under Search Target Machine. `Property` denotes the name of the condition, which will be set to the value of the Registry entry specified by the `MajorVersion` entry in the `RegKey` property. This gives excellent flexibility, but does require a certain amount of knowledge about the organization of the Windows Registry.

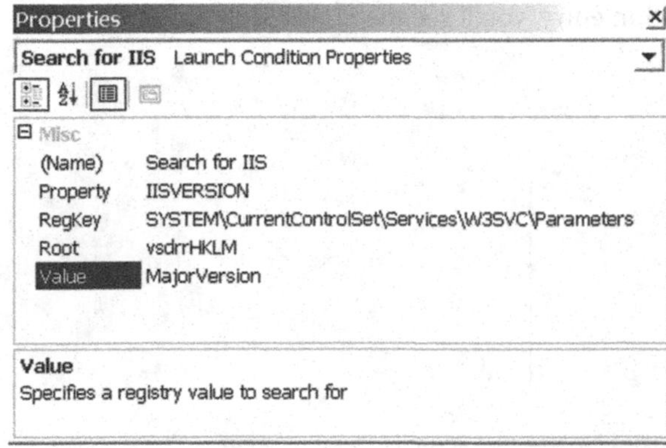

Figure 13-21. *Properties for the Search for IIS entry under Search Target Machine*

The `Root` property (`vsdrrHKLM`) that is specified informs the installer to start looking under the `HKey_Local_Machine` (`HKLM`) node within the root of the Registry. You would need to supply alternative values to search within other root nodes, such as the current user's settings (`HKey_Current_User`).

Try It Out: Search for SQL Server or MSDE Installations In our installer, we need to attach a database to a SQL Server or MSDE running on the local machine. This makes for an excellent opportunity to check for that condition by searching the Registry.

1. Right-click the Search Target Machine and select Add Registry Search. Rename the entry to `Search for MSSQL`.
2. Set the following properties on the entry:
   - (Name): `Search for MSSQL`
   - Property: `MSSQL`
   - RegKey: `SOFTWARE\Microsoft\Microsoft SQL Server`
   - Root: `vsdrrHKLM`
   - Value: `InstalledInstances`

How It Works

When the MSI file launches, the Registry will be searched for the value you specified. The key you're looking at is created by both SQL Server and MSDE, and specifies the different installations that exist on the machine. By assigning this search the property name `MSSQL`, you can refer to it later, as you'll do in the next exercise.

Now that you know how to perform a search, you need to know how to use the result to change the installer behavior. That's the role of the Launch Conditions node of the Launch Conditions Editor.

Setting Up the Launch Condition

Searches for items on the target machine are always performed before the processing of the launch conditions in this section, so any properties set by searches can be used here. If you again check the properties of the IIS Condition entry, you'll see the `IISVERSION` property in use, as shown in Figure 13-22.

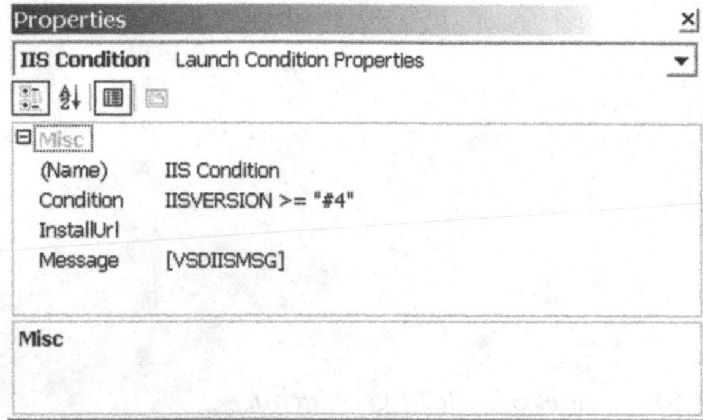

Figure 13-22. *The IIS Condition properties*

All launch conditions must evaluate to `True` if the installation is to take place, so the `#4` in Figure 13-22 represents the minimum version number of IIS required in order to install the web application. The # is used to denote that the value stored in the Registry is a hexadecimal value, and that a conversion is required when performing a comparison. If the condition is simply a reference to a search value and the value is not found, it evaluates to `False`.

The `Message` property indicates the message to display if the condition is not met. As used by this condition, it's a message stored in a resource and referenced by placing the name of it within square brackets, such as the standard IIS message `[VSDIISMSG]`. You can use a literal string also.

Try It Out: Set a Launch Condition to Check for SQL Server or MSDE Let's add a condition that ensures SQL Server or MSDE is installed, using the Registry search you created in the previous section.

1. Right-click Launch Conditions in the editor, choose Add Launch Condition, and give it the name `MSSQL Condition`.

2. Set the following properties on the entry:
    - (Name): `MSSQL Condition`
    - Condition: `MSSQL`
    - InstallUrl: Leave blank
    - Message: **Either Microsoft SQL Server or Microsoft Desktop Engine must be installed.**

That's all that's required. When you now rebuild the setup project, the MSI file it creates will proceed with the installation only if a previous installation of SQL Server or MSDE created the Registry entry you searched for before.

How It Works

A condition pointing to a search alone means that if it didn't found the desired value, the condition has failed. You're not limited to checking for values' existence, as you've already seen for the IIS search. A search for ASP.NET, for example, could also check that the version installed equals a certain value expected by your application. In that case, you could use direct value comparisons within the `Condition` property. The configuration for such a search (using the Search Target Machine section of the Launch Conditions Editor) would be as follows:

- `Property`: `ASPNETVERSION`
- `RegKey`: `SOFTWARE\Microsoft\ASP.Net`
- `Value`: `RootVer`

The Launch Condition properties would be set like this:

- `Condition`: `ASPNETVERSION="1.1.4322.0"`
- `Message`: **This application requires version 1.1 of ASP.NET.**

If you run the MSI file with this condition, it will not proceed with the installation if a different version of ASP.NET is detected on the host machine.

Summary

We began this chapter by looking at .NET application deployment methods. You saw that a web project can be published manually using XCOPY deployment, seeing how and where the files should be placed.

Next, we looked at setup and deployment projects, which are the .NET approach to distributing applications. Creating one of these projects allows you to transfer your application to a remote server in a professional manner, such as a single compressed archive.

You then learned about adding customizations to a deployment project. First, you saw how to add the database from the Friends Reunion application as a custom file, demonstrating in the process how your entire application, including all of the external resources that it requires, can be installed as part of the same process. You customized the installation wizard UI to account for the new values you needed for your application, and you learned how to pass values from the wizard into your custom installation components.

We discussed installer classes and how to take advantage of them to perform some complex operations, such as attaching a database to a server and setting file-access permissions on files. We also discussed the trade-offs of overusing custom actions and installer classes.

Finally, we explored launch conditions, which allow you to check that the environment to which you are installing your application meets criteria that you can specify using the IDE.

Throughout this book, we've dissected how a real-world application is designed, developed, debugged, improved, and deployed—covering almost every aspect of its lifecycle. With these concepts, you're ready to take over new projects leveraging this incredible powerful and revolutionary platform for developing web applications.

Web Applications—An Overview

At the end of this chapter, and consequently the end of this book, it seems fitting to present an outline of the process of developing and then preparing a web application for deployment and installation, with an obvious focus on the areas we've been discussing most recently. Figure 13-23 presents this outline.

Over the course of the book, we've addressed the end-to-end development of an application—from the creation of the solution in Chapter 3 to the deployment of the application on remote servers. The best way to take things forward is to experiment with what you've learned throughout the book. For further information and updates for the book, check the Apress web site at `http://www.apress.com`. You can also check out the Apress forums at `http://forums.apress.com`—you never know what you might find. Good luck!

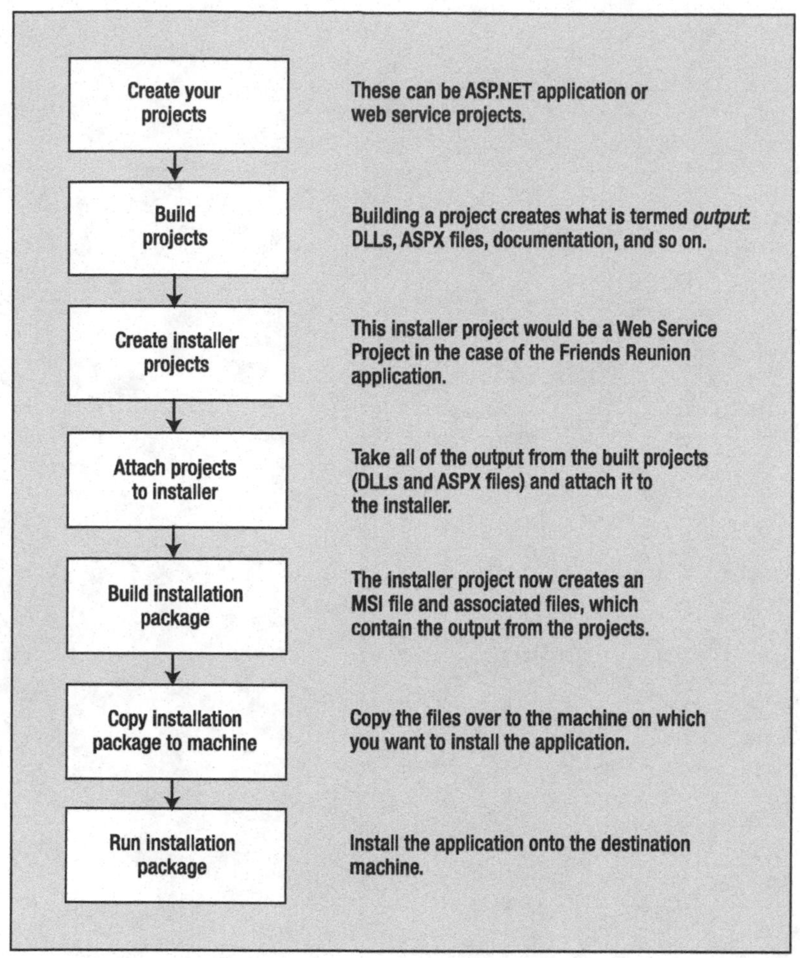

Figure 13-23. *The web application development and deployment process*

APPENDIX A

The Friends Reunion Application

Throughout this book, we developed an application called *Friends Reunion* to apply the concepts we explore in each chapter. The sample application provides a web site where registered users can get in touch with other users who have attended the same schools or worked in the same location.

We include many features in Friends Reunion: counters, search engines, web services, and so on. As is common in real-life web applications, Friends Reunion uses a database to store and retrieve information.

Friends Reunion Database Design

The database tables involved in storing user information for the Friends Reunion application are shown in Figure A-1.

The institutions (schools, colleges, and other places where users may have been) are located in the `Place` table, which uses the `PlaceType` lookup table to specify the type of place (school, university, business, and so on). The users can register their attendance at different institutions into the `TimeLapse` table, in which they specify a friendly name for the time lapse period (such as "Systems Engineer Career"), the year/month in, and the year/month out. There's also a free-form `Notes` field for any comments they wish to add.

When users have matching or overlapping time lapse periods, they can submit a request for contact with the other user. This is represented as a row in the `Contact` table, whose `IsApproved` flag is initially set to `0`, to indicate a pending request. The destination user (that is, the user receiving this request for contact) can optionally accept this request, and from there, the requester's details are unveiled, allowing a direct contact.

Early in the book, we build a registration form, a login form, and a couple of report forms, which show a list of approved and pending contacts, as well as list of places and users for administrator users (those who have the `IsAdministrator` flag set to `1` in the `User` table) to view. A `Place` has an `Administrator`, who usually is the user who registered the place. This user will be able to modify the place details later on.

We also build search functionality into the application, so that users can search for different matches, such as first and last name, place, type, and time lapse. The `Counter` table has a single field, `Visitors`, which is used to store a global counter for the number of visitors and preserve application state.

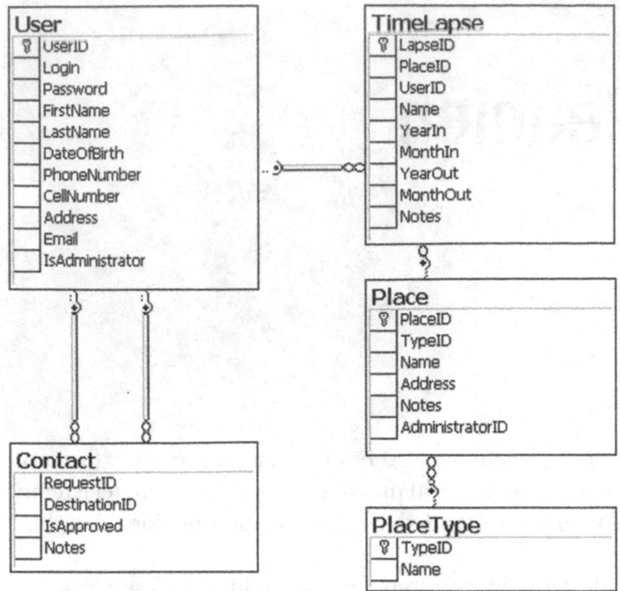

Figure A-1. *The tables in the FriendsData database*

How to Set Up the Code Download Package

The code download package from the Downloads section of the Apress web site (`http://www.apress.com`) contains a folder for each chapter (except for the first two) and also a `Db` folder, with a detached SQL Server database (a file that contains a fully operational database that only needs to be attached to a server).

Setting Up the Database

The `Db` folder contains four files:

- `Friends_Data.MDF`
- `Friends_Log.LDF`
- `MixedMode.vbs`
- `Setup.txt`

The `Setup.txt` file contains instructions on how to get the latest version of the Microsoft SQL Server Desktop Engine (MSDE), as well as how to attach the database using the command-line `osql` utility.

If you already have MSDE installed, it's possible that its default security mode, Windows Integrated Security, is enabled. However, you need to set up the database so that database-configured users are also allowed to log in; that is, you need to be able to pass specific non-Windows credentials to the database and be able to log in. In this book's examples, you do that by using the apress user name and password.

To configure mixed-mode authentication, rather than the default mode, we've provided the `MixedMode.vbs` script, which you can run on your machine. Simply double-click the script to run it and change the authentication mode to support both approaches.

Once you have the database attached, you can add the connection to the Visual Studio .NET (VS. NET) Server Explorer by right-clicking the Data Connections node and choosing Add New Connection from the context menu, or by clicking the Connect to Database icon. This connection can be used to administer the database, much as you can with SQL Server Enterprise Manager.

Setting Up the Code Samples

Inside the chapter folders, there's a `FriendsReunion` folder containing the code developed during the chapter. For the third chapter, when you start coding the sample application, you'll need to configure this folder as a web application in Internet Information Services (IIS). For subsequent chapters, you just point the web application to the new folder. Here's how:

1. To access the code for Chapter 3, right-click the chapter's folder and select Properties to open the folder Properties dialog box. In the Web Sharing tab, enable sharing and accept the default name suggested, which matches the folder name. This procedure is illustrated in Figure A-2. By default, enabling sharing configures the folder with IIS and sets Windows Integrated authentication for it. In the book, we'll add Anonymous access to leverage the new authentication and authorization features of ASP.NET. We'll do so by modifying the application configuration through the IIS management console. This is discussed in Appendix B.

2. Double-click the `FriendsReunion.sln` solution file inside the `FriendsReunion` folder, which contains the project code for Chapter 3.

3. When you move to the next chapter, point the web application to the new folder. This is done through the IIS management console (Administrative Tools ➤ Internet Information Services). Locate the `FriendsReunion` node inside the Default Web Site, right-click it, and select Properties to see the dialog box shown in Figure A-3. In the dialog box that appears, specify the appropriate chapter in the Local Path field to point to the new location. This requires changing only the chapter number.

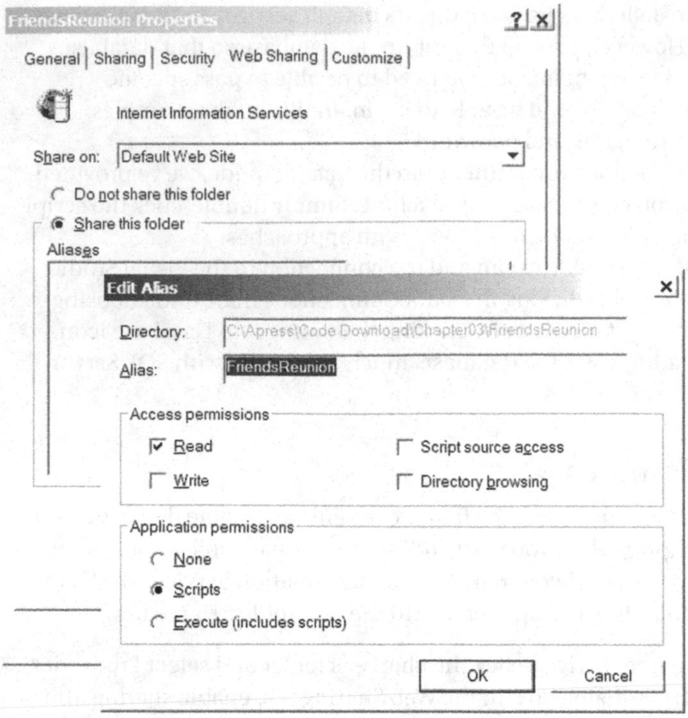

Figure A-2. *Configuring a folder as a web application in IIS*

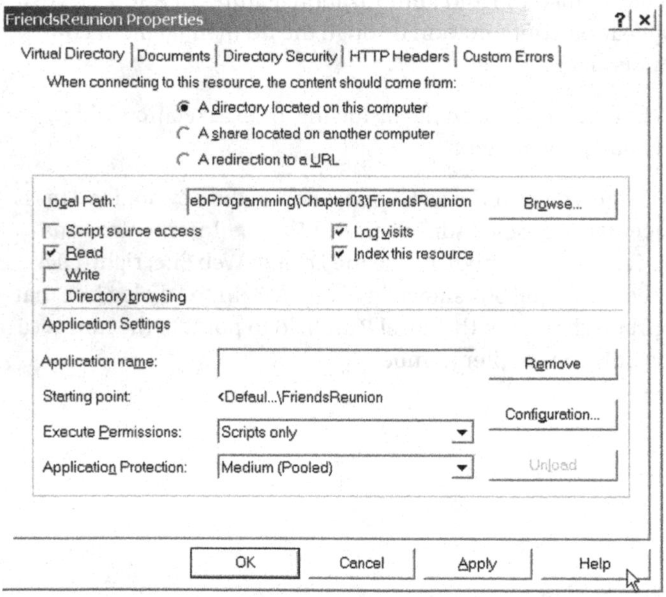

Figure A-3. *Pointing the web application to a chapter's folder*

4. Now you can open the `FriendsReunion.sln` solution file in the new folder. This time, when VS .NET opens, it will display the dialog box shown in Figure A-4.

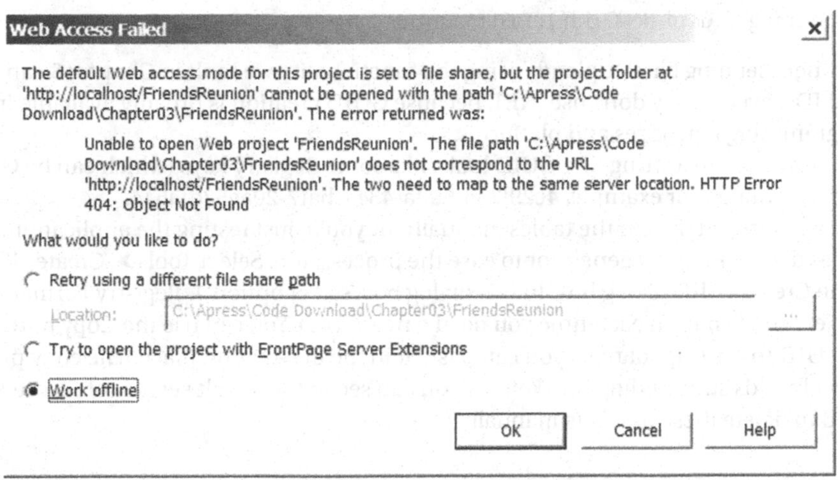

Figure A-4. *VS .NET indicates that it couldn't access the folder.*

5. This happens because VS .NET caches files from web sites, as well as the location where they were opened last time. In this case, you can see that it's trying to open Friends Reunion from the Chapter03 folder, which no longer maps to the web application. This is easily solved by selecting the "Retry using a different file share path" radio button, and replacing the chapter number with the new one, just as you did in IIS. This will cause VS .NET to refresh its cache and synchronize with the new files.

How to Create GUIDs for Database Keys

All the primary keys in our database use GUIDs, a fixed-length (`char` type) string of 36 characters. A *GUID* is a unique value calculated using a complex algorithm that includes the network adapter ID and a timestamp. This ensures its uniqueness, even across machines. The main benefit of this approach is that keys can be generated on the client machine, or in a middle-tier component, prior to posting data to the database.

In the scenario analyzed in Chapters 7 and 8, which are about XML, using GUIDs allows a partner institution to upload a file containing information about its attendees, with their IDs already assigned even before uploading the file, and it can save these values for future reference in its own system. If you use auto-numeric fields, for example, you would need to send back the assigned IDs for every new row inserted.

Note SQL Server provides a `uniqueidentifier` type that can also be used to store GUIDs. We used a `char` type because that allows you to export the database structure and re-create it on a database server other than SQL Server.

The best news is that .NET has a class that can be used to generate these GUIDs: the `System.Guid` class. Only one line of code is required to generate a new ID and turn it into a string through the `ToString` method:

```
Dim id As String = Guid.NewGuid().ToString()
```

Customers sending batch uploads using the functionality we built in Chapter 8 can generate valid IDs, even if they don't use .NET, because GUID creation is broadly available in other programming languages and platforms.

Once converted to a string, the GUID looks like some Registry keys (which can be GUIDs themselves) or values; for example, 4e29f256-5ada-4344-baf7-20ae52dfa544.

If you want to add data to the tables manually, or you're just testing the application, VS .NET has a built-in GUID generator to ease the process, too. Select Tools ➤ Create GUID to open the Create GUID dialog box. In this dialog box, select option 4. Registry Format, and click the New GUID button each time you need a new GUID. You can use the Copy button to copy the GUID to the Clipboard so you can paste it in the destination place. The copy process automatically adds surrounding brackets, as you can see in the Result section of Figure A-5. You'll need to delete these brackets manually.

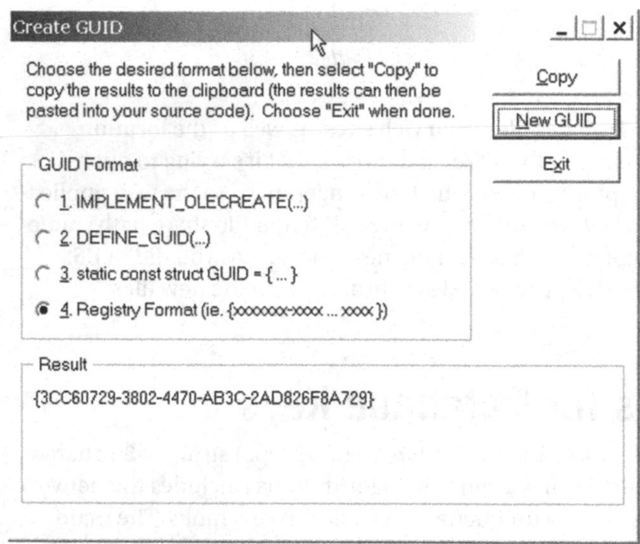

Figure A-5. *Creating a new GUID*

This appendix explained how to work with the files for the Friends Reunion application, the web application developed in this book. The next appendix provides information about configuring IIS and MSDE, which will be useful for developing Friends Reunion and, of course, your own web applications.

APPENDIX B

Management of IIS and MSDE

This appendix is intended to supplement the coverage of Internet Information Services (IIS) and the Microsoft SQL Server Desktop Engine (MSDE) in this book, providing tips on configuration and on how to perform common tasks. This appendix covers the following topics:

- Configuration options for IIS 5.*x*, including site-wide settings, application-specific settings, and locking down IIS
- Impersonation when working with ASP.NET and IIS
- An introduction to IIS 6.0 and its new features
- MSDE database management in Visual Studio .NET (VS .NET)

IIS Configuration

You can apply many different settings to the virtual directories on your system. Site-wide settings configure the defaults. You can then override those settings on a per-application basis. In the following sections, we'll look at the IIS settings for the site, and then examine how to override them. Finally, we'll cover how to close down potential IIS security holes.

We are not going to discuss every IIS configuration option available, but we suggest that you do look through the tabs and dialog boxes to see what's possible. IIS configuration is something of an art, and balancing performance configuration, security settings, and application load settings is a tricky job for system administrators.

Configuring Site-Wide Settings

To access the settings for a web site, in the IIS management console, right-click the Default Web Site node and select Properties. You will see the Default Web Site Properties dialog box, with the Web Site tab displayed, as shown in Figure B-1.

The settings that you apply in this Properties dialog box are the default settings for *all* web applications on this web site. An individual application can override the defaults, but these settings will provide the starting point.

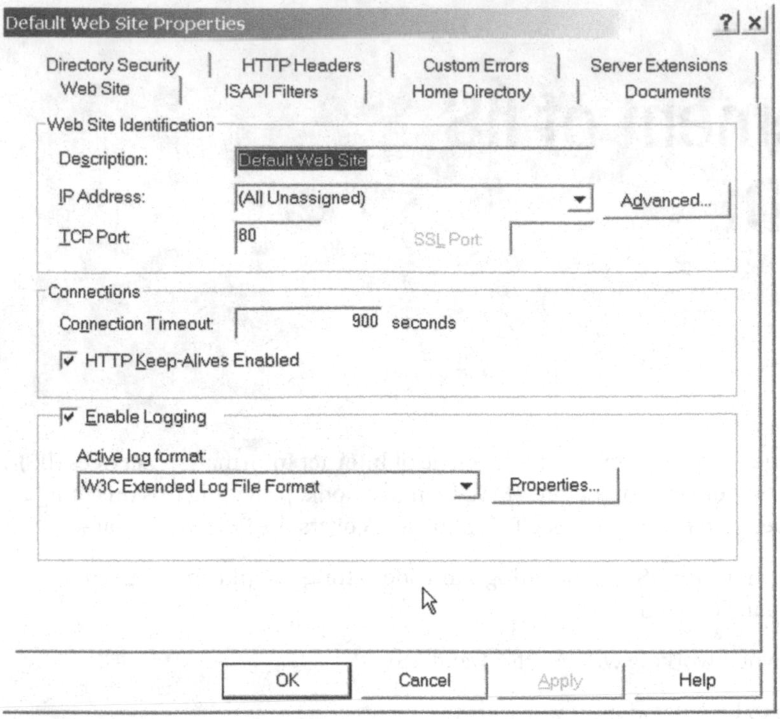

Figure B-1. *Properties for a web site*

If you're using Windows Server 2003, you'll see another tab, called Performance, where you can tweak settings that affect the performance of the server, such as the available bandwidth and connections.

Logging User Activity

One item to notice in the web site's Properties dialog box is the Logging facility. IIS will keep a log of all requests to the web server, unless you configure it not to. Click the Properties button in the Logging section to open a dialog box that allows you to customize the type of information logged and the frequency of generation of log files, as shown in Figure B-2.

The IIS logs are stored in the specified folder, with the file name shown in the label below the field. The content of such a log file might look something like this:

```
#Software: Microsoft Internet Information Services 5.0
#Version: 1.0
#Date: 2004-07-31 12:31:54
#Fields: time c-ip cs-method cs-uri-stem sc-status
12:31:54 127.0.0.1 GET /FriendsReunion/default.aspx 200
12:32:05 127.0.0.1 POST / FriendsReunion /default.aspx 200
12:33:01 192.168.202.185 GET / FriendsReunion /default.aspx 200
12:33:08 192.168.202.185 POST / FriendsReunion /default.aspx 200
12:34:50 192.168.0.121 GET / FriendsReunion /default.aspx 200
12:35:00 192.168.0.121 POST / FriendsReunion /default.aspx 200
```

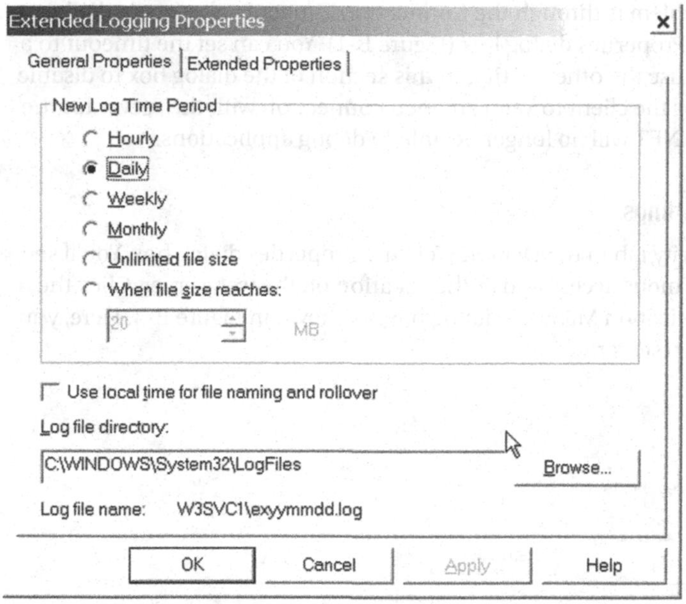

Figure B-2. *IIS Logging settings*

This sample log shows a request for the main page of the Friends Reunion application, `Default.aspx`, originating from the local machine (the request was made by the 127.0.0.1 loopback IP address). It also shows a couple of other requests for the same page from other machines on the local network. The IP addresses of all requesting machines are listed, along with the name of the resource requested from the client, either by using the HTTP `GET` verb or the HTTP `POST` verb. The number 200 at the end of each entry is an HTTP response code, which indicates that the operation was successful.

Logging hits to the web server is a great way to watch for malicious activity and to track general usage of your site, so usually you should leave it turned on.

Handling Simultaneous Connections

In non-server Windows versions, such as Windows XP, IIS allows for a maximum of ten simultaneous connections by default. While this may be enough in most cases, if you're developing many web services and debugging several at the same time, as well as developing and debugging a couple client web applications, you may run out of connections rather quickly. This results in HTTP result code 403.9 (usually with the description "Access Forbidden: Too Many Users Are Connected").

Tip The default of 10 connections can be bumped up to 40 (but not higher) by using a script included with IIS. Locate the `adsutil.vbs script` (by default in `C:\Inetpub\AdminScripts`). Open a command prompt in that folder and issue the following statement: `adsutil set w3svc/MaxConnections 40`.

One way of solving this problem is through the Connection Timeout value on the Web Site tab of the Default Web Site Properties dialog box (Figure B-1). You can set the timeout to a lower value. You cannot simply use the other setting in this section of the dialog box to disable HTTP Keep-Alives (which allows the client to keep an open connection with the server for the specified timeout), because VS .NET will no longer be able to debug applications.

Managing General Security Settings

Now look at the Directory Security tab in the Default Web Site Properties dialog box. You'll see a section for configuring Anonymous access and authentication on the web server. Click the Edit button to open the Authentication Methods dialog box, as shown in Figure B-3. Here, you can configure access to your web server.

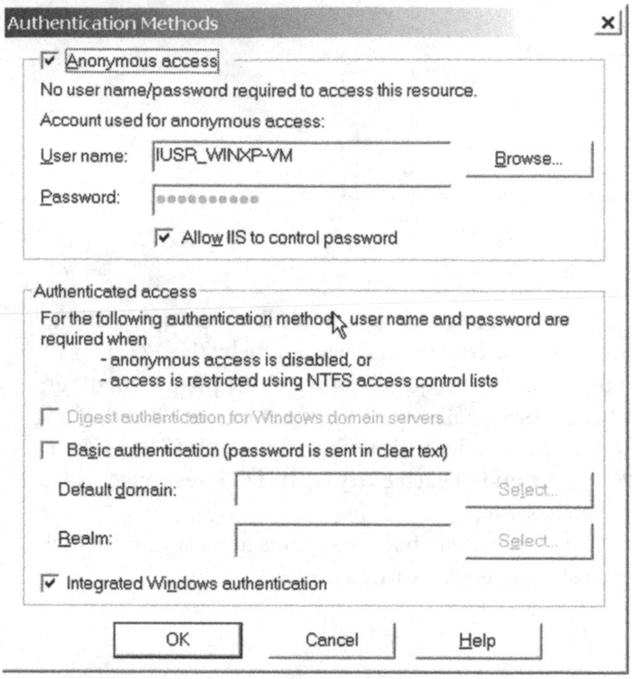

Figure B-3. *Configuring web server access*

By default, Anonymous access to your web server is enabled. This is a logical choice in an Internet environment, particularly for web applications that are intended to serve web pages to unknown users. When users access the site via Anonymous access, they are still authenticated by the web server; all such users are authenticated under an account defined for that purpose. The default account used in that case by IIS is called `IUSR_MachineName`, and it defines the basic rights assigned to all Anonymous access users.

Note Along with `IUSR_MachineName`, there are several other special accounts you might come across when using IIS. `IWAM_MachineName` is an account used when the application runs out of process. `ASPNET` is a user account under which the ASP.NET worker process runs and the one used for Anonymous access to ASP.NET applications. It has very few privileges on the local machine, and therefore limits the chances that ASP.NET code is exploited for malicious purposes on the server. In Windows Server 2003, another account named `NETWORK SERVICE` is used for the same purpose.

Anonymous access is great for public web sites, but it's not always the best solution for an intranet scenario or for other "restricted" sites for which you want to have more fine-grained control of access to your web server. In those cases, you can use the other authentication options:

Basic authentication: This method prompts the user for a valid user name and password, and these are transmitted to the server in a Base64-encoded, unencrypted format. (Base64 encoding is a standard used for sending binary information over a network.) This isn't a very secure technique, but it's standards-compliant, and it's compatible with almost all browsers. If you're sure that the connection between your server and your client is secure, then Basic authentication should be sufficient. The Secure Sockets Layer (SSL) is commonly used alongside basic authentication to provide a secure communication channel.

Digest authentication: This method works in a similar way to basic authentication, except that all transmitted information is encrypted using a hashing technique, which makes it harder for a malicious user to intercept the data and decrypt it. This method of authentication can pass data through firewalls and proxy servers, so it's great in an Internet scenario. However, it relies on HTTP version 1.1, which excludes some older browsers, and more important, it's dependent on the server residing in a domain with a Windows 2000 domain controller.

Integrated Windows authentication: With this method, user details are encrypted before being transmitted to and from the server, so information exchange is much more secure. Users are not prompted for their details, as the current login credentials for the client machine are sent automatically when requested. If the credentials are not valid or the user does not have enough privileges for the operation the user is attempting, the user is prompted to enter a user name and password, but the information will still be transmitted using this scheme. Integrated Windows authentication is dependent on the end user having a compatible browser. It's great for intranet environments in which the clients and server reside on the same domain, because it makes it simple for users to log in to a site and gain access to the information they require. The drawback of this method is that it cannot reliably pass data through firewalls and routers, so it's best to keep it only for intranets.

If both Basic authentication and Integrated Windows authentication are selected in the Authentication Methods dialog box, and the browser supports Windows authentication, it will attempt to use Windows authentication first.

THE ROLE OF SECURE SOCKETS LAYER

It's also possible to configure the web server to work with *SSL certificates*, in order to enable secure communication between the server and the client. SSL was created by Netscape, and is designed to run between the root level of communication over the Web (TCP), and the application-level communication (HTTP). An SSL-enabled server and an SSL-enabled client can authenticate each other and establish an encrypted connection.

You may be familiar with this process if you've ever purchased anything online. By default, your browser will warn you whenever you switch between secure and "unsecure" connections. When you're in a secure area, you'll see a padlock icon somewhere in the window. Here are examples of this icon in Mozilla Firefox (left) and Internet Explorer (right):

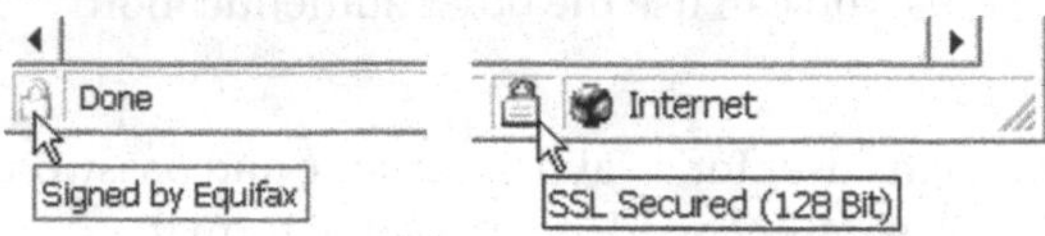

SSL uses *public key cryptography* to establish a secure connection between the client and the server. The server side of the connection must be equipped with an SSL certificate. These are available from various vendors. A good explanation of public key cryptography can be found at `http://www.sun.com/blueprints/0801/publickey.pdf`.

Note For more information about IIS authentication, see `http://msdn.microsoft.com/library/en-us/vsent7/html/vxconIISAuthentication.asp`.

Configuring ASP.NET Applications in IIS

We've examined some of the options available for the site-wide configuration of IIS. Now let's explore how you can specify properties that apply to an individual application. To set an application's properties, right-click the virtual directory for that application and select Properties. You'll see the Properties dialog box for that directory. The Virtual Directory tab, shown in Figure B-4, has several settings that you can alter.

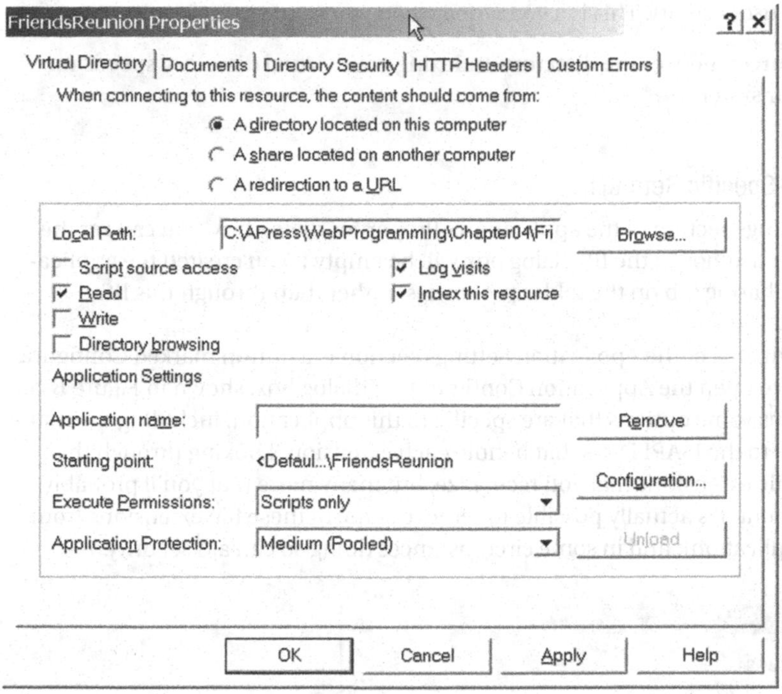

Figure B-4. *Properties for a web application*

Setting Application Permissions

The Local Path section contains check boxes that determine the basic permissions for your application:

- **Script source access:** Determines whether the client can view the source code for server-side applications. This is normally left unchecked, because it's unlikely that you'll want to allow users to view your source code. Note that this permission can be set only if Read or Write permission is also set.
- **Read:** Enables browsers to read or download files in the virtual directory. This option should be left checked for published web applications. Unchecking it will mean that clients requesting the page will see an error message.
- **Write:** Allows users to create or modify files within the directory. In most situations, this should be left turned off.
- **Directory browsing:** Allow users to browse the contents of a directory. This is a useful feature when you're working with an application that contains many files. In most cases, however, it's recommended that you leave this turned off on production sites in order to hide as much of your site as possible from prying eyes.

- **Log visits:** Logs user activity. This is a good idea when you want to track users.
- **Index this resource:** Indexes the directory. Indexing your virtual directory speeds up searches on your system.

Choosing Application-Specific Settings

In the Application Settings section of the application's Properties dialog box, you can set the Application Name (this text box in the IIS dialog box will be empty if you created the application through the Web Sharing tab on the folder properties, rather than through this IIS management console).

In the bottom-right area of the Application Settings section is a button marked Configuration. Click this button to open the Application Configuration dialog box, shown in Figure B-5. This dialog box contains some options that are specific to this application, including the mappings of file extensions to the ISAPI DLLs that handle each extension. Looking through this list, you'll see several file extensions that you recognize, but many more that you'll probably never have to worry about. It's actually possible to remove some of these file extensions from IIS (or just from an application), and in some circumstances doing so can aid security.

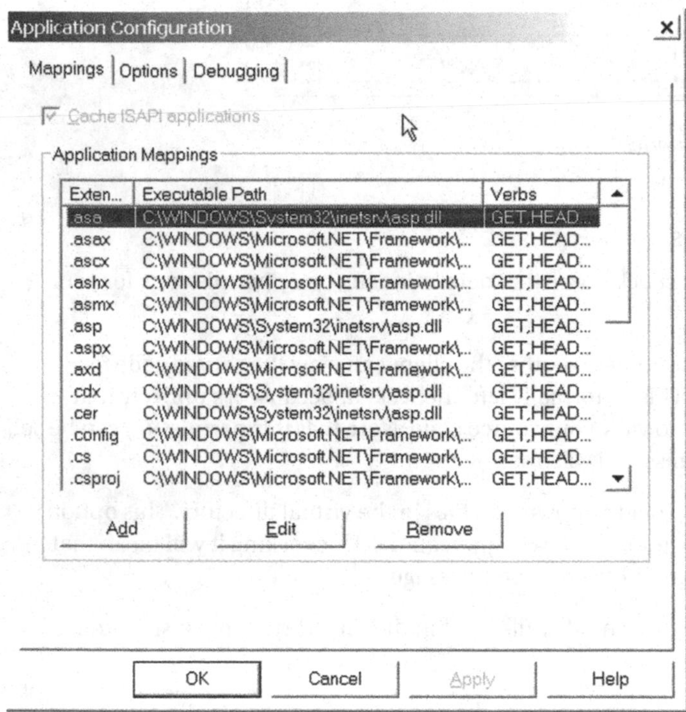

Figure B-5. *Application-specific configuration settings*

THE ROLE OF ISAPI

ISAPI is an acronym for *Internet Server Application Programming Interface*. ISAPI is a low-level interface that resides beneath higher-level abstractions like ASP.NET. In many ways, you can think of ASP.NET as a developer-friendly way of working with ISAPI. It's possible to work with ISAPI directly, but it's much easier if you can find an alternative approach! Every web development technology that's compatible with IIS must be able to communicate with ISAPI, which provides the ability to process page requests and send responses.

An ISAPI extension, such as the ASP.NET ISAPI extension, is the go-between that can process and make sense of code written in a given programming language, and process it so that it's possible to send an appropriate response to the client browser. IIS has a list of allowed file extensions that it can handle, and each file extension maps to an ISAPI extension designed to handle that type of request.

ASP.NET pages have the extension `.aspx`, and the ASP.NET ISAPI extension is `aspnet_isapi.dll`, which is located in the `%WinDir%\Microsoft.NET\Framework\v1.1.4322` folder. When IIS receives a request, the file extension will tell IIS which extension to pass the request to for processing. This extension will then pass the request on to the ASP.NET worker process to be processed.

The ASP.NET ISAPI extension passes requests for ASP.NET pages to `aspnet_wp.exe` (`w3wp.exe` in Windows Server 2003), which runs as a system process. Here, you can see this process highlighted in the list that's produced by the Windows Task Manager on a Windows 2000/XP machine:

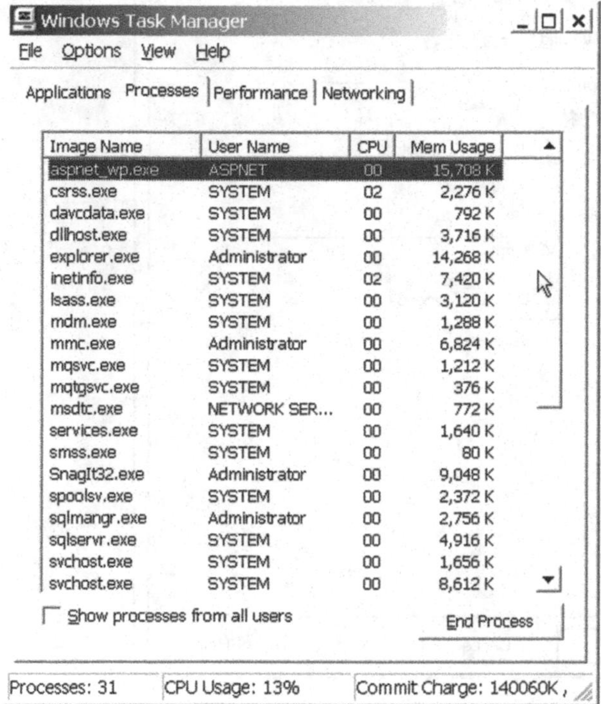

On a Windows Server 2003 machine, you would see a w3wp.exe process running with the NETWORK SERVICE account.

On the first request for an .aspx page, this process is started automatically. (This is one reason why the first hit on an .aspx page can take so long.) Subsequent hits to the same page benefit not only from the fact that there is a cached, compiled version of the page stored on the server, but also from the fact that the ASP.NET process is already started.

Note that there's also an entry in the list some lines below the aspnet_wp.exe, called inetinfo.exe. This is the name of the process that IIS runs as, and it will appear in the list whenever the web server is up and running.

The Options tab of the Application Configuration dialog box provides an option to configure session timeout length, as shown in Figure B-6. This setting will affect any ASP.NET application that relies on session state. This overrides the defaults that you specified in the site-wide settings, giving you the ability to work with different timeouts for each application on the server.

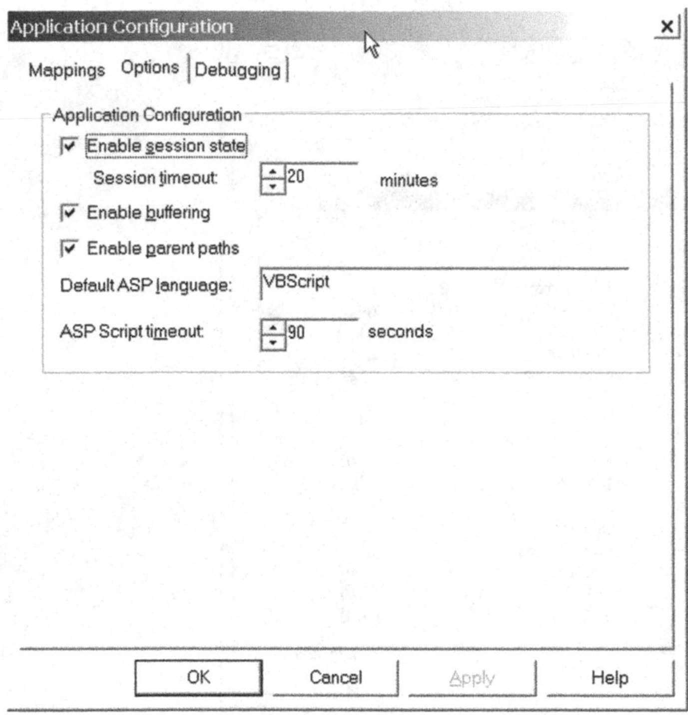

Figure B-6. *The Options tab of the Application Configuration dialog box*

Locking Down IIS

In general, there are a lot of things that you can do on a day-to-day basis to close down potential security holes on your IIS server. You can install all the security patches and hotfixes, turn off directory browsing on sites, enable logging, remove IIS samples, and install antivirus software. You should always make sure that your IIS installation is as patched and up-to-date as possible, to prevent newly discovered security holes from affecting your server.

To simplify this process, Microsoft has released a very useful tool that helps to secure IIS 5, called the *IIS Lockdown Tool*. This tool is used to turn off unnecessary features and disable some loopholes in IIS. At the time of writing, the Lockdown Tool is available for download from `http://www.microsoft.com/downloads/release.asp?ReleaseID=43955`. It's recommended that you read the instructions very carefully and understand each step in the process before proceeding to download and use this tool. If you proceed too hastily, you can end up turning off too many features, rendering your web server nonfunctional.

Impersonation Configuration

When hosting a web application for general public consumption, it's usually acceptable to allow Anonymous access to your web server. But what if you wanted to enable more functionality (requiring greater permissions) for *certain* users? What if certain users need Write permissions on a target folder on the web server or need to write to an event log? ASP.NET can handle this situation by using a technique known as *impersonation*.

In any situation that involves Windows Integrated security (in an intranet or extranet application, for example), you can enable impersonation on your ASP.NET application. This means ASP.NET will use the authentication token determined by IIS instead of its own mechanism, so your users can be authenticated as local or domain accounts that have more privileges than the standard `ASPNET/NETWORK SERVICE` account or the `IUSR_MachineName` account.

With impersonation turned off, there's an entry in the `Machine.config` file that determines which account is used for Anonymous access. The entry is `<processModel>`, and the default setting is `username="Machine"`, `password="AutoGenerate"`. This special `"Machine"` value maps to the `ASPNET` or `NETWORK SERVICE` account.

Impersonation can be turned on by adding the following to the `system.web` section of either the `Machine.config` or `Web.config` file:

```
<identity impersonate="true" />
```

Using this setting, if Anonymous access is enabled on IIS, your anonymous ASP.NET users are now authenticated using the `IUSR_MachineName` account, instead of the `ASPNET` or `NETWORK SERVICE` account. You can configure impersonation further by adding to this definition:

```
<identity impersonate="true" username="name" password="password"/>
```

Here, the user name and password must relate to a valid account on the web server. This setting affects *only* the account under which the ASP.NET process itself is run; it doesn't affect Anonymous access to any other IIS-based application.

Implementing impersonation gives users of your application a specific set of permissions for performing tasks that the basic `ASPNET` user account cannot perform.

This is a two-phase process:

- **IIS authentication:** IIS determines the Windows identity depending on authentication settings or uses the account set for the Anonymous access, if it's enabled.
- **ASP.NET impersonation:** For the request execution, the ASP.NET engine impersonates the account set in the `<identity>` element or the one received from IIS, if no particular one is set. The one received from IIS may be the `IUSR_MachineName` account or the actual Windows local/domain account the user logged in with, depending on the IIS authentication settings.

Try It Out: Establish Identity Let's take a look at how to use impersonation with a quick example that declares the user account under which ASP.NET is currently authenticated.

1. Open VS .NET and create a new web application called `ImpersonationExample`.
2. Create a new web form in your application by right-clicking the application in the Solution Explorer and selecting Add ➤ Add Web Form. Call the new form `ImpersonateMe.aspx`.
3. Delete `WebForm1.aspx` from the project, right-click `ImpersonateMe.aspx`, and select Set As Start Page from the context menu.
4. View the code-behind file for `ImpersonateMe.aspx` and enter the following code into the `Page_Load()` event handler:

```
Private Sub Page_Load(ByVal sender As System.Object, _
  ByVal e As System.EventArgs) Handles MyBase.Load
  Response.Write("I am authenticated as: " + _
    WindowsIdentity.GetCurrent().Name)
End Sub
```

5. In order to get access to the `WindowsIdentity` class, you need to tell your web page to reference the classes in the `System.Security` namespace. Add the following line to the top of the code-behind page, before the class definition:

```
Imports System.Security.Principal
```

6. Run the project, and view the results. (In Windows Server 2003, you will see `NT AUTHORITY\NETWORK SERVICE` instead.)

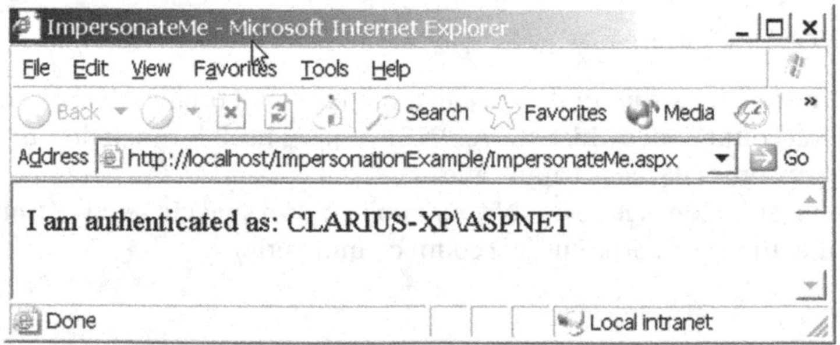

How It Works

So far, you have not done anything too complex. You just confirmed the fact that ASP.NET pages are run under an account on the web server called ASPNET (NETWORK SERVICE in Windows Server 2003):

```
Response.Write("I am authenticated as: " + _
  WindowsIdentity.GetCurrent().Name)
```

Here, you've output a simple line of text on your browser that gathers information from the local system, using functionality provided by the System.Security namespace.

Try It Out: Enable Impersonation with Anonymous Access Let's now extend the example to see how you can enable impersonation for anonymous users and what effect this has on your application.

1. In the ImpersonationExample application, open the Web.config file and add the following line near the top:

```
<?xml version="1.0" encoding="utf-8" ?>
<configuration>
  <system.web>
    ...
    <identity impersonate="true" />
    ...
  </system.web>
</configuration>
```

2. Run the application again, and you'll see something similar to the following page.

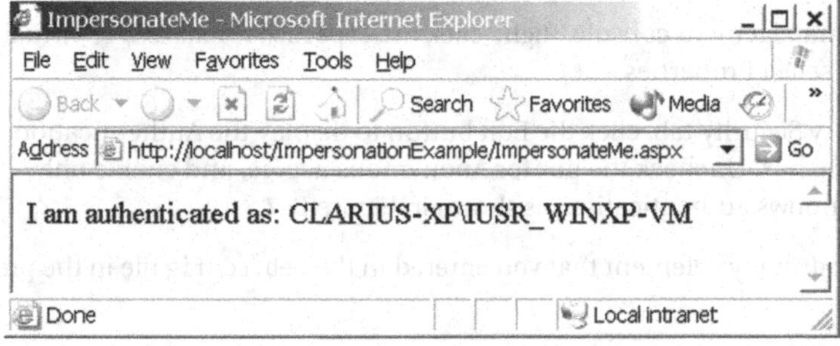

How It Works

The <identity> tag that you added to the Web.config file has changed the default user account for Anonymous access to your ASP.NET application. The application has reverted to the default user account for all IIS Anonymous access, which is IUSR_MachineName (IUSR_WINXP-VM in the example). If you had configured IIS to use a different account for standard Anonymous access, the details of that account would be displayed instead.

To log in as a specific user in this example, you need to have a user account on your local system that you can use. Let's suppose that you've set up a temporary account called `TestUser`, with an eminently hackable password: `letmein`. Let's also imagine this account is a member of the Power Users group on the local machine. Here's what the line in the `Web.config` file needs to look like:

```
<identity impersonate="true" userName="TestUser" password="letmein" />
```

With the configuration you've set up, you would end up with the following result.

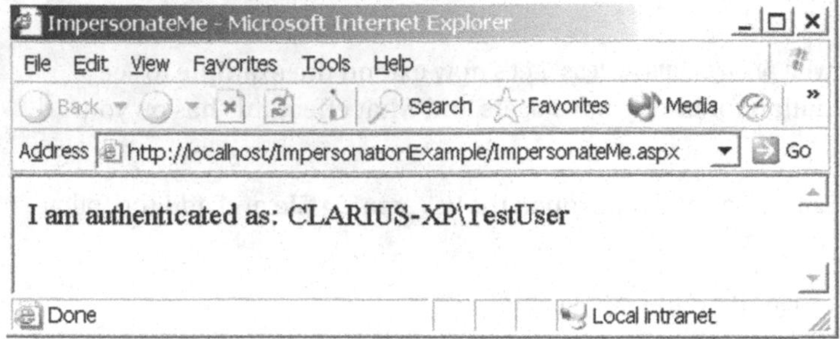

Since this user has more privileges on the local machine than the basic anonymous users, your applications have more flexibility. For example, code in your ASP.NET application could now create and modify files as required, provided the current user has the appropriate permissions on the target folder or files.

Try It Out: Use Impersonation and Integrated Windows Authentication While you have an example, let's take a quick peek at what happens when Integrated Windows authentication is switched on for your application.

1. Open the IIS management console. Right-click the `ImpersonationExample` virtual directory and select Properties.

2. In the Directory Security tab, click the Edit button to display the Authentication Methods dialog box. Uncheck the box for Anonymous access, and enable only Integrated Windows authentication, as shown in Figure B-7.

3. Remove the `<identity>` element that you entered in the `Web.config` file in the previous exercise.

4. Run the application, and you'll find that ASP.NET will revert to using the `ASPNET` account for authentication.

5. Now reinsert the `<identity>` element in the `Web.config` file as follows:

```
<identity impersonate="true" />
```

Authentication Methods

Anonymous access

No user name/password required to access this resource.

Account used for anonymous access:

User name: IUSR_WINXP-VM Browse...

Password: ••••••••••

Allow IIS to control password

Authenticated access

For the following authentication methods, user name and password are required when

- anonymous access is disabled, or
- access is restricted using NTFS access control lists

Digest authentication for Windows domain servers

Basic authentication (password is sent in clear text)

Default domain: Select...

Realm: Select...

Integrated Windows authentication

OK Cancel Help

Figure B-7. *Using Integrated Windows authentication*

6. Run the application again, and ASP.NET will attempt to use the currently logged-in user's account for authentication.

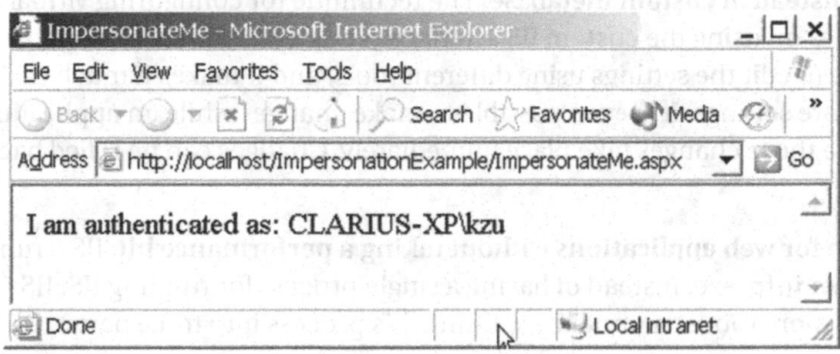

How It Works

As a result of the switch to Windows Integrated authentication, ASP.NET pages are now running under the current Windows user's account (this Windows user is logged in as `kzu`, in the `CLARIUS-XP` machine/domain). Access to your application is now controlled by the access control lists (ACLs) maintained by the operating system, moving the authentication portion of your exchange to the underlying security settings of the system, rather than IIS. This is useful if you need to access to resources managed by the operating system, such as files, the Registry, or the event log.

When using impersonation, you should always consider what it is you're trying to achieve. You need to take care to restrict access to the minimum possible privileges for each user, and you will rarely need to give any user full administrative capacity on your server.

An Introduction to IIS 6

IIS 6 is part of Windows Server 2003, which is quite different from the Windows 2000 Server family, mainly because of the introduction of the Windows Server 2003 Web Edition. IIS 6 is installed by default on Windows Server 2003 Web Edition, and it is an optional installation for the rest of the product family.

Note Windows Server 2003 Web Edition is designed solely for hosting web applications, and, as a result, lacks a lot of the functionality contained within the other Windows Server 2003 editions (the full list is Web Edition, Standard Edition, Enterprise Edition, and Datacenter Edition). It doesn't include functionality to act as a domain controller, and you won't be able to install many server products on it.

IIS 6 is designed to be more secure than IIS 5 by default. The default settings you get with an IIS 6 installation have been chosen with security issues foremost, with the potential loopholes disabled (so you need to opt in, rather than opt out). ASP, ASP.NET, and technologies such as WebDAV and FrontPage Server Extensions are disabled in a default IIS 6 installation; if you need them, you must enable them explicitly. Also, IIS 6 installs security patches automatically by default, so you need to opt *out* of this process if you don't want it.

The major changes and new features of IIS 6 can be summarized as follows:

XML metabase instead of custom metabase: The technique for configuring virtual directories in IIS 5 relies on using the custom IIS interface. The new XML-based metabase makes it possible to edit the settings using different tools, and it makes it much easier to back up and restore settings. It is even possible to make changes while an application is running and have those changes take place immediately. Changes can be rolled back if necessary.

Process isolation for web applications without taking a performance hit: IIS 5 runs in a process called `inetinfo.exe`. Instead of having a single process for running IIS, IIS 6 hosts applications in a more robust manner by splitting this process into three parts:

- The *HTTP.sys* part runs in kernel mode and serves the requests. This part alone will give you a performance boost, especially for static or cached content.
- The *Web Admin Service (WAS)* part is used to configure HTTP.sys and manage the lifecycle of worker processes. The WAS is what looks after the memory allocation needs of your applications, and detects crashes and protects the server from failure. (Note that this is *not* the Web Application Stress tool introduced in Chapter 12 of this book!)

- The *W3 core* part is where your applications actually are loaded. This is where ISAPI extensions and filters are loaded. The W3 core isolates each application in its own process, so if an application crashes, there is less chance that it will take the whole web server down with it.

Secure by default installation: IIS 6 removes security holes and black spots that seemed to plague IIS 5. IIS 6's defaults should help to ensure that hackers who have been used to exploiting vulnerable servers will have a much harder job.

The IIS 6 management console also has some changes, as shown in Figure B-8. It has some new nodes, such as Application Pools, which corresponds to the new application process model. A new feature of the IIS 6 management console is the ability to save a particular site or even an individual web application configuration to a file, so you can import it later on another server.

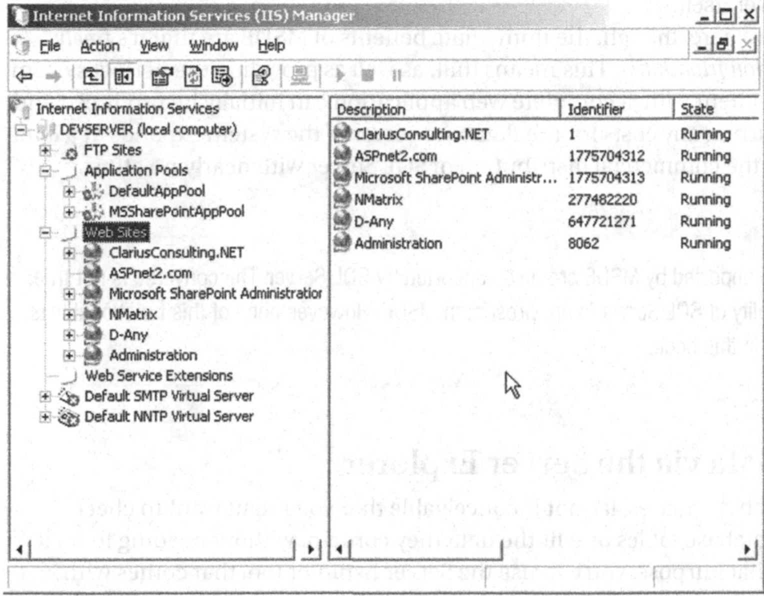

Figure B-8. *The IIS 6 management console*

Also, by default, there is nothing under the Default Web Site node. This is very different from an IIS 5 server, which has several default directories and virtual directories when it is first installed. You will also notice that requesting your default page from this newly installed web server produces an error instead of a detailed IIS page. These all reflect the new "secure by default" aims of IIS 6: a lot of the functionality that you have seen previously is removed or disabled.

Note You can find more information about the different versions and the features of IIS 6 at `http://www.microsoft.com/windowsserver2003/`.

MSDE Management

One of most important ingredients of a dynamic web application is the ability to store data in and retrieve data from a database, and several of the examples in the chapters in this book involve this functionality. For that, of course, you need a database. In this book, we choose to use the Microsoft SQL Server Desktop Engine (MSDE), which is a specialized version of SQL Server 2000.

Using MSDE

MSDE is entirely compatible with and behaves in the same way as Microsoft SQL Server, which is truly an enterprise-class database server. (The only differences from the full version of SQL Server are that MSDE is optimized for—but not limited to—up to five connections at a time, the maximum database size is limited to 2GB, and some enterprise features are absent.) This means that the things you learn while using MSDE will stand you in good stead when you move on to use SQL Server itself.

From our perspective here, though, the immediate benefits of MSDE are that it's *freely distributable* and *freely downloadable*. This means that, as well as providing the perfect system for us to learn and experiment with, a complete web application can initially be produced and distributed without incurring any costs for the database server. If the system expands at a later date, it can be ported to the commercial distribution of SQL Server with nearly no effort.

Note All of the features supported by MSDE are also supported by SQL Server. The converse is not true; some of the richer functionality of SQL Server is not present in MSDE. However, none of this functionality is required by any of the code in this book.

Administering Data via the Server Explorer

When you're working with databases, it's not inconceivable that you might want to check what's going on in the database tables or edit the data they contain, without needing to do it through ADO.NET. For that purpose, you can use the Server Explorer tool that comes with VS .NET. If you already feel comfortable with this tool, or you'll be using SQL Server's Enterprise Manager to administer the database, feel free to skip this section. If not, choose the View ➤ Server Explorer menu item to open the Server Explorer window, which will look something like this:

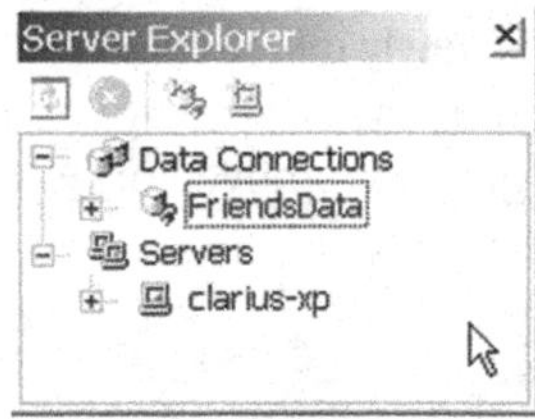

Note If the Server Explorer hasn't been used before, there may be nothing at all underneath the Data Connections root node. We'll address that right away.

The Data Connections node maintains a list of configured database connections, to which you can add new connections.

In the Professional and Enterprise versions of VS .NET, the Server Explorer allows you to connect to just about any database you might want to manipulate. Once a connection has been established, its node can be expanded, and the features of the database then appear as child nodes. In the version that comes with the Standard Edition of Visual Basic .NET, your options are more limited—you can connect to only MSDE and Microsoft Access databases, but that's more than adequate for the examples in this book.

To see how it works, we'll add a connection to the database for Friends Reunion, the application that we work with in this book.

Try It Out: Add a Connection to the Friends Reunion Database As explained in Appendix A, you attach the `FriendsData` database by following the instructions in the `Setup.txt` file in the `Db` folder of the code you've downloaded for this book (from the Downloads section of `http://www.apress.com`). You will now connect to this database and manipulate its data.

1. Right-click the Server Explorer's Data Connections node and select Add Connection. You'll see the Data Link Properties dialog box.

2. Set the server name to the machine on which you installed the Friends Reunion database.

3. Select the Use Windows NT Integrated security radio button.

4. Select the `FriendsData` database from the drop-down menu. The Data Link Properties dialog box should look something like the one shown in Figure B-9.

How It Works

VS .NET assumes, by default, that you want to make a connection to a SQL Server database (if you need to, you can change this by clicking the Provider tab). By using Windows NT Integrated security to log on, you don't need to enter a separate user name or password to connect to the database.

You used the actual machine name for the server name field, but you can also replace it with the special value `(local)`, which means the local machine.

Now let's see how to use the Server Explorer to edit the data contained in a database table.

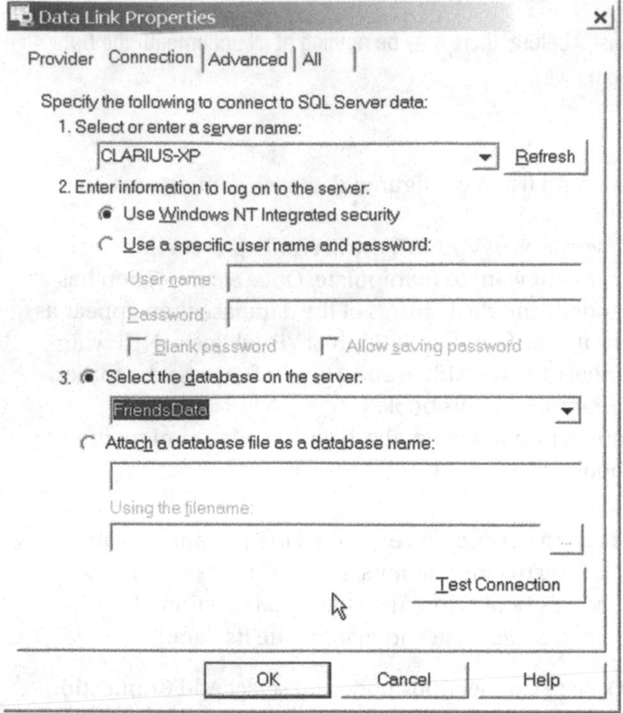

Figure B-9. *The Data Link Properties dialog box in the Server Explorer*

Try It Out: Change Data and Perform Queries with the Server Explorer In this example, you'll use the Server Explorer to take a look at the `FriendsData` database that you just connected to, and perform some simple operations on it through the interface that VS .NET provides.

1. In the Server Explorer, go to the `FriendsData` connection and open the Tables node.
2. Right-click the `User` table and select Retrieve Data from Table (or simply double-click the `User` table). The main Server Explorer window will look similar to Figure B-10. Also, a new toolbar, called the Query toolbar, will appear at the top left of the window, as well as a new Query menu, which presents most of the button actions as menu items.
3. At this stage, any change you make to the data will be sent to the database as soon as you move the cursor to another row, just as if you were working in Microsoft Access. For example, locate Robert De Niro in the table and set his birth date to August 17, 1943. Move the cursor to the next row, and the change will be applied.
4. With the cursor positioned anywhere inside the table, click the Show SQL Pane button in the Query toolbar (the one with the letters *SQL* on it) to display the SQL code that was executed in order to produce the data you see.

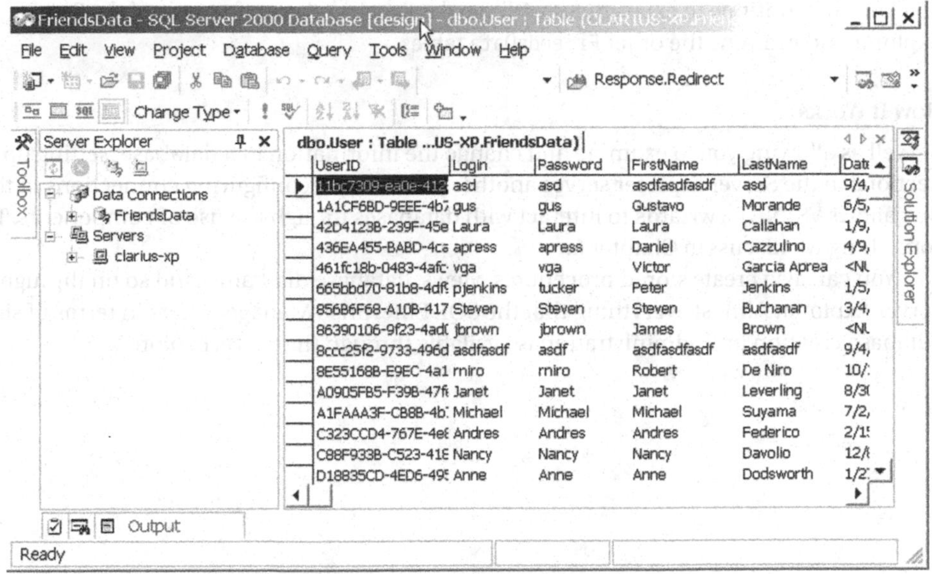

Figure B-10. *The User table displayed in the Server Explorer*

5. In the new pane, you can write any valid SQL statement, such as `SELECT * FROM [Users]` and click the Run Query button in the Query toolbar (the one with an exclamation point) to show the results. You can also check the validity of the statements you enter by clicking the Verify SQL Syntax button (the one with small *SQL* letters and a check sign), as shown in Figure B-11.

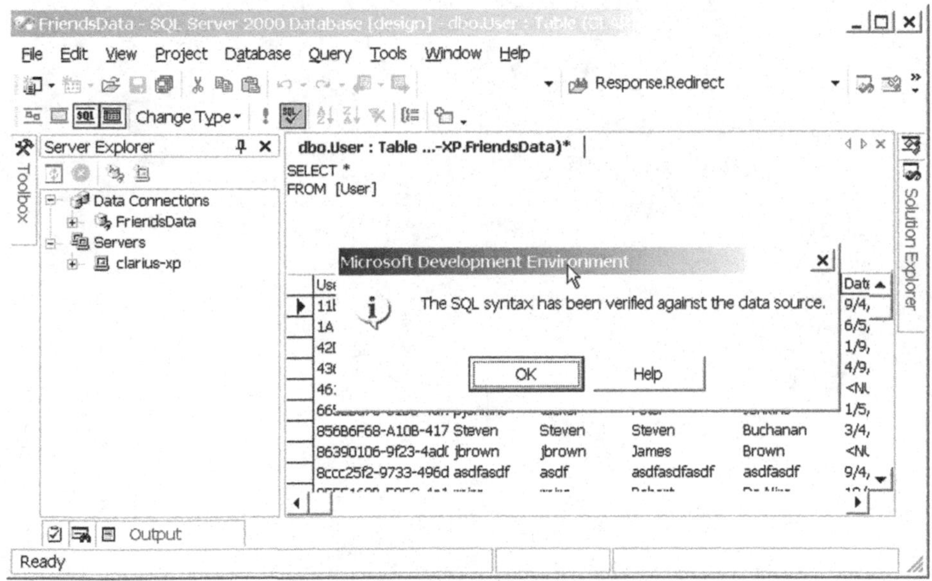

Figure B-11. *Checking SQL syntax*

You can continue to experiment with the data-manipulation features of the Server Explorer and examine the other `FriendsData` tables.

How It Works

As well as allowing you to examine and change the information in a database, setting up connections in the Server Explorer serves another purpose: preconfiguring connections in this way allows VS .NET's wizards to interact with databases though the use of components. This is something we discuss in Chapter 5.

You can also create stored procedures, views, database diagrams, and so on through the Server Explorer. Almost everything that the SQL Enterprise Manager offers in terms of simple database creation and administration is available through the ServerExplorer.

Index

Special Characters

A

B

D

F

G

H

I

J

L

M

N

O

P

S

T

U

V

W

X